Introduction to Hebrew Bible

A Guided Tour of Israel's Sacred Library

James E. Bowley

Millsaps College

PEARSON

Prentice
Hall

UPPER SADDLE RIVER, NEW JERSEY 07458

Library of Congress Cataloging-in-Publication Data

Bowley, James E.
  Introduction to Hebrew Bible : a guided tour of Israel's sacred
library / James E. Bowley.—1st ed.
    p. cm.
  ISBN 0-13-045357-9
  1. Bible. O.T.—Study and teaching.   I. Title.
  BS1193.B69 2007
  221.6'1—dc22

                              2006037234

Editor-in-Chief: Sarah Touborg
Senior Editor: Mical Moser
Editorial Assistant: Carla Worner
Assistant Marketing Manager: Andrea Messineo
Production Liaison: Marianne Peters-Riordan
Manufacturing Buyer: Christina Amato
Cover Art Director: Jayne Conte
Interior Art Director: Kathryn Foot
Cover Design: Bruce Kenselaar
Cover Illustration/Photo: David Harris/The Israel
Museum, Jerusalem

Director, Image Resource Center: Melinda Patelli
Manager, Rights and Permissions: Zina Arabia
Manager, Visual Research: Beth Brenzel
**Manager, Cover Visual Research &
  Permissions:** Karen Sanatar
Image Permission Coordinator: Craig A. Jones
**Composition/Full-Service Project
  Management:** Sarvesh Mehrotra/Techbooks
Printer/Binder: R.R. Donnelley & Sons
Cover Printer: The Lehigh Press, Inc.

Credits and acknowledgments borrowed from other sources and reproduced, with permission, in this
textbook appear on appropriate page within text.

Pearson Prentice Hall™ is a trademark of Pearson Education, Inc.
Pearson® is a registered trademark of Pearson plc
Prentice Hall® is a registered trademark of Pearson Education, Inc.

Pearson Education LTD.
Pearson Education Singapore, Pte. Ltd
Pearson Education, Canada, Ltd
Pearson Education–Japan
Pearson Education Australia PTY, Limited

Pearson Education North Asia Ltd
Pearson Educación de Mexico, S.A. de C.V.
Pearson Education Malaysia, Pte. Ltd
Pearson Education, Upper Saddle
  River, New Jersey

10 9 8 7 6 5 4 3 2 1
ISBN 13: 978-0-13-045357-0
ISBN 10: 0-13-045357-9

To my teachers,
D. Brent Sandy, Weston Fields,
Ben Zion Wacholder, and Adam Kamesar
With admiration and gratitude.

בקש קהלת למצא דברי חפץ
וכתוב ישר דברי אמת

Contents

IN THE LIBRARY

CHAPTER 8 Writings Ketuvim   325

AFTER THE TOUR

A Note to Teachers

Welcome (back) to school, my fellow teacher. I wanted to let you know a few things up front about this book. This guided tour of the Hebrew Bible is unapologetically written to be accessible to, and understood by, a broad spectrum of undergraduate students in colleges and universities, including those with no prior knowledge of the Bible. This accessibility should also make it good for individual readers. In my years of teaching, I have used many other introductory books and have found that many of them, which seem to me to be full of great information, are too advanced for my students. In our classrooms of the twenty-first century, biblical literacy cannot be assumed, because students come to us from so many different cultural traditions, including those where biblical literature may have played little or no role in a student's education. Also, a student with some commendable knowledge of biblical content may know little or nothing about biblical history, cultural settings, or literary analysis.

This guide is also an introduction, not a full-scale explanation: a taste, not a meal; a trailer, not the whole movie. Its purpose is breadth—to survey all the material in a manageable manner for college students, many of whom have no experience in biblical studies and who are taking your course as part of a broad educational requirement. I'm trying to get people in the door and whisk them through this great library we call Bible in an enjoyable way, so that they'll come back later and read more. If I imagine meeting the perfect reader of my guided tour, I can think of no greater compliment than to hear that a previously disinterested student had her curiosity awakened, that she began to read biblical literature with new understanding, and that she went on to read more advanced studies on biblical subjects, perhaps ones that you have written. With that reader in mind, I have also kept the book as brief as possible, so that reading my guided tour would not stand in the way of reading the real thing—the ancient texts themselves.

This is an eclectic guide; you will see several methodologies at work. Sometimes it seemed useful to be overt about the method in use and at other times it seemed overly repetitious. You no doubt have your own approaches and expertise, and it is my hope that this eclectic approach will serve you well by allowing you to head off in your own direction for discussions or lectures and encouraging your students to explore areas that I simply didn't have time and space to cover, as I and my reviewers know. In the questions at the end of each section, I have tried to engage students in a wide variety of issues, which I hope will provide something for everyone's taste.

And finally, a word about style: I have strayed from formal academic parlance somewhat in this book because students encountering a subject for the first time often think standard text books are dry and stiff. This guided tour is meant to engage students—to invite them in, to get them into the library—and so in much of this work I have written in a more informal, conversational style—as a tour guide might speak. I hope that this will make the material more accessible to all my readers. Of course, it is never meant to sound trite or condescending! Instead, I hope it allows my own passion and personal fascination with this literature to come through loudly and clearly. I love this literature and the ancient world that we have the privilege of studying.

So, good luck, *mazal tov*, and blessings to you. I hope you enjoy teaching the fascinating ancient literature as much as I do, and I hope this guided tour aids you and your students in your quest. I would love to have your suggestions and comments for future reference and improvement.

Guide to Displays, Posters, Study Rooms, and Community Reflections

Displays: Artifacts, Art, Photographs

Posters: Quotations, Charts, and Maps

Study Rooms: Opportunities for Interesting Investigations

Community Reflections: Jewish ✡, Christian ✝, and Muslim ☪

Preface

Welcome to the Library

You are now entering one of the most ancient and famous libraries in the world. Millions have come here before you to browse, look something up, sing or pray, read a good story, or hear a poem. This library goes by many names in many different languages; the most common name in English is probably *The Bible*. The book that you are looking at right now, *Introduction to Hebrew Bible,* is intended to be like one of those informative brochures (a thick one!) that you might pick up as you enter a museum to help you find your way around the galleries and to point out interesting facts about the displays you encounter. If you have never been to the biblical "museum" before, that is, if you have never read a Bible before, you will learn a lot from this guide about the collection's history and the volumes it contains, and I hope you will come in and see why it is so famous. If you have been here before, perhaps many times, this guide will still provide you with new information about the library's history, formation, librarians, and its frequent users. Even a regular visitor will probably find that some of the books are well known, but others are almost foreign, having been rarely checked out. Our tour in the following pages will stop and consider them all.

Easy Access for All

While the library is ancient and may even sometimes be called sacred or holy (more on those adjectives in Chapter 2, in the section called "Valuing the Scrolls"), there are no restrictions on who may enter. You need not be of a certain religion—or even be religious at all—to be interested in a tour of this collection; you only need to be curious. And don't worry, this guide has not been written for library experts, that is, biblical scholars, but for all visitors of any background, even for those who has not been here before. I've written this guide primarily with college/university students in mind, and I find it delightful that college classes are a colorful blend of cultures and perspectives. You may have come for this tour of the Hebrew Bible without any familiarity or interest, or, conversely, you may already be an avid reader. No matter; I have found all that one really needs to enjoy this tour is wide-eyed curiosity about any number of subjects, including art, God, sex, history, tragedy, ancient customs, dramatic stories, violence, and dozens of others.

As you probably already know, this collection has been around for centuries, and there have been many people who have been reading its books, writing about them, and instructing others on how to understand them. Today in the United States you can turn on the television or radio at any hour of the day or night and find someone, usually from the Christian tradition, preaching about the Bible. A trip to a bookstore will present you with a plethora of Bible-related books from different religious perspectives. In fact, as our tour proceeds we will sometimes pause to consider how biblical ideas and books are understood differently in the various religious traditions that embrace this biblical literature. But it is important to point out up front that this guided tour is "sponsored by" the high ideals of free and rigorous academic inquiry, and it does not advocate for any single religious tradition's understandings.

Three broad religious traditions of the modern world—each one with a great deal of internal diversity—relate directly to the library we are about to enter: Judaism, Christianity, and Islam (see more in Chapter 10, "Meeting the Librarians"). During our tour we will explore interpretations and traditions within all of these religions in the feature entitled "Community Reflections." As we consider various ideas, we will not employ discrediting mechanisms that suggest that a certain biblical text can be understood only one way or that differing interpretations are illegitimate because other people are spiritually blind or lack our interpretive gifts. All are welcome to this guided tour, and all we need is some healthy curiosity for the tour to be enjoyable. My hope is that persons of all backgrounds will find this guide useful for understanding as they peruse the stacks and read the volumes of this most fascinating, inspiring, sometimes even shocking, library.

Why a "Library"?

Approaching the Hebrew Bible as a library, is, I believe, the best way of accounting for and appreciating the realities of this book. Many people today and in the past have recognized that what we hold in our hand when we pick up a Bible is a collection of diverse books from many different authors and from many different times and places—that sounds like a library to me. While these books now usually come packaged in one convenient volume, the texts are separate entities in their origin and integrity. So, as it turns out, this library analogy is not really an analogy at all. It is an appropriate and accurate description of what we encounter every time we read a Bible.

If you took me on a tour of a library in your town or city, we might hear briefly about the collection's history and the way it is arranged. We might be led from one room to another, and, going from shelf to shelf, the librarian would pull books off and tell us interesting things about their history, form, or content. This guided tour progresses essentially that same way. We might call this a literary approach—treating each book as an artifact to be explored and perused through literary questions and investigations about history, religion, sociology and the like. Academic disciplines, such as history, religion, sociology, and others, add much to our discussion and are vital to academic understanding of texts, but they do not provide the organizational model for our study. History, for example, has often been used as the guiding paradigm for biblical studies. Many introductory textbooks are organized around the history of the ancient Jews (Israelites), and the advantage for the historical approach is that the reader is constantly aware of the historical context of biblical literature. Among the drawbacks of the historical approach are that we often do not know the specific historical situation in which a book was written, and many of the books themselves register little interest in history. Other authors have elected to organize their introduction to the Bible around an important idea or theme, such as covenant or story. While fascinating insights often result from the thematic approach, it often does not account adequately for the great diversity of thought and form encountered in the various texts of the library, not all of which share themes. Take the "story" theme, for instance. No single storyline unifies all of this literature or provides a narrative to which all the books can be naturally linked. The various books use different defining (crucial, generative) stories, and some books do not engage an Israelite story at all; they seem to eschew it.

But all of this—different stories, different relations to history, different kinds of literature, different themes—sounds perfectly natural for many libraries, where diversity abounds and variety is a hallmark of the shelves. So, let's begin our tour with a short presentation about the library's development and arrangement (Chapter 1). These are matters that are vital in their own right and will help us find our way around later, when we enter the stacks and begin perusing the books themselves.

How This Guide Works

Arrangement

In an introductory text it is impossible to cover everything that should be covered, and it is equally impossible to explore every valuable approach and perspective. Above all else, I hope that you will read the biblical books for yourself and *not* settle for a second-hand encounter with these fascinating writings. And when you do read the ancient texts, you will immediately see that no brief introductory textbook such as this could possibly do justice to all the material that deserves our attention. So I hope your curiosity takes you well beyond this brief tour, deep into the biblical scrolls and into more detailed works of scholarship.

Looking at the table of contents, you will notice that we stop in the entrance to the library for a series of four short chapters that deal with important but preliminary matters—basic concepts that we need to know if we want to understand these writings in their own world. Chapters 1–4 bring up all kinds of important preliminary information that Bible readers need in order to see the biblical books as the ancient documents that they are. I suggest that the entrance section be read quickly, perhaps in just a couple of weeks, so that you have plenty of time for the major part of the tour.

Leaving the entrance, we walk through the main library and look individually at all the books of the Hebrew Bible, following the order of modern Jewish Bibles (Chapters 5–8). We also deal with some of the additional scrolls that are found in Roman Catholic and Eastern Orthodox traditions (Chapter 9). As we leave the main library, we have some pertinent information about the communities who have preserved and interpreted the scrolls (Chapter 10). Just as in a library, you can skip some books and go straight to others, each scroll's presentation can stand alone. Of course you would miss out on some things, but reading some is better than reading none! In such cases, perhaps different people in the class could be assigned different scrolls and then report back for the benefit of others. Check out the Glossary too, its brief identifications should be useful.

Literature and History

As you read the material about each scroll of the Hebrew Bible, you will also notice that literary concerns—format and literary movement, themes, rhetoric—are slightly favored over historical concerns, such as attempting to recreate the historical context of the author(s) or exploring all the historical data that may be found in a scroll. No manageable introductory book can do everything, so this one leans toward literary matters. By favoring literary matters I do not want to suggest that historical questions are less important. This tour reflects growing scholarly interest in literary matters, thanks to the work of writers such as Robert Alter. It also reflects the realities of modern historical research: we are often unable to identify with any confidence the historical circumstances and contexts in which a given scroll originated. For these reasons, historical concerns are not our major focus.

Dead Sea Scrolls

There is, however, one historical development that is of major and unique importance for our tour, namely the discovery of a great cache of ancient manuscripts, known today as the Dead Sea Scrolls, between 1947 and 1956. About one-quarter of these scrolls, just over 200 of them, are copies of the ancient writings that are now a part of our modern Bibles. We have copies of books that are over 2,000 years old in the library we are about to tour. Unlike most other introductions, I have attempted to make significant use of these copies because they tell us so much about the condition, form, and use of biblical literature at a time so much closer to the original writings. The Dead Sea Scrolls give of a glimpse of our Bibles before there were Bibles, and so they provide fascinating details and insights that are often overlooked. But not on *this* tour.

Questions

Asking and investigating interesting questions is the essence of curiosity, and I hope we have a lot of it. At the end of each chapter I have a "Questions for Further Study" section, some of which will give opportunity for more advanced study in the discipline of biblical studies. In addition, I often find in class or on museum tours that excellent questions come up in the middle of a lecture or discussion and it doesn't always make sense to wait to the end to ask; it seems poor pedagogy to me. Thus, throughout the chapters I sometimes raise questions in the middle of discussions, and along the way I have also included "Study Rooms," boxes in the text that provide longer queries for investigation.

Bibliographies

Also at the end of sections are brief bibliographies of works in English that I thought would be useful especially to students. These are not advanced bibliographies, but they will be helpful to most undergraduates.

A Library and Time for All

When dealing with ancient history, every author must choose a system of chronological notation. In the sixth-century work of a Christian monk named Dionysius Exiguus in Rome, the Latin term A.D. *Anno Domini* ("year of our Lord") was coined and the influential writings of ninth-century English scholar St. Bede first used the term B.C., "before Christ," both of which have been used by many writers in English cultures. However, since the twentieth century, many writers have opted for abbreviations that are not tied to exclusively Christian theological claims. In this guided tour, for which I am keen to signal a welcoming attitude to all, I will use the abbreviations, BCE, "Before the Common Era," and CE, "Common Era." Using CE and BCE is a way of trying to be respectful of all my readers and students, and to present information in a neutral and fair way.

Acknowledgments

We all know that "it takes a village" to write a book or do anything! I'll never be able to come close to mentioning all those who should be thanked. I'm happy to acknowledge the many wonderful students of my Hebrew Bible courses at Millsaps College. It is, after all, for students that we do what we do. Some who made specific contributions were Mary Buntin, Livia Eckhardt, Ben Ross, Justin Sledge, Anne Long, Elizabeth Olds, and my student assistants, Jessica Hoffpauir and Matt Marston who aided me at several levels of this project. Also, my colleagues at Millsaps: Hollis Robbins, William Storey, Laura Franey, Steve Smith, Connie Campbell, and Darby Ray have all offered helpful feedback or inspiration along the way. I am also thankful for the aid of other scholars, Annalisa Azzoni, John C. Reeves, J. Edward Wright, and John Kaltner. I must also thank the Prentice Hall reviewers who made many excellent criticisms and suggestions—some of them precisely opposing each other—that I have used to improve this work. I am truly grateful for their hours and insights. In the summers of 2003 and 2004, a grant from the Hearin Foundation allowed the work on this project to continue. Of course, my Prentice Hall editors and staff have made it possible and better—Mical Moser, Jennifer Murtoff, Carla Worner, Sarvesh Mehrotra, and Ross Miller. The gifts of perspective and patience have been provided by Bonnie, Spencer, Karissa, Austin, Sophia, and my friends Craig, and Jenn even when they didn't know it.

And now the requisite disclaimer: All the errors in the following pages are mine, and can't be blamed on anyone else. And all the brilliant ideas are mine too, except for the ones that I learned from so many other scholars and teachers over the years. In fact, this book is dedicated to four of my beloved teachers; I know full well that they let me stand on their shoulders, and still I often don't see as far as they.

James Bowley

What Is a Bible?

CHAPTER OUTLINE

The Bible Is Not a Book

The first thing we should make clear as we begin this tour is that the Bible you may have on the desk or table next to you is not a book. Allow me to explain. Our word *bible* comes from a plural form of the ancient Greek word *biblion*, which is properly translated "book" and is used in ancient literature to refer to a treatise, much like our word *book*, or a subdivision of a treatise, much like our word *volume. Biblion* derives from *byblos*, the Greek name for the stalk of the papyrus plant from which sheets of paper were made in ancient Egypt. The plural form of *biblion* is *biblia*, and it is from the plural *biblia* that the English (through Latin) word *bible* comes. But, today its original plural sense is not maintained; everyone thinks *bible* is singular. In fact, even before the English use of the word *bible*, the Latin form of the word *biblia* was used as if it were singular. This shift from plural to singular occurred gradually; however, it was completed prior to the ninth century CE. This linguistic shift—one that occurred long after all parts of the biblical

P OSTER 1.1

The making of scrolls has no end, and much study makes one tired.

—QOHELET (JEWISH SCHOLAR, FOURTH CENTURY BCE)

A big scroll is a big evil.

—CALLIMACHUS (GREEK SCHOLAR, THIRD CENTURY BCE)

library were written—is just one facet of the conceptual change in which the many *biblia* came to be regarded as one work. A Bible is a collection of books.

Books and Scrolls

Even the ancient *biblion* or *biblos* was not quite a book as we in the modern world think of it. All of the writings now contained in anyone's Bible were composed in the days before the invention of the codex. *Codex* is the Latin word for *book*, the physical entity in which sheets of papyrus or parchment (processed animal hide) were folded or stacked together and fixed, in order, between two covers, which were usually made of a sturdier material such as leather. The invention of codex in the late first and early second centuries CE and its development changed the world— and you have proof in your hands right now. You are reading a codex, a stack of sheets of paper between two covers.

In Jewish culture prior to the codex, books were written in the scroll format. Scrolls were rolls of papyrus or tanned leather that were divided into columns. They could be long or short, wide or narrow. They were usually rolled from just one end, starting with the last of the book's content so that the book's beginning was seen first by anyone who picked it up to read. Short rolls may be less than a foot in length, with only a column or two of writing; long rolls may be as long as 25 to 30 feet (7.62 to 9.14 m) with dozens of columns. Anything much more than that could become somewhat unwieldy to use. If we want to think about biblical writings in their original form, we should imagine holding, rolling, and reading scrolls that are 5 to 30 feet (1.52 to 9.14 m) long. In the greatest manuscript discovery of ancient Jewish scrolls, found from 1947 to 1956 in caves near the Dead Sea at a site called **Qumran,** the two longest rolls are the scroll of Isaiah and the scroll known as the Temple Scroll. The first of these measures about 24 feet, 4 inches (7.42 m) by 1 foot (.3 m) wide with 54 columns, and the second measures about 26 feet, 8 inches (8.13 m) with 67 columns (Burrows 1954, 19; Yadin 1983, 1:8).

For some users, very long scrolls seemed just too impractical, and so for the sake of convenience, Greek and Roman scroll makers commonly divided a single composition into two or more rolls—the equivalent of our multivolume composition. For example, if you open your Bible and scan the table of contents, you will see the books called 1 Samuel and 2 Samuel, which are really one composition divided into two scrolls so as not to create one long, unwieldy scroll. Three works, Samuel, Kings, and Chronicles, are by far the longest compositions in our library and after they were translated into Greek, they were divided into two scrolls. However, no **Hebrew** manuscripts until the fifteenth century CE divide them. Among the Dead Sea Scrolls manuscripts is a copy of Samuel with what we call 1 and 2 Samuel on the same roll. Also, Hebrew codices of the tenth and eleventh centuries CE do not make the book divisions. So we can see that in regard to these three books, modern Bibles have all followed the Greek and Latin traditions.

But what about a really short composition? Couldn't a small piece of papyrus or leather quite easily be misplaced or damaged? Have you ever lost a one-page homework assignment in a stack of papers on your desk? The answer to the first question (you answer the second) is yes, and one solution was to copy several small compositions onto one roll. By the second century BCE, the writings now known as the twelve minor prophets (Hosea, Joel, Amos, Obadiah, Jonah, Micah, Nahum, Habakkuk, Zephaniah, Haggai, Zechariah, Malachi) were already sometimes combined onto one single scroll.

So as we imagine the early days of the library we are entering, we should think of separate scrolls, each one independently written and copied by hand. When we come to Chapter 3 we'll review the historical situations of the people of **Israel,** or **Jews,** but for now, imagine that we are on a tour of the scrollery (similar to a library) of the temple in Jerusalem in the first century BCE. As we stand in the doorway, what do we see? There are a few tables about a foot high with writing implements and unused rolls of parchment and papyrus on them; there are knives for cutting papyrus sheets or animal skin and for scoring the scroll with guidelines or marks for columns and lines within columns. We notice thin leather strings, used for sewing pieces of the "paper" together to make longer scrolls. We see already written scrolls, some wrapped in linen, in clay jars, cupboards, or wooden boxes by the walls. Some of these boxes are labeled with names of scrolls or persons. In some cases the name or title of the scroll is written directly on the outside of the roll for easy identification. On the floor in one corner are some pieces of broken pottery and some sheets of leather that have random letters and words on them—obviously the doodles of scribes or trainees practicing or trying out a new stylus on "scratch paper" (Discoveries 2000, 341). A scribe sits on the floor, legs crossed, with a flat board in his lap. He is looking back and forth between two texts, apparently recopying the contents of a rather ragged looking scroll that lies on the floor beside him onto a new piece of parchment in his lap. Another seated scribe is copying portions of several scrolls onto the roll on the low table in front of him. About every four or five words, he dips his stylus, a pen made of a reed or stick, into one of the several small pots of black or reddish brown ink, made from a mixture of charcoal (or iron oxide), gum, and oil (King and Stager 2001, 310). Most conspicuous to the modern time traveler, there is not a true book, that is, a codex, anywhere to be seen. And now we can begin to see why the Bible is much more like a library than it is like a single book.

Of course, in the modern world Bibles do exist as single books for most people, but there are exceptions. In Jewish synagogues, for example, scrolls are still valued

DISPLAY 1.1 | EGYPTIAN SCRIBES AT WORK

and used for public reading. But in most places in our society, the codex has replaced the roll, and so the Bible is thought of as a single book. However, for the purpose of understanding the ancient books themselves *as they were written historically,* and not as "chapters" of one book, it is important that they be studied in such a way that their *individual integrity* is not compromised. This is because, in actuality, over the course of hundreds of years, dozens of different authors wrote distinct compositions. Certainly some connections exist among some of the scrolls, including common ideas and expressions, but it would not reflect the historical reality to assume or expect some sort of unity among the scrolls, such as one might expect of a book by a single author.

In any number of settings, you've probably heard someone say, "The Bible says . . . " Upon reflection, such a statement becomes quite problematic. It would not make much sense to stand in front of our local library and declare, "The library says . . . " and then go on to quote from *one* book, as if by citing words from *one* book we are a quoting *the library.* (I suppose it is remotely possible that the person may be trying to make a point about the librarian's selections or agenda, but that is rarely the point when we hear the words "The Bible says . . . ") We know that the books in our local library say different things and that what one of them says should not be credited to the others, both for the sake of accuracy and for the sake of recognizing each book's individuality and integrity. So too, it is crucial to remember that our Bibles do not comprise one book and that the current form of most Bibles (pages between two covers) is simply a convenient way of presenting individual scrolls written during many centuries by dozens of authors in various forms and genres. If we remember this, we will be more likely to respect the integrity of each individual composition, and we also will be in a more suitable frame of mind for considering and understanding each writing's unique historical reality and unique meanings.

The Bible or Bibles?

Before viewing more of the ancient library, we should pause to consider the modern state of the Bible. For most people today, *the Bible* connotes a tangible, definable entity. People carry the Bible to a college class, read from the Bible in **synagogue** or **church,** or see the Bible in the hands of television preachers. In the United States, presidents and public officials are sworn into office with their right hands on a Bible. It seems clear that the Bible is an important cultural icon, yet there is really no single entity that everyone agrees is *the* Bible. If we stopped to compare what is really between the covers of the world's Bibles, we would immediately discover a wide variety of formats that feature conflicting tables of contents, different books, books having the same name but very different content, and divergent arrangements of parts or groups of texts. These discrepancies are by no means minor, and so if we are to explore this thing called the Bible, we must determine the destination of our tour. The undeniable reality is that there is no such thing as *the* Bible; there are only Bibl*es*. That is to say, books with *Bible* on the cover have significantly different contents inside the covers. The dozens of particular forms and arrangements displayed in our Bibles today have been decided upon by the various religious communities that use them or by the organizations that publish them: There is no worldwide standard for Bibles. Here too, thinking of the Bible as a library can be helpful. The collection of books in my neighborhood library may be similar to other libraries in my city, but I'm sure there are differences also. So, too, the biblical libraries of different religious communities, such as Jewish, Catholic, **Orthodox,** and Protestant groups, all have similarities but also many differences.

The list of books that are in any particular community's Bible is sometimes known as the **canon** of that tradition. *Canon* used this way means a list of books that are considered holy or in some sense authoritative. A list of books necessarily includes some and excludes others and, unless there is an understanding to the contrary, it always implies the closing of the canon simply by ending. So, for example, it might be asked, "What books are in the Christian canon?" Put another way, this question could read, "What books does **Christianity** revere as sacred or as having authority?" Having introduced the frequently used term *canon*, I must immediately add that it is not such a good term to use for the early history of our biblical library because it too is an anachronistic idea. *Canon*, in the sense of a list of books

Study Room 1.1 ANCIENT LIBRARIES

We know that libraries or writing depositories existed throughout the ancient world of the Fertile Crescent. They are nearly always found in part of a royal complex.

In Ebla, now in northwest Syria, more than 17,000 well-preserved clay tablets of bureaucratic and literary texts dating to around 2500 BCE were found by archaeologists in the 1970s.

Mesopotamian cultures (e.g., Babylonia and Assyria) also boasted libraries. Assyrians started libraries at least by the thirteenth century BCE. Perhaps the most famous is that of the Assyrian king Ashurbanipal (ruled from 668 to 627 BCE) at Nineveh. The clay tablets there number over 1,500. We even have a copy of his instructions to go throughout the land searching for specific books and gathering them for his library. (Apparently the king thought his interlibrary loan privileges were unlimited!) The patron God of the library and scribes was Nabu. His shrine in Borsippa was called Ezida and so, by extension, that became the name of other libraries. These libraries have become a great boon for our knowledge of ancient **Mesopotamia.**

Although there are some references in various sources to libraries in Egypt prior to the arrival of the Greek rulers, no actual library has been found. However, the most famous and likely the largest library in the ancient world, containing about 75,000 individual works, was founded in Alexandria, Egypt, in the late fourth century BCE. This library became a famous study center throughout the Hellenistic period and drew many Greek scholars. The librarians collected works in Greek and sponsored the translation of works in other languages into Greek. For example, the Torah (Genesis, Exodus, Leviticus, Numbers, and Deuteronomy) of the Jews, who lived in Alexandria in large numbers, was translated for the library according to a second-century BCE account. The collection was mostly on papyrus.

Unfortunately, the library at Alexandria and its contents were eventually destroyed. Scholars are still debating the reasons for the destruction.

The largest discovered cache of Hebrew writings is the **Dead Sea Scrolls,** which were found in 11 different caves near an abandoned settlement at the northwest corner of the Dead Sea. It is highly probable that the scrolls (mostly treated skins) were placed in the caves by members of the nearby Qumran settlement. The more than 900 scrolls, many in fragmentary condition, date from the third century BCE to the first century CE.

What other ancient libraries do you know of? How do these numbers compare to modern libraries? What can be said about civilizations that maintain libraries?

For this information and more, see:

Casson, Lionel. *Libraries in the Ancient World.*
New Haven, CT.: Yale, 2001.

POSTER 1.2

The Bible does not exist; there are only Bibles.

regarded as authoritative or holy, was not used until the late fourth century CE, and then only by Christians. As we think of the scrolls of our biblical library being written, we should not imagine that the authors wondered or hoped that their work might make it into the canon or into the Bible. There is no evidence of such a list or of some sort of broadly and officially accepted and restrictive collection until *long after* all the scrolls of our library were written. But in the modern world, many communities have a definite canon, a definite list of books that they have selected and accepted as authoritative, a bible with a set number of books.

So, if *the* Bible does not exist, that is, if there is not just one thing that is called the Bible, what are these different Bibles we see? I once sat in a Presbyterian church awaiting the beginning of a Friday night orchestral concert. Behind me two people thumbed through a Bible in the pew rack. I overheard one remark to the other, "Look, this Bible has a book called Zephaniah. It must be just in the Presbyterian Bible because it's not in the Baptist Bible." In this case the gentleman was wrong, but he was not completely off the mark; he was at least aware of the existence of different canons and different Bibles. Presbyterian and Baptist Bibles both have the book of Zephaniah. In fact, because both groups are Protestants, all 66 of their books are the same. But there are some canon differences among various Christian groups, as we will see shortly. The most widely known difference in modern Bibles is that between Jewish Bibles and Christian Bibles. The Jewish biblical library contains 24 books, whereas Christian libraries contain more. How many more? The answer depends on which Christian community. But this is only the beginning of the subject. For example, ancient and modern Samaritans (a small religious group living in Israel, closely related to the Jews) and the ancient and modern Ethiopian Christian Church both hold what we would call "the Bible" as sacred. But the Samaritan Bible contains only five books and the Ethiopian Orthodox Bible more than 80! If we think of a Bible as a library instead of a single book, this great divergence and all of those in between are easily grasped. If we go into a Jewish library, we find 24 books on the shelves, but when we go next door to the Roman Catholic library we find 73 volumes, and they are divided into two major sections—the **Old Testament** and the **New Testament.** When we visit a Protestant friend's sacred library, we notice that it, too, is divided into Old and New Testaments, but it only has 66 books, seven fewer than the Roman Catholic Bible. When we enter a library of the Orthodox Christian Churches down the block, such as a Greek Orthodox Church, we find that its "shelves" hold 76 different books, and we might be told by the librarian that even within the various Orthodox churches the number varies. So, the Bible is clearly many different things.

There are even more differences beyond just the numbers of books. The Jewish Bible's 24 books are counted differently than the same writings in Christian Bibles.

For example, the Jewish Bible has three large books commonly known by the English titles of Samuel, Kings, and Chronicles. They are counted as just one book each. However, in Christian Bibles, each one is divided into two parts for a total of six books. Somewhere in the scrolls' copying history a scribe decided to divide them into two parts, probably for the sake of physical convenience in a scroll format, because an overly long scroll could be unmanageable. (Remember, however, that one of the Dead Sea scrolls of Samuel was not divided into two.) But the division is retained even in the codex format where the division serves no similar usefulness. Ezra-Nehemiah is counted as one book in Jewish Bibles, but it is split into two distinct works in Christian Bibles, Ezra and Nehemiah (This division is not because of length; see Chapter 3). Similarly, the Jewish Bible contains a book known as The Twelve, which is subdivided in Christian Bibles into 12 separate books; the so-called minor prophets.

In addition to these differences of division, the books in the library are arranged differently, too. The last book of most Jewish Bibles is Chronicles, while most Christian Bibles close the Old Testament with the book of Malachi. This is just one of numerous arrangement differences. So, the Bible is a collection of writings that can be divided and arranged in many different ways.

And that is not all the differences. All Christian Bibles, whether Catholic, Orthodox, Ethiopian, or Protestant, include books, usually 27 of them, in a section called the New Testament. These books, composed in Greek in the mid- to late first century, all reflect distinctly Christian ideas and are not a part of any Jewish or Samaritan Bible. When we look at the first section of a Christian Bible, the Old Testament, we find that many of its books match the 24 books of the Jewish Bible. But things get complicated when we realize that not all Christian Bibles have the same books in the Old Testament. Bibles printed by and for Protestant Christians since the eighteenth century usually contain only 39 books in the Old Testaments seven fewer than the 46 books of the Roman Catholic Old Testament and ten fewer than the 49 books of Orthodox Churches. The seven books left out of most Protestant Bibles are Tobit, Judith, Wisdom of Solomon, Ecclesiasticus (also known as Sirach or Ben Sira), Baruch, and 1 and 2 Maccabees. Protestants call these "extra" books the **Apocrypha** and have sometimes included them as a separate section in a Bible edition. (For example, see the original 1611 King James Version and Martin Luther's Bible of 1534.) The Orthodox Bible contains these seven and also 3 and 4 Maccabees and the Letter of Jeremiah. So, the Christian Bible contains a New Testament, and it may contain books such as Tobit or 3 Maccabees. The Jewish and Samaritan Bibles contain none of these.

But we need to go still deeper. Unlike the Samaritan Bible, Jewish and Christian Bibles contain a book named Daniel. If we open up that book we find that not all Daniels are the same. In Jewish and Protestant libraries, Daniel is a relatively short book of 12 chapters. But in Catholic and Orthodox Bibles it has three other lengthy chapters. Something similar occurs with the book called Esther. In Catholic and Orthodox Bibles, Esther contains six major components (107 verses) not found in the Esther of Jewish or Protestant Bibles, and there are other significant textual differences. All in all, the additions and differences are so dramatic that the character of the book is radically altered. In the longer version used by Catholics and Orthodox Christians, the story is a very religious drama with frequent mentions of

Poster 1.3
Many Bibles[a]

#	Samaritan Library	Jewish Library	Roman Catholic Library	Orthodox Library[b]	Ethiopic Orthodox Library[c]	Protestant Library
1	Genesis	Genesis	Genesis	Genesis	Genesis	Genesis
2	Exodus	Exodus	Exodus	Exodus	Exodus	Exodus
3	Leviticus	Leviticus	Leviticus	Leviticus	Leviticus	Leviticus
4	Numbers	Numbers	Numbers	Numbers	Numbers	Numbers
5	Deuteronomy	Deuteronomy	Deuteronomy	Deuteronomy	Deuteronomy	Deuteronomy
6		Joshua	Joshua	Joshua	Joshua	Joshua
7		Judges	Judges	Judges	Judges	Judges
8		Samuel	Ruth	Ruth	Ruth	Ruth
9		Kings	1 Samuel	1 Samuel	Samuel	1 Samuel
10		Isaiah	2 Samuel	2 Samuel	Kings	2 Samuel
11		Jeremiah (long)	1 Kings	1 Kings	Chronicles	1 Kings
12		Ezekiel	2 Kings	2 Kings	Ezra-Nehemiah	2 Kings
13		The Twelve (Hosea, Joel, Amos, Obadiah, Jonah, Micah, Nahum, Habakkuk, Zephaniah, Haggai, Zechariah, Malachi)	1 Chronicles	1 Chronicles	Tobit	1 Chronicles
14		Psalms (150)	2 Chronicles	2 Chronicles	Judith	2 Chronicles
15		Job	Ezra	1 Esdras	Esther (long)	Ezra
16		Proverbs	Nehemiah	2 Esdras (Ezra)	1 Maccabees	Nehemiah
17		Ruth	Tobit	Nehemiah	2 Maccabees	Esther (short)
18			Judith	Tobit	Job	Job
19			Esther (long)	Judith	Psalms	Psalms (150)
20			1 Maccabees	Esther (long)	Proverbs	Proverbs
21			2 Maccabees	1 Maccabees	Ecclesiastes	Ecclesiastes
22			Job	2 Maccabees	Song of Songs	Song of Songs
23			Psalms (150)	3 Maccabees	Wisdom of Solomon	Isaiah
24			Proverbs	Psalms (151)	Sirach (Ecclesiasticus, or Ben Sira)	Jeremiah (long)
25			Ecclesiastes	Job		Lamentations

Samaritan Library	Jewish Library	Roman Catholic Library	Orthodox Library[b]	Ethiopic Orthodox Library[c]	Protestant Library
	18. Song of Songs	26. Song of Songs	26. Proverbs	26. Isaiah	26. Ezekiel
	19. Ecclesiastes	27. Wisdom of Solomon	27. Ecclesiastes	27. Jeremiah	27. Daniel (short)
	20. Lamentations	28. Sirach (Ecclesiasticus or Ben Sira)	28. Song of Songs	28. Lamentations	28. Hosea
	21. Esther (short)	29. Isaiah	29. Wisdom of Solomon	29. Baruch (includes Letter of Jeremiah)	29. Joel
	22. Daniel (short)	30. Jeremiah (long)	30. Sirach (Ecclesiasticus or Ben Sira)	30. Ezekiel	30. Amos
	23. Ezra-Nehemiah	31. Lamentations	31. Hosea	31. Daniel (long)	31. Obadiah
	24. Chronicles	32. Baruch (with Letter of Jeremiah)	32. Amos	32. Hosea	32. Jonah
		33. Ezekiel	33. Micah	33. Joel	33. Micah
		34. Daniel (long)	34. Joel	34. Amos	34. Nahum
		35. Hosea	35. Obadiah	35. Obadiah	35. Habakkuk
		36. Joel	36. Jonah	36. Jonah	36. Zephaniah
		37. Amos	37. Nahum	37. Micah	37. Haggai
		38. Obadiah	38. Habakkuk	38. Nahum	38. Zechariah
		39. Jonah	39. Zephaniah	39. Habakkuk	39. Malachi
		40. Micah	40. Haggai	40. Zephaniah	40. Matthew
		41. Nahum	41. Zechariah	41. Haggai	41. Mark
		42. Habakkuk	42. Malachi	42. Zechariah	42. Luke
		43. Zephaniah	43. Isaiah	43. Malachi	43. John
		44. Haggai	44. Jeremiah (short)	44. Jubilees	44. Acts
		45. Zechariah	45. Baruch	45. 1 Enoch	45. Romans
		46. Malachi	46. Lamentations	46. Josippon's History of the Jews	46. 1 Corinthians
		47. Matthew	47. Letter of Jeremiah	47. Matthew	47. 2 Corinthians
		48. Mark	48. Ezekiel	48. Mark	48. Galatians
		49. Luke	49. Daniel (long)	49. Luke	49. Ephesians
		50. John	50. Matthew	50. John	50. Philippians
		51. Acts	51. Mark	51. Acts	51. Colossians
		52. Romans	52. Luke	52. Romans	52. 1 Thessalonians
		53. 1 Corinthians	53. John	53. 1 Corinthians	53. 2 Thessalonians
		54. 2 Corinthians	54. Acts	54. 2 Corinthians	54. 1 Timothy

55. Galatians	55. Romans	55. Galatians	55. 2 Timothy
56. Ephesians	56. 1 Corinthians	56. Ephesians	56. Titus
57. Philippians	57. 2 Corinthians	57. Philippians	57. Philemon
58. Colossians	58. Galatians	58. Colossians	58. Hebrews
59. 1 Thessalonians	59. Ephesians	59. 1 Thessalonians	59. James
60. 2 Thessalonians	60. Philippians	60. 2 Thessalonians	60. 1 Peter
61. 1 Timothy	61. Colossians	61. 1 Timothy	61. 2 Peter
62. 2 Timothy	62. 1 Thessalonians	62. 2 Timothy	62. 1 John
63. Titus	63. 2 Thessalonians	63. Titus	63. 2 John
64. Philemon	64. 1 Timothy	64. Philemon	64. 3 John
65. Hebrews	65. 2 Timothy	65. Hebrews	65. Jude
66. James	66. Titus	66. James	66. Revelation
67. 1 Peter	67. Philemon	67. 1 Peter	
68. 2 Peter	68. Hebrews	68. 2 Peter	
69. 1 John	69. James	69. 1 John	
70. 2 John	70. 1 Peter	70. 2 John	
71. 3 John	71. 2 Peter	71. 3 John	
72. Jude	72. 1 John	72. Jude	
73. Revelation	73. 2 John	73. Revelation	
	74. 3 John	74. Sinodos	
	75. Jude	75. 2 Simodos	
	76. Revelation	76. 3 Simodos	
		77. 4 Simodos	
		78. 1 Book of the Covenant	
		79. 2 Book of the Covenant	
		80. Clement	
		81. Didascalia	

aBased on Alexander, Kusko, Decker-Lucke, Ernest, and Petersen, eds. 1999, Appendix D.

bThis list refers to the Greek and Russian Orthodox churches. An appendix includes 4 Maccabees, Prayer of Manasseh, and, in Slavonic Orthodox tradition, 3 Esdras.

cThere are actually at least three different canon traditions in the Ethiopic Orthodox tradition; though the number 81 is standard, it is arrived at in different ways.

God. In the shorter version found in Jewish and Protestant Bibles, God is not mentioned at all and the book is often considered completely secular. Of course, in each community, the form used is accepted as the "right" one. So, the Bible may have a long, pious Esther a short, secular Esther, or no Esther at all.

We could mention other differences, but we'll stop here with one final example to demonstrate that there is no single entity called the Bible. When we compare the long book called Jeremiah in various English Bibles, we find that in Bibles of the Orthodox tradition it is not nearly as long (about one-sixth shorter, or 50 pages instead of 60) (Tov 2001, 320), and many chapters and verses are found in a different order from that in the Jeremiah in Jewish, Catholic, and Protestant Bibles. A little investigation reveals that the Orthodox Jeremiah has been translated from a different ancient version of Jeremiah—a Greek one instead of a Hebrew one. We will talk more about this when we discuss the famous Dead Sea scrolls. So, the Bible may have one of two versions of Jeremiah or may not have Jeremiah at all.

Which Library Are We Touring?

A very practical question! Since there are many Bibles, we must choose which Bible—which library—to tour. This *Guided Tour* might be called primarily an exploration of the 24 scrolls of the Jewish library, also known as the Hebrew Bible, because we will not stop after the five books of the Samaritan Bible and we will not venture into the New Testament part of Christian Bibles. However, we will briefly consider some Jewish writing beyond the Hebrew Bible. For the following reasons then, our tour cannot properly be called simply a tour of the (modern) Jewish Bible:

- We will stop briefly to look at books and forms of books that are in some Christian Old Testaments but that are not in the modern Jewish library. These additional books were all composed by Jews before the advent of Christianity and were at one time revered by Jewish communities, but they have not been included in the Bibles of **rabbinic Judaism,** the dominant Jewish tradition since the third century BCE.

- As we investigate individual books, we will often talk about the different versions of one book that existed in antiquity, and so our study will not be limited to the modern form of a Jewish (or any other) Bible, in much the same way an English literature class might study and compare the various editions, early and late, short and long, of Walt Whitman's *Leaves of Grass.*

- Finally, as we make our way on our library tour, we will have occasion to consider interesting readings and interpretations of our scrolls from Muslim, Christian, and Jewish sources. All three of these world religions are inextricably linked to this great library and to each other, and they offer us fascinating material to enhance our experience and our historical and religious awareness.

Because of the diversity of format and content that Bibles display, we will avoid using the rather inaccurate term *the Bible.* Instead, we will use the terms *biblical literature* or *library* or even just *Bible* to designate this large body of ancient Jewish literature not strictly limited by any tradition's official canon.

Naming the Library

Through the centuries, this library has been called many different things, depending on which community or individual is using the library. *Bible* is certainly not the oldest title.

In the second century BCE the Jewish author of the prologue to the book of Sirach, also called Ben Sira or Ecclesiasticus, refers three times to a collection of Jewish writings as "the law, the prophets, and the other writings" or "the rest of the books." This shows that the scrolls were probably grouped, and the recurrence of the phrase suggests that this is the author's preferred way of referring to this literary heritage, though "law, prophets, and other writings" may not be an official title. One of the most fascinating documents among the Dead Sea Scrolls, a formal letter of sorts, refers to some writings as "the book of Moses, the books of the prophets, and David" (4QMMT C.10). Similarly, **Philo,** a prolific Jewish philosopher of Alexandria (ca. 20 BCE to 40 CE) speaks of "laws, oracles through prophets, and hymns, and others" (*Contemplative Life* 25). Luke, an author in the Christian New Testament, writes in the first century of the "law of Moses, the prophets, and the psalms" (Luke 24.44). Frequently the collective sense of Jewish writings is given the two-part division "law and prophets," both in New Testament writings (e.g., Matthew 5.17; 7.12; 22.40; Luke 16.16) and in the Dead Sea Scrolls (e.g., 1QS 1.2–3). Recall that the content of these categories may not match what we think of today as being in those same categories, and the ancient sources do not give us a list. In centuries past, Moses was considered the author of numerous books that are not part of Bibles today, and what books were considered prophetic or authoritative for any given Jewish group is not at all definite. Now we must be clear that these designations do not imply the existence or crystallization of a canon, nor the establishment of an official and formal collection, nor an official title for a collection. Certainly there is no listing of the scrolls that might be grouped under each of the headings *law, prophets,* and *other writings.* For those reasons I have not capitalized them as titles in this paragraph.

Other more generic terms were also used by Jews and Christians in antiquity to refer to their special books. In Greek, probably the closest to the modern term *Bible,* was *graphé,* "writing" (*graphai,* plural). Some use *hierai graphai,* "sacred writings" (Josephus, *On Antiquity of the Jews* 2.45). *Graphai* could also be used without an adjective to refer to Jewish (and later Christian) sacred texts (e.g., Matthew 21.42) and, though the plural form is more common when speaking of more than one scroll, occasionally the singular is used as a collective plural for the group (e.g., 2 Timothy 3.16; 2 Peter 1.20). *Graphé* was translated literally into Latin as *scriptura* and eventually into English as the word *scripture,* which to this day is used in singular or plural to refer to the collection of Jewish and Christian sacred texts. A similar designation in Greek was *hiera gramata,* "sacred writings." This term was used for the sacred writings of any people; already in the fifth century BCE the famed Greek historian Herodotus spoke of the *hiera gramata* of the Egyptians (2.36). Centuries later, Jews and Christians used the term to refer to hallowed writings, with or without the adjective "sacred" (Josephus, *Against Apion* 1.42, 2 Timothy 3.15).

In Hebrew the equivalent term, *kitvé ha-qodesh,* "writings of holiness, holy writings," is found in the Mishna (ca. 200 CE) to refer to the collection of Jewish scriptures (*Yadayim* 3.5). The Greek term *bibliotheca,* "collection of books," was used in the early first century BCE by the Jewish author of 2 Maccabees (2.13) in reference to the book-gathering activity of Nehemiah. Centuries later, the Christian scholar Jerome (342 to 420 CE) would use the equivalent Latin term to refer to the sacred library of scripture.

A specifically Jewish designation is *Miqra,* a Hebrew word literally meaning "reading, recitation, or calling," which has been used to describe the collection of scriptures at least since times of the **Talmud** (ca. 500 CE, see *Babylonian Talmud Taanit* 68a). The word *Miqra* shares its origin with the Arabic word *Qur'an,* which means "recitation." Another common title within **Judaism** is *Tanakh* or *Tanak.* This name is based on an acronym (T-N-K) using the heading of the divisions of the library: **Torah** (Instruction), **Neviim** (Prophets), **Ketuvim** (Writings).

The terms *Old Testament* and *New Testament* are exclusively Christian theological designations in their origin. They arose in the late second century as part of an internal Christian dispute regarding the Christian use of Jewish scriptures. *Testament* is used in the sense of "covenant" and the *Old* and *New* aspects of the names seem to have been originally intended to show both the continuity of the covenant (God's arranged relationship with his people) and to stress the distinctly Christian possession of God's new and superior covenantal work. Today there is an ongoing discussion among some people in the Christian community about the nature and usefulness of these terms and about alternative titles, such as *First Testament* and *Second Testament.* In academic discussions of biblical literature, many people make genuine attempts to be as open, respectful, and unprejudiced as possible in the naming of the biblical literature. Although *Old Testament* became the most common term in those parts of the world dominated by Christianity, this Christian theological term may be considered objectionable in an educational context that seeks to welcome participants from all perspectives. As a result, the rather generic term *Hebrew Bible* has come to be widely used, and I use it in this book. *Hebrew,* of course, refers to the original language of nearly all the texts and so distinguishes these books from the writings of the Christian New Testament, which were penned in Greek. The philosophical and religious point is worth making that biblical literature is not owned by any one religious community, and so using terms that are descriptive and as non-prejudicial and nonsectarian as possible is appropriate. In classrooms today, people of every background are welcomed to the lively conversation about this great literature and, in a setting of free inquiry, no religion should claim control or exclusive possession of these texts. This *Guided Tour* is certainly intended to warmly welcome *all* who are curious about this great library, and I see great merit in using a title that attempts to reflect that openness.

Arranging the Library

Different libraries in the modern world use different systems to bring order to their books. We use the Library of Congress system; a few might still use the Dewey decimal classification system, and there are others too. Similarly, biblical libraries have been arranged differently in different times and places. Of course, all of these fixed arrangements are necessitated by the use of the codex, where different books must be bound together in a certain order. When all these books existed on separate scrolls, physically ordering them was much less important and much more variable. True, the content of some scrolls naturally followed that of others (e.g., Exodus after Genesis), and sometimes the contents of short scrolls were written consecutively on one roll, presumably for the sake of convenience. But every time a codex was used, it was necessary to fix an arrangement of the entire library. If you look back at our charts of scrolls on pp. 9–11, you will see the variations in modern Christian traditions by comparing the Old Testament order of the Roman Catholic Bible with the order found in a Protestant Bible. Our oldest Jewish codex evidence also gives a varied picture. The first nine books in Jewish codices, which more or less carry a continuous storyline, are found always in the following order: Genesis, Exodus, Leviticus, Numbers, Deuteronomy, Joshua, Judges, Samuel, Kings. After that the order varies greatly depending on the list or manuscript. This variety should remind us that each of these works began as individual scrolls that should be read with awareness of their individual integrity.

Subsections in the Library

We know from evidence in various sources that long before the advent of the codex the scrolls were sometimes mentally (and likely in physical scroll rooms also) divided into groups, or subgroups. For example, we hear of the books of Moses or the books of the prophets and The Twelve as early as the second century BCE. This practice continued and was eventually ingrained in Jewish tradition. For pragmatic purposes, this *Guided Tour* will follow the traditional order that one finds in most modern editions of Tanakh.

The Rare Books Room: Our Oldest Manuscripts

If you are a book collector, you may own some original editions. Unfortunately, we do not have any of the original editions of any form of any biblical scroll. Just what the "original" is of any particular biblical book is quite complicated due to the growth through time of many scrolls. Even without the originals, our "rare books room," that is, the collection of the oldest copies of biblical books, is quite fascinating. I love going into rare books rooms of museums or libraries, and here in our library a quick look at a few displays is well worth the time because, ultimately, all the thousands of forms and translations of Bibles that exist in our modern world go back to these manuscripts, which are preserved in several different libraries throughout the world.

The Dead Sea Scrolls

Our oldest forms of any book now in the biblical library come from what are now called the Dead Sea Scrolls (DSS). These famous manuscripts, which date from about 200 BCE to 50 CE, were discovered in caves near the Dead Sea from 1947 to

DISPLAY 1.2 | UNROLLED SILVER AMULET SCROLL OF PRIESTLY BLESSING

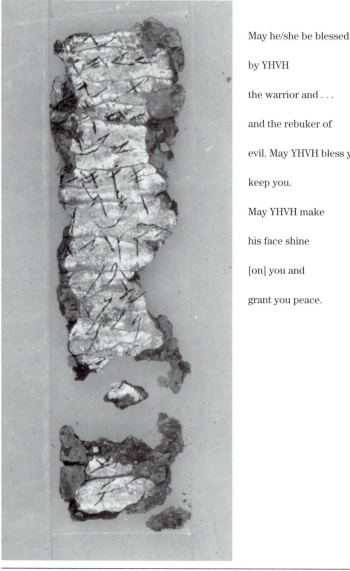

May he/she be blessed

by YHVH

the warrior and . . .

and the rebuker of

evil. May YHVH bless you,

keep you.

May YHVH make

his face shine

[on] you and

grant you peace.

Translation of Barkay, 334 modified.

1956 at a site called Qumran. Of the about 900 scrolls discovered (some very fragmentary), slightly more than 200 scrolls are of books that are included in the modern Hebrew Bible (see Display 7.1). It is clear, though, that the devout Jewish community who produced the scrolls also highly valued and considered other books authoritative that are not in modern Hebrew Bibles. In addition, they probably valued only slightly or not at all some books of current Bibles, such as Esther and Chronicles. In fact, as you already know, they had no such designation as *Bible*. They used the scroll format exclusively, and they have no preserved list of holy books or even an explicit notion of canon. Thus, it is misleading to apply terms such as *Bible* or *canon* to literature of this community and of this period.

Furthermore, frequently we have found that among these manuscripts there are several different forms of the same book. For instance, six texts were found for the book of Jeremiah, including fragments of both a long version and an older short version. Finally, we must point out that these manuscripts are a thousand or more years older than any Hebrew Bible texts that we had prior to 1947, and so they are of exceptional value. They provide direct evidence of "biblical" texts as they existed in antiquity. For the study of biblical texts, the Dead Sea Scrolls could hardly be overrated, especially when we consider that up until about 1500 CE all manuscripts had to be copied by hand, a daunting task fraught with numerous pitfalls. Most of these scrolls are now carefully preserved in the Israel Museum and the Palestine Archaeology Museum, both of which are located in Jerusalem.

A Rare Find

Even older than the Dead Sea Scrolls are two tiny silver amulets that were discovered in the burial chamber of a **priest** near Jerusalem of the sixth century BCE. These amulets, probably worn around the neck on a string, were tiny scrolls made of finely pounded silver inscribed with a poem of blessing now contained in Numbers 6. It is clear that this poem was of great importance to the priests of Jerusalem before the amulets were meticulously crafted and long before the book of Numbers was composed. Here we have yet another example of the use of older traditional material for the composition of our biblical books. (Display 1.2)

Greek Translations

Beginning probably in the third century BCE, Jews living in the Greek-speaking Hellenistic empires translated important scrolls into Greek. Those scrolls translated into Greek that were later included in Bible codices came to be known as the **Septuagint** (abbreviated *LXX*), an anglicized Greek word that means "seventy." This unusual designation arises from an ancient story about the number of translators for the five books of the Torah. (You can read an early form of the story in a book called *Letter of Aristaeus.*) The Greek versions were eventually transmitted only by Christian communities, but for prior centuries they had been composed, copied, edited, and revised in Jewish communities. Except for a few Greek compositions, most books in LXX collections are only translations of more ancient Hebrew texts, and so, given the inherent difficulties of translation, the LXX texts are of less utility for our understanding of their Hebrew originals. However, for much of Christianity this Greek text served as the base text of Scriptures for centuries, and it is through Christian monasteries and churches that these texts were preserved. Early complete manuscripts of the LXX are the oldest codex forms of biblical books. The three oldest copies come from the fourth and fifth centuries CE and are now housed in the libraries at the Vatican and the British Museum. These Christian Bibles all contain more books than the 24 of the Hebrew Bible in their Old Testament, and they show varying arrangements of the books and differences in their New Testament canons also. (Display 1.3)

DISPLAY 1.3 | FOURTH-CENTURY CE GREEK BIBLE PAGE

Samaritan Hebrew Manuscripts

A group closely akin to Jews known as the Samaritans has maintained copies of the scrolls of Genesis, Exodus, Leviticus, Numbers, and Deuteronomy for thousands of years. For the Samaritans, none of the other Hebrew scrolls are valued as authoritative texts. But the five books that they do preserve are very important. In some cases the Samaritan texts match the Dead Sea Scroll manuscripts, indicating that their textual tradition is very old. The oldest surviving copies come from the twelfth to fourteenth centuries CE, and scholars now use them extensively for doing the work of textual **criticism**; that is, trying to understand the ancient history of writing and copying texts.

Medieval Hebrew Manuscripts

Finally, and most important for understanding modern Bibles, we come to the best preserved, though not the oldest, Hebrew manuscripts. These manuscripts are part of what is known as Masoretic texts (MT). The **Masoretes** were Jewish scholars who carefully studied and copied biblical manuscripts in the city of Tiberias on the Lake

DISPLAY 1.4 | FACSIMILE OF AN ELEVENTH-CENTURY CE MASORETIC TEXT, THE LENINGRAD CODEX

Ancient Biblical Manuscript Center

of **Galilee** from the sixth to the ninth century CE. The earliest Masoretic biblical manuscripts that survive are from the late ninth to early eleventh centuries CE. The Masoretes served the Jewish communities of their own day, and in time their reputation for accuracy grew outside the Jewish community as well. Their texts were seen as desirable by Christian scholars who favored access to the original language of their Old Testament texts. Today, Masoretic texts provided the basis for the majority of modern Bibles, Jewish and Christian (Old Testament). In the Jewish tradition and in modern Bibles of Roman Catholics and Protestants, a Masoretic text is translated into English or some other language. Popular translations such as the New Revised Standard Version, the Jewish Publication Society's Tanakh, the New International Version, as well as the seventeenth-century King James Version, are all based on Masoretic texts. This widespread use is best explained by

1. the completeness of the Masoretic texts (many of the DSS, because of natural decay, do not preserve the entire scroll),
2. the fact that they are in Hebrew (the LXX texts are translations from Hebrew into Greek); and
3. and the reputation of the Masoretes for careful textual copying. (Display 1.4)

POSTER 1.4

TEXTUAL COMPARISON OF 1 SAMUEL 10.27–11.1

LXX	MT	DSSᵃ
And destructive men said, "How will this man save us?" And they dishonored him and did not bring to him a gift.	And men of destruction said, "How will this man save us?" And they despised him and did not bring to him a gift. But he was as a deaf man. And Nahash	And men of destruction sai[d, "How will this man save us?" And] they despise[d] him and did not bring to him a gift. [And N]ahash, king of the sons of Ammon, he was oppressing the sons of Gad and the sons of Reuben with vicious-ness, and he gouged out from them a[ll] their right eyes and he brought ter[ror and fear] on [I]srael. and no man remained among the sons of Israel beyo[nd the Jordan wh]om Naha[sh, king] of the sons of Ammon, did not gouge out every right eye, except for 7,000 men who escaped the sons of Ammon and went to Jabesh-Gilead. And it was about a month later and Nahash the Ammonite went up and besieged Jabesh-[gilead].
And it was about a month later and Nahash the Ammonite went up and besieged Jabesh-gilead.	the Ammonite went up and besieged Jabesh-gilead.	

ᵃThe brackets in the DSS text show where the manuscript is damaged and has to be filled in by modern scholars.

The two oldest and most important editions of the MT come from the tenth and eleventh centuries. The Leningrad Codex was copied in 1008 CE and is now in St. Petersburg Russia. The Aleppo Codex, now in Jerusalem at the Hebrew University, was copied around 925 CE.

Comparing Manuscripts

Modern translators and biblical scholars are still wondering how to make the best use of the various manuscript traditions. Among widely used English Bibles, the

New Revised Standard Version (1989) is currently the translation that most utilizes the Dead Sea Scrolls, with their 1,000-year gain over the MT. The Jewish Publication Society's Tanakh (1985) and the New International Version (1978) also make some use of these new discoveries. Which texts would you use? Should modern Bible publishers select only one particular ancient manuscript, or should these various manuscript traditions be combined to produce modern Bibles? When the texts are different, how does one decide which text is "better" in a given situation?

Because we are here in the rare books room, surrounded by all these ancient manuscripts, let's illustrate the problem. Open up a copy of the LXX to 1 Samuel 10.27–11.1 and read a Greek text such as I have translated in the first column of Poster 1.4. If you open up the Hebrew MT (second column) to the same passage, you will find something very similar. But now if you use the much older Hebrew Dead Sea Scroll (4Q51) you will find a striking difference. I have translated all the texts quite literally for the sake of comparison.

What should a modern translator or text scholar do? Should the "extra" paragraph be included or excluded from modern Bibles? How might the differences between the MT, LXX, and DSS be explained? Is the "extra" paragraph really "extra"—that is, has it been added to an earlier composition? Or is it a "missing" paragraph—a paragraph that had been removed or lost? Was it a later addition to the DSS, or was it omitted from the MT and LXX traditions? As it turns out, so far the NRSV is the only modern translation that follows the DSS in 1 Samuel 10.27–11.1. Some individuals would argue for inclusions because of the following:

- The longer version is a much older, carefully produced text; older usually means better in textual transmission.
- There is a good textual explanation for how the paragraph was inadvertently omitted in the other texts, perhaps by a common copyist visual error of jumping from the first occurrence of a word or phrase to a later occurrence of the same (or similar) word or phrase.
- There is corroborative evidence from antiquity in the writings of the first-century Jewish historian Josephus (*Jewish Antiquities* 6.68–71) that the paragraph was in his text of Samuel.
- From a literary point of view, the story that follows in 1 Samuel 11 makes much more sense with this paragraph as its opening. Without it there is no motivation given for Nahash, and without it he does not receive an introduction in the narrative that is typical of the author of Samuel.

Textual comparisons like this can be done with ancient manuscripts for every line of every scroll in the biblical library. Later in our tour we will look at other interesting examples from specific scrolls, for example, a famous case of missing numbers in Samuel 9. Sometimes the differences are minor; sometimes, such as in Jeremiah, they are much larger than our example from 1 Samuel 10.27–11.1. Textual scholars who work on these sorts of questions in the field known as textual criticism are really historical detectives trying to recreate the process of textual development. Perhaps to some of you this brief excursion into the dusty world of old manuscripts

Study Room 1.2

TEXTUAL COMPARISON OF EXODUS 1.1–5

LXX	**MT**	**DSS**
These are the names of the sons of Israel who came to Egypt with Jacob, their father —each with his household came:	And these are the names of the sons of Israel which came to Egypt with Jacob —each and his household came:	And these are the names of the sons of Israel which came to Egypt with Jacob, their father—each and his household came:
Reuben, Simeon, Levi, Judah, Issachar Zebulun and Benjamin, Dan and Naphtali, Gad and Asher. And Joseph was in Egypt. And all the persons from Jacob were seventy-five.	Reuben, Simeon, Levi and Judah, Issachar, Zebulun and Benjamin, Dan and Naphtali, Gad and Asher. And it was that all the persons coming out of the loins of Jacob [were] seventy persons. And Joseph was in Egypt.	Reuben, Simeon, Levi and Judah, Issachar, Zebulun, Joseph and Benjamin, Dan and Naphtali, Gad and Asher. And it was that all the persons of Jacob were seventy-five persons.

This comparison is not atypical of what textual scholars encounter when comparing texts. Read the texts very carefully and compare them word by word. Note that in two texts it is explained who Jacob is. What are other differences? Check the lists of names. Where does Joseph fit? What components are in a different order? How is the summary statement at the end different? What about the difference in the total number of persons? Notice that in some places the LXX matches the MT against the DSS, in other places the MT and DSS agree against the LXX, and in still others the LXX and DSS agree against the MT. What differences do you consider major, and which are minor? Now look up Exodus 1.1–5 in a Bible and see which textual tradition is being followed. If you have a Christian New Testament, look up Acts 7.14, which refers to this passage, and speculate what tradition the author of that book followed.

might seem unnecessary. "I just want to study the Bible!" you might be thinking. However, every single modern Bible depends on decisions made by textual scholars for every line and every word, even if that decision is simply to follow one particular tradition (MT or LXX). Even then the decision is not so simple because within various copies of the individual traditions there are many differences. That is, not all LXX (or MT) manuscripts agree. Sometimes alternative readings are even noted in the margins of one text. Our oldest biblical manuscripts—remember, older nearly always means better in textual criticism—are the DSS, and they display a good deal of textual variety. Modern readers of biblical texts should be informed of the textual riches that the archeological spade and religious communities have bequeathed to us. The appearance of every word of every modern Bible is not a matter of fate or the simple reproduction of a single "original" Bible. Every word is the direct result of *choices* by generations of writers, copyists, scholars, and translators who ultimately determine for each of us what a Bible is.

Because most modern Bibles use the MT tradition as a basis, so too this *Guided Tour* will function on that basis. But don't worry, we won't stop there. As we said earlier, we will often pull off of the library shelves other editions of a scroll in order to have a look at several of its different ancient forms. If we really want to understand this literature in its ancient environment, we must make the most of the ancient forms and all the ancient evidence we can find. If we really want to know what a biblical scroll says, we must look at what the ancient manuscripts have (or don't have).

Questions for Further Study

1. What would be different about approaches to and uses of the Bible if the codex had not been invented?

2. Look at the introductory material in a Bible that you use. Does it tell you about the manuscripts it relies on? What does it say about ancient texts? What do you think Bible producers should inform their readers of?

3. Try to find as many different Bibles as possible from different religious traditions and compare them, their introductions, their table of contents, their order, and the translations of passages. What do you observe? How are they different? How are they the same?

4. How do you think the differences in manuscripts, such as those in 1 Samuel 10 or Exodus 1, should be represented in modern Bibles?

References

Abegg, Martin Jr., Peter Flint, and Eugene Ulrich. The Dead Sea Scrolls Bible. San Francisco: Harper, 1999.

Alexander, Patrick H., John F. Kusko, Shirley Decker-Lucke, James Ernest, and David Petersen, eds. *The SBL Handbook of Style*. Peabody, MA: Hendrickson, 1999.

Barkay, Gabriel, Marilyn J. Lundberg, Andrew G. Vaughn, and Bruce Zuckerman. "The Amulets from Ketef Hinnom: A New Edition and Evaluation," *Bulletin of the American Schools of Oriental Research* 334 (2004): 41–71.

Bowley, James E., ed., *Living Traditions of the Bible*. St. Louis, MD: Chalice, 1999.

————, and John C. Reeves. "Rethinking the Concept of 'Bible': Some Theses and Proposals," *Henoch: Historical and Philological Studies on Judaism* 25 (2003): 3–18.

Burrows, Millar. *The Dead Sea Scrolls,* New York: Viking, 1954.

Casson, Lionel. *Libraries in the Ancient World.* New Haven, CT: Yale, 2001.

Davies, Phillip. *Whose Bible Is It Anyway?* 2nd ed. London: T. & T. Clark, 2004.

Discoveries In the Judaean Desert vol XXXVI. Ed. by S. Pfann and P. Alexander, Oxford: Oxford University Press, 2000.

Grayson, A. K. in *Cambridge Ancient History,* III.2, 227–28 New York: Cambridge University Press, 1991.

Hallo, William W. ed. *The Context of John Knox.* 3 vols. Leiden: E. J. Beill, 2003.

Katz, Bill. *Dahl's History of the Book.* 3rd ed. London: Scarecrow Press, 1995.

King, Philip J., and Lawrence E Stager. *Life in Biblical Israel.* Lavisville, KY: Westminster Scripture, 2001.

Knapp, A. Bernard. "Mesopotamia," in *Anchor Bible Dictionary.* New York: Doubleday, 1992.

McDonald, Lee Martin, and James A. Sanders. *The Canon Debate.* Peabody, MA: Hendrickson, 2002.

Roberts, Colin, and T. C. Skeat. *Birth of the Codex.* New York: Oxford, 1987.

Tov, Emanuel. *Textual Criticism of the Hebrew Bible.* 2nd ed. Minneapolis, MN: Fortress, 2001.

VanderKam, James, and Peter Flint. *The Meaning of the Dead Sea Scrolls: Their Significance for Understanding the Bible, Judaism, Jesus, and Christianity.* San Francisco: HarperCollins, 2002.

Yadin, Yigael. *The Temple Scroll,* vol. 1. Jerusalem: Israel Exploration Society, 1983.

Preliminary Matters of Interpretation

Translations

According to a very old story, in the late third century BCE Greek speakers in the cosmopolitan city, Alexandria, wanted a translation of the Hebrew sacred texts. Even today most Bible readers have the same desire for translation of the Hebrew texts into their language. The differences between ancient Hebrew and modern English (and many other modern languages) are so vast that the work of translating from one language to another is beset on every side with barriers that seem to make the task impossible. As we enter the library at the beginning of the twenty-first century with our multicultural and multilingual sensitivities, we are well aware of the many differences in languages. The old joke about the tourist asking for directions and being told by a local, "Sorry, you can't get there from here," applies quite well when one is attempting to go from one language to another. No language, with its complexities of words, syntax, connotations, and denotations, is the same as any other, and the result is that it is impossible for any translator to render the *exact* equivalent of a source language into a receptor, or target, language. Compared to English, the Hebrew of our scrolls is in some ways more precise: Verbal forms designate specific person (first, second, third), gender (feminine, masculine), and number (singular, plural). On the other hand, in some ways Hebrew appears more flexible (e.g., in syntax) and more ambiguous (e.g., in verb tenses). The wealth of literary forms are equally difficult to translate: figures, metaphors, aesthetics, wordplay (paranomasia), and poetic rhythms and styles. These usually cannot be directly moved from one language to another without some change.

Some perplexing translation issues that must be faced by every translator have to do with translation habits of later cultures. If you open nearly every modern English translations of the Hebrew Bible you would think that many Israelite men had names starting with the "J" sound—Joseph, Judah, Jeremiah, and many more. But Hebrew has no "J" sound, and it is only a rather late and unfortunate twist of linguistic history that has resulted in renaming all those ancient people, at least in modern English. Similar pronunciation problems happen with other names also. On this *Guided Tour* I would prefer to always speak of Yᵉhoshua and Shᵉlomo and Yirmiyahu, but how many people would recognize these as Joshua, Solomon, and Jeremiah?

On the other hand, there is much more to representing an ancient name than simply trying to approximate sound. Our scrolls have numerous wordplays based on the meaning of names—some overtly pointed out by the author, some only

POSTER 2.1

HEBREW NAMES

Common English	Approximate Hebrew	Common English	Approximate Hebrew
Abraham	Avraham	Jonathan	Yᵉhonatan
David	Dahveed	Joseph	Yoseph
Egypt	Mitzrayim	Jordan	Yardain
Elijah	Eliyahu	Joshua	Yᵉhoshua
Ezekiel	Yᵉhezqel	Moses	Moshe
Isaac	Yitzak	Rachel	Rahkhel
Isaiah	Yᵉshayahu	Rebecca	Rivkah
Israel	Yisrael	Ruth	Rut
Jacob	Ya'akov	Samuel	Shᵉmuel
Jeremiah	Yirmᵉyahu	Sarah	Sahrah
Jerusalem	Yᵉrushalayim	Saul	Shaul
Job	Eyyov	Solomon	Shᵉlomo

noticeable to a reader of Hebrew. For example, *Isaac/Yitzak* is a name explicitly tied to the meaning "laughter/to laugh," and, if you look at Genesis 18 and 21, the author makes a major point that the story of his birth is very much a laughing matter. But the reader who is unaware of this obvious wordplay would miss out completely. Should a modern translator provide something like *Isaac/Yitzak/Laughter* every time she comes across the name? But wouldn't that be awkward, make the text harder to read, and make for really long sentences?

A specific tradition has arisen for the translation of the name of God. Just as we have personal names that distinguish us from other persons, the ancient scrolls use for the God of Israel a personal name, and it's not *God*. The most frequently encountered personal name for the Israelite God is probably best spelled in English as *Yahveh* (or *Yahweh*) or, to better reflect the absence of vowels in written Hebrew, **YHVH** (or *YHWH*). At some point in ancient Jewish tradition and in early Christian tradition, it was considered disrespectful to pronounce this name, even when reading biblical texts. In that name's place the Hebrew word for "master, lord," *adonai*, is pronounced. But the letters of the personal name, YHVH (יהוה), are certainly still there in the printed texts, over 6,800 times in fact, far more than any other name. Among the Dead Sea Scrolls, there are some scrolls that print the name in a special ancient script, again as a sign of respect. Many English Bibles since the time of the King James edition of 1611 have represented the personal name for God as Lᴏʀᴅ (large capital *L*, small capitals ᴏʀᴅ. Unfortunately, because Lᴏʀᴅ is not a personal name, the personal aspect of all these occurrences is lost on the modern English reader. And if we just use *God,* the sense is much too generic and fails to recognize that in the ancient social reality of Israel there were many Gods, and for the Israelite authors of our library, YHVH was their distinct, national God, not just some generic deity. For the remainder of our *Guided Tour* we will usually print the name as *YHVH*. But when you read modern translations of the Bible, you'll just have to remember that every time you come to the word printed as Lᴏʀᴅ, it is a substitute for the personal name of Israel's God, *YHVH*. Printing the name as *YHVH* is actually truer to the Hebrew scrolls, and any reader is welcome to articulate it in any suitable form.

In addition to the personal name, more generic terms, more like our word *God,* are also used. In Hebrew, **Elohim** is the most common and **El** is also used. They are sometimes employed for deities and beings other than the God of Israel, and there was an important local god named *El.* Hebrew does not have capital letters, and so biblical scrolls never distinguish between *God(s)* and *god(s)* the way many modern translations do. The same is true of pronouns referring to God; there is no *Him* vs. *him.* If you were a modern translator, what would you do—maintain an English tradition, or try to better represent the Hebrew?

In biblical literature the God of Israel is consistently referred to using masculine pronouns and masculine forms of verbs. However, we also find expressions and metaphors that indicate that Israelite authors sometimes employed female imagery to speak of their God. Modern writers refer to the God of biblical literature in a variety of ways, using *he,* or *she,* or by avoiding the use of any gender-specific language. What language and pronouns do you use? What you think is appropriate terminology for this God will be greatly influenced by your religious upbringing and study and your valuation of diverse religious traditions, including biblical literature and

POSTER 2.2

DARE TO TRANSLATE?

He who translates a verse literally is a liar; he who translates loosely is a blasphemer.

—RABBI JEHUDA BEN ILAI (SECOND CENTURY CE; *TOSEFTA MEGILLAH*)

Traduttore traditore. The translator is a traitor.

—OLD ITALIAN PROVERB

the religious groups that use it. This *Guided Tour*, however, attempting to be a descriptive study of ancient literature and not a prescriptive statement on how a modern reader should conceive of God(s), will reflect the practice of each particular piece of literature that we encounter and so will generally use the masculine pronoun in reference to the God of Israel (see Trible 1978).

In addition to these peculiarities of names and gender, there are also all the ordinary problems of translation. Wordplay is usually lost, rhymes and assonance are impossible to reproduce, and subtle nuances require delicate treatment by a translator. What should we do with metaphors or similes that don't have meaning in our culture, such as the apparently romantic complement, "Your teeth are like a flock of sheep . . ." (Song of Songs 6.6) or the frequent use of internal body organs, such as heart (Genesis 8.21), kidneys (Jeremiah 12.2), and bowels (Isaiah 16.11), for what we today thing of as mental or emotional aspects of humans? How can the translator be accurate and literary and still capture meaning? Just because we metaphorically use the word *heart*, it does not mean that the ancient Hebrew metaphor held the equivalent meaning. And what about euphemisms used by ancient writers? *Covering the feet* actually referred to urinating or defecating (1 Samuel 24.3–4). The sentiments of the Jewish **rabbi** and the old Italian proverb quoted in Poster 2.2 match modern understandings of the tricky business of translation. This information should not lead us to give up, but I hope it encourages at least some to learn Hebrew; translation is certainly worth the effort. Of course, some kinds of texts are more difficult to translate than others. Lists of names of persons (Genesis 10) or cities (Joshua 15), are quite easy, though pronunciation may be difficult. Although all ancient Hebrew narratives display peculiar traits foreign to modern readers, some prose narratives may be more or less straightforward, whereas others are quite complex and thus quite difficult for us to understand.

As with most languages, perhaps the most thorny translation problems come in poetry, and our library is full of poems! Wendell Berry, a modern American writer, has put the problem of translating poetry this way:

"The problem is that the poetry is in the language, or is the language. We can certainly translate the 'sense' of one language to another, but the question of how to

translate a poem from one language to another is the same question as how to translate a language from one language to another, which cannot be done" (Berry 2000, 116).

But translate we must! And, of course, it is well worth the attempt to bring the great poetry of ancient and foreign cultures to our own culture. (We will talk more about ancient Hebrew narrative and poetry in Chapter 7.)

In both narrative and poetic writings, a translator must be concerned with linguistic and aesthetic dimensions. The literature we are reading here is not a grocery list or a series of uniformly produced propositions. Each scroll is a distinct piece of art and rhetoric, and proper translation should consider all its dimensions. The "meaning" of each scroll is not something merely "contained in" the artistic form of the texts, as if we can peel away the form like a banana skin and find the meaning. Artistry is integral to meaning. A poem in any language is not truly translated when its supposed "meaning" is explained in prose propositions. Aesthetics and meanings are inextricably bound. A translator should attempt not to *explain* the meaning of a poem but to *artistically render* the aesthetic sense into the receptor language.

To see what I'm trying to get at, look at my drawing in Display 2.1. You probably figured out right away that it is a representation, a "translation," of Michelangelo's famous Creation of Adam in the Sistine Chapel of the Vatican. But something has been lost in translation! The basic lines, the angles, the proportions are similar enough to the original that you could identify it, but the "meaning" of the painting is almost totally lost. What of the grandeur, the beauty, the artistry, even the sense, remains? Any biblical translation that aims for translating some supposed "basic meaning" contained in a literary form—like cereal in a box—while ignoring the literary artistry is doomed to "re-present," or translate, the meaning and beauty of the original text in a manner similar to the way my drawing "represents" the meaning and beauty of Michelangelo—that is, badly.

As we proceed through the library, pulling the books and looking at them individually, I think you will find the wide variety of artistic styles fascinating. Therefore, the job of any translator attempting to do justice to the literature varies greatly depending on the book, and it should be the case that the style in English (or any other modern language) varies accordingly. For example, if we read an artistically attuned translation we would find that the poetry of Job is much more stately, refined, "high-brow," and even more difficult than that of Song of Songs. Similar distinctions could be made for many other scrolls, narrative and poetic, in our library.

It seems clear to me that most modern English translations err on the side of clarity of information and so do not adequately represent creative artistry or ambiguity of ancient Jewish poets or narrators. To extend the visual art analogy, "translators" might take a Monet impressionistic masterpiece and turn it into a black-and-white, clearly defined picture. Clarity has been gained, but the original artistry, beauty, content, and form have been lost. A few translations are beginning to appear that take into account the artistry of texts to a greater extent, but none of these has been published for the entire Hebrew Bible. Everret Fox's *The Five Books of Moses* is a beautifully produced edition of the first five books of the library, which pays admirable attention to matters of literary artistry and makes readers feel they have entered a foreign and fascinating world. So too Robert Alter's translation of Genesis aids English readers in getting a sense of the Hebrew artistry and meaning. I must admit that my own translations in this *Guided Tour* are not exactly great works of art. I have attempted to be artistically sensitive, but my translations are still probably several steps removed from the literary caliber that an official translation should have.

Having said all that, your tour guide must face a certain reality: An introductory guide such as this will be most helpful if its biblical translations can at least be recognized by students in their own copies of biblical texts. So, throughout the book, I nearly always translate the Hebrew text myself, but you should have no trouble following along in the text of a published Bible, such as the Jewish Publication Society's *Tanakh*, the *New Revised Standard Version*, or the *New Jerusalem Bible*, all of which are readily available good English translations. Even if I reprint another translation, I will modify one aspect for the sake of accuracy; namely, I will print the English consonants *YHVH* wherever the personal name of the God of Israel occurs in the Hebrew texts, instead of following the more problematic procedure of substituting the article and title *the Lord*.

I have one final word about a reality of modern Bibles that does not represent the ancient scrolls. Open almost any Bible and you will see a system of numbers. Within each book large sections, called *chapters*, are numbered, and within each chapter smaller sections, called *verses*, are numbered. None of our ancient manuscripts uses such a numbering system, and my guess is that ancient readers would find them intrusive. Ancient Jews and Christians did not write in numbered verses or even chapters. How would any modern writer or poet like it if her work were divided into hundreds of separate segments by someone else, sometimes even splitting up sentences, and then labeled with numbers? Does that numbering atomize the text, obstruct continuity, and even subtly reinterpret it? This penchant for numbering is a relatively late phenomenon in our library's history, arising from the desire to find a particular portion of text easily and to facilitate quotation. But, as scholars of ancient writing have pointed out, "in the ancient world there was no such thing as exact quotation in the sense of giving the precise location of a particular passage" (Roberts and Skeat 1987, 50). The numbers of most modern Bibles follows the numbering system devised by Robert Estienne (also known as Stephanus), a famous Bible printer of the sixteenth century, who was the first to use versification for the whole Bible (Black 1963, 3:442). It is easy to recognize how different a poem or narrative might read without this late intrusion of numbers, especially for those modern versions, such as the King James Version, which treat each of Estienne's verses as if it were a new paragraph. Often, many of the chapter and verse divisions do not fit well with the flow of the composition. For these reasons I prefer those modern Bibles that, if they use numbers, at least make them as unobtrusive as possible. Finally, because the modern numbering system of most Bibles produced in Christian communities varies slightly from the numbering of most Hebrew editions, I will usually indicate in parentheses the English equivalents where they are different.

Valuing the Scrolls

In our pluralistic societies, where people of cultures worldwide often interact meaningfully and peacefully about religion, literature, history, and many other subjects, one will find many different ways in which Bibles are valued and used. Unfortunately, sometimes violence and hatred also exist among different groups, and at times violence and hatred are related, at least in part, to views of "the Bible." In my classrooms through the years I have had Hindus and Sikhs who have never opened a Bible sitting side by side with Jews and Christians who have read Bibles or heard them their entire lives. On the other hand, I know some Christians who rarely read their Bible and some Jews who hardly know it, while others have studied it daily in Hebrew for a lifetime. Some nonreligious people know it extremely well; others are quite illiterate regarding it. And people often change in their attitude toward biblical literature as they move through life, depending on their experiences. We could ask all these people on any given day what the Bible means to them, that is, how do they value it? We would get a wide variety of answers. Some hear it from pulpits and value it as "the Word of God," whereas others who are very devout in their religious faith might not even associate the Bible with God. Some consider biblical literature of immense personal or social benefit; for others it is of little or no benefit.

Even within the religions that prize biblical literature, Judaism and Christianity especially, its valuation and status vary greatly and always have. For some adherents of these religions, a Bible is considered to *be* the Word of God; others would say it *contains* the Word of God. Many would describe a Bible as the *revelation* of God, which to some would mean that it reveals God and to others would mean that each word is God's exact revelation. For some people it is instruction from the mouth of God; whereas for others it is the classic voice(s) of tradition, in the same way that ancient Greek authors could speak of Homer. Some do not value all the books the same way—the New Testament, for example, is often more highly valued among Christians than the Old Testament books. Some consider a Bible to be inerrant. This word, too, means different things to different people; for some it means absolute, total, perfection, and for others it means that the message of salvation they believe is taught in their Bible is without error. Others who highly value the Bible conceive of it as a highly esteemed classic, even though they may perceive many errors. Sometimes it is said to be inspired by God or inspiring. For some, divine inspiration is exclusive to biblical texts; for others divine inspiration may be credited to other great works of art and literature as well. Many of these terms show that people invest their Bibles with some kind of authority, but that, too, can mean many different things. For some people, biblical authority means one should attempt complete submission to a Bible as submission to the command of God, whereas others would say that biblical authority must also take into account human freedom and reason. Anyone who has read much about this or discussed the issues will know that I've only scratched the surface of the possibilities.

In the academic spirit of this *Guided Tour*, everyone is welcome, mainly because our objective is not to articulate a certain position on the value of biblical texts. How you choose to value that book called Bible is up to you. Your valuation is likely to be different from that of the person next to you. What traditions and experiences have you had that have influenced your choices? Again our answers will be different. Printed Bibles do not have an authoritarian power that forces a person to decide only one way, as, say a powerful wind might authoritatively force a boat to move north. The kind of authority that a Bible possesses in a person's or religious community's life is a matter of each person's and community's reflections and decisions. All writings, whether the **Qur'an,** the United States Constitution, or a book by Willa Cather or Dr. Seuss, are objects that individuals, groups, and traditions engage with and *evaluate;* that is, make decisions about and decide the *value* of. We encounter texts as children or adults in various places: houses of worship, homes, classes, and courtrooms. Our encounters and our reflections on those encounters shape our decisions and attitudes about all texts. How useful or important are they? What purpose(s) do we ascribe to them? Why should we study them? We consciously (or not consciously) answer these and many other questions about all sorts of texts. So, as our tour is about to commence, we could ask, "Who and what has been influential in your evaluations and your ideas about 'the Bible'? What traditions are you familiar with and which ones are new? What valuations have you chosen? What does *Bible* mean to you?"

This *Guided Tour* of the library is *not* intended just for people who answer those questions a particular way. Whatever our individual answers as we begin our study, entering a Bible as a library can be an enjoyable and enlightening experience for anyone because, as I've found from experience, for any thought-ful valuation of a Bible, there is much to be gained from engaging the individual compositions of the library in their integrity and uniqueness. Perhaps we will find that our valuation of scrolls in the library varies from scroll to scroll. Perhaps new information we encounter about each scroll will alter our previous perceptions and valuations.

Many of us are accustomed to hearing the evaluative term *Holy Bible.* Now, if we take the word *holy* in a generic sort of way, meaning "set apart, distinct, separate," it is easy to see that by simply forming a library, which always means including some books and excluding others, we are creating distinctions among books and so ren-dering some holy (separate) and others, those not in the library, not holy. In this sense, I suppose, a Bible is holy for everyone who encounters it in a form separated from other books. But beyond that, what other claims we might make for the library (inspired, classic, worthless, etc.) will depend a great deal on our experience in the world: our cultures, subcultures, traditions, and socially reinforced valuations of our environments.

If you look around the United States, symbols of the Bible's valuation are every-where. Look in courtrooms and watch inauguration ceremonies of presidents and judges; you will see people placing their right hands on a Bible (but which one, we might ask?) to be sworn into their offices. I recently saw a book entitled *The Body Sculpting Bible for Women* and, of course, a companion volume for men. Search any booksellers catalogue for "Bible" and you will discover many more "Bibles" of this or that. All of these examples demonstrate that Bible long ago became a cultural icon. It symbolizes authority for any given topic and stands for stern divine author-ity before which one must pledge truthfulness and integrity. By studying the history of the United States, it is easy to understand how the Bible, usually a Protestant form, came to be such an icon and why its status as a great symbol of authority stands even though the U.S. Constitution, states that there is to be "no law respect-ing an establishment of religion." Sometimes it is clear that a Bible is a public sym-bol, devoid of real governing power, such as when it is used in inaugural cere-monies, given that no one opens the book and begins dictating law. On the other hand, citizens of the United States have long been involved in a cultural debate about the authority of the icon and of its interpreters. For example, in 1925, John T. Scopes was indicted and convicted in Tennessee for violating a state law that for-bade teaching theories denying the biblical account of the creation of man. How should Bibles be valued and used as public symbols?

So where does all that leave us as we begin our *Guided Tour?* You might value bib-lical literature highly for a variety of reasons, while the student sitting next to you hardly values it at all. You might value some scrolls of our library highly or read some of them frequently, while others you do not value or use as much. Many teachers have found that differences in valuation do not necessarily hinder the fruitful study of biblical literature in our rich pluralistic classrooms. There are some basic human issues to understanding all kinds of literature. Learning its languages and under-standing its **genres** and messages does not require a certain kind of religious or nonreligious valuation. Nothing about the Bible's valuation is magically marked on it to ward off some readers and invite others. Despite legends to the contrary,

DISPLAY 2.2 | U.S. PRESIDENT GEORGE W. BUSH, 20 JANUARY 2001, SWEARING ON A BIBLE

printed Bibles do not stop bullets any better than copies of the Communist Manifesto or the Analects of Confucius. The ancient Hebrew scrolls do not glow with some sort of divinity, and to study them profitably does not require divinely installed specialized brain cells. Instead, the texts of all Bibles all speak in human languages and use human alphabets, words, styles, and metaphors. Their textual history is like that of other human books: They were copied by human hands through the ages and today are printed by human printers. Therefore, to better understand this literature requires the same sorts of skills that the understanding of other literature requires, including learning languages and asking questions about history, authors, figures of speech, or contexts. While some religious communities maintain that only their adherents or certain members can properly read and understand a Bible through their own particular system of ideas, the assumption of this academic tour will be that insight and understanding can come from and reside in anyone. Remember, biblical literature is not owned by anyone, and in an open and free environment no one has a monopoly on its study or meanings. The practice of nonsectarian biblical studies can be an enriching humanistic, even spiritual enterprise for participants of all traditions—I've seen it in book clubs, elder hostels, colleges, and universities. Through the ages, whatever methods of study have been applied to other books, people inside and outside of religious communities have also applied them to books of the Bible—sometimes with success, sometimes without; sometimes with objections from others, sometimes with widespread approval.

You may have noticed that I have *not* used the term "secular" to characterize our *Tour*; this is for good reason. Much of the Hebrew Bible is concerned with what we would call deeply religious issues. The same can be said for a great deal of classic literature—consider the works of Homer, Dante, Milton, and Dostoyevsky—and to deal with any of these writers adequately, one must take up what are usually considered religious issues. In that broad sense, this *Tour* is religious. However, this academic study does not advocate for any sectarian or particular religious understandings or valuations of these texts. As we explore together, guided by freedom and curiosity, we will enlighten our understandings of this literature, no matter what our heritage or personal beliefs.

Ways of Studying the Scrolls

There have always been many different ways to study writings. These different methods of study arise because people want to know different things and have different interests. Some people want to know about the history, author, or themes and writing style of a book. Some study biblical texts for spiritual reasons, to learn timeless wisdom, or even for mystical guidance. These and many other purposes are expressed by different methods of studying; each method is really asking certain kinds of questions about a text and then trying to find the answers. Among scholars, these sets of questions—these different methods of reading any writing—are called criticisms. This does not mean that people criticize a text; it just means they are asking and trying to answer particular *critical* questions about a text in a disciplined, rational, and systematic way. Of course, as in all branches of learning, the results are mixed. Sometimes the methods seem to work well to achieve the desired results, while at other times they do not. Sometimes the answers convince a few scholars but not others. Some answers that satisfied scholars 100 years ago no longer satisfy. Furthermore, the questions change as our own societies and interests change. One hundred years ago very few biblical scholars asked questions about the role of women (who compose half of the human race) in the ancient world or in biblical literature. Today, happily, questions about women are a thriving part of biblical studies; many of them are raised especially in a field called feminist criticism. At its heart, biblical scholarship is basically quite simple: it is posing any and every question one might possibly think to ask about a text (*no* questions are off limits) and then seeking to devise methods that will help us answer the questions.

Here are some of the major sets of questions, in alphabetical order, that are used to study texts:

- *Canonical criticism* is concerned with the relationship of a religiously sacred text and the community that chose it for its canon. How did or does the community shape the form and meaning of the text? How does the text influence the community? How does one text function in relation to other canonical books? What is the hierarchy?

- *Comparative approaches* may be used in the fields such as religion, literature, and social sciences. Here the scholar is interested in learning how one culture or society compares to another. How do views of Gods differ? How do literary styles and content compare? How are the cultural values and taboos similar or different? Is there any evidence of contact? What anthropological models can be used in both?

- *Devotional study* of texts by those devoted to a religious faith asks how one can become closer to God or how one can better love God and others. Devotional study will sometimes move into mystical categories and ask about the mysteries of God and God's creation. These questions usually assume a particular religious viewpoint and are pursued within a particular religious community. Questions might be ethical (e.g., what does God want me to do?) or theological (e.g., what is the proper relationship between God and humans?).

- *Ecocriticism* asks about the relationship of a writing to its physical setting and the earth. How does the author conceive of nature? How are nature metaphors used, and what do they reveal about an author's view of nature? How is the text related to land and place, and how are these ideas about location used in a text? How does the author value earth and land and relate to it?

- *Feminist criticism* asks sociological and historical questions. What were the roles of Israelite women in village social structure during the seventh century BCE? It can also involve literary of questions. How is the female character represented in this narrative, what assumptions are made about women by the author, and how does an author's treatment of women differ from that of men?

- *Form criticism* asks question about the social setting of parts of texts prior to their incorporation in biblical texts. Do the formal language patterns of text reveal an original oral use? Does a poem or a phrase represent a part of temple liturgy? Was the text recited at certain social or holy day settings?

- *Historical criticism* asks all kinds of question having to do with historical events and how they are perceived and presented. What is the relationship between historical events and what an author says? What really happened and what was really said? How does one reconstruct history using all the available evidence from archaeology and the texts? Historical criticism has been used extensively to try to determine the history of the text itself, giving rise to more focused criticisms such as form and source criticism.

- *Literary criticism* asks about all those topics that are common in other studies of literature. How do we describe the genre? What is the structure of the writing, and how does it develop? What is the plot? Does it use poetic forms, structures, and figures of speech?

- *Reader-response criticism* is a newer form of criticism that asks questions about how a text interacts with its intended audience(s) and later readers. What do readers bring to the text that affects its reading? What are readers' limitations? What gaps in content do the readers fill in? How do communities make some interpretations plausible and others implausible?

- *Redaction criticism* acknowledges the use of earlier sources in the formation of biblical texts and focuses on the work of editors who brought material together, edited it, and redacted it. What were the principles and goals of the redactor? What is his social situation, and what traditions did he inherit and champion? Can seams in the text be detected?

- *Rhetorical criticism* asks how an author seeks to persuade. What is the author's appeal and what are the methods and strategies the author uses to convince the assumed audience? This is one of the oldest forms of criticism, following from the insights of Aristotle.

- *Social-scientific criticism* involves history but more specifically asks questions from the fields of anthropology, sociology, and ethnography. What are the social norms and hierarchies assumed by the author? What sociological power is involved and represented or questioned? What are the population and ethnographic patterns revealed by archaeology and how do they impact the study of the texts? How do illiterate and peasant peoples relate to the texts? How does the material culture of agriculture, architecture, village and city patterns affect our understanding of the texts?

- *Source criticism* asks questions about the origins of a work. What sources, if any, may have been used by the author(s) of this scroll? Are they oral sources or written sources? Were they sources used in a certain place in the culture (e.g., a temple or king's court)?

- *Textual criticism* is all about the study of manuscripts and how best to explain the many different forms of an ancient text. Which manuscript traditions are older, and how and why did the changes develop? Why and when did a copyist change a text?

- *Theological criticism* is a broad category that interests many readers for many different reasons. Theology proper is the study about a God, and within the biblical field, theological study can be done by historians interested in the religious ideas of ancient Israelites and also by modern religious communities who look to biblical literature as a guide for their own religious beliefs and practices. What beliefs about the God did the author have? What are the doctrines about the God that are taught in the text? How do different ideas about the God and the God's relation to humanity and the world that are found in the texts relate to each other?

All in all, the lines of inquiry in biblical study are endless, and the possible answers impossible to count. And that's why some of us think it's so much fun: studying is seeking to satisfy our curiosity about ancient times and people, texts, and even life. Later on our tour (Chapter 4), we will have a more detailed overview of the literary forms of ancient biblical texts, and throughout our study we have occasion to mention or use many of these sets of questions too. In fact, almost any of these methods of study can be applied to almost any text, so feel free to experiment!

Thinking About Meaning

We already discussed the question "What does 'the Bible' mean?" in connection with the ways we value "the Bible." We can also talk about meaning in another way. We could ask, "What is the meaning of this word, this verse, this paragraph, or this scroll?" And of course you are aware we would not get a uniform answer. The books written about the meanings of biblical literature are innumerable, and it seems as if 1,000 people would give you 1,000 different answers about the meanings of Bible texts. Even biblical scholars or other persons reasonably acquainted with the literature often disagree. This is no surprise. Wise observers have been telling us for centuries that "Good literature in any language or culture has a high degree of multivalency, [multiple meanings] especially poetry" (Sanders 1999, 19). The myriad interpretations by the hundreds of communities that have highly valued biblical writings through the centuries prove beyond any doubt that this literature must be really good.

So the aim of this book is not to go through the library and give you the final word on what each scroll "means," nor is this a survey of what it has meant to different people through the centuries. Though we will pause briefly on occasion to observe interpretations of various communities, this is not a history of interpretation, nor a guide to modern interpretation. Rather, this *Guided Tour* is a modern academic historical study of this ancient literature as literature, with modern academic interpretive values, such as rational inquiry, literary sensibility, and philological study. I am not claiming a timeless, value-free, "bird's eye" stance from which I alone can tell you what it all means. All observations and readings I make of any scroll are interpretations that must stand up or fall down in the courts of evidence and the mentalities of other readers. Experts in various fields of biblical studies will recognize that my readings are hardly unique to me. An introductory textbook such as this is hardly the place to present new or idiosyncratic viewpoints. Our *Guided Tour* contains a good amount of historical information, but it is not simply using these texts as evidence for reconstructing events of ancient history. This introduction is both historical *and* literary (and does not consider them antithetical) because of guiding questions such as these: How was this literature produced, intended, read, and understood in the society of ancient Israel? What would these writings have meant to people of that world? How does each piece of literature work as literature? How is it designed? What sources, ideas, appeals, aesthetics, values, and so forth do we find in it?

These and many other questions are sometimes hard to answer; sometimes we must hypothesize. Modern scholarship had developed many tools and methods to help answer such questions, and this tour will make use of many of those. These methods include all the forms of criticism that we already mentioned. The questions guiding this *Guided Tour* are not about what input biblical literature should have in our modern communities or how you as a reader ought to react to its ideas. Each of us will have to answer such things for ourselves. You will have to decide how our

*C*ommunity *R*eflections 2.1

MANY MEANINGS

Religious traditions have long dealt with the problem or the blessing of multiple interpretations. Here are two sentiments from Jewish and Christian traditions published around the fifth century CE.

Jewish

> Rabbi Abbaye said, "The text says, 'One thing spoke the LORD, two things I heard: that power belongs to God and faithfulness is yours, O LORD.' (Psalm 62.12.) A single verse results in several meanings, but a single meaning does not result from several texts."

> Rabbi Ishmael taught, " 'Behold, like fire is my word declares the LORD, and like a hammer that shatters rock' (Jeremiah 23.29). Just as a hammer produces many sparks, so also one text has several meanings."

> –BABYLONIAN TALMUD, SANHEDRIN 34A (CA. 450 CE)

Christian

> For what more liberal and more fruitful provision could God have made in regard to the Sacred Scriptures than that the same words might be understood in several senses, all of which are sanctioned by the concurring testimony of other passages equally divine?

> –SAINT AUGUSTINE (354 TO 430 CE), ON CHRISTIAN DOCTRINE III.27

explorations in this ancient literature impact your current thinking about Bibles, religion, history, faith, or society. Your answers will be influenced by the choices that you (and others) have made about the biblical library's valuation and usefulness, its literary genres, and its religious and philosophical appeals and questions. People and groups of people make choices about what they value most, and those choices dramatically affect the way we read and behave. In a sense, our behavior can't be blamed on an old book, whether a Bible or any other one. In our modern settings, where we can pursue knowledge openly, we can often be very active in choosing (and changing) our religious ideals, authorities, and actions. This great library and the individual scrolls within it have always provided inspiration for a whole range of actions in our world, some of them in direct opposition to others. Why? It is because people come to the same library but with different moral ideals, different religious priorities, different assumptions, and so they leave with different meanings that they have found.

But regardless of what Bible means to you now, I believe that our historical and literary study can capture the attention of all. I'm just crazy enough to think that despite some reputation to the contrary, biblical literature is intrinsically fascinating even for modern students and that modern scholarship offers much to help make our tour interesting and enjoyable. For one thing, I've found that these old scrolls are seldom what people on my tours expect of "holy scripture." So many things in any Bible are downright weird to the honest contemporary reader, such as a God having casual conversation with humans, people getting eaten by fish, donkeys talking, bathroom humor, boys calling an old **prophet** "baldy" only to have the prophet get mad and sic bears on them, a woman taking off her sandal in court and spitting in a man's face, a vaunted patriarch lying to save his own skin at the expense of his wife's, strange regulations about priests wearing underwear, and rules about women's menstrual cycles and mildew on walls. And don't forget all that wildly passionate poetry—some in despair, some in the throes of sexual fantasy wild enough to catch Dr. Ruth's attention. This is the stuff of biblical literature, and it often makes for fascinating reading for those with even a modicum of curiosity.

As a tour guide, my hope is that our exploration of these scrolls' ancient meanings will enrich and enlighten our understanding and will be useful as we consider the contemporary use of biblical literature in our pluralistic world.

History Then and Now

Two topics that definitely have different ancient and modern understandings are history and religion. Just how much "history" is contained in our library is a matter of great debate. It is a debate partly about genre—what kind of writings were the various authors intending to write?—and partly about issues of how history "should" be written—what standards of historiography should we apply when we attempt to determine the historical accuracy of any of these scrolls? But what is not debatable is that the various scrolls of our library have been appreciated and valued through the ages for many things besides history. Their historical valuation has varied a great deal over time, but even people who have not considered biblical books to be historical have still highly valued the writings, even considered them divine. The reason for this, of course, is that many readers have sought things other than history, such as spiritual wisdom, instruction, or some other religious objective. And certainly the scrolls themselves show that their authors were interested in many things besides history! The ways in which a writing seems useful to historians has and will continue to differ depending on the objectives, principles, and assumptions of each historian.

Simply put, the modern academic study of history is, in one way or another, an attempt to reconstruct and explain in our minds the events of the past. The study of history is not a science that can reproduce what happened. Instead, it is an attempt to explain data, all the evidence of the material culture that we can find or that we can read in texts. If you wanted to write a history of ancient Israel, Canaan, **Mesopotamia,** or Egypt, trying to answer questions about what happened at a certain time you would probably use as many relevant sources as you could find. You would dig in the dirt for material evidence and check the latest anthropological studies; you would try to support your narrative of what happened with as many pieces of evidence as you could find. Data for your historical inquiry would come from environmental, geological, botanical, and zoological studies. You would also, of course, study socio-economic, political, ideological, and religious systems, and you would attempt to view all levels of human society. You would try to be aware of a wide range of differences among peoples and groups. Depending on the level of evidence, you might label parts of your reconstruction "highly probable," "less probable," "possible," "unlikely," "speculation," or "nearly impossible." You might even conclude that some things we would like to know are beyond the reach of current knowledge altogether. For the historian, the rules of history, that is, the criteria by which she determines the probability of her reconstruction, ought to be the same, regardless of the popularity a certain event or country may have in our culture. So too, the archaeologist attempts to use methods that are fair to all evidence and best explain all the data. While some events or periods in the past attract the attention of many people (e.g., ancient Israel) others attract only a relatively small amount of interest (e.g., ancient Moab). Have you ever heard of Moab? Some readers will answer "yes," but many others, "no." But the academic study of history tries to find out as much as possible about any ancient culture, whether it is famous or not, because modern familiarity says nothing about the relative importance or worth of events that occurred in ancient Moab and Israel. Now, if I were to announce that I was holding a news conference to give a brand new interpretation of the life of Mesha (a Moabite king from the ninth century BCE), few people would attend because there are no large groups or major institutions interested in supporting (or challenging) Moabite history and tradition. But if I announced a major new interpretation of the life of Abraham, Moses, David, Solomon, or Jesus, the response would be different because there are many institutions and individuals in the modern world that take a great deal of interest in those figures from the past. But for the historian trying to be consistent with all her sources, whatever criteria she uses, she must apply them as equitably as possible. (For a simple list of more commonsense historical rules, see Dever 2001, 106–08.)

When it comes to ancient texts, a modern academic historian often reads narratives of actions taken by Gods. For example, suppose an Egyptian text says that, in a great battle with an Asian enemy, the Egyptian God Horus gave the victory to the Egyptian king. A text written by the Egyptians' Asian enemy said the Egyptians actually lost the battle. What would you write in your history? Wouldn't you try to find out as much as possible about the battle from all possible sources in order to determine which account was more historically accurate and which one was mostly propaganda? You would also include in your history that the Egyptian royal public viewpoint was different from that of the enemy, and you would attempt to explain these differences. That's the way modern historical study works. It goes to great lengths to check on battle strategies, weapons, the geography of the area, the supplies needed to sustain troops, and many other factors, all in an effort to determine what details of the accounts seem credible.

By carrying out their study this way, modern historical investigators are following certain general rules of the discipline. Rational investigators assume that contradictory sources can't be absolutely right in all areas. This is the law of noncontradiction. However, in this case a historical investigator will consider the possibility that the Egyptian king might have won in some respects and lost in others, because battles do not always end with clarity and historical events are often open to various interpretations. On the other hand, authors may present honest but incorrect information, and that they are capable of stretching the truth or even lying. As human beings, all authors have limited perspectives and biases and those limitations and biases may be more or less of a factor in any given writing or passage. We know these things are based on the rule of historical analogy, that human beings in the past were capable of the same sorts of human motivations and actions as we humans are today. An ancient author might not be reporting things exactly the way they transpired in the eye of the unbiased observer. Furthermore, people may write narratives for many different reasons, not just for straightforward historical reporting, and so one must consider the possible motives, goals, and purposes of a piece of writing in order to use it appropriately. In this way, a reader must be aware of the "rules" of a genres language game.

What about the Egyptian God Horus's part in the battle? Although perhaps being theoretically open to the possibility, the vast majority of modern historians would not send an archaeological expedition to look for Horus's footprints on the battlefield or other historical evidence of his participation. Why not? Our historical investigation into many ancient sources would show us clearly that Gods are everywhere in ancient texts—and modern historians have found it impossible to take them all as historical beings or actors. How do we propose to investigate what Horus was thinking, what he actually did on the battlefield, how he moved in for the victory, and how he got away? The best we can do is to investigate what ancient people said and thought about Horus's actions on that day. Perhaps the most widely reported miracle from antiquity is the appearance of the Greek God Apollo in 279 BCE to save the Greek defenders of the temple Delphi from the invading Gauls. Contemporary inscriptions, sacred assemblies to honor Apollo, official decrees, and reports by numerous later historians demonstrate that without doubt thousands of people believed in this miracle. Do you? Claims of divine intervention and miracles number in the thousands and are so frequent that historians have come to take them as an important part of the social and psychological makeup of both ancient and modern cultures. As Herodias remarks in Oscar Wilde's *Salome,* p. 23, "I don't believe in miracles because I have seen too many." How can the modern historian take *all* of these claims seriously and fairly? There are many serious attestations for miracles in the ancient literature of cultures, but belief (ancient or modern) in a miracle, no matter how sincere, does not make the miracle a fact of history. Some people tend to grant the miracles of their tradition but deny those of other traditions. But any historian attempting to be honest and fair cannot do this; it is precisely this sort of bias a historian attempts to avoid by consistently using impartial criteria.

Sometimes people today discuss this issue as if it were merely a choice between a naturalistic and a theistic view of faith. If you are theistic, and have faith in God, then you will be open to believing that miracles recounted in biblical narratives were actual historical events, but if you adopt a naturalistic stance, you will not be open to miracles. But this is a wholly inadequate and simplistic way of thinking about the matter: the issue is much more complex.

- First, by definition, theists do not necessarily believe in all miracles reported in a Bible. A person may have strong religious convictions about a God and still not accept every ancient (or modern) report of miraculous activity. Some reports may be accepted, others may not, and the difference will be determined by criteria of historical research, not by religious presuppositions. There have been thousands of individuals of sincere religious faith through the centuries who have not accepted many miracle reports as historical.

- Second, a theist who is consistent and does consider miracle reports to be historically accurate on the basis of arguments of historical evidence will use the same criteria about miracles from all traditions and all sources. Some theists in fact do this, accepting miracles (and Gods) of many traditions. In some ways, this position best reflects many writers of antiquity, including many of our library. For many ancient Israelites, YHVH's miracles were believed as real events, but other Gods had supernatural powers as well (e.g., Exodus 7.1–24).

- Third, even for the theist who is open to the possibility that miracles could be historical, the miracle itself is in some sense beyond the reach of historical research, because miracles are not subject to any of the laws of physics or normal reality. Gods in miracle stories don't leave footprints that historians can trace by systematic and consistent criteria.

But all this is not to say that miraculous claims should not be taken seriously. Modern historians attempting to treat all evidence fairly and to take religious claims seriously, have solved the problem in a sense by recognizing (1) the power and seriousness of beliefs in the ancient (and modern) world and (2) that the divine realm(s) is off limits to modern empirical inquiry of historians, because we are not in a position to investigate the heavens (or wherever Gods are) or to inquire of the God(s). Such an approach is not a denigration of religion or faith; it is simply an admission of the limitations of rational historical research. It is beyond the tools of rational historical investigation to determine what a deity has done. All we have are written narratives of what humans said happened, evidence of the material culture, and whatever else we can dig up. We do not have videotapes of events, and few historians will claim to have access to God's mind. But if a modern academic historian claimed fellow historians should accept her history as fact because God told her in a dream exactly what happened in 1986 or 1586 or 586 BCE, would she be taken seriously as a historian? If a professor came into class and told you that last night God had told him what questions to put on today's history exam, would you believe him? How would you investigate? Would you believe him if he claimed the revelation came from Horus or Athena? If your teacher said that everyone in the class would be getting a grade of D because the God had told him to do so, would you accept it? Would you argue about the legitimacy of this revelation?

If free, ethical, academic inquiry means anything, it means that a historian's evidence and arguments must be open to anyone else's investigation; the rules of falsification and replication must apply. He or she cannot claim exclusive and privileged truth. Question-stopping, special-revelation pronouncements, such as "God told me to . . . " or "You just have to accept it on faith" are not a part of open inquiry. In modern historical inquiry, all of the past must be treated according to fair and open principles, and all our reconstructions of the past are a matter of rational probability, because that is the only way we have of treating all evidence fairly. In historical inquiry into biblical matters, we are trying to find all possible evidence from texts and from the material culture unearthed by archaeologists. Then we put it all on the table and ask, "What best explains all this?" As one seasoned biblical scholar, James Barr, put it, "there are only two ways to go: either the straight fundamentalist way, i.e., that everything is historically true because it is in the Bible, or a historical-critical way, which will assess the historicity of reports point by point" (Barr 2000, 76).

Here's a helpful way of thinking about it: modern academic historical study applies the same methods and rules of study to biblical texts that it applies to any other texts. Ideally, all evidence gets treated consistently. This is part of what I call the ethics of interpretation. We must always attempt to be fair, just, and honest in our readings and not use double standards or forced interpretations. To do so would be disrespectful of ancient authors and unfair in our modern academies. As we brought to light in the last chapter, the biblical texts themselves display all the physical and natural human traits of other ancient literature that has survived from antiquity, and so there is every reason to investigate our scrolls using the same sorts of questions that are applied to other texts. Following the lead of the Jewish philosopher and scholar Spinoza (1634 to 1677) who articulated this ideal, many religious and nonreligious scholars have sought to read these texts using normal methods of interpretation. In fact, you might say that this is the crucial difference between open academic inquiry and many non-open approaches to studying. In a truly open inquiry into any text, no questions are off limits, no lines of inquiry are taboo, no conclusions are predetermined, and no results are ruled out. It is not even accurate to say that modern rational scholarship has predetermined that miracles are always impossibilities. It is entirely a matter of explaining the evidence. What is the best explanation for the hundreds of thousands of miracle reports that come to us in the thousands of texts from antiquity? Is the best explanation that they all happened? Are there fair ways of making distinctions? The answers will vary.

Now we all know, scholars included, that we do not always live up to our ideals, or that our ideals may even change. That is why scholarship is always ongoing, theories come and go, and methods are created, considered, critiqued, modified, or abandoned. What we think of today as a sound method of discerning history in texts or artifacts will be critiqued and perhaps changed in years to come. Openness to new possibilities and better understanding is as vital as the conservation of ancient learning, evidence, and proven methods. Scholarship on ancient Israel and biblical literature is never finished.

What is clear to everyone is that Israel's ancient narratives about the past, some of which are found in the biblical library, do not share the conventions of modern academic historiography. The narratives of Genesis, Kings, Chronicles, and all the rest are not written as contemporary rational investigations into historical events. They do not declare in their narrative what is historically probable and what is speculation. They do not give various possibilities or cite the various pieces of archaeological evidence to counter opposing views. Biblical texts, even those that are narratives about the past, are written with different conventions, different purposes, and different values

Study Room 2.1

TRUE OR FALSE?

What do you make of this old European saying?

"A country is a group of people united by a common misconception about their ancestry and a common dislike of their neighbors" (*National Geographic Atlas of the World 1995,* 50).

Is there truth in this statement, or is it just a cynical overstatement? Is this true of modern countries? What are common misconceptions of the ancestry of the United States or other countries? How might it apply to any ancient countries?

than modern academic historiography. Why should we expect an ancient author to subscribe to modern conventions?

Recognizing this gulf of purpose and convention that separates many a modern historian from the ancient Israelite is crucial for a proper assessment of the literature and has several ramifications. First, these ancient narratives about Israel's past are not the same things as a modern conception of the history of Israel. To write a modern history of ancient Israel would mean that one would use these ancient texts as one source among others (other texts, archaeological and anthropological evidence, etc.) to determine as best as possible what happened and how life was lived in a particular period and place. Biblical narratives would not necessarily be the controlling paradigm or outline of Israel's past any more than one archaeological excavation would be. All potential pieces of evidence would need to be evaluated for their historical accuracy and relevance, including each line of our biblical scrolls. A historical investigation open to all sources would also recognize that the literature of Israel that survives in our library does not represent all levels of society. It is instead a selected and highly edited literature, reflecting the values and interests of literate individuals and groups. It does not provide the direct access to Israelite society that we might imagine or desire for our historical curiosity.

So what does this all have to do with our tour? This *Guided Tour* is *not* a history of ancient Israel or an investigation into the historicity of each scroll. This is a broadly interested library tour of Israel's formally preserved library. Thus, when we deal with narratives in Genesis or other books, our primary questions will not be "Did this really happen?" or "What evidence can we find for or against this event?" Reconstructing Israel's history is not our goal, and the value of our tour and the worth of the scrolls themselves do not depend on the historicity of the narratives. It is not that your tour guide thinks the texts are worthless in the field of history. On the contrary, during our tour we will encounter many texts that I believe have a great deal of historical information in them. Sometimes this is the case in what they intend to communicate, for example, that there was a king of Judah named Josiah

(2 Kings 22). Sometimes they disclose historical information without intention. That is, all authors communicate many things about their ideas of history simply by the way they write. So we often will have occasion to speak of history along the way, but it is by no means the preeminent value of this tour.

The library that we are about to enter has numerous reports of miracles, and through the ages these reports have been interpreted in many different ways—historically, allegorically, mythically, as parables, or as stories to be rationalized. Those of us on the tour may understand them in different ways, and in the context of ancient Israel's societies and literature, these stories served many functions and likely had many interpretations, too. Because this tour is not primarily a historical investigation, our focus will be on these stories in the context of literature—how they function. We will focus more on what people said and wrote and very little on the historicity of what they describe. From this literary point of view, miracle stories are not problematic at all—they are among the most common kinds of stories in all literature, and there is no need to flatten or rationalize them. Often modern attempts to rationalize miracle stories by "explaining" a reported action of YHVH as an natural event—for example explaining the burning bush as just a bush of Exodus 3.2 with brightly colored leaves—end up destroying the story's attempt to highlight YHVH's power and mystery.

In some places of our culture, you can observe an unfortunate side effect of the great strides of historical research in the last few centuries, namely the devaluing of narratives about the past that do not share the goals of modern historical writings. Or, to put it another way, a narrative that is not historical is considered untrue. A story is often said to be true if the events narrated in it really happened. But this is a most unfortunate equation and one that has been lamented by many.

Let's illustrate what we mean by using a narrative from ancient Greece. One of Æsop's most famous fables is The Fox and the Crow. One day while walking through the woods, Fox noticed Crow high in a tree, holding a delicious piece of cheese in her beak. Hungry and sly Fox began to make conversation with Crow so as to get her to respond and thus drop the cheese. Fox started with flattery, calling her plumage the most beautiful he had ever seen and begged Crow to sing a song so that she would be hailed as the queen of birds. Lured by compliments and the promise of glory, Crow opened her mouth to sing, and the cheese fell down to Fox who thanked Crow and walked away satisfied.

After telling this story in class, I often take a vote: "How many of you think this story is true?" "How many of you think it is false?" Almost 100% usually answer "false," and by so doing they merely follow the commonly accepted equation that truth = history. But really, I could hardly think of a truer story than this fable of Æsop. The reasons the story is true are several. Æsop is not writing a historical narrative about the dietary habits of foxes or crows. He is not writing about the communication between foxes and crows or whether they could really speak Greek (or English!). He is not recounting a miraculous event that he witnessed one day while strolling in the woods of Athens; in fact, he is not really talking about foxes and crows and cheese at all. Æsop is talking about human social interaction and behavior, and his story is as true today as it was 2,500 years ago, because humans still flatter each other and fall prey to flattery every day. The story is certainly *true*. It is certainly *not history.* Its concluding moral, "Flatterers live at the expense of those who trust them" or "Never trust a flatterer," is as relevant and as truly good advice as there ever was.

But what would you think if someone attempted to use this story for history, for what really happened? Does this story prove that in ancient Greece foxes ate cheese? Should we send a notice to biologists across campus that we have discovered that at one time foxes and crows could actually speak to each other (in Greek, of course)? If we are religious, should we be compelled to believe this story because, after all, God can do anything (so they say), including make animals talk, and who are we to question the worthy sage Æsop? Should we conclude that there must have been an eyewitness in the forest who observed this conversation or that Æsop must have had divine inspiration to tell him exactly what transpired? Most importantly, does this story lose any of its value or any of its truth (however one might define that), just because all of its historical facts are entirely fictional? Clearly the answer to all these questions is an emphatic "no!" A narrative's worth may have nothing to do with its historical value. Historicity is not the only criterion for the evaluation of literature. If we think it is, we impoverish ourselves by our devaluing of parables, myths, epics, poetry, metaphors, and many other literary forms.

For our *Guided Tour* of Israel's library, the point is not that biblical scrolls are the Hebrew equivalent of Æsop's fables. The point is that narratives, whatever their specific type, may have value, purposes, and meanings that are unrelated to their historical worth. The moral or religious value of a piece of literature may be unrelated to its historical worth. Literature in general plays many roles in societies. Religious communities through the centuries have used the scrolls of our biblical library for many purposes other than reconstructing history. In some eras, the historicity of biblical narratives seemed the least interesting or valuable, at least to a significant number of writers. When it comes to reconstructing a verifiable detailed political history of Israel, archaeology has been of limited value—no royal or official temple archives have been found—and so we must learn to live with a good deal of uncertainty and lack of knowledge. But because we are interested in far more than history on our tour, we will find ourselves exploring many other fascinating aspects of these rich texts.

Religion in Ancient Israel

Just as a modern historical investigation of the history of Israel is not the same thing as any narrative we find in any biblical scroll, so also we do not have in our Hebrew Bible a history or description of religion in ancient Israel. The library we are about to enter does not reflect all the views of God(s) that ancient Israelites held. The library does show some diversity, but it does not reflect the religious viewpoints and practices of all Israelites at all levels of society. Furthermore, our library does not consist of literature that was voted in as most important based on a scientifically designed Gallup poll on religion and literature of ancient Jews. So, if we want to study the actual religion and religious practices of ancient Israelites (or any other people group), we would need to use all the sources available, including archaeology and anthropology, not just scrolls from our library.

When we put all the evidence together, what do we find? Historians and archaeologists have been uncovering a good deal of evidence about Israelite religion. For starters, the archaeological spade has revealed thousands of goddess figurines apparently in use in popular Israelite religion, yet the texts of our library reflect mostly anti-goddess viewpoints. In fact there is no doubt that many Israelites regularly honored deities in addition to YHVH; archaeology and biblical texts make this clear. Some Israelite leaders, especially in the periods when our library's scrolls were taking shape, opposed this worship and advocated for worship of YHVH only. Another example is that the personal God of Israel, YHVH, is found in texts outside of Israelite biblical texts and even outside of Israelite tradition, so he seems to have a history beyond what one can learn from our library. Finally, for many centuries religious practices among Israelites were centered socially in the family tribe and physically in household, village, and regional shrines. More centralized practices with larger temples and priesthoods, and later with one centralized temple in Jerusalem, were complex developments over time from the tenth to fifth centuries BCE. Our library, however, often reflects the centralized temple forms of cultic practices that evolved later, because the formative stages of these scrolls come from the later periods of that development and are, generally speaking, the products of individuals and groups who were supportive of the more developed religion.

DISPLAY 2.3 | AN ISRAELITE GODDESS FIGURINE

But what about the God of Israel? In the ancient world, cultures almost invariably acknowledged and honored more than one deity; **monotheism** was not common. But when historians attempt to discern the religious ideas and developments that are behind the current forms of monotheism in Jewish, Christian, and Muslim traditions, our library is an important place to go. Our library attests to several aspects of this development, and if we want to understand this history of this God, we cannot simplistically assume that modern ideas of monotheism were current in ancient Israel. The first point must be that the Israelites lived in a culture where many different Gods were a part of the cultural landscape and there was no agreed-upon, centralized, single, universal God. When an ancient Israelite said "YHVH," she or he was referring to a specific, distinguishable, national deity, not to a generic universalized "God," as we so often use the term in modern conversations. As we progress on our tour, I will attempt to reflect the reality of this situation by referring to YHVH, the God of the Israelites, or the God, instead of to a generic God. The question, "Do you believe in God?" would not have made much sense to most Israelites. This is also the reason that I will capitalize all references to all Gods: in the ancient world of the Israelites we are always referring to individual deities with personal, proper names. Hebrew manuscripts make no cosmetic distinctions—such as capitalizing *God*—when writing *Elohim*, "God," for Israel's God in contrast to other Gods. For this reason in this *Guided Tour* we will follow the more authentic practice and always recognize the word *God* or *Gods* as a proper, formal designation.

DISPLAY 2.4 | ISRAELITE PICTURE AND INSCRIPTION "YHVH OF SHOMRON [SAMARIA] AND HIS CONSORT ASHERAH." (EIGHTH CENTURY BCE)

In addition, religious scholars have developed the following terms to show some of the various possibilities of thinking about Gods:

- henotheism—the idea that there are many Gods, but one God is singled out by a person or group for worship or commitment. This God may be thought of as primary or chief among others.
- monolatry—the worship of only one God, without denial of other Gods
- monotheism—the idea that there is only one God
- polytheism—the idea that there are many Gods
- theism—the idea that God (or Gods) exist; usually involves the idea that God(s) created the world and is (are) involved in ruling it.
- theology—the ideas or statements about God(s) and how they/she/he/it is relate to the world. The word may be applied to the study of these ideas or to formal explanations of religious beliefs.

All these terms can be helpful, but we should be careful to realize that they are modern terms and categories, not the topics of our ancient library. The literature of our library

Community Reflections 2.2

✡ ✝ ☪

Forms of Monotheism

Today three religious traditions, Judaism, Christianity, and Islam, are often known as the "three great monotheistic faiths," and they all developed out of the traditions of this library. Monotheism is a religious and theological term that refers to the idea that there is one, and only one, deity. The importance of one God is especially stressed in the constantly repeated liturgical and prayer formulas of Judaism, such as the *She'ma*.

Hear, O Israel, the Lord our God, the Lord is one.

So also in Islam, a frequent recitation begins:

There is no God but God.

The Christian idea of God as a Trinity (God as Father, Son, and Holy Spirit) developed alongside the idea of monotheism. Many declarations from the Christian tradition therefore affirm both Trinitarian and monotheistic images.

In addition we should mention that monotheism became a standard idea in Western philosophy, even outside of the rise and spread of these three religions. Philosophical monotheism is the idea that there is a single and ultimate God/Power/Mover in the universe. This idea is not dependent on the three major monotheistic religions, and through the centuries many who have espoused philosophical monotheism have not espoused these religious. Aristotle, the Greek philosopher, for example, was a philosophical monotheist. Philosophical monotheism also differs from the three religions in that it does not picture God as personal.

is mostly narrative and poetic and is certainly not formal philosophical or religious propositional treatises (Levenson 1985, 56–70). For this reason I prefer to use the term *Yahwists* to describe the Israelite authors who are sometimes called monotheists.

In our library we can see a variety of ideas about Israel's God, but it is still a selective library, not a "democratic" library reflecting the entire cross section of Israelite religious thought. It is diverse in many ways, but it is still limited by the priests, scribes, rabbis, and other social leaders who influenced the writing and selection of literature that they valued highly. As we conduct our tour, we will occasionally have reason to consider popular religious ideas and practices that are not enshrined in our scrolls, but this tour is by no means a full-fledged account of the religion(s) of ancient Jews. That would require a very different sort of guide, and there are several excellent books on the subject. But of course our *Tour* will have much to say about the religious ideas that we do find in our scrolls. Here at the outset, just before we enter and start pulling scrolls off the shelves, it is worthwhile to point out a few things about what we will find.

First of all, we must remember that our library is an ancient one and the religious views it reflects are not those of our world. Even if we are a part of religious traditions that make frequent use of the biblical literature, there are still vast differences between the religious culture of ancient Israel and its neighbors and that of our twenty-first century. Whether it is animal **sacrifices,** religious sexual taboos, or conceptions of the mechanics of the universe and how it relates to God(s), the religious realities of ancient Israel were different from those of our world. If we want to attempt to read these scrolls as ancient witnesses to a fascinating world, assumptions that are commonly made about religion today—for example, about the afterlife, or salvation, or God's nature—must not be automatically applied to the authors of our scrolls. As we explore, we should expect divergences from modern religious ideas, and in the field of religion in particular, we must do our best to understand the words of the ancient authors in light of *their* culture, not ours.

Let's consider one example of an important difference that we encounter in our library, a topic that is often today considered central to religion, namely salvation and the afterlife. For many people a fundamental and essential ingredient of religion is the idea that personal "salvation" involves going to heaven instead of hell, a place of punishment. However, thoughtful readers, not just academic scholars, have long noted that the concepts of an afterlife and salvation in our library are vastly different from those of many modern religious traditions. When our scrolls are read as if they referred to salvation in heaven, it becomes a classic case of forcing later conventions and modes of thought on ancient authors. This is not the place to trace the history of heaven and hell (it is a fascinating history!), but though our scrolls may talk about salvation, it is an earth-centered concept and operative in this life, not the next. Israelites did not pray to YHVH or any other God to be saved from hell; they prayed to YHVH to be saved from drought, sickness, enemy invasions, premature deaths, family discord, despair, and bad harvests. These ancient Israelite writings do not attest to the modern conception of a heaven or hell where people went after death. Our literature shows relatively little interest in an afterlife and when it does so, it usually speaks of *Sheol,* a murky, dark place of quasi-existence, the realm of the dead. **Sheol** is used only 66 times in the

Study Room 2.2

YHVH AND THE GODS

The best way to gain some sense of the ways the ancient writers thought about God(s) is to carefully read their expressions. Consider the following selections, and try to determine what sort of viewpoints they represent. How would you describe them? What do the authors assume or not assume?

Exodus 18.11 Deuteronomy 4.19; 32.8–9
1 Kings 18.20–29 Isaiah 46.5–7 Psalm 82
Psalm 89.6–9 (or 5–7) Job 1.1–6

whole library, and was a common Hebrew name for the place of the dead. Here humans seem to exist but not live, and eventually they seem to fade out of existence all together. *Sheol* is variously described; it was not a place of joy or happiness, yet it was not a place of punishment either. Eventually all would go there, but one tried to avoid going there prematurely! Our scrolls of Psalms, Job, and Qohelet (Ecclesiastes) speak of *Sheol* the most.

Finally, this is a good time to point out a major historical reality that is crucial for understanding how this library relates to ancient Israelites. It is inaccurate and reductionistic to speak of the Israelite way of thinking, Israel's view of God, or Israel's view of just about anything, for that matter. Israelites did not all hold a certain view or set of views. The diversity of our library and the even greater diversity of social, ethical, political, religious ideas among ancient groups of Israelites during their many centuries of existence, is vast. We do their memory no justice and our own understanding no honest service by reducing the historical diversity or imposing some modern theological or religious uniformity on them. Like all historical study, studying ancient Israel is an untidy business. Our library, the historical record, and the mass of evidential remains from the material culture are rich, vast, and messy, and so in this *Guided Tour* we will pay attention this diversity and resist the temptation to simplistic models of Israelite thought.

We spend this time prior to proceeding into our library essentially for this reason: Biblical literature comes from a distant and different world, not from our own. The world that produced the literature of our library is not the twenty-first century, and no matter what modern technology does to make Bibles familiar and easy to access, no matter how many times biblical stories are simplified and told to children, and no matter how systematic and graspable "the biblical message" is made, the scrolls still originated in a distant land and retain a foreignness for anyone who desires a honest understanding of how they were written and read in antiquity. My colleague and friend, Michael Gleason, once brought together two observations about ancient history that are fitting for our biblical study. The first is "The past is never dead. It's not even past," penned by William Faulkner in *Requiem for a Nun* (1951). Novelist L. P. Hartley made the second point in *The*

Go-Between: "The past is a foreign country; they do things differently there" (1953,). Indeed, biblical literature is a huge part of our modern world and cultures; it certainly is not dead or past. On the other hand, exactly because biblical texts occur in so many places and forms of modern religious culture (especially in the United States), its true foreign nature is often forgotten. It is so easy to domesticate biblical stories and texts as if they really speak in our language, as if they are of our world, as if their authors shared modern assumptions about the universe, God(s), or cultures. These scrolls have often been domesticated by selective readings, by theological or ideological systems, or a few simplistic ideas. Part of the purpose of this *Guided Tour* is to de-domesticate biblical literature for modern readers. This guide is an attempt to view this fascinating literature in its ancient context, without reducing it to themes, lessons, or history.

Questions for Further Study

1. What are different purposes for translating an ancient text? How might different translation methods and styles work better or worse for different purposes?

2. How do you value the scrolls of the biblical library? Who has been most influential in these value choices? What would be some good guidelines for a having a beneficial discussion about the Bible among people who value it differently?

3. What methods of study, or criticism, have you used? Which ones sound most interesting and why? In what ways do they overlap?

4. What topics concerning biblical scrolls have piqued your curiosity?

5. Doing history properly requires commitment to high ethical ideals and principles of justice. In what ways can historians and honest readers of the Bible be fair to all sources and not use double standards for making historical judgments? What are fair ways of dealing with reports of miracles?

6. All religions develop and change over time. How should historians of religion trace the developments of ancient Israelite religion(s)? What methods, principles, and sources would be important? How would biblical literature figure into the study?

References

Alter, Robert. *Genesis.* New York: Norton, 1996.
———— *The Five Books of Moses.* New York: W. W. Norton, 2004.
Barr, James. *History and Ideology in the Old Testament.* Oxford: Oxford University Press, 2000.
Barton, John. *Reading the Old Testament.* Philadelphia: Westminster Press, 1984.
Berry, Wendell. *Life is a Miracle.* New York: Counterpoint, 2000.
Black, M. H. "The Printed Bible," in *Cambridge History of the Bible.* 3 vols. Ed. by S. Greenslade. 3:408–75. Cambridge: Cambridge University, 1963.
Coogan, Michael, ed., *The Oxford History of the Biblical World.* New York: Oxford University, 1998.
Dever, William. *Did God Have a Wife? Archaeology and Folk Religion in Ancient Israel.* Grand Rapids, MI: Eerdmans, 2005.

Dever, William. *What Did the Biblical Writers Know and When Did They Know It?* Grand Rapids, MI: Eerdmans, 2001.

Dever, William. *Who Were the Early Israelites and Where Did They Come From?* Grand Rapids, MI: Eerdmans, 2003.

Edelman, Diana Vikander, ed. *The Triumph of Elohim: From Yahwisms to Judaisms.* Grand Rapids, MI: Eerdmans, 1995.

Faulkner, William. *Requiem for a Nun.* New York: Random House, 1951.

Fox, Everett. *The Five Books of Moses.* New York: Schocken, 1995.

Gillingham, Susan E. *One Bible, Many Voices: Different Approaches to Biblical Study.* Grand Rapids, MI: Eerdmans, 1998.

Hallo, William, and K. Lawson Younger, Jr. *The Context of Scripture.* 3 vols. Leiden: E. J. Brill, 1997.

Hartley, L. P. *The Go-Between.* London: Hamish Hamilton Ltd., 1953.

King, Philip J., and Lawrence E. Stager. *Life in Biblical Israel,* Louisville, KY: Westminster/John Knox, 2001.

Levenson, Jon. *Sinai and Zion,* San Francisco: Harper, 1985.

McKenzie, Steven, and Stephen R. Haynes. *To Each Its Own Meaning: An Introduction to Biblical Criticisms and Their Application.* Rev. ed. Louisville, KY: Westminster/John Knox, 1999.

Meyers, Carol. *Households and Holiness: The Religious Culture of Israelite Women.* Minneapolis, MN: Augsburg Fortress, 2005.

Millard, Alan. "Amorites," in *Dictionary of the Ancient Near East,* edited by Philadelphia: University of Pennsylvania, 2000.

National Geographic Atlas of the World. 6th ed. Washington, D.C.: National Geographic Society, 1995.

Niditch, Susan. *Ancient Israelite Religion.* New York: Oxford, 1997.

Pritchard, James. *Ancient Near Eastern Texts Relating to the Old Testament.* 3rd ed. Princeton, NJ: Princeton University, 1969.

Redford, Donald. *Egypt, Canaan, and Israel in Ancient Times.* Princeton: Princeton University Press, 1912.

Roberts, Colin H. and T. C. Skeat, *The Birth of the Codex.* London: British Academy, 1987.

Rogerson, John, et al., *Beginning Old Testament Study.* St Louis, MO: Chalice, 1998.

Sanders, James A. "The Scrolls and the Canonical Process," in *The Dead Sea Scrolls after Fifty Years,* ed. by P. Flint and J. VanderKam. 2:1–23. Leiden: E. J. Brill, 1999.

Smith, Mark. *The Early History of God: Yahweh and the Other Deities in Ancient Israel.* San Francisco: Harper & Row, 1990.

Smith, Mark. *The Memoirs of God: History, Memory, and the Experience of the Divine in Ancient Israel.* Minneapolis, MN: Fortress, 2004.

Spinoza, Benedict de, *Theologic-Political Treatise.* Trans. R. Elwes. New York: Dover, 1951.

Trible, Phyllis. *God and the Rhetoric of Sexuality.* Philadelphia: Fortress, 1978.

Wilde, Oscar. *Salomé.* New York: Heritage Press, 1945.

Zevit, Ziony. *The Religions of Ancient Israel.* London: Continuum, 2001.

Preliminary Matters of Ancient History

Where Are We Going and Why?

Our destination holds the oldest known civilizations of human history. We are going to what is commonly and appropriately known as the Fertile Crescent, a crescent-shaped area anchored in the east by the Persian Gulf and in the west by Egypt. It is a large swath of arable land, home to many rich cultures today,

DISPLAY 3.1 | SATELLITE PHOTOGRAPH OF THE FERTILE CRESCENT
WITH MODERN BORDERS

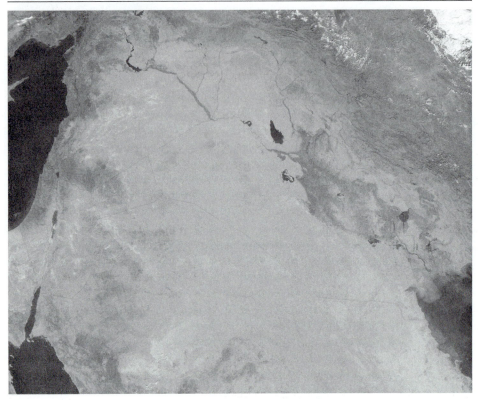

and dotted with the impressive remains of ancient human civilizations. It
includes parts of the modern countries of Iraq, Syria, Turkey, Jordan, Lebanon,
Saudi Arabia, Israel, and Egypt. This is our destination because every word of the
literature in our library arose not in our world, but in this ancient world—its
foods, notions of Gods, roads, clothes, sacred rituals, crops, kings, and ideas of
family. Our scrolls, in all their aspects—language, genres, forms, content—
reflect the culture(s) of what is often now called the ancient Near East (ANE). In
their cultural development, Israelites were not isolated from others; instead, they
were constantly interacting with other peoples. Therefore, if we are trying to
understand the contents of these scrolls as they would have been understood by
ancient readers, then we need to consider those parts of ANE culture that are
relevant to those contents. For example, to understand Israelite **creation** stories
as they were understood in ancient Israel, it will be helpful to know about the
many popular creation stories that circulated in ancient cultures and were
aspects of Israel's larger culture. The scroll of Genesis contains a famous
creation narrative, and like all the other books, it is not a writing that fell out of
the sky with no connections to the real world. It has an ancient cultural context;

that culture is *not* twentieth- or twenty-first century writings about creation or universe origins.

Though both Genesis and modern science may address the origin of the world, they are in very different worlds. So, when we get to Genesis, we will investigate the ANE stories of universe origins, and we will find how Israelite versions compare with other stories and poems of the ancient world. When we study the library's scrolls this way, by asking questions about their cultural context and about comparative literature of their time, we will find that the authors were engaged in their culture, not isolated from it.

Ancient Near-Eastern Political History

Sumer: In the Beginning

Ancient Near-Eastern history begins in southern Mesopotamia with the Sumerian civilization, a group of city-states were loosely organized around the southern reaches of the Tigris and Euphrates river valleys near the Persian Gulf, flourished for several centuries from about 3300 BCE. The Sumerians developed many cultural forms that are still familiar today. They formed a nonalphabetic writing system and an organized government and kingship with laws, courts, and structured economies. Education, math, record keeping, agricultural science, and visual and literary arts all existed and flourished in Sumer. The earliest-known story of a great flood that is caused by a God and survived by a human on a boat, comes from a clay tablet found by archaeologists in the Sumerian city of Nippur. It is dated to the late third millennium BCE.

Egypt: Nile's Gift

On the other side of Fertile Crescent, around the same time as the Sumerians, Egyptians were developing a high level of civilization that lasted for more than 2,500 years (3100 to 500 BCE). As the ancient Greek explorer Herodotus said Egypt was the "gift of the Nile" (*History*, 2.5; see Display 3.2), and what a gift! The stability of the Nile, with its abundant supply of water for flourishing agriculture in the midst of the desert of northern Africa, produced a long-lasting civilization. The magnificence and advanced stature of ancient Egyptian culture is still visible in the form of stunning monuments and temples. Egyptian writing, called *hieroglyphics* by the Greeks, developed into an advanced writing system. It's probably safe to assume that almost everyone on this tour has seen a video or television documentary about ancient Egypt. Egypt also had formal education, highly organized governmental structures, advanced engineering and agricultural techniques, medicine, science, and many arts. And, of course, these are the pyramids—those massive burial monuments that date from the middle centuries of the second millennium (2700 to 2300 BCE)—never fail to impress even today. Built around 2650 BCE, the tallest of them (482 ft/146 m) remained the highest human construction until the completion of the Eiffel Tower in Paris in 1897. The wealth and opulence of Egyptian royalty is apparent to anyone who has been to the National Museum of Egypt in Cairo or seen a video about the treasures of the tomb of King Tutankhamen, popularly known as King Tut, who reigned from 1352 to 1344 BCE.

Back to Mesopotamia

In the area of Mesopotamia, other city-based nation-states arose, rivaled, and eventually replaced the Sumerian powers. These were the early Babylonians who, with other people groups, dominated the eastern part of the Crescent from about 2350 to 1750 BCE. During this period, **Semitic** peoples known as Amorites came into upper Mesopotamia by 2000 BCE and then spread to other parts of the Fertile Crescent. They were a powerful influence and integrated with the local population, adopting much of its culture, including the Akkadian language. The most famous of their kings was Hammurabi, who reigned from 1792 to 1750 BCE and whose code of 282 laws was inscribed on a large stone monument, discovered by archaeologists in 1901 (see Display 5.1). Hammurabi achieved fame as just and righteous. Even after his death around 1750 BCE, his law code was published in many manuscripts in the cities of Mesopotamia.

In addition to the city of **Babylon,** one of the most impressive Mesopotamian centers of this period was Mari, a now-excavated ancient city located in modern Syria, which yielded a great treasure trove of texts—more that 20,000 tablets!—and many other artifacts. Amorites and related groups also moved into the western branch of the Fertile Crescent, some settling in Syria-Palestine: they are referred to in Numbers 13:29 and Joshua 24:15. Their language and culture mixed with that of other Semitic peoples of the region and eventually the Amorites lost their distinctiveness

DISPLAY 3.2 | EGYPT: GIFT OF THE NILE

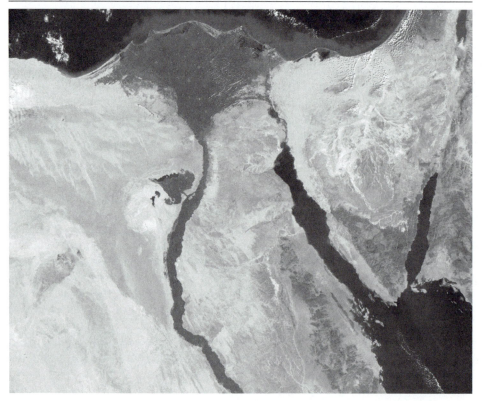

as a separate people group. Some went as far as Egypt by the seventeenth century where they were known as Hyksos (see Millard 2000).

Beginning in the ninth century (the 800s BCE), Assyria (ancient form: Asshur) arose as the most powerful state that part of the ancient world had ever seen and maintained power in much of the Fertile Crescent until 612 BCE. During much of this time, Assyria also controlled the western arm of the Fertile Crescent, including land that had been locally controlled by Israelites, as a result of many military campaigns to the Mediterranean coast and even into Egypt. The final Assyrian conquest of the Northern Kingdom of Israel came in 722 BCE, but they did not completely devastate the Southern Kingdom of Judah. The Assyrians too built an impressive and large-scale civilization. In their conquests, they seem to have relished the propaganda value of their reputation for cruelty. After conquest, the Assyrian policy of control consisted of deporting people to other regions of its vast empire, encouraging or forcing acculturation and assimilation, and establishing directly governed Assyrian provinces in newly acquired territory (King and Stager 2001, 384). Their royal residences and most important cities were first Ashur and later the famous Nineveh. There was a great deal of cultural continuity between the ancient Babylonians and Assyrians; in many ways we might think of them as rival city-states vying for power in the same cultural world. The remains of several impressive Assyrian libraries contain thousands of Babylonian texts in the dominant Semitic language of Akkadian.

Eventually Babylon's fortunes rose again and it dominated nearly the entire Fertile Crescent for a short time, approximately 612 to 539 BCE, after the demise of the Assyrian Empire (with Babylon's help!) in 612 to 605 BCE. The short and final period of Babylonian rule saw the reign of the great warrior and empire-builder **Nebuchadezzar II** (reigned 605 to 562 BCE), who conquered Jerusalem and the entire region in the first two decades of the sixth century. The Babylonians also deported some of those they conquered in order to strengthen other areas of the empire, but they allowed the conquered people to maintain their own ancestral customs and traditions. They also left large areas of conquered territory underpopulated (King and Stager 2001, 384). Their most famous and capital city was Bavel, now known best by its Greek name, Babylon. Renowned the world over for their astronomical learning, the influence of Babylonians is still felt today by anyone who divides their days into 24 hours and their hours into 60 minutes. Hundreds of years later the city of Bavel was famous in the Greek world for its hanging gardens, which the Greeks labeled as one of the seven wonders of the world. Because Babylonian sources do not mention these gardens, we are unsure to what the Greek traditions may be referring. But there are plenty of other impressive remains of the material culture of Babylon. The Babylonians supported many kinds of learning and literature as well, some of which we will read later in our library tour. Jewish life fared relatively well in Babylon, as they adapted and maintained their own Jewish traditions in this exilic environment. As it turned out, Jews in Babylon became among the first of many Jews who lived outside of the homeland of Israel. All such Jews are called diaspora Jews.

Persia: Conquest from the East

Babylonian rule in Mesopotamia ended with the rise of the Persian Empire under the leadership of **Cyrus the Great** in 539 BCE, the year he conquered Bavel. Persia, which is east of Mesopotamia, now modern Iran, had its own culture and language, Persian,

DISPLAY 3.3 | THE AMAZING EGYPTIAN KARNAK TEMPLE COMPLEX

but respected and encouraged the cultures of the peoples it conquered in the west. As a result, Aramaic became the lingua franca of the massive Persian Empire, which by the sixth century BCE stretched from east of the Indus River to Egypt to Western Asia Minor in the west. Like no other empire before, Persia expanded its control taking Egypt and Asia Minor, now modern Turkey, and even attempting a conquest of Greece. It is at this point that ancient and modern historians speak of the final demise of ancient Egyptian power, because after the Persians, Egypt was ruled first by the Greeks and then by the Romans. The Persian emperor Cyrus in 539 BCE reversed the deportation policy of the Babylonians before them and allowed—even encouraged and funded—the return of people to their homelands and the maintenance of ancestral traditions. Some Jews chose to return home, but many did not because the regions outside of Syria-Palestine had become home to them, and they were able to maintain their Jewish identity even as a minority population in Persian Empire.

This massive yet relatively free Persian Empire was governed by an efficient and direct system in which, according to the Greek historian Herodotus (*History* 3.89),

POSTER 3.1

PROLOGUE TO HAMMURABI'S LAWS

When the august God Anu, kin of the Anunnaku deities and the God Enlil, Lord of Heaven and Earth, who determines the destines of the land, allotted supreme power over all peoples to the God Marduk, the firstborn son of the God Ea, exalted him among the Igigu deities, named the city of Babylon with its august name and made it supreme within the regions of the world, and established for him within it eternal kingship whose foundations are as fixed as heaven and earth, at that time, the Gods Anu and Enlil, for the enhancement of the well-being of the people, named me by my name: Hammurabi, the pious prince, who venerates the Gods, to make justice prevail in the land, to abolish the wicked and the evil, to prevent the strong from oppressing the weak, to rise like the Sun-God Shamash over all humankind, to illuminate the land.

I am Hammurabi, the shepherd . . . the capable king . . . seed of royalty . . . humble and talented . . . discerning king, obedient to the God Shamash . . . the warrior who shows mercy . . . the judicious one . . . the pure prince . . . wise one . . . leader of kings . . . the pious prince who brightens the countenance of the God Tishpak . . . who sustains his people in crisis, who secures their foundations in peace . . . shepherd of the people . . . who proclaims the truth . . . who guides the population properly . . . the pious one, who prays ceaselessly . . . favored of the Goddess Ishtar, am I.

When the God Marduk commanded me to provide just ways for the people of the land (in order to attain) appropriate behavior, I established truth and justice as the declaration of the land, I enhanced the well-being of the people.

—Translation of Martha Roth in Hallo 2003 II:336–37; modified

there were twenty states, or satrapies, each one overseen by an aristocrat called the satrap, who was appointed by the king. Within these satrapies local people groups and towns were granted a large measure of autonomy in matters of culture and religion; of course support and tribute for the Persian Empire was expected. The local leaders, governors, or kings served at the pleasure of the Persian satrap and ultimately of the king. The last historically based narratives of our library tell stories of Jews in Syria-Palestine of this period. The region around Jerusalem was the Persian province of Yehud and was overseen by Persian-appointed Jewish governors.

POSTER 3.2

TWO SIDES OF ASSYRIA

Nearly all civilizations have displayed both a violent face and a nurturing, cultured face, sometimes simultaneously. These two quotations from Assyrian royal archives show both: one king's cruelty to humans and another's love of learning.

I built a pillar over against his city gate, and I flayed all the chiefs who had revolted, and I covered the pillar with their skin. Some I walled up within the pillar, some I impaled upon the pillar on stakes, and others I bound to stakes round about the pillar . . . And I cut the limbs of the officers, of the royal officers who had rebelled . . .

Many captives from among them I burned with fire, and many I took as living captives. From some I cut off their noses, their ears and their fingers, of many I put out the eyes. I made one pillar of the living and another of heads, and I bound their heads to tree trunks round about the city. Their young men and maidens I burned in the fire.

—Document of Ashurnasirpal II (883 to 859 BCE); cited from Georges Roux, *Ancient Iraq*, 1980, 269–70.

When you receive this letter, take with you these three men and the learned men of the city of Barsippa, and seek out all the tablets, all those that are in the houses and all those that are deposited in the temple Ezida . . .

Hunt for the valuable tablets which are in your archives and which do not exist in Assyria and send them to me. I have written to the officials and overseers . . . and no one shall withhold a tablet from you; and when you see any tablet or ritual about which I have not written to you, but which you perceive may be profitable for my palace, seek it out, pick it up, and send it to me.

—Letter of King Ashurbanipal (668–631 BCE); cited from Georges Roux, *Ancient Iraq*, 1980, 328–29.

Greece: Conquest from the West

The next great conquest came from the opposite direction. Alexander the Great, the famous Macedonian warrior, led his Greek and other western soldiers in a lightning-fast conquest of Asia Minor, the entire Fertile Crescent and Egypt, Persia, and beyond (333 to 323 BCE). During the Persian reign, Greek travelers and traders were frequent in many regions, including Syria-Palestine, so the invading Greeks

POSTER 3.3

ARCHAEOLOGICAL TIME PERIODS (BCE)

Neolithic ("new stone") Age		8500 to 4500
Chalcolithic ("copper/stone") Age		4500 to 3500
Early Bronze Age		3500 to 2250
Middle Bronze Age		2250 to 1550
Late Bronze Age		1550 to 1200
Iron Age		1200 to 586
	Iron Age I	1200 to1000
	Iron Age II	1000 to 586

To this point the time periods are named for the kinds of tools that were developed and used in these time periods. For post–Iron Age periods, historians and archaeologists use the dates of political empires for basic periodization. The following periods are standard.

First Israelite Temple Period		ca. 970
Babylonian Exile Period		586 to 539
Persian Period		539 to 332
Second Israelite Temple Period	ca. 520 BCE to 70 CE	
Hellenistic Period		332 to 63
	Ptolemaic Greek Period	323 to 198
	Seleucid Greek Period	198 to 164
Roman Period		63 BCE to 330 CE

—Mazar, Amihai, *Archaeology of the Land of the Bible 10,000–586. BCE* 1990.

were not seen as an alien people. In later centuries, stories are told of Alexander's largely peaceful conquest of the region of Syria-Palestine where Jerusalem, then under control of Persians, was located. As Alexander moved east in conquest, he established garrisons and cities based on Greek institutions in order for the newly immigrating Greek-speaking colonists to thrive.

Alexander died while only in his thirties, and his empire immediately became a prize to be ripped apart by his generals. As Alexander had done, his successors established many Greek cities for the support of their countrymen who spread into all corners of the empire. In the last decades of the fourth century (323 to 300 BCE) the vast regions Alexander conquered were split into several smaller empires. This era, until the rise of Rome, is known as the Hellenistic Era.

The cultural interaction between those from Greece and the inhabitants of Egypt and Asia was always a two-way street; interaction and intermarriage was common. Generally speaking the Greek immigrants, who held the upper hand politically and militarily, were influenced by local cultures, but some of them were also devoted to maintaining aspects of their own rich Greek culture, such as educational and cultural institutions even far from home. The blending of cultures at times took place relatively peacefully—Hellenistic rulers were not bent on destruction of people or cultures—and at other times conflicts arose.

One of the many cities established by Alexander was Alexandria, Egypt, home of the ancient world's most renowned library, a learning center that boasted thousands of scrolls and was the home and visiting quarters of many scholars, poets, philosophers, and writers. This library and the thriving culture that it represented was ruled by a family called the Ptolemies, after the first king, Ptolemy. The Ptolemies ruled most of Syria-Palestine from about 315 to 198 BCE. Many Jews lived in Alexandria and developed a thriving culture there that exhibited both distinctly Jewish traditions and Greek ways. Around 198 BCE, the Greek empire that was based in Syria and Mesopotamia, the Seleucid Empire, finally succeeded in conquering all of Syria-Palestine, including Jerusalem. The Ptolemies and Seleucids had been fighting over this strategic "land between," which was a land between continents and between major kingdoms, for over a century, and the Jews of the region were divided about which kingdom was better for their own political, social, and economic interests. It was during this period, as the Seleucid Empire waned, that violent and revolutionary conflicts developed, and the Jews of Judea gained their independence for a brief time, prior to the Roman conquest of the entire region in the middle of the first century BCE.

Where We Are

It's hard to decide what we should call this land between during our tour. The land that comprises the western leg of the Fertile Crescent and is northeast of Egypt has gone by many names through its history. The Egyptians called the area Retenu or land of the Hurru. In antiquity it was designated by various titles in various periods by various people: Canaan, Palestine, Israel, Phoenicia, Greater Syria, Yehud, and more. Starting in the European medieval period, all the lands on the eastern coast of the Mediterranean region have been called the Levant. For the sake of geographic inclusivity, not for modern political purposes, on this *Guided Tour* I will usually use the term Syria-Palestine for the entire western area of the Fertile Crescent, including territory from the modern states of Israel, Jordan, Syria, Lebanon, and Egypt. More specifically, it is the southern half of this region of Syria-Palestine in which much of the history of ancient Israel unfolds. I will call this southern region by various names, including Canaan, Palestine, Israel, Judah, and Yehud, depending on which seems most appropriate in the context.

Syria-Palestine has seen its varied landscape populated by many different small groups of people. In antiquity, many of these peoples spoke Semitic languages and originally were related ethnically and culturally. There were numerous large migrations of Semitic peoples, such as the Amorites, in and out of the western Fertile Crescent, Mesopotamia, and Arabia. The second millennium (2000 to 1001 BCE) saw the arrival of many of these Semitic peoples in Syria-Palestine. These related groups came to be known by names such as Canaanites, Arameans, Jebusites, Phoenicians, Moabites, Edomites, and Israelites. The name *Canaanites* is sometimes used generally to refer to any of these Semitic people of

POSTER 3.4

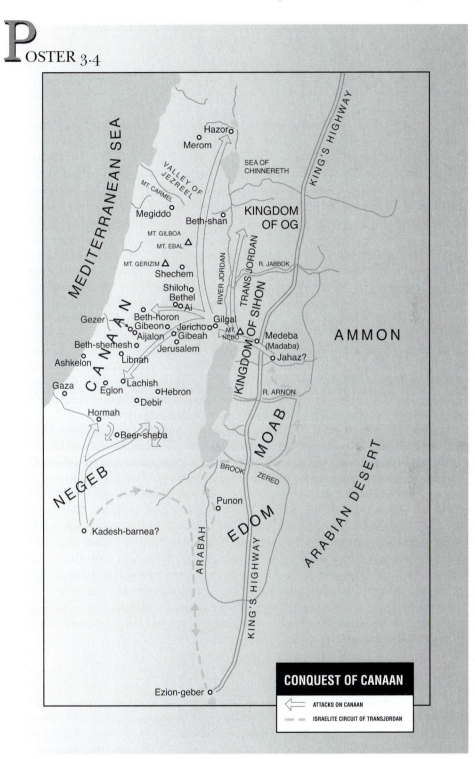

MEDITERRANEAN SEA

Hazor
Merom

VALLEY OF JEZREEL

MT. CARMEL

SEA OF CHINNERETH

KING'S HIGHWAY

Megiddo

Beth-shan

KINGDOM OF OG

MT. GILBOA

MT. EBAL

MT. GERIZIM

Shechem

RIVER JORDAN

TRANSJORDAN

R. JABBOK

Shiloh
Bethel
Ai

Beth-horon
Gibeon   Jericho   Gilgal
Gezer
Aijalon   Gibeah
Beth-shemesh
Libnah   Jerusalem

MT. NEBO

KINGDOM OF SIHON

Medeba (Madaba)

AMMON

Jahaz?

CANAAN

Ashkelon
Gaza   Eglon   Lachish
Hebron
Debir

R. ARNON

Hormah

Beer-sheba

MOAB

NEGEB

BROOK   ZERED

ARABIAN DESERT

Punon

ARABAH

Kadesh-barnea?

EDOM

KING'S HIGHWAY

Ezion-geber

CONQUEST OF CANAAN

⇐ ATTACKS ON CANAAN

– – – ISRAELITE CIRCUIT OF TRANSJORDAN

this area. When we try to imagine these peoples moving from one area to another, we should not think in terms of large modern nations or random collections of refugees, but of the movement of large extended families or tribes, who practice subsistence agriculture and animal husbandry. They inhabited towns in places still on our world maps, such as Damascus, Jerusalem, Megiddo, and many others.

One large non-Semitic group that came to this area was the Philistines. They were part of larger movement of people from Asia Minor and Greece, known as the Sea Peoples Movement, dated to around 1200 BCE. They devastated many towns in their path, including the now famous city of Ugarit and its affiliated towns (ca. 1180 BCE). Their invasion of Egypt was not successful, but the group known as the Philistines did settle northwest of Egypt in the southern coastal plains of the western leg of the Fertile Crescent. They came to control five major towns and the areas around them: Gath, Gaza, Ekron, Ashdod, and Ashkelon. Gaza, of course, is still a part of our modern history and is the home of many Palestinians, and the name *Ashkelon* exists today in the word *scallion,* which is a green onion named for this famous ancient town.

The Phoenicians were the great seafaring traders of the Mediterranean, and their maritime interests led them to establish settlements in Cyprus, north Africa, Asia Minor, Greece, Italy, and as far west as Spain. Their main cites in Syria-Palestine were Byblos, Tyre, and Sidon. Tyre was famous for its coastal fortress that was unconquerable for centuries until the invasion of Alexander the Great. During the Persian period, the Phoenicians also moved to the southern port cities of Ashkelon and Ashdod, displacing the Philistines. Just inland from the Phoenicians during the Iron Age were the Arameans. Their central city was Damascus, now capital of Syria, one of the oldest continuously inhabited cities of the entire world.

Other groups and clans of Canaanites, in the broad sense, will be mentioned during our *Guided Tour* because they play roles in the narratives of our library, but now we should mention the Israelites. Archaeologists have detected an influx of what many scholars believe to be Israelite settlers in the middle and southern hill country of Canaan in the thirteenth and twelfth centuries BCE. These settlers established about 300 small villages in the region. Archaeologist William Dever indicates that the region's population grew from around 12,000 (thirteenth century) to about 55,000 (twelfth century) to about 75,000 (eleventh century) (Dever, 110). Some of these were Israelites whose settlements were situated in the central hill country, away from the major travel zones of the coast and Jordan Rift valley and this section of the country was their primary territory throughout their history. Culturally and ethnically, continuity existed between the Israelites and the other Semitic peoples of the area, but there were also contrasts, perhaps especially in religious matters.

Canaan: The Land Between

The nations of Egypt, Assyria, Babylon, Phoenicia, and others are not just background noise for the history of Israel. They play major roles in ANE history, and their entire culture—fortunes, expansions, material goods, technologies, foods, literatures, religions, architecture—affected Israel and the authors of our texts dramatically. Look at the map of the Fertile Crescent (Display 3.1) again and notice that the area the ancient Jews inhabited is part of the prime real estate on the route between the superpowers of ancient civilization, Egypt and Mesopotamia. Not only that, but this area is the only land bridge between the three continents of Africa, Asia, and Europe. To control the travel zones of this land was to control and profit from a great deal of trade. For Egypt especially it meant controlling the only avenue of access by which the powerful nations of Mesopotamia might invade. Those desiring to attack Egypt would have seen it as Egypt's front door and those desiring to travel for diplomacy, trade, or other business would have to traverse this land. The area also served as a buffer zone between the eastern or northern superpowers in Mesopotamia/Asia and Egypt at the southwest end of the Fertile Crescent. It is no wonder then that with the geopolitical significance of this territory, people of many nations are constantly traversing the area in the stories of ancient Israel's library; that interaction was a constant historical reality.

This land between was not home to the massive cultures and dense populations of Egypt and Mesopotamia. Nevertheless, its various interrelated cultures thrived and boasted several outstanding developments. Canaanite people developed the first-known widely used alphabet, a 22-letter writing system. The Canaanite alphabet was probably linked to alphabetic writing found in Egyptian mines in southern Sinai and Amorite developments, and may have been used as early as the eighteenth century BCE. In the fourteenth century, Ugarit, a thriving city-state located not far north of later Israelite settlements, seems to have been the first to use an alphabetic script for state purposes. Soon thereafter others of the region, such as the Arameans, Moabites, and Israelites, were using the Canaanite alphabet. The Phoenicians spread the Canaanite alphabet along their sea-bound trade routes. It was adopted successively by the Greeks, Etruscans, Romans, nearly all Europeans, and finally us! Along the way there were numerous adaptations made by different people, but the 26-letter alphabet used to write this book traces it history back to this land between. And beyond the alphabet, does it go without saying that this land produced much of the literature (our library) and religious heritage of millions of people in the Jewish, Christian, and Muslim traditions?

Topography and Travel

It is not surprising, given its strategic importance, that this land boasted major routes between the centers of civilization that were bustling with travelers from many countries. These international highways of the ANE carried trade caravans that were beneficial to the local economy, but also to armies and bandits. Such strategically valuable land was of great interest to the governments of surrounding states, and the superpowers took great interest in the stability, control, and political leanings of the small nations that occupied this land. It is not surprising, therefore, that the strategic cities that grew up along these routes were often the objects of warfare. As it turns out, the oldest detailed recording of a battle comes from the annals of the Egyptian king Thutmose III, who attacked and triumphed over the unified forces of rulers of Canaanite towns and villages at the site known as Har-Megiddo, "Hill of Megiddo," around 1482 BCE. Megiddo sits overlooking a picturesque valley and guards an important pass through the mountains along the coastal route from Egypt. Megiddo remained a strategic site for many centuries and an intriguing literary and religious symbol in Christian cultures until today; *Armageddon* is the Greek form of *Har-Megiddo.*

The topography and climate of the land between, the southern portion of the western leg of the Fertile Crescent, displays a great deal of variety. The area is a narrow strip of land sandwiched between the Mediterranean Sea to the west and the Arabian Desert to the east. This narrow strip, 50–80 miles (80.47– 128.75 km) wide, is topographically further subdivided into the following narrow north-south ribbons:

- *The coastal plain:* This usually dry land was used for travel to and from Egypt and was known in Roman times as the *Via Maris,* "Way of the Sea." The five major Philistine towns were in this heavily traveled area. Moving up the coast from Egypt, travelers were forced to cross the mountains, which came to meet the sea at the modern city of Haifa.

- *The low hill country or shephelah:* From the coastal plain the land gently moves to low, rich soil and well-watered hills, easily accessible but off the major international thoroughfare.

- *The mountainous central hill country:* The low hills give way to more mountainous and forested terrain. The mountainous region becomes broader to the north. Travel in this region is difficult; travelers generally follow the east–west valleys and a north–south ridge route from Jerusalem to Hebron. Rainfall is good, and with hard work the rocky soil is very productive. In the north especially, the broad, rich valleys and plentiful rainfall allow for excellent crop production.

- *The mountainous wilderness:* Little or no rainfall combines with steep, rocky ravines and mountains up to 3,000 feet to form the wilderness region, where raising crops is virtually impossible, but ancient and modern Bedouin pasture sheep and goats in this area.

- *The Jordan Rift Valley:* The South's hill country and wilderness dramatically give way to a large, broad valley. In the north, the valley contains the Lake of Galilee, out of which flows the Jordan River, which empties into the Salt Sea, or Dead Sea, about 35 miles (56.33 km) to the south. The Dead Sea is the lowest point on earth, some 1200 feet (365.76 m) below sea level. The Jordan Rift Valley, which receives little or no rainfall, was hospitable to tropical agriculture where oases provided ample water supply, such as Jericho, one of the oldest cities on earth. The Jordan Rift Valley's flat surface was excellent for travel, and it was an important regional thoroughfare.

- *The high eastern plateau:* The land rises steeply east from the Jordan Rift Valley to the high tableland of Transjordan. Here ample rainfall and relatively easy passage provided convenient locations for ancient settlements, such as Amman, the current capital of the state of Jordan. The major north–south route was known in antiquity as the King's Highway, and it connected Syria with Arabia, the Red Sea, and ultimately Egypt. East of this highland plateau the terrain fades into the Syrian-Arabian Desert and is thus open to the desert winds and any armies or raiders that may have braved the vast sands that separate the two legs of the great Fertile Crescent.

Poster 3.5

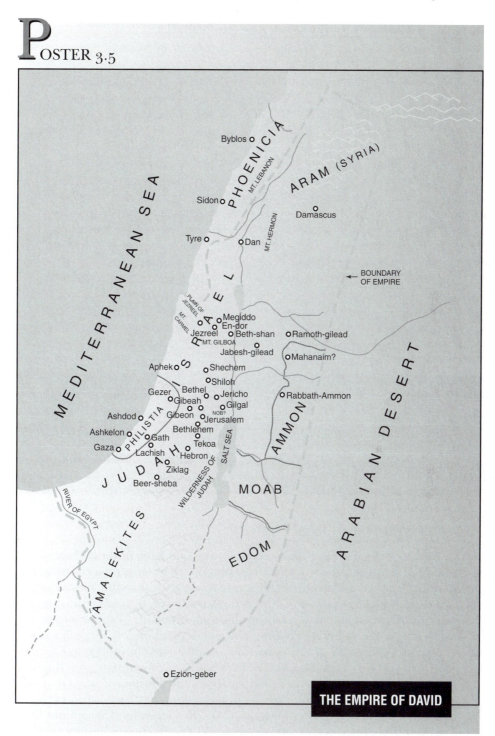

THE EMPIRE OF DAVID

DISPLAY 3.4 | JORDAN RIVER VALLEY IN THE NORTH

Ancient Israel's Political History

For the purposes of our *Guided Tour*—in order to get our basic historical bearings—a summary of Israelite history will suffice. Because the archaeological data that unequivocally pertain to Israelite history is very scarce until about the ninth century BCE, a wide range of historical reconstructions is offered by modern historians. Because history is not our main focus on this tour, our study of the scrolls in the biblical library in the following chapters will not depend on any single historical interpretation. For the sake of clarity, we will use a standard chronology as found in Coogan's *Oxford History of the Biblical World,* 1998, 447–52. Right now we will simply provide a simple, historically centrist, and widely accepted history of Israel that uses archaeological data, biblical literature, and other cultural artifacts. (You can read much more about this history in the works of Coogan, Dever, and Stager and King listed in the references.) In later chapters, we will discuss specific historical information that relates to each of the biblical scrolls.

POSTER 3.6

IT'S NOT ALL GREEK (BUT A LOT IS)

Ancient Greek travelers and writers explored far beyond their own borders, and their writings have been influential in the study of ancient history, especially for European-based cultures. Still today, many of the words and phrases we use in modern study and standard practice derive from ancient Greek authors. Here are a few examples:

alphabet The English name for the list of letters reflects the first two letters in the Greek list of letters, alpha and beta.

Egypt This English name reflects the Greek form, *Aiguptos*. In antiquity several names were used for the land we call Egypt, including the ancestor of the modern Arabic word *Misr*.

gift of the Nile This phrase was coined by the Greek historian Herodotus in the fifth century BCE, signifying Egypt's dependence on the Nile River.

hieroglyphics This is the Greek word for "sacred writing"; it was used by Greeks to refer to the writing of the Egyptian scribes and priests.

Mesopotamia This Greek term means "between the rivers" and refers to the land between the Tigris and Euphrates.

Moses Though the name Moses first appears in Hebrew texts, the way we say this name in English reflects the Greek translations of the Hebrew name. The Hebrew form is transliterated as *Moshe;* the Greek form is Μωυσης, transliterated as *Mouses*.

Solomon This is an anglicized form of the Greek pronunciation. The Hebrew pronunciation would be Sh^elomo.

synagogue This Greek word, meaning "gathering" or "gathering place," was used in Jewish texts to refer to a meeting or place for study and or prayer.

Thebes Greeks gave this name to the Egyptian city apparently because it reminded them of a Greek city by that name. The ancient Egyptian name for the area was Waset.

POSTER 3.7

THE EARLIEST KNOWN MENTION OF ISRAEL CA. 1210 BCE

. . . Plundered is (the Canaan) with every evil;

Carried off is Ashkelon; seized upon is Gezer;

Yanoam is made as that which does not exist;

Israel is laid waste, his seed is not;

Hurru is become a widow for Egypt!

All lands together, they are pacified;

Everyone who was restless, he has been bound by the King of Upper and Lower Egypt: Ba-en-Re Meri-Amon; the Son of Re: Mer-ne-Ptah Hotep-hir-Maat, given life like Re every day.

—Translation of J. Wilson in Pritchard, 378

Israelites first seem to appear as a distinct tribal confederation in the thirteenth and twelfth centuries. The Egyptian king Merneptah, who ruled from approximately 1213 to 1203 BCE, set up a stone monument in Egypt poetically commemorating his military victories over a variety of enemies, including the Israelites in Canaan. This is the earliest mention of Israel among any of the thousands of ancient records that have been unearthed. The inscription's terminology recognizes these Israelites as a distinct people group, but not as a distinct nation, kingdom, or city-state. We should imagine a loose network of small tribes and clans, mostly related by family ties. They were related by genealogy, culture, and language to other Semitic Canaanites who lived in Syria-Palestine. At the end of the Bronze Age and the beginning of the Iron Age, many of these loosely united groups that we can call proto-Israelites moved away from larger population centers in the easily accessible and populated areas of Canaan. They went into the central hill country away from the well-traversed plains, and the archaeological record demonstrates a dramatic increase in the number of small villages in the central and nearly inaccessible hill country. For several centuries these settlements continued to grow in a non-centralized manner with periods of rise and decline. Though somewhat removed, they were not completely isolated from other Canaanites in the larger region with whom they had much in common. Hebrew and other Canaanite languages are nearly identical, as we will discuss in Chapter 4, and the cultures are also very similar. The Israelites rubbed shoulders (sometimes in conflict, sometimes joining arms) with Phoenicians, Arameans, Amorites, Moabites, Edomites, Philistines, and Hittites. This region, the coastal plain and trade routes especially, but also the hill country, was under the watchful eye of larger nations, especially Egypt.

Israelite society was actually an amalgam of related tribes, organized by clans and extended families, with authority residing in the patriarchs of the social divisions, such as family leaders, clan leaders, and tribal leaders. Numerous stories in Genesis, Joshua, and Judges display aspects of this social reality. By immigration and association, clans joined with each other at different times. When we try to picture these groups that eventually came to be Israel, we should picture hundreds of small villages and a few larger towns in the central hill country.

If we consider the cultural advancements of these people, we should not think of modern cultures or of primitive, stone-age conditions. There is little doubt that the culture of these early settlements employed *oral tradition,* with stories, traditions, customs, and group moral codes being articulated and passed on by clan elders, parents, storytellers, priests, and holy persons. Some of the earliest parts of our library are poems that come from these centuries, such as we find in Genesis 49, Exodus 15, Numbers 23–24, Deuteronomy 33, and Judges 5 (see Poster 4.3). If we had been there to listen, we would have heard stories of origins of the various groups reflected in the oral traditions of the varying clans, and we would see how they are now echoed in many texts of our library. But it is notoriously difficult for modern scholars to sort out by consensus the historical kernels in the existing written records of Israelites who lived centuries later.

In the eleventh and tenth centuries BCE, pressures from neighboring peoples and city-states led these hill-country dwellers to seek greater political and cultural unity, eventually leading to the establishment of a unified kingdom. An initial and failed monarchy arose under a king named Saul (ca. 1025 BCE). The first successful king was David who, after a bitter rivalry with the family of Saul, succeeded in uniting the tribes around the year 1005 BCE.

The unification created stability and the growth of formal social institutions, and written records and traditions became more important. The Israelites began to store, copy, maintain, and collect scrolls and other forms of writing. But the unification lasted only through the reign of his David's Solomon, after which the kingdom divided into two parts along tribal lines around the year 928 BCE. But this period of the divided monarchy was culturally quite stable, and scribes, priests, and prophets continued writing.

The Northern Kingdom possessed the larger, more prosperous, more internationally strategic territory. Its strongest capital was **Samaria.** It lasted for a little more than two centuries and was ruled by a series of about twenty kings from several different families, the dynastic line of succession having never been firmly established. The Southern Kingdom continued the dynasty of David, was smaller and more secluded in the central hill country, and centered around Jerusalem. It lasted about 340 years and was also ruled by 20 kings. Both kingdoms had their moments of strength in the regional context of the numerous city-states of Canaan, especially during years of relative weakness on the part of the large nations-states in Egypt and Mesopotamia. Both kingdoms had individuals and institutions that fostered the writing of records and literature. But both of them, like their neighboring kingdoms, eventually fell to the larger superpowers of the time, as mentioned previously. Israel fell to the mighty Assyrians in 722 BCE. Many of her people were killed or exiled to the eastern portion of the vast empire, and history has been unable to trace them further. Numerous refugees fled south to Judah, some bringing writings with them. Judah collapsed under the onslaught of the Babylonian Empire in 586 BCE. Many but not all Judahites were taken captive to Babylonia, where writing traditions continued.

The forced resettlement in Babylon lasted less than 50 years. In 539 BCE Babylon fell to Cyrus the Great and his Persian forces, who liberated many exiles, allowing Judahites (the word behind the modern word *Jews*) to make the 1,000-plus mile (1,609.34 km) journey back to their homeland. With Persian royal support and a Persian appointed governor, the area around Jerusalem became a Persian province called Yehud, which is the Persian version of *Judah*. The Jewish temple of Jerusalem was rebuilt, and society in Yehud was governed along the lines of Jewish custom. By this time, Jewish enclaves were scattered in various parts of the Persian Empire and this spreading of Jewish groups who maintained in one form or another their Jewish traditions was continued throughout the succeeding periods of history. In 323 BCE the **Greek** armies of Alexander the Great took over all of Syria-Palestine, as well as all other places where Jews lived. The Greeks, like the Persians, generally allowed people to live according to their ancestral ways. Near the beginning of the second century BCE there was one remarkable exception to this policy of freedom, namely the policies the Greek king Antiochus Epiphanes IV. He persecuted the Jewish people, which led to a revolt of Jews in Syria-Palestine under the leadership of the Hasmonean family, known as the **Maccabees,** and their initial success (in 167 to 164 BCE) led to near independence for the Jews of Syria-Palestine during the waning decades of the Greek empires. But Roman military might was advancing in the east, and in 63 BCE the Roman general and statesman Pompey captured Jerusalem. The Jewish nation, with fellow Jews now living far and wide across the empire, was once again a small part of a massive empire. Generally speaking, Rome allowed a significant amount of self-rule, but the hardships of Roman taxation and a series of incompetent or callous governors led to a Jewish revolt in 68 CE. The outcome was the destruction of Jerusalem and its temple by the Roman legions in 70 CE. A second revolt in 132 CE brought an end to the dominant Jewish habitation in and around Jerusalem. The Roman Emperor Hadrian renamed Jerusalem *Aelia Capitolina.*

We have taken our political historical tour to this point in time because, as noted in the last chapter, even though most of the books of our library had all been written in some form by the end of the period of Greek rule (ca. 140 BCE), some of them existed in many different forms well into the Roman era. The work of collecting and selecting continued among various Jewish groups in the last two centuries BCE and first two centuries CE. We possess the actual physical remains of such a collection from one group of Jews from the Roman period (first century CE), thanks to the fortunate discovery of the Dead Sea Scrolls. It is also during this Roman period (late second century CE) that influential Jewish leaders settled on a particular collection of books as sacred for Jews under their influence. It is also during this period that the use of the codex began to spread, eventually making possible the publication of Bibles as we know them—in a single book.

Many things, both positive and negative, might be said in reflection on this brief and rapid historical overview, but for now I have only these two observations: the Israelites (or Judahites or Jews)—exhibited a remarkable ability to survive and conserve and transform their own traditions; so much so that these traditions have always been alive and are part of living communities to this day. Secondly, as a small nation of Syria-Palestine, like all of their neighbors, the Israelites' political fortunes and their daily lives were always lived out *under* the power or threats of the great empires, the superpowers of the ancient world. Many ancient Israelites must have lived with a sense of vulnerability, threat, fear, and tenuousness of existence. Israel was no superpower, and as modern readers we should be aware of this significant difference.

Everybody's History

The political events of Israel and ancient Near Eastern history impacted every individual who lived in these lands. But in another sense, it is the daily histories—the normal existence of individuals—which are equally (or more?) important for our trip into the world that produced biblical literature. Let's put it this way: If we want to understand the world of a modern author living in the United States, knowing who is president or which governmental actions are being talked about in the newspapers may not be as important to us as knowing about his or her daily life. How does she live, what are the ordinary things and phenomena of this person's existence? These are the sorts of things we often already know about most modern writers from our own culture, simply because we live in the same world and so have a great deal of knowledge in common. The question is not so much about the individual personal lives of writers but about the realities of daily existence in a given culture. Simply by knowing that an author wrote in New York from 2000 to 2002, many facts about his or her real world can be safely assumed. The scrolls of our library are full of the references and allusions to the stuff of daily existence—crops, water, weather, topography, family and clan life, physical ailments, and much more.

How was life lived among ancient Israelites? To answer such a question in detail I recommend the books *Life in Biblical Israel* by Philip King and Lawrence Stager and *Daily Life in Biblical Times* by Oded Borowski. There are many other helpful books by historians, archaeologists, and anthropologists as well. In the next few pages we will spend a few brief minutes in ancient Israelite culture. As we already noted, in the 1200s and 1100s BCE Israelites lived mostly in small villages dotting the central hill country with populations usually under 300. Over the centuries, their population grew and so did their towns and cities, a few of which may have reached between 20,000 and 40,000. Frequent wars against immediate neighbors or larger and more distant superpowers and forced exiles brought the population down. The average life span, due to disease and general hardship, was around 40. The society was organized around extended families then larger clans, and then tribes, headed by patriarchs at every level. Parents typically arranged their children's marriages to blood relatives. Girls were married in their early to mid teens and boys in their early twenties. Women often died in childbirth and infant and child mortality was high, so family size was small, with perhaps two or three children reaching adulthood. A larger family was considered advantageous in many ways, and so society often allowed a man to marry more than one woman in an effort to increase the family size.

All ancient Israelites lived much "closer to the ground" than most modern urban dwellers, meaning they depended daily on their own skills to obtain food and shelter. The vast majority of Israelites were agro-pastoral, that is, small-crop farmers and keepers of small flocks. Typical houses were small, often with walls of mud brick or plastered stones, dirt floors, and roofs made of wooden beams covered with plastered woven branches. A wooden door with a wooden lock opened to reveal two to four rooms separated by stone pillars; there was often a second story for sleeping and eating, the first floor being used for animals and work. Windows never had glass and were only small slits in the walls. Animals were often kept inside the house, so the dwelling also served as a barn. The house served as the primary work space: grain was crushed into flour, meals were prepared, flax was woven and made into cloth, cloth was made into clothing, animals were fed and watered. It was also the storage area: oils, wines and water were stored in clay or stone jars; solid foods in baskets or jars. Some staple provisions could be stored in plastered pits. Cooking was done in stone pits or in ovens constructed of baked clay, either in a small courtyard in front of the house or on the first floor of the house. Beds consisted of mats, blankets, or even one's tunic, which were placed on the floor at night. Do we need to mention that there was no bathroom?! In one house there might reside a man and his wife or wives, their unmarried children, unwed or widowed aunts and uncles, widowed parents, and sometimes married children. As families outgrew a dwelling, wedded children might move out and establish their own house, often attached to that of their parents. Significant physical labor was done by everyone in the family who was capable; survival required it.

In most areas in which Israelites lived, agriculture depended on rainfall. There was no luxury of a Nile to consistently flood the plain and water the land. In Syria-Palestine there were two seasons: dry, from approximately May or June to September, and wet, from October to May. The agricultural seasons, often reflected in writings of our library, are actually the subject of oldest surviving Hebrew inscription, from the tenth century BCE (Display 3.5). It is a planting and harvesting **calendar** of sorts, starting in what we call autumn, around August or September. In the fall was the olive harvest, followed by several plantings; grain first (e.g., wheat and barley), then legumes (e.g., lentils, beans, chickpeas) and vegetables and fruits (e.g., cucumbers, melons, onions, leeks, garlic). Of the larger crops, flax (for cloth

DISPLAY 3.5

His two months are (olive) harvest,

His two months are planting (grain),

His two months are late planting;

His month is hoeing up of flax,

His month is harvest of barley,

His month is harvest and feasting;

His two months are vine-tending,

His month is summer fruit.

–Translated by W. F. Albright, in Pritchard 1969, 320.

Agricultural Calendar, the Oldest Known Hebrew Inscription, ca. 900 BCE.

production) was harvested first, then came the barley harvest, followed by wheat. The dry months brought the work of vine tending and then fruit harvesting (e.g., grapes, figs). Again, everyone who was physically capable—children, men, and women—did physical labor.

There is, of course, much more that could be said about daily life, but we'll stop there so we can move on to a brief history of the biblical scrolls themselves. Having in our imaginations a sense of how the Israelites and other people really lived their lives will improve our reading of biblical scrolls dramatically, especially because our modern technologies and modes of living are so different and far removed from the land.

Questions for Further Study

1. In what ways do you think superpowers interacted with lesser nations?
2. From the perspective of a superpower nation, how would the history of Israel (or another lesser nation) read and sound differently?
3. What difference does the identity and perspective of the author make when we read an ancient historical source?
4. What aspects of ancient Near-Eastern culture do you see in your culture? What differences do you see?
5. In what ways might it be true that geography determines history?
6. Make a list of the differences in national life, daily life, military actions, and culture before the development of modern travel technology.
7. The ancient people of the cultures of Syria-Palestine lived much "closer to the ground" than modern urban dwellers. What does this mean, and how should it affect the way we imagine their lives and history? How should it affect the way we read biblical scrolls?

References

Anderson, Bernhard. *Understanding the Old Testament.* 4th ed. Upper Saddle River, NJ: Prentice Hall, 1998.

Berquist, Jon. *Judaism in Persia's Shadow.* Minneapolis, MN: Fortress, 1995.

Boardman, John, et al. *The Oxford History of the Classical World.* New York: Oxford, 1986.

Borowski, Oded. *Daily Life in Biblical Times.* Atlanta, GA: Society of Biblical Literature, 2003.

Coogan, Michael, ed. *The Oxford History of the Biblical World.* New York: Oxford University, 1998.

Cook, J. M. *The Persian Empire.* New York: Schocken, 1983.

Dever, William. *What Did the Biblical Writers Know & When Did They Know It?* Grand Rapids, MI: Eerdmans. 2001.

Dever, William. *Who Were the Early Israelites and Where Did They Come From?* Grand Rapids, MI: Eerdmans, 2003.

Green, Peter. *Alexander of Macedon, 356-323.* Berkeley, CA: University of California, 1991.

Hallo, William. *The Context of Scripture.* 3 vols. Leiden: E. J. Brill, 2003.

Hoerth, Alfred J., et al. *Peoples of the Old Testament World.* Grand Rapids, MI: Baker, 1994.

King, Philip J., and Lawrence E. Stager. *Life in Biblical Israel.* Louisville, KY: Westminster John Knox, 2001.

Markoe, Glenn E. *Phoenicians.* Berkeley, CA: University of California, 2000.

Mazar Amihai, *Archaeology of the Land of the Bible 10,000–586 BCE.* New York: Doubleday, 1990.

Mendenhall, George E. *Ancient Israel's Faith and History.* Louisville, KY: Westminster John Knox, 2001.

Meyers, Eric M., ed. *The Oxford Encyclopedia of Archaeology in the Near East.* 5 vols. New York: Oxford University, 1997.

Millard, Alan. "Amorites," in *Dictionary of the Ancient Near East.* Philadelphia: University of Pennsylvania, 2000.

Roux, Georges. *Ancient Iraq.* 2nd ed. New York: Penguin, 1980.

Pritchard, James. *The Ancient Near East In Pictures Relating to the Old Testament.* 2nd ed. Princeton, NJ: Princeton University, 1969.

Pritchard, James. *Ancient Near Eastern Texts Relating to the Old Testament.* 3rd ed. Princeton, NJ: Princeton University, 1969.

Saggs, H. W. F. *Everyday Life in Ancient Babylonia and Assyria.* New York: Dorset, 1987.

Soden, Wolfram von. *The Ancient Orient.* Grand Rapids, MI: Eerdmans, 1994.

Tubb, Jonathan N. *Canaanites.* Norman: University of Oklahoma, 1998.

Wallbank, F. W. *The Hellenistic World.* Cambridge, MA: Harvard, 1981.

The Composition of Biblical Scrolls

Hebrew Language

As we in the twenty-first century enter this library, we are entering foreign territory. Its foreign nature is perhaps most obvious as we consider the language of biblical writings; we've already noted some of the difficulties of translating. The scrolls of this ancient Jewish library were composed by people who thought and spoke in Hebrew. The vast majority of the writings are in Hebrew, with a few sections of two books in a closely related language, Aramaic. Linguists and other language scholars have learned much about the usage, history, and development of many ancient languages including Hebrew, one of the large family of Semitic languages. This language family was spread throughout the Fertile Crescent (see the table) and remains the longest-running language family—dialects of it have been spoken since at least 2500 BCE until today.

POSTER 4.1
THE SEMITIC LANGUAGE FAMILY

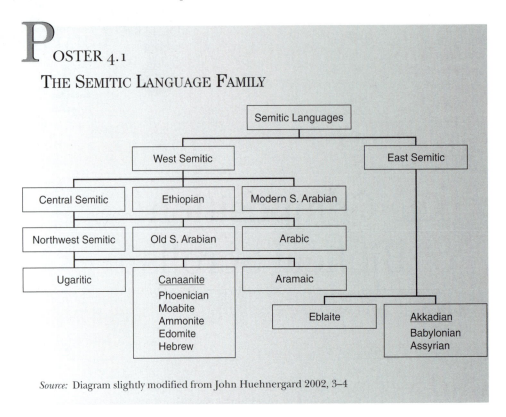

Source: Diagram slightly modified from John Huehnergard 2002, 3–4

As we mentioned in the last chapter, Semitic peoples of the western Fertile Crescent, the various Canaanite nations, were among the first to use and spread the 22-letter alphabet. That alphabet is the one used in the Hebrew scrolls of our library. There are also other ancient Hebrew writings preserved.

The earliest inscriptions in Hebrew date from the tenth century (900s) BCE. The form of Hebrew preserved in most of the compositions in our library biblical literature is somewhat later and varies depending on which scroll we read. For any library that contains writings from different periods, the variance in linguistic forms is perfectly normal and expected. All languages evolve over times with usage, and linguists and language scholars have detected early and later forms of the Hebrew preserved in our texts. Some poems found in our scrolls, for example, may preserve ancient forms of Hebrew that were used before the tenth century BCE. At the other end of the spectrum, late forms of Hebrew (e.g., in Ecclesiastes, Song of Songs, Daniel) are often dated to the fourth to second centuries BCE.

Time Periods of Composing the Scrolls

We have one more piece of history to review before we move on, and that is a simple basic history of the composition of the scrolls we are about to study. For each of our scrolls we will address this question more specifically later, but for now we will establish a general timeframe. When were they written? We know it was before the invention

Poster 4.2

A History and Comparison of the Alphabet

the alphabet

Sinai script, proto-Canaanite, 1500 BCE

Proto-Canaanite, 13th-12th. Century

Phoenician, 1000 BCE

Gezer Calendar, Hebrew, late 10th Cent.

Mesha Steele, Hebrew, mid 9th Cent.

Phoenician, late 9th Cent.

Siloam Inscription, Hebrew, late 8th Cent.

Hebrew Seals, 7th Cent.

Arad Ostraca, Hebrew, 6th Cent.

Elephantine Papyrus, Aramaic, late 5th Cent.

Qumran, Leviticus scroll, late 2nd Cent.

Samaritan Manuscript, 13th Cent. CE

Qumran, Isaiah scroll, late 2nd Cent. BCE

Classical Greek Script

Latin Script

Nabataean Script, 1st Cent. BCE

Classical Arabic Script

the israel museum, jerusalem, 1981

POSTER 4.3

EARLY HEBREW SONGS AND POEMS

The dates presented here are currently debated by scholars, but they are a credible estimate of the date of composition of the earliest pieces of literature found in biblical texts. Other scholars argue for dates not quite so old. Some believe that these older dates apply only to oral forms of the poems, but the written forms come from the eighth century BCE or later.

Poem	Composition Date, by Century
Genesis 49	11th
Exodus 15	12th
Numbers 23–24	11th
Deuteronomy 33	11th
Judges 5	12th

Source: Based on D.N. Freedman 1980.

of the codex, before "the Bible," but when and by whom? Who began collecting them? What is the precise history behind the many different compositions in our Bibles today? We must first acknowledge that we do not have detailed answers to these and hundreds of other questions that we often ask about the history of our Bibles. But we do have a substantial amount of historical data that enable us to reconstruct a plausible account of the development of biblical literature. These questions are essentially historical in nature and so for the modern investigator they require historical evidence. We do not have the minutes from the "library acquisition meetings," but we do have much telling evidence in the scrolls themselves and in the material evidence that archaeologists have uncovered. For example, we have the fantastic discovery of the Dead Sea Scrolls that gives us an invaluable first-century BCE and CE snapshot of the development and condition of biblical scrolls.

First we should point out that the building of the library is a stage neither chronologically nor logically separated from the writing and editing of individual documents within that library. It did not happen that all the scrolls had been written and then someone decided to start a museum collection. The collecting of scrolls in various places of the social structure in ancient Israel was just one aspect of the social, religious, and political fabric of time. The background and development of this library is intimately tied to the community of ancient Jews, the Israelites.

In speaking of the development of a library, ancient Israel did not have one official library. The historical situation is much more complicated than that. As we discussed in Chapter 3, Israelites first appear in the historical record of the ancient world in the late thirteenth century BCE. The 1200s to about 1000 saw this loose amalgam of tribes and clans become a more or less stable, politically organized, and land-holding group. These gains became firmly established during the tenth to eighth centuries BCE with the rise of the centralized monarchies of Judah and Israel. It was in such settled situations, with the growth of formal social institutions, that Israelite society was afforded the luxury of storing, copying, maintaining, and collecting scrolls or other recorded media (clay or stone tablets, for example). Indeed, as divided village and clan politics gave way to regional unification and control under the rule of kings, the demands of governmental bureaucracy would have encouraged and sponsored such activity. It is not that Israel was an entirely illiterate people prior to this time. Certainly, Israelite traditions such as folktales and poetic songs, like many others in the ancient world, existed orally in their culture, and some may have been put in a written form prior to the rise of the more centrally organized state. In fact, Hebrew language scholars speculate that the oldest texts embedded in biblical literature go back to the centuries just prior to the rise of the monarchy (see Poster 4.3).

However, there are no direct Israelite textual records of these texts preserved from the twelfth through the ninth centuries BCE. As the monarchy grew, other institutions or loosely organized groups also flourished, such as scribes, priests, and prophetic groups. It is during this period that the Israelite inscriptions and other artifacts began appearing in the archaeological record.

Many of the scrolls of our Bibles are a product of this unifying process at several different levels. In some cases, older oral traditions of different clans would have been lost, while others were carried on and mixed with traditions of other clans, thus creating new traditions. Cultural traditions developed and were shared, including common religious traditions. Archaeological and biblical evidence shows that YHVH was the dominant deity of Israelite clans but not the only one. (Recall the brief discussion in Chapter 3.) Later this developed into YHVH-only traditions, and deities worshipped earlier were put aside. So also, stories about the past came to be shared and held in common and often served to unify various clans. For example, a common tradition in many of the scrolls of our library is a story of Israelites living in and then escaping from Egypt. This had become a dominant story in the oral traditions by the time the scrolls of our library were written. Modern historians have often compared this "adoption" of originally independent traditions about the past by a larger society to the way American history is told and celebrated. In the United States, stories of the 102 English Puritans of the Mayflower and their Thanksgiving Day in 1621 are recounted and celebrated as the common heritage of all Americans, even though historically speaking these traditions are the actual genealogical heritage of a very small number of people. Even though most people in the United States today are descendents of immigrants from much later times and completely different places, these stories are still held in common and are often spoken of as "our" stories. This is a good example of a national "myth," and of one that began with a small group but was later adopted for a much wider culture.

From about 1000 to 586 BCE, many documents were likely produced by scribes of the royal courts and the temples. Writing was not an activity of everyone in the population, but it was becoming important in the management of a more centralized bureaucracy. One clue that writing was a bureaucratic is provided by the many documents mentioned in the scrolls of Kings and Chronicles as historical sources (e.g., the Book of the Acts of Solomon, 1 Kings 11:41). None of these source documents have been preserved in their original form, but it is probable that parts of them were

POSTER 4.4

I CAN READ ALL BY MYSELF!

The following translation is the first part of a letter sent by a Jewish military commander at Lachish to his superior commander around 589 BCE.

Your servant Hoshayahu (hereby) reports to my lord Haush. May Yahweh give you the very best possible news.

And now, please explain to your servant the meaning of the letter which you sent to our servant yesterday evening. For your servant has been sick at heart ever since you sent (that letter) to your servant. In it my lord said: "Don't you know how to read a letter?" As Yahweh lives, no one has ever tried to read me a letter! Moreover, whenever any letter comes to me and I have read it, I can repeat it down to the smallest detail.

–Translation of Dennis Pardee, in Hallo 1997, 3:79

incorporated into scrolls that now form part of modern Bibles. From the eighth century onward, archaeologists have turned up a remarkable amount of writing activity even on a more popular level: One scholar calls it "truly astonishing" (Stern 2001, 2:169) and another calls it an "epigraphic explosion" (Schniedewind 2004, 98). In the early centuries of the monarchy, most writers would have been centered in the royal court and would have produced mainly, but not exclusively, administrative documents and records for the affairs of state, including those of political and religious interests. But in subsequent centuries of the monarchy, as urbanization dramatically increased, especially in Jerusalem, so did writing, including many kinds of literature, which became increasingly important in Jewish culture (Schneidewind 2004, 93–6). We also find remains of economic and military communications in this period, often written on clay potsherds, as was common. In one letter of the early sixth century, a mid-level Jewish military commander vigorously insists that he has no need of a scribe to read his commander's written communications; he can read well himself (see Poster 4.4). Thus, a growing number of scrolls or tablets were produced in royal offices, temples and shrines, and later educational and prophetic scribal houses. These writings contained an indeterminate number of narratives about the past, traditional myths and tales, songs and hymns, rituals, oracular pronouncements and visions, royal annals and tax rolls, epigrams, legal compilations, event chronicles, and genealogical records. Depending on the setting, some of these were more highly valued and had more authority than others. The king and his court were interested in promulgating laws and traditions that promoted social stability and the royal interests; other groups, such as priest and prophets, would have had their own interests and favorite scrolls. Fortunately, the Jewish literature that has survived does not have a monolithic character or outlook that reflects only one of these groups; it is quite diverse.

Another example of divergent viewpoints in biblical literature arose from the division of the nation of Israel into two separate nation-states around 928 BCE. The royal court in Southern Jerusalem had interests and viewpoints distinct from those of the Northern court at Samaria. Indeed, such distinctions in the origin of sources can

Display 4.1 | A MODERN PHOTOGRAPH OF RECENTLY PREPARED
PARCHMENT ROLLS

be observed in narratives such as 1 Kings 15:29–21:30 (North) and most of 2 Kings (South) and in the names of sources such as the Book of the Chronicles of the Kings of Israel (North, 1 Kings 14:19) and the Book of the Annals of the Kings of Judah (South, 1 Kings 14:29). Scholars have reasonably speculated that when the Northern Kingdom of Israel fell to Assyrian forces in 722 BCE, some persons with access to northern writings must have escaped to the South, bringing with them not only oral traditions but probably some written sources as well. Parts of these traditions, oral or written, were eventually incorporated into writings composed after 722 BCE in the Southern Kingdom, some of which survive today in the biblical library.

In our modern world we think of written documents as vitally important, but we should never assume that an ancient culture valued the written text in the same manner as we do. It is fascinating to study ancient cultures and see developments and shifts in attitudes toward and use of various media. The growing importance of written tradition in religious affairs is observed in the late history of the Southern Kingdom, and an excellent illustration of its growth is found in the scroll now called 2 Kings. In 2 Kings 22–23, one of the South's most famous kings, Josiah (who reigned 640 to 609 BCE), is reported to have launched a religious reform based on the interpretation by Huldah, a prophetess, of a scroll found in the temple by a

P OSTER 4.5

SUMMARY SO FAR

To summarize our compositional history so far, it is in the tenth to sixth centuries BCE, and especially in the eighth to sixth, that ancient Jewish culture had the requisite means and cultural desire for written documents to promote the production of many written texts. During this period monarchies of ancient Jews many of the scrolls that now appear in our modern Bibles began taking shape.

priest (ca. 621 BCE). We should point out the authority of oral pronouncement, Huldah's words, in this story. What scroll was this? Many scholars believe that the text interpreted by Huldah was an early version of what we now know as Deuteronomy, because Josiah's reforms seem to be in accord with that book. Regardless of the exact identity of the text, the valuation and use of a scroll for religiouspolitical purposes in this seventh-century-BCE context is certainly credible and gives us a sense of the function of the written word and oral word at that time: a scroll is found in the sacred temple and so a word from the deity is sought to determine what should be done. An *oral* authoritative pronouncement by a prophetess/prophet in the name of the God is made that confirms the legitimacy of the *written* scroll. Once the scroll is valued by a community as a document that represents divine will, it is not likely to be discarded by any who considered the oral pronouncement genuine. But, if communal voices arise that question the authority of part or all of the text, then adjustments may well be made to the tradition. So, in this story of Huldah and the scroll we can see that the written scroll is valuable as a source for knowing God's will, but we also see that the relationship between oral and written authority could be complex. Sometimes oral and written authorities were cooperative, but sometimes they were contentious. In every case, however, the written word's authority depends on the valuation of living persons who affirm or disaffirm the text in speech and practice.

From the end of the period of monarchy (sixth century BCE), another book that provides us some interesting evidence about the practice of writing in ancient Israel is the one named for the famous Jewish prophet Jeremiah. The scroll now called Jeremiah, which had several different forms even in antiquity, is a fascinating and rambling literary conglomeration from the last desperate decades before Jerusalem's fall to invading armies of the powerful Babylonian Empire in 586 BCE. Look at the different kinds of writings and media referred to in Jeremiah.

- writings of scribes, priests, and other prophets (Jeremiah 7:22; 8:8–9; 29:24–31)
- the written scrolls of Jeremiah, penned by his scribe Baruch (Jeremiah 29:1–31; 36:1–32)
- the oral proclamations of Jeremiah (Jeremiah 37:38)
- **oracles** of other prophets, reports of which have been preserved in written form (Jeremiah 23:16–32; 29:8–9)

This list represents the kinds of religious communications taking place in the days of Jeremiah.

When Jerusalem and the small country of Judah were decimated by Nebuchadnezzar's Babylonian forces in 597 and 586 BCE, many documents were lost to the flames, undoubtedly forever. But some, including some of Jeremiah's writings, survived and were apparently transferred to Babylon with Judean exiles. Many scholars hold that in those years of exile, some segments of Jewish society were motivated to preserve scrolls and even to create new ones that would provide written witness to their legal, cultic, narrative, and prophetic heritage. Such a scenario is plausible because evidence suggests that in Babylon Jews were allowed to retain their own cultural practices and that their community was economically viable enough to carry out such a literary enterprise. It also shows that by this time Jewish literary activity was not entirely dependent on royal Israelite support, for there no longer was an Israelite kingdom. It seems likely that the sixth to fifth centuries BCE witnessed a crucial literary output by Jewish authors and scribes and that many of the books in modern Bibles were substantially formed during those years. Scrolls written during those formative centuries incorporate oral traditions and even written sources that were older and available. For example, the scroll called by the name of Ezekiel, a prophet of the sixth-century exile to Babylon, uses material now contained in the books of Exodus and Leviticus (Friedman, 1987 161–73). Substantial portions of those two scrolls likely come from a period before the exile. However, there are no indications that the content of the scrolls of this period had so crystallized in the minds of their readers and writers that they could never be changed; changes and emendations by later scribes or authors were common and were not thought objectionable. Remember, modern sensibilities about authorship rights had no bearing.

When the exiled Jews were allowed to travel the 500 plus miles (805 km) (a 2–3 month trip) back to their homeland beginning in 538 BCE under the more liberally minded Persian empire, the Persian-appointed Jewish governors were charged with shaping the newly constituted Persian-controlled Jewish state according to ancestral law in a written form and in harmony with Persian policy and with royal financial support (Ezra 7:11–26). Listen to the way these traditions are presented; it tells us a lot about the perceived value and function of ancient scrolls for Jewish social leaders at this time when we see references to God's "commands through his prophets" (Ezra 9:10–11), the written "torah which YHVH commanded through Moses" (Nehemiah 8:14), and the "scroll of the torah of God" (Nehemiah 8:18). The writings referred to are clearly works that one group of Jewish returnees from Babylon in the fifth century led by Ezra undoubtedly viewed as peculiarly authoritative.

So, what scrolls was the author referring to, and do we still have them? In the two instances where these authoritative works are actually quoted (Ezra 9:11–12 quoting "prophets" and Nehemiah 8:15 quoting the "instruction of Moses"), the quotations do not match any passages that are still preserved in our modern Bibles. This tells us several things.

1. Jews of the sixth and fifth centuries possessed documents that they considered to have the authority of God through Moses and prophets.

2. Some of the authoritative documents quoted or referred to in Ezra-Nehemiah are similar to some books that we have in our Bibles (e.g., Leviticus and Deuteronomy), based on a general similarity of contents of the quotations with other scrolls we have and the widespread practice of using earlier traditions.

3. However similar they may be, it is equally clear that the evolution of such writings had not ground to a halt; the creative inspiration still flourished, creating new writings and preserving and revising older ones.

4. The traditions of Moses, hero of liberation, as recipient of revelations from Israel's God, were taking on heightened status in this later period.

In relative security and in a culture in which writing and literature had now become important on many levels, Jews of the Persian and Greek periods continued to produce literature of great variety, even though the Jewish settlement in Syria-Palestine was not always thriving economically. In addition to scrolls known as *Torah,* "Instruction" (of God and/or Moses), there was a host of other literary products of the Jewish communities. Written collections of prophetic oracles from the persons and disciples of Isaiah, Jeremiah, Ezekiel, and others had been compiled, edited, supplemented, copied, and preserved through the exile. Narratives of earlier tribal times, monarchies, civil wars, and national demise, all of which likely had their oral and written forms prior to exile, also survived the destruction. Some of these narratives would be major components of later works. And the writing never stopped.

The fourth century BCE through the first centuries CE saw a large output of scrolls from many different Jewish communities. Many of these writings are still extant, either due to continuous preservation in Jewish or Christian communities or by virtue of having been discovered by archaeologists, such as the Dead Sea Scrolls. Not surprisingly, Jewish writings of the fourth century BCE through the first centuries CE continued the practice of using older materials, both written and oral. The book called Daniel, which survives in various forms stemming from the second century BCE, quotes (in verse 9.2) Jeremiah 25:11–12 and 29:10 as an important but cryptic revelation about the future of the world. A book known now as **Jubilees,** which was important in antiquity and now part of the Ethiopic Christian Bible, claims divine origin and Mosaic authorship and was supremely valued by the vigorous and prolific Jewish community that produced the Dead Sea Scrolls. So also, scrolls of Isaiah, Deuteronomy, and Psalms were used by Jewish communities, and they are frequently quoted in literature of the second century BCE to first century CE.

Collecting the Scrolls

So who were the Jews who were keeping these various writings? Since the eighth-century Assyrian monarchy, Jewish communities had spread to many parts of ancient Near Eastern world (e.g., Persia, Babylon, Syria, Egypt, Cyprus, Greece), and no single group was always the universal authority over all other Jews, especially after the fall of Jerusalem in the sixth century. In the realm of literature, there was no governing body with the power to decide and impose a canonical scripture for all Jews, dispersed as they were over a vast geographic and cultural expanse. We are not even close to talking about a Bible. In the fourth century BCE, Ezra may have established or propounded some form of a Torah as the formal repository of ancestral narrative and law, but in the centuries to come this did not result in a world-wide authoritative Judaism controlled by a Jerusalem priesthood or governor. Although the Jerusalem temple priesthood and political leaders had significant influence among Jews from the sixth century BCE to the first century CE, they were in no position to define or regulate international Jewish life and religion. Neither could they control the multiple developments of what some scholars have come to call the "Judaisms" of the culturally fertile Hellenistic world. When we look at the variety of Jewish expressions in the fifth to second centuries BCE, we discover that the designation *Jewish* must include, for example,

- the separatist *Yahad* community near the Dead Sea (second century BCE to first century CE). This community valued many writings as authoritative revelations from God to Moses or other prophets that are not part of any Bibles today.

- the Jewish military colony on Elephantine Island in southern Egypt serving the Persian king fifth to fourth century BCE. This Jewish colony built its own temple and held sacrifices there.

- the many Jews influenced by aspects of Greek culture and ideals after the campaigns of Alexander the Great (late fourth century BCE). An example is Philo (ca. 20 BCE–50 CE), the Jewish-Greek philosopher who wrote extensively on Genesis, Exodus, Leviticus, Numbers, and Deuteronomy as allegories of Platonic ideas.

- the Jewish author of the *Letter of Aristaeus* (first century BCE). This writer said that Greeks and Jews worship the same God, only using different names.

- Jews who penned and used books as if written by ancient heroes such as Enoch and Abraham, though not used by any Jewish communities today.

- the more well-known groups. Some examples include the **Essenes, Sadducees, and Pharisees.**

- the **Samaritans,** who later came to be distinguished from Jews, but have always been closely related. Samaritans for a time had their own alternative temple, and accepted as their holy books only the scrolls of Genesis, Exodus, Leviticus, Numbers, and Deuteronomy in a form slightly different from their Jewish neighbors.

And these are just some of the groups of Jews who maintained collections of writings. By the first century CE, large and diverse Jewish communities thrived—using the hyperbole of a first Christian document called Acts (2:5)—in "every nation under heaven," and many of these communities had access to written forms of their Jewish traditions.

No doubt various Jewish communities collected scrolls. In Hellenistic and Roman times, libraries were becoming more and more numerous. Jewish literature from this period clues us in to a few of these. One author from 180 BCE shows awareness of a collection of The Twelve, which may well be the same prophets listed as The Twelve in modern Jewish Bibles (Sirach 49:10). Another composition, 2 Maccabees, speaks of Judas the Hasmonean in the second century BCE collecting the "books that had been lost on account of the war," even as Nehemiah in the fifth century BCE was thought to have "founded a library and collected books concerning the kings and prophets and books of David, and letters of kings about votive offerings" (2 Maccabees 2:13–14). The report of Nehemiah's activity is not corroborated by our older sources about Nehemiah—though it is by no means incredible—but we at least gain a sense of library building as conceived in the second century. Also in the second century, the very influential composition called Jubilees (45:15) makes reference to the collection, preservation, and recopying (or re-editing) of scrolls. The Jewish author of the *Letter of Aristaeus* in the first century BCE speaks of the library and librarians of Alexandria and also of scrolls under the care of the high priest in Jerusalem.

In speaking of the growth of a library we ought not to think that there was only expansion. Even as some books were being added to collections and enjoying some authority by virtue of their use in Jewish communities, other scrolls that had once been authoritative were losing their force, perhaps being partially incorporated into other scrolls and then replaced. There are clear references in our biblical writings to texts that were sacred or authoritative to one degree or another in earlier times but that were discarded later. We have a few fragments of some of those texts because later authors quoted them. For example, lines of poetry are quoted from the no longer extant Book of Yashar, twice invoked as an authoritative source for knowing about God's actions on behalf of Israel (Joshua 10:13; 2 Samuel 1:18). Also, the Book of the Wars of YHVH is also used in Numbers 21:14. The books of Kings and Chronicles name many sources, and although we are not sure what to make of their status vis-à-vis other writings, we do know that these books, whatever they were, were not retained by later generations from any Jewish community and so are lost to us. And here's another example: if the **Book of the Covenant,** or mentioned in Exodus 24:7 ever existed as a separate document, as it likely did, it certainly held authoritative status for some. Today its contents form part of our book of Exodus. It is clear then that the books of modern Bibles were not Israel's first sacred and authoritative texts; there were earlier authoritative scrolls that were highly valued, and some were even seen as divinely sanctioned. What remains in modern day Bibles is the result of the continuous choices of Jewish authors and communities, and later Christian ones, through the ages.

The group(s) that likely had the most direct influence on the particular collections that led more or less directly to our contemporary Bibles were likely the scribes and priests associated with the Jerusalem temple during the last few centuries BCE and the first century CE, during the Persian, Greek, Hasmonean, and early Roman periods of Jerusalem's history. But we know very little about their practices of scroll writing and collecting. We know a lot about some neighboring Jews, the ones who wrote and collected the Dead Sea Scrolls, but unfortunately we have not found a cache of scrolls from Jerusalem. But this is not surprising, really, because in the first and second centuries CE, Jewish revolts in the oppressive Roman Empire met with severe military actions in Jerusalem and **Palestine** (68 to 70 and 132 to 135 CE) and in the Diaspora (areas outside of the land of Israel), including Alexandria (115 CE). One result of the complex and tortuous history of that time period was the loss of flourishing diversity among Jewish communities and the ascendancy of what would later be called rabbinic Judaism. Rabbinic Judaism, the historical foundation of modern forms of Judaism, drew heavily from the rich heritage of the Pharisees. It featured a strong regard for temple traditions and was guided by gifted and forward-looking rabbis. In these same two centuries, another prominent group evolved—first within Judaism and later outside of it—which came to be known as Christians. Jewish and Christian leaders and communities of this period had a major impact on Bibles that we still read today.

We have some evidence from the end of the first century CE regarding the collecting of scrolls from the point of view of Pharisees living in Rome. After the destruction of the temple and the devastation of Jerusalem in 70 CE, the Jewish historian Josephus (ca. 95 CE) writes in his work *On the Antiquity of the Jews* (a.k.a. *Against Apion* that Jews do not have myriad books, but rather "just 22 properly accredited books" 1:37–38). This is our first explicit record of a formal accounting of what one Jew considered to be the complete list of sacred Jewish books. Josephus reveals much about the status of these works in his mind. He considers them the product of prophets, and their perfection is due to the "inspiration of God." He also uses a threefold division of Moses (5 books), prophetic history (13 books), and "hymns to God and advice to men about life" (4 books). We can make reasonable conjectures about his categorization of most books, but we cannot be certain of what he included in each category, because he does not list them by name. It should also be noted that in writing his own history of the Jews, Josephus did not always use the same parts of the Hebrew Bible and form of books that we now use. For example, he used a Greek version of Ezra's activity (known today as 1 Esdras) rather than the Ezra-Nehemiah version found in the Hebrew Bible. This fact shows us we should be wary of simply identifying Josephus's 22 books with forms that we know of from the Hebrew Bible, because even if a book title is the same, the book itself may be different.

We have another piece of evidence about the collection of Jewish scrolls in this period. A writing called 4 Ezra is a fascinating Jewish work from around 100 CE. Of Jewish origin—but used later in Christian circles—it refers to a legend about all the ancient authoritative scrolls having been destroyed, an event that then required Ezra, by divine inspiration, to dictate the words of 94 books. Ezra made 24 of the books available to the public but retained the 70 others for later dissemination (4 Ezra 14:19–48). Do these 24 books represent 24 books that the 4 Ezra author thought of as the public collection of sacred scrolls, similar to Josephus's 22 books? Many think there is continuity between them. On the other hand, the additional 70 books, which for the author of 4 Ezra are the more important ones, demonstrate that in the second century CE some Jews considered it perfectly appropriate to add more books to the sacred library. But what were those 70 books? And did they even exist outside the 4 Ezra author's imagination?

Josephus and 4 Ezra are helpful, but they tantalize us by not revealing as much about the process of selecting scrolls as we might wish. The end result is well known, but our knowledge of the process still contains a good deal of speculation. For the newly established rabbinic Jewish leadership of the second century CE—if we are to judge from extant rabbinic writings—the matter of which scrolls were considered holy seems quite settled, with only a few possible question marks, though we have no list from this early rabbinic period. The great literary product of second-century Judaism was the **Mishna,** a codification of rabbinic thought and discussion. Nothing is said directly in this large work about putting books in the library of Judaism or confirming those that were there, but in one section, Yadayim 3:5, there is an enigmatic report about the sacredness of Song of Songs and Qohelet (Ecclesiastes). Some scholars think this may be an echo of discussions about the appropriateness for the collection of authoritative writings of various books. A roughly contemporary rabbinic work, the Tosefta (Yadayim 2:13), similarly discusses the book of Ben Sira (Sirach).

A 24-scroll library of Hebrew compositions (with a few Aramaic sections) emerged from rabbinic Judaism and came to dominate Jewish tradition after that time. By the time of the Babylonian Talmud (ca. 500 CE), a great compendium of Jewish learning of the time, the 24 books were commonly divided into three sections (Law, Prophets, and Writings), though the books of Prophets and Writings are listed in a variety of orders when we compare talmudic lists and other manuscript witnesses. We cannot be sure that all these 24 texts were originally housed in the temple prior to its destruction in 70 CE, though such a scenario is possible. It does not surprise us that no archaeological remains of the Jerusalem library have been found, given Jerusalem's tumultuous history. Historical disasters have brought the demise of many other ancient libraries too, such as Augustus Caesar's library at the temple of Apollo on the Palatine Hill and the even more famed library of Alexandria. We also cannot demonstrate that the historical process of selecting the books that resulted in the 24-book canon was an intentional one centered in only one location, nor do we know that those involved had a particular end in view. The last point is important because it is a common fallacy to assume that what resulted was in fact a common goal throughout the library's formation.

So, after all these negatives—all the things we don't know—how might we summarize what we can know from the historical evidence? Of course, all our knowledge must be open to further modification and deliberation, but the following points provide solidly supported history.

We can be quite certain that

- ancient Israelites maintained ancient oral traditions and later, in the early half of the first millennium BCE, used texts that they considered authoritative and divine, even as the scrolls later collected for our Bibles were being written;
- significant writing was done in the monarchic period of Israel's history (ca. 1000–586 BCE) and that some scrolls of our Bibles emerged as honored literature beginning at least in the fifth century BCE, but not necessarily in only one version;
- written texts were becoming more and more important for many Jewish groups, a trend that continued in the fifth through first centuries BCE.
- in the last centuries BCE and first century CE there was a variety of Jewish groups who valued a variety of different scrolls as authoritative, with some overlap among groups;
- due to the consolidation of Jewish leadership after 70 CE, the end result for most forms of Judaism, as early as 200 CE and certainly by 500, was a list of 24 books (and no more) that constituted the most sacred literature; and
- this resulting library exhibits an impressive variety of religious, historical, literary viewpoints and styles, and clearly was *not* the product of ideologically motivated decisions aiming for uniformity or singularity.

If we were to go on and consider the Christian traditions and developments regarding writings considered authoritative, the matter would become even more complicated. For our purposes here, we must be content with saying that the earliest Christian canon lists do not mirror the 24-scroll library of rabbinic Judaism. Why would we expect them to? The living voices of authority for developing Christian communities were not the same as of Jews. By the second century, most Christians were not of Jewish origin, had separated themselves from Jewish communities, and were developing their own distinct traditions that centered on their understandings of Jesus **Christ.** They did not look to rabbinic Jewish leadership for authority. Instead,

P OSTER 4.6

We really have no direct evidence for how the scrolls were chosen and how their content affected the choice; we simply know the result.

Christian communities naturally decided to add distinctly Christian books, and thus the New Testament developed. But Christian communities were also not obligated to follow the 24-scroll rabbinic tradition, even though they highly regarded the holy writings of the Jews, because Christianity grew out of Judaism. Christian communities tended to use more than the 24 books for what they came to call the Old Testament. All of these developments in the first centuries of Christianity are still reflected in the canons of all Christian communities, with the addition of the specifically Christian New Testament books and, for most Christians today, additional Old Testament books as well. In time Christian leaders and scholars began to ask questions about the difference between the Jewish collection and their own. A minority of Christians, among whom was the scholar Jerome (342 to 420 CE), preferred the smaller 24-book Jewish collection with the addition of the New Testament, whereas most others, such as the theologian Augustine (354 to 430 CE), argued for a larger collection that included the Maccabees, Tobit, Judith, Wisdom of Solomon, Ecclesiasticus, and Baruch. Early Christian canons all reflect a larger canon supported by Augustine, and they include the books called **Deuterocanonicals** by Catholic or Orthodox and Apocrypha by Protestants. Centuries later, Protestant churches adopted the smaller canon of Jerome and so removed the Deuterocanonicals from their Bibles.

Looking at the forms of Bible evidenced in Christianity since the early centuries of its history, we can clearly see that the canon has always had some variety within Christianity as a whole. Since the time of Jerome, some church leaders and bodies have sought compromise by creating a middle category of books that are deemed good for reading and moral edification, but not for the establishment of Christian doctrine. In this tradition stand the early editions of the King James Version (1611), which included all the books of the Apocrypha but placed them in a separate section between the Old and New Testaments.

All of this history about the building of this library may seem unduly long, but it is crucial for understanding why what one group calls Bible may be very different from what another group calls Bible. Which Bible do you have? Maybe you have more than one, and maybe they are really quite different.

Authoring a Scroll

The last two chapters have provided historical surveys, but now we can move beyond those and talk more about literature. If we want to understand these scrolls in their ancient world context, we must recognize some of the major differences between our culture and ancient Israel's; we must let go of some of our modern conceptions of books and book making. For starters, the majority of scrolls in the biblical library were written anonymously. Anonymous authorship is not unknown today, but it is certainly unusual. Ancient Israelite culture did not value authorship in the manner we do. Our notions of copyrights, royalties, plagiarism, and ownership of expression are wildly out of place in ancient Israel. Although this surely seems obvious to anyone who has studied these texts at all, the implications for our understanding of biblical literature are by no means insignificant; they are profound. As much as we would like to know who wrote the book of Genesis, for example, the book itself does not say. Unlike a typical Greek historian of antiquity, the Israelite author of Genesis did not begin with an autobiographical note. Genesis and the other four books of Moses are all presented anonymously and though the association with Moses in later tradition is easily understood, the books themselves actually carry no claim of Mosaic authorship. The anonymity of so many books complicates our understanding of their authorship, but it also opens our minds to a manner of book writing different from our own. Books were not owned by their authors; there was a more communal notion to scroll production and ownership.

Another reality of biblical literature that diverges from the way we publish books is the common practice of using the words of other authors without attribution. In a few cases sources are cited (e.g., Joshua 10:13), but more frequently they are not. For example, there is a nine-line poem (or part of a poem) in Micah (4:1–3) that is nearly identical to a poem of Isaiah (2:2–4). One of these texts has obviously been borrowed from the other, or, perhaps, the two authors both borrowed from a third and older source. The same is true of thousands of other passages in our biblical library; for example, Chronicles borrows heavily from Samuel and Kings. In a modern classroom, such blatant plagiarism is disapproved; yet modern scholars or writers do not even mildly criticize the biblical authors for such behavior. It would be ludicrous to expect ancient authors to follow our modern conventions of copyright and book writing.

The common practice of borrowing from other writings introduces us to the ancient practice of composite authorship. This simply means that a given scroll may be the product of more than one author, just as it is clear that much of Chronicles originated in Samuel and Kings. Modern scholars make some general distinctions by using the terms *editor* and **redactor,** and *copyist*. An editor is considered a writer who supplements, revises, or arranges a received piece of literature. A redactor is considered a writer who does the same work of an editor but who is responsible for the final shaping and overall perspective of the composition. A copyist was a scribe who worked simply with the intention of reproducing or copying the words of one scroll onto another. Because the work of some editors and redactors was so extensive and even creative (e.g., Chronicles), they can legitimately be thought of as authors themselves. For this reason, as we peruse the scrolls on our tour, I will often refer to whomever was responsible for the last form of the scroll as the author.

In any given scroll, the amount of material that is culled from earlier sources may vary from nearly everything to next to nothing, but the composite nature of many biblical books is a standard feature explaining the history of many biblical texts. For example, the traditional prophetic books, such as Isaiah and Amos, frequently reflect distinct historical and political realities indicating different periods of composition for different sections of the same book. An obvious implication of composite authorship is that books were composed diachronically. They were supplemented, altered, and edited over time. According to the social book-writing conventions of ancient Israel, diachronic composition explains what scholars often call

POSTER 4.7

Political History	Composition History
1300 BCE	
Origins of Israelite clans and tribes	
	Oral traditions of Israelite clans and tribes
Movement of clans and tribes to central hill country	
Israel mentioned in Egyptian record of Merneptah **ca. 1210**	
	Forms of early Israelite poetry and the Exodus; e.g., Exodus 15, Judges 5
Monarchy of David **ca. 1010 to 965**	Development and growth of written traditions in royal and other cultural institutions
1000 BCE	
Monarchy of Solomon **ca. 968 to 928**	
Division of kingdom into North (Israel) and South (Judah) **ca. 928**	Oral liturgies and earliest know Hebrew inscription, the Gezer calendar
	ca. 900 Early written *sources* for scrolls: Genesis, Exodus, Leviticus, Numbers
	Oral speeches of prophets and beginnings of written prophetic traditions
Conquest of North by Assyria and exile to Mesopotamia **722**	Northern Refugees flee South with texts
	Early forms of Genesis, Exodus, Leviticus, Numbers
King Josiah in Judah **ca. 639 to 609**	Early forms of Deuteronomy, Judges, Joshua, Samuel
Conquest of Judah by Babylon and exile to Mesopotamia **586**	
	Growth of documents for conservation and expansion of narratives, liturgical collections, prophetic collections, wisdom literature
Persia allows Jews to return to Judah **538**	
Completion of Second Temple in Jerusalem **ca. 515**	Early narratives of monarchy; Kings
500 BCE	
Persian-appointed governors Ezra and Nehemiah	Development and completion of scrolls of Torah, Joshua, Judges, Samuel, Kings, Isaiah, Jeremiah, Ezekiel, individual documents and collection of The Twelve, Ruth
	Composition of EzraNehemiah, Chronicles

(contineud)

POSTER 4.7 *(Contd.)*

Political History	Composition History
	Composition of Esther, Qohelet (Ecclesiastes), Song of Songs
Conquest by Alexander, Greek Empire **323**	
Ptolemaic rule **310 to 198**	
Seleucid rule **198**	
Seleucid persecution and Jewish revolt **167**	Formation of scroll of Daniel
Jewish rededication of Temple **164**	
Conquest by Pompey, Roman rule **63**	Composition of 1 Maccabees & 2 Maccabees

layers of a text, each layer coming from a different period. This also helps to explain the numerous anachronisms and editorial remarks in biblical texts. An anachronism is the use of a term or phrase that does not fit in the period being described. For example, Abram (later called Abraham) is said to come from **Ur** of the Chaldeans (Genesis 11:28), but the name *Chaldean* is an ethnic term that comes from a time much later (eighth to sixth century BCE) than the setting of Abram, and it helps historians date the writing of the text. Therefore, at least this line of Genesis comes from a later time when the Chaldeans were active.

Another evidence of later writing is editorial comments. For example, an editor of 1 Samuel seems have added a note of explanation for his readers about a word from an older source that his modern readers might find confusing (1 Samuel 9:9). Similarly, an editor of the book of Psalms, a great collection of prayers and poems, has added major clues for the history of that book with statements about the extent of the collection at certain points. For example, after the concluding line of Psalm 72 we have the editorial remark, "Thus ends the prayers of David, son of Jesse."

Another difference between ancient and modern convention is the ancient literary device of writing in the name of another, or **pseudepigraphy.** In Jewish antiquity this was not an uncommon practice, variously motivated and not necessarily censured as deception, especially in the late centuries BCE and early centuries CE. A text could be penned as if written by an ancient ancestor, such as Enoch, Abraham, or even Moses. There are many examples of this practice, preserved in both Jewish and Christian provenance. It is within this tradition that books (or parts of books) such as Ecclesiastes, Proverbs, Song of Songs, and Wisdom of Solomon are considered Solomonic. This possibility must be considered in all evaluations of authorship. In one sense, the practice of pseudepigraphy is an extension of the practice of supplementing the writings of an earlier author, such as Isaiah, and it is a practice that once again underscores the living and dynamic nature of the tradition. Once the commonality of this ancient convention is understood, a modern reader will not devalue a writing just because it uses differing conventions. Why should ancient authors follow our customs?

These are some of the crucial differences between modern writing conventions and those of ancient Israel. The actual process for every book of the sacred library must be investigated on an individual basis—words such as *composite* or *pseudepigraphic* cannot be indiscriminately applied. It has been my experience, as a frequent tour guide of this library, that expecting these ancient authors to follow modern conventions of writing and book making is one of the major impediments to exploring biblical literature. When the ancient writers are freed from the bonds of our modern customs, they obtain liberty to live and write as ancient Jews.

Literary Forms

Beyond the question of language, all readers in the library must at some point answer basic questions about literary form. We always have some guiding thoughts in mind as we begin to read. Do you read a math textbook the same way you read a poem? When you open any book, do you read it

1. by assuming that all of its data are accurate, as if it were a phone book or mathematical formula or a computer-programming manual?
2. with the healthy skepticism with which you read advertisements for cars, diets, or clothes?
3. by granting it great poetic and artistic license, the way you would approach poetry or fantasy literature?

When we see or hear the words "Roses are red, violets are blue," what do we expect to come next? How many lines do we expect? Which lines do we expect to rhyme at the end? What do we expect about the content and meaning? Why do we not expect phone books to rhyme on every second and fourth line? What does this imply about our knowledge of literary forms?

Why does the following sentence sound strange? "The stars will fall from heaven, and the sun will cease its shining, the moon will be turned to blood, and fire mingled with hail will fall from the heavens, and the rest of the country will have sunny intervals and scattered showers" (Barton 1984, 17). We chuckle because we recognize the incongruity in this mixture of literary types. There was a jarring genre shift—from a doomsday apocalyptic prophecy, which we would probably not take literally, to the weather forecast, which we would like to take literally, and the weather forcaster wants us to take literally (but we have learned that we should not).

All texts belong to some genre of writing. No one can write just a text, and no one reads all texts the same way. Even unconventional, unique texts are considered unique because they stand out against conventions (Barton 1984, 16). We can describe different literary conventions as "language games," using the term of the philosopher Ludwig Wittgenstein. Different literary "games" (poetry, narrative, etc.) are played by writers and have different purposes and rules. I like the way W. Placher summarized Wittgenstein:

> Just as we use a ball in different ways in soccer, baseball, and tennis, so we use language in different ways in different "language games"—in giving an order, reporting an event, lying, testing a hypothesis and so on. Philosophers [and Bible readers] go

astray when they try to impose one set of rules on all forms of language. It makes no sense for scientists to condemn poets because their statements cannot be empirically tested, for instance, just as it makes no sense for a soccer fan to condemn basketball players for picking up the ball with their hands—that would be judging by the rules of the wrong game. (Placher 1989, 58)

This concept of language games helps us in thinking about a writer's approach to her or his writing, and it also helps us to understand better our own assumptions and thinking as we approach and read texts.

The first point to be made is that ancient Hebrew authors did not write according to the rules of modern language games, and why would they? Their civilization had its own literary genres, its own language games, by which it played. Everyone who is now reading this *Guided Tour is* a sophisticated reader who automatically has different rules in mind when reading telephone books, novels, histories, advertisements, or birthday cards. In the rest of this section, let's consider some of the essential characteristics of Hebrew literature so that, whether we are reading in Hebrew or English, we can be better prepared for the kind of literature we will encounter in this library and the kind of rules of the game we should have in mind. These can be roughly divided into two overarching categories that cover virtually the entire biblical collection: narrative and poetry.

A second point, which is becoming widely acknowledged in recent years, is that whatever else one desires to find in the Bible, such as history, doctrine, morality, theology, philosophy, worldview, faith principles, and so on, biblical writings are, above all else, literature. By *literature* here we mean that our scrolls are intentionally and artistically crafted compositions. Whatever historical, moral, or religious meanings the texts may have, those ideas are completely bound to literary artistry; the rhetoric, figures, styles, forms, syntax, and vocabulary. To speak of Bible as literature has been rightly compared to speaking of Leonardo's *Mona Lisa* as art. It should not need to be said at all. Biblical texts may have to do with ethics, religion, or history, but they are all in literary formats; they are not mathematical formulas in verse. Though they might abound with theological or philosophical ideas, they are not some kind of theological propositional documents listing doctrines, nor are they like modern rigid, legal documentation. Even the lists of names or laws in our scrolls are all embedded in narrative texts. I am not at all saying that a Bible is simply literature, whatever that means. Far from it! It's doubtful that the ancient writers or readers would resonate with any clear distinctions among such categories as literary, religious, or historical texts. All of these subjects and more are intertwined and interfused by the craft of artistic literary creation. It is by careful literary observation of the woven threads—such as style, vocabulary, figures—in their various narrative and poetic manifestations that we come to understand most clearly the visions and ideas of the ancient authors.

Hebrew Narrative

A narrative is basically a story, a consecutive telling of events that may or may not be historical. Of course, there are many different kinds of narrative, written for different audiences, different purposes, and different styles. The narrative games of the Hebrew Bible are generally have different sets of rules than English narratives. What we describe as rules are descriptions of observable general practices or conventions. Students of literature are familiar with terms such as *theme, motif, characterization, plot, denouement, resolution, irony, metaphor,* and others. These are some of the standard categories of the study of literature that help us answer questions about the function, form, and meaning of a work. These are questions fruitfully asked of all literature, including the scrolls in our library. At the risk of oversimplifying, the following five observations about Hebrew narrative, reflecting insights especially of Robert Alter, are among the most important:

1. Hebrew narrative tends strongly toward economy of expression. These Jewish prose writers avoided long descriptions of places, persons, background, and contexts. The narrators do not give expansive treatment of lush green hillsides or detailed explanations of a character's inner feelings, society, or sunsets. One does not usually find descriptive embellishments; instead, conciseness is highly valued. Perhaps the utter contrast of two of the most famous whale tales, *Moby Dick* and *Jonah,* illustrates this well. Herman Melville, the nineteenth century author of *Moby Dick* describes everything, it seems; the Hebrew scroll of Jonah, in contrast, is sparse, with a few carefully planted details. The conciseness of Hebrew narrative results is an unparalleled immediacy for the reader, a constant focus on the main event stripped of all distractions. There is a crisis on nearly every page; with no long descriptive pauses in the movement of the plot, every word becomes crucial; the descriptors that are found are often pregnant with meaning.

2. A second feature of Hebrew narrative is the frequent use of wordplay and leading words (*leitwort*). To a degree not at all typical of English prose, the ancient Jewish authors seem to delight in both obvious (for readers of Hebrew) and subtle wordplay. Puns and alliterations, homophones, and a host of other kinds of paranomasia pepper and enrich biblical texts, and it's not all just for fun. Nearly every modern commentator on Genesis will make the point that the author of Genesis 2, through narrative wordplay but not through overt lesson or commentary, stresses the intimate connection between the man and the ground. This connection is, in a sense, enshrined in the Hebrew language because the word for "earth" is *adama* and for "human" is *adam.* In Genesis 2:7 the wordplay goes something like this: "YHVH God shaped the *adam,* dust from the *adama . . .*" Later **Adam** is used as the name of this first male human, and his wife is given the name *Chava,* poorly rendered in English as Eve. But her name is also a wordplay, easily recognizable in ancient and modern Hebrew. *Chava* looks and sounds like the feminine form for the verb that means "to give life/be alive," and is closely associated with the word for "life." It's as if her name is Lifer, for she is the mother of all life (Genesis 3:20). Genesis 2–4 and many other passages, too, are full of puns and wordplays such as these, which both enliven the telling with creativity and often carry a great deal of narrative and religious meaning.

Leitworter, a German word meaning "leading words" or "guide words," refers to words or groups of related words that a narrator uses repeatedly in sections or subsections of a composition to move a narrative along and to signal connections, reflections, and complexities in a narrative. One might think of it as a theme, but not in the sense of some grand idea with which the text is concerned. For example, someone might say that the book of Genesis is about beginnings. But we're talking about something much more specific than that, something intimately tied to the actual mode of expression. Hebrew words for "beginning" or "to begin" do not play a large role in the scroll of Genesis, but words related to blessing (*berakhah*) often do. They appear frequently at crucial junctures in the story line, and they seem to carry a great deal of narrative weight and provide important linkage. Furthermore, there is a wordplay between this *leitwort* and another guide word of Genesis, *bekhorah*, "birthright," and in the narrative they are often intertwined (Alter 1981, 94).

3. Another point is that in contrast to much modern plot-driven narrative, speech and dialogue perform a central role in Hebrew narrative. It is often the dialogue of characters (including God) around which a story is built, and in this way the actors themselves—rather than a narrator's descriptions—demonstrate character, suggest motives, make crucial observations, and give direction to the story. This "narration-through-dialogue" (Alter 1981, 69) to some degree "silences" the narrator by keeping the characters' voices immediately in the listener's ear.

4. A fourth characteristic of Hebrew narrative is the frequent mixing of genres and sources. In many modern English translations, some of this mixing can be seen when the text type switches from prose to poetic form. For example, in many Bibles Genesis 1:27, 2:23, and 3:14–19 are printed as poetry because the translators are attempting to reflect the Hebrew poetry in those places. Some Hebrew narratives also weave together or juxtapose different prose sources, lists, proverbs, laws, or genealogies to create a form of narrative artistry that may strike a modern reader who values smooth consistent narrative as disconnected or disturbed. Although it is certainly possible that an ancient Hebrew text may show signs of disruption, it is sometimes possible that what seems like a stylistic disturbance to us may have seemed perfectly normal to an ancient person.

5. A final reality must be stressed not so much in contrast to modern literature but in contrast to the way Bible stories are often presented in modern settings. Hebrew narrative contains a high degree of ambiguity. Ambiguity in a text may be the result of several things, including

a. the normal obscurity that comes with the gap between the time of the writing of biblical literature and the time of modern readers. For example, in Genesis 29:17, Leah's eyes are said to be soft. Was that a compliment or a disparagement in the ancient writer's world? Scholars and translators do not really know, and the variety of translations reflects the confusion. Older English versions tend to go with a negative meaning, but more modern ones tend toward a positive meaning.

b. textual corruption in the transmission process. For example, a literal translation of the Masoretic text of Genesis 4:8 begins "And Cain said to Abel his brother, and it was while they were in the field. . . ." Most textual scholars think that Cain's words—the quotation of what he said—were somehow inadvertently omitted in the transmission process.

Community Reflections 4.1

WHY WERE HUMANS CREATED?

Do you think that this should be a basic question answered in creation stories? The most popular ancient Mesopotamian story, Ennuma Elish, tells us that the God Marduk created the first humans to do the work of the Divine Assembly. Other creation stories also provide an answer to the question.

But if you read the stories of Genesis carefully, there is no mention of YHVH's motive. We are told why YHVH was sorry that he made people (Genesis 6:5–7), but the narrator does not speak explicitly of the God's motive(s) for making humans in the first place. Why this silence? Can some answers be inferred from Genesis 1:26 and 2:5–8? What can be implied from the narrator's silence? Why the elusiveness? Why is such a question left open?

A History of Answers

The reticence of the narrator opens the door for many answers from many readers. It is certainly a worthy consideration of the religious traditions that read these texts—why were we created? In the Abrahamic religious traditions from different centuries, we find many different reflections on this question. A few are given here. What connections might they have with the Genesis stories?

A homiletic rabbinic legend answers the question with its own story, though it slightly changes the question. You might recognize part of this from the closing scene of the movie Schindler's List!

"The reason Adam was created alone in the world is to teach you that whoever destroys a single soul, scripture imputes it to him as though he had destroyed the entire world; and whoever keeps alive a single soul, scripture imputes it to him as though he had preserved the entire world."

—BABYLONIAN TALMUD, SANHEDRIN 37A

The following translation of a Sura (51:56–58) from the Qur'an presents a paradox of sorts:

I have only created
Jinns and men, that
They may serve Me.
No Sustenance do I require
Of them, nor do I
Require that they should
Feed Me.

For God is He Who
Gives (all) Sustenance,—
Lord of Power,—
Steadfast (forever).

✠

Karl Barth was a Swiss Protestant theologian in the mid-twentieth century who put the purpose of creation in the following Christian terms, using words of the sixteenth-century Christian reformer Martin Luther.

He (God) does not wish to exist for Himself only and therefore to be alone. He does not grudge the world, distinct from Himself, its own reality, nature and freedom. . . . God has no need of us, . . . He is rich in Himself. He has fullness of life; all glory, all beauty, all goodness and holiness reside in Him. . . . To what end, then, the world? Here in fact there is everything, here in the living God. How can there be something alongside God, of which He has no need? This is the riddle of creation. And the doctrine of creation answers that God, who does not need us, created heaven and earth and myself, of "'sheer fatherly kindness and compassion . . .'"

—Karl Barth, *Dogmatics in Outline*, 1949, 50–4.

    c. didactic reticence. Frequently Hebrew narrative tends toward ambiguity and "indeterminacy of meaning, especially in regard to motive, moral character, and psychology" (Alter 1981, 12). An author rarely gives a moral or lesson and seldom pauses to pass judgment. Instead, these narrators often pull the reader into the midst of conflicted and complex human relationships and into the conundrum of relationship with a sometimes mysterious deity and then move on without resolution of explicit and implicit issues. In this way the narrative characters, including God, and the stories themselves remain elusive, open, and undefined. This enshrined openness has also left the narratives open to generations of interpreters who suggest or dictate for their followers answers to the galaxy of questions. In fact, myriad later interpreters of these stories can often be divided according to how their religious authorities have answered the questions left open by the narrators.

Hebrew Poetry

In many cultures, ancient and modern, poetry has been considered the highest form of artistic verbal expression. In ancient Greece, where poets were often thought to be divinely inspired, four of the nine muses, divine daughters of Mnemosyne, were muses of poetry. Frederick Buechner, a modern novelist and essayist, has written that poetry is "a language made up of metaphors and music, of great intensity of feeling and great inventiveness. It is the language that man always uses when he tries to talk about the real mysteries of existence . . ." (Buechner 1985, 20). Though we do not possess extensive reflections on the art of poetry from ancient Israel, there is no doubt that it was highly esteemed; our biblical literature is bursting with poetry. Poems large and small are diffusely scattered throughout books that are predominantly narrative (e.g., Genesis, Kings) and poetry itself predominates in other mixed-genre books (e.g., Isaiah, The Twelve), and still other books

Poster 4.8

Parallel Patterns

Antithetic Parallelism: contrasting ideas are set side by side

A wise son makes a father glad,

But a foolish son grieves his mother.

(Proverbs 10:1)

Developmental Parallelism: the second (sometimes a third) verset subtly develops the meaning of the first verset, bringing more specification, adding example or concreteness, or even pointing in another direction. In some cases the the differences are extremely subtle, so that scholars have often used the term *synonymous parallelism* for those cases where two versets seem to mean the same thing. However, all changes in vocabulary and syntax create difference, and so there is always some kind of purposeful modification or development. The developments and specifications are quite clear in these lines:

> For this I praise you among the nations,
> YHVH, and to your name I sing.
> He makes great the victories for his king,
> And shows loving-loyalty to his anointed,
> To David and to his line for all time.
> (Psalm 18:50–51 or 18:49–50)

are completely poetic (e.g., Psalms, Lamentations, Song of Songs). We would do well to consider a few basics of Hebrew poetry before we actually begin reading individual books. We can go into more detail when we come to particular books.

Just as rhythm and end-of-line rhyming are basic characteristics of a great deal of modern children's poetry, or nursery rhymes, poetry of our library is generally marked by *parallelism* and *cadence*. Parallelism might be loosely defined as the arrangement of brief lines of text, usually two lines, sometimes three or more, in which each line is parallel to the other in its meaning. An example will make this clearer than an attempt at definition. Following the Hebrew word order generally, we find the following in Genesis 1:27:

> And created God the human in his image,
> In the image of God he created him,
> Male and female he created them.

In this case we have three lines in the parallel structure. In analytical language we might say, this forms one *verse*, and each line of the verse can be called a *verset*, sometimes called a *colon*. It is easy to see that the meanings of these lines are parallel, being closely related to each other and having great similarity. This basic pattern

Study Room 4.1

STUDYING HEBREW POETRY

One of our finest listeners to the sounds of Hebrew poetry is the literary scholar Robert Alter, who writes the following about poetry:

> There is in all genres of biblical poetry . . . an expressive music whose fine pulsations have continued to be heard through the ages. The most impressive testimony to the continuing ability of many readers to hear that music is in the creations of later writers who have responded poetically to biblical poetry. . . . We cannot all be poets, but what some are privileged to grasp through an act of imaginative penetration others may accomplish more prosaically, step by step through patient analysis. We will of course never be able to hear these poems again precisely as they were once heard in ancient Israel, but the effort to set aside certain literary and religious prejudices and recover what we can of biblical poetics is abundantly warranted. Even a limited success in the enterprise of recovery should help us take in more fully the extraordinary force of these ancient poems, the intricate substantive links between the poetic vehicle and the religious vision of the poets, and the crucial place of the corpus of biblical poetry in the complex growth of the Western literary tradition (Alter 1985, 213–14).

Describe what you think might be meant by the paradoxical statement "Poetry is quintessentially the mode of expression in which *the surface is the depth.* [italics mine]" (Alter, 1985, 205)

Where have you seen the influence of biblical poetry? Is it a part of your religious culture? Is it a part of your popular culture?

allows for great flexibility. What is stated in one line is not usually simply restated in the next. Meanings of the first verset are further developed, inverted, or played with in the following verset. Literary scholars have classified these variations in several ways. Two basic examples are shown in Poster 4.8.

A second general characteristic is the rhythm or cadence of Hebrew poetry. This has to do with how the poetry was read aloud or chanted—how it sounded. Without recordings of ancient chanters or readers we cannot be overly confident, but there are clues to the rhythm in Hebrew textual traditions, though it is virtually impossible to render the cadence or rhythm into English. Versets are invariably short, usually three to five separate word units in Hebrew with usually three vocalic stresses in each verset. Combined with the normal two-verset pattern of parallelism, this often seems to create a 3 + 3 cadence for each verse. Within this common pattern, which is sometimes modified or completely abandoned, all sorts of creative sound devices can be used, such as alliteration, assonance, acrostic, and creative word order.

By briefly describing these characteristics of parallelism and cadence, I do not intend to suggest that we have now defined or somehow grasped Hebrew poetry. Later on we will talk more about poetry when we discuss the famous poetic scrolls of our library, especially Psalms, Job, and Proverbs. Good poetry in any culture is a creative, intricate art, the work of imaginative wordsmiths. So also the poetry of ancient Israel is artistically dynamic; there is no formula, no exact science, no unbreakable logic to its construction. Furthermore, as we might have guessed from the poetic license that is granted to poets elsewhere, so too this ancient Jewish poetry must be granted a wide swath. There must be room for ambiguity and subtle, delicate wordplay. We must expect a wide range of poetic expression, including metaphor, simile, shifting devices, changes in voice, exaggeration, and unusual vocabulary. After all, this is poetry, not scientific, philosophical, or theological propositions. Poetry, with all its nuance and flair, is greatly in danger of being overinterpreted by readers zealous to find religious dogma in literature that was not written for the purpose of constructing theological codes. By mentioning these basic issues now, we are more prepared to read appropriately, according to a proper language game, when we encounter poems in our scrolls.

Questions for Further Study

1. Consider the practices of a mostly oral culture. How would information and traditions be spread? How would it change perceptions of authority?

2. What would be the results, advantages, and disadvantages of a growing literate and writing culture? Who would be empowered?

3. What practices of ancient authoring that seem the most significant for the way we understand the writing of biblical texts? Do they impact your perceptions of ways we should or should not read these texts?

4. How do the traits of Hebrew narrators compare to those of your favorite prose authors? What do you think is most significant for the way we understand narratives?

5. What do you now see as major dilemmas of modern translators of Hebrew narrative and poetry? What priorities would you suggest for biblical translators?

References

Aaron, David. *Biblical Ambiguities*. Leiden: E. J. Brill, 2002.

Alter, Robert. *The Art of Biblical Narrative*. New York: Basic Books, 1981.

———— *The Art of Biblical Poetry*. New York: Basic Books, 1985.

Auerbach, Erich. "Odysseus' Scar," in *Mimesis*. Trans. by W. Trask. Princeton, NJ: Princeton University, 1953.

Barth, Karl *Dogmatics in Outline*. Trans. by G. Thomson. London: SCM, 1949.

Barton, John. *Reading the Old Testament*. Philadelphia: Westminster, 1984.

Boadt, Lawrence. *Reading the Old Testament*. New York: Paulist, 1984.

Freedman, David Noel. *The Anchor Bible Dictionary*. 5 vols. New York: Doubleday, 1992.

————"The Earliest Bible," in *Backgrounds for the Bible*, ed. M. O'Connor and D. Freedman, Winona Lake, IN: Eisenbrauns, 1987.

————*Pottery, Poetry, and Prophecy*. Winona Lake, IN: Eisenbrauns, 1980.

Friedman, Richard Elliott. *The Bible with Sources Revealed*. San Francisco: HarperCollins, 2003.

————*Who Wrote the Bible?* San Francisco: HarperCollins, 1987.

Gabel, John B., Charles B. Wheeler, and Anthony D. York. *The Bible as Literature*. 3rd ed. New York: Oxford University, 1996.

Hallo, William, and K. Lawson Younger Jr. *The Context of Scripture*. 3 vols. Leiden: E. J. Brill, 1997.

Huehnergard, John. "Introduction," in *Beyond Babel*, ed. J. Kaltner and S. McKenzie. Atlanta: Society of Biblical Literature, 2002.

Huehnergard, John. "Languages," in *Anchor Bible Dictionary*, vol. 4. New York: Doubleday, 1992.

Placher, William. *Unapologetic Theology*. Louisville, KY: Westminster/John Knox, 1989.

Pritchard, James. *Ancient Near Eastern Tests Relating to the Old Testament*. 3rd ed. Princeton, NJ: Princeton University, 1969.

Schniedewind, William M. *How the Bible Became a Book*. Cambridge: Cambridge University, 2004.

Stern, Ephraim. *Archaeology of the Land of the Bible*. Vol. 2. New York: Doubleday, 2001.

Trolling, Lionel. *The Liberal Imagination*. New York: Viking, 1950.

Wilder, Amos. *The Bible and the Literary Critic*. Philadelphia: Fortress, 1991.

Instruction *Torah*

The First Five Scrolls

The first five books in every Bible, no matter how many volumes it contains, are Genesis, Exodus, Leviticus, Numbers, and Deuteronomy. Recall that in Jewish Bibles (or *Tanakh*) these five are called *Torah*, which means "instruction." Sometimes these five are referred to as the Five Books of Moses or the **Pentateuch,** from a Greek word meaning five scrolls. Are they the most important scrolls in the library? That is a question with different answers, depending on whom you ask. The answer has varied historically and certainly does today among Bible readers. Within the Jewish tradition, at least since the first century CE, these books might be said to overshadow the rest of the library; the Torah is supreme. In Christian and Muslim religions, it could be argued that traditions from these scrolls are crucial. Think about the importance of the following ideas

POSTER 5.1

Traditional English Titles	Hebrew Title and Translation	Greek Title and Translation
Genesis	בראשית *Bᵉreshit* "in beginning"	*Genesis* "beginning"
Exodus	שמות *Shᵉmot* "names"	*Exodos* "departure"
Leviticus	ויקרא *Vayyikra* "and he called"	*Leuitikon* "levitical"
Numbers	במדבר *Bᵉmidbar* "in the wilderness"	*Arithmoi* "numbers"
Deuteronomy	דברים *Dᵉvarim* "words"	*Deuteronomion* "second law"

or stories, all from the Torah: the creation of the world, first humans, first human failures, first covenants, divine rescue from Egypt by YHVH through Moses, and divine revelation of instruction to Moses at Mt. Sinai. If we think of these three religions as houses, these ideas are certainly among the most important pieces of furniture in the houses.

Within the Torah we find two dominating literary shapes: narrative and legal code. The first scroll is entirely narrative, and the last four all contain large sections of social and religious laws. But even the laws are framed by narrative sections with the result that we clearly are presented with narratives into which authors have incorporated a great deal of legal material. To read the law codes of Exodus and Deuteronomy is not like reading a court document simply listing rules and housed in an official archive. All of these scrolls are works of literature first that have as part of their story ancient legal material.

As a cautionary note, we must not assume that because these scrolls come first in the library, they must be the oldest. We also cannot assume that the authors of the scrolls that we will come to later in the library must have known the content of these first five scrolls. Their order in the library or in a table of contents page was created centuries after they were written and so says nothing about which scrolls were composed first.

You can see from the above chart that the traditional English titles follow the Greek tradition, not the Hebrew. Whereas the Greek titles seem to have been chosen to reflect a main theme or subject of the scroll, the Hebrew tradition simply calls each book after the first noun or verb of the scroll. Our earliest manuscript with a title is a Dead Sea Scroll of Genesis (4Q8c) entitled בראשית, "bᵉreshit," using the same first-word custom.

Moses *Moshe*

In keeping with the common practice of the most of the preserved literature of ancient Israel and Judaism, all five of these scrolls are presented anonymously. They contain no authorial claim, though later traditions did credit them to Moses. Moses, whom we can also call by his Hebrew name, Moshe, pronounced "moe-*shay*," is surely one of the most famous personages of ancient literature. (The *s* at the end of the English *Moses* reflects the Greek spelling, not the Hebrew.) Although Moshe is not associated with the first scroll, Genesis, he is mentioned throughout the next four. Of all the human characters, his character dominates the narratives of the last four books, and in a few places the anonymous narrators depict him as writing (e.g., Exodus 24.4; Numbers 33.2; Deuteronomy 31.22). Moshe is heroic and larger than life yet intensely human as well. He is YHVH's hand in rescuing the Israelites and YHVH's mouth in speaking YHVH's instructions. Only YHVH appears more times in our library than Moshe. But Moshe never is identified as the author of these five books in the forms we have.

We should also point out, remembering the commonly accepted convention of pseudepigraphy, that there are several other writings from antiquity that are credited to Moses. Early Christian authors refer to two books, the Testament of Moses and the Assumption of Moses (*assumption* means being transferred to heaven instead of dying). Even earlier, a book now known as Jubilees (third to second century BCE) is Mosaic in that it begins with a narrative of Moses receiving revelation from God delivered by an angel on Mt. Sinai and then being instructed to write a scroll—the content of which is the book of Jubilees. This Mosaic work was influential in some Jewish groups and for some early Christians. In the Jewish documents known as the Dead Sea Scrolls, there were at least four more writings directly credited to Moses in the first person, but they are only fragmentarily preserved. Additionally, some Dead Sea Scrolls give Moses credit for saying things that cannot be found in any currently existing Mosaic book. Similarly, we also have to mention that in the fifth and fourth centuries BCE there existed works credited to Moses that no longer exist. A small book much later in our library from that century, Nehemiah (8.14), contains a quotation of a writing credited to Moshe that we no longer have. In other words, if we were on this tour of Jewish or Christian libraries in the last centuries BCE or first or second century CE, prior to the final shaping of the current Jewish and Christian sacred libraries, we would undoubtedly come upon several more than five Mosaic books. These other Mosaic books were considered legitimate and authoritative works of Moses. But over the centuries certain communities decided against keeping some of these works. Some books didn't survive simply because the communities that cherished them were destroyed or died out. In our day, beyond the five books of Torah contained in most Bibles, the book of Jubilees is the only Mosaic work that remains in a current canon, the canon of the Orthodox Ethiopic Christian Church.

We could stop here and trace the figure of Moses in the history of Israelite and Jewish thought. It is an exciting study, but also a long and complicated one. Moses does not loom large in *all* ancient Jewish traditions or even in large portions of our library. For example, most of the classical prophetic writings, Isaiah through Malachi, do not even mention Moses. The figure of Moshe became especially important in much of Jewish thought, as best we can recover it, from the sixth century BCE down through the period of the first and second centuries CE. And even though there were traditions within Judaism that did not focus so heavily on Moses, he did become the central human figure in traditional rabbinic Judaism starting in the first century until today.

In summary, then, as we proceed to open our scrolls we should be ready for a great deal of attention to Moshe beginning in our second scroll, Exodus. We could never say enough about Moshe as a literary figure and a figure in religious traditions. When we start asking historical questions, we will find that historians are divided in several directions about Moses. Questions arise about when he lived, just what he actually did, and even if he was an actual historical figure. The questions arise mostly because there is no external historical evidence of Moses outside of our library. All the non-Jewish authors who mention Moses come much later, long after our scrolls were written and many centuries after Moses would have lived, which was probably the thirteenth century BCE. To sort out all the questions—not to mention arriving at evidence-supported answers—would require many pages, and so I will simply recommend the historical books at the end of Chapter 3 and repeat that the historical questions are not our main focus on this tour; the valuation of our scrolls is not logically tied to the simple questions of historicity. No matter what you conclude about Moshe's historical reality, he is extremely real in several of the scrolls we are about to encounter and he is a figure who looms large in much of later Jewish, Christian, and Muslim traditions. Regardless of our historical conclusions, as we read the last four scrolls of the Torah and a few other scrolls later in the library, we will benefit greatly by listening carefully to the authors' presentations of Moshe. By so doing we will see fascinating portraits painted of this most human hero, and we will learn a great deal about how various authors of our library conceived of the role of Moshe in their national and religious memory. In some he will dominate; in some he will be missing.

One Story Begins

To this point I have repeatedly stressed that the books of our library are essentially separate entities that, if they are to be understood as documents of their own time, need to be read with an awareness of their own individual integrity and point of view. With this emphasis I am attempting to correct an anachronistic tendency to see these originally separate documents as simply chapters in one ancient book. At the same time, and without violating the integrity of each scroll, it can be observed from historical study that some of our scrolls were structurally related prior to their being placed in a codex. Some scrolls in our library form a loosely continuous narrative. In classical literature, Virgil, the first-century BCE Roman author, makes his epic the *Aeneid* sequential to the much earlier Greek epic of Homer, the *Iliad*. Similarly, the book of Exodus as it stands now takes up a narrative thread about the Israelites that is a continuation of the Genesis narrative. That storyline continues through other scrolls of our library, down to the scroll of Kings. But the connections among the scrolls certainly do not indicate that the whole thing was planned from the beginning as a nine-volume set—far from it. The scrolls do not all have the same point of view, identical theology or ideology, literary traits, or basic vocabulary. They also do not all use a common chronological or dating system, and later parts (of the storyline) do not all show knowledge of or agreement with earlier parts. The scroll of Leviticus is in some sense an interruption in the continuous narrative. In short, the individual scrolls have unique origins, perspectives, and themes. Their continuity comes not because they all flow from a single mind, but because the scrolls were selected and in their final version were edited by those who desired to preserve a general narrative of Israel's past.

Within each scroll, the storyline itself is highly episodic, not a smooth comprehensive historical account. In addition, these books do not present the only version of Israel's past that was told and retold through Israel's history. The book of Chronicles also surveys Israel's past, from creation to exile. And there are numerous clues in these nine books that signal to the attentive reader the existence of even more stories of the past that are not contained in our library. For example, in the book of Joshua (24.2) the author says that Abraham, his father Terah, and his brother Nahor lived beyond the Euphrates River (in Mesopotamia) and worshiped different Gods, Gods other than YHVH. But in the book of Genesis, where we find a few remarks about Abraham's life in Mesopotamia, there is no mention of his family's worship of other Gods. Clearly, the author of Joshua knew of such stories about his Jewish ancestors, but the author of Genesis does not speak of them. At some point in time in the history of our library, some authors and editors arranged the content of a series of scrolls so as to form a roughly continuous narrative of dozens of generations and thousands of years which runs from Genesis through Kings.

Explaining the Composition of Torah

When we study U.S. history, we are accustomed to knowing something about the time and place of writings and documents that we use. We place *Uncle Tom's Cabin* in our discussion of slavery and the Civil War and not in our discussion of the Constitutional Convention or with World War II because we know that Harriet Beecher Stowe's great work is historically associated with the mid-nineteenth century. Most would agree that knowing relevant details about the historical time period can be helpful in reading and understanding the literature from that period. The same would certainly be true for every scroll of our library. If we knew the identity and associations of the authors and the time of their writing, then we would have a great deal more historical understanding for each writing. But providing such historical information was clearly not the purpose and priority of authors represented in our ancient Jewish library; they rarely give their names, or dates, or historical associations. As a result, readers today who want to gain a historical understanding of the composition of these scrolls must do detective work to collect clues about dates and authors.

Historical study is by no means the only kind of legitimate study of texts. Historical questions do not have to be top priority. We might want to ask other kinds of questions; for example, literary understandings (e.g., motifs, style, speech, poetic form) may be a top priority for some. Others might be primarily interested in the long interpretive traditions in both Jewish and Christian communities, whose religious understandings, perhaps through **allegory** or *midrash,* do not directly concern historical issues. Clearly there are a variety of interpretive strategies and priorities, and they have different sets of questions to bring to texts. The Torah is also a fascinating place to engage social understandings such as feminism. Genesis provides fascinating examples of colorful female characters, and the laws in Exodus, Leviticus, Numbers, and Deuteronomy reveal much about the status of women in Israelite antiquity.

As we go through the library on this *Guided Tour* we will not primarily concentrate on the historical situation in which the scrolls were written or on whether the narrative content of the scrolls accurately reflects historical facts, though these historical questions provide excellent lines of enlightening inquiry. For many of our scrolls, those questions are extremely complex and difficult to answer precisely because the ancient authors had different priorities and values in writing than do modern historians. In the case of five books of the Torah, there has been a long tradition of interpreters asking about how these books came to be in the shape they are in, when they were written, and by whom. Even though Moshe had widely come to be identified as author of the scrolls of Torah, even in antiquity commentators pointed to evidence in the texts themselves that indicates they must have been written long after Moses. In recent centuries, there have been important advances in our knowledge of the history of biblical texts. First, evidence from the close study of many different biblical manuscripts made us aware of a wide variety of textual differences that go back to antiquity. Second, the discovery of texts of the ancient world—some of ancient Israel and many more from surrounding cultures—provided us with direct knowledge of how ancient texts were composed. Third, a great deal of internal evidence, such as identical repetitions of lines or paragraphs, changes in laws, anachronisms, simply cannot be accounted for by simple, one-author explanations. It is now commonly recognized among biblical scholars, and to some degree in popular circles, that these five scrolls of the Torah were composed using earlier sources that were assembled, copied, and edited by later persons. Even the texts themselves explicitly name sources, for example in Exodus 24.7 and Numbers 21.14. Today the discussion among scholars has moved to determining what are appropriate criteria for recognizing the earlier sources—and there is much disagreement!

There have been many attempts to reconstruct the history of the composition of the scrolls of the Torah in a manner that best fits the evidence. The best-known theory goes by the name documentary hypothesis or JEDP. This theory is most closely associated in its origin with a scholar named Julius Wellhausen, who wrote in the second half of the nineteenth century in Germany. Over the years it has been critiqued and revised from many angles by hundreds of scholars; Some have offered competing theories, and others have abandoned all attempts at getting a clearer picture of what sources were used. Here I will offer a widely regarded and probably the most widely used modern incarnation of the documentary hypothesis, put forward by Richard Elliott Friedman in his best seller, *Who Wrote the Bible?*

J A text now designated J was composed sometime during the divided monarchy in the Southern Kingdom of Judah (ca. 928 to 722 BCE). It is called J because the author preferred to use the personal name YHVH when referring to Israel's God; YHVH in Wellhausen's German was spelled *Jahwe.* This text was mostly narrative and included many of the famous stories now contained in Genesis. Most of Genesis 2.4b–4.24 is credited to J. Its author seems to have a special interest in female characters and one literary scholar, Harold Bloom, has proposed that the author was a woman.

E This text was also composed during the divided monarchy (ca. 928–722) but is thought to come from the Northern Kingdom of Israel. Its author, supposedly a priest, preferred to use the more generic term *Elohim* or *El* for Israel's God, until his story reached the time of Moses, where he begins to use YHVH.

P This source comes not long after J and E from priests in Jerusalem, probably early in the late eighth or early seventh century BCE (700 to 600s), after the Northern Kingdom had fallen. The P document presumably was written by priests. It comprises much of the material in Exodus, Numbers, and nearly all of Leviticus. P also used the name YHVH beginning in the time of Moses. Genesis 1.1–2.3 is credited to this author.

The idea that ancient Jewish authors differed regarding the time that the name YHVH came into usage is not a wild invention by modern scholars. If we look in Exodus 6.2–3 we will see the one piece of evidence behind this idea:

> And Elohim spoke to Moshe and said to him, "I am YHVH. But I revealed myself to Abraham, to Isaac, and to Jacob as "El Shaddai," but my name YHVH I did not make known to them.

This statement in Exodus is exactly consistent with the way YHVH is introduced to Abram in Genesis 17.1 as El Shaddai. However, it is not consistent with statements earlier in Genesis. The writer responsible for J (in this scheme) used YHVH in his story long before he reached Moses; he writes these words when his story is just a few generations beyond Adam (Genesis 4.26b):

> At this time [people] began to call on the name YHVH.

And in Genesis 12.8, we find this (cf. 13.2–4):

> [Abram] built there an alter to YHVH and called on the name YHVH.

How should we explain these statements? In one place it says that the name YHVH became known only at the time of Moses, while another says YHVH was used by people long before Moses. Is there a historical, rational manner to account for this? Scholars who study the compositional history of Genesis are attempting to provide a theory that accounts for this kind of evidence. Thus, it seems that two different documents, one of which held that the name YHVH became known only to Moses (P) and the one that held that YHVH was known long before Moses (J), were intertwined by a later writer.

D This work is named for Deuteronomy and was formed in the second half of the seventh century in Jerusalem, around the time of Judah's king Josiah (639 to 609 BCE). It exalts Moses greatly and is found now mostly in the scroll called

Deuteronomy. However, Deuteronomy is related to the works which immediately follow it—Joshua, Judges, Samuel, Kings—because the editors of those works share a powerful religious outlook with the creator(s) of Deuteronomy. In Wellhausen's view, D came before P (thus the order JEDP); but Friedman has argued quite successfully for their reversal.

However, these four works, JEPD, are just one part of the documentary hypothesis. First of all, these four authors also used sources, some oral, some written, and some archival, to compose their works. Perhaps the most important work is that of editors or a series of editors, sometimes called **redactors,** who put together the sources in the sixth and fifth centuries BCE. It is these editors who began to shape the scrolls into their modern forms. Archaeological evidence begins to help us with the period of these later stages of editing. Unfortunately we have scant textual finds dating before the sixth century BCE. As mentioned in Chapter 1, the Dead Sea Scrolls and other ancient manuscript traditions testify brilliantly and unequivocally to the practices of Jewish editors who both conserved and altered their important texts. The documentary hypothesis is certainly in keeping with the demonstrable practices of ancient Israel's writers, but we do not have any archaeological discoveries of the source texts of JEDP. Thus, the theory right now stands or falls based on how well it explains the evidence from the Hebrew manuscripts of the Torah, as do all other theories. (Some people have criticized the "documentary hypothesis" because they object to certain religious and philosophical ideas of Wellhausen, but such arguments are red herrings because they miss the reality that this textual-historical theory is not logically dependent on his other ideas.) Needless to say, not everyone agrees with the documentary hypothesis. Other scholars have come up with different scenarios, and many have declared that we simply do not have enough ancient evidence to reconstruct the compositional history of the scrolls.

As we proceed in our library tour, I will rarely refer back to this hypothesis. My reason is simply that I want to provide a more broadly focused tour that works largely with the forms of texts that we actually do have and that asks a range of other questions beyond the historical composition of the scrolls. Furthermore, the scrolls as we have them, even in the variety of their manuscript forms, are not crudely cobbled together or cut and pasted collections of clippings. Instead, they are thoughtfully designed narratives, and there is great benefit in analyzing them as whole works. For this reason we will usually speak of a work's author(s), instead of just a compiler. On the other hand, we will sometimes refer to general ideas of sources and editors, because these are well-established realities of ancient Israelite compositions, and they are useful even when we cannot be more certain about the specifics.

Questions for Further Study

1. How does it change our understanding of the five scrolls of Torah if we think of them being composed in generally the same time period that other books of our library were composed, instead of much earlier?

2. What are the anachronisms in the following passages and how would you explain them? Genesis 14.14; 21.34; 26.14, 18; 36:31; Exodus 13.17; Deuteronomy 1.1; 33.22 (see Judges 18.29).

References

Boadt, Lawrence. *Reading the Old Testament.* New York: Paulist, 1984.

Dever, William G. *Who Were the Early Israelites and Where Did They Come From?* Grand Rapids, MI: Eerdmans, 2003.

Fox, Everett. *The Five Books of Moses.* New York: Schocken, 1995.

Friedman, Richard Elliott. *Who Wrote the Bible?* New York: HarperCollins, 1997.

——— *Commentary on the Torah.* New York: HarperCollins, 2001.

——— *The Bible with Sources Revealed.* New York: HarperCollins, 2003.

Laffey, Alice. *An Introduction to the Old Testament: A Feminist Perspective.* Philadelphia: Fortress, 1988.

Kaltner, John. *Ishmael Instructs Isaac.* Collegeville, MN: Liturgical Press, 1999.

Kassis, Hanna *A Concordance of the Qur'an.* Berkeley, CA: University of California, 1983.

The New Interpreter's Bible. 2 vols. Nashville, TN: Abingdon, 1994–98.

The Torah: A Modern Commentary. Plaut, Gunther, ed. New York: Union of American Hebrew Congregations, 1981.

Rosenberg, David, and Harold Bloom. *The Book of J.* New York: Grove Weidenfeld, 1990.

בְּרֵאשִׁית

Genesis B^ereshit

SECTION OUTLINE

I suppose that everyone on this tour has heard of this first book. It is probably the most famous one. Its stories and characters—creation, Adam, Eve, Abraham, Jacob/Israel, Joseph—are frequently referred to, and Genesis 1.1—"In the beginning God created . . ."—is certainly one of the most familiar lines in all of literature. Go into any American bookstore, and you will find many wonderful (and some not so wonderful) translations and interpretations of Genesis. This fame is not hard to explain; Genesis is the first book you come to when you open any Bible, Jewish or Christian. But that, of course, has only been true since the time of the widespread use of the codex. Because Genesis was placed first in the codex form of the Bible, Genesis is the beginning for anyone who likes to begin reading books at the beginning! Such was not always the case. For example, the authors of the Christian New Testament, all of whom wrote before the invention of the codex, quote other scrolls, in particular Exodus, Deuteronomy, Isaiah, and Psalms, much more often than B^ereshit. Similarly, the Qumran community of Jews in the first centuries BCE and CE, authors of the Dead Sea Scrolls, referred to many other ancient scrolls more frequently. And although it seems that everyone today has heard of Adam and Eve, they were not famous to any authors of our Hebrew Bible, outside of Genesis they are almost never mentioned. None of that is meant to suggest that Genesis is not justly famous; it is one of the most intriguing and compelling pieces of literature in our library and beyond it as well.

*L*ITERARY FORMAT AND MOVEMENT

B^e^reshit is long—the fifth longest of our library. It is a delightfully diverse yet simply organized work. It has its obscurities, ambiguities, and sophisticated literary execution, yet it is in many ways deceptively straightforward. Its compelling storylines have made many of its episodes among the most memorable in all of literature. In short, B^e^reshit is a literary masterwork about world and Israelite beginnings. It is mostly narrative in form but is punctuated at crucial points with poetic segments. Most of the narrative is organized biographically as stories of men and their relations to their God and their kin. These biographies are episodic and are often only loosely tied in sequence. However, they are thematically connected, and the deity is so important in all these narratives that one is tempted to say the composition is a story of the God of Israel and his relationship to the world and the Jewish ancestors.

It is not difficult to divide the scroll into large sections, but upon closer inspection the shifts are generally smooth, not abrupt. The first large section of the scroll, approximately one-fifth of the whole, is the preliminary material leading up to the main stories of Abraham, Isaac, and Jacob. But besides these larger narrative shifts, the composition contains a repeated literary signpost—likely from an earlier source document—that divides the work into a series of stories of a patriarch and his descendants, and shows a generational organizing principle. Often translated by something like "these are the generations of . . . ," these markers introduce narratives or genealogies about a specific male ancestor and his descendants: Adam (5.1), Noah (6.9), sons of Noah (10.1), Shem (11.10), Terah (11.27), Ishmael (25.12), Isaac (25.9), Esau (36.1,9), Jacob (37.2). The first time the formula is used (2.4), the referent is both peculiar and appropriate, for the stories are not of a person but instead are of the "the heavens and the earth." And of course the story of the creation of the heavens and earth has just been told (1.1–2.3), and the story of the earth's descendants is about to be told; in 2.7, *adam* (Hebrew has no capitals) is formed from the ground, *adama*, and so he is in a very literary and real way its descendant. If we count carefully the generations we find that in the primordial history (chapters 1 through 11), they are arranged schematically: ten generations before Noah back to Adam, and ten generations after Noah to Abraham. But the overall movement of the narrative is also organized temporally and geographically. It takes the reader from the beginning of God's creating of the world though about 2,300 years by its own reckoning. Most of this time passes by a recording of genealogies. Geographically the story travels from the primordial Garden of Eden, to Mesopotamia where Abraham is chosen. The narrative then follows its protagonists to Canaan and eventually to Egypt, where the story closes. Thus not only is the story tied to the land of the Israelites, it is also connected to the major centers of civilization known to the ancient Israelites, Mesopotamia and Egypt.

1.1–11.32 *Primordial stories*	12.1–25.11 *Stories of Abraham*	25.12–27.46 *Stories of Isaac*	28.1–50.26 *Stories of Jacob and his sons*
creation; first humans; survivors of universal flood	move from Mesopotamia to Canaan	centered in Canaan	focus on Joseph in 37, 39–50; move from Canaan to Egypt

The English title *Genesis* comes from Greek manuscripts and simply means "origin" or "generation," a word that is used in Genesis 2.4 and elsewhere to introduce large narrative sections. The Hebrew title, as we will see is true of many scrolls in our library, comes from the first words of the scroll. In Hebrew it is really two joined words, *B*^{e} and *reshit*" which is pronounced "b^{e}ray-*sheet*" and means "in beginning." Our scroll is certainly a composition of origins, generations, and beginnings. It is famous, of course, for its multifaceted story of creation, but much more important to the author, judging by the space used, are the stories of the beginnings of the Israelite people. After setting the universal stage by carefully putting together some Israelite narratives about primordial events, the main drama of the God of Israel and the Israelite ancestors begins in Chapter 12, introducing characters such as Abraham, Sarah, Jacob, and Joseph.

Composition of B^{e}reshit

There have been so many fascinating studies about how this scroll was composed. Based on what we saw about the general practices of ancient scroll writing in Israel in the previous two chapters, what sort of compositional history would you expect for this anonymously written document? Despite their differences, most modern studies recognize the demonstrated realities of scroll writing, and so they understand an oral background for many of the stories of B^{e}reshit, they recognize the use of previously written sources, and they understand that the scroll was produced diachronically. The writing stages of B^{e}reshit are usually placed during the era of Israel's monarchic state(s), from the tenth to sixth centuries BCE, with some late activity coming even after this. Clues for dating the work are found, for example, in the several anachronisms of the scroll, such as the use of Chaldean (12.9), a people who first appear on the scene in the ninth century and come to prominence in the seventh, and the reference to Israel's kings in 36.31.

B^{e}reshit and History

The author of B^{e}reshit writes from the point of view of an omniscient writer; someone who seemingly knows everything about the earliest creation and the next 2,000 years as well. Yet for such knowledge, our author cites no verifiable evidence, gives no historiographic proofs, and makes no evidential supporting claims. But why should he? He is not a modern academic historian arguing according to modern historiographic conventions. Our ancient author follows only ancient Israelite customs. So what are we to do if we want to ask modern historical questions of our scroll? We must first recognize the many differences between the ancient writer's conventions and our own. We must next gather all possible evidence from every ancient source, both written sources and material, and attempt to carefully correlate it all. We must then have a good look at our own scroll in an attempt to determine what time periods various portions of it reflect, because we know that ancient Israelites often composed diachronically. If we can identify a fairly precise time period for a particular passage, then we may well discover that items in the narrative reflect the time period of its composition. And finally we must learn to live with a great deal of uncertainty for the following reason: the large amounts of material evidence from Egypt, Mesopotamia, and Syria-Palestine provide us with very few direct, story-corroborating details. Later we will find in non-Torah scrolls of our library that historical evidence from other sources is much more helpful in our quest to answer modern historical questions. On the other hand, for B^ereshit, we find a fair number of historical trivia, such as similar names, social and religious customs, or historical traces that lead us to think that traditions narrated in B^ereshit are not just inventions of late of, the seventh or sixth centuries BCE. But there is not nearly enough corroborating evidence to treat B^ereshit as if it were some verified historical document. This is not a great disappointment, unless one values narratives only when they can be confirmed as historical. Instead, B^ereshit offers us a narrative composed from oral and written traditions that stem from different times and places in Israelite history, some of which may be quite ancient, going back to the second millennium BCE. The antiquity of most of these traditions is extremely difficult to determine, in part because B^ereshit is a well-written narrative tapestry whose ancient strands are not easy to unravel and date. From a historical point of view, B^ereshit is of immense value not because the narrative it recounts is evidential history, but because it gives us direct evidence of some of Israel's most important traditions about their past—how leading social groups understood their national identity, their ancestral relations, and the origins of their relationship to their God.

Setting the Stage: Creation

If we approach our scroll as a knowledgeable Israelite would have, we will be aware of other creation stories in their larger culture, and, emphatically, we will not be aware of modern scientific ideas about universe origins. Stories about the making of the world by deities were commonly told and retold in all areas of the Fertile Crescent. Modern scholars of ancient societies often refer to them as creation myths because of the way the stories functioned in many societies. In this case, *myth* does not mean "false" or "untrue." Instead, this academic use of *myth* refers to important stories that serve an orientation function; a myth is a story that provides a basic vision of the structure of reality and informs people about themselves and about their relation to God(s), nature, and destiny (Barbour 1974, 17–23). Creation stories serve this function because they illustrate the basic structure of the world, how the Gods relate to each other, which Gods are dominant, how Gods and humans relate, and often how social structures are impacted. In the most famous Babylonian version of the creation story, called **Enuma Elish,** the reader learns how divine forces brought order out of the primal **chaos,** how the chief God Marduk triumphed, and also that Marduk created humans from divine blood in order to do work for the Gods. These ideas can provide basic mental orientations to ancient reality that were likely held by many and, therefore, enshrined in this famous story. To put it another way, B^ereshit begins with a grand religious and theological vision of the Israelite God and humanity, not at all with the goals, outlook, or values of a modern historical and evidence-driven scientific account.

But creation stories do not come with interpretive guidelines or footnotes for figuring out the important social ideals, nor do we find an appended list of "five things this story means." And it is a much too simplistic view of ancient literature that would just look for the supposed lessons or social functions of a work of literature. In the case of Israel's stories of origins, B^ereshit 1–3 provides one ancient Israelite example of a creation story that is so fascinating from so many angles that we could easily spend the rest of this book talking about it. So let's ask some basic questions about how the literature is working in its ancient context, and let's also consider several of the rhetorical points that seem to be clearly made.

Episode One

B^ereshit 1.1–2.3 is commonly taken to be the first episode of this creation narrative, and it presents the most orderly sort of creation one could imagine. In contrast to *Enuma Elish*, there is no violence here and no opposition to the will of the sovereign God. Similar to *Enuma Elish* and many other creation stories, there was a murky chaos prior to Elohim's actions (1.2), but this dark waste was no challenge to this Elohim, who merely speaks and his orders are fulfilled. The entire story follows a highly structured pattern, with repeated formulas set in the rhythm of the seven-day week. This format serves to underline the orderliness of the entire episode and the absolute power and majesty of this God. The high point of the story comes on day six when Elohim creates the pinnacle of his creation: humans. They are not named and are in both male and female form. This is the only creation that is said to be in the "form/image of Elohim," and the humans are intended to have a position over all creatures on earth. Now notice how this apogee is highlighted in literary form by the appearance of three poetic lines in verse 27:

> And God created the human in his image,
> In the image of God he created him,
> Male and female he created them.

And one last point of rhetoric, notice the stress on the **Sabbath,** the seventh day of rest at the end of the story. Although the Sabbath will not be a factor in any other stories in B^ereshit, it is a major factor in following scrolls of Exodus, Leviticus, Numbers, and Deuteronomy, all of which come from priestly circles that stressed the keeping of the Sabbath in Israelite religious and social practice. Might this be reason to think that this story of creation also stems from priestly circles?

*C*ommunity *R*eflections 5.1

✡ ✝ ☾

ADAM AND THE ANGELS

For many centuries, one of the most intriguing and significant details of this story is that the humans were created in God's image. What does that mean or imply? How do humans bear God's image? Just studying the Jewish, Christian, and Muslim interpretations of this one line could fill several volumes! One idea that was common to some Jewish and Christian authors was that the first human was a hermaphrodite, that is, a human having both male and female physical characteristics. Another common idea in the early centuries CE is that the first human was a physical image of God, whom the angels were supposed to worship!

Jewish Tradition

From the Life of Adam and Eve (ca. 100 CE?)
(The Devil is speaking to Adam) . . . It is because of you that I have been thrown out of there (heaven). When you were created, I was cast out from the presence of God and was sent out from the fellowship of the angels. When God blew into you the breath of life and your countenance and likeness were made in the image of God, Michael (the chief angel) brought you and made us worship you in the sight of God, and the Lord God said, "Behold Adam! I have made you in our image and likeness." And Michael went out and called all the angels, saying, "Worship the image of the Lord God, as the Lord God has instructed." And Michael himself worshiped first, and called me and said, "Worship the image of God, Yahweh." And I answered, "I do not worship Adam." And when Michael kept forcing me to worship, I said to him, "Why do you compel me? I will not worship one inferior and subsequent to me. I am prior to him in creation; before he was made, I was already made. He ought to worship me."

—Translated by M. Johnson in Charlesworth 1985, 2:262. Items in parenthesis are mine.

Christian Tradition

From the Gospel of Bartholomew (ca. 200 CE)
(The Devil is speaking to Bartholomew, a Christian apostle) . . . But the devil said: Allow me to tell you how I was cast down here, and how God made man. I wandered to and fro in the world, and God said to Michael: Bring me earth from the four ends of the world and water out of the four rivers of paradise. And when Michael had brought them to him, he (God) formed Adam in the east, and gave form to the shapeless earth, and stretched sinews and veins, and united everything into a harmonious whole. And he showed him reverence for his own sake, because he was his image.

And Michael also worshipped him. And when I came from the ends of the world, Michael said to me: Worship the image of God which he has made in his own likeness. But I said: I am fire of fire, I was the first angel to be formed, and shall I worship clay and matter? And Michael said to me: Worship, lest God be angry with you. I answered; God will not be angry with me, but I will set up my throne over against his throne, and shall be as he is. Then God was angry with me and cast me down, after he had commanded the windows of heaven to be opened. When I was thrown down, he asked the 600 angels that stood under me, whether they would worship (Adam). They replied: As we saw our leader do, we also will not worship him who is less than ourselves.

—E. Hennecke, *New Testament Apocrypha*, 1963, 1:500.

Muslim Tradition

Translation of Qur'an 15.28–34, 600s CE
Behold! The Lord said/ To the angels: "I am about/ To create man, from sounding clay/ From mud molded into shape;/ "When I have fashioned him / (In due proportion) and breathed/ Into him of My spirit,/ Fall ye down in obeisance/ Unto him./ So the angels prostrated themselves,/ All of them together:/ Not so Iblis: he refused to be/ Among those who prostrated themselves./ (God) said: "O Iblis (Satan)!/ What is your reason/ For not being among those/ Who prostrated themselves?"/ (Iblis) said: "I am not one/ To prostrate myself to man,/ Whom Thou didst create/ From sounding clay, from mud/ Molded into shape."/ (God) said: "Then get thee out/ From here; for thou art/ Rejected, accursed.

—Abdullah Yusef Ali, *The Holy Qur'an*, 1987.

Episode Two

Since antiquity, it has been noted by some readers that this first creation story seems to be followed by a different creation story. (Remember, the chapter and verse divisions should often be ignored; they were only put in many centuries after the composition.) It is now commonly thought by scholars that at one time B^{e}reshit 1.1–2.3 comprised an originally separate creation story told about Elohim, the only name for God used therein, whereas B^{e}reshit 2.4–25 presents a second story told about the God named YHVH and always refers to him as "YHVH God." Look in your translations and see where the capitalized "LORD" appears—you recall that's the name YHVH in the Hebrew—and you will see that it only occurs in the second story. The first sentence of verse 4, "These are the records of . . . ," is often thought to be that of a later editor who used those words to introduce new segments, such as in 5.1, 6.9, and 10.1. There are many differences between the two stories besides the names of God. For example, the second story unequivocally and emphatically states that the first human was created before any plant had come up from the ground

(2.5–9): *when there were no* plants YHVH God formed the man, *after* YHVH God made the human from the dirt, he then planted the plants, next he made the animals, and finally he formed the first woman out of the rib of the man. But the first episode, Genesis 1.1–2.3, clearly has plants, on day three, *before* humans—male and female created together—on day six. Perhaps the greatest difference lies in the way YHVH creates in the second story. There is no creation by spoken word here! The descriptive terminology is much different. Here we find YHVH working like a potter and a gardener, using the ground as raw material. Then, in the longest description of all, we find the unique forming of woman by YHVH acting as a surgeon, using a rib of the man. Here woman is specially featured, unlike any other creation story of the surrounding cultures; notice the poetic highpoint in 2.23. At the same time, this author does make fascinating use of common features from ancient literature, what I like to call story props—be they ideas or objects, such as the tree of life; an idyllic garden of perfection; a snake; and the idea of humans fashioned from dirt or clay by a God. All of these can be found in other ancient Near Eastern literatures.

From an ancient literary and rhetorical point of view, setting these two stories side by side is not difficult; in fact it can be considered a brilliant stroke. Perhaps someone attempting to read this literature as modern science or modern academic history might object, but those are clearly not the genres of our scroll. Together the stories present a fuller and more complex—perhaps even mysterious—depiction of the transcendent power and intimacy of YHVH God. Whatever the origins of the stories might have been, they now form one larger story, told in a distinctly ancient form. This second episode, which really runs through all of Chapter 3 also, focuses on humanity and adds significantly to what we might call the myth function, the social and mental orientation to the world that the story provides. Unlike the first episode, issues of morality, human choices, human shame, sexuality, the limits of human knowledge, and death are prominently featured. These issues are raised in a narrative about symbolic or magic fruit trees, one whose fruit makes you live forever and one which gives you knowledge like a God. YHVH God commands the humans not to eat of the first tree because "on the day you eat of it you will die" (2.17). The story involves animals, a nude man and woman, and, of course, a sly talking snake (not Satan!), who approaches the woman with a quote from YHVH God. The turning point sees the woman and the man choosing to eat of the tree of knowledge against YHVH God's instructions. There follows YHVH walking around looking for the couple, interviewing them, cursing the snake and the ground, and finally evicting them from the garden now guarded by two monsters. Commentators are still trying to unravel the meanings of this narrative! This is no simplistic morality tale. This narrative is terse, elliptical, and, most of all, it raises so many questions and leaves so much open that the imagination is loosed to wonder about many things. This is not a philosophical or religious text of propositions and definitions. It is much more subtle and ambiguous, much more mysterious, enthralling, and beautiful.

Sometimes when a story is so popular and has been told so many times in a culture, its original details and events are easily confused with later retellings and interpretations. Whether it is the idea that the snake was the devil or Satan or that Chapter 3 is about the fall of the human race, many people in our modern culture assume things about these stories that just are not there in any straightforward

Study Room 5.1

STUDYING OTHER CREATION STORIES

There are several fine translations of ancient creation stories available from the Fertile Crescent and Egypt. All sorts of questions may help us better understand how such stories were read and understood in their own pre-scientific cultures. We would find, for example, that the same culture preserved wildly differing accounts, that authors never argue about evidence or materialist proof for their stories and are illogical from modern scientific and historical points of view. It is not long until we see that these ancient creation myths are not playing the same word games as modern scientists and historians attempting to discover what really happened. Even in antiquity readers did not understand these stories as we might think of historical events.

The most common version of the Babylonian *Enuma Elish* begins with only the murky, watery chaos. In this story the first Gods, **Apsu** and his wife **Tiamat,** represent fresh water and salt water respectively, and their swirling together—pictured as waters and bodies—produces children, who are also parts of creation—other Gods who also procreate. Eventually Apsu is disturbed by his boisterous clan and, in an effort to bring about rest and peace, decides to destroy them all. But Ea, the earth God, heard of the plot of his forefather Apsu and so launches a preemptive strike, killing Apsu. He uses Apsu's body to create a shrine and palace and there, in this divinely filled home, Ea and his wife, earth Goddess Damkina, conceive the great Marduk. Marduk's birth is very auspicious, and he is declared the greatest of all Gods, omniscient, with divine light radiating from eyes. Meanwhile, Tiamat has raised a large army of divine monsters to avenge the death of Apsu, and so a mighty war ensues with Tiamat and Marduk as the leading protagonists. In the end, Marduk subdues Tiamat with an arrow. He then splits her body and uses it to create the dome of the earthly sky—remember her body is water— and bring order to the earth by arranging and dividing world. Divine beings are set as stars and constellations under the dome and the moon placed there to rule the night. Finally, because the Gods are eager for someone to do their work, Marduk decides to make humans in order to serve the Gods. The first human is created out of the blood of the now killed God Kingu, a leader on the loosing side of Tiamat's battle against Marduk. And thus humans are fashioned by the divine, and the Gods have rest.

How do you think this myth reflects the current worldview of its culture? How does it illustrate the relationship among Gods, the material world, and humans? Given that Babylon's chief God was Marduk, what political and social implications may the story carry?

For this and many other stories that relate to Israelite literature in a very accessible and affordable form, see Matthews and Benjamin 1997.

reading of the original Genesis. These opening columns of our scroll have a long and fascinating history of interpretation in Jewish, Christian, and Islamic traditions that is well worth our study, but if we want to attempt to read this scroll as an ancient document before the development of so much later tradition, we should train ourselves to read exactly what is actually said and not said. These chapters hint at nothing about Satan, nor do they refer to something called the fall or original sin. In fact, the narrator doesn't even use the Hebrew word closest to "sin." And it does not say that Adam and Eve were removed from the garden as punishment for their sin. Instead, it explicitly states that YHVH God banished them because the human had become like God in his knowledge, because he ate the fruit, and YHVH God wanted to prevent the human from now eating of the tree of life, which would give him eternal life (3.22–23)! My main point is that we should work hard to read very carefully in order to find out just what this fascinating story actually says. What else do you see is there or not there when you read carefully?

What we can say to summarize the stage setting for Bᵉreshit so far is that the creation has been divinely made and is controlled by God, that is, YHVH. The first humans are in some sense free and morally responsible and are making choices for good and ill. YHVH, who appears as an active character in the narrative of their daily lives, takes them seriously as moral agents, and requires obedience. We must admit, though, that the author does not state the matter in such abstract inferences. But for all the threats YHVH made ("You will die!"), the couple is not dead, and in fact YHVH has shown them great care (3.21). The story and the generations of the earth continue.

Setting the Stage: From Creation to Abraham

The stories so far, and those that follow in Genesis 4–11, illustrate for the ancient Israelite hearer the beginnings of human society with its conventions and dangers. Some of the episodes must come from oral traditions, and they have been placed here to show in some ancient sense why the world is the way it is. We find the beginnings of clothes, pain in childbirth, agriculture, feelings of estrangement from God, weaponry, cities, sacrificial worship, sibling rivalry, murder, city and geographical names, development of languages, and much more. These stories also link Israelite traditions to those of other peoples. For example, genealogical lists link the various peoples of Israel's world to ancestors and cities. As elsewhere, we find stories of fantastically long life spans and a long story of a great universal flood. Anyone who has read much ancient literature has probably encountered the Mesopotamian flood story, most famously known from the **Gilgamesh Epic.** It is in fact in Mesopotamia, not in Israel's land in Syria-Palestine, that major flooding wreaked havoc on human civilization, and it is not surprising to find stories of universal floods from Sumerian times (second millennium BCE) to Hellenistic times (third century BCE). The Gilgamesh version has been discovered not only in Mesopotamia, but also in Syria-Palestine at the site of Megiddo. All of these rather discrete episodes of the twenty generations between Adam and Abraham serve in the narrative to set the stage onto which Israel's storied ancestors will soon arrive. We also find that they often function to introduce themes that are important later in the narrative.

POSTER 5.2

SUMMARY OF A FLOOD STORY

The story of Utnapishtim surviving a worldwide flood is just part of a larger epic of Gilgamesh. Gilgamesh has been sent to Utnapishtim to find out how he became immortal. Utnapishtim then tells Gilgamesh how the Gods had determined to destroy all humanity with a great flood. But one God, Ea, mercifully informed Utnapishtim of the plan and instructed him to build a large roofed boat and to take onto it specimens of all living things. Utnapishtim worries about what he will tell his fellow citizens of Shuruppak, his home town, but he obeys. He constructs a seven-story boat (ark) sealed by bitumen and tar and loads it with his family, gold and silver, wild and domestic animals, and craft workers. The Gods create a frightening storm lasting for six days and nights in which every living thing drowns. On the seventh day when the storm has subsided, Utnapishtim opens a window and sees that his boat has landed on a mountain. Seven days later he releases a dove, but it returns, having found no place to land. On subsequent days he releases a swallow, which returns as well, and then a raven, which found dry land and did not return. Utnapishtim then sets all the animals free and prepares a sacrifice in order to worship, the smell of which is appreciated by the Gods. When the chief architect of the plan to destroy humans, the God Enlil, discovers that Utnapishtim had ingeniously survived, he is furious with Ea for revealing his plan. But Ea credits Utnapishtim by saying he had actually divined the plan through a dream. At that point, Enlil enters the boat and declares that Utnapishtim and his wife will be immortal.

Upon reading B^ereshit 6.11–9.29, we will not only see many similarities, we will also see many differences. This Israelite version, clearly uses older popular traditions but also transforms them to create a distinctly Israelite version in which the Israelite God is the only God of the story, and Noah is saved not because he is lucky enough to be informed by a deity of the impending cataclysm, but because Elohim appreciates his righteous, blameless life, while everyone else was so horribly violent that God regretted creating humans in the first place.

Abraham Our Great Father

In B^ereshit Chapter 12 the story gains a specific focus as it begins to follow one family. The ancient listeners would not be surprised to find themselves in Mesopotamia for the beginning of Abraham's story. They were well aware of their own Mesopotamian heritage; after all, their language, their culture, their traditions were similar to those of the Mesopotamians. But the story of Abraham, whose given name was Abram, is not intended to highlight continuity, but rather to narrate a gigantic change: YHVH's new creation of a specific family and future nation to be his chosen people. Abram is commanded by YHVH to take his family and move to a place YHVH will show him. He is promised prosperity and a far-flung and long-lasting

Community Reflections 5.2

✡ ✝ ☪

ABRAHAM OUR FATHER

It is probably common knowledge that the three monotheistic religions traditions, which in some nominal sense comprise about half of the world's population, claim Abraham as their father. That's one big family!

In Jewish traditions, "Abraham our father" is mentioned in many prayers and is the supreme patriarch. He is most important because he is the one first called by YHVH and the first to form the family covenant with YHVH (B'reshit 12–17).

In Christian traditions, even for **Gentiles,** people without Jewish heritage, Abraham has been considered the father of all who share the spiritual link of faith with him (see Romans 4.16–21).

In Muslim traditions, Abraham is considered the first submitter, that is, the first muslim, (the Arabic word *muslim* means "one who submits") because he, amidst the polytheism of his day, stood up and submitted to the one and only God, and so is the father of all those who also submit (Qur'an 2.63, 3.67).

reputation of greatness. Abram does as he is told without question. Again the narrator brings a spotlight to his narrative by utilizing the parallel poetic format:

I will make you into a great nation,
And I will bless you,
And make great your name.
And you will be [or must be] a blessing.
And the one who harms you I will curse
And all the families of the earth shall be blessed by you (12.2–3).

It is in this section that the author of B'reshit gathers many traditions about the great ancestor Abraham and his wife Sarah. The major storyline is of YHVH establishing a permanent relationship—a **covenant**—with Abraham and all his descendants. This covenant involves the loyalty of Abraham and his house and the promise of YHVH for a land of their own in Canaan (see B'reshit 15). The major geographical shift from Mesopotamia to Canaan occurs in Chapter 12. This also reinforces the religious shift of Abram, now the follower of YHVH.

These traditions are fascinating from so many vantage points. If we ask first about the basic plot, we soon see that on almost every page the covenant and promises are threatened or doomed by enemies, lack of heirs, barrenness of wives, famines, and sometimes by YHVH himself, such as when he commands Abraham to offer his son Isaac as a sacrifice (22.1–24).

If we follow feminist literary criticism, we will find women officially playing out very limited roles of child-bearers in polygamous and patriarchal families. But there is also a substratum to the stories with subplots of rivalry between women, episodes where women subtly spar with men, and cases where YHVH intervenes especially on behalf of women.

We might investigate religious traditions because we notice that these stories contain religious practices and aspects foreign to other scrolls of our library. Names and title of God are different here, such as *El-roi*, "El, God of seeing" (16.13), and *El Elyon*, "El the Highest" (14.18–22), and numerous practices described do not match Israelite law traditions, such as setting up worship at sacred trees and stones (21.33 and 28.18; see Leviticus 26.1 and Deuteronomy 16.21). Also, Abraham calls on YHVH to account for his unjust plans (18.25), and Abraham's God commands a human sacrifice as a test (22.2). What might we discover about the development of Israelite religious traditions and their diversities and complexities? What time period and level of society might these traditions reflect? One thing that becomes clear is that editors did not edit our scroll of B^ereshit in such a way as to make it conform to notions found in other scrolls of our library.

Stories of Isaac and Jacob

The brief episodes that focus on Isaac (25.12–27.46) serve in the larger narrative mostly as a link between the larger collections of Abraham and Jacob stories. It could be argued that Isaac's wife Rebekah is a more potent character than he. But Isaac is a vital link who is crucial to the movement of the plot and the maintenance of the covenant with YHVH (26.4–5), as well as the continuity with the next generation. Danger lies in the feud between the twin sons of Isaac, Esau and Jacob, the first of whom seems prone to abandon YHVH and the second of whom seems highly at risk of an early death. Israelite listeners likely reveled in these stories, because Esau was seen as the ancestor of their neighboring rivals the Edomites.

Jacob is perhaps the most complex and developed human character in the entire scroll. He is a fighter from the womb and a frequent trickster and alternately a scoundrel and a saint. Again, the main themes of YHVH's covenant and promises are included in this gathering of Jacob stories. In the case of Jacob, the primary threat lies not in external adversaries, but in Jacob himself, whose behavior is sometimes so outrageous that the reader wonders if he will get what he deserves. But Jacob always fights his way through. In one of the most compelling and mysterious passages (B^ereshit 32), Jacob literally is attacked by and fights with God, a figure that could be a man or an angel. The story is extraordinary, full of delightful wordplay and deliberate ambiguity—after all, it is set in the dark of night at a muddy, strange, dangerous river crossing. In the end, Jacob is sure that he has seen the face of God (32.30), and the reader is assured that Jacob has fought once more, even against God, and has triumphed. His new name, "Isra-El," which the author takes to mean "fought with God," becomes the **eponym** for all his descendants. Whatever might be said about Abraham as their father, they are not Abrahamites. The author here enshrines the tradition that their name and their identity lie in an unforgettable, mysterious struggle with this God.

The last half of the Israel/Jacob collection of stories is mostly the story of Joseph, one of Israel's sons. It is found in Chapters 37 to 50 and is briefly interrupted in 38 with a story that thematically links it to earlier narratives. It reads quite differently from the episodic, more discrete story collections of Abraham, Isaac,

Community Reflections 5.3

☸ ☪

ISAAC AND ISHMAEL

The presentation of the relationship between the two sons of Abraham in the scroll of B^ereshit and later Jewish (and Christian) traditions differ significantly from the presentations in the Qur'an. The main thematic difference is that the Qur'an does not depict any rivalry between them or their mothers. The most famous difference has to do with the story of Genesis 22, the binding and near sacrifice of Isaac. In the Qur'anic version (37.100–112), the name of the son is not mentioned, and later Islamic commentators through the ages have disagreed; most early writers preferred Isaac, but today the majority says it was Ishmael. Equally interesting is that the test of faith was not just for Abraham but also for the son, because Abraham told him that he had dreamed that he should sacrifice him and asked, "What do you think of that?" The son replied that Abraham should do whatever he had been commanded and that he, the son, would willingly cooperate. It is at that point that God intervenes and commends both for their faith. This gracious provision by God is commemorated in the festival of *Eid al-Adha* at the culmination of the annual pilgrimage to Mecca.

Another important Islamic tradition is that Abraham and Ishmael set up the Ka'ba, the house of God, as an altar in Mecca (Qur'an 2.125–127). This altar or house was later lost to polytheistic worshippers but was then regained and purified by Muhammad.

For more on these traditions see Kaltner 1999, pp. 118–131.

and Jacob. You will see why scholars usually think of the Joseph material as one continuous narrative or independent short story that has been incorporated into our scroll. YHVH is much less active in this section compared to the rest of the scroll. He is more of a behind-the-scenes operator. In regard to the major plot lines, the Joseph narrative introduces the traditional tribal identities that were so important at some points in Israelite history, and it occurs within the second major geographical shift in the scroll—from Canaan to Egypt. Because of Joseph, Jacob and all his children are living in Egypt at the end of the scroll.

This ending leaves unfulfilled YHVH's promise of a homeland in Canaan for Abraham, Isaac, and Jacob. Undoubtedly there were one or several scrolls that could continue the story, using a variety of traditions. But what was eventually preserved in our library is the scroll of Exodus, which picks up the story's thread in Egypt.

Themes of B^ereshit

Throughout our discussion we have mentioned the prominent appearance of covenants, the formal establishment of relationship between the God of Israel and Abraham and his descendants. The theme is actually introduced before Abraham, back in the story of Noah (Bᵉreshit 9). After Noah disembarks from the ark, God makes a covenant with him, requiring that Noah and his descendants respect life and be fruitful, and God promises never again to destroy the world by flood. This is indeed a covenant with all humanity, for according to Bᵉreshit Noah and his family were the only survivors of the inundation. Noah acts as a second Adam, made clear by the narrative parallels between the two men, such as the wording of 1.28 and 9.7.

It might be said that the covenant theme is part of an even broader theme of blessing and God's care; at the very least they are integrally connected. In addition to many acts of compassion (e.g., 3.21; 29.31), formal words of divine blessing occur throughout the scroll including in the covenant episodes. These blessing are always physical and concrete in their outlook—fruitfulness, longevity, well-being, and familial success. Already on days five and six in the earliest creation story, God is blessing the creatures and humans (1.22, 28). The words of blessing come as Noah begins life anew (9.1) and resonate in the covenant affirmations with Abraham, Isaac, and Jacob. Blessing is the central focus of the entire Jacob–Esau dispute in the pathos-filled Chapter 27. And it is a blessing ceremony that provides the final great poems of the scroll, in Chapters 48 and 49.

The Bᵉreshit narrative is beautifully messy and the characters who march across its columns are not the shallow, pious paper cutouts so often represented in our modern culture's depiction of biblical characters. There is a rich thickness in the stories from the standpoint of literature and religion. Our author seems to delight in reversals of expectations, such as the cultural convention that the firstborn always got the primary rights and benefits. The characters can be found fighting and arguing with each other and their God. They can be seen worshiping and lying, sacrificing to YHVH and maintaining their household Gods. Bizarre and enigmatic episodes dot the landscape, often reflecting ancient traditions to which we no longer have full access (e.g., 4.1–26; 6.1–4). But ultimately, through and in all the mess, the narrator has woven a story of the workings of a divine plan and promise.

The Main Character

We could place under the heading *themes* the idea that Israel's God (represented as El, Elohim, YHVH) is in complete control and that his presence is a constant factor. Perhaps it is better to put it in even stronger terms. Bᵉreshit has one character that towers over all, and that is its God. The stories of this God have been culled from various traditions, but here they are woven together to create a single God whose power is unstoppable but not predictable. From the first words of the scroll he is clearly in charge:

> "Elohim said, "There must be light!" And there was light." (1.3)

And the scroll's closing words about Elohim's action that Joseph speaks to his brothers:

> "What you planned to do to me for harm, Elohim planned it for good to cause on this day the survival of a great people!" (50.20)

Here, in the end we find our themes of God's care and control wedded through the mess of human failings.

Equally intriguing are the numerous and unpredictable ways this God appears in the narrative. Here are just a few examples:

- working and walking around like anyone else (e.g., Chapters 2–3)
- appearing mysteriously as an angel or a man (e.g., Chapters 18, 32)
- appearing only like a voice with no discernible source (e.g., 12.1; 22.1)
- manifesting himself more visibly than we might imagine (e.g., 15.1–19)
- remaining behind the scenes as in much of the Joseph story (Chapters 39–50)

On two occasions, the narrator declares overtly that YHVH was with someone, both in situations of despair, once with Ishmael (21.20) and once with Joseph (39.21). But just what sort of presence this is, is unclear. In the end it must be said that our narrator is telling a story about the God of Israel working out his designs and is presenting him as vitally involved in the lives of the characters in ways that are sometimes clear and sometimes mysterious.

Questions for Further Study

1. Asking questions as a feminist critic, how do you perceive the roles of the matriarchs of B^ereshit Sarah, Hagar, Rebecca, Rachel, and Leah? How do they function in the stories?

2. From a comparative approach, what are the roles of Gods and humans in different cultures' creation stories? How are they similar or different from B^ereshit?

3. B^ereshit 22, the binding of Isaac story, is one of the most famous in all of literature and has been written about an untold number of times through the centuries. What does it suggest about the author's view of human sacrifice? of God? How does the episode function in the scroll? Does it change the way God and Abraham interact? How has it been interpreted in your experience?

4. For a study in the variability of honest interpretation, read though B^ereshit 1–3, looking for evidence of a *hierarchical* view of gender relations. Read the same material again, this time looking for evidence of an *egalitarian* view of gender relations.

References

Ali, Abdullah Yusef. *The Holy Qu'ran.* Elmhurst, NY: Tahrike Tarsile Qu'ran, 1987.

Barbour, Ian. *Myths, Models, and Paradigms.* New York: Harper and Row, 1974.

Charlesworth, James H. *The Old Testament Pseudepigrapha.* 2 vols. Garden City, NJ: Doubleday, 1985.

Hallo, William W, and K. Lawson Younger, Jr. *The Context of Scripture.* 3 vols. Leiden: E. J. Brill, 1997.

Hennecke, E. *New Testament Apocrypha.* 2 vols. Philadelphia: Westminster, 1963.

Kaltner, John. *Ishmael Instructs Isaac.* Collegeville, MN: Liturgical Press, 1999.

Matthews, Victor, and Don Benjamin. *Old Testament Paralllels.* 2nd ed. Mahwah, NJ: Paulist, 1997.

Pritchard, James. *Ancient Near Eastern Texts.* 3rd ed. Princeton: Princeton University, 1969.

——. *Ancient Near East in Pictures.* 2nd ed. Princeton: Princeton University, 1969.

Sarna, Nahum. *Genesis, The JPS Torah Commentary.* Philadelphia: The Jewish Publication Society, 1989.

שמות

Exodus *Sh^emot*

SECTION OUTLINE

Literary Format and Movement

Date, Composition, and Manuscripts

Exodus and Historiography

The Dramatic Liberation

God, Moses, and YHVH

Women and the Rescue

Who Was Rescued?

The Celebration

The Instruction on the Mountain

How Shall YHVH Live with Israel?

Questions for Further Study

References

We could make the argument that this second scroll of our library is even more important than the first. That's not a claim about the relative value of the writings, just an observation about some realities in religious traditions. For example, Exodus introduces us to Moses, arguably the most important figure in our library and in much of later Jewish tradition. Also, the story of the exodus of the Israelites from Egypt, one of the two major events of our scroll's narrative, is easily the story to which our library refers most. One scholar has counted no less than 120 references to it in our 24 Hebrew scrolls (Sarna, *Exodus* xiv). The second major event of the Exodus narrative, YHVH's giving of instructions (*torah*) for the Israelites at Mt. Sinai, is equally famous and also plays a major role in other scrolls of our library. And, of course, if one looks beyond the 24 scrolls of our library to many later Jewish traditions, the exodus from Egypt, and the Torah are very important ideas. Even beyond Jewish tradition, these stories loom large; they include Ten Commandments.

The scroll's common name in Hebrew is Sh^emot, pronounced "sh^e-*mote*," which means "names." It is a shorthand version of the first words of the scroll: "And these are the names of the sons of Israel." The English title, Exodus, comes from Greek tradition, *Exodos* being a Greek word for "departure." In later Jewish tradition there was also a Hebrew equivalent to this "leaving Egypt" name.

LITERARY FORMAT AND MOVEMENT

Intricate describes the style and composition of this scroll. For scholars investigating its compositional history, Sh^emot has provided a complex puzzle. Researchers recognize the author's use of earlier sources, and the seams of these sources is in some places quite clear. Nevertheless, the scroll exhibits unity, tightly woven themes, and intricately formed artistry. Scholars interested in this literary artistry have found in this scroll much to consider, admire, and ponder. The scroll is fundamentally a prose narrative, but poetry (Chapter 15) and a great deal of legal instructional material have been woven into the story. Within these instructions there is great diversity as well—holiday celebrations, cultic sacrifices, social and personal moral codes, and directions for building a portable shrine. Yet the storyline seems always present—not lost in a forest of detail.

The scroll can be divided various ways, as you will see if you look at different scholarly attempts to outline the content. This variety is a testimony to smooth movement in much of the scroll and the thematic weaving that ties together the material. Essentially there are two major events: YHVH's rescue of his people, the Israelites, from slavery in Egypt and YHVH's instructions to them for living up to the standards of the God who now dwells with them. The scroll opens by setting the stage for the drama of the rescue: the ordeal of slavery and certain death. Moshe himself must first be rescued from this horror and then he is called to be YHVH's representative in a dramatic and emotional story of calling, hostility, plagues, death, defeat, and triumph. The rescue is capped by a celebratory ancient poem of YHVH's victory and kingship, known often as the Song of the Sea. In the narrative it divides the book geographically, in Egypt and out of Egypt at Mt. Sinai. The instruction section also begins dramatically with YHVH's appearance at the mountain. The author masterfully weaves narrative and law in these chapters to produce not only a great many instructions but also a riveting story. The storyline concerns YHVH's desire to dwell with his people, their impatience and abandonment of the covenant, and their punishment and repentance. The story and scroll close at the high point of the dwelling being built for YHVH and, most importantly, YHVH's coming to dwell with his people.

Setting the Stage
1.1–22 Oppression of Israel in Egypt

YHVH's Rescue of Israel from Egypt
2.1–4.31 Rescue and calling of Moses

5.1–7.7 Calling of Moses and dispute with Pharaoh

7.8–10.29 YHVH's nine victories over Pharaoh and Egypt

11.1–14.31 YHVH's final victory, Passover inaugurated, death for Egyptians and freedom for Israelites

15.1–21 Songs of YHVH's victory

Traveling to the Mountain
15.22–19.2 Journey from Sea of Reeds to Mt. Sinai

YHVH's Instructions at Mt. Sinai
19.3–25 Encountering YHVH

20.1–23.33 YHVH's commands and covenant

24.1–18 Concluding covenantal ceremonies

25.1–31.18 Instructions for building a dwelling for YHVH

32.1–34.35 Israel's breach of covenant and restoration

35.1–40.38 Building of YHVH's dwelling; YHVH is present

Date, Composition, and Manuscripts

Discoveries of ancient scrolls and manuscripts have shown what was normal for scrolls of ancient Israel, namely, changes and additions through time. Sh^{e}mot, too, was composed diachronically, and scholars attempting to excavate the layers of this text have hypothesized many stages of development. Furthermore, we have a wealth of ancient manuscript evidence exhibiting significant variants: the medieval Masoretic texts that are the basis of most modern Bibles, nearly 20 manuscripts from the Dead Sea Scrolls, Greek translations, and the Samaritan manuscript tradition, also in Hebrew. The form of Sh^{e}mot I outlined above is the Masoretic text, and its basic form probably took shape in the sixth or fifth century BCE. But the writing clearly was not crystallized at that time; the later manuscript evidence testifies loudly and clearly to continued changes. Equally important is the realization that the author(s) even in the sixth and fifth centuries were working with older materials, some written and some oral. Indeed, the poem of Sh^{e}mot 15 is often thought to be one of the oldest compositions preserved in our library.

Exodus and Historiography

When we begin to read carefully and ask the questions of a modern historical researcher, we notice that this fascinating scroll is something different than a straightforward historical account. It is highly episodic: In passing remarks we learn that it covers more than 80 years, yet only about two of those years get any narrative. In fact the chronology of the scroll is very unclear and clearly not a priority of the author. The author's interests also differ from a historian's regarding personal identities. He names few persons that should be named in a historical account, especially the kings of Egypt. The king, who is the main antagonist of the drama of Chapters 5–14, is never mentioned by name. What king was it? No modern historian would fail to mention it. This would be like writing a "history" of World War II and never mentioning the name Hitler or identifying him! But this is no mistake; the author has religious and literary reasons for completely snubbing the Egyptian king in this way.

If, as historians, we look for all the historical evidence we can find, we will discover that there is little to help us. In all the huge amounts of evidence of ancient Egypt, there is no indication of the Israelites ever being in Egypt. There is no distinct evidence of their presence, and no record of the Egyptian national catastrophes that are spoken of in early chapters of Sh^{e}mot. The first reference to Israel in all of Egyptian records is the famous Merneptah stele, which comes from the end of the thirteenth century, about 1210, and it testifies that Israelites are living in the area of Syria-Palestine at that time. A look at the scroll of Sh^{e}mot shows that the author is not concerned with providing the kind of chronological data and specific information that a modern historian needs to reconstruct history with confidence. Sh^{e}mot 1.11 is the best we can do—the cities of Pithom and Ramses are said to have been built by Israelite slaves. Egyptian archaeological work has indicated that these cities of the Egyptian Delta region were being built in the thirteenth century. If a historical correlation is to be made, it would indicate that the Israelites were there in Egypt during that period (1200s) and then left Egypt by the mid- to late 1200s. This would likely place the Israelites in Egypt at the time of **Ramses II,** the famous king who reigned from about 1290 to 1224 BCE. But this placement is just conjecture, and clearly our scroll is not focused on such details. An Israelite audience of the sixth century probably would not know anything about Ramses II from about 700 years prior. Trying to figure out an actual geographical itinerary for the Israelites traveling from Egypt according the narrative of Sh^emot has proved impossible—there are at least a dozen or so educated guesses, and the locations of even key places such as Mt. Sinai are disputed.

Thus the historical search leaves us without much evidence, and a full appreciation of our scroll will not come from trying to read it as a critical history to be united with other historical records. We can also approach it with questions that are not historical ones and as a writing with different goals and priorities. Sh^emot is a record of Israelite traditions about the past, but in what ways those traditions correlate with the actual events is beyond our ability to judge as historians at this time, given the lack of information. The scroll's lack of attention to historical essentials, the style of the composition—with its historical schematizations and hyperbole, the overt interest in the religious life of the audience centuries after the events—all suggest other types of questions we could productively ask about the scroll.

The Dramatic Liberation

The first story of Sh^emot is a story of liberation from intolerable slavery that is meant to inspire loyalty to the God who rescued. Slavery, a social custom whereby a person is allowed to maintain ownership rights over another, was a common and accepted reality in the ancient world of the Israelites, and as an institution it is not condemned by Israelite authors. As modern readers we have read about more recent forms of slavery, including that practiced in the United States from colonial times until the mid-nineteenth century. But in ancient Israel and the ancient Near Eastern world in general, slavery was not identical to the American version. Slavery was not a racial issue, and there were not large segments of the economy, such as farming, that depended on slavery. Debt repayment and military conquest were common reasons for slavery. Household slaves were the most common. A slave might be another Israelite or a foreigner, and there were various ways out of slavery. Authors of our library (and the Christian New Testament, too) accepted the reality of slavery, but we do find numerous places where inhumane treatment and overwork are condemned (e.g., Exodus 20.10). Furthermore, biblical texts advocate a slave's participation in communal events and a basic sense of respect (e.g., Deuteronomy 12.12). Of course, we cannot know from texts the actual practices of most individual slave owners, though the several laws that concern slaves give us some clues.

Sh^emot begins by setting the stage for YHVH's mighty acts of liberation. The horrendous plight of the Israelite slaves is severe oppression. The story depicts the Egyptian masters as cruel and ruthless. The Israelites as a nation are slaves—a huge slave labor camp. Slavery turns from cruelty to genocide, and the Israelites face extinction because every male born is to be executed by being drowned in the Nile (1.22). This oppression continues to get even worse throughout the next episodes. (Notice the poetic justice when the Egyptian warriors are finally defeated by drowning! 14.26–28) In these early chapters, the author keeps heightening the desperation of the situation as he builds toward a dramatic confrontation (see 1.8–14, 22; 2.23; 5.4–21). The author has planted the seeds of possibility with the birth of Moses (Chapter 2), but the real hope is spoken of only at the end of Chapter 2:

> And God [Elohim] listened to their groans and God attended to his covenant with Abraham, with Isaac, and with Jacob. And God saw the children of Israel and God knew. (Sh^emot 2.24–25)

This turning point signals the future by looking to the past—the traditions and stories of God's covenant with the three great patriarchs, of which we read in Genesis, are invoked. The God of Israel hears the pain of his people and is moved. The tension of the entire liberation narrative has now been introduced. What can the Israelite God do? How will the promises of covenant made to those patriarchs be kept? Will this God be able to overcome the Egyptian's seemingly unlimited power over his people? The course of conflict is set, and in the next chapters the battle is engaged between the God of the Israelites and the Gods and the king of Egypt. In a spectacular revelation, coming through a flaming bush, God chooses a sympathetic yet reluctant leader for his side, Moses. At this time the author begins to use the name YHVH, revealing that YHVH is in fact the same God who appeared to their ancestors.

Moses's efforts are at times heroic yet ineffective, and the battle goes back and forth. As YHVH strikes the Egyptians with a series of nine supernatural disasters, traditionally called plagues, Egyptian power and oppression intensifies, and the Egyptian king is more hardened against the Israelites than ever.

Sh^emot is clearly insiders' literature; the outcome of the fight is never in doubt by the audience. Through dramatic irony—the audience knows what the characters do not—the God of Israel is clearly presented as always in control even though Moses and the Israelites in Egypt may doubt it (5.15–23) and even though the king himself is fully confident that he is in charge. The author assumes that the audience knows the significance of God's remembering the covenant with the patriarchs—the promise of blessing and land in Canaan, as narrated in Genesis 12.1–3, 15.1–21, and elsewhere.

In the end, the God of Israel triumphs through the use of a final dark miracle: the death of every Egyptian first-born male, including the prince (Sh^emot 12.29). The Israelites are officially released, but the king has second thoughts and chases after them. Pharaoh soon finds his army fighting against an angel of the God of Israel and YHVH himself incapacitating their chariots and finally drowning the army in a miraculous display of power. The outcome of the battle and the rhetorical emphasis of the author is summarized just as the Israelites make it safely to the mountain of God in the words of Moses's father in-in-law, *Yitro* in Hebrew, a Midianite foreigner and an impartial observer of sorts:

Yitro said, Blessed by YHVH,

who rescued you [plural] from the hand of Egypt and from the hand of Pharaoh;
who rescued the people from under the hand of Egypt.

So now I know that YHVH is greater than all the Gods, indeed even in their [the
Gods] arrogant raging against them [the people]. (Sh^emot 18.11)

God, Moses, and YHVH

You may wonder why at the beginning of this chapter I usually referred to God
instead of YHVH. That is just what ancient Sh^emot's readers may have wondered!
Attentive readers for centuries have noted that the name YHVH is studiously
avoided at the beginning of the scroll; instead we only find the more generic *God*,
Hebrew *Elohim*. YHVH occurs for the first time in Chapter 3. This is the famous
story of Moshe in the desert being surprised by a blazing bush and a divine voice
that calls him to the mission of deliverance. Moshe naturally asks the deity which
God is sending him:

> And Moshe said to the God, "Now when I come to the sons of Israel and I say to them,
> 'the God of your fathers sent me to you,' and they say to me, 'What is his name?' what
> shall I say to them?" And God said to Moshe, "*Ehyeh asher ehyeh.*" And he said, "Thus
> you shall say to the sons of Israel, '*Ehyeh* has sent me to you.'" (Sh^emot 3.13–14)

I didn't translate the key words *Ehyeh asher ehyeh*, but we will discuss their meaning later. First, observe a similar scene later in the narrative, when YHVH reaffirms
his own commitment to honor his promises to Israel's ancestors and again speaks
about his name:

> God spoke to Moshe and said to him, "I am YHVH. I appeared to Abraham, to Isaac,"
> and to Jacob as *El Shaddai* and my name YHVH I did not make known to them.
> (Sh^emot 6.2–3)

Here the narrator again links his story to the past—the God now speaking to
Moses is in fact the same God known to the ancestors of the Israelites, the God of
Abraham, Isaac, and Jacob. The author is also explaining something about the history of Israelite religion, namely that YHVH was *not* known by his name YHVH to
the ancestors; instead he was known by the name *El Shaddai*. Indeed we find this
latter name in stories about the patriarchs, for example Genesis 17.1–8 and
35.11–12. *El* in Israelite literature can be a generic title, like *God,* but it can also be a
specific name. El in fact was an important God of Canaanite culture, and so once
again we see that the Israelite traditions are closely connected other Canaanite cultures. When we investigate the use of the term *Shaddai* we find it is quite rare and
difficult for scholars to translate. Its use in prose narrative in our library is limited
almost exclusively to the book of Genesis. Other uses are in poetic texts, and
Hebrew poetry characteristically draws on archaic words and forms. It has also been
found in non-Israelite sources prior to the rise of Israel. In other words, historically
focused research indicates that *El Shaddai* is a very old title that fell into disuse by
the Israelites and was replaced by YHVH. Its meaning is even more difficult. It

seems likely to many that that *Shaddai* is related to an Akkadian word for "mountain" and that it may have referred to a mountain God, El of the Mountain(s). But nearly all scholars acknowledge that we need more evidence before we can have confidence in this suggestion or any other, including the traditional older English translation of "almighty."

Whatever the meaning of the old name, the author associates *El Shaddai* with the ancestors and YHVH with Moses and explains that *El Shaddai* is an older name for YHVH. If you go back through Genesis, you will find that names other than YHVH are frequently used to a greater degree than in other scrolls. However, another Israelite tradition seems to have understood this aspect of the history of Israelite religion differently. The author(s) of Genesis 4.26, 12.8, and 13.4 write(s) that the name of YHVH was used and known by patriarchs long before Moses. Modern researchers have dealt with these traditions in various ways. The common explanation described at the beginning of this Chapter is that the tradition that YHVH was not known by the patriarchs (Sh^emot 6.2–3) and the tradition that YHVH was known by the patriarchs (Genesis 4.26; 12.8; 13.4) represent different sources. No later editor changed the differences in the perspectives. In fact, this weaving together supports the continuity theme of the author of Sh^emot 3 and 6.

Now we come to the meaning of the name YHVH. Sh^emot 3.14 is perhaps the most famous line from the scroll, except for the Ten Commandments. What does the name YHVH—in Hebrew, יהוה—mean? Discovering the source and historically original meaning of any name is difficult and often the evidence is quite sparse, but

Study Room 5.2

STUDYING SEVERAL PLAGUE TRADITIONS

In writings and oral retellings, Israelites kept alive multiple traditions about their past. In many cases we possess only one record of one of the versions that existed long ago. In some cases, however, our library preserves multiple accounts. This is the case with the tradition about the disasters with which YHVH defeated Israel. We have the long prose version in Sh^emot 7.8–14.31 and two poetic versions in Psalms 78.42–51 and Psalms 105.28–36. It makes for a fascinating study to compare these three artistic retellings; there are numerous sets of questions we could ask. Write or print the three retellings so you can read them side by side, and then compare. What differences in content and order to you find? What seems to be unique in emphasis or perspective about each? Are there any direct quotations? Can you make any arguments about which came first? How does the story fit into the larger work?

it is a fascinating exploration. On the other hand, if we ask *literary* questions about the meaning of the name in the burning bush story of Sh^emot, we will find several different answers. The author presents the name as a form of the Hebrew verb *h-y-h* (or *h-w-h*), which can mean "to be, to become, to be present" and in another form "to cause to be." Interpreters have used all of these options. The form *y-h-v-h* looks like a third person form of the verb and is similar to the English future tense "he will be" or "he will cause to be." The translators of the JPS Tanakh and the NRSV are forthright enough to include a footnote indicating that the meaning is uncertain and has been taken various ways.

1. It has been related to the hope and promise for oppressed Israel's future: "The-One-Who-Will Be" or "He-Causes-To-Be."
2. Others have taken it as referring to YHVH's promise to be present with Israel, to be with them: "The-One-Who-Will-Be-There."
3. Much less likely is the more philosophical reading, which sees it as a statement of eternal being: "The-One-Who-Is."

So, choosing the second option, we would translate Sh^emot 3.14 this way:

And God said to Moshe, "I will be there how I will be there." And he said, "Thus you shall say to the sons of Israel, 'I-Will-Be-There has sent me to you.'"

The ambiguity and subsequent possibilities are certainly apparent for honest modern translators: perhaps ambiguity and multivalence were there for ancient writers and readers as well. When you read Chapters 1–6, what significance of YHVH's name do you see in the narrative? How might the meaning relate to the story?

Sh^emot is a fascinating story about Moshe. He was rescued from death at birth by a resourceful and hopeful mother who floats him on the Nile in a basket and is then rescued by the princess of Egypt and raised in the palace. He murders an Egyptian trying to defend an enslaved Israelite and flees to the desert and marries a foreign woman. He is overwhelmed by an encounter with YHVH speaking from a blazing bush, returns to Egypt, and eventually leads the Israelites out of their slavery. But even with all that attention paid to Moshe, which includes a lot of character conflict and development and ample attention given to the supporting role of Moshe's brother Aaron, the hero of the story is clearly not Moshe. The hero and main character is YHVH. Moshe is more human than heroic and often a reluctant though dedicated leader. But the great conflict of the story is YHVH versus the Gods and King of Egypt to rescue his people, whose cries of suffering he heard. The God of Sh^emot is not presented as a remote, distant, heaven-dwelling being. This God is passionate, involved in the fray of battle, a partisan for his people, emotive in love and anger, using tricks and direct action. The language of the story presents him as present, constantly speaking to Moshe anywhere. YHVH's presence is a theme that runs through the entire scroll.

It would be worthwhile here to pause for an aside, especially for modern readers who may have heard what we might call naturalistic interpretations of the plagues. These are modern explanations of the plagues that describe them as natural occurrences of, for example, muddy water resembling blood or infestations of frogs or flies. But these explanations seem to miss the whole point of the narrative, namely that this is a contest between the God of Israel and the Gods and the king of Egypt, and these naturalistic explanations seem completely foreign to the ancient literary and religious context of the ancient Near East. Trying to somehow remove the supernatural from the story also removes a crucial objective of the story. The frequent actions of YHVH in speaking, striking, fooling, fighting, and more make him immediately active in the narrative and therefore difficult to remove. If one is really trying to provide strictly rationalistic explanations for the narrative of this scroll, there is a whole lot more to explain than just the ten plagues. Should a modern reader take such a story so full of direct, divine action as historical, literal, metaphorical, or allegorical? Should such a story be valued as relevant, meaningful, or worthless? Answers will vary with each reader. For many modern readers and traditions with differing views of its historicity, it is one of the classic stories of liberation.

Women and the Rescue

The dominating male perspective and interests are a reality of most texts in our library, which reflects some of the social realities of life in ancient Israel. Female characters are much less frequent and rarely prominent in the narratives of this library. And for that reason, the early stories of Moshe are exceptional. Moshe, by responding to the call of YHVH, may have saved the Israelites from Egypt, but it was women who saved Moshe. We can read through Shemot asking feminist questions that have to do with women, such as their function and power in narratives, their roles as writers and readers, and the author's perspective on them. It is remarkable that the author gave so much attention to women. The Hebrew midwives perform the scroll's first deeds of salvation, courageously defying the king's orders to kill the Israelite boys at birth (1.15–21). It is no incidental aside or mistake that the author tells the names of the midwives, Shiphrah and Puah, but the name of the Egyptian king is never so much as mentioned; his name is denigrated and studiously obliterated from the story. Saved once by the midwives, Moshe is next rescued by his mother and sister and then by the daughter of the Pharaoh himself (Chapter 2). With great irony on several levels, it is in fact the princess who gives Moshe his name. The name is Egyptian, a rather common name meaning "son," which you can see in other Egyptian names, such as Thut-*mose*. But our author relates the name to a Hebrew word, *m-sh-h*, meaning "to draw out," and has the Egyptian princess explain the Hebrew meaning. The Hebrew meaning describes not only what she did to save Moshe from floating down stream, but also foreshadows what Moshe is destined to do: draw the Israelites out of Egypt. Another scroll in our library also has this wordplay in poetic form (Isaiah 63.11).

The roles of women continue. When Moshe flees to Midian, he meets seven daughters, one of whom becomes his wife (Chapter 2). Later in one of the most mysterious episodes in our library, his wife Zipporah saves him from YHVH's attempt on his life (4.24–26). And let's mention one more episode. Miriam,

Moshe's sister, and the women of Israel are the ones we see in the last major scene of the celebration of the rescue, dancing and singing (15.20–21). It is appropriate to include Miriam in the last scene because it was she who at the beginning of this story of this salvation helped save her little brother (Chapter 2).

Who Was Rescued?

Just as the plot of his dramatic escape story begins to climax, the scroll seems to lose focus and stumble into another genre, legislation. We can see this clearly by reading from Chapter 12.1 to 13.16. Much of this section is comprised of rules about the calendar and how to celebrate Passover, the Jewish holiday commemorating deliverance from Egypt. It is unlikely that the author has lost his focus. Instead the material is deliberately placed and reveals more of the author's

POSTER 5.3   ISRAELITE CALENDER

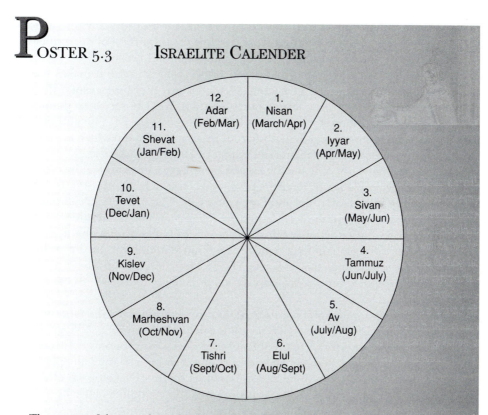

The names of the month used in the Hebrew Bible were originally Babylonian names. These were adopted by the Jews after 586 BCE, and because our literature took its final form after that time, the authors and editors used the Babylonian names. The earlier Hebrew names are known only for four months: Aviv for Nisan (Exodus 23.15); Ziv for Iyyar (1 Kings 6.1); Etanim for Tishri (1 Kings 8.2); Bul for Marheshvan (1 Kings 6.38).

religious purpose. The author is not writing a critical historical record or just telling a good story; he is involving his own audience in the story by placing the detailed regulations for *their own* celebration and calendar right here in the climax of the great rescue. The author has future generations in mind, which is evident from 13.14:

> And in the future when your son asks you saying, "What does this (mean)?" you will say, "With a strong hand YHVH brought us out from Egypt."

By integrating the rituals and practices of later generations into the narrative, the author has from a literary perspective involved later generations in the story and made them participants. This seem to me a likely explanation of the manner of writing.

The Celebration

Completing the festive mood introduced by the inclusion of so many instructions for the festival of Passover, the author closes his first major portion of the scroll with a poem of victory, found in Chapter 15. The poem that was used here was credited to Moses, with the opening lines attributed to his sister Miriam. It makes use of themes that were widespread in ancient Near Eastern literature, especially the theme of a divine warrior who defeats one's enemies. You can see these themes in other Israelite song literature as well, such as Psalms 77 and 78. The author also uses it to anticipate stories that he has not told in his narrative but which are known to him and his audience, namely the settlement of Israelites in Canaan.

The celebration is not only for the escape from Egypt, but also for the crossing of the *Yam Suf*, that is "Sea of Reeds" (13.18; 15.22), which signifies the Israelites have crossed the line of safety beyond Egyptian attack. The intended location is not at all clear; the meaning of the term is not the Red Sea, which is a tradition started by ancient Greek translators of Exodus, but *Sea of Reeds*, likely referring to marshy grounds east of the Egyptian delta region. Much more important for the author is the great demonstration of the power of YHVH over the Pharaoh, the Egyptians, and their Gods, a point repeatedly emphasized and celebrated (14.4, 8–14, 17–18, 23–25, 27–31; 15.1–21).

Like *Yam Suf*, the geographic location of their next destination, the mountain of God (e.g., Sh^emot 3.1, Numbers 10.33), often called Mt. Sinai (e.g., Sh^emot 19.11 Deuteronomy 33.2) or Horeb (e.g., Sh^emot 3.1; 17.6, Deuteronomy 4.10), is not clear from the narratives. Perhaps these different names refer to the same place, or maybe different traditions have been combined. Is there archaeological evidence for the location? Hundreds of books by historians and geographers have been written about these topics, but we can summarize the results this way.

1. There is no consus on these matters. The site(s) idenification remains uncertain.
2. The traditional site of Mt. Sinai on the southern end of the Sinai pennisula, known as *Jebul Musa* (Arabic for "Mount of Moses"), goes back only to the third or forth century CE.

3. There are dozens of other proposed locations, some near Palestine, some in modern Jordan or Saudi Arabia.

The Instruction on the Mountain

Perhaps the most famous lines from this scroll are the Ten Commandments, which come in Chapter 20. They are represented in many synagogues and churches. Moses holding the famous tablets is depicted on the east portico of the United States Supreme Court building along with Solon and Confucius, and of course there is the Hollywood movie *The Ten Commandments* from 1956. Signs with the Ten Commandments appear in American front yards, and in 2005 in the state of Alabama there was a legal battle over a display of them in a courthouse. Clearly this passage from Sh^{e}mot 20 has a life far beyond this scroll. In Sh^{e}mot, however, these ten are not separated from their literary context as if they were not part of a much larger document. Before he writes about any instructions given by YHVH, the author spends a good deal of time on the ominous atmosphere of thunder, lightning, and dense clouds. Here at the mountain of God, where Moshe had his own flaming bush encounter with YHVH (see 3.1 and 18.5), the rest of the Israelites have their own mysterious encounter. They hear YHVH's voice speak the first commands and beg Moshe to intercede for them because the experience is too frightening (20.1–21). At that point, the scroll launches into a lengthy section of legal rulings about such things as capital crimes, slaves, property damage, care of the poor, husbandry, judicial procedure, and religious festivals. This section runs through 23.33 and is known today as the Covenant Code. It is often thought to have existed independently prior to the composition of our scroll. As we would expect, given that we recognize that Israelite culture and writers were a part of a larger culture of Canaan, Mesopotamia, and Egypt, many of these particular laws have parallels in law codes of other nations, some of which are cited in the following chart (Poster 5.4).

The specific laws themselves provide a fascinating picture of ancient Israelite legal thinking. First of all, the laws reflect and assume a settled, agriculturally based society, not large urban centers and not a wandering, landless community. The laws collected here are representative of Israelite social and religious legal thinking as developed by priestly authorities and written into a literary composition by our authors. Israel's laws were constantly evolving in divinely directed ways, and this is reflected in stories such as Sh^{e}mot 18.13–27, Leviticus 24.10–16, Numbers 27.1–11, Deuteronomy 17.8–13, and 1 Samuel 30.21–25. The fact that the laws are rooted in the social reality of ancient Israelite society explains why so many Israelite laws are similar to laws of neighboring societies. The laws are moved from their original social, legal, and oral settings to the literary settings of our library. The authors of Sh^{e}mot, as well as those of Leviticus, Numbers, and Deuteronomy, place known laws and collections of laws of their own choosing into this literary scenario of YHVH speaking with Moses and Israel. Contests of such claims can be seen in Jeremiah 7.21–23 and 8.8–9. The kinds of laws include **case law**—rulings that begin with a certain situation and then prescribe a penalty, often using the formula "If/when a

DISPLAY 5.1 | THE GOD SHAMASH GIVING THE LAWS TO KING HAMMURABI, EIGHTEENTH CENTURY BCE

person does _____, he shall be punished by _____" (e.g., Sh^emot 21.2–22.27). Other laws are stated without reference to specific cases: "You shall/shall not do _____" (e.g., Sh^emot 20.1–17 and 23.1–19). Historians of ancient Israel have attempted to figure out the specific historical contexts behind the different laws in the literature, an extremely difficult task because archaeologists have not discovered legal documents or other sources dated to specific periods.

More important for our questions about the literary make-up of Sh^emot is the narrative context of these laws and the way they fit within it. These laws are not found independently inscribed on a stele standing as a record of some ancient legislation. They are a part of literary composition that is retelling Israelite traditions about YHVH's actions on behalf of Israel's ancestors and their covenant with him. Within this narrative composition of YHVH's covenant, compassion, and

Poster 5.4

Similar Ancient Near Eastern Laws

Hammurabi's Law Code (ca. 1770 BCE)

117. If an obligation is outstanding against a man and he sells or gives into debt service his wife, his son, or his daughter, they shall perform service in the house of their buyer or of the one who holds them in debt service for three years; their release shall be secured in the fourth year.

195. If a child should strike his father, they shall cut off his hand. (trans Roth COS 2:348)

125. If a man give his property for safekeeping and his property together with the householder's property is lost either by (theft achieved through) a breach or by scaling over a wall, the householder who was careless shall make restitution and shall continue to search for his own lost property, and he shall take it from the one who stole it from him.

Shᵉmot

21.7 If a man sells his daughter as a maid, she shall not go out just as slaves go out. . . .

21.15 Whoever strikes his father or his mother, he must be put to death.

22.6–7 (or 7) If a man give to his neighbor money or goods for safekeeping and it is stolen from the house of the man, if the thief is found he shall pay double; if the thief is not found the house owner shall be taken near the God (to inquire if) he took the property of his neighbor.

One of the most fascinating comparative historical studies one can undertake is a comparison of many different ancient law codes. Of course each document must be read in light the context of the literature in which it is preserved, and rarely is there evidence of exact borrowings. But there is much to learn about ancient conceptions of justice, morality, and religion in the many fascinating codes that have been preserved. We are fortunate to have many of these translated into English, for example Pritchard, Hallo, and Matthews and Benjamin, listed in the references.

presence, we find a lively story of YHVH's commands, given on a dark, mysterious mountain, involving Moshe, Aaron, clan elders, and all of Israel. The individual laws are important to the author, but there is no claim and likely no ancient expectation that they are a complete collection of the laws of Israel. As we would expect, the composer undoubtedly drew on other sources for these lists of laws for his literary creation. Furthermore, there is clear manuscript evidence that the ancient laws vary in different manuscripts; the composition of these laws in this literary environment continued for centuries. For the sake of understanding the literary unity of the scroll, it is crucial to see all the laws as the instructions of YHVH for his people whom he rescued from slavery.

And Moshe went up to the God and YHVH called to him from the mountain saying, "Thus you will say to the house of Jacob, and you will tell the sons of Israel, 'You yourselves say what I did to Egypt and that I carried you on eagles' wings and brought you to me. And now if you listen to my voice and keep my covenant, they you will be to me a treasure from among the peoples. Yes, all the earth is mine. And you will be for me a kingdom of priests, and a distinct nation.'" (19.3–6)

How Shall YHVH Live with Israel?

Nearly a third of this scroll is spent on this question, which relates directly to one of its major theme. The largest part of the legal section of Sh^{e}mot (25.1–31.18) is YHVH's instructions for building a portable dwelling for YHVH:

> "They must build for me a holy shrine so that I may dwell in among you [plural]." (25.8)

This dwelling is meticulously described and the details of these chapters may seen tiresome to many readers. Using some diverse materials, the author lavished a great deal of artistic attention on his depiction of this tent for YHVH. For example, he makes YHVH's instructions for the shrine read as a mirror image to the description of the building of the shrine (25.1–31.18). YHVH gives instructions starting from the inside of the structure and moving out. The building of the shrine (Chapters 35–40) moves in just the opposite order, from the outside in, concluding their work in the most sacred space of all. This portable shrine is presented as a constant reminder of YHVH's presence and the place in which Moshe is to seek Counsel from YHVH (33.7–11). YHVH's presence would be most powerfully felt in the center. There we find the **ark of the covenant,** a portable wooden chest overlaid with gold, where YHVH was enthroned invisibly between golden statues of figures that were a mix of human, animal, and bird, called *cherubim,* in a completely covered sacred tent (25.10–22). A cloudy pillar that descended and rose over the tent signaled his presence externally (40.34–38).

Between YHVH's instructions for his dwelling and the actual building of it comes a famous narrative about Israel's impatience with Moshe and their disobedience to the command not to represent YHVH with a physical form. This is the incident of the making and worshiping of a golden calf, which caused Moshe to lash out, to break YHVH's tablets, and to initiate a violent punishment by death for many. The author has placed this very negative story (Chapters 32–34) right in the middle of the narrative about YHVH's sacred tent, demonstrating that even such an offense does not deter YHVH from dwelling with his people. The scroll ends on this triumphant note after the dwelling is completed:

> And the cloud covered the meeting tent and YHVH's glory filled the dwelling. And not even Moshe was able to enter the meeting tent because the cloud dwelled on it and YHVH's glory filled the dwelling. And whenever the cloud arose from the dwelling, the sons of Israel traveled on in their travelings. And if the cloud did not arise, they did not travel until the day of its rising. Because YHVH's cloud was on the dwelling by day and fire was in it (cloud) by night, in the sight of all the house of Israel in all their traveling.

Questions for Further Study

1. Looking through the scroll, where do you find the laws placed in the narrative? How do the laws relate to the story being told?

2. From a social point of view, what kind of society do these laws reflect? What do they assume about humans, hierarchies, economies, and ethnic groups?

3. Reading Chapters 20–40 carefully, who goes up the mountain, and how many times? How does the narrator present the mountain-top experience? Do you see clues to sources or redactors?

4. As a redaction and source critic, what seams that give clues about sources and editing do you observe in the text?

References

Brueggemann, Walter. "The Book of Exodus." In *The New Interpreter's Bible*. Vol. 1:1.677–981. Nashville, TN: Abingdon, 1994.

Greengus, Samuel. "Law." In *The Anchor Bible Dictionary*, ed. by David Noel Freedman, 4:242–52. New York: Doubleday, 1992.

Sarna, Nahum. *Exodus, The JPS Torah Commentary*. Philadelphia: The Jewish Publication Society, 1991.

Sarna, Nahum. *Exploring Exodus*. New York: Schocken, 1986.

Redford, D. "Pharaoh," in *The Anchor Bible Dictionary*, ed. by David Noel Freedman. New York: Doubleday, 1990.

ויקרא
Leviticus *Vayyikra*

Section Outline

My own attitude about Leviticus has changed drastically over the years. At one point I thought the book was extremely pedantic and rather dry. But my opinion changed while I was reading some fine scholarship on the book—anthropology and commentaries—which attempted to understand the ancient cultural mindset that gives this scroll a certain logic. These studies introduced me to a group of ideas about Israelite antiquity that helped me understand the scroll. But before we get there, let's mention the names and see how the book is arranged.

The Hebrew title, *Vayyikra,* is simply the first words of the scroll and means "and he called/summoned." It is pronounced as "vah-yik-*rah*." The *v* is the Hebrew word "and." The English title, *Leviticus,* derives ultimately from the name in Greek manuscripts, which named the scroll for the tribe of Levites who were designated priests in many Israelite narratives. We might think *Leviticus* a rather unfortunate title because Levites are only mentioned in Chapter 25, and then only in passing. But the designation probably reflects a time period when *Levite* was essentially a synonym for *priest,* and this book deals with the work of priests.

LITERARY FORMAT AND MOVEMENT

Vayyikra, the shortest book of Moses—a little more than half the size of Genesis—has been edited to be a continuation of the Exodus scroll; it has no introduction of its own. But unlike Exodus, it contains only a sparse narrative and entails no movement of the Israelites in the larger storyline that runs from Genesis to Joshua. Vayyikra is set at the foot of Mt. Sinai, though the mountain is not mentioned until Chapter 25. Usually the author simply says that YHVH was speaking to Moses at the sacred meeting tent. Most of the material is presented as YHVH's direct words to Moses and consists mostly of ethical code. In some sense, the book interrupts a storyline, or perhaps we should say it is not tightly tied to the surrounding books. It does not date events or YHVH's speeches as does Exodus before it (40.2, 17) and Numbers after it (1.1). In that sense it is atemporal. So its literary form is essentially instructional speech situated in a definite but thin narrative frame.

YHVH Instructs Moses About Sacrifices

1.1–17 Burnt animal offerings

2.1–16 Grain offerings

3.1–17 Well-being offerings

4.1–5.13 Forgiveness offerings

5.14–6.7 Guilt offerings

6.8–7.38 Offering rituals

YHVH Instructs Moses About Food and Body Purification Rites

11.1–47 Permitted and forbidden foods

12.1–15.32 Purification rites for Israelites

YHVH Instructs Moses About Holiness in Israelite Life

17.1–16 Issues of blood

18.1–30 Holiness in sexual relations

19.1–20.27 Holiness in daily life

21.1–22.33 Holiness for priests

23.1–44 Holiness in festivals

24.1–9 Priestly laws

24.10–24 Example and laws

25.1–26.2 Holiness for land and slaves

Per YHVH's Instruction, Moses Consecrates Priests

8.1–9.24 Setting apart Aaron and sons

10.1–20 Sons of Aaron make unauthorized offering and are destroyed by YHVH

16.1–34 YHVH Instructs Moses About Purification Rites for Sacred Tent, Priest, Day of Atonement Ritual

YHVH's Concluding Summary on a Life of Holiness

26.3–13 Obedience leads to YHVH's blessing

26.14–46 Disobedience leads to YHVH's curse

27.1–34 Appendix on Sacred Vows

Vayyikra as Literature

Now of all the books we have come to so far, this one may raise the most questions in our minds about what sort of writing it is. The majority of its content would generically be called legal material because it consists of commands. However, there is a thin narrative framework into which the laws are cast; it is not a simple list. The scroll begins is as a narrative that describes YHVH's conversation with Moses, but already by the second sentence we move to law.

> YHVH called to Moshe and spoke to him from the meeting tent saying, "Speak to the people [literally *sons*] of Israel and say to them, 'Any man that brings a livestock offering to YHVH, must bring the offering from the herd or flock.'" (1.1–2)

And YHVH's speech, consisting only of legal instructions, continues, without another interruption for several columns. As the scroll progresses, the narrator occasionally inserts commentary, but usually just enough to echo the scroll's introduction in phrases such as "YHVH spoke to Moshe saying, speak to the people [literally *sons*] of Israel and say to them . . . " as in 4.1; 5.14; 6.1, 8, 19, 24, and others. But after this briefest of introductions, we immediately encounter a long list of regulations. Is this literature? An observation that might help us answer the question is that the scroll is not a kind of law book, as if it were a list of laws straight from a courtroom register of legislation approved by a governing body, a king, or a God. If we were to conduct a careful structural analysis of the entire scroll, we would notice a certain scaffolding, or frame. The frame, or organization, of the document, however thin, is *always* the conversation between Moses and YHVH, with YHVH giving Moses instruction (*torah*) about what Israelites are to do. This conversation is sometime interrupted. At one point in particular, about a third of the way through the scroll (Chapters 8–10), the narrator breaks in and actually provides a continuous narrative about the ordination of priests and the downfall of two of them. A much shorter interruption is found in 24.10–23. But the remainder of the scroll is presented as YHVH's instructional conversation with Moses, with many junctures where the reader is reminded that it is YHVH speaking to Moses, and sometimes Aaron, too, and directing the Israelites. With these constantly repeated introductory formulas, approximately 30 times over the course of the entire book, the narrator never allows his audience to forget the dramatic setting of YHVH instructing Moshe and the Israelites.

Dating Vayyikra

Of course the dramatic setting of any narrative does not tell us when the story was written. We already have learned that we cannot just ask "When was this book written?" and expect a clear and definite answer from our scrolls, as we might from a title page of our favorite English novel or history book. By ancient Israelite custom, Vayyikra too was written diachronically. Many scholars attempting to unravel the history of the scroll's composition through source criticism have concluded that

Vayyikra was composed from different sources. Some contend that it was put into roughly the form that we have it in during the eighth to seventh centuries BCE, while the Southern Kingdom of Judah was still extant. Many others argue for a somewhat later period, the sixth and fifth centuries BCE, during and after the exile of the Southern Kingdom. In any case, all would agree that the document was composed by priests, who were involved in and concerned with the function of the Israelite temple and **cult** in Jerusalem. Thus, according to one common reconstruction of the compositional history, the vast majority of the scroll is credited to priestly (P) authors. But the priests did not see themselves as starting a new cult or temple for YHVH; their interests were also in preserving the past and a heritage. They undoubtedly used documents and other oral and written traditions to create this scroll. So, some of the laws or sections of text may be quite ancient, reflecting codes during the period of the **First Temple** or even before. Because the authors were not bound by the conventions or interests of modern historians, they did not carefully document which sections were old and which were new. Like so much of Israel's literature, this scroll was a living text, growing and expanding according to the desires of its keepers completely in harmony with the conventions of the time. The scroll's dramatic setting at Mt. Sinai is centuries before its present composition, and the authors were free to add contemporary material to the ancient drama. By this practice the authors support the continuity and pliability of their social and cultic traditions, and their own authority is sustained.

Sources and Sections in Vayyikra

There are numerous textual clues to the distinct sources that were incorporated into the scroll as we now have it. For example, Vayyikra 7.37–38 is a concluding summary to the instructions for the sacrifices presented in Chapters 6 and 7. Clearly there is a segment break here, and possibly this at one time concluded an independent writing. Interestingly, one of the sacrifices mentioned in the closing summary, the ordination sacrifice, is omitted in the body of the text and from Vayyikra as a whole. It is, however, explained in Exodus 29. The omission may well indicate that an editor has (re)moved that particular instruction from the body.

Scholars frequently refer to Chapters 17–26 as the **Holiness Code,** and it is quite possible that this section at one time existed independently. Based on overlaps and repetitions in Chapters 17–26, some scholars believe that this section, too, is made up of smaller preexisting units. The Holiness Code is characterized by stress on holiness, or perhaps better, separateness, as the mark and motivation of Israelite personal and social practices, and by the repeated use of several formulas, such as "Separate you must be, because separate am I, YHVH, your God" (19.2; 20.7, 26; 21.8); "I am YHVH, I separate you" (20.8, 24, 26; 21.8, 15, 23; 22.9, 16); and especially the refrains "I am YHVH" or "I am YHVH your God" (18.2, 4, 5, 6, 21, 30 and dozens more).

If we look at the lines found in 26.46 (see Poster 5.5), we find two sentences that at one time were quite clearly at the end of a collection of instructions from

POSTER 5.5

A CONCLUDING SUMMARY (NO LONGER AT THE END!)

These are the commands and judgments and the instructions (*torah*) that YHVH arranged between himself and the sons of Israel at Mt. Sinai by the hand of Moses. (Vayyikra 26.46)

YHVH. In fact, Chapter 26, beginning at verse 3, is a motivational epilogue for the entire section, even for the entire book. Here we find no new laws, but a grand concluding speech by YHVH to the Israelites telling them that if they live according to his instructions then YHVH, who rescued them from slavery in Egypt, will bless them with plentiful harvests, peace in their land, victory over enemies, harmony in their covenant with YHVH, and YHVH's presence with them (26.3–13). However, if they do not abide by YHVH's commands, "I will do this to you," says YHVH. "I will bring plagues and military defeat. And if still you do not repent, I will bring more and more disasters, even to the point of destroying the nation and making the people exiles, scattered in foreign lands" (26.14–39). But, even then, YHVH continues, hope is not lost, for if the people repent of not following YHVH's commands, then YHVH will remember and be faithful to the covenant made with Abraham, Isaac, and Jacob and will again be their God (26.40–45). (For similar concluding prose speeches, each with its own unique rhetoric, see Exodus 23.22–33, Deuteronomy 28–30, and Joshua 24.1–28.) And then come the closing, scroll-ending words of verse 26.46. The last section, Chapter 27, then is anticlimactic, because it returns to giving specific commands; these are about different kinds of vows. Most scholars attempting to understand the book's organization see this last segment as an appendix that was added at a later time. At some point, a second concluding editorial postscript, 27.34, was added, and this now closes the entire scroll of Vayyikra.

Now, to return to the great closing epilogue of 26.3–46, it sounds to many readers like a theological review of Jewish history from the point of view of an author aware of Israel's exile yet still advocating dedication to YHVH and hope for a future. It can readily be compared to similar perspectives of prophetic and narrative scrolls from the time after the Jewish exile in Babylon. Thus, one of the later historical stages of the Leviticus scroll's history is likely in a period of Jewish exile or after it, that is, the sixth to fifth century BCE. But that is not to say that many specific laws or many ideas contained in the scroll did not exist earlier. The later authors combine a variety of materials and presentation all as the instructions spoken by YHVH at Mt. Sinai. Here in the Vayyikra scroll, in the dramatic setting of Mt. Sinai and a time long before the Exile, YHVH speaks to Moses, giving Jews of centuries later instructions and hope.

Holiness and the Main Ideas of Vayyikra

Holiness, or, as translated previously, *separateness,* is not a subject that only occurs in the holiness code (Chapters 17–26). It is certainly stressed there, but it also appears in many other places in our scroll. What is holiness? The English word is not uncommon in modern times—Holy Bible, holy day/holiday, even the exclamation "Holy cow!" In the scroll of Vayyikra and in the rest of our library's scrolls, too, the Hebrew adjective form is *qa-dosh* and might best be translated with something like "distinct, apart, separate, and differentiated." The verb form would mean "to set apart, to separate, to distinguish, to differentiate." Now, it is fairly easy to see how these meanings relate to *holy,* though it is unfortunate that modern English word *holy* has no usable verb form; *to sanctify* is the closest. But Hebrew words related to *holy* and *separate* are used in a less restrictive manner than our normal usage of *holy.*

Searching out the ideological and religious underpinnings of this scroll, there is a certain underlying issue that is being worked out in much of the text, and the notion of separateness is explicitly central to it. Vayyikra presents YHVH as unequivocally the God identified with the Israelites. The preceding narrative of Exodus had concluded with the building of YHVH's sacred shrine, YHVH's dwelling place with the Israelites and "the glory of YHVH filled the dwelling" (Exodus 40.35). Vayyikra begins with YHVH speaking with Moses at the meeting tent. It is quite apparent that YHVH is *present* and among *them*; he meets with Israel. Yet, the Leviticus scroll repeatedly emphasizes YHVH's *separateness.* YHVH is distinct, set apart, and separated from all else. How is it possible to have it both ways? How is it possible to conceive of living *with* a God who is so *separate?*

The scroll of Vayyikra provides a priestly model of just how an ancient Jew might answer such a question. In the instructions contained here—remember the scroll's dramatic setting is of YHVH instructing Moses—we find prescribed the ways in which Israelites are to honor both YHVH's presence among them and his separateness from them. Such a way of life involves every possible deed and bears upon personal and social realms at all levels. Vayyikra is concerned with the **cult** and priests as well as with the daily life of common Israelites and even resident aliens.

Perhaps the first principle of this way of living is that interaction with YHVH, and indeed all of life, must be carefully ordered. YHVH may be present in the tent next door, or in Jerusalem's temple, but that does not mean that one deals with him as one might with any other neighbor. YHVH is different, separate, holy, and so engaging this distinct deity involves all manner of carefully ordered activities. Separation always involves orderings, arrangements, partitions, drawing lines, and making boundaries. This system of separation involves degrees of holiness, or what we might think of as a carefully laid-out grid of partitions into which all Israelites and all of life fit. Another helpful way to imagine it, as presented by the anthropologist Mary Douglas, is as a system of concentric circles, with the most sacred, YHVH and YHVH's dwelling, at the middle and many borders between regions of holiness all the way around. Each section or area and each person or object within it is thought of as a whole, with a certain natural completeness and perfection. The notion of separations between all entities is applied to *persons, space, time,* and *actions.* For example, the leading priest is conceived of as the most holy, but nonpriestly Israelite men, then women, are less so. Of course the most sacred *space* is the sacred dwelling of YHVH, and after it comes the holy precinct for sacrifices and ritual washings. But the legally and mentally constructed special boundaries are drawn further out, between Israelites and surrounding non-Israelite peoples also. *Time* too is partitioned so that holy days are marked off as separate and distinct. This would include annual holidays as well as the weekly separation of one day, Shabbat, from the rest of the week. In regard to *activities,* the rituals performed by priests in the cult are separated from ordinary daily chores, but even daily acts of average Israelite peasants, such as sowing one's field, making a garment, and eating food, are subject to careful ordering, distinctions, and degrees of separation. To live all of life this way is to live with constant physical reminders of YHVH's separateness and in constant recognition of his presence and holiness. In short, the scroll of Vayyikra instructs the Israelites to create a life and culture of holiness, because they are identified with their God who is separate and holy.

Any such system of separation will necessarily involve attention to the boundaries. Time moves back and forth from more to less sacred, priests interact daily with regular Israelites, people move constantly between places that are more or less holy. Boundaries are natural and socially common: male/female, night/day, alive/dead, parent/child, married/unmarried/widowed, priest/nonpriest. Understandably then, Vayyikra often considers ways in which people are to negotiate the many boundaries they encounter. If the separations and holiness are to be valued and honored, then there must be ways to honor and recognize the boundaries and, at the same time, ways to accommodate required movements across boundaries. Such recognitions and accommodations are frequently accomplished by ritual acts. For example, a task of the leading priest is explained in Vayyikra 16. On the most distinct day of the year, called **Yom Kippur,** or the **Day of Atonement**) when he enters the most holy space, he must perform special ritual acts of bathing and dressing at the beginning and end of his duties, in recognition of the boundaries he has crossed in both directions.

Within this system of ordered separateness, notions of purity/impurity and clean/unclean repeatedly appear. I'm sure you noticed that sort of terminology as you read from our scroll. To pick a few examples out of hundreds, in the scroll of Leviticus we find that a raven is considered impure (11.15), as are women after childbirth (12.1–6), a priest who has touched a corpse (21.1-3), and a man with a rash on his bald spot (13.42–45) or who ejaculates (15.1-3). What does all this mean? First we must emphasize what it does not mean. Uncleanness does not mean sin in Vayyikra. When the scroll considers something unclean, it is not a statement about what we might consider morality or intrinsic worth. A priest or a common Israelite at any given moment may be considered impure or pure, but such a declaration says nothing about whether they have done something morally wrong by the standards of the ancient scroll writers and readers. By the standards of Vayyikra, there is nothing morally wrong with giving birth or having a rash. Certainly some wrong acts, such as murder, may make one unclean, but the purity/impurity distinction has to do with a differing system of ideas than a moral/immoral distinction. Another incorrect meaning of *impure* would be "physically dirty." It is unfortunate that in modern English *impure, unclean,* and *pollution* all bear very physical connotations and we simply do not have a good word to cover the Hebrew in this case. An object or person that is impure is ritually or symbolically unclean, though I hesitate to use *ritually* or *symbolically* because for many modern readers that implies something of less importance or even less real.

Purity and cleanness in Vayyikra have to do with the order of holiness and the system of separations, and it is enlightening to observe just how purity operates in the system envisioned in our scroll. Impure or unclean situations seem to arise in ways that modern analysis might describe in three basic categories: *mixings, imperfections/incompletions,* and *disorderly events.* There is some conceptual overlap in the three, and some situations might be categorized in more than one category, but anthropological and cultural studies of ancient Israelite taboos yield this basic descriptive analysis. First, impurity results from the crossing of boundaries or the mixture of separated objects or groups; we can call these *mixings.* For example, different kinds of thread are not to be woven into the same garment and different kinds of seed are not to be sown in the same field (19.19), not because certain kinds of threads or seeds are somehow wrong, but because even clothing and fields and seeds are to reflect YHVH's holiness and separateness. Similarly, married couples are not to have sex during a wife's menstruation (15.24; 18.19; 20.18), which was likely thought to mix the fluid of life, semen, with a fluid symbolizing death, menstrual blood. The one most holy priest is not supposed to marry a widow because her status as a widow, which relates her to death, imperfection, and a previous marital union, should not be mixed with the status of the most holy person who has duties in the most holy space. He is also not allowed to be in the same room as a corpse, even that of his mother or father (21.10–15). Chapter 18 lists many improper sexual unions, such as a man with his mother, or a man with his son's wife. Improper mixture rules apply to animals that were used for food as well. If you brought a sacrificial animal to the sacred precinct of YHVH and so crossed a holiness border, you could not return it to the less holy realm for your consumption (7.18–21). Those animals that in ancient Israelite society were thought to have odd physical combinations were not to be eaten or even touched, because they were mixed. Consider the lobster. It is hard and almost bug-like, yet it lives in the sea like a fish. Proper water animals were thought to be fish with fins and scales, so water creatures without these were deemed mixed and unsuitable (11.9–11). Some mixings were to be avoided altogether; other proper border crossings or mixings, such as a husband and wife having sex (15.18), were ritually marked and separation was reinstated after the mixing by ritual washing.

Another category that describes some impurities we can call *imperfections/incompletions.* This would apply to land animals that did not meet the criteria of perfect animals, which was apparently provided by the common domestic animals that Israelites kept, namely sheep, goats, and cattle. All of these animals had a split hooves and chewed their food a second time in the form of a cud (11.1–8). Imperfect animals were not to be eaten. Notice how the fish versus. lobster example could fit this category, too. People with physical deformities or something incomplete about their status, such as widowhood, were in a separate category for holiness purposes, and their contact with persons of greater holiness, such as priests, was limited (21.10–24). In this category we can also place the several skin imperfections mentioned. Rashes make one impure, restrict one's interaction with others, and require rituals of purification, which usually involve time and washings. These skin conditions have sometimes been translated as "leprosy," a most unfortunate choice given that they do not refer to disfiguring disease of leprosy, know today as Hanson's disease, but instead to any number of surface skin imperfections, such as rashes and boils. Even walls and cloth can be described as having this leprosy in Hebrew, meaning mold, fungus, or mildew. Even walls and cloth are to be inspected by a priest and treated by a ritual act once the imperfection is gone (13.47–14.53). Remember, all aspects of life are involved in the honoring of YHVH's holiness.

A third major kind of impurity arises from what we can call *disorderly events.* Recall that orderliness is a powerful concept in Vayyikra, yet life, both ancient and modern, is full of natural disorder. To the minds behind Vayyikra, a woman's menstrual period and giving birth were such events and required certain rituals to put her status back to the proper ritual order (12.1–8; 15.19–33). So also was a man's ejaculation of semen even when not having sex with a woman (15.1–18).

Areas Covered by Holiness Laws

Chapters 18 to 25 contain more instructions that are presented as ways of living according to holiness and ways in which Israelites can identify with YHVH their separate God. Several of these are repeated from earlier in Vayyikra, sometimes with alterations. The thematic key to everything remains the command "Separate you must be, because separate am I, YHVH your God" (19.2).

This includes, perhaps obviously, not worshiping other Gods or making images of Gods—that would surely be an improper mixture for YHVH's people (19.4). It also includes the following matters that may not seem as obvious:

- respecting one's mother and father (19.3);
- eating one's sacrificial offering at the proper time (19.5–8);
- leaving some grain and grapes in the field for the poor to harvest (19.9–10);
- not stealing, lying, falsely testifying (19.11–12);
- not insulting the deaf or harming the blind (19.14);
- not hating or revenging one's fellow, but loving one's neighbor as oneself (19.17–18);
- not allowing different kinds of animals to mate (19.19);
- treating a foreigner with love just like one's neighbor (19.33–34);
- not committing adultery (20.10);
- not living by laws of neighboring peoples (20.24);
- dividing between clean and unclean animals (20.25);

- ensuring that the leading priest remains separated within the holy shrine (21.10–12);
- separating a priest who has had an ejaculation or rash from sacred food and rites (22.4–8);
- working on six days, but ceasing work on Shabbat (23.3);
- observing **Pesach** (**Passover**) (23.4–8);
- giving the first of the grain harvest to YHVH (23.9–14);
- observing **Yom Kippur** and **Sukkot** (23.26–44);
- not killing another person (24.17);
- allowing the land to rest and enjoy Shabbat by not planting every seventh year (25.1–7);
- allowing land to rest and proclaiming freedom from debts every fiftieth year, the year of Jubilee (25.1–24);
- redeeming, or purchasing for restoration, an impoverished family member (25.25–28); and
- not enslaving fellow Israelites; but foreign slaves are allowed (25.39–46).

The purpose of this long list is simply to give some notion of the kinds of instructions found in these chapters. By modern standards of categorization, they seem to be very mixed up—ethics, priestly rituals, holidays, and economic policy all combined. They are certainly not arranged according to modern categories. When we describe the laws of Vayyikra, it is potentially harmful to distinguish categories of laws such as religious, ethical, cultic, personal, ceremonial, ritual, or social. The text itself makes no such distinctions, and if we rank these categories in some sort of hierarchy of religious or moral importance, we misrepresent the scroll itself. For Vayyikra, the single primary category is YHVH's holiness. On the other hand, if we use such categories with an awareness that they are our later constructions and not reflective of an ancient author's valuations, then they may serve a useful purpose of descriptive analysis. The instructions in Vayyikra concern religious, cultic, ritual, ethical, personal, and social arenas of life, but those distinctions probably were not compelling for the ancient Israelites, and they are not the organizing ideas in this scroll.

As with Exodus, Numbers, and Deuteronomy, Vayyikra is not a collection of laws carefully edited to remove repetition and provide complete and comprehensive coverage of Israel's laws from a certain period of time. This is narrative into which priestly instructions for ancient Jews were incorporated, and it shows numerous signs of a work that was supplemented and edited through time. It exhibits shifts, repetitions, and conflicts. Israel almost undoubtedly had other laws about holiness, such as a law against incest between father and daughter, which that Vayyikra strangely omits from its long list of forbidden sexual unions. Repetitions are seen; for example Leviticus 19.9–10 is nearly identical to 23.22. We can see differences also, for example, in the treatment of sex during menstruation. In 15.24 it is assumed, not forbidden, and ritually marked, but in 18.19 and 20.18 it is forbidden. Repetitions may reflect different original sources, a later author's or editor's point of emphasis, or an aspect of literary structure. Omissions in this literary text cannot be assumed to have been absent in Israelite law. Differences, or shifts in commands, reflect an

DISPLAY 5.2 | LET FREEDOM RING!

Pennsylvania colonists were proud of their religious freedom and the Speaker of the House in 1751 wanted to celebrate that freedom by putting the following text, including a quotation from Vayyikra, on the new State House Bell:
"Proclaim liberty throughout all the land unto all the inhabitants thereof - Lev. XXV, v. x. By order of the Assembly of the Province of Pensylvania [sic] for the State House in Philada."
The command to proclaim liberty is taken from Vayyikra 25.10. Originally the bell was used to announce meetings and special events. In the 1800s it was chosen by a group trying to outlaw slavery as a symbol, and it was by them that it was first called the Liberty Bell.

author's awareness of the always living nature of Israelite law and practice, as does the very composition of this and other texts of Israelite priests through the centuries.

Vayyikra and Other Nations

Whatever we modern readers might think about the subjects covered by laws in Leviticus, they would not have seemed extraordinary to neighboring peoples of the time. Sacrifices and purification rituals were commonplace in the ancient Near East and ancient Mediterranean cultures. Food taboos, sexual regulations, and religious festivals were widespread. Many cultures had rituals for overcoming impurities associated with death or blood. The unique aspects of Israel's laws of this kind lie in the details. For example, you will notice that in Vayyikra, YHVH is the only God considered proper to worship. Israel's food taboos may have had similarities with other people, but they certainly had peculiarities, too. And though people from other ancient cultures would disagree on the specifics, they would understand all of these notions of purity. Ritual purifications and ritual boundaries were extremely common in the ancient world, as historians and anthropologists have demonstrated many times.

Behind-the-Scenes Observations

There are still a few important things to add about the notion of holiness and other underlying cultural basics that will help make Vayyikra more accessible for a modern reader. Vayyikra's system of holiness is envisioned and textualized in an ancient culture, with ancient Near Eastern cultural values, categories, symbols, and assumptions. We might think of it like this: modern economic systems rely on certain unspoken cultural agreements about the relationship among ideas and objects. For example, every time I go to a gas station, a U.S. dollar is worth a certain amount of gasoline, but there is nothing intrinsic to the dollar bill that makes it worth that certain amount of gasoline, and I cannot put the dollar bill in my gas tank and expect it to work. The money is only worth the gas, or anything else I want to buy, because our society has agreed on the value of that object. The piece of paper that we call a dollar has become a symbol, with distinct meaning and worth unlike any other piece of paper. Unlike other pieces of paper, my dollar bill is set apart or holy. Religious systems, like all cultural systems, ancient and modern, also have objects or tools with agreed-upon values. A Christian cross, a pulpit, a masjid, and a **menorah** are examples of objects vested with special worth in a given culture or subculture. A cup of wine in a church sanctuary is not simply a container with a beverage inside it, anymore than a dollar is simply a piece of paper with fancy writing on it. They both carry an agreed upon value, or worth, for the community they are serving.

Another example from some modern cultures is the necktie, which men in many parts of the world wear whenever they dress up. The necktie is a highly valued piece of material that men wear tied with a knot around their necks, and it is one of the crucial objects with which a male must appear in certain cultural settings in the United States. It is a symbol that carries meaning. And the necktie system also involves degrees of sacredness—different levels of specialness have been ascribed to different strips of cloth men wear around their necks. The black bow tie is probably the most holy of all, is required at some very important occasions, and would be thought "out of place" at most others. These pieces of cloth are not important because of their practical or intrinsic value; they are important because of widespread assumptions and understandings about their cultural worth and meaning.

Understanding the cultural systems of a foreign culture is difficult, especially if no one is around to explain them. Regardless of any claims of unbroken traditions, there are no ancient Israelites available to explain things, so sometimes we are not sure of the underlying cultural valuations. This difficulty is made acute not only because of the wide expanse of time between us and ancient Israel, but also because texts, ancient or modern, rarely explain their underlying cultural values and systems of their own culture. Authors often assume the reader shares their same values and systems, and so explanations are unnecessary. So as modern readers of these ancient scrolls, we attempt to use our methods of textual analysis, anthropology, and archaeology to get beneath the surface of the writings.

Let's consider an example of a highly valuable object. Among ancient Israelites and other ancient peoples, blood was of enormous cultural value and worth. Blood was not simply a circulatory fluid; it might better be described as the life force of the human and animal world and seems to have had a certain "radioactive" quality to it. There are many sacrificial rituals that highly value animal blood and carefully control it. Vayyikra assumes and values an economy of sacrifice, as did all of Israel's neighbors. In the mindset of Vayyikra, death comes into life as the ultimate improper mixing, imperfection, and disorderliness, and blood symbolized both life, by being in the body, and death, by leaving the body. This polarity gave it a unique worth. On the one hand, some attempts were made to avoid contact with blood, but on the other hand, because so much of life was tied directly to blood, great care was taken when dealing with it. Thus, in the instructions of Vayyikra blood was to be treated specially, whether from animals to be eaten or sacrificed, from human corpses or injuries, or from female menstruation or childbirth. It is no wonder that childbirth, involving loss of blood, mixing of bodily fluids, beginning of a new life, or death of mother or child on many occasions, was a highly charged event that required numerous rituals honoring its deep meanings.

There are other underlying cultural basics, values, categories, symbols, and assumptions that account for many of the laws on the surface of Vayyikra. We should also note another polarity, similar to the life-and-death polarity, that of order and disorder. The text seems to create a kind of utopian system whereby all the messiness of reality, with its life and death and order and disorder, can be properly accounted for, avoided in some cases, and negotiated and ordered in others. Through these instructions are presented as YHVH's words to Moses, the priestly authors present in this scroll a manner of living with YHVH, who is both present and separate, or holy. This system of orderliness and holiness reaches into the daily life of every Israelite and even into the physical world of animals, seeds, and land. Many scholars have linked this scroll, with its overwhelming concern for order, to the opening chapter of Genesis. There, too, God is presented as vigorously interested in bringing order by making separations at the very beginning of creation. If you look back at Genesis 1, you'll notice that all sorts of separations and divisions are applied to all of creation. On the first day the chaotic mass of earth is separated into day and night, then follows the division of waters and land and the creation of various creatures, all of which are created as specific separate kinds. As the week concludes, God separates, or sanctifies and makes holy, the seventh day, Shabbat. Thus, the first creation story of Genesis harmonizes with the priestly holiness-centered outlook of our Vayyikra scroll. For this very reason, many scholars believe that the authorship of the two texts must be linked; perhaps it was not written by the same individual but likely individuals within the same priestly group.

Questions for Further Study

1. Notions of purity, taboo, and separation are common in many cultures, ancient and modern. How would you compare these ideas in Vayyikra to other cultures or literature you have studied?

2. Reading Leviticus 18–19, what do you perceive as the arrangement and order of these laws? How does it compare with the way you would arrange them?

References

Damrosch, David. "Leviticus" in *The Literary Guide to the Bible,* ed. by Robert Alter and Frank Kermode, 66–77. Cambridge, MA: Harvard, 1987.

Douglas, Mary. *Purity and Danger.* New York: Routledge, 1966.

Fox, Everett. *The Five Books of Moses.* New York: Schocken, 1995.

Levine, Baruch. *Leviticus, The JPS Torah Commentary.* Philadelphia: The Jewish Publication Society, 1989.

Plaut, Gunther, ed. *The Torah: A Modern Commentary.* New York: Union of American Hebrew Congregations, 1981.

במדבר

Numbers *B^emidbar*

SECTION OUTLINE

Literary Format and Movement

Date and Composition

The Behavior and Punishment of One Generation

YHVH's Blessings

Numbers and History

Laws in B^emidbar

Questions for Further Study

References

This scroll is one of the more oddly fascinating and least known of our library. It has some intriguing stories and some puzzling and peculiar features. Yet is has its share of familiar elements, too, the most prominent being the famous priestly blessing that we talked about in our first chapter (Display 1.2), which has been recited in more places and times than perhaps any text of our library. It is necessary to realize that the ancient authors and preservers of this literature were not simply interested in telling flattering stories about their own past. Whatever their specific purposes were for writing, there is no hero worship here. The stories and their characters, including YHVH, Moses, priests, and many others, are complex, and sometimes seemingly inexplicable. It's a narrative that often seems unpredictable, and I'm always surprised by some of the ways in which its characters act.

The title in our English versions, Numbers, derives from the Greek translation's *Arithmoi*, a word from which we also get "arithmetic." That name reflects two stories in the scroll in which the people of the tribes of Israel are counted. The Hebrew title comes from words in the first line, but not the very first words in this case. *B^emidbar,* pronounced "b'mid-*bar,*" is the first part of the phrase *B^emidbar Seenai,* "in the wilderness of Sinai," so the scroll's Hebrew name is "In the wilderness." As in the Hebrew title *B^ereshit* (Genesis), the *b* is the preposition "in." This Hebrew title happens to be appropriate given the content of the scroll, because the large prose body of the scroll narrates national stories about experience in the wilderness.

The last scroll we examined, Leviticus, contained little narrative and did not advance the larger story line of the Israelite movement from Egypt to Canaan. It consisted mostly of instructions and regulations stemming from priestly circles. Much of B^emidbar is also thought to stem from priestly circles, but it is a very different kind of literary text than Leviticus. Here narrative predominates, and the

LITERARY FORMAT AND MOVEMENT

B^emidbar is a travel narrative that the author has organized and marked with formulas and significant use of dating. But the scroll is not entirely narrative. Woven into a basic storyline of travel from Mount Sinai to Canaan are lists of tribes and clans, laws about the priestly duties, and matters of cultic liturgy and vows. The material is quite diverse, and reader sometimes have difficulty seeing the logic behind some of the material. Some people have seen many thematic connections, and others have wondered if the scroll was in some way a repository of miscellaneous traditions. For a literary scholar, these are pressing questions. How do various pieces of the scroll intellectually and thematically cohere? Regardless of how one characterizes the non-narrative inclusions, the author clearly presents progressive, though the temporal markers are not all in chronological order. In the first sentence of the scroll, he puts the dramatic setting exactly one month after the story at the end of Exodus. There Moses had set up YHVH's sacred dwelling on the first day of the month in the second year after escaping from Egypt (Exodus 40.2, 17), and now it is exactly one month later (Numbers 1.1) at the same place, Mount Sinai. The first major section relates to preparations for leaving Mount Sinai beginning with a census of the people, but it also includes a flashback to a month before the story began (see 7.1.). The first major literary and geographical move is in Chapter 10, where the Israelites begin their journey north. This long section comprises stories and other traditions about their travels. In Chapter 22 the tribes arrive at Moab, their last stopping point, and in 26 the author records a final census, mirroring that of Chapter 1, which serves as a summary of those who had left Egypt. From this point the text seems mostly focused on preparations for entering, conquering, and allocating land in Canaan. In fact, Numbers contains a fair number of military stories of land reconnaissance, bloody campaigns, and holy war conquests.

Israel at Mount Sinai

1.1–54 YHVH's command and Moses' census taking

2.1–34 Arrangement of tribal tents for travel

3.1–4.49 Priestly organization and census

5.1–6.27 Instructions from YHVH for Israelites about specific issues, such as adultery, vows, corpses

7.1–10.10 Tribal sacrifices at time of sacred tent building; Levite consecration; laws

Traveling to Canaan

10.11–11.35 People's complaints

12.1–16 Dispute about Moses' authority

13.1–14.45 Spying in Canaan; desire to return to Egypt; YHVH refuses to allow the current Israelites to enter the land

15.1–41 Instructions about offerings

16.1–50 Revolt against Moses' authority

17.1–18.24 Aaron, priests, and Levites

19.1–22 Instructions about Israel's purity

20.1–29 Moses and Aaron punished

21.1–35 Plagues; opposition in travel; wars

Preparing to enter Canaan

22.1–24.25 Arrival at Moab; encounter with Baalam the prophet

25.1–17 Worshiping other Gods in Moab

26.1–65 YHVH's command and Moses' census taking; entire exodus generation dead

27.1–11 YHVH instructs about inheritance

27.12–23 YHVH instructs about Moses' successor Joshua

28.1–30.16 YHVH instructs about offerings and vows

31.1–54 Holy war against Midianites

32.1–42 Land east of Jordan River conquered by tribes

33.1–49 Summary of travel: Mt. Sinai to Moab

33.50–36.2 Instructions for entering Canaan: boundaries, Levitical cities, murder, inheritance

613 Editorial conclusion

larger storyline moves forward considerably. B^e^midbar is a wilderness travelogue that contains stories of about Israelite tribes traveling in the barren lands from Mount Sinai to Canaan. Like other scrolls, there are signs that it comes from various other sources. As it stands now, an editor has made the scroll begin where Exodus left off, in fact, exactly one month after the end of Exodus.

Date and Composition

Much of B^e^midbar reflects the interests of priests not only for cultic activity proper, but also for the relationships of various priestly groups. As Israel's religious institutions and traditions developed, different groups emerged within the priesthood. This is not at all surprising. In ancient Egypt, for example, one reads of numerous cooperative and competing priestly groups. In ancient Israel in the Iron Age (1200–586 BCE) we know from physical remains and from scrolls in our library that there were temples and shrines at various places and different priestly groups. B^e^midbar overwhelmingly reflects the interests of priestly groups: those who claimed descent from Moses or from his brother Aaron, Levites, and subgroups such as Kohathites. And just what were the relations between these priests and the nonpriests of the Israelite tribes? Historically interested scholars have attempted to sort out all the various priestly traditions in B^e^midbar and elsewhere, but here we will only observe that the priestly traditions contained here are complex, many of them seem to be quite ancient, and the textual evidence is quite ambiguous regarding identification of particular priestly groups from particular times. Many scholars date much of the material in the scroll, especially the priestly material, to the seventh or sixth centuries BCE, and many recognize that older sources were used, and that there is evidence of some later smaller-scale editing.

As we will explore further on, stories of the ancestors traveling in the wilderness seem to have been quite prominent in Israelites' thinking in the eighth through sixth centuries BCE, much more so than stories of the patriarchs from Genesis. Prophets and poets from this period often refer to wilderness traditions. B^e^midbar

Study Room 5.3

A POPULAR POEM ABOUT YHVH

YHVH, slow in anger, and great in kindness.
Forgiving sin and guilt,
While not leaving unpunished,
And avenging guilt of fathers on sons,
To the third and fourth (generation).

This often quoted statement about YHVH was apparently well known and popular. It is of considerable interest for many reasons. Just what does it mean? Read and consider its meaning in our library, Exodus 34. What do you make of the balance or tension found in the poem between judgment and mercy? In what sort of oral setting in ancient Israel could it have been used? What rhetorical use does it serve in Exodus and in other texts in which it is quoted, such as Bᵉmidbar 14.18; Jeremiah 32.18; Joel 2.13; Jonah 4.2; Micah 7.18–20; Nahum 1.3; Psalms 86.15, 145.8, and 103.8; and Nehemiah 9.17 and 31? How is the wording different in these passages? How do the differences affect meaning? How does it show what some people thought about the character of YHVH?

is the primary repository of those wilderness stories in our library, and it tells us with the most detail how writers of this time desired readers to imagine Israel's corporate past. These are community stories that reflect and forge corporate identity in much the same way that modern nations, communities, families, and institutions present and repeat stories of the past that serve to unite people. The wilderness journey is a key ingredient in unifying story of ancient Israel.

Bᵉmidbar contains a wide diversity of material—lists, laws, poems, stories—and so those interested in reconstruction the compositional history of the scroll have searched it for clues using these diverse forms. Some of the clues are subtle, but in other cases there is explicit evidence that the scroll incorporates older traditions. A few of the many examples will suffice. If we look at 21.14 we find a footnote to an older source from which a couple lines of poetry are taken. The name of the source is the scroll of YHVH's wars. A few lines later another poem is quoted (21.17–18) and then another (21.27–30), but their sources, if they were different, are not named. In 14.18 we find a quotation of an old and popular religious tradition of Israel that we also saw in Exodus 34.5–8 (see also Study Room 5.3).

Other clues involve the flow of the narrative. For example, readers have also noted that Numbers 7.1 and 9.1 both begin an episode of the narrative that is set chronologically prior to the narrative dated in 1.1. To explain this backtracking, some have reasonably suggested that the author began to use another source right at this point. There is also something interesting about the narratives dealing with Aaron's death in 33.38–39 and Moshe's death in 27.12–14 and Deuteronomy 32.48–52 and 34.1–6. Many have noted that the form and vocabulary of the two accounts are very similar. They conclude that the author of Deuteronomy 32.48–52 is using what is now Numbers 27.12–14 and that the text of Deuteronomy 34.1–6 was at one time actually a part of Bᵉmidbar's narrative but was placed at the end of Deuteronomy by a later editor. Finally, the editorial remark that concludes the scroll (36.13) may well have been the conclusion to an independent tradition about YHVH's commands to Moses in Moab. A lot more could be said, but these examples indicate that the compositional history of the scroll is complicated and fascinating, and that, without the discovery of much earlier manuscripts, we will have to learn to live with some uncertainty regarding specifics of the text's history.

The Behavior and Punishment of One Generation

This travelogue of Bᵉmidbar displays some prominent themes that give contour to the travel narrative. Far from giving us pious stories about their communal past, those responsible for Bᵉmidbar depict a group of people who complain against Moses and YHVH, fight among themselves, and worship other deities. In regard to the last in that list, many commentators have noted that the separation of Israelites from other peoples is a strong priority of the author, one that is emphasized in many ways throughout the scroll and likely reflects social polemical issues of the author's day. In Bᵉmidbar, the Israelites go so far as to state that they wish they were back in Egypt (e.g., Chapter 11), which the author clearly sees as a slap in the face of YHVH who rescued them from slavery and death there. To the author such actions are frequent and deserving of severe punishment. In fact, one might think that the overriding plot of the travel narrative is a story of the frequent rebellion of the Israelites who departed from Egypt. YHVH's anger with them culminates in 14.20–35, where in vociferous language he condemns them all to die in the wilderness and to never reach the land they were promised. Then follows a long wait for every one of that generation to die, which finally occurs in Chapter 26.

Only when they are all dead can the story move along and can their children be prepared to enter Canaan. It is no surprise to find out in the summary, Chapter 33, that this period of traveling in the wilderness is presented as lasting exactly the generalized traditional amount of 40 years, even though the actual narratives only speak of events in about two of these years. Thus in many ways the travel narrative is not a 'happy' one; though there are many positive traditions included too, crime and punishment is the controlling motif of this one wilderness generation. One might ask how this punishment of the one generation and the better fortune for their descendants relate to the classic poem of YHVH's mercy and judgment in 14.18. Is there irony to be seen here? We should also point out that this wilderness period loomed large in Israelite thought, as indicated by the many other writings that reflect on it, both positively and negatively. As the Israelites imagined their communal past, stories of their desert experience powerfully influence and reflect their corporate identity and relationship with their God YHVH. What do you think is the appeal and power of such stories of wandering for an individual or nation? We find these wilderness traditions in other narratives too, such as Exodus 15.22–17.15 and Deuteronomy 1.19–3.29; in poetic liturgy such as Psalms 78; 95.8–11, 105, 106, 135.10–12, and 136.16–22; and in the poetry of prophetic literature, such as Jeremiah 2.2–6, Ezekiel 20.10–26, Hosea 2:14–15, 13:4–5, and Amos 2:10 and 5:25. If we had time, it would be very interesting to see how wilderness traditions differ from scroll to scroll and how they are used in rhetoric.

But it is not just masses of Israelites who are presented in less than flattering ways; the same is true of leaders, such as the priests, Aaron, and Moses. Moses is shown impatient and angry, doubting the ability of YHVH and pitying himself. True, at other times he is heroic and a tireless servant of YHVH and the people, but this is no romantic hero's tale. In one of the most discussed stories of our scroll, 20.1–13, YHVH punishes Moses and Aaron, forbidding this incomparable leader and his brother to enter the land to which he was leading the Israelites. The story does not state unambiguously what Moshe's fault was in this case, and readers are often baffled as to why YHVH would be so hard on Moses. Most interpreters have felt that Moshe's error lay in striking a rock to perform a miracle instead of speaking to it, as YHVH had instructed him. Others have thought that Moses' error was claiming personal credit for the miracle. The ambiguity is intriguing and I think intentional. In any case, YHVH cites their lack of trust and failure to treat YHVH as holy (20.12). Holiness was a grave concern, especially in priestly circles. We have already learned from our last scroll, Leviticus, and here that concern comes to the fore again. With this story, the author makes the major point that no one, not even Moses and Aaron, can get away with offending YHVH's sense of holiness.

There are other leadership crises as well. In two different episodes Moshe's authority is questioned by others; in one case by Miriam and Aaron, his brother and sister (12.1–13), and in another by the men of a clan of Levitical priests, the Korahites (16.1–50). In both cases, YHVH intervenes angrily and dramatically on Moshe's behalf. In the first instance, he smites Miriam with a skin disease, and in the second case, YHVH is so angry that he open the ground and sends fire to devour the entire clan, including the women and children. With the first story the author makes the clear point that Moses is the unequaled prophet of Israel; his words have the sanction of YHVH because

> When there is a prophet of YHVH among you,
> in a vision I make myself know to him,
> in a dream I speak with him.
> Not so with my servant Moshe. In all my house he is trusted.
> Mouth to mouth I speak to him;
> Clearly and not in visions
> And the form of YHVH he sees (12.6–8).

In this Bᵉmidbar narrative, Miriam and Aaron are put in their place below Moses, and not without some irony from the previous chapter (see 11.26–29). In

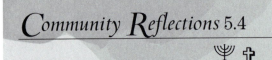

*C*ommunity *R*eflections 5.4

NO ORDINARY ROCK

B^emidbar 20 and Exodus 17 both contain stories of a very special rock—a rock from which water flows. In these miracle stories YHVH uses a rock to sustain the Israelites in the hostile dry deserts of their wilderness journey. Centuries later, both Jewish and Christian readers of these stories reflected on their contemporary meaning— the meaning for their own communities. Jewish commentators playfully imagined that this rock was in fact movable. After all, it appears among the earliest stories of the wilderness time (Exodus 17) and among very latest (B^emidbar 20). And surely the Israelites needed water the entire forty years in between the two stories! Rabbinic commentators concluded that the same rock is in both stories, which they called "the well," and actually followed the Israelites around in their forty-year jour- ney. The homiletical point was that God takes care of God's people *all* the time and can be counted on to provide. Some writers had even more fun, imagining that the water from the rock produced rivers and lakes on which the Israelites boated and swam.

The Christian writer Paul, whose background was in Jewish learning, also reflected on these rock stories and talks about the rock in one of his letters to Christians in the Greek city of Corinth (1 Corinthians 10.1–4). He, too, and perhaps his audience, is well aware of the tradition that the rock actually followed the Israelites, and he repeats the story. Paul put a distinctly Christian spin on the story by an allegorical interpreta- tion: He says that the rock that followed them around was actually Christ. Paul's Christian homiletical point is that Christ has always been present providing sustenance for his people.

For the many stories from Jewish tradition, see Ginzberg 1909, 3:51–54.

the world of the authors and editors of B^emidbar, what polemic might have been involved? In the seventh to fifth centuries BCE prophetic claims were being made and prophetic scrolls were being composed. Look at the first couple lines of the scrolls of Isaiah, Hosea, Amos, Obadiah, and Micah for example, and you'll see claims of YHVH speaking through visions. Some prophets clearly challenged priestly traditions and claims. See for example Jeremiah (2.8; 8.8), Hosea (6.6–9), Amos (5.21–25), and Micah (6.1–8). But this story of B^emidbar puts Moses above all those. And who mediates and proclaims the words of Moses? Remember that scrolls like Leviticus and B^emidbar contain a great deal of *priestly* material, and it is invari- ably presented as the words of YHVH to Moses. But see also an intriguing alterna- tive prophecy story in 11.16–30.

There is likely another polemic active in Numbers. To return to our second story of YHVH's defense of Moshe from Chapter 16, there the point was forcefully made that *only* Aaron's descendents, not all Levites, are allowed to perform certain priestly rites and those who violate this privilege risk the wrath of YHVH on themselves and their families. This, too, was likely a polemic in a dispute among priests at some point during the time of the scroll's composition.

If you read these stories you may be surprised because YHVH is not at all represented as an aloof God of the philosophers or as a more modern God, distant, dispassionate, and dignified. YHVH is there, in the middle of every mess. He directs every move in their journey by the physical sign of his presence among them, a cloud over the sacred tent (9.15–23). He speaks constantly to Moshe and sometimes to others. He interacts, responds, and is directly associated with the sacred tent that was built for him. Moses and the priests move his tent carefully to the next location so that he will return to it (see 10.33–36), and if it does not go with them into battle, the result is disaster (14.44). We have already noted YHVH's anger, and sometimes he must be talked out of overly harsh punishments (Chapter 14). At other times such pleas come too late, for example when he overhear's some individuals complaining, and in spontaneous anger he burned up some of them (11.1–3).

YHVH's Blessings

YHVH is complex and multifaceted in Bᵉmidbar; there is much more to him than anger. My favorite part of the entire scroll is the fascinating and delightfully entertaining story about the foreign prophet Balaam, son of Beor, whom the tribes of Israel encounter just as they near Canaan in Chapter 22. Here we have a deftly told story with careful attention to detail, serving to demonstrate YHVH's care and blessing even in adverse circumstances. The Israelites have arrived in the land of the Moab, which is just east of the Jordan River, and the king of Moab, Balak, sends word to a famous prophet to come and curse the new immigrants. The story is full of polarized motifs such as blessing/anger, blessing/cursing, seeing/not seeing, speaking/not speaking and has generous doses of irony. In the end, regardless of Balaam's attempts to curse, YHVH controls his mouth, and he can only bless the Israelites. As the comedy of the story builds so does the overabundance of YHVH's blessing, and one is left with the sense that YHVH's ultimate disposition to his people is one of blessing and that ultimately he controls even foreign prophets. This extended story (Chapters 22–24) picks up the theme of the famous priestly blessing in 6.22–27 (see Display 1.2). There YHVH had promised that he would bless them, and later in Chapters 22–24 that promise is being fulfilled through the mouth of a foreign, reluctant, out-of-control prophet!

To add one more intriguing element to this episode, we must explore a fascinating archaeological find in 1967 at a site in modern Jordan called Deir 'Alla. An inscription from about 800 BCE in plaster on a wall tells the tale of a prophet named Balaam, son of Beor. It was apparently from a collection of stories about Balaam recorded as the Book of Balaam. Written in a Canaanite dialect, it is a different story about Balaam than we have in our Bᵉmidbar scroll, but there are many similar associations with Balaam. In both he is a prophet, apparently well known for his visions and communication with Gods. In both he speaks his oracles in poetic form, and both are

POSTER 5.6

BALAAM THE SEER

Here is the beginning of the ancient inscription about Balaam.
The misfortunes of the Book of Balaam, son of Beor.

A divine seer was he.
The Gods came to him at night,
And he beheld a vision in accordance with El's utterance.
They said to Balaam, son of Beor:
"So will it be done, with nothing surviving?
No one has see [the likes of] what you have heard!"
Balaam arose on the morrow;
He summoned the heads of the assembly unto him,
And for two days he fasted, and wept bitterly.
Then his intimates entered into his presence,
And they said to Balaam, son of Beor:
"Why do you fast,
And why do you weep?"
Then he said to them:
"Be seated, and I will relate to you what the
Shaddai-Gods have planned,
And go, see the acts of the Gods!"

Modified translation of B. Levine, in Hallo and Younger 1997, II:142.

concerned with future events of great important and fortune. In the Canaanite story, Balaam serves the Gods of the pantheon of El, who is chief. Interestingly, both stories use the name *Shaddai* for deities (Numbers 24.4, 16) and in B^emidbar Balaam himself frequently uses the names *El* and *YHVH*. There is much to say about how this ancient inscription might enrich our understanding of the literary meanings of B^emidbar 22–24, and also of the impact it has on our understanding of historical and religious realities in ancient Israel. This is yet one more exciting indication of the many connections within the Canaanite cultures, of which Israel was one. If you are interested in reading more about the topic, see the books cited in the References section. Maybe they will inspire you to become an archaeologist!

B^emidbar and History

Modern historians searching for evidence of historical events in the scroll of B^emidbar and in the written and material remains of surrounding cultures and geographical area have little to go on. The events depicted here would have to be placed in the early to mid-thirteenth century BCE, prior to the earliest known mention of the Israelites on the ca. 1210 inscription of the Egyptian king Merneptah (see p. 135). Modern academic historians have myriad questions about these traditions. For example, the colossal number of Israelites—about two million—given in the censuses of Chapters 1 and 26 is impossibly large for a desert existence if taken as literal numbers. Many readers have offered other explanations, such as numerical symbolism, hyperbole, or other meanings for words. But interpreters through the ages have found the scroll of B^emidbar meaningful in various ways. Like all the other narrative scrolls of our library, its valuation by readers is not necessarily dependent on the historicity of its content. The authors and editors of this scroll were providing communal traditions of Israel's past that were rich in religious and literary value to be told and passed on to later generations. What uses each generation and individual makes of these and other stories is clearly their own decision.

Laws in B^emidbar

Even though to this point I have talked mostly about narrative matters, we need to address the laws and instructions contained in the scroll, presented as spoken by YHVH to Moshe. As in Exodus, the laws of B^emidbar are set within a narrative framework, but here they are much more spread out throughout the prose. You will find them scattered in Chapters 1 to 6, 8 to 10, 15, 18, 19, 28 to 30, 35, and 36. Even more than in Leviticus, the laws primarily concern priestly matters. In some cases it is easy to relate the laws to their surrounding narrative, but in other cases the relationship is much less clear. This presentation indicates that in the author's mind YHVH's instructions to Moses did not come in a one-time event at Mount Sinai. The *torah* continues to grow through the years as Moses seeks new guidance (9.9) and new instructions are presented. The opening line of the scroll has YHVH instructing Moses at Mount Sinai, and the last line of the book, forty years later, has YHVH instructing Moses at Moab. Thus, from beginning to end this is a scroll of *torah*, instruction from YHVH.

Questions for Further Study

1. B^emidbar has some of the most intriguing episodes. Pick your favorite and then, as a literary critic, see how it fits with the rest of the scroll. Does it have common themes? Does it play a pivotal role?

2. How do the themes of 'land' and 'others' (non-Israelites) relate to each other in this scroll? How would Israelite readers who may be exiles in a foreign land read the scroll?

References

Ackerman, James S. "Numbers" In *The Literary Guide to the Bible,* ed. by Robert Alter and Frank Kermode. Cambridge, MA: Harvard, 1987.

Barkay, Gabriel, Marilyn J. Lundberg, Andrew G. Vaughn, and Bruce Zuakerman. "The Amulets from Ketef Hinnom: A New Edition and Evaluation." *Bulletin of the American Schools for Oriental Research* 334 (2004): 41–71.

Fox, Everett. *The Five Books of Moses.* New York: Schocken, 1995.

Ginzberg, Louis. *The Legends of the Jews.* 7 vols. Philadelphia: Jewish Publication Society, 1909.

Hallo, William W., and K. Lawson Younger, Jr. *The Context of Scripture.* 3 vols. Leiden: E.J. Brill, 1997.

Milgrom, Jacob. *Numbers, The JPS Torah Commentary.* Philadelphia: The Jewish Publication Society, 1994.

Plaut, Gunther, ed. *The Torah: A Modern Commentary.* New York: Union of American Hebrew Congregations, 1981.

דבדיס
Deuteronomy D^evarim

Have you ever read a book or watched a movie where the heroine or hero, before dying, gives a great speech, the famous last words? It's a common literary scene, and we see it a lot in our library too: Jacob/Israel (Genesis 49), Joshua (Joshua 24), David (1 Kings 2). It was also common in literature of cultures surrounding Israel. The scroll we are examining contains a great example of a final speech. It also contains some famous passages that you are likely to recognize even if you haven't read the scroll before.

The English title of this book comes straight from the title in Greek manuscripts. *Deuteronomy* means "second law" and likely reflects the idea that this scroll is Moshe's restatement of instructions given first, according to Exodus, at Mount Sinai. It likely arose from the ancient Greek translation of Deuteronomy 17.18, which translates a Hebrew phrase meaning "copy of torah" with one word, *deuteronomion*. The Hebrew phrase *mishneh torah* is used in some ancient Jewish writings as the title of the scroll. But the Hebrew name most often used today is *D^evarim*, pronounced "d^eva-*reem*," meaning "words" or "speeches." It comes from the opening line of the scroll, "These are the words that Moses spoke . . ."

Composition and Date

Although much of D^evarim is the first-person speech of Moshe with occasional references to recording his instructions in writing, those speeches are still encased in the narrative of an anonymous writer. We do not know with certainty when this author lived, but most scholars today recognize that this scroll, was composed according to ancient Jewish customs, in stages by several different hands. The two poems at the end of the scroll in Chapters 32 and 33

LITERARY FORMAT AND MOVEMENT

D^evarim has the most straightforward structure of the five scrolls of the Torah; D^evarim is speech. An anonymous narrator introduces the scroll and occasionally appears again, but the vast majority of the scroll is presented as the direct speech of Moshe, mostly in the first person. It is Moshe giving a history lesson of Israel, Moshe reporting conversations with YHVH, Moshe foretelling the future, Moshe stating YHVH's commands, Moshe reciting a song he composed, Moshe speaking a final blessing on Israel. About the only thing Moses doesn't narrate is his own death! Now much of the time the scroll is quoting Moshe quoting YHVH, so rhetorically the sense of authority projected by the scroll is extreme—Moshe himself, Israel's supreme teacher, quoting YHVH himself, Israel's God.

The dramatic setting of the book, which is described in the first paragraph, fits within the larger story of the Israelites having left Mt. Sinai (Numbers 10.11), though it is known by the name *Horeb* in Deuteronomy. Israel has arrived on the eastern side of the Jordan River in Moab, and they are on the edge of the land they are on the edge of the land they are to attempt to conquer west of the Jordan. According our scroll, it is now 40 years later and Moshe stands up for the last time to instruct Israel. The scroll divides his instruction into three long speeches, followed by a two-part conclusion, a song and formal blessing.

Moshe's speeches also show a particular design and movement. The first speech is a history lesson of the last 40 years with the clear objective of showing how YHVH guided and cared for his people Israel. The second speech contains YHVH's instructions on how Israel is to live in faithfulness to the covenant with YHVH. The third and shortest speech is a grand summary of YHVH's care, a view of Israel's future, and a final exhortation to obedience. In his speaking Moshe moves back and forth between past and present, or "that day"/"that time" at Horeb and "this day" in Moab. Rhetorically these shifts are important, for they provide an authoritative symbol and presentation of the ongoing nature of divine instruction to Israel; here is Moshe himself, long after those events, reporting the past, interpreting the past, and speaking authoritatively now for the sake of the present generation. The narrator too, in his small segments, can move between then and now, but the references are shifted. For the narrator then is the time of Moshe and now is the narrator's own time. Again, the moves are important for they bring the sympathetic audience of the scroll into an imaginative parallel with Moshe's audience. Both Moshe and the author of the scroll are instructing a new generation what the traditions of the past mean for them now. The speeches of Moshe climax in the two long poems of Chapters 32 and 33 that are words of warning, instruction, hope, and promise. Chapter 34, the last, is really a brief epilogue narrating Moshe's death and eulogizing him as incomparable to any before or after him.

1.1–5 Narrator's introduction	**4.40–5.1a Narrator's report**	**28.69–29.1a (or 29.1–2a) Narrator's conclusion and introduction**
1.6–4.40 Moshe's first address	Refuge cities and introduction to second address	**29.1b–30.20 (or 29.2b–30.20) Moshe's third address**
Historical review of Israel's past with YHVH, with narrator's comments in 2.10–12, 20–23; 3.9, 11	**5.1b–28.68 Moshe's second address** Instructions for present living with YHVH, with narrator's comments in: 27.1, 9, 11	Exhortation for faithfulness to covenant

31.1–30 Narrative	**32.1–43 Moshe recites** song	**32.44–33.1 Narrative**	**33.2–29 Moshe's final poem**	**34.1–12 Moshe's death and eulogy**
Moshe's final deeds and words		Moshe's farewell and final view of land	blessing for Israel by tribes	

seem significantly older in language that other parts of the scroll—perhaps from the tenth or ninth century BCE—and they were likely well-known poems, which were included with the rest of the book at some point. Individual laws in the central section of the scroll have individual histories in the legal and religious traditions of Israel. Many scholars today also posit that the double introductions—compare 1.1–5 with 4.44–49—signal that at one time the earlier section (1.1–4.40) was a separate document from the large second address of Moses (5.1–28.68). And you'll remember from our discussion of Numbers that the style and vocabulary of the episode of Moshe's death in D^evarim 34.1–6 seems to have been at one time a continuation of the narrative now contained in Numbers 33.38–39 that has been moved to this scroll. There are numerous modern books that address other sections that may reveal information helpful for analyzing the scroll's composition.

Attempting to discover the time period of D^evarim's more or less final composition has proved to be one of the more fascinating of historical study of our scrolls. Because the scrolls of Joshua, Judges, Samuel, and Kings share some important ideals with aspects of Deuteronomy, the history of their composition is often tied into the discussion of D^evarim's composition. There are also interesting similarities with some prophetic scrolls, especially Jeremiah (seventh or sixth centuries BCE) and Hosea (eighth century BCE), and so the history of those two books is sometimes tied to the story of D^evarim's composition. Many investigators today believe that an early form of D^evarim was the scroll used in the temple by the Jerusalem King Josiah who ruled from 639 to 609 BCE. In 2 Kings 22–23 the scroll is called the record of torah or record of the covenant, and the religious reforms undertaken by Josiah match quite well with teachings of D^evarim. But because we do not have ancient scrolls to document the stages of growth, there are several possible scenarios presented by scholars. Links have been made to the period of King Hezekiah of Jerusalem (early seventh century BCE) and with King Josiah (late seventh century BCE).

The author of D^evarim seems to assume knowledge of traditions now contained in Exodus and Numbers (e.g., D^evarim 4.3; 8.3; 24.9). It is widely agreed that additions and modifications continued after the seventh century as well. For example, D^evarim 30.1–10 speaks from the point of view *after* Jews had been exiled in the sixth century. Other editorial additions can be seen in 2.10–12 and 3.11. In summary, we can say that D^evarim exhibits many indications of a complicated diachronic history of composition, just as we should expect. Some form of the scroll was available in the seventh century, and it continued to be modified after that.

Because so much of D^evarim is presented as a first-person account of Moses and several times Moses or the narrator refers to the writing of a scroll (28.58; 31.9, 19, 24), we should briefly review a few basics about this tradition. It was acceptable to expand, edit, and rewrite scrolls in the name of Moses. All this activity was conventional compositional practice, and Moses was one of the most common personages under whose name to write. One scroll of our library from the fifth century quotes from a written "torah that YHVH had commanded to Moshe" (Nehemiah 8.14–15), but the citation is not from any writing still preserved today. Undoubtedly there were other writings in the name of Moses that are no longer preserved, some of which were older than D^evarim and some of which were younger. Among the Dead Sea Scrolls are several writings credited to Moshe, such as the Book of Jubilees. D^evarim, like works before and after it, invokes Moses as its foremost source and enjoins Israelites to be faithful to the covenant with YHVH by obeying the instructions contained in the scroll.

The Unique Voice of Moshe in D^evarim

How might we summarize the themes and emphases of the final words of the great character Moshe? There is no mistaking D^evarim; anyone can hear its unique characteristics simply by reading several chapters. In D^evarim the rhetoric of Moshe is not subtle or indirect. Moses is constantly appealing passionately to his audience to heed, listen, and obey. The scroll's most famous words illustrate this well:

> Listen, O Israel!
> YHVH (is) our God, YHVH alone.
> [alternate reading: YHVH our God, YHVH (is) one.]
> And you must love YHVH your God
> With all your heart, and all your being, and all your power (Deuteronomy 6.4–5)

These lines, known in Jewish liturgy as the **She'ma**, the Hebrew word for "hear!" stress deeply committed love as the proper attitude toward YHVH. In the chapters before this, Moshe had been reminding his listeners of YHVH's care, and now he presents love as the way they should respond. Far beyond legal obedience, D^evarim repeatedly stress the spiritual, personal, and emotional ideal of love between YHVH and his people (7.7–9; 13.3; 19.9; 30.6, 16). Furthermore, in addition to the care lavished upon Israel, Moshe makes the point that YHVH loves the stranger, that is the non-Israelites who live in their towns and villages, and Israelites are to do the same (10.12–18). Here in D^evarim, YHVH is said to have chosen the Israelites to be his people because of his love for them (4.37). D^evarim is full of language of emotion, sympathy, love, and gratitude, evident in the large legal section, especially in the motivation clauses that are given for specific laws. Why should a person obey a law? Modern law codes and ancient ones might stress punishment that awaits violators, or perhaps the authority, divine or human, of the lawgiver is stressed. In the scroll of Leviticus, we saw the frequent refrain "I am holy," which served as a general motivation; obedience was the way to live in accord with YHVH's holiness. But in Dᵉvarim well over half of the laws have specific motivation clauses—more than any other of the scrolls with extensive lists of laws (Exodus, Leviticus, Numbers). Dᵉvarim motivates by appealing to gratitude (e.g., 15.12–15), sympathy or empathy (e.g., 5.13–15), a sense of justice or equity (e.g., 16.19–20), or healthy self-interest— obedience is the way to life and blessing (e.g., 30.11–20).

It has also been noted that the scroll's stress on just and compassionate treatment of others is strong. Individual non-Israelites living in Israelite towns, orphans, and widows are often mentioned as needing and deserving special protection and care. Societal laws of Dᵉvarim make formal provision for welfare of poor and disadvantaged (14.28–29; 15.1–18; 24.10–13, 17–22). Slavery of some foreigners is allowed, but there are laws requiring humanitarian treatment and communal involvement (12.12; 16.11, 14). Escaped slaves from other places are protected and not to be returned (23.15–16). Animals, too, are to receive basic humane treatment (22.6–7; 25.4). Again, much of this humanitarian treatment is compelled on the basis of YHVH's justice and love for the weak and disadvantaged (e.g., 10.17–22; 24.22). We will see later in our library that scrolls of prophets will take up this pursuit of justice (16.20).

Dᵉvarim also stresses in unique ways a YHVH-only approach to Israelite religion. YHVH is not just the greatest God—"God of all Gods" (10.17); Dᵉvarim goes farther than the other scrolls of the Torah by speaking of YHVH as the only God. Consider Dᵉvarim 4.35 (see also 39), where it says of YHVH that "he is God; no more beside him."

Religion scholars and theologians have argued about whether this statement would qualify its author as a monotheist. Recall that a distinction is made in religious discussions between monolatry, the worship of only one God while recognizing the existence of other Gods, and monotheism, the belief that there is only one God. Authors in our library do not use these categories, and scholars are not united on how these categories fit with the ancient rhetoric. The scrolls in our library often sound as if the authors would acknowledge other Gods but would advocate for Israelites a YHVH-only approach—that only YHVH should be served, that YHVH was superior to all Gods, and that YHVH alone was Israel's God. Do you think that the author a few lines earlier is acknowledging other deities when he writes

> . . . has a people heard a voice of a God speaking from the midst of a fire as you have and lived? Or has a God gone forth to take for himself a people from the middle of (another) people . . . ? (4.33–34)

I prefer to use the term *YHVH-only* to describe the attitude and approach of many Israelite authors because I think it better reflects their own rhetoric and language. YHVH-only, which would cover both monotheistic and monolatric positions, can accurately describe many of our scrolls. Going beyond that, we can then attempt to understand more specifically by studying particular statements, arguments, and

Study Room 5.4

YHVH, GODS, AND MANUSCRIPTS

The ending of Moshe's song (D^evarim 32.43) is interesting because there are different forms. In the oldest form of the verse, the Dead Sea Scroll 4QDeut^q, which happens to essentially match the oldest Greek version of the song, we find this:

> Rejoice **heavens, with him!**
> **Bow down to him all you Gods,**
> For the blood of his **sons** he will avenge,
> Returning vengeance on his enemies,
> **And will repay those who hate him,**
> And will atone for the land of his people.

But now here is what we read in the medieval Hebrew and Samaritan manuscripts, from which most modern English Bibles derive:

> Rejoice nations, his people!
> For the blood of his servants he will avenge,
> Returning vengeance on his enemies,
> And cleansing his land (for) his people.

The general tone is the same, but there are significant differences. I have set in bold the text in the longer version that is missing or different in the shorter version. Perhaps most obvious is that the shorter, later version has removed the reference to YHVH's preeminence over other Gods. How does this change the religious outlook of the song? What other differences do you see, and how significant are they? Why do you think such changes were made?

particular understandings of the God or Gods that we find in the scrolls. All authors should be considered in all their rhetorical, religious, and poetic diversity. But whatever modern theological or religious categories we might use, we can say that this scroll of D^evarim, especially here in the concluding words of Moshe's first great speech (4.32–40), argues passionately that YHVH has done more wondrous deeds for Israel than any God has done for anyone, his love for them is strong and proven, and they should respond with loyal obedience. Loyalty to YHVH is perhaps the most valued ideal of the scroll; the idea appears frequently as the basis of many injunctions and as the objective of many exhortations. It is the ideal behind the command to exterminate other Canaanites upon entering the new homeland (e.g. 7.1–4; 20.16–18) and to put to death Israelites who worship other Gods (17.2-5), as well as key to a prosperous future (11.13–17; 28.1–68).

Another teaching of Moshe that is unique to D^evarim is the strong and repeated ruling that the sacrificial worship of YHVH was to be done only at one place (e.g., 12.1–27; 14.23–25; 16.2–15; 26.2).

> Be careful that you not sacrifice your offerings in any place that you see, but only at the place that YHVH will choose in one of your tribal territories; there you are to sacrifice your offerings and there you are to do all that I command you. (12.13–14)

The ruling is easy enough to understand and is found in several places in Dᵉvarim. But complications arise when we probe a bit deeper into its uniqueness. This ruling is a significant clue for scholars investigating the religious history of Israel and the history of various biblical scrolls. This ruling is especially conspicuous because even though Exodus, Leviticus, and Numbers all refer frequently to sacrificial offerings, they never mention a specific site. Why not? There are numerous stories and traditions of the Israelites having many altars to YHVH, and great prophets such as the tenth-century Samuel (1 Samuel 1.3; 7.5–11; 7.17; 16.5) and ninth-century Elijah sacrifice at many different places. Both the prophet and YHVH clearly consider it proper to do so. Elijah considers YHVH's enemies to be those who destroy his altars (1 Kings 19.10, 14). By way of explanation, scholars in the nineteenth century noted that Dᵉvarim's ruling concerning one place of sacrifice matched well the religious reforms of later seventh-century kings of Judah, Hezekiah (2 Kings 18) and Josiah (2 Kings 23), who removed sacrificial shrines other than Jerusalem. Furthermore, this removal of other shrines, called *high places* in the ancient Hebrew wording, was one of the major criterion by which the author of the scroll of Kings evaluated the kings of Israel and Judah (e.g., 1 Kings 22.42). What might explain this correspondence as well as several other similarities between Dᵉvarim and Josiah's massive religious reform? Putting all these pieces together, many historians are persuaded that much of Dᵉvarim, including its regulations concerning are place of sacrifice, comes from a later time (seventh century BCE) and that the scroll reflects the views of those persons influential for Hezekiah and Josiah and for the writers of Kings.

The Covenant of YHVH and Israel

How did ancient writers of our library conceive of the relationship between YHVH and the Israelites? The answers vary from scroll to scroll and from time to time, and undoubtedly the range of answers would increase if views outside of our library were included. But if we began a study of each scroll on this topic, we would find that one of the most commonly used metaphors was covenant, *b'rit* in Hebrew, and that Dᵉvarim is one of the scrolls in which it is most prominent. A covenant is essentially the terms of a relational arrangement between two parties and can be expressed in more specific English terms such as "promise," "compact," "agreement," or "contract." We find a summary of it in 26.16–19.

> This day YHVH your God commands you to do these laws and regulations and you will keep and do them with all your heart and all your being. YHVH you have declared today to be your God and to walk in his ways and to keep his laws and commands and regulations and to listen to his voice. And YHVH declares today that you are for him a treasured people even as he said to you and [for you?] to keep all his commands and to set you high over all peoples, whom he made, for praise and for fame and for honor and for you to be a people separated to YHVH your God even as he said.

The whole idea of covenant has long been a rich and pregnant concept in Jewish and Christian religious thought, but only in modern times has our understanding of the metaphor also been enriched by archaeological discoveries. The covenantal language and structure that we find in Dᵉvarim and other scrolls reflects to some degree the language and structure of some ancient international treaties, especially between the Hittites and Assyrians from the Bronze Age and later Iron Age. In other words, the metaphor of covenant was drawn from the realm of international politics and became a favored way of expressing the way of Israel's relationship to YHVH. These treaties can be divided into two types: parity treaties between equals and suzerainty treaties between a superior state and an inferior one, in which the stronger of the two sets the terms of the agreement. In the latter case, which has the most similarities with Dᵉvarim, there were usually certain basic components that formed the structure of the covenant:

1. Introduction of the ruler and covenant giver, stating that the following covenant is the message of the ruler to his vassal
2. Historical review of relationship, emphasizing the benevolence of the covenant giver
3. Requirements and laws for the vassal
4. Arrangement for written record and public reading of the covenant
5. Naming of divine witness to treaty
6. List of blessings and curses to be brought by Gods for obedience or disobedience
7. Arrangement for an acceptance ceremony on the part of the vassal

Now, if we read through Dᵉvarim with this basic structure in mind, we see that all the components are in our scroll. Dᵉvarim is not an actual covenant legal document; it is a literary creation by authors who knew the covenantal form well and used its format extensively: (1) Moshe speaks YHVH's *message* and (2) the historical *review* is contained in Chapters 1–11. (3) There is an extensive list of *laws* in the Moshe's second address. (5) YHVH is the only *witness*, and (6) YHNH also the one to bring to the *curses and blessings* listed in Chapters 27–28. (7) Chapter 28 includes instructions for an *acceptance ceremony* by the Israelites. Of course Moshe is providing a public recitation in Dᵉvarim, just as Josiah does in 2 Kings 23.

Dᵉvarim and Other Scrolls of Moses

We have already mention that among ancient Jews there were numerous writings other than Exodus, Leviticus, and Numbers associated with Moses, some of which we have copies or fragments of, and some of which are lost entirely. Having read the other three, many questions arise in our minds when we read through Dᵉvarim. A large percentage of Dᵉvarim is composed of laws, and many of them are similar or identical to laws found in the three scrolls prior to this one in our library. This is not surprising for readers paying attention to the dramatic setting of the scroll: Moshe is in Moab reminding the Israelites of YHVH's instructions to them 40 years earlier at Horeb (Mount Sinai). In fact, Dᵉvarim adds an interesting episode to the plot when Moshe says that back at Horeb the Israelites themselves heard YHVH speak the first ten commands, and then, out of fear for their own safety—hearing YHVH was a terrifying event—they instructed Moshe to go and listen to YHVH without them and then report

P OSTER 5.7

ANOTHER INTERESTING SCROLL OF . . . MOSHE?

Among the fascinating manuscripts found among the Dead Sea Scrolls were copies of a scroll that scholars called the Temple Scroll or the Qumranic Torah. One copy is actually the longest of all the scrolls found, about nine meters long, divided into 67 columns. It is written as a direct address from YHVH to Moses and was likely composed in the late second century BCE. It was clearly an important scroll for this group of religious Jews, and it claims the highest authority and YHVH's direct speech. Its content, much like the four books of Moses in our library, is primarily laws for living in accord with YHVH's covenant. And, just as we might expect from our study of scrolls in our library, it is not a free, original composition. The author uses extensively the texts of Exodus, Leviticus, Numbers, and especially D^evarim and combines them with new regulations to form a coherent organized law code dealing with sacred objects, sacrifices, purity, and rules for kings and others. One of the intriguing aspects of the scroll is that when quoting from D^evarim, it always attributes the direct speech to YHVH rather than Moses, as in D^evarim. Compare these texts for example:

D^evarim 17.16 presents Moses as saying: . . . he (the king) . . . must not acquire many horses for himself or return the people to Egypt in order to obtain more horses, <u>since YHVH has said to you,</u> "You must never return that way again."

Qumranic Torah (11QT 56.15–8) presents God as saying: . . . he (the king) must not multiply horses for himself, or cause the people to return to Egypt for war, in order to multiply horses for himself, <u>since I said to you,</u> "You must never return that way again."

Unfortunately, the first column of the scroll is too damaged to read, so we cannot be sure of the dramatic narrative setting it may have created. In any case, like D^evarim, this scroll is a fascinating example of the ongoing process of composing the instructions of Moshe and YHVH in Jewish tradition. D^evarim, too, is a part of that ongoing process and has much in common with later books attributed to Moses, such as Jubilees and the Qumranic Torah.

back to them (5.22–33). In D^evarim we find the first commands singled out as the **Decalogue,** "the ten words" (4.13; 10.4) better known as the Ten Commandments.

Many fascinating studies have been conducted about the relationship of the laws in Exodus, Leviticus, Numbers, and D^evarim, and, generally speaking, D^evarim seems to represent a later development in the history of Israel's written laws than the codes contained in Exodus, Leviticus, or Numbers. But the tradition of writing instructions and attributing them to YHVH or Moses did not stop with D^evarim. Later codes, such as a very interesting scroll known as the Temple Scroll found among the Dead Sea Scrolls, came after D^evarim (see Poster 5.7).

DISPLAY 5.3 | THE SCROLL OF MOSES KNOWN AS THE TEMPLE SCROLL

If we compare the laws in Dᵉvarim with those in Exodus, Leviticus, and Numbers, we will find that many laws in Dᵉvarim are identical to those in earlier collections, such as "You must not murder," found in both Dᵉvarim 5.17 and Exodus 20.13. Laws about resting on Shabbat, the seventh day of the week, are found in all four scrolls and even mentioned in Genesis (Genesis 2.1–3; Exodus 16.23–29; 31.12–7; 34.21; 35.3; Leviticus 19.3; Numbers 15.32–36; Deuteronomy 5.12–15). Comparing these texts, as well as references to Shabbat in other books, makes for an absorbing study about developments and variations of an Israelite tradition. For example, consider the distinctive form of the Shabbat command, especially reasons given for observing Shabbat in Exodus and Dᵉvarim. Although much of the wording is identical, which is easily explained by saying that the author of Dᵉvarim used the tradition found in Exodus, other aspects, especially the rationale, can be explained as part of Dᵉvarim's strong tendency toward sympathy and empathy of which we spoke earlier. There are dozens, even hundreds of other interesting comparisons to be made about every kind of law among the different scrolls, such as the laws about Israelite slaves in Exodus 21.2–11, Leviticus 25.42–43, and Deuteronomy 15.12–18. These types of comparison demonstrate yet again that the librarians of our collection did not edit for uniformity.

One of the most striking differences between Dᵉvarim and the scrolls Exodus, Leviticus, and Numbers is the way in which the **Ark of the Covenant,** and the portable shrine, or **tent of meeting,** are treated. In Exodus, Leviticus, and Numbers, a great deal of attention is given to these physical objects—the terms seem interchangeable most of the time—in both prose narratives and legal regulations. The box is YHVH's dwelling on earth and the official site of YHVH's ongoing revelations to Moshe. It is crucial for Israelite success in battle. But in Dᵉvarim, which is full of revelations from YHVH and

P OSTER 5.8

SIMILAR ANCIENT NEAR EASTERN LAWS

Hammurabi's Code (ca. 1770 BCE)

16: If a man should harbor a fugitive slave or slave woman of either the palace or of a commoner in his house and not bring him out at the herald's public proclamation, that householder shall be killed.

17. If a man seizes a fugitive slave or slave woman in the open country and leads him back to his owner, the slave owner shall give him two shekels of silver.

117. If an obligation is outstanding against a man and he sells or gives into debt service his wife, his son, or his daughter, they shall perform service in the house of their buyer or of the one who holds them in debt service for three years; their release shall be secured in the fourth year.

130. If a man pins down another man's virgin wife who is still residing in her father's house, and they seize him lying with her, that man shall be killed; that woman shall be released.

–Translated by Martha Roth in Hallo and Younger 1997, 2:338–44

Hittite Code (ca. 1500 BCE)

193. If a man has a wife, and the man dies, his brother shall take his widow as wife. (If the brother dies,) his father shall take her. When afterwards his father dies, his (father's) brother shall take the woman whom he had.

–Translated by H. Hoffner, Jr., in Hallo and Younger 1997, 2:118

Dᵉvarim

23.16–17 (15–16 in some versions): You must not return a (foreign) slave to his master who has escaped to you from his master. With you he may live he may settle in your midst, in the place he may choose in one of your towns that pleases him; you must not ill-treat him.

15.12 If a fellow Hebrew is sold to you, a male or female slave, and he works for you six years, in the seventh year you must set him free.

22.23–24a: If a young woman, a virgin, is engaged to a man and a man comes to her in the town and lies with her, then you must take the two of them to the gate of that town and stone them to death; the young woman because she did not cry out in the town and the man because he violated the wife of another man.

25.5: If two brothers dwell together and one dies without a son, the wife of the deceased must not be married outside the family to a stranger; he (living brother) must have relations with her and take her as his wife and his duty for her. . . .

Knowing of Israel's close interaction with neighboring cultures, we are not surprised to find similar laws. At the same time we recognize unique aspects of Israelite legal outlooks and laws.

instructions about how Israelites are to fight, the box and portable shrine play no major role. It is not presented as the place of YHVH's presence and it is not a powerful force or symbol in battle; it is only a storage container for the tablets on which YHVH's commands are written (10.1–5; 31.9). For the author of D^evarim, this container was not YHVH's home on earth, and it seems that the author's conception of YHVH was different than it was for the authors other scrolls. YHVH is never spoken of as directly dwelling with Israel; he is more removed when physical language is used (compare Exodus 19.9–20 with D^evarim 4.36); YHVH dwells in the skies (26.15).

All in all, D^evarim is a grand sermon proclaiming the instructions of YHVH to Moses with the passion and verve of a prophet. And, in fact, that is just the image presented for Moses at the conclusion of the scroll. The last words of the scroll depict Moshe as the greatest prophet of Israel (34.10–12). Unlike the more priestly interests of earlier scrolls of Moshe, this scroll emphasized Moshe as the greatest and most authoritative prophetic voice of the tradition.

Questions for Further Study

1. Historians have found many clues to the age of monarchy in D^evarim. As a historian, what do you see?

2. In this scroll the author has Moses dominate. How do you evaluate Moses's rhetoric? How would you evaluate the rhetoric of the author for his audience? How does he appeal? On what authority? How does the rhetoric of this scroll sound different from that of Exodus through Numbers?

References

Fox, Everett. *The Five Books of Moses.* New York: Schocken, 1995.

Mendenhall, George E. and Gary A. Herion. "Covenant" in *The Anchor Bible Dictionary,* ed. by David Noel Freedman, 1:1179–202. New York: Doubleday, 1992.

Polzin, Robert. "Deuteronomy" in *The Literary Guide to the Bible,* ed. by Robert Alter and Frank Kermode. Cambridge, MA: Harvard, 1987.

Strugnell, John. "Moses-Pseudepigrapha at Qumran: 4Q375, 4Q376, and Similar Works," in *Archaeology and History in the Dead Sea Scrolls,* edited by L. Schiffman. Sheffield, England: Journal for the Study of the Pseudepigrapha, 1990.

Tigay, Jeffrey H. *Deuteronomy, The JPS Torah Commentary.* Philadelphia: The Jewish Publication Society, 1996.

Plaut, W. Gunther, ed. *The Torah: A Modern Commentary.* New York: Union of American Hebrew Congregations, 1981.

Chapter 6

Prophets *Neviim* Part I

Narratives: Four Scrolls

Unlike Deuteronomy's great speeches, our next four scrolls, Joshua, Judges, Samuel, and Kings, are basically strict narratives in format. However, as was explained when we talked about the Torah section, they are related to Deuteronomy because of the work of an editor, they share certain important components of its religious outlook. They also provide a somewhat continuous narrative, taking the story of the Israelites from conquest of land in Canaan to exile away from the land centuries later. Most likely the name for the section, *Neviim*, pronounced "neh-vee-*eem*," which means "prophets," comes from the scrolls that follow these first four, which are made up mostly of prophetic oracles. However, especially in Samuel and Kings, individuals known as prophets play major roles in the narratives. We will talk more about what a prophet was in ancient Israel at the beginning of Neviim Part II, Chapter 7.

POSTER 6.1

THE DEUTERONOMIC HISTORY

Joshua Yᵉhoshua	Judges Shophtim	Samuel Shᵉmuel	Kings Mᵉlakhim
After Moshe's death, Joshua becomes Israel's leader; Israel begins conquest of land; Joshua dies	After Joshua's death, Israel is led by local, tribal warlords (judges); Israelite tribes fight for territories; social and religious disorder	Under leadership of Samuel, Israel moves from tribal disorder to kingship; first king, Saul; second and greatest king, David	David dies; third king: Solomon; kingdom is divided into North and South; North conquered and exiled by Assyria; South conquered and exiled by Babylon

These four scrolls are often called the **Deuteronomic history,** even though they were not originally composed as a four-volume unity. What they share is some shaping by an editor after their own stages of individual composition, probably in the seventh or sixth century BCE. This editor was interested in telling the story of Israel as one of obedience or disobedience to the laws of YHVH. For him everything—military success or failure, disasters of nature, human actions, foreign superpowers, and enemy clans—can be related to the proper keeping of covenant with YHVH, just as Moses says in his great final speeches in Deuteronomy 27–30. Thus the latter narratives are seen as a working out of the vision of Moses in Deuteronomy. This ideological link to Deuteronomy is what inspired scholars to refer to these scrolls as the Deuteronomic History.

References

Dever, William G. *Who Were the Early Israelites and Where Did They Come From?* Grand Rapids, MI: Eerdmans, 2003.

Fretheim, Terence E. *Deuteronomic History.* Nashville, TN: Abingdon, 1983.

Halpern, Baruch. *The First Historians.* San Francisco: Harper & Row, 1988.

The New Interpreter's Bible, vols. 2, 3. Nashville, TN: Abingdon, 1998, 1999.

McKenzie, Steven L. "Deuteronomic History" in *The Anchor Bible Dictionary,* edited by David Nuet Freedman, 2:160–8. New York: Doubleday, 1992.

Polzin, Robert. *Moses and the Deuteronomist: A Literary Study of the Deuteronomic History, Part 1: Deuteronomy/Joshua/Judges.* Terra Haute, IN: Indiana University, 1993.

——. *Samuel and the Deuteronomist: A Literary Study of the Deuteronomic History, Part 2: I Samuel.* Terra Haute, IN: Indiana University, 1993.

——. *David and the Deuteronomist: A Literary Study of the Deuteronomic History, Part 3: 2 Samuel.* Terra Haute, IN: Indiana University, 1993.

יהושע

Joshua Y^ehoshua

Section Outline

Literary Format and Movement
A Familiar Story Continues
Y^ehoshua and History
Complexity and Reality in Narrative
Questions for Further Study
References

In one sense this sixth scroll of our library is a culmination of the first five. It has been edited so that its story begins right where Deuteronomy's ends—immediately following the death of Moses. What will happen without this incomparable leader who has dominated the last four books, leading the tribes of Israelites out of Egypt, bringing them YHVH's direct instructions, and building their sacred shrine and society? Will they become residents of Canaan? The name of the scroll is pronounced "ye-ho-*shu*-uh," after the name of Moses successor, rendered in English as *Joshua.* It is in this narrative that YHVH's promise to Abraham, as recorded in Genesis 17.7–8, finally reaches some sort of fulfillment. But we shall soon see that from a literary perspective there are more complexities than one might at first notice, and from a historical perspective there are a host of complications. Regarding the history, this scroll in its current form is an idealistic story of Israelite tribal conquest of their homeland and the storyteller or major final editors are from a time many centuries after Israelites first appeared in Syria-Palestine in the thirteenth century BCE. It might resemble an early European American storyteller weaving threads of history and legend to tell an idealistic story of the westward expansion of the United States. The goal is not an objective chronicle that incorporates perspectives of the conquered; the methods do not attempt to approach evidential exactness. Many aspects of this Israelite story in Y^ehoshua are likely very old, because stories were handed down from one generation to another, but other parts seem to have originated only in later times. Regardless of how far back some may go, these narratives, in the form we have them, reflect the past as seen by some Jewish writers of the late Judahite (sixth-century-BCE) monarchy and exilic periods. But Y^ehoshua is much more than a simplistic straightforward narrative. Let's have a look.

LITERARY FORMAT AND MOVEMENT

Yᵉhoshua combines stories of a group of tribes conquering territory in the region of Canaan, led and directed by their God YHVH and supervised by his ordained leader Yᵉhoshua, with boundary descriptions. The conclusion makes clear the ultimate aims of the authors—that Jews should live according to their covenant with YHVH.

Conquest of Canaan	Distribution of Canaan for Tribes	Joshua's Farewell and Covenant Renewal
1.1–18 Introduction of Yᵉhoshua	13.1–33 Settlement overview	23.1–16 Yᵉhoshua's farewell speech
2.1–24 Spies sent to Jericho	14.1–19.48 Tribal allotments	24.1–28 Joshua leads tribes in confirming covenant at Shechem.
3.1–5.12 Crossing Jordan River	20.1–9 Cities of refuge	24.29–33 Yᵉhoshua dies; concluding editorial remarks
5.13–6.27 Conquest of Jericho	21.1–42 Cities of Levite tribe	
7.1–8.35 Loss and conquest at Ai	21.43–45 Summary	
9.1–27 Trick of Gideonites	22.1–34 Tribes east of Jordan River	
10.1–43 Conquest in south		
11.1–23 Conquest in north		
12.1–24 Summary of conquest		

A Familiar Story Continues

When you start reading this scroll after having read the previous five, you know exactly where you are. The editor has picked up the narrative right where the editor of Deuteronomy left it: "after Moses' death . . ." Repeated ideas of this narrative will also sound familiar, and there will be numerous connections to things we read in Genesis, Exodus, Numbers and Deuteronomy. Traditions about Yᵉhoshua had already been included in Exodus, where we find him as a leading warrior and in one story as Moses's assistant who accompanied him up the mountain of God (Exodus 17.9–13; 24.13). The scroll of Numbers has him as one of the tribal leaders who goes to spy out the land of Canaan (Numbers 13–14). Also important are the traditions that Yᵉhoshua is YHVH's designated successor to Moses (Numbers 27.12–23; Deuteronomy 3.23–28). We could even say that the author of Yᵉhoshua paints his hero as a second Moses in many ways: YHVH speaks directly to Yᵉhoshua; Yᵉhoshua speaks to and for YHVH; YHVH is with him in a special way as he was with

Moses (Y^ehoshua 1.5; 3.7); Y^ehoshua has a unique and mysterious physical encounter with YHVH like Moses (Y^ehoshua 5.13–15; Exodus 3.1–6); he performs similar deeds (Y^ehoshua 4.23) and issues YHVH's commands (Y^ehoshua 8.27); and, again like Moses at the end of Deuteronomy, the narrator concludes the scroll with Y^ehoshua, before he dies, giving a rousing call to the Israelites to maintain their covenantal responsibilities with YHVH (Y^ehoshua 23–24).

In the first sentences of the scroll, YHVH is presented as telling Y^ehoshua that YHVH's promises to Moses will be fulfilled and the land promised to, but not received by, his ancestors will be given to Y^ehoshua and the Israelites under his command. Of course we saw that these ideas of promise, covenant, and land are common themes in the scrolls of Genesis, Exodus, Numbers, and Deuteronomy. And, perhaps the most important continuity is that the author makes YHVH, who is mentioned in the scroll many more times than even Y^ehoshua, central to the entire story. Thus, the narrator begins, "After Moses's death . . . YHVH spoke to Y^ehoshua . . . ."

A summary of the basic plot of the drama of the Y^ehoshua scroll is quite simple.

1. YHVH, Israel's God, covenant partner, and giver of law through Moses, had promised to Abraham and sons the land of Canaan.
2. YHVH instructs and brings victory to Joshua in the conquest of that land, taking it from other peoples.
3. YHVH is angered and brings defeat to Joshua when the Israelites fail to obey his instructions.
4. The conquest mission is a success and the land is divided among Israelite tribes.
5. Joshua leads the people in reaffirming their commitment to YHVH's covenant.

This summary shows the idealism of the scroll's author and his commitment to understanding Israel's past as a successful story controlled by YHVH and as a continuous demonstration that YHVH prospers the nation when Israel upholds its covenantal responsibilities. We will encounter this same plot line in several more scrolls of our library. This principle is presented in the sphere of the tribes and nation; it is not presented as a failsafe means of individual success. Recall also, if you will, that this national viewpoint is laid out explicitly in Moses's last speeches in Deuteronomy; it is basically shared by the final composers of Y^ehoshua, Judges, Samuel, and Kings. Within these scrolls we often find the repeated sequence of disobedience, disaster, repentance, and success, which I call the Deuteronomic narrative pattern (DNP). We will see it explicitly and succinctly stated in Judges and illustrated throughout all these scrolls.

Y^ehoshua and History

The composer of Y^ehoshua undoubtedly had materials to work with for his story; there were oral traditions and written records from various periods. The lists of towns and villages allotted to each tribe in Chapters 13–19 seem to reflect

Study Room 6.1

STUDYING THE PROMISED LAND IN OTHER TEXTS

The scroll of Yᵉhoshua is only one of the many texts of our library that speak of Israel and its land. YHVH's giving of the land of Canaan was for many Jewish writers a central chapter in their national story. For example, Israelite poems and prayers from the book of Psalms often speak at length about the land, and in many of these references the land is seen as YHVH's gift of freedom and hope to the previously enslaved and homeless people.

It is a profitable and interesting study to read poems such as Psalms 44, 78, 80, 106, 114, and 135 and to notice how these poets use this Promised Land tradition (see also Jeremiah 31, Ezekiel 37). How does the land relate to ideas of covenant, promise, justice, and mercy? What is different and what is similar among the various retellings of the story, and how do they differ from the scroll of Yᵉhoshua? How does the author use the Promised Land tradition for his contemporary audience? Why is the land story mentioned in prayers? Have you ever observed this Promised Land story being used in your life experience?

geographical locations and divisions during the period of Israel's divided monarchy (tenth to seventh centuries BCE), and official records from that period also may have been used. In 10.12–13, the author quotes an ancient poem and even names the source, the Scroll of Yashar, which seems to have been a collection of poems about Israel's divine warrior. There is a much longer quote from this book in 2 Samuel 1.18–27. Yᵉhoshua 24.11–12 seems to come from a source that relates the victory over Jericho differently than Yᵉhoshua 5–6, and the information in 24.2 about Abraham is from a tradition not reflected in the book of Genesis. Modern scholars have done considerable work attempting to distinguish and describe many more possible sources for this scroll, especially attempting to link a specific narrative with a particular tribe.

But this use of divergent sources does not make the author or editor of the scroll a modern historian seeking all available ancient evidence to reconstruct events of the past in a dispassionate manner. This story about Israel's past is idealistic because it uses selected communal traditions and available documents to illustrate YHVH's actions on behalf of Israel and to record the relevance of loyalty to the covenant for Israel's communal life of the author's own day. On the other hand, modern historians, archaeologists, and anthropologists have different purposes and, naturally, their methods and results are much different. Historically, as we saw above in Chapter 3, Israelite tribes and clans are beginning to emerge as distinct entities during the thirteenth and twelfth centuries BCE, a time of tumult and large-scale movement of many tribes and clans in the region of Syria-Palestine. The archaeological record for this period is complex and yields massive amounts of data from hundreds of excavations throughout the area. As we said before we should think of Israel as an amalgam of related tribes, showing various degrees of federation at different times, organized by clans and extended families, with authority residing in the patriarchs of the several layers, such as family leaders, clan leaders, and tribal leaders. The entire population—not just Israelites—of the hill country grew from approximately 12,000 at the end of the twelfth century to about 75,000 in eleventh century. This complexity in some sense matches a subcurrent in the narrative of Y^ehoshua.

Complexity and Reality in Narrative

On a literary level, Y^ehoshua is not quite the straightforward, smooth story the preceding basic plot summary above seems to imply. If we read Y^ehoshua 1–12 without a map, we might think that the entire land of Canaan was conquered, due to summaries such 11.23: "And Y^ehoshua captured the entire land in accord with all that YHVH had spoken to Moses."

But if we read the lists of villages and areas defeated or not defeated in Chapter 1–12 and mark them on a map, we discover that most of captured villages are in the hill country; much territory of Syria-Palestine is not covered. (On the other hand, the lists of tribal allotments in 13–19 are much more broadly spread.) In some places the narrative itself explicitly mentions territories and towns that remained unconquered.

> This is the remaining land: all regions of the Philistines, and all of the Geshurites—from the Shihor, which borders Egypt, north to the boundary of Ekron is considered Canaanite . . . —and of Avim, from the south all Canaanite land and from Mearah of the Sidonians to Aphek to the Amorite boarder, and the Gebalite land and all Lebanon, east from Baal-Gad below Mount Hermon to Lebo-Hamath. (Joshua 13.2–5; see also 13.13; 15.63; 16.10; 17.11–13; 17.16–18)

Finally, we see that our scroll contains what we might consider intriguing oddities and ironies. Spies are sent to view the land, but they only go a few miles (kilometers) to Jericho and hill country. In Jericho they go straight to a prostitute's house, and she gives them a lecture demonstrating that she knows all about YHVH and his plan for the land, as if Deuteronomy had been her reading material the day they arrived (2.1–14). It is no wonder that in later Jewish literature she is pictured as a great proselyte. Chapter 5 has interesting stories about how, upon crossing the Jordan River, before any conquest, the Israelites celebrated **Pesach (Passover)** and made sure all the males had undergone **circumcision.** Surely such narrative placement of these two rituals signals some contemporary concerns of the author. A seemingly independent story of Y^ehoshua's encounter with an obscure being, the commander of YHVH's army (5.13–15), has intrigued many. Similarly Y^ehoshua's cursing of Jericho (6.26) is unique and not really explained in the context, making it a matter of much speculation through the centuries. For the curious reader and literary scholar, these episodes become interesting challenges for incorporating into the structure and themes of the scroll.

Community Reflections 6.1

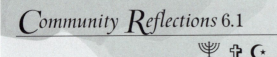

HOLY LAND, BLOODY LAND

The scroll of Y^ehoshua contains a great deal of violence that is inextricably linked in the text to religion; Chapters 2–12 run with blood. For example, "So Y^ehoshua defeated the entire land, the hill country, the **Negev,** the Shephelah, the slopes, and all their kings. He left no survivor and all that breathed he religiously annihilated just as YHVH, God of Israel, commanded." (10.40)

The verb I have translated as "religiously annihilated" is difficult to put into English. It is *kh-r-m,* and it is means to "devote, put under a ban, destroy" with strong religious overtones. And our scroll is only one of many graphic battles through the centuries for this holy land.

This scroll is not the only one in our library with violence, and this land is not the only land that is bloody. The author of Y^ehoshua knew of earlier traditions of YHVH commanding Israelites to utterly destroy Canaanite inhabitants, and we can read some of those in Deuteronomy 20. There are many violent passages in later Jewish, Christian, and Muslim sacred texts as well. Recall from our discussion entitled "Valuing the Library" in chapter 2 that how one values the various scrolls of this library will determine how one reacts to these violent images. A historian accustomed to reading ancient texts would not be surprised at all to find such accounts of warfare, nor would she be startled to read that the warfare is commanded and directed by the God. She would also not be surprised that the archaeological record or other historical data suggest that the claims of massive victory or total annihilation are overstated. In the case of the Israelites conquest—even as noted in other parts of our Y^ehoshua scroll—clearly there were many tribes of people who survived and were not threatened by Israelites: Canaanites, Philistines, and many others thrived alongside Israelites for centuries, and texts, both ancient and modern, often exaggerate victories.

As sacred texts with some sort of authority in Jewish and Christian communities, these passages stand alongside other passages in our library that speak of peaceful negotiations, being merciful to all, or loving enemies. All these texts are interpreted for their contemporary relevance and what to do with the texts is clearly the decision of distinct individuals or communities.

Through the centuries religious communities and nations in the Jewish, Christian, and Muslims traditions have often committed violent acts against others and have justified those acts as divinely sanctioned by appealing to texts such as Y^ehoshua. This happens today, too; many believe in divine approval of national violence and war because of their valuation and interpretation of sacred texts. But these same religious communities also have alternative traditions and interpretive strategies available to them that do not lead to violence. Communities and individuals choose how the various texts are to be read relevant to one another and which texts are controlling and which are subsumed under higher principles. It is impossible for readers to get out of the tasks of interpreting and deciding. Each community and individual must face the issues of dealing with their sacred texts and traditions *and* with their fellow humans. In the end, it is not an ancient scroll that commits acts of violence or peace. Instead, humans determine values personally and communally, decide priorities, select and prioritize texts, and choose what actions to take.

Questions for Further Study

1. As an ecocritic, how would you understand this scroll's attitude to themes of land? Who owns it? How is it utilized?

2. How do the many lists of Yᵉhoshua function in the narrative?

3. How does the Promised Land story line of Exodus through Deuteronomy have its fulfillment, or dénouement, in Yᵉhoshua? Even though Yᵉhoshua is in some sense the concluding pinnacle of the story, the scroll itself did not become part of the Torah in Jewish tradition. We have a Pentateuch not a Hexateuch. Why might this be? What difference does this make for a community that reads this story concluding at Deuteronomy?

References

Boling, Robert G. "Joshua, Book of," in *The Anchor Bible Dictionary*, edited by New York: David N. Freedman; 3:1002–015. Doubleday, 1992.

Boling, Robert G. and G. Ernest Wright. *Joshua*. Garden City, NY: Doubleday, 1982.

Gunn, David M. "Joshua and Judges," in *The Literary Guide to the Bible*, edited by Robert Alter and Frank Kermode, 102–21. Cambridge, MA: Harvard, 1987.

Nelson, Richard D. *Joshua*. Louisville, KY: Westminster/John Knox, 1997.

Sanders, James A. *Torah and Canon*. Philadelphia: Fortress, 1972.

Stager, Lawrence E. "Forging an Identity: The Emergence of Ancient Israel," in *The Oxford History of the Biblical World*, edited by Michael D. Coogan, 90–131. New York: Oxford, 1988.

שפטים

Judges *Shophtim*

SECTION OUTLINE

Formation and Dating
Literary Format and Movement
What's the Point?
A Literary Genius
Shophtim and History
Questions for Further Study
References

Joshua presents a story of a mostly successful military campaign of YHVH's Israelite tribes under his chosen leader Joshua, but the next scroll, Judges, which in Hebrew is *Shophtim,* pronounced "shof-*teem,*" has a profoundly different perspective on the Israelite incursion into Syria-Palestine. The scroll we have here provides a conclusion to the continuing narrative of the Israelites gaining control of villages and arable land in the hills of Canaan. This scroll is a fascinating compilation of stories filled with local color and historically curious details, actions both fabulously heroic and unspeakably evil. Furthermore, the accounts are drawn up in an artistically thoughtful and fascinating manner. As a final introductory comment, *judge* here does not refer to a person who presides in a court of law. The word is a more general term indicating tribal leadership.

Formation and Dating

The Shophtim scroll strings together stories that likely existed in oral forms long before the writing of the book. These stories of Israelite warrior folk heroes come from diverse geographical and tribal sources, many of the longer stories stemming from the northern part of the Israelite settlement. The stories seem

LITERARY FORMAT AND MOVEMENT

Shophtim is a collection of stories that have been gathered from various tribal traditions, most likely with oral backgrounds, and placed within a political-religious, or Deuteronomic, framework to make a basic religious or political point. Thus the book is like an anthology. However, many of the individual stories are told with considerable rhetorical skill, and the work as a whole coheres well to support the editor's major point. We will discuss that skill and the literary adroitness of the compiler.

1.1–2.5 General Political and Religious Introduction

The ordained warrior Joshua has died

Various Israelite tribes, led by YHVH, continue fighting for territory in Canaan with some success;

Israelite tribes also have failures and fail to obey YHVH.

2.6–3.6 Deuteronomic Introduction—Israelite Cycle of Failure Explained

1 People do evil in sight of YHVH.

2 YHVH, in anger, causes them to lose to enemy.

3 People cry out to YHVH.

4 YHVH sends military hero to deliver them.

5 The land has peace until the cycle begins again.

The Cycle Illustrated in Stories of Military Heroes

3.7–11 Othniel fights Arameans.

3.15–30 Ehud fights Moabites.

3.31 Shamgar fights Philistines.

4.1–24 Deborah and Barak fight Canaanites (prose version).

5.1–31 Deborah and Barak fight Canaanites (poetic version).

6.1–8.35 Gideon fights Midianites.

9.1–57 Abimelech wars with Shechem.

10.1–5 Heroes Tola and Jair.

10.6–12.7 Jephthah fights other Israelites, Ammonites, and sacrifices his daughter.

12.8–15 Heroes Ibzan, Elon, Abdon

13.1–16.31 Samson, the last hero of book, fights Philistines; his greatest victory is in death.

The Cycle Ends: Stories of Precipitous Decline

17.1–18.31 A Northerner and Southerner (Levite priest) lead in worship of metal idol; Tribe of Dan moves North due to failure to defeat Philistines and takes idol and priest.

19.1–21.24 Tribe of Benjamin's atrocious gang rape and murder, the resulting civil war, and Israelite-style justice.

21.25 Concluding refrain: "There was no king, everyone did what seemed right to him/her."

mostly independent in origin, as opposed to coming from one continuous united narrative. The poetic form of the story of the warrior Deborah and her right-hand man Barak (Judges 4) is very old, among the oldest of all texts in our library, as evidenced by its ancient forms of Hebrew.

Probably in the seventh century BCE someone selected some of the ancient stories about the days before Israel had kings (see 21.25) and put them in one collection with an editorial framework. Many of these stories have their setting in the northern regions of Israelite settlements, and this northern perspective likely indicates the origin or interests of the first editor. The modern scroll certainly comes from after the year 722 BCE; notice that Shophtim 18.30 refers to the captivity of the Northern Kingdom of Israel, which occurred in that year. It seems that the scroll was supplemented by a few authors or editors in the next several centuries. It is clear from the textual evidence that the book continued to pass through stages of transmission. Among the ancient Dead Sea Scrolls there is a copy of Shophtim from the last centuries BCE without the editorial addition of what in English Bibles is Shophtim 6.7–10 (Tov 2001, 344–345).

What's the Point?

But the collection was not haphazard nor was it simply an effort to preserve a sampling of ancient tales for posterity. The political and religious purpose of the author is clear from the introduction and the many editorial remarks made along the way. The scroll begins with an introduction of the period—a time in Israel after Joshua but before the Israelites had kings. Joshua's death is recounted and the rise of a new generation remarked (2.6–10). How does Israel fare in its new environment with new leaders, surrounded by hostile people as intent on capturing Israelite lands as the Israelites are on capturing theirs? In the first few paragraphs (1.1–15) one might conclude that the Israelites thrived under new leadership. But the author of Shophtim soon indicates that the situation is to the contrary; the Israelites are floundering militarily.

The early chapters (1.1–3.6) set up what I referred to in the section on Joshua as the Deuteronomic narrative pattern (DNP). The entire five-step DNP (see p. xx) is laid out explicitly in Shophtim 2.11–22 and clearly illustrated almost everywhere, including the following section:

> The Israelites did what was evil in the sight of YHVH, forgetting YHVH their God, and worshiping the **Baals** and the Asherahs. Therefore the anger of YHVH was kindled against Israel, and he sold them into the hand of King Cushan-rishathaim of Aram-naharaim; and the Israelites served Cushan-rishathaim eight years. But when the Israelites cried out to YHVH, YHVH raised up a deliverer for the Israelites, who delivered them, Othniel son of Kenaz, Caleb's younger brother. The spirit of YHVH came upon him, and he judged Israel; he went out to war, and YHVH gave King Cushan-rishathaim of **Aram** into his hand; and his hand prevailed over Cushan-rishathaim. So the land had rest forty years. Then Othniel son of Kenaz died. The Israelites again did what was evil in the sight of YHVH . . . (Shophtim 3.7–12)

The reader could not miss the point that no matter how many times YHVH sends his spirit to raise up a new leader to save a tribe of Israelites, they again fail to obey YHVH. For the author this means primarily the worship of foreign Gods (2.11–13, 19; 3.7; 10.10) or of images (17.3–6; 18.30–31) and maintenance of close associations with the non-YHVH worshipping foreigners (2.2), including intermarriage (3.5–6).

By weaving the originally tribal stories together and referring frequently to the Israelites en masse, the author has turned these accounts of local heroes and distinct tribal events into a general national history of Israel.

This narrative pattern unifies an otherwise diverse collection to make its general religious point.

But the author does not stop with illustrating the DNP. The last military hero raised up by YHVH comes three-quarters of the way through the scroll (Chapter 16), and the remaining columns present stories bereft of heroes. Localized personal tragedies in Chapter 19 lead to widespread tribal feuds and bloody revenge (Chapters 20–21). The fighting changes from fighting foreign enemies to warring among Israelite tribes and chaotic civil war. According to our author, Israelite society, due to abandoning the proper ways of following YHVH, has destroyed itself.

A Literary Genius

In the first century CE, the literary critic Longinus noted how the Greek literary genius Homer would shape his language and literary expression to match the events he was describing (*On the Sublime* 10.6). I think Shophtim would have impressed Longinus, too. By the end of Shophtim, the narrator has described downfall of the Israelite tribes into a state of unmitigated disaster, religiously and socially. This degradation—from the days of Joshua to the arrival of kingship—is the content of this scroll. Much like Homer, the author brilliantly illustrates this social and religious breakdown in the way he writes. Consider the following:

- The structure provided in the first half of the book by the repeated and distinctive DNP is lost in the second half. The narrator opts to abandon the pattern in the final columns, and thus as the society becomes more chaotic, so does the narrative form.

- The order in which the author chooses to present the judges is generally from better to worse on religious and moral grounds. The early judges are pleasing to YHVH, but later ones are progressively questionable or corrupt. Jepthah sacrifices his own daughter (11.29–40) and Samson, the last of all the heroes, is presented as much as a villain as a hero, except in his death, which was the greatest thing he ever did (16.30).

- At the end of his narrative there are no more judges, only mob rule.

- The mob mentality and lack of leadership are signified in the loss of all personal names. In the brutal and horrific penultimate story in Chapter 19, the actors are a certain Levite, his concubine, the old man, his daughter, and the men of the city.

- In narrating the civil war that follows in Chapters 20–21, there still are no personal names, just mobs from tribes and villages marauding the land, deliberating anonymously on justice, and killing. Now the narrative has no responsible individuals, just mad mobs.

- Finally, though the ordering control of the DNP is long gone by the end of the scroll, the author utilizes a much smaller and unobtrusive repeated device to strike a memorable chord that is first sounded in 17.6, then again in 18.1, 19.1, and finally to conclude the entire scroll (21.25): "In those days there was not a king in Israel, a person did the right of his own eyes."

In the chaos of the concluding narrative, this is the one fact the narrator sets apart as clear.

Shophtim and History

A historian eager to reconstruct the past can make judicious use of Shophtim. Though the scroll's editor completed collected and composed 400 years or more after the period described, he seems to have had a rather light hand as an editor. As already mentioned, the poem of Chapter 5 retains an ancient form, and other chapters also seem not to have been heavily rewritten at a later time. Of course, the antiquity of a story does not guarantee accuracy of information, but it does indicate that the author was interested to some degree in preservation, and that is beneficial to the modern historian working on pre-monarchical Israel. Historians must be aware of legendary folk traditions that grow up around ancient persons and places; for example, fantastic elements of the Samson stories in Shophtim 14–16. A modern historian will also find interesting the several editorial asides in Shophtim where the editor tells his audience of certain reports or facts of the editor's own day (1.21, 26; 6.24; 10.4; 11.39–40).

In the centuries before the development of the monarchy in Israel (roughly 1200 to 1000 BCE), tribal groups and clans battled and skirmished with other tribal groups and clans, as portrayed in Shophtim. Egyptian hegemony over Canaan, what Egyptian sources often call *Retenu,* was on the decline since the death of Ramses III in 1153 BCE. The Philistines, part of the wave of immigration known as the Sea Peoples Movement, invaded Egypt but were repulsed by Ramses III in the early decades of the twelfth century, forcing the Philistines to move to Canaan. The Philistine came beginning in about 1180 and grew in power from their region of dominance on the coastal plain anchored by their five towns, Gaza, Gath, Ashdod, Ashkelon, and Ekron. Their increasing strength can be correlated to the migration of the tribe of Dan, unable to displace the Philistines, from the south to the north (Chapter 18) and is reflected in the local legends of Samson (Chapters 14–16). The growing strength and threat of the Philistines that led to the conclusion among Israelite clan leaders that a new form of defense and organization was needed—Israel needed a king (Stager 113–116). But for the author of Shophtim the problem is not the Philistines. The only problem is that the Israelites did not properly obey YHVH and so YHVH brought them military and social failure.

Finally, the singular perspective of the author that guided his selection and arrangement of stories must be taken into account. By the end of the scroll, the reader has the impression that life among these people must have been nightmarish, especially for women. But Shophtim does not bring us *all* the stories and *all* the facts. Ruth, another story of our library, is also set in this period of Shophtim, and

Study Room 6.2

MAKING MOVIES

The stories of Shophtim are some of the most unusual and shocking in ancient Israelite literature. They are not what comes to mind for most modern people when they think of a Bible story. The story of Ehud reaches its apex as the obese King Eglon is imagined to be defecating (Chapter 3). A rare story of female power has a woman pounding a tent peg through a sleeping general's skull (Chapters 4–5). One hero actually performs a child sacrifice of his own daughter (Chapter 11). The gang rape of a woman is particularly brutal and even graphic, but it is surpassed in its shock value by the horrific dismemberment of her body by her husband and local priest (Chapter 19). The mob violence that ensues from this in the name of justice is a grotesque and senseless travesty (Chapters 20–21).

It is an interesting exercise to compare these stories with similar material from one's own culture. What books or movies or news stories would you use to make comparisons? If you were to make a motion picture based on these stories, what rating would be given to your film? How does the violence of the stories serve the author's larger purpose, and what purpose does it serve in the books or movies you chose to compare?

under its impression, the period takes on a completely different atmosphere, and the author's attitude toward foreigners and intermarriage is distinctly different.

Questions for Further Study

1. Try to imagine these stories as they were told before being written down. How would they be told? What regional or clan characteristics would you hear? What settings would fit for their original telling? How might an audience react?

2. Try to imagine being the editor or compiler of these stories. What kind of stories would you want? What might be your selection criteria?

3. How would Israelite readers of the seventh and sixth centuries BCE who lived with troubled kingships or exiled kings engage these stories?

References

Ackerman, Susan. *Warrior, Dancer, Seductress, Queen: Women in Judges and Biblical Israel.* New York: Doubleday, 1988.

Boling, Robert G. *Judges.* Garden City, NY: Doubleday, 1975.

Boling, Robert G. "Judges" in *The Anchor Bible Dictionary,* edited by David N. Freedman, 3:1107–17. New York: Doubleday, 1992.

Gunn, David M. "Joshua and Judges," in *The Literary Guide to the Bible,* edited by Robert Alter and Frank Kermode. 102–21. Cambridge, MA: Harvard, 1987.

Hackett, Jo Ann. "'There Was No King in Israel': The Era of the Judges," in *The Oxford History of the Biblical World,* edited by Michael D. Coogan. 132–64. New York: Oxford, 1988.

Halpern, Baruch. *The First Historians.* San Francisco, Harper & Row, 1988.

Tov, Emanuel. *Textual Criticism of the Hebrew Bible.* 2nd ed. Minneapolis: Fortress, 2001.

Trible, Phyllis. *Texts of Terror: Literary-Feminist Readings of Biblical Narratives.* Philadelphia: Fortress, 1984.

שמואל

Samuel *Sh^emuel*

Section Outline

History and Composition
Literary Format and Movement
The Man Sh^emuel
Saul
David
The Text of Sh^emuel
Questions for Further Study
References

Joshua and Judges were narratives about the past that depicted from an ancient Israelite's perspective the early centuries of Israelite tribal confederacy and land occupation in Canaan. In our next scroll, *Sh^emuel*, pronounced "sheh-moo-*el*," another Israelite writes a narrative reflecting the succeeding years that saw increasing stability and the formation of a monarchy. The story told here is of a period with rich extra-biblical archaeological and historical records. The historical time frame covers roughly 75 years, the end of the eleventh century to the beginning of the tenth century BCE (ca. 1040 to 965 BCE). From the ancient author's perspective, his narrative shows the growing cooperation among groups of Israelites, YHVH's people, in the form of the establishment of kingship.

This scroll, the third longest in the library, might be of interest for several reasons.

- It houses the oldest preserved stories about David, the great hero of Jewish tradition, whose name is mentioned more often in the scrolls of our library than any human except Moses.
- Some historical events documented in other sources can be correlated with events in Sh^emuel.
- The ancient texts of Sh^emuel, including medieval Hebrew, ancient Greek, and the Dead Sea Scrolls, display hundreds of divergences; therefore, for anyone interested in the way ancient manuscripts were copied and altered, and errors were introduced, this scroll provides a lifetime of exploration.

- Recent literary scholars have shown the skilled craftsmanship with which many of these narratives were composed, weaving poetry, folklore, and other materials into an elaborate narrative. Careful reading can reveal much more than simple history.

We should remember from the opening chapter of this *Guided Tour* that Sh^emuel is really one long composition—only in later Greek and Latin forms was it divided into 1 and 2 Sh^emuel for the sake of convenience. Among the Dead Sea Scrolls is a copy of Sh^emuel (4Q51) from the first century BCE that does not split the book. But the division is followed in all modern Bibles and so for numbering purposes, we will follow it too. But for reading and analysis, it's all one book.

History and Composition

Egypt and the empires of Mesopotamia were not a major factor in the region of Canaan during this time. Instead, the major forces were local peoples—tribes, clans, and tribal federations—vying for control of towns, arable land, water resources, trade routes, and power. The Philistines, centered in the southern coastal plain, were growing in power and expanding east and north. The organizing Israelites spread out mostly in the central hill region. Our scroll presents an ancient

*L*ITERARY FORMAT AND MOVEMENT

The ancient author narrates Israel's movement toward kingship by focusing on three individuals, Sh^emuel, Saul, and David, and their complex interactions and clashes. Of the three, Sh^emuel and David are presented heroically, though tempered with an earthy realism. Saul, who has a love/hate relationships with both Sh^emuel and David, is a much more tragic figure. The narrative's larger plot centers on the nation of Israel and its God YHVH, who is in some sense the main character.

Sh^emuel	Saul	David
1 Sh^emuel 1.1–4.1a Birth and rise of YHVH's priest and prophet	1 Sh^emuel 13.1–31.13 First king's rise and fall—David's rise; stories of Saul's military defeat, YHVH's rejection; David anointed; David as hero; King Saul and the growing threat of David; death of Saul in battle with Philistines	2 Sh^emuel 1.1–8.18 Victory over Saul's house, expansion of power and kingdom
4.1b–7.2 War with Philistines and loss of Israel's sacred covenant box		9.1–20.26 Domestic failures and royal successes of David; David flees Jerusalem during civil war; David returns; royal sons vie for succession
7.3–12.25 Sh^emuel as judge leads Israel; choosing Saul as king		21.1–24.25 David's final acts and words

Jewish view of how the eleventh-century tribes of YHVH fought with surrounding tribes and how they came to organize themselves under leadership of a king. Religiously, the various people groups worshipped local Gods who were associated with people, towns, clans, and homes. Israelites, too, had various local shrines for the worship of YHVH, a few of which are mentioned in our scroll (1 Sh^emuel 1.3; 3.21; 7.5–11, 17; 16.1–3). As we learned from our historical review of Israelite religions in Chapter 2, some groups of Israelites also honored other deities, though the much later author of Sh^emuel did not approve and presented this history from a more ideal YHVH-only perspective.

The Man Sh^emuel

The man Sh^emuel serves as the author's major transition figure, bringing the Israelite story of disparate tribes to a unified nation. His introduction is as the miraculously born son of Hannah, using a motif common to Israelite authors, an aging, barren woman gifted by YHVH with a son (compare to Sarah in Genesis 17, Rebekah in Genesis 25, Rachel in Genesis 29, Samson's mother in Judges 13). Hannah, grateful for YHVH's blessing, dedicates her son Sh^emuel to the cultic service of YHVH, and as a boy priest Sh^emuel receives his first audible message and revelation from YHVH. Subsequent stories depict Sh^emuel in his role as priest as he conducts sacrifices and comes to oversee the important shrine at Shiloh, where he eclipses the sons of the priest Eli. But the author soon begins to add to Samuel's character dimension by depicting him as a *navi,* pronounced "nah-*vee,*" "prophet," which for our author means one who receives messages from YHVH (see Sh^emuel Chapter 3). As one to whom YHVH appears and speaks, Sh^emuel develops a growing reputation among Israelites as a trustworthy prophet.

Having built up this first protagonist's religious reputation, our scroll then turns to the war with the Philistines and the loss of Israel's sacred covenant box in Chapters 4–6, where Sh^emuel is strangely absent. This seemingly abrupt shift to a curious tale about the loss and return of a portable shrine with supernatural powers is a clue to a change in sources, but for the larger plot it serves to introduce to the story Israel's perennial enemy in the rest of the scroll and to demonstrate YHVH's power over Israel's enemies. Sh^emuel returns to the action in 7.3 and begins to play his large role as national leader and YHVH's chief prophet. But his task, pressed upon him and all Israel by the onslaught of the Philistines, is to lead the tribes in choosing a king who will organize and defend them. Scholars have long studied the section from 7.3–12.25 and noted the ambivalence of the narrator, his character Sh^emuel, and YHVH himself, toward the institution of kingship. Compare 1 Sh^emuel 9.1–20; 10.1–16; 11.1–15 with 8.1–22; 10.17–27; 12.1–25, the pro-kingship and anti-kingship passages. And indeed, kingship for Israel, both in its later reflective literature and in its history, turned out to be both blessing and curse. In our scroll specifically, the tension is seen with Saul, whose presentation leans to the negative, and no less in David, whose presentation leans to the positive. From a religious or theological standpoint, the narrative is a subtle tracing of the messiness of attempting to live under the rule of YHVH amid the geo-political realities of enemies, human ambitions, and human failings.

Community Reflections 6.2

☰ ✝

THE SONG OF HANNAH AND THE SONG OF MARY

Commentators noted long ago that Mary's *Magnificat,* the poem in the Christian New Testament book of Luke (1.46–55), is modeled after the poem presented as Hannah's in this scroll of Sh^emuel (1 Sh^emuel 2.1–10). Luke writes in Greek and, like most other early Christian writings, when he cites Jewish scriptures he naturally uses Greek translations of those books. Mary's song of Luke 1 was modeled after a Greek translation of Hannah's song in 1 Sh^emuel 2. In their respective stories, both Hannah and Mary are mothers whose children are miraculously conceived. Both poems use language that is much broader in scope than a single childbirth. Sh^emuel's poem is in typical Hebrew poetic form, and Luke's, though apparently composed in Greek, also exhibits some classical Hebrew form characteristics. Both poems likely existed independently at one time and were then placed into their respective narratives. In these two columns I have translated the first part of the Greek text of Hannah's song, on the left, and also the Greek texts of Mary's song, on the right. Note that if you compare the Sh^emuel column with an English translation of the Hebrew Sh^emuel, you will see several differences. The lines that are most similar are in bold.

. . . she (Hannah) prayed to Lord and said,	And Mary said,
My heart is strong in (the) Lord; my strength is exalted in my God.	**My soul magnifies the Lord;**
Over my enemies my mouth boasts,	**And my spirit rejoices in God my Savior,**
I rejoice in your salvation.	For he has looked with favor on the lowliness of his servant.
There is none holy as (the) Lord,	Surely, from now on all generations will call me blessed;
And there is none just as our God;	For the Mighty One has done great
None holy beside you.	things for me, and **holy is his name.**
Do not boast, and do not speak arrogance,	His mercy is for those who fear him
Do not let out words of greatness from your mouth,	from generation to generation.
Because a God of knowledge is (the) Lord,	**He has shown strength with his arm; he has scattered the proud in the thoughts of their hearts.**
And a God preparing his own plan.	**He has brought down the powerful from their thrones, and lifted up the lowly; he**
The bow of the mighty ones is weakened, and the weak ones gird on strength.	**has filled the hungry with good things, and sent the rich away empty.**
Those full of bread are brought low, and those hungry are furnish land,	He has helped his servant Israel, in remembrance of his mercy, according
Because a barren one has borne seven, and the one with many children is weakened.	to the promise he made to our ancestors, to Abraham and to his descendants forever.
	—Luke 1.46–55

(The) Lord kills and brings to life; he brings down to Hades/death and raises up.
(The) Lord makes poor and makes rich; he brings low, he exalts.
He raises up the poor from the dust; and from the dunghill he lifts the needy to sit with the princes of the people, bequeathing to them a throne of glory . . .
—1 Sh^emuel 2.1–7 (Greek)

Notice the similarity of forms, especially the opening lines. Even more significant are the shared motifs of the God humbling the rich and powerful and raising up the poor and weak. Both poems celebrate the power of the God on a broad social—even national—scale, and both women see the birth of their child as a manifestation of their God's great might. Both speak of God as the one who has brought them salvation. In fact the similarities go beyond the poems. Some commentators have noted other similarities in the childhood stories of Samuel and Jesus. For example,

Now the boy Samuel continued to grow both in stature and in favor with YHVH and with the people.
—1 Samuel 2.26

And Jesus increased in wisdom and in years, and in divine and human favor.
—Luke 2.52

Saul

Perhaps a more tragic figure is not encountered in our library than the character of Saul, or Shaul, pronounced "shah-ool," who is known traditionally as the first king of Israelite tribes. From the beginning of our scroll, he is presented as both great and defective and admirable and pitiful. In the complex character development of this scroll, Sh^emuel and YHVH at once favor him, yet his relationships with the prophet and Israel's God become irredeemably broken. Although David honors and respects Saul, their relationship becomes one of legendary rivalry and revenge. The author presents him as both high and low and often as a man of conflicted personality. Inspired by God's spirit, he leads Israelites in a great military victory (1 Sh^emuel 11), yet he commits suicide during a battle with the Philistines and his body is hung in disgrace on the walls of the Beth-Shan (1 Sh^emuel 31). Saul proves to be one the most fascinating character in ancient Israelite literature.

David

But David (pronounced "dah-*veed*" in Hebrew) would be an excellent choice for a character study, too! Historically, David's reign as a king can be placed at about 1005 to 965 BCE. The depiction of Israel's most inspiring and legendary king in Sh^emuel has been called nothing short of brilliant and among the best examples of ancient Hebrew prose. The long and intriguing story of David's rise to power is carefully plotted in accord with Saul's downfall. The two are inextricably intertwined. Shᵉmuel, YHVH's spokesperson in Israel, anoints David secretly in a ceremony of kingship, even while Saul is still king (1 Shᵉmuel 16). The conflict between the two anointed leaders is played out on many levels in the subsequent narrative.

David is presented as pious, charismatic, politically astute, and patient. He can also be a calculating and ruthless outlaw, and when necessary he is willing to align himself with Israelite enemies, the Philistines. From a large and most important tribe, Judah, he is also able to gain the support of other tribes and clans, and so he is capable of uniting Israelites as no one before him could. He captures the city of Jerusalem from the Jebusites, making it for the first time a Israelite town and a constant reminder of his own military prowess. He astutely chooses the site for his own capital, making the most of its previous independence from any Israelite tribe; the location is also important because it is between the tribal lands of Judah, David's tribe, and Benjamin, Saul's tribe. David had made a major stride toward kingship by marrying Saul's daughter, and his ambition enables him to obtain the throne. After Saul's death, he shrewdly and forcefully overcomes Saul's descendents and establishes himself as Israel's sole leader. For this small kingdom, he establishes some permanent institutions, such as a foreign bodyguard, scribes, a chancellor, and harem. Aware of the power of the priesthood, he makes his own sons priests, but he is also depicted as one genuinely devoted to YHVH. In the absence of international powers such as Egypt, David manages to defeat neighboring peoples, especially the Philistines, and so he establishes a small area of political and military influence outside of the hill country. Decades later, with the dynasty still intact, the kingdom of Judah is regarded by its neighbors as the "house of David," quoting a late-ninth-century inscription of the powerful Damascus king Hazael. With such success, is it any wonder that this story includes a tradition of YHVH selecting David and his descendants to reign forever in Jerusalem (2 Shᵉmuel 7.4–17)?

But David's ascent is not simplistically recounted; complexities and compromises abound. David is painted as a man of internal conflict, as a look at his relations with Saul will demonstrate. Consider, for example, one of the most hauntingly beautiful poems of our library, presented as David's eulogy to the fallen Saul in 2 Shᵉmuel 1. All is not well in the house of David. Even after Saul's death, David's kingdom still seems split along tribal lines just below the surface. He sometimes appears weak, unable to stand up to powerful men below him; sometimes he is pathetic. A secret sexual affair with a married woman leads him to arrange the murder of her husband, one of his most loyal soldiers. Ever concerned about his successor—after all, he had engaged in a long civil war to wrest the throne from the sons of Saul—he is unable to stop the violence among his own children, and the reader encounters painful stories of rape, murder, intrigue, and grief. Eventually David himself is forced to flee his own capital when his son Absalom attacks. The David portrayed by our author is great, heroic even, but he is not a flat, perfect, iconic David. The author is not just interested in character depiction; primary in the author's mind are the ways in which this newly founded monarchy lives in relation to YHVH. And David, in this regard, with all his failings, is presented as YHVH's chosen and, in contrast to Saul, he is never rejected as king. Such a view reinforces the legitimacy of David's royal descendants.

DISPLAY 6.1 | NINTH-CENTURY ARAMAIC INSCRIPTION OF BEN HADAD, KING OF ARAM, MENTIONING THE "HOUSE OF DAVID" FOUND AT TEL DAN IN NORTHERN ISRAEL

The Text of Sh‍ᵉmuel

You will recall from our entryway remarks (Chapter 1) that there are various ancient manuscripts from which modern Bibles are made, including Hebrew texts around 1000 CE, known as the Masoretic Texts (MT) the Dead Sea Scrolls in Hebrew that are not as complete but are about 1000 years older than MT, and the Septuagint from the fourth and fifth centuries. In the case of Shᵉmuel, students of the ancient manuscripts have for centuries noted that the medieval Hebrew texts, which provide the basis for most modern English Bible, have a much higher number of transmission problems and errors than most other texts of our library. For example, words or whole lines are missing, and there are some major content differences between the Hebrew manuscripts and ancient Greek ones. Some of these are easy to see in translations. Scholars also noted centuries ago that the Greek translations improved the situation and solved numerous problems. It was a great fortune when the discovery of the Dead Sea Scrolls brought to light several copies of the scroll of Shᵉmuel, one of which is quite extensive (4Q51), with parts of 47 out of 57 different columns.

These much older Hebrew manuscripts frequently match the Greek translations and disagree with the much later medieval Hebrew texts. They clearly indicate that at some point in the course of being copied through the centuries, many problems and errors became a part of the MT tradition in Sh^emuel that were not part of the Hebrew texts or the Dead Sea Scrolls. It is also clear that the Greek translations and the Dead Sea Scrolls do not solve all the problems—we'd love to have some more textual discoveries. If we look at just a few examples, we will see what kind of work is involved in textual criticism and what sort of decisions are constantly being made by producers and translators of modern Bibles.

Two Missing Numbers? 1 Sh^emuel 13.1

If you open many modern Bibles to 1 Sh^emuel 13.1, you will find a footnote or indication in the text alerting the reader to a problem in the Hebrew text. This is true, for example, of the New Revised Standard Version from the National Council of Churches (NRSV), the Jewish Publication Society's *Tanakh* (JPS), the Roman Catholic New Jerusalem Bible (NJB), and the New International Version from Christian evangelicals (NIV). Even the King James Version (KJV) in its original 1611 edition has a marginal notation of the difficulty. Unfortunately, the popular KJV editions of our time, which stem from the revised 1769 edition of the KJV, do not include many of the marginal notations. The problem is that a straight literal reading of the Hebrew words makes little sense, as you can see: "*A year old* was Saul when he began to reign; and *two years* he reigned over Israel." Obviously the correct numbers are missing, because Saul was not one year old when he became king, and he was not three when he died. So the translations indicate this problem in various ways, often by leaving blanks for the years. In this case, unfortunately, the Dead Sea Scrolls are of no help because this segment of Sh^emuel is not preserved, and the oldest Greek texts do not even have this verse; Greek versions moves directly from what in English Bibles is 12.25 to 13.2. Commentators and translators have been puzzling over these missing words for centuries. Some suggest that the original and sensible numbers were somehow lost. Others suggest that an early editor who inserted such chronological notices (see, for example, 2 Sh^emuel 2.10; 5.4) had actually left blanks to be filled in later. In later transmissions the blanks were not left in the new scroll—the scribe just ran all the words together even though the sense was not clear. In the case of "a year old," the Hebrew could easily make sense by inserting a number prior to *year,* such as *twenty,* which would then be rendered in English as "Saul was twenty years old . . ." The case of the "two years" is more complicated but, to simplify, it seems as if an original blank before "years" was filled by a simple and not uncommon copying mistake of repeating the Hebrew word for *years,* which is just one letter different from the Hebrew word for *two.*

A Missing Paragraph: 1 Sh^emuel 10–11

Probably the most dramatic example of missing text in Sh^emuel is the one we talked about in the "Rare Books Room" in Chapter 1 (Poster 1.4, page 20) There we saw that the much older edition of Sh^emuel from the Dead Sea Scrolls preserves a superior text, and so the editors of the New Revised Standard Version have included this older paragraph in their edition of Sh^emuel. Apparently, an ancient scribe had inadvertently omitted about 50 words from the middle of a military narrative, words that are vital for understanding the actions of King Saul and the Israelites.

A Difficult Difference: 1 Sh^emuel 1.23

The story at the beginning of Sh^emuel about Hannah is well worth reading for many reasons. A textual question arises about a conversation in the story: Does Hannah's husband say to her, (1) "may YHVH fulfill *his* word," or does he say, (2) "may YHVH fulfill what comes out of *your* mouth"?

The difference in meaning for the immediate context is quite significant: Whose word is to be fulfilled? In this case the medieval MT has (1), "his," and the Dead Sea Scroll and the Greek translation record (2), "your." The JPS, NRSV, and NIV all go with the MT's "his word," but all have footnotes indicating the alternative. Personally, I prefer (2) because I think it is easier to explain why a later scribe would change the reading from (2) to (1) than the reverse, and because the Dead Sea Scroll is so much older and has the support of the ancient Greek manuscripts. The major question textual critics have to answer in every decision is this: "What best explains all the evidence, including the differences in the manuscripts?"

Tall or Grande? 1 Sh^emuel 17.4

Less significant for the history of composition, but of interest to anyone who has heard of the story of David and Goliath, is another difference in the ancient manuscripts. In the Greek and Dead Sea Scroll (4Q51), Goliath in 1 Sh^emuel 17.4 measures up to four cubits and a span (over six feet), whereas in the MT and most English traditions he measures to six cubits and a span (over nine feet). This change likely came centuries ago when a scribe in the MT tradition probably added two cubits to Goliath's height by committing a fairly common copying mistake of transferring a nearby number (*six* in verse 7) associated with a nearly identical word (*cubit* in Hebrew is easily confused with *hundred* in Hebrew). A footnote in the NRSV points out the difference. Cultures using the major Greek texts, such as most early Christian communities and currently the Orthodox churches, have never had a nine-foot Goliath. A modern translator must decide whether to go with the older DSS scroll's and Greek's "four" or with the younger and English traditional "six."

Editorial Remark: 1 Sh^emuel 9.9

This last case has nothing to do with textual transmission difficulties or different text forms. Instead, it's about one simple sentence, most likely inserted by an editor, meant to explain a Hebrew word that he thought his readers might have difficulty understanding. The word that the editor thought archaic—or perhaps had negative connotations in his mind—was *roeh*, "seer," and he provides a parenthetical explanation, translating it as *navi*, "prophet." This indicates that by the time of the editor, the word *roeh* was thought to be old fashioned, though not necessarily obsolete. In this case, instead of simply updating the language by changing every *roeh* to *navi*, this remark was inserted. What might be the reason(s)?

These are just a few of the hundreds of examples of differences between the ancient manuscripts of Sh^emuel; they exist on every page. The NRSV, JPS, and NIV translations indicate many of the divergences among the medieval Hebrew, Greek, and Qumran texts, but by no means all. We should not think that the whole text is flawed or give up any claim to having a good sense of the ancient content of our scroll of Samuel. In fact, we have a very good sense of the contents of two ancient versions of Samuel. On the other hand, the textual realities—hard facts preserved in ancient manuscripts—are complex and sometimes confusing, and we should give up all dogmatic claims of knowing with certainty how the "original" text of Samuel read. Textual realities, not ideological bias, render such claims simply unwarranted. All modern text makers and translators are forced make decisions about which ancient text to represent in their modern editions.

Questions for Further Study

1. How do the roles of prophet, priest, and king interact in the narrative of Sh^emuel? What are the conflicts? What suggests underlying social tensions? Could these correspond with different sources?

2. If the author of Judges declares that Israel needs a king, does kingship work according to the author of Sh^emuel?

3. The science or art of textual criticism is exceedingly complex for the scroll of Sh^emuel. What are the questions about the textual history that intrigue you most? What difference does this complexity make for your understanding of the compositional history of biblical scrolls?

References

Alter, Robert. *The Art of Biblical Narrative.* New York: Basic Books, 1981.

Brenton, Lanulot. *The Septuagint with Apocrypha.* Reprinted. Peabody, MA: Hendrickson, 1986.

Klein, Ralph W. *1 Samuel.* Waco, TX: Word Books, 1983.

Levenson, Jon D. *Sinai and Zion.* San Francisco: HarperCollins, 1985.

McCarter, P. Kyle, Jr. *I Samuel,* Garden City, NY: Doubleday, 1980.

———. *Samuel,* Garden City, NY: Doubleday, 1984.

Rosenberg, Joel. "1 and 2 Samuel," in *The Literary Guide to the Bible,* edited by Robert Alter and Frank Kermode. 122–45. Cambridge, MA: Harvard, 1987.

Stager, Lawrence E. "Forging an Identity: The Emergence of Ancient Israel," in *The Oxford History of the Biblical World,* edited by Michael D. Coogan. 90–131. New York: Oxford, 1988.

Tanakh-The Holy Scriptures. New York: Jewish Publication Society, 1988.

Tov, Emanuel. "The Composition of 1 Samuel 16–18 in the Light of the Septuagint Version," in *Empirical Models for Biblical Criticism*, edited by Jeffrey H. Tigay. 97–130. Philadelphia: University of Pennsylvania, 1985.

——. *Textual Criticism of the Hebrew Bible.* 2nd ed. Minneapolis: Fortress, 2001.

Zevit, Ziony. *The Religions of Ancient Israel.* London: Continuum, 2001.

מלכים

Kings M*elakhim*

SECTION OUTLINE

Literary Format and Movement
Composition and Sources
History and Historiography
Organizing the Religious History
Prophets in M^elakhim
Religion and Writing
Questions for Further Study
References

This is the longest of all the scrolls in our library. If you like fast-moving history, with hundreds of years passing in the space of several pages, and curious and fascinating stories about kings, prophets, and Gods, this scroll will fascinate you, though it is not considered one of the most famous books. The scroll of Kings is a grand narrative covering a wide expanse of time, compiled and composed by an ancient Jewish historian with a story to tell from a particular perspective. The time period it is intended to cover corresponds to a period of history—approximately from the mid-tenth century to the mid-sixth century BCE—for which there are many sources available for the ancient Near Eastern scholar. If your interest is ancient history or archaeology, it means there are many ways to relate this scroll to other ancient writings and aspects of material culture unearthed by myriad archaeological discoveries. We may even call this scroll political history. But we must not expect modern academic historical research. Instead, we might call the scroll of M^elakhim an ancient religious history of the kings of Israel and Judah, or better, a review and evaluation of the kings and kingdoms Northern and Southern Israel, according to certain religious and theological ideals of some Jews dedicated to YHVH in the sixth or fifth century BCE.

The name of the book in Hebrew is M^e*lakhim*, pronounced "m'lah-*kheem*," with *kh* pronounced *ch* as in *Bach*, which simply means "kings." In this case the English and Hebrew names have the same meaning. In Greek manuscripts the

LITERARY FORMAT AND MOVEMENT

This fascinating scroll is sprawling in size and coverage and diverse in sources and genres, yet Mᶜlakhim is a highly organized and structured literary work. By its own counting it covers over 400 years and dozens of kings, and most of the time it moves quite rapidly. It is episodic in that it devotes much more time to some persons than to others, and there is no attempt to give equal space to all periods. But the ordered arrangement and massive coverage does not make for a pedantic or flat narrative. There are still surprising turns, riveting well-told stories, ambiguities reflecting a certain realism, and artistically textured individual episodes. Unlike the Samuel scroll, Mᶜlakhim is not structured around particular individuals, though there are some standouts.

- David functions as a remembered hero and model.
- Solomon, portrayed as magnificent, pious, and wise but also seriously flawed, is a major focus.
- Elijah the prophet is centralized in the narrative and stands out as the character who dramatically voices the narrator's religious outlook.
- Ahab, a king of the North, is vilified yet sympathetically and pathetically portrayed.
- Hezekiah, a king of the South, is praised for his YHVH-only faith and receives YHVH's miraculous protection, yet compromise and defeat are his, too.
- Josiah, a late king of the South, is presented by the author as the best thing since David, yet his depiction does not lack irony.

But the single character who dominates the narrative more than anyone else is YHVH. The narrator depicts him speaking and acting; he is on the lips of characters and in the author's historiographic evaluations. Without hesitancy, qualification or proffered verification, the author presents himself as knowing intimately YHVH's will, desire, and thoughts. The author fits all these fascinating characters into a chronologically demarcated narrative formation that marches along at a steady pace. This movement begins in hoary days of an independent kingdom of David and Solomon and ends in days of exile in Babylon.

Solomon
1 Kings 1.1–2.46 Death of David; Solomon's contest and triumph for throne
1 Kings 3.1–11.43 Reign of Solomon over all Israel

Division
1 Kings 12.1–14.31 Division of kingdom into two: Israel, the Northern Kingdom with King Jeroboam; and Judah, the Southern Kingdom, with King Rehoboam, Solomon's son

Early Kings
1 Kings 15.1–16.34 Kings of South and North; introduction of Ahab, King of Israel

Elijah and Elisha
1 Kings 17.1–2 Kings 9.37 Elijah the prophet of YHVH and Elisha his successor and their conflicts with Ahab of Israel

Fall of Israel
2 Kings 10.1–17.41 Northern and Southern Kingdoms until the fall of Israel to Assyria

Fall of Judah
2 Kings 18.1–25.30 Southern Kingdom until the fall of Judah to Babylon

name *Kingdoms* applies to what English Bibles have as 1 and 2 Samuel and 1 and 2 Kings: 1–4 Kingdoms. From one standpoint, the practice of linking them together is understandable: Mᶜlakhim does continue the storyline of Samuel. On the other hand, this scroll of Mᶜlakhim is quite different from Samuel in style, outlook, and approach to its subjects. The same person(s) did not do the major composition of the two scrolls. The fact that it continues the storyline of Samuel is indicative of the work of an editor or editors at some point fairly late in the scroll's history.

Composition and Sources

As you might expect with such a massive work from ancient Israel, a discussion about the sources used and the various levels of composition could be long and complicated but also fascinating if you like doing detective work with ancient manuscripts. Ancient Greek manuscripts do show significant variances from Hebrew manuscripts, though the differences are not as great as in the scroll of Samuel. As luck would have it, manuscripts of Mᶜlakhim found among the Dead Sea Scrolls, unlike those of Shemuel, are too fragmentary and minimal to be of much help in giving us our most ancient picture of this scroll. But because the primary goal of our *Guided Tour* is not to excavate the compositional history of each writing, we will not pursue the textual history and compositional questions at length, interesting and valuable though they are.

There are several competing ideas about the details of when and how the scroll was composed. Everyone recognizes that the last paragraph of the work brings the story down to about 560 BCE with the Jews in exile in Babylon, so obviously the work was concluded sometime after that, in the late decades of exile in Babylon or after the end of the exile in 538 BCE. Most scholars also hold that a good deal of the book was composed before this time and that the composition involved the utilization of older written resources, some of which are named in the text itself. Here are some of the citations:

- Book of the Deeds/Events of Solomon (1 Kings 11:41)
- Book of the Daily Deeds of the Kings of Judah (e.g., 1 Kings 14.29; 15.7, 23; 22.45)
- Book of the Daily Deeds of the Kings of Israel (e.g., 1 Kings 14.19; 15.31; 16.5, 14)

It is hard to know if these are all different works or if they are just descriptive titles, perhaps of just one or two scrolls. The books are usually cited at the conclusion of a narrative about a particular king and usually using formulaic text, such as "And more of the deeds of Yarabom, regarding warring and reigning, are written in the Book of the Daily Deeds of the Kings of Israel" (1 Kings 14.19).

The purpose of the notation is to indicate a source for specific and additional information. Unfortunately, none of these source documents were passed down, and excavations in Israel have not uncovered any documents that even resemble such a description. In other places of the ancient Near East, such as Assyria and Babylonia, many such state archives have come to light by the work of archaeologists. Therefore, it is easy for us to imagine similar accounts in Israel, both in Jerusalem and in Samaria, the capital cities of the Southern and Northern Kingdoms of Israel.

Besides these cited sources, investigators have detected others as well. Many scholars have thought that the first two chapters of Kings are from the same document as Samuel 9–20, an early court history of the Southern Kingdom and a literary gem. There is even a Greek version that divides Samuel and Kings differently; Samuel ends with the death of David, what we know as 1 Kings 2.11. Many scholars consider the middle section of the scroll, 1 Kings 17 through 2 Kings 9, to consist of prophetic traditions from a Northern source that was brought to Judah with refugees following the fall of the Northern Kingdom in 722. Some hold that a large part of the M^{e}lakhim scroll was compiled and written during the reign of Josiah (639 to 609 BCE) by leaders of a strong YHVH-only group that influenced Josiah toward his many religious reforms. Some have stressed the role of a Deuteronomic editor(s) who may have had a hand in editing major portions of Joshua, Judges, Samuel, and Kings. All these works are thought to reflect major religious tenets of the book of Deuteronomy. In all cases, researchers recognize that in keeping with writing conventions of ancient Israel the compilation, authoring, and editing of this scroll was a diachronic process involving many hands and that the final product presents Israel's past through the eyes of a Southern kingdom, strong YHVH-only, Jerusalem-centered author.

History and Historiography

Modern historians trying to reconstruct the actual events of 400 plus years covered by M^{e}lakhim need to use all of the sources at their disposal. A great deal of detailed evidence of the material culture of Israel unearthed by archaeologists comes from this period, including the oldest known Israelite inscriptions and several inscriptions of neighboring cultures that mention Israel. If you like to excavate, study artifacts, and read old documents, this is a period of Israel's history that can easily draw you in. This material can also enlighten your reading of Kings, especially if you are curious about the historical realities behind literary texts.

One of the oldest Hebrew writings we have from Israel does not help us much with political history in the scroll of M^{e}lakhim, but it does remind and reinforce for us the importance of agriculture. Remember the Israelite agricultural calendar we looked at in Chapter 3 (page 76)? It is dated to about 900 BCE. Ancient Israelites of this period were part of an agrarian society in which most people were involved in food production. Therefore, historians writing about politics, religion, poetry, or any thing else must always bear in mind the agricultural issues that affected every aspect of culture, from cult offerings and royal land holdings, to poetic metaphors and ideas about God and covenant.

DISPLAY 6.2 | INSCRIPTION OF SHALMANESAR III, KING OF ASSYRIA

> . . . I approached the city of Qarqar. I razed, destroyed and burned the city of Qarqar, his royal city. 1,200 chariots, 1,200 cavalry, (and) 20,000 troops of Hadad-ezer of Damascus; 700 chariots, 700 cavalry, (and) 10,000 troops of Irhuleni, the Hamathite; **2000 chariots, (and) 10,000 troops of Ahab the Israelite . . .**

Translated by K. Lawson Younger, Jr., in Hallo 2003, 2:261–4.

There is also a significant amount of material evidence regarding realities of the religious situation during these centuries of Israelite monarchies. There are local shrines, household deities, and figurines of bulls, horses, Goddesses, and Gods. Other deities were honored along with YHVH; for example the Goddess Asherah is often mentioned either by name or as a figurine, also called an asherah, as are the Gods Baal and El. But the scroll of Mᵉlakhim derives from segments of society that argued that YHVH alone was to be regarded as the God for peoples of Israel. In fact, we could go so far as to say that Mᵉlakhim is a historical polemic against honoring any other Gods, with the story of Elijah the prophet of YHVH versus the prophets of another Canaanite God, Baal, being a classic example of polemic in narrative (1 Kings 18). This argument is also clear in the narrator's evaluation of every king (see below, "Organizing the Religious History"). Clearly what produced such a sustained polemic were the common practices of many individuals in the Northern and Southern Kingdoms in homes, local shrines, and royal properties. For more information, see especially Smith 2003 and Zevit 2001.

In addition to these artifacts from within the lands of Israel and Judah, several inscriptions from outside Israel are also of great importance if we want to reconstruct Jewish history during this time period. For example, one of the largest battles of the ancient Fertile Crescent was the Battle of Qarqar in 853 BCE, which pitted the expanding Assyrian empire of Shalmaneser III (reigned 858 to 824) against a coalition of forces from across Syria-Palestine. One of the leaders of the coalition was the Israelite king Ahab, who led the largest contingent of chariots to the battle. In typical Assyrian fashion, Shalmaneser claimed a great victory, but in fact Ahab and the coalition managed to stave off Assyrian aggression for some time; however, the Assyrian presence was now a reality in

Syria-Palestine. We learn of Ahab's participation not from Israelite sources, but from Assyrian records, on a stele found on the northern Tigris at Kurkh, in present-day Turkey (Display 6.2).

We should also mention Mesha, king of Moab, who set up a monument to commemorate victories over the Israelite kings Ahab and his father Omri during the ninth century BCE (Display 6.3). Our scroll also speaks of these conflicts, but from a later Jewish point of view (see 2 Kings 3). This meter-high stele gives an excellent look at how ancient Moabites viewed their relations to Israel and allows many comparisons with Israelite thought. For example, the Moabite writer believed that a recent Israelite military victory over Moab was allowed by the Moabite God Khemosh because he was angry with the people of Moab. But later victories over Israel are credited to Khemosh, and the dwelling place of Khemosh is restored. Similar to narratives in the scroll of Joshua, Mesha practices *kherem,* the complete destruction of all human life in enemy towns, dedicating and massacring them to God. As was common practice, Israelite prisoners of war are put to work in Moab. Khemosh, like YHVH (e.g., 1 Samuel 15.3, 1 Kings 22) is though to give direct commands to go to battle. Finally, we also see that even in the ninth century, Moab knows of tribal distinctions within Israel.

But the authors of our scroll are not concerned about compiling all the available evidence and providing a broad overview of what Israelite life was like during this long period. For a modern historian, it would be astonishing and inexcusable to write a history of the reign of King Ahab (reigned 873 to 852 BCE) and not mention his participation and leadership in the great Battle of Qarqar. Yet even though the author of our scroll dedicates a great deal of time to Ahab (1 Kings 16–22), he gives not the slightest hint of this great battle. Clearly this is not a typical political history. The historiographic objective of Mᵉlakhim was to narrate how the kings of Israel and Judah displeased YHVH their God and, despite the warnings of prophets and many disciplinary acts of YHVH, how they violated YHVH's covenant by allowing the worship of other Gods, thus leading to the ultimate destruction of both kingdoms as YHVH's punishment. In writing about Ahab, the events that serve the purpose of the narrator are not the king's domestic or foreign triumphs; what matters are his conflicts with YHVH's prophets, his marriage to a Phoenician princess who advocated the worship of Baal in Israel, and his support of non-YHVH cults. The major history of Mᵉlakhim is the storyline that unites the entire work: Israel and Judah displease YHVH and so they are punished. Although there are many fascinating stories along the way, this central theme is never lost.

Organizing the Religious History

Mᵉlakhim begins with the famed and beloved David about to die. By the time Mᵉlakhim nears completion, hundreds of years after David, Israel's first successful king is a distant and venerated hero in many Jewish memories, farther back in time George Washington is from us today. Who could possibly fill his shoes? What will become of his kingdom? Will his successor(s) relate to YHVH as he was supposed to

DISPLAY 6.3 | MESHA'S MONUMENT

I am Mesha . . . king of Moab . . . And I made this high place *(sanctuary)* for Kemosh . . . because he delivered me from all kings (?), and because he had made me look down on all my enemies. Omri was the king of Israel, and he oppressed Moab for many days, for Kemosh was angry with his land. And his son *(Ahab)* succeeded him, and he said—he too— "I will oppress Moab!" In my days did he say [so], but I looked down on him and on his house, and Israel has gone to ruin, yes, it has gone to ruin forever! And Omri had taken possession of the whole lan[n]d of Medeba, and he lived there (in) his days and half the days of his son, forty years, but Kemosh [resto]red it in my days . . .

And the men of Gad *(Israelite tribe)* lived in the land of Ataroth from ancient times, and the king of Israel built Ataroth for himself, and I fought against the city, and I captured it, and I killed all the people [from] the city as a sacrifice (?) for Kemosh and for Moab . . .
And Kemosh said to me: "Go, take Nebo from Israel!". . . and I took it, and I killed [its] whole population, . . . for I had put it to the ban for Ashtar Kemosh. And the king of Israel had built Jahaz . . . and Kemosh drove him away before my face . . .
And I cut out the moat (?) for Karchoh by means of prisoners from Israel . . .

Translated by K. A. D. Smelik in Hallo, 2003, 2:137–38. Items in italics are mine.

Poster 6.2

Israel and Judah's Monarchs Mentioned in MeLakhim

Approximate Dates BCE

Monarchs of United Israel

David	1005 to 965
Solomon	968-928

Southern Monarchs

Northern Monarchs
Founders of dynasties are underlined.

Southern Monarchs		Northern Monarchs	
Rehoboam (son of Solomon)	924-907	Jeroboam I (son of Nebat)	924-903
Abijah	907-906	Nadab	903-902
Asa	905-874	Baasha	902-886
Jehoshaphat	874-850	Elah	886-885
Jehoram	850-843	Zimri	885
Queen Athaliah (wife of Jehoram)	843-837	Omri	885-873
		Ahab	873-851
Joash	837-?	Ahaziah	851-849
Amaziah	?-?	Jehoram	849-843
Azariah	?-?	Ahaziah	843
Jotham	?-742	Jehu	843-816
Jehoahaz I	742-727	Jehoahaz	816-800
Hezekiah	727-698	Joash	800-785
Manasseh	697-642	Jeroboam II	785-745
Amon	642-640	Zechariah	745
Josiah	639-609	Shallum	745
Jehoahaz II	609	Menahem	745-736
Jehoiachin	608-598	Pekahiah	736-735
Jehoiakim	598-597	Pekah	735-732
Zedekiah	597-586	Hoshea	732-722
Babylonian destruction and exile		Assyrian destruction and exile	

Dates reflect Miller in *Oxford Companion to the Bible*, 391, modified.

have done? An intriguing story is told of Solomon's fight for the throne against David's oldest son Adonijah followed by a long account of Solomon's 40-year reign. Solomon—in Hebrew it is Sheomo—is depicted as magnificent and pleasing to YHVH in many ways, most notably in his building of YHVH's magnificent temple in Jerusalem. Yet the author does not shy away from also describing another side of

Sh^{c}omo; he allowed the worship of other Gods in his kingdom, and this was the worst of all sins for our author. For this reason "YHVH was mad at Solomon" (1 Kings 11.9) and began to punish him by raising up enemies against him. In the eyes of the M^{c}lakhim author, the ripping apart of the kingdom between Solomon's son Rehoboam and a rival, Jeroboam, was YHVH's punishment of Solomon's sins. This depiction of Solomon sets the tone and prefigures the events for the rest of the scroll. The rest of the book is an evaluation of 20 Southern rulers and 19 Northern kings, based on their faithfulness to YHVH as measured by their advocacy for and enforcement of YHVH-only worship and their honoring of YHVH's cult in Jerusalem.

The writer of M^{c}lakhim usually follows a formula to introduce and evaluate each king. These formulas provided the constant ordering—both chronological and religious—to the entire scroll. His chronological scheme uses a relative dating system of the kings of Israel and Judah, as we can see in the following example. The kings of the Northern Kingdom, Israel, are introduced this way:

> In the _____ year of King _____ of Judah, _____, the son of _____, began to reign over all Israel at Samaria [or another capital], and he reigned for _____ years. He did evil in the eyes of YHVH, and he walked in the ways of Jeroboam and in the sin that he instigated in Israel.

For examples, including variations, see 1 Kings 15.33, 16.8, 15, 29–30; 2 Kings 3.1; 13.1–2. Northern kings are also given a concluding formulaic summary of their reigns at their death.

> And more of the deeds of _____ and all that he did are written in the Book of the Daily Deeds of the Kings of Israel. And _____ slept with his fathers and was buried at _____; and _____ his son reigned after him.

For examples, including variations, see 1 Kings 14.29; 15.31; 22.39–40; 2 Kings 10.34–35.

This line of succession was often broken by coups during the approximately 220 years of the separate existence of the Northern Kingdom. What is crucial to note about all of these Northern kings is that not one of the 19 receives a favorable evaluation from YHVH according to the author of M^{c}lakhim. And this is not surprising, for the kings of the Northern Kingdom did not worship or advocate worship at the temple in Jerusalem, which was not even in their territory. They had their own shrines to YHVH and associate deities in the towns of Dan and Bethel, the last of which was a sacred site in ancient Israelite tradition, associated with the patriarchs Abraham and Jacob (see Genesis 12.8; 31.13). For M^{c}lakhim, the perfect and exact explanation of Israel's destruction by Assyria is this: YHVH destroyed them for their unfaithfulness to the covenant he had made with them. This religious claim is spelled out clearly and at length at the end of the narrative about Israel. As you read the following passage, notice how the central message of the scroll is restated and encapsulated here:

> And the king of Assyria attacked all the land and he attacked Samaria and he besieged it three years. In the ninth year of Hoshea [king of Israel] the king of Assyria captured

Samaria and exiled Israel to Assyria and settled them in Halah and at Habor, the River Gorzan, and the towns in Media. And this was because the Israelites sinned against YHVH their God who had brought them from the land of Egypt from under the hand of Pharaoh king of Egypt, and they honored other Gods and they walked in the customs of the peoples which YHVH dispossessed right before the Israelites and [because of] the what the kings of Israel did. And they committed things not right against YHVH their God: They built high places (shrines) in all their towns, from watchtower to fortified town; and they set up for themselves images and figurines/asherahs on every high hill and under every leafy tree; and they sacrificed there at all the high places (shrines) as the peoples that YHVH exiled before them; and they did evil things to provoke YHVH. And they served fetishes that YHVH had told them not to do.

And YHVH warned Israel and Judah through every prophet and every seer saying, "Return from your evil ways and keep my commands and my laws according to the instruction which I commanded your fathers and which I sent to you through my servants the prophets." And they did not listen and they stiffened their necks as their fathers who were not faithful to YHVH their God. And they despised his laws and his covenant that he made with their fathers and his warnings with which he warned them. And they walked after delusions and were deluded, and after the peoples who surrounded them whom YHVH commanded them not to do as they did . . .

So YHVH was very angry at Israel and removed them from before him; none remains except the tribe of Judah alone. (2 Kings 17.5–15, 18)

Southern kings do not fare much better according to our scroll. Though they all worshipped in Jerusalem at the shrine built by Solomon, most of them also continued Solomon's tradition of allowing for the worship of other deities. However, the Southern kings, according to M^elakhim, have a continuous unbroken line of succession from David all the way through the 400 years of the narrative, and so our author is most interested in them and usually provides more information about them in his introductions:

> In the __ year of _____, king of Israel, _____ began to reign over Judah. He reigned for ___ years in Jerusalem. And the name of his mother was _____, daughter of _____. And he did what was right/wrong in the eyes of YHVH . . .

The last sentence usually ends with a particular comparison; bad kings are said to "walk in the ways of the kings of Israel" or "in the way of Ahab," and good ones are often compared to David. For examples and variations, see I Kings 14.21; 15.9–11; 2 Kings 8.16, 25; 14.1–3. The concluding formula generally follows this pattern:

> More of the deeds of _____ and all that he did are written in the Record of the Daily Deeds of the Kings of Judah. And _____ slept with his fathers and they buried him in the city of David and _____ his son reigned after him.

For examples and variations, see 1 Kings 5.7–8; 2 Kings 8.23–24; 14.18; 15.6–7. Judah's list of 20 rulers includes one queen, Athaliah, who ruled for not much more than five years around 840 BCE. The author did not approve of her at all; nor of many others. The rulers of Judah fall into three basic categories.

- Twelve who do what is evil by supporting non-YHVH worship and non-Jerusalem shrines
- Six who are personally devoted to YHVH but nevertheless allow non-YHVH worship and non-Jerusalem shrines to exist during their reigns
- Two who work to reform Judah by destroying all non-YHVH worship and all non-Jerusalem shrines. These two were Hezekiah (ca. 715 to 687) and Josiah (639 to 609 BCE), both of whom are highly praised. The praise of these two kings (see 2 Kings 18.5 and 23.25) has led many to speculate that a significant portion of M\u1d49lakhim had its origin during the days of Hezekiah or Josiah. Notice how Josiah's good works are described in detail, his faithfulness to YHVH's covenant is highlighted, and this conclusion is given:

> There was no king before him like him, who turned to YHVH with all his heart, and all soul, and all his strength, according to all the instruction of Moses; nor did any arise after him like him. (2 Kings 23.25)

It seems particularly noteworthy that David is not even mentioned; Josiah seems to outrank even him on the scale of total dedication to YHVH. Does this language sound familiar? If we go now and compare this quote and several others in the Josiah narrative with passages in Deuteronomy such as 6.5 and 17.17–20, 29.1–20, we will see why many people think that there are strong connections between parts of M\u1d49lakhim and Deuteronomy.

But no matter how good Hezekiah and Josiah might have been, the Judaites in M\u1d49lakhim are marching inevitably toward destruction. In fact, the narrator's major theological and religious explanation of Judah's downfall comes right on the heels of the pious description of Josiah.

> But YHVH did not turn from the burning of his great wrath that blazed against Judah because of all the torments done by Manasseh. And YHVH said, "Judah also I will remove from before my face even as I removed Israel, and I will reject this city which I chose, Jerusalem, and the house in which I said my name would be." (2 Kings 23.26–27)

After this notice, the narrative of the final collapse of Judah begins. This is the end to which the book has been driving. The chronology and record of kings is not done for the sake of academic research. In fact, M\u1d49lakhim seems to use a couple different counting systems that do not coincide. For example, the numbers in 2 Kings 3.1 cannot be reconciled with those of 2 Kings 1.17 because Jehoram could not have begun his reign in both the second and the eighteenth year of Jehoshaphat. But such discrepancies mean nothing for the major purpose of the writing: to show how Judah and Israel were unfaithful to YHVH.

Prophets in M\u1d49lakhim

Throughout this narrative about kings, hundreds of prophets frequently appear. The good ones always function to bring the message of YHVH, and they are frequently sought out for a word from YHVH by the kings. They have a range of knowledge and experience unequalled by anyone else in the narratives: They know YHVH's will intimately; see visions; are transported; and interact with great kings, foreign and domestic, as well as destitute widows. In most stories they are accorded great respect as spokespersons for YHVH, and some of the most curious and fascinating stories of all of M^elakhim are told about them. It might be said that a continuous subplot of the narrative is the actions and conflicts of prophets. They are sometimes pitted against other prophets, such as those of the Canaanite God Baal who contests with Elijah on the top of a mountain. The long section in the middle of the scroll focuses on the Northern prophets Elijah and Elisha, and Elijah in particular is presented as another Moses, who was the greatest of all prophets according to Deuteronomy. The prophets here do not so much function as critics of social justice systems; they are most often predictors of YHVH's punishments, which are subsequently fulfilled in the narrative, and they are courageous advocates for YHVH-only worship (e.g., 1 Kings 18). They are often depicted as persons of power and authority. Huldah, for example, was the prophetess to whom the heroic Josiah and temple priest looked for an authoritative word from YHVH and for an interpretation of a sacred scroll (2 Kings 22). At other times their power is more spectacular and miraculous—outlandish, even—as when Elijah calls down fire from heaven (1 Kings 18.20–40), and Elisha curses a group of small boys who were making fun of his baldness so that two bears come out of the woods and maul 42 of them (2 Kings 2.23–24). Such stories function in the narrative as reinforcements of prophetic power, their YHVH-granted authority, and of course, of YHVH's power over other Gods.

One other story we should mention demonstrates that M^elakhim is not blind to the fact that prophets of YHVH disagreed among themselves about YHVH's messages. Just because a prophet spoke what she or he claimed was a message from YHVH, did not make her or him immune from the charge that he did not speak accurately or with authority. 1 Kings 22 contains an intriguing story of 400 prophets of YHVH led by Zedekiah who are opposed by one prophet of YHVH named Micaiah. Micaiah dramatically claims that YHVH himself sent a lying spirit to trick his own prophets, except for Micaiah, of course! Well, the 400 certainly would not accept the idea that YHVH deliberately lied to them, and they accused Micaiah of not even having a legitimate message from the spirit of YHVH. The story is so fascinating and reveals many things, including the reality that in ancient Israel there were many prophets who claimed to have messages from YHVH, yet their messages could often be contradictory. It was no easy matter for kings, priests, and commoners to know whom to believe. Who was speaking the true words of YHVH? The claims were many; the proofs were elusive.

Finally we must mention that it is a matter of great curiosity that hardly any of the 15 so-called classical prophets are mentioned in this extensive narrative that deal frequently with other prophets. Only Isaiah (2 Kings 19–20) and Jonah (2 Kings 14.25) find their way in. The literature of these classical prophets was being collected and written during the same period that Kings is being composed, and it is hardly conceivable that those involved with the formation of M^elakhim were unaware of some of these public figures. Isaiah and Jeremiah, for example, were prominent individuals in Jerusalem, and the scrolls that bear their names have many passages that depict them as deeply involved in the events in M^elakhim. In several cases one author has directly borrowed from another. Yet to read M^elakhim one would never know that they even existed. Such silence may be explained several ways, and a variety of disputes between prophets and authors can be reasonably imagined. In any case, it should certainly give us pause before we entertain the idea that we have anything like an integrated and complete picture in our scroll of ancient Israel and her prophets and priests. There are likely polemics involved here and different conceptions of what constituted proper prophecy. In any case, our scrolls reflect distinct perspectives and do not necessarily attempt to incorporate all other perspectives, even ones that may have been contemporary.

Religion and Writing

M^elakhim's overall viewpoint and religious conclusion could hardly be clearer: failure to serve only YHVH resulted in the downfall of both kingdoms. Even so on religious and literary levels, the scroll is not without its subtleties. David, Solomon, Elijah, and even the evil Ahab are complex characters, not cartoon figures. Yes, true prophets speak YHVH's words directly, but the author knows it is no simple matter. Even prophets of YHVH disagree and must sometimes resort to claiming that YHVH himself is responsible for the false words of others (1 Kings 22). Josiah is as obedient to YHVH as one could be, yet he meets a bitter bloody end in battle (2 Kings 23.29–30), not the peaceful end predicted by the prophetess (2 Kings 22.18–20).YHVH engages in deception and his words through his prophets do not always come true At the end of M^elakhim's long march to destruction and exile, the scroll closes with a faint flicker of hope. The last paragraph, an epilogue of sorts, reveals that Judah's last king has not died. He is alive, out of prison, and being well treated by the king of Babylon. The point is not explicit, only subtle, and open to various interpretations. There are no celebrations, and no optimistic theological commentary to tell the audience the meaning. But, a king of Judah is still alive. And our author too, despite the disasters that had befallen his people, had hope for a future for his community.

Questions for Further Study

1. For what sorts of people is this scroll? Who will read it? How does the author view various types of people, such as women, royalty, peasants, and farmers, and what social hierarchies are assumed or advocated?

2. Religiously what is important to the author? What are his priorities?

3. What do you think of the scroll's conclusion? How does it fit? What response or emotion does it evoke?

References

Fritz, Volkmar. *1 & 2 Kings*. Translated by Anselm Hagedorn. Minneapolis: Augsburg Fortress, 2003.

Jones, G. H. *1 and 2 Kings*. 2 vols. Grand Rapids, MI: Eerdmans, 1984.

Cogan, Mordechai. *1 Kings*. Garden City, NY: Doubleday, 2001.

Cogan, Mordechai and Hayim Tadmor. *2 Kings*. Garden City, NY: Doubleday, 1988.

Hallo, William W. *The Context of Scripture*. 3rd ed. Leiden: E. J. Brill, 2003.

Holloway, Steven W. "Kings, Book of," in *The Anchor Bible Dictionary*, edited by David N. Freedman, 4:69–83. New York: Doubleday, 1992.

Savran, George. "1 and 2 Kings" in *The Literary Guide to the Bible*, edited by Robert Alter and Frank Kermode. 146–64. Cambridge, MA: Harvard, 1987.

Smith, Mark S. *The Origins of Biblical Monotheism*. New York: Oxford University, 2003.

Zevit, Ziony. *The Religions of Ancient Israel*. New York: Continuum, 2001.

7

Prophets *Neviim* Part II

CHAPTER OUTLINE

Prophetic Oracles

We could spend a long time talking about the figure of the prophet in ancient Israel and in surrounding lands. It is a fascinating study from many angles. It can involve historical detective work, sociological and anthropological models, and rhetorical and literary questions. But we'll just stop for a moment to present a few background historical realities about ancient prophets that will help us before we start reading the next four scrolls, which are mostly prophetic oracles.

Like many cultures, the Israelites had members of society who claimed to know and speak messages from their God(s). Besides priests and ocassionally kings, the most common group of people who made such claims were known as prophets. In Hebrew several designations were used for what we think of as a prophet: *navi,* "called one, speaker"; or *roeh,* "seer"; and *khozeh,* "visionary." Although *navi* predominates in our scrolls, clearly in ancient Israel there were some contentions about which terms were best suited (1 Samuel 9.9, Amos 7.14). Our English word *prophet* actually comes from a Greek word with the same meaning. If we had to give a descriptive definition for prophets in ancient Israel, we might say that prophets were public poets who proclaimed messages they credited to a God, usually YHVH, in the towns and villages of Israel. They numbered in the hundreds—many more than for which we have names—and included both men and women. They were not unique to Israel; all surrounding peoples also had prophets who spoke messages credited to their Gods. Many of them seemed to have possessed impressive poetic and oratorical skills—they were more artists with a mission than screaming preachers. Some were a part of the temple establishment or part of the royal court advisors. Others seem to have been independent. 1 Kings 22 illustrates both kinds. There were schools to train prophets, and many had official status in society. They often delivered oral messages, or oracles, with great flair and creativity, and sometimes their words were accompanied by startling symbolic gestures or acts, nudity, and music. Some seem to have spoken from a state of ecstasy or frenzy. Some spoke at great personal risk against powerful kings, priests, or influential members of society. They could be popular and entertaining, but they could also be despised and endangered because of their willingness to offend. They often spoke out against other prophets with whose messages they disagreed. Finally, we should mention that, unlike the popular understanding of prophecy today that we might gain from tabloids, television preachers, and prophecy conferences in evangelical churches, ancient prophecy in Israel was so much more than telling the future. A prophet would often speak of the past or the present, delivering a message about YHVH's action or about matters of social concern.

The scrolls that come next are not transcripts of the oral presentations of prophets. Instead, we can think of the development of these scrolls this way: some prophets made such an impression that their oracles or speeches were sometimes written down, probably by other people such as students or scribes. The vast majority of these oracles are written in poetic form, which seems likely to reflect an earlier oral form. This process of writing and collecting oracles seems to have begun in the eighth century BCE. Later groups of speeches were collected and placed in a larger collection, a sort of anthology, which was sometimes given an editorial framework. These anthologies were constantly in process in an effort to make them current and relevant to a new generation. Their editors were not inhibited by our modern concerns with copyright or authorship. These collections could be shaped, edited, supplemented by students or later prophets of later generations. Whole new poems might even be composed and added. In some cases, narratives and editorial frameworks were combined with the oracles. Updating of prophetic oracles can often be observed if we know what to look for. The scribes, editors, and prophets were not collecting the museum documents of a great speaker of the past; they were providing written forms of YHVH's message for their own time.

Community Reflections 7.1

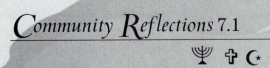

THE GREATEST PROPHET

The designation of prophet is used by all three of the Abrahamic religions and can be applied to numerous persons, including Moses, Jesus, and Muhammad. Although those three have other important designations as well, that of prophet is certainly among the most prominent and important in the traditions, especially with the meaning of "one who speaks God's will." Not surprisingly, each religion presents its particular prophet as the greatest of all.

Judaism

The scroll of Deuteronomy contains the first example from any Abrahamic tradition for the claim that Moses is the greatest prophet. Likely stemming from the sixth or seventh century BCE, the entire scroll is presented as Moses, final words, and the concluding paragraph declares that Moses is the greatest prophet Israel has ever seen.

> No prophet like Moses has ever arisen in Israel, whom YHVH knew face to face, with all the signs and marvels that YHVH sent him to do in the land of Egypt to Pharaoh and all his servants and all his land, and with all the strong might and all the great power that Moses displayed before the eyes of all Israel. (Deuteronomy 34.10–12)

Christianity

In the New Testament a succinct, easily quoted statement to the effect that Jesus is the greatest prophet is not to be found. However, in numerous passages the Gospel writers present him as a prophet, and in numerous ways his primacy is presented. Matthew's Gospel presents him as the new and great Moses, John's presents him as the great "word of God" (John 1), and a story in mark links him with the prophets Moses and Elijah, with special instructions from heaven to listen to Jesus (Mark 9.2–8). For Christian authors, Jesus is the one foretold by the earlier prophets and the one they point to as God's greatest spokesperson (e.g., Luke 24.27; John 1.45; Acts 3.22). It is clear that Jesus is a greater revealer of God's will than Moses.

> Long ago at many times and in many ways God spoke to our ancestors through the prophets, in these last days he has spoken to us by a son [Jesus] . . . (Hebrews 1.1–2)

Islam

The Qur'an speaks often of the importance of earlier prophets and of the continuous chain of God's mouthpieces on earth. But Muhammad, often called The Prophet, is presented as the last and greatest in the line of prophets (5.21), God's universal messenger (34.28), foretold by earlier prophets, including Jesus (61.6). Consider also this statement:

> Muhammad is not the father of any of your men, but he is The Apostle of God, and the Seal of the Prophets . . . (Qur'an 33.40)

The next four scrolls—sometimes called the latter or classical prophets—contain some of the most fascinating poetry and some of the most interesting messages involving YHVH, social issues of the day, the past, and the future. These prophets often use great powers of imagination to paint spectacular pictures of the past, present, or future in ways that still capture our attention today. Have you ever heard the phrases "the lion shall lie down with the lamb," "beating swords into plowshares," **"the Day of the Lord"** *(YOM YHVH),* or "let justice flow down like water"? These are all phrases from these scrolls. Given the variety of viewpoints among prophets, we should also expect that a great deal of variety on many issues to be found in these scrolls. Three of the scrolls are named after three individual prophets, Isaiah, Jeremiah, and Ezekiel. The fourth scroll is called The Twelve because it actually is a collection of twelve originally separate compositions, which, because they were so short, were written onto one physical scroll for better convenience and preservation. These twelve are sometimes called the minor prophets, not because they or their works are unimportant, but because these twelve writings are so short. In fact, the twelve combined are not as long as any one of the three major prophets. On the other hand, each one of these short writings has its own history and integrity, and so in the following discussion, we will be sure to treat each of these twelve with the individual treatment they merit.

References

Blenkinsopp, Joseph. *A History of Prophecy in Israel,* rev. ed. Louisville, KY: Westminster/John Knox, 1996.

Brueggemann. *The Prophetic Imagination.* Philadelphia: Fortress, 1978.

Heschel, Abraham J. *The Prophets.* 2 vols. New York: Harper, 1962.

Koch, Klaus. *The Prophets.* 2 vols. Translated by Margaret Kohl, Philadelphia: Fortress, 1982.

Lang, Bernhard. *Monotheism and the Prophetic Minority.* Sheffield, England: Almond, 1983.

The New Interpreter's Bible, Vols. 6, 7. Nashville, TN: Abingdon, 1996, 2001.

Nissinen, Martti. *Prophets and Prophecy in the Ancient Near East.* Atlanta: Society of Biblical Literature, 1993.

Petersen, David L., ed. *Prophecy in Israel.* Philadelphia: Fortress, 1987.

ישעיהו

Isaiah *Yᵉshayahu*

SECTION OUTLINE

Literary Format and Movement

Compositional History

The World of Yᵉshayahu of Yᵉrushalayim

The World of Yᵉshayahu of Babylon

Oracles of Criticism

Oracles Inspiring Trust and Hope

Poetry and Pictures

Questions for Further Study

References

This scroll is a goldmine. Probably the most famous of Israel's classical prophetic writings, words from this scroll have echoed through the ages in minds, poems, religious writings, and music. This undoubtedly has to do with the compelling quality and content of poetry found in the scroll, which has attracted many readers and interpreters in later times. In the first centuries after it was penned, it was already a favorite composition among some Jews, such as the authors of several of the Dead Sea Scrolls, and also several early Christian authors.

The scroll is named after the a prophet Yᵉshayahu, pronounced "yᵉshah-ya-hoo," who, historians believe, lived in Jerusalem at the end of the eighth century. The author of 2 Kings (Chapters 19–20) writes about him. This is significant because none of the other classical prophets is mentioned in the narratives of our library, except for Jonah. The author of Chronicles also mentions Yᵉshayahu as an author of a work about Hezekiah (2 Chronicles 32.32), who ruled as king in Judah from about 727 to 698 BCE. Our scroll does contain some narrative about Hezekiah, but is our scroll the one the chronicler has in mind? Hezekiah is a main figure in the narrative section in Isaiah 36–39. But many scholars doubt that our scroll is the one referred to because the material we have about Hezekiah in Yᵉshayahu is not at all complete. Interestingly, the author of Chronicles also says that Isaiah also wrote a full account of the life of Uzziah, an earlier king in Jerusalem (2 Chronicles 26.22), but our scroll is certainly not that

LITERARY FORMAT AND MOVEMENT

On a literary level the scroll is quite mixed. It is mostly made up of oracles, frequently introduced with formal claims of YHVH's authority. These oracles are mostly poetic, as we expect from prophetic literature. But there are prose narrative segments also, some of which are historically oriented, while other prose segments are part of oracles. There is also some first-person narrative of the prophet (Chapters 6 and 8) as well as some third-person prose about Yᵉshayahu (e.g., 7.3). The content and subject matter of the scroll do not move in some obvious pattern that readers can easily see, and many wonder if it had an overall plan or design; therefore, the scroll can be difficult and confusing. It seems to many scholars that the content of the scroll evolved over a long period, and there was not a heavy-handed final editor shaping the work into a clear pattern. This gives the scroll its goldmine quality, for much of the content is extremely rich from a religious and literary viewpoint. Isaiah, by its evocative and hope inspiring imagery, has provided some of the most stirring poetic moments and memorable phrases in western literature.

Most scholars divide the book into three large sections; Chapters 1–39, Chapters 40–55, and Chapters 56–66. These are thought to roughly correspond to three historical periods from which much, but not necessarily all, of the material in that section comes. Such divisions reflect the likely compositional history of the scroll, as reconstructed by modern historical analysis. It should be noted that the prophet Yᵉshayahu is mentioned quite regularly, but only in the first 39 chapters.

But for our literary analysis, we must consider how the work as a whole moves. In the first section, we see some of the standard components of preserved Israelite prophetic literature: denunciation of the people of Israel and oracles against foreign nations. There are also some oracles of a future; some of them are hopeful, both for Israel and other nations. At the end of this section are some prose narratives about some political events during the life of Yᵉshayahu in Jerusalem at the end of the eighth century BCE. The second and smaller segment (Chapters 40–55) contains lengthy oracles of comfort and hope, supplied by visions of good news coming to Israel for release from exile. Some of these provide the most memorable selections. Here we find fewer formulas claiming "thus says YHVH." The speech format is sometimes that of YHVH addressing his people and sometimes the prophet speaking to the people about YHVH in the third person. The final section (Chapters 56–66) is again mixed in tone; it includes not only oracles of hope for the future, but also oracles criticizing the author's contemporaries for worshiping other Gods, injustice, and dishonesty. This section seems to come from after the Jews had returned from exile in 536 BCE.

1.1 Editor's introduction 1.2–12.6 Oracles of judgment on Judah/Jerusalem and words of hope	13.1–23.18 Oracles against foreign nations and words of hope	24.1–27.13 Depictions YHVH's future universal judgments, psalms, words of hope	28.1–35.10 Oracles of judgment on Judah/Jerusalem and others; words of hope
36.1–39.8 Narrative of King Hezekiah's and Y^eshayahu's involvement; poems		40.1–55.13 Oracles of YHVH's forgiveness and future hope of release	56.1–66.24 Oracles of judgment and hope; prayers

one. Regardless of what other scrolls Y^eshayahu might have written, this is the only scroll that tradition and history have preserved for us.

Compositional History

When asking historical questions about how this scroll was composed, we need first to look at the various manuscript traditions to see what our textual evidence looks like. In the case of Y^eshayahu, the ancient Greek manuscripts, medieval Hebrew texts, and more ancient Dead Sea Scrolls are all basically the same. Of course there are minor differences that would be expected in any handwritten text being copied over hundreds of years, but unlike our next scroll, Jeremiah, we do not find large content shifts, revisions, or additions in any of the extant manuscripts. So it seems that whatever developments took place in the compositional history of the scroll, they occurred prior to the second century BCE.

Our best understanding of that development must come from our careful reading of the scroll and must be in accord with the known writing conventions of ancient Israel. The idea that the scroll developed over time is a normal possibility, easily demonstrated from other texts. In the case of Y^eshayahu, most scholars think that a large portion of the material in Chapters 1–39 stems from Y^eshayahu of Jerusalem, a historically significant prophet who was active in the Jerusalem court in the second part of the eighth century (700s) BCE and who was active during the period of Assyrian supremacy, which lasted until about 605 BCE. Some headings in the scroll indicate the work of an editor, such as at 1.1, 2.1, and 13.1. Other individual units of material are identified as being younger, such as the material in Chapters 24–27, which nearly all compositional historians take as a more recent addition because of differences in tone and outlook. The large historical section in Chapters 36–39, which shares some identical narratives with parts of 2 Kings 18–20, has clearly been taken from another scroll. It may have been added at one time to close the scroll, just as a historical section closes the scroll of Jeremiah. Only later were materials added after it.

The next major section brings us ahead about a century and a half. Chapters 40–55 are often thought of as a complete unit, composed in the mid-sixth century BCE, as the Persian King Cyrus was beginning to conquer the Babylonian

DISPLAY 7.1 | THE DEAD SEA SCROLL OF ISAIAH

Empire under which the Jews lived. Its consistent message of hope and forgiveness and its lively poetry have led many to view it as the work of a single poet, known as the Second Y^eshayahu, or the Y^eshayahu of Babylon. Unlike material from Isaiah of Jerusalem, this author knows the fall of Jerusalem to the Babylonians and the exiling of Jews as past events (e.g. 40.1; 43.14; 47.1–6; 48.20). And, most importantly, he knows of the fall of Babylon to Cyrus (45.1). He is exuberant in his hope that YHVH has worked to dramatically alter the fate of the exiles.

The final section (Chapters 56–66)—oracles of condemnation, hope, consolation, and prayers—is often thought to reflect the words of several different prophets. Unlike the second section, it seems to come from a perspective of people living in Jerusalem, after exile, that is, after the late sixth century BCE. So, to summarize, it seems that our scroll's composition likely spans a couple of centuries, beginning with words originating in the eighth century BCE, but also incorporating material from the sixth and fifth centuries BCE.

The World of Y^eshayahu of Y^erushalayim

Unlike some prophetic scrolls, this scroll overtly ties some of its oracles to particular events in Israel's history. The opening editorial line sets the work of Y^eshayahu in the days of four Jerusalem kings, Uzziah, Jotham, Ahaz, and Hezekiah, who reigned consecutively, according to historical reconstructions, from about 783 to 698 BCE. These were tumultuous years in Syria-Palestine; the Assyrian empire was attacking and overtaking the small city-based local kingdoms of the region, including the

DISPLAY 7.2 | PHOENICIAN SEAL WITH A FOUR- OR SIX-WINGED CREATURE. SEE ISAIAH 6.2.

Northern Kingdom of Israel, which fell in 722 BCE. Other city-states also came under Assyrian domination, including Damascus, Tyre, Sidon, Ashkelon, Gaza, Moab, and Edom. Eventually Egypt, too, would be controlled by Assyrian interests. In the years before its final destruction, the Northern Kingdom attempted several times to lead a rebellion against the growing Assyrian presence and tried to force the smaller Southern Kingdom of Judah to participate. The Assyrian reputation for atrocities was well known—people had seen and heard what had happened to neighboring towns. These decades were times of excruciatingly painful political uncertainty and fear, with personal and national life under the sword and little chance of escape. The advice of pundits and prophets must have been an unending cacophony of earnest voices. Some counseled submission to Assyria, some rebellion; some looked to Egypt, some sought a neutral position. Most would have in one way or another claimed the support of YHVH. Yeshayahu was one of those voices.

Our scroll reflects Yeshayahu's oracles about two major Assyrian-caused crises during this time: whether to join the Northern Kingdom in armed resistance

Display 7.3 | RELIEF SCULPTURE FROM A PALACE IN NINEVEH DEPICTING SENNACHERIB'S CAPTURE OF LACHISH IN 701 BCE

(730s and 720 BCE) and King Sennacherib's invasion of 701 BCE. Judah avoided the destruction that came to Israel in 722 BCE, though for all practical purposes she became a vassal of Assyria. Times improved as Judah actually experienced benefits of the Assyrian empire and the loss of competition from now destroyed neighboring states. But in 701 BCE the Assyrian King Sennacherib led a campaign to put down the anti-Assyrian rebellion of Judah and surrounding states in the region that had broken out with unexpected death of the Assyrian King Sargon II in 705 BCE. The invasion devastated the kingdom of Judah. The result was that the now quite small hill-country kingdom was spared her capital, Jerusalem, but much of her territory was under Assyrian control, including her important outlying towns, such as the fortress of Lachish to the south. Assyrian records indicated the fall of the Judean town of Lachish (see Display 7.3), the containment of Hezekiah to Jerusalem, and the harsh terms of tribute to which he submitted.

DISPLAY 7.4 | A MONUMENTAL INSCRIPTION THAT INCLUDES SENNACHERIB'S RECORD OF HEZEKIAH'S SUBMISSION, WRITTEN 700 BCE

Sennacherib speaks of Hezekiah: "... As for Hezekiah, the Judean, I besieged forty-six of his fortified walled cities and surrounding smaller towns, which were without number. Using packed-down ramps and applying battering rams, infantry attacks by mines, breeches, and siege machines, I conquered (them). I took out 200,150 people, young and old, male and female, horses, mules, donkeys, camels, cattle, and sheep, without number, and counted them as spoil. He himself, I locked up within Jerusalem, his royal city, like a bird in a cage. I surrounded him with earthworks, and made it unthinkable for him to exist by the city gate. . . . I imposed dues and gifts for my lordship upon him, in addition to the former tribute, their yearly payment. He, Hezekiah, was overwhelmed by the awesome splendor of my lordship . . ."

Translated by M. Cogan in Hallo 2003, 2:303.

Although all of these events form the backdrop for the early chapters of Y^eshayahu and are helpful for our understanding, our scroll does not relate the events and their associated oracles in a clear chronological order, nor does it always indicate the events behind certain oracles. Often, it is downright confusing in this regard. For those who compiled and preserved the scroll, it was not so much a historical commentary by Y^eshayahu, but a deposit of oracles and other prophetic material that could not simply to be tied to a few political events. Although Y^eshayahu counseled King Ahaz not to join the revolt but also not to actively seek Assyrian aid because soon the threat would pass (Chapters 7–8), Y^eshayahu's visions for the future looked long past any immediate threat and encompassed the whole world. The perception that these words were relevant beyond their own times led to their preservation.

Study Room 7.1

ONE BATTLE, MANY VIEWS

Battles and wars look very different depending on a person's viewpoint and ideology. Various accounts are available our scroll shows one view of Hezekiah's conflict with the Assyrian Sennacherib: the scrolls of Y^eshayahu, Kings, Chronicles and the official account of the royal scribe of Sennacherib, which comes from about 700 BCE. Find the following accounts and consider the various perspectives. What is unique to each one? What is shared? What religious, national, and ideological viewpoints do they display? As a historian, how would you evaluate their usefulness for reconstructing the actual events? How would you evaluate the historiographic values and priorities of each author? As a literary and religious scholar, how would you evaluate the rhetorical aims of each text?

> 2 Kings 18.1–19.37
> Isaiah 36.1–37.38
> 2 Chronicles 32.1–33

> Sennacherib's account is in Hallo 2003, 2:302–04, and
>   Pritchard 1969, 287–88.

The World of Y^eshayahu of Babylon

Although the foreign power looming over Israel is Assyria in the first part of our scroll, when we come to Chapter 40 we find that Assyria is gone and Babylon is now the enemy (e.g., Isaiah 46–48). Historically, this change came about at the end of the seventh century BCE; the Assyrian capital fell to Babylonian forces in 612 BCE. And in fact, Babylon, too, is falling—being replace by the rising Persian Empire, a huge change that came in 539 BCE. The prophetic speech of these chapters is not addressed to people living in Jerusalem, but instead to people living as exile in Babylon, who now have the opportunity to return. The massive political shifts are mirrored in the charges in tone and outlook in this middle part of our scroll, and the differences have been observed through the centuries by many readers. The sixth-century poet, who is never named in Chapters 40–55, composes poems that are buoyant words of hope for exiles, anticipating Israel's restoration to its land and renewed celebration of YHVH's faithfulness to Israel.

Oracles of Criticism

As we progress through our prophetic scrolls, it is not surprising that there are strident speeches against the behavior of persons or groups of Israelites. Y^eshayahu of Jerusalem, during the time of the fallen Northern Kingdom, points the finger of accusation at an audience made up of those from Judah and perhaps some refugees from the north. More importantly, authors and editors who came after him present these criticisms for later generations; the scroll begins with a denunciation of a sinful nation that has forsaken YHVH (1.4). It is not long before the poet gives some substance to the charge.

> Hear a message of YHVH, rulers of Sodom!/Listen to the instruction of our God, people of Gomorrah!/"What to me are all these sacrifices?" says YHVH./"I am full of your offerings of lambs and fat of animals./And in blood of bulls and lambs and goats I do not delight./When you enter to see my face,/Who requested this from your hand?/Trampling my courts, stop doing it!/To bring an offering is worthless,/Incense—it's offensive to me!/New moon [rituals], Sabbath, called convocation,/I will not endure injustice and assembly!/Your new moon [rites] and holy days my soul hates!/They are a burden to me; I am tired of bearing them./And when you lift your hands, I will turn my eyes away from you./Even when you make long prayer, I am not listening!/Your hands are full of blood. Wash! Come clean!/Take the evil of your actions away from my eyes/Stop the evil! Learn how to do good!/Seek justice! Stride against the oppressor!/Advocate for the orphan! Argue for the widow!/Come, let's argue," says YHVH./If your sins are red, they can be white like snow./If they are reddish as dyed wool, they can be like fleece./If you consent and listen, you will eat the good of the land./And if you refuse and rebel, you will be devoured by a sword./For the mouth of YHVH has spoken. (Y⁰SHAYAHU 1.10–20)

Could a call for social concern and justice be put in any stronger language? Is not the very idea of YHVH loathing the prayers, sacrifices, and holy days of his people among the most radical messages a prophet could speak in the middle of Jerusalem, the sacred city of YHVH's temple and priesthood? How do you think priests and YHVH worshippers reacted, in the prophet's day or in later generations?

The scroll of Yᵉshayahu does not only contain radical pronouncements. There are many more acceptable calls for right action and the proper keeping of holy days (see 56.2–6; 58.1–14), though each oracle should be allowed its full voice in its own context. Yᵉshayahu contains scathing rebukes of other social ills (e.g., 5.1–30) and of those worshipping other Gods (57.1–13). As part of long poems of hope and encouragement, the writer of the central chapters of consolation (Isaiah 40–55) mocks those who worship Gods at other cult sites and asks, "To whom can you equate me, to whom can I be compared?" (40.25).

Like the scrolls of other prophet-poets, our scroll speaks out frequently against what was perceived as unrighteousness, or better, acts lacking right-ness in relation to YHVH and fellow humans. Like the prophets Amos and Micah especially, our scroll often puts a premium emphasis on social justice as a requirement for proper conduct for the nation and individuals within it.

Oracles Inspiring Trust and Hope

One theme common to many prophets of YHVH was that their God was the master of all nations. For Yᵉshayahu of Jerusalem this meant that Judah and her king should not look to foreign nations such as Egypt or Assyria for aid or support. Throughout the scroll, statements of YHVH's supremacy abound. This is the central thesis of the oracles against foreign nations in Chapters 13–23; the poet is not actually addressing the leaders of Assyria, Babylon, or Tyre when he proclaims their downfall. It is easy to see how authors of various times could add oracles of this type to the collection, depending on the political events of the times. Thus, long after the days of Y^{e}shayahu of Jerusalem and the dominance of Assyria (see 14.24–27), the nation of Babylonia rose and fell (ca. 615 to 539 BCE), and Israel's poetic writers were there to observe and interpret the events through the lens—a peculiar Israelite religious ideal and claim—of YHVH's sovereignty over all national affairs. The rhetoric of all the oracles making such claims is explicitly meant to inspire hope and to encourage people to faithfully trust YHVH. For authors of our scroll, YHVH was in charge at all times and his people should always be faithful and look forward with hope. Y^{e}shayahu of Babylon, speaking as prophetic historian, looks at the Assyrian aggression against the Northern Kingdom and sees it as YHVH's action—Assyria is his "rod of anger"—to punish his people for their social inequities (10.1–5). Yet Assyria's downfall is also YHVH's plan, as is Babylon's demise (14.3–23). Assyria is YHVH's tool but so is Cyrus, the Persian king of centuries later who brings freedom from the Babylonian exile (538 BCE). The poet paints Cyrus as YHVH's designated conqueror, his **messiah**—the scroll's only use of the term—and though Cyrus may have thought he was fighting for his own gain, our poet declares that YHVH raised him up for the sake of the good people of Israel (45.1–4). Perhaps the best-known and most beautiful expressions of YHVH's supremacy come in the central poems of consolation.

Who has measured in his palm the waters,
And the skies calculated with a span?
And contained with a measure the earth's dust?
And weighed mountains in a scale? And hills in a balance?
Who has calculated the mind/spirit of YHVH
And what man can tell him his [YHVH's] plan?
With whom does he consult? Who instructs him? Teaches him the right way?
And teaches him knowledge and tells him the path of understanding?
Notice! the nations are a mere drop from a bucket,
And are considered like dust on scales.
Notice! Islands he lifts like powder.
Lebanon is not enough wood-fuel
Its animals are not enough for a sacrifice.
All the nations are like nothing before him,
Less than zero, and empty. . .
Why Jacob do you say, and Israel do you declare,
"Hidden from YHVH is my path,
And by my God my right acts are ignored"?
Don't you know? Did you not hear?
The God of every-time is YHVH.
Creator of the extent of the earth.
He does not faint or get tired.
There is no limit to his understanding.
He gives to the tired one strength,
For the one without power he provides vigor. . . .
Those who trust in YHVH will renew strength . . .
(Y^{E}SHAYAHU 40.12–17, 27–29, 31)

Study Room 7.2

MANY MESSIAHS?

Most people know the word *messiah*, which is actually a Anglicized form of the Hebrew word *meshiach*, pronounced, "m^e-*she*-akh." In Greek it is translated by the word *kristos*, and from the Greek form we get the word *Christ*. Obviously this became an extremely important term later in Christianity. But how is the term *meshiach* used throughout our library, long before the rise of Christianity?

First of all, the word is a title that means "anointed one," and it refers to a person who had oil poured on his head in a ceremony that set him apart as special, much as some countries have a coronation ceremony for their new queen or king. Read 1 Samuel 16 for a story with an anointing ceremony in it.

A study of all of the uses of this title in our library—there are fewer than 40—reveals that the word is never used to refer to a future savior, a coming Jewish king, or a longed-for rescuer. The word *meshiach* is used most often for the king, that is, the person who had been crowned, anointed, as king of Israel (Psalms 2, 45, 89). It is often used of David (2 Samuel 1.14, 16, 21; 19.22) but also of Saul (1 Samuel 12.5; 24.6) and Solomon (2 Chronicles 6.42). It could also be used for priests (Leviticus 4.3, 5, 16; 6.22) or prophets (1 Kings 19.16, Y^{e}shayahu 61.1). The *meshiach* could also be a non-Israelite king, as we will see when we come to Isaiah 45.1. In that poem the writer sees Cyrus, king of the Persians, as anointed by Israel's God to do his work of freeing the Jewish exiles in Babylonia.

In later Jewish literature during the period of Greek rule (third to first centuries BCE) in writings not contained in our library, the title *meshiach* became for some Jewish authors the title of a future royal hero and savior that they hoped their God would use in order to stop oppression and restore their national fortune. But in this later time period, there was no single pan-Jewish idea of who or what a *meshiach* was, or even if there was such a future figure. Some authors talk about two coming *meshiachs*, but others have no notion of or need for a coming *meshiach*.

Obviously the understanding of many early Christians that Jesus was the *meshiach* utilized some of these older Jewish concepts and also created some new distinctly Christian ones. Doing some basic research on the use of the concept of messiah in Judaism and early Christianity can be very enlightening. A good Bible dictionary would be a good place to start, along with the following basic treatments: de Jonge 1992, "Christ," 1:914–21 and "Messiah," 4.777–88; and Neusner, Green, and Frerichs 1987.

Poetry and Pictures

But the cause for hope offered by the scroll of Yᵉshayahu was not merely that YHVH ruled history and the world. Our scroll contains dozens of portraits of a future for Israel, portraits of peace, prosperity, and triumph, some of which focus on Judah or Jerusalem and some of which expand to encompass the world. An example from early in the scroll comes from the Chapters 8–11, which envision the royal dynasty of David being continued and exalted to greatness because of YHVH and the justness and equity of David's descendant. Such visions put into compelling poetry provided listeners with a motivation to remain devoted to YHVH. Near the end of the scroll, Chapters 54–56, the language of covenant and YHVH's eternal unbreakable love are used to present a picture of coming establishment of the reign of righteousness for YHVH's people, including foreigners. Similarly, early on the poet calls his audience to envision this:

> It will happen in days ahead,
> The mount of YHVH's house,
>   shall stand at the top of the mountains,/and shall be lifted above hills,
> And all the nations shall stream to it,/And many peoples will travel saying,
> "Come, let's go to YHVH's mount, to the house of Jacob's God.
> And he will instruct us in his ways and we will walk in his paths.
> For from **Zion** instruction goes forth/And YHVH speaks from Jerusalem.
> (Yᵉshayahu 2.2–3)

The poem goes on to speak of complete harmony among the nations. You will see later that this passage is also used by another prophet and poet, Micah: a peaceful world is a longing of many, both now and then.

In the passage previously quoted, the future geography is focused on Jerusalem, but in another intriguing passage an altar to YHVH is set up in Egypt, YHVH will rescue oppressed Egyptians, and Egyptians and Assyrians, too, will worship YHVH together with Israel. Here the author smashes stereotypes of exclusivity and gives a most original religious and artistic image:

> In that day Israel will be a third part with Egypt and Assyria,
> A blessing in the middle of the earth
> Whom YHVH of armies blessed saying,
> "Blessed are my people Egypt, Assyria, the work of my hands,
> and my inheritance Israel."
> (Yᵉshayahu 19.24–25)

Undoubtedly such poetic visions were meant to inspire hope; they must have raised some nationalistic eyebrows too. Intended to capture the imagination, the poems are filled with details, not vague generalities or overused clichés. The poetic imagination is fully engaged in an effort to fully engage the spirit of the listener. We must resist attempts to somehow systematize the hundreds of details of the future we find in this scroll. In one future picture the lions lie down with lambs (11.6–9) but in another future, the lions are apparently still dangerous (35.8–10). Yᵉshayahu is a storehouse of beautiful poetry, the authors are painters envisioning a longed-for world and attempt to provide comfort and hope to their hearers.

Perhaps the most famous words of consolation in the scroll open what is now Chapter 40. Thanks to the oratorio *Messiah* by Handel, which was composed in 1742 and drew on several parts of Yᵉshayahu, many people are familiar with these lines:

Comfort, comfort my people, says your God.
Speak gently to Jerusalem and cry to her,
That her term is fulfilled,
That her guilt is paid,
That she received from YHVH double for all her sins (40.1–2).

The historical scholar would indicate that this poem likely had its origin at the time that the exile was ending (538 BCE). But just as our scroll's denunciations of injustice continue to ring through the centuries, so do these words of comfort and forgiveness. For many the words carry significance far beyond their first utterance.

One of the most intriguing of all the pictures painted in our scroll is the recurring image of the servant found in the section sometimes called Second Yᵉshayahu (Chapters 40–55), especially, though not exclusively, in four poems that are often referred to as the Servant Songs because they all depict this servant in YHVH's service (42.1–4; 49.1–6; 50.4–11; 52.13–53.12). In the majority of the references it is clear that this servant is the nation of Israel itself (e.g., 44.1–2). But the poems contain subtle allegory and at times intriguing ambiguity as they tell of the life of this servant of YHVH in the world. In some cases later interpreters saw the servant as Yᵉshayahu, Moses, or as one group of Jews within the larger national group. If you are familiar with Christian traditions, you will recognize right away that words of the fourth servant song (Isaiah 52.13–53.12) were applied to Jesus starting with early Christian authors contained in the New Testament, even though the song never speaks about a messiah. Recall that Yᵉshayahu's only reference to a messiah is in 45.1 where Cyrus is the messiah. These are songs of encouragement and hope deeply meaningful to suffering or forgotten Jewish exiles and those of later centuries. The fourth song, the longest of all, is a fascinating portrayal of victory through defeat and honor out of humiliation. Rhetorically, for the poet's original sixth-century audience, what could have been more compelling to a nation devastated by war and exile than a song that recognized their suffering and gave it redemptive value?

Questions for Further Study

1. Read through the scroll and look for various attitudes and engagements with non-Israelites. When do you find hostility and when not? How would you describe the attitude toward foreigners behind various passages?

2. Read Second Isaiah (Isaiah 40–55) and note especially the uses of the term *servant* and any related words. Now consider later interpretations, Jewish and Christian, that apply these words to later events or persons. For example, see Daniel 11.33–12.10, Matthew 8.17, and 1 Peter 2.21–25. What interpretive strategies to you find? How has the poem of Isaiah been used to support the later author's point?

References

Blenkinsopp, Joseph. *Isaiah 1–39*. New York: Doubleday, 2000.

——. *Isaiah 40–55*. New York: Doubleday, 2002.

——. *Isaiah 56–66*. New York: Doubleday, 2003.

de Jonge, Marinus. "Christ." In *The Anchor Bible Dictionary*, edited by David N. Freedman, 1:914–21. New York: Doubleday, 1992.

de Jonge, Marinus. "Messiah." In *The Anchor Bible Dictionary*, edited by David N Freedman, 4.777–88. New York: Doubleday, 1992.

Hallo, William W. *The Context of Scripture*, 3 vols. Leiden: E. J. Brill, 2003.

Hayes, John H. and Stuart A. Irvine. *Isaiah*. Nashville, TN: Abingdon, 1987.

Neusner, Jacob, William Scott Green, and Ernest Frerichs. *Judaisms & Their Messiahs at the Turn of the Christian Era*. Cambridge: Cambridge University, 1987.

Pritchard, James B. *Ancient Near Eastern Texts,* 3rd ed. Princeton: Princeton University, 1969.

Schökel, Luis Alonso. "Isaiah," in *The Literary Guide to the Bible*, edited by Robert Alter and Frank Kermode. 165–83. Cambridge, MA: Harvard, 1987.

Seitz, Christopher R. William R. Millar, and Richard J. Clifford "Isaiah, Book of," in *The Anchor Bible Dictionary*, edited by David N. Freedman 3:472–507. New York: Doubleday, 1992.

יִרְמִיְהוּ

Jeremiah *Yirmᵉyahu*

SECTION OUTLINE

Literary Format and Movement
The Scrolls of Yirmᵉyahu
The Life and Times of Yirmᵉyahu
Baruch: Scribe and Associate
Yirmᵉyahu's Poetic Preaching
Questions for Further Study
References

After the narratives of Kings, Chronicles, and Samuel, Jeremiah is the longest, by word count, of all the scrolls of our library. It is a fascinating and rambling literary conglomeration from the last desperate decades before Jerusalem's fall to invading armies of the powerful Babylonian Empire (586). The scroll is mixed in genre and format, and the plan of its arrangement is seemingly inscrutable. Nevertheless, I find the figure of Jeremiah and this scroll compelling in many ways. In Hebrew, Jeremiah is *Yirmᵉyahu,* pronounced "year-mᵉ*yah*-hoo." There is a rich amount to be learned from a wide variety of methodologies about Yirmᵉyahu the person and Yermᵉyahu the scroll. If you are interested in biographical history then you will find that archaeology, the scroll's autobiographical sections, and narrative portions combine to give us fascinating material about Yirmᵉyahu as historical person—more material than we have on any other prophet of these fifteen classical prophets. If you have broader historical interests, you will find plenty about the traumatic times of Yirmᵉyahu, who personally experienced the fall of Jerusalem and the Babylonian takeover. If the study of ancient scroll writing and the history of a biblical writing is your interest, then Yirmᵉyahu is rich for your consideration because, unlike most of our other scrolls, it talks explicitly about scribes and writing practices, and the Dead Sea Scrolls provide some intriguing direct evidence of its textual evolution. Or what about religion? Yirmᵉyahu the prophet seems to have been in the middle of major religious conversations and debates of his day. He seems often to have been under fire from the royal administration and other religious interests, yet he seems to have exhibited a great deal of independence and courage. He often speaks directly about his opponents and provides a wealth of material about the realities of life in ancient Judah before and after the destruction of the Southern Kingdom. So there certainly is something for everyone in Yirmᵉyahu.

*L*ITERARY FORMAT AND MOVEMENT

As we discussed in Chapter One, Yirm^eyahu comes to us in two different literary formats. The Hebrew edition that is translated in most modern English Bibles (NRSV, JPS, NIV, KJV) represents the Masoretic texts from about 1000 CE. But ancient Greek manuscripts are much shorter, and parts of the texts are in a different order. With the discovery of the Dead Sea Scrolls, it has now been confirmed that the shorter Greek form comes from an even earlier Hebrew form. In fact, the longer Hebrew edition is most likely an expanded version of this short form, and both short and long forms are represented among the texts of the Dead Sea Scrolls. The two texts run generally together until Chapter 25, and then they diverge greatly. Because the editions are so different even in their literary format, I will provide a synopsis of the literary organization and movement for both. Both texts could be described as very mixed in terms of genre and style. They both have long poetic and prose sections; use first-person writings presented as Yirm^eyahu's and also third-person accounts about Jeremiah; and contain oracles with numerous "Thus says YHVH" formulas. In both, Yirm^eyahu addresses fellow Israelites and speaks to YHVH in prayers. Finally, both have many oracles that are dated to a certain time, but they are not presented in chronological order. Trying to track the arrangement of the scroll and see a detailed scheme or pattern is extremely problematic. The word *conglomeration* keeps coming to mind! Because most readers have only a modern Bible that is a translation of the longer form of Yirm^eyahu, I have used the numbering system from that edition in both of the following descriptions. This will enable you to look up the passages in most modern translations. In addition, I have indicated the major rearrangement of material in the longer version by setting those sections in bold.

The Shorter, Older Yirm^eyahu I

1.1–3 Editor's superscription	7.1–8.3 Temple sermon	11.1–17 Prose narrative of Yirm^eyahu's interaction with YHVH	12.14–15.9 Oracles (poetic, prose) against Jerusalem and Judah	17.14–18 Yirm^eyahu's lament
1.4–19 YHVH calls Yirm^eyahu	8.4–10.22 Oracles (mostly poetic) against Jerusalem and Judah			17.19–18.17 Oracles (poetic, prose) against Jerusalem and Judah
2.1–6.30 Oracles (mostly poetic) against Jerusalem and Judah	10.23–25 Prayer	11.18–12.6 Yirm^eyahu's lament	15.10–21 Yirm^eyahu's lament and YHVH's response	18.18–23 Yirm^eyahu's lament
		12.7–13 YHVH's lament	16.11–17.13 Oracles (poetic, prose) against Jerusalem and Judah	

19.1–13 Oracle (prose) against Jerusalem and Judah	**51.59–64** Yirmᵉyahu's scroll and his scribe Seraiah	**30.1–34, 37, 35, 36, 38–40** **31.1–40** Oracles of restoration	**42.1–44.30** Narratives about Yirmᵉyahu and journey to Egypt	
19.14–20.6 Narrative: conflict with priest	**47.1–7;** **49.7–22;** **49.1–5, 28–33, 23–27; 48.1–47** Oracles (poetic, prose) against foreign nations	**32.1–35.19** Narratives and prose oracles	**45.1–5** YHVH's word to Baruch	
20.7–18 Yirmᵉyahu's lament	25.15–38 Oracle (prose) against Jerusalem and Judah	36.1–32 Yirmᵉyahu's scroll and scribe, Baruch	**52.1–34** Historical appendix	
21.1–25.13; **49.34–39** Oracles (poetic, prose) dated by kings	26.1–28.17 Narratives and prose oracles	**37.1–41.17** Narratives about Yirmᵉyahu and fall of Jerusalem		
46.2–28; **50.1–51.58** Oracles (poetic, prose) against foreign nations	29.1–32 Yirmᵉyahu's letter to Babylonian exiles			

The Longer, Younger Yirmᵉyahu II (MT)

1.1–3 Editor's superscription	7.1–8.3 Temple sermon	11.1–17 Prose narrative of Yirmᵉyahu's interaction with YHVH	12.14–15.9 Oracles (poetic, prose) against Jerusalem and Judah	17.14–18 Yirmᵉyahu's lament
1.4–19 YHVH calls Yirmᵉyahu	8.4–10.22 Oracles (mostly poetic) against Jerusalem and Judah	11.18–12.6 Yirmᵉyahu's lament	15.10–21 Yirmᵉyahu's lament and YHVH's response	17.19–18.17 Oracles (poetic, prose) against Jerusalem and Judah
2.1–6.30 Oracles (mostly poetic) against Jerusalem and Judah	10.23–25 Prayer	12.7–13 YHVH's lament	16.11–17.13 Oracles (poetic, prose) against Jerusalem and Judah	18.18–23 Yirmᵉyahu's lament
19.1–13 Oracle (prose) against Jerusalem and Judah	**21.1–25.38** Oracles (poetic, prose) dated by kings	**30.1–31.40** Oracles of restoration	**37.1–41.17** Narratives about Yirmᵉyahu and fall of Jerusalem	**46.1–51.58** Oracles (poetic, prose) against foreign nations

19.14–20.6	26.1–28.17	32.1–35.19	42.1–44.30	51.59–64
Narrative: conflict with priest	Narratives and prose oracles	Narratives and prose oracles	Narratives about Yirmᵉyahu and journey to Egypt	Yirmᵉyahu's scroll and his scribe, Seraiah
20.7–18 Yirmᵉyahu's lament	**29.1–32** Yirmᵉyahu's letter to Babylonian exiles	**36.1–32** Yirmᵉyahu's scroll and scribe, Baruch	**45.1–5 YHVH's** word to Baruch	**52.1–34** Historical appendix

The Scrolls of Yirmᵉyahu

The study of the history of the writing of this scroll is rich with evidence. Of course a plethora of evidence does not mean that all our questions are answered or that we have common agreement on everything; it just gives us more to work with, more to understand, better foundations of knowledge, more questions to ask, and more fun to have! Many modern Bible readers might be surprised that there is more than one book associated with Yirmᵉyohu—after all, many modern Bibles only have one. However, in antiquity there are other references to a plurality of Yirmᵉyahu books, such as in 2 Maccabees 2. The Dead Sea Scrolls include other works credited to Yirmᵉyahu that are not in any Bibles today, which are called the **Apocalypse** of Yirmᵉyahu. And the authors of ancient books about Baruch contain stories and oracles of Yirmᵉyahu that are not found in the Yirmᵉyahu of modern Bibles. So what really existed in antiquity was similar to a portfolio, of which most modern Bibles have one sample.

Unlike most books of our library, the scroll of Yirmᵉyahu refers to practices of scroll writing. The composition of scrolls is mentioned several times, and these may refer to specific scrolls of which the author knew, such as the scroll with good news mentioned in 30.1–3, the letters of 29.1, the multiple scrolls of Chapter 36, and the scroll with bad news mentioned in 51.60. We are told that Yirmᵉyahu had an aid who wrote down oracles. In fact the scroll refers to six people as scribes, working in different places, most of them as members of royal administration (Shaphan, Elishama, Baruch, Jonathan, Seraiah, and an unnamed army scribe). More than just a secretary, his aid Baruch is pictured more as an assistant, especially in Yirmᵉyahu I, and perhaps was being groomed to follow Yirmᵉyahu. In fact, there is plenty of ancient literature with stories and traditions about Baruch becoming a prophetic leader in the Jewish community. According to the narrative in Chapter 36, Baruch writes the words of Yirmᵉyahu, but we do not know which scroll it was or if we still have it.

Many scholars have concluded that the scroll referred to in Yirmᵉyahu 36 is actually found in the early chapters of Yirmᵉyahu, the first 20 or 25 chapters of modern editions. If you read through Yirmᵉyahu I or II, you will notice that the early chapters are mostly oracles, whereas most of the biographical narratives about Yirmᵉyahu come in Chapters 26–45. These biographical narratives are thought by many to be Baruch's own composition about the life of his mentor. There are several different explanations of when these major sections of Yirmᵉyahu were composed and were brought together. Dates, range from the late seventh century to the fifth century BCE.

The biggest change of textual arrangement between Yirm^eyahu I and II is the movement of a large block material, the oracles against foreign nations, from its original position preceding the biographical narratives (see Yirm^eyahu I), to nearly the end of the scroll—Chapters 46–51 in Jeremiah II. We can see an editor's remark at the end of the oracles against foreign nations in last line of Chapter 51: "Until here, the words of Yirm^eyahu." There is also an introduction; notice that the first part of 25.13 reads as an introduction to those oracles against foreign nations: "I will bring on that land [Babylon] all the words I spoke against her, all which is written in this book . . ." Following all those oracles, Yirm^eyahu I has this postscript editorial notation: "These things Yirm^eyahu proclaimed against all the nations." The editor of Yirm^eyahu II turned this postscript into the final relative clause of 25.13: "which Yirm^eyahu proclaimed against all the nations." Then he added 25.14 to serve as a bridge to the material that begins in 25.15. The story and oracles that followed in 25.15–38 are also perfectly suited as follow-up to the foreign nation oracles. It is hard to know why the editor responsible for Yirm^eyahu II would have moved these oracles. It seems perfectly plausible and likely that the block of oracles against foreign nations existed independently at one time and was a block of material that was easily shifted. Perhaps material about foreign nations was less important to the editor of Yirm^eyahu II, and so it was put at the end.

There are hundreds of additions made in Yirm^eyahu II—many are very small; a few are quite large. For example, consider these additions: 94 words in 27.19–22; 254 words in 33.14–26; 227 words in 39.4–13; and 55 words in 48.45–47. In other cases certain material occurs twice in Yirm^eyahu II but only once in Yirm^eyahu I, such as 6.13–15, which is repeated in 8.10b–12, and 15.13–15, which is repeated in 17.3–4. Some additions in Yirm^eyahu II significantly change the meaning in certain contexts. For example, read these two versions in Poster 7.1 and consider who is being held directly responsible of Jeremiah's near starvation.

There are hundreds of interesting questions concerning the differences between these two editions, and you can try to find answers by careful reading. This longer version of Jeremiah does not radically alter the religious tone of the scroll. But that is not to say that the differences are insignificant. For example, Baruch is cast differently in the two editions. In Yirm^eyahu I he is more independent—a prophet coming into his own. In fact, in Yirm^eyahu I Baruch is never called a scribe, and he is the one who receives the last revelation of the scroll (45.1–5). But in Yirm^eyahu II he is only a scribe, the scroll does not end with a revelation to Baruch, and Baruch is more of an assistant to Yirm^eyahu. These differences of depiction can be related to other Yirm^eyahu and Baruch documents, and their literary relationship can be traced for centuries.

One last observation about scroll making is that both editions end with an appendix that has been taken from another scroll, and in this case we know which one. Yirm^eyahu Chapter 52 is essentially a duplication of 2 Kings 24.18–25.30, with slight modifications. It is a narrative report about the fall of Jerusalem and the exile of the Jewish people to Babylon. Editors of editions I and II apparently thought it a fitting epilogue to the oracles and stories of the famous prophet Yirm^eyahu. A read through the proclamations that are credited to him makes this easy to understand.

POSTER 7.1

TWO SCROLLS, TWO DIFFERENT VIEWS

| Yirm^eyahu I | Yirm^eyahu II |

Yirmᵉyahu I

Yirmᵉyahu II

Ebed-melek went to him and spoke to the king [Zedekiah] and said, *You* acted wickedly, doing what you did to kill this man by starvation . . . (from LXX, 45.8–9)

Ebed-melek left the king's house and spoke to the king [Zedekiah] saying, My Lord King, *these men* have acted wickedly, in all they did to Yirmᵉyahu the prophet, putting him in pit to die of hunger . . . (from MT, 38.8–9)

In this case the speaker blames different people for putting Jeremiah in prison, depending on which version you read. Was it the king or "these men"?

The Life and Times of Yirmᵉyahu

No other prophet has as much biographical material in his scroll as does Yirmᵉyahu. In contrast to most other prophetic books, both editions of the Yirmᵉyahu scroll show a marked interest in giving a depiction of the scroll's protagonist throughout his work. The scroll first sets the period of Yirmᵉyahu's words (ca. 626 to 586) and then gives a long story of YHVH calling Yirmᵉyahu to be a prophet while he is still a boy. The decades of Yirmᵉyahu's activity are tumultuous, both on the grand scale of Fertile Crescent geo-politics and on the local scale of the Yirmᵉyahu's small homeland of Judah. These are desperate and dangerous times. Assyria is still attempting to assert her hegemony over Syria-Palestine, though she is being torn apart by internal and external strife. In the final decade of the 600s, Assyria falls but is soon replaced by an equally able military power from Mesopotamia, the Babylonians under their great king Nebuchadrezzar II (604 to 562); spelled Nebuchadnezzar in modern biblical texts. Babylon soon asserts her control; and when Nebuchadnezzar perceives rebellion, he wastes no time in a complete conquest of Judah; Jerusalem is demolished, with thousands killed, and thousands exiled to Babylon. Judah is no more by 586 BCE. This is Yirmᵉyahu's world.

The author uses this first episode of Yirmᵉyahu's calling to prefigure many of the difficulties the prophet will experience in the course of the book. We might even say that the depictions of Yirmᵉyahu's conflicts, sorrows, sufferings and his deeply personal reactions to them are prime objectives of the scroll. Yirmᵉyahu is from a family of priests, but they fell out of favor with King Solomon back in the tenth century and had been banished (see 1 Kings 2.26–27). Such royal–priestly conflicts and power struggles were (and are!) common. Yirmᵉyahu is depicted as constantly at odds with kings, priests, and many other prophets of his day.

Yirmᵉyahu's conflict with these authority figures is apparent throughout the scroll. Priests and prophets oppose his oracles of condemning Judah's religious and social establishment and of coming military defeat brought by YHVH. He was not an armchair critic, shooting off critical missiles from a safe distance at no personal risk. Just the opposite is true; he is pictured as being in the middle of the cultural fray, with opposition all around. He dared to question royal and military authorities, was considered an unpatriotic rabble-rouser, and was frequently denounced. There are several stories where he is almost put to death for his outspoken opposition, including that of discouraging Jerusalem's soldiers from defending their city (see Chapter 38). At another time he is nearly executed by the king but barely escapes due to a well-positioned friend in the royal court; another prophet, Uriah, who preached the same message as Yirmᵉyahu, was not so lucky (see Yirmᵉyahu 26). The king burns Yirmᵉyahu's writings in Chapter 36, and another attempt is made on his life.

Conflicts with priests are not uncommon in prophetic literature, but they seem to be raised to new levels in Yirmᵉyahu. Priests are frequently denounced in generalities (see 2.8, 26; 8.10; 14.18), but at times the text is more specific. Chapter 7 is introduced as a sermon that Yirmᵉyahu delivered in the temple of YHVH in Jerusalem, where the priests presided. He mocks those who believe in YHVH's protection and instructs his listeners not to trust those who say, "this is the house of YHVH." He condemns what he considers their lack of concern for widows, orphans, and justice and their worship of other Gods. He says that YHVH will destroy this temple, just as an earlier temple at Shiloh (see 1 Samuel 4–6) was destroyed by the Philistines. Perhaps even more startling, he says that YHVH did not command their ancestors to offer sacrifices in the years after they left Egypt (7.21–22). These words directly contradict priestly traditions in Exodus, Leviticus, and Numbers, where sacrifices are exactly what YHVH does command. If we go back to our Leviticus scroll we see the first words that that author credits to YHVH are all about sacrifices. Traditions like these may be what Yirmᵉyahu has in mind when he dismisses the teachings of those who claim that "YHVH's *torah* is with us," but in fact, says Yirmᵉyahu, they have nothing but the "lying pen of the scribes" (8.8). We are witnessing here a struggle for religious traditions, ideas about the past and future, and ideologies about YHVH's presence and covenant. The text even claims that YHVH told Yirmᵉyahu not to pray for the welfare of his people (7.16; 14.11). It is no wonder that Yirmᵉyahu was banished from the temple (36.5) and experienced, according to the scroll, repeated opposition from Judah's religious and political leadership; Yirmᵉyahu was anything but patriotic!

But perhaps the worst conflicts of Yirmᵉyahu's life came with other prophets of YHVH. More so than the writing of any other prophet, this scroll gives us the image of a Yirmᵉyahu who is frequently opposed to others who claimed to speak for YHVH. While Yirmᵉyahu proclaims disaster and punishment,

- they speak messages of hope and peace and comfort (6.14; 8.11; 14.13);
- they are sure YHVH will protect Judah (5.31);
- they speak oracles people love to hear (5.31);

POSTER 7.2

A PROPHET SCOFFS

Yirm^eyahu's words are often strikingly bold, direct, and sardonic. Here he mocks a priestly tradition that because the temple was YHVH's it was therefore inviolable. Perhaps his words sarcastically echo priestly liturgy.

Don't trust the deceptive words saying,/"The temple of YHVH,

The temple of YHVH,/The temple of YHVH . . ." (JEREMIAH 7.4)

- they claim to know YHVH's words, but they are ignorant (14.18); and
- they are deluded liars who speak their own words, not YHVH's, claims Yirm^eyahu (26.16–22).

We can be sure that the charges went both ways and that prophets on each side of the issues claimed their own genuineness and charged others with fraud. There is even a story in this regard in Chapter 28. After Babylon's destruction of Jerusalem and the Babylonian exile some prophets encouraged the people with a message of hope and imminent action by YHVH to restore them to their land. But Yirm^eyahu writes to them and instructs them not to listen to their dreams and instead to get settled in Babylon, to pray to YHVH on behalf of Babylon, and to be prepared to be there several generations (Chapter 29). The scroll's author pictures Israelites having to choose between the radical ideas of Yirm^eyahu and the established ideas of the status quo. But why should anyone accept Yirm^eyahu's claims? Were there not traditional stories, instructions, psalms, and national poetry that were full of promises from YHVH? Who had the authority to interpret national traditions and to represent YHVH? Would it not be wiser to side with the majority of YHVH's representatives? Who really speaks for YHVH?

Given all the conflict presented in the scroll, it is not surprising to learn of Yirm^eyahu's inner turmoil, though the frankness of the expression in the poetic texts known as Yirm^eyahu's autobiographical laments or confessions may startle us. These segments of poetry, which we noted as Yirm^eyahu's lament in the scroll's summary at the beginning of this section, are some of the most intimate poetic expressions of our library. Later on our tour we will find similar agonizing language from Job.

Damned be the day I was born,

The day that my mother birthed me, let it never be blessed.

Damned be the man who brought news to my father, saying, "A son is born to you," making him rejoice.

May that man be like the cites that YHVH destroyed without mercy,

May he hear a cry in the morning,

And an alarm at noon.

Poster 7.3

COUNTERING A PROPHET

The scroll of Yirm^eyahu sometimes represents the ideas or sentiments of his opposition. Here we find a candid summary of those who spoke against Yirm^eyahu as defenders of traditions of YHVH's *torah*, traditional wisdom, and prophetic utterances.

> And they said, "Come, let us devise countermeasures against Yirm^eyahu, because *torah* is not lost from a priest, and counsel from wise man, nor oracle from prophet. Come, let us speak out against him and let us not listen to his words." (YIRM^EYAHU 18.18)

Because he did not kill me in the womb,
And my mother would be my tomb.
And her womb great forever.
Why did I come from the womb
To see toil and sorrow,
And to complete my days in shame? (JEREMIAH 20.14–18)

In these painful texts Yirm^eyahu is shown weeping and complaining to YHVH about his oppressed and depressing situation. Is it any wonder that the very name Yirm^eyahu has given English the noun *jeremiad*—a recitation of complaint and woe? According to the scrolls of Yirm^eyahu, the personal story of Yirm^eyahu does not take a dramatic turn and end happily ever after. His brushes with death are followed by the complete collapse of Judah and Jerusalem, a traumatic and tragic experience for any who survived. Yirm^eyahu survives only to be taken against his will to Egypt by other Jewish refugees. The last words we here of him are excoriating sermons against those refugees (Chapters 43–44).

Baruch: Scribe and Associate

There are many reasons to think that Baruch was actually much more than simply a scribal secretary to Yirm^eyahu. We have already mentioned some of the differences between the depictions of Baruch in the two different editions of our Yirm^eyahu scroll. The perception of conflict between the two is not a modern invention: it is already an idea overtly mentioned in Yirm^eyahu 43.3. It makes a fascinating study to trace the relationship of these two as literary figures into later Jewish, Christian, and Islamic traditions. Baruch is sometimes a great prophet, in other places a dangerous false prophet, or even equated with Zoroaster, the great Persian religious leader. As with Yirm^eyahu, there are also other writings associated with Baruch, one of which, now simply called Baruch, has always immediately followed the book of

DISPLAY 7.5 | THE SUPPOSEDLY PERSONAL SEAL (BULLA) OF BARUCH

Yirm^eyahu in biblical Greek manuscripts. We will consider the scroll of Baruch at the end of this chapter.

Baruch is also of interest for historians and archaeologists of ancient material culture because archaeologists discovered a clay bulla (see Display 7.5) with the inscription

"(Property) of Barukhyahu son of Neriyahu, the scribe."

This is the same name as the Baruch of our scroll (see 36.4) with a common variation for the name. This clay seal would have been pressed onto a scroll in order to seal it closed, and then Baruch's metal seal, like a modern rubber stamp, was pressed onto the soft clay to mark ownership of the document. Unfortunately, the seal is a forgery. This is indeed what ancient seals look like and how they were used, but this one is not authentic. In the years that I was writing this book, this artifact of Yirm^eyahu's scribe Baruch and several other supposedly ancient Israelite artifacts and inscriptions were shown to be forgeries, or at least grave doubts were cast upon them. For the sake of truth and history, forgery is a catastrophe. Scholars and the public must be able base their understanding of the past on authentic artifacts and documents. The primary impetus for such forgery in our day is the strong desire of some to see biblical history proven by archaeological facts and the desires of others to profit monetarily. Put these two together and the result is pious fraud and historical disaster. For more on the controversy, see the article by Silberman and Goren.

Yirm^eyahu's Poetic Preaching

The scroll of Yirm^eyahu is not lacking for prophetic denunciation. We have already mentioned condemnation of leadership for improper teaching and reliance on traditions of YHVH's protection of Jerusalem and her temple. A detailed study would reveal many more nuances besides his disapproval of social injustice and the worship of Gods besides YHVH. It would also show that Yirm^eyahu's foretelling of destruction to come upon Judah is presented not as future telling, or prediction, but as a catalyst for current change. Unlike the "anti-prophet" Jonah (see in "The Twelve") who actually wanted his destructive prophecies to come true, Yirm^eyahu's hope is that his listeners will listen and heed and that crisis will be averted.

> For if you truly improve your ways and your actions,
> If you create justice between each man and another,
> A stranger, orphan, and widow you do not oppress
> And innocent blood you do not shed in this place,
> And after other Gods you do not go, to your own harm,
> Then I will dwell with you in this place, in the land to your ancestors for all time.
> (YIRM^EYAHU 7.5–7)

But the scroll does not present the prophet Yirm^eyahu as being successful; the crisis was not averted. However, it is equally important to ask about the rhetoric of the scroll, which was made for readers or listeners in the exile or post-exilic period long after Yirm^eyahu. How would they hear and heed these words?

Yirm^eyahu's boldness is matched by his creativity and free use of traditions. In an echo of the first lines of Genesis, he pictures the earth returning to "formless and void" and "darkness." Yirmeyahu is telling a "de-creation" story (4.23–26). In another case, he repeats the tradition that YHVH is with them, and then boldly asks YHVH why he is like a warrior who cannot fight. He imagines YHVH as a wandering stranger among the people; confused and stumbling and not aware enough to help (see 14.7–9). A couple of places Yirm^eyahu uses a device called an *atbash*. In this clever device the letters of the alphabet are reversed for spelling words. In English, for example, every *A* would become a *Z*, and every *B* would become a *Y*, and so on for the entire alphabet. We find these curious literary figures 25.26 and 51.1 and 41 for Babylon and Chaldea. These and many other expressions are the product of an agile and inventive poet.

Finally, the scroll of Yirm^eyahu is not all negative in regard to the future. True, as he sees the kingdom fall, he declares that no offspring of David will ever again rule (22.30). But in fact, other oracles present a picture of hope for the future (e.g., 23.5–6). We can say that some of the scroll's most famous lines are expressions of hope for the future. In Chapters 30–31, for example, a picture of the future is imagined with Israel and Judah restored and a **new covenant** established with their God. How these words of hope related to Yirm^eyahu's condemnation of other prophets who preached hope is a question the scroll does not overtly address. Do these ideas reflect a different time in the life of the prophet Yirm^eyahu? Are they the words of Baruch or a later writer that have been added here? Are they meant to bring hope to those who experienced national destruction? One way that a future is envisioned is by the use of earlier traditions regarding a covenant between YHVH and his people. Yirm^eyahu imagines a day when there is no need for anyone such as priests and prophets to teach, for everyone will have YHVH's *torah*/instruction written internally on their hearts. This vision of perfect natural obedience to this new covenant—new in the sense that it is now impressed on the heart, not on a scroll—brings with it a perfect creation and eternal restoration of all the blessings of Israel's covenant with YHVH (see Yirm^eyahu 31.26–37).

Before we move on to another scroll, we might well reflect on this scroll's criticism of royal, priestly, and prophetic establishment and its inclusion in our library. There are many directions our questions could go. What words, ideas, institutions would be modern analogies of Yirmᵉyahu's? How do or can modern religious traditions make use of the subverting notions of the scroll? Is there not major irony in the inclusion of this book side by side with other priestly books in this library? What does that inclusion say about the vision and ideas of those who collected our library?

Questions for Further Study

1. The picture of Yirmᵉyahu the scroll gives is a rather tragic figure. How does this affect the rhetoric, or persuasive quality, of the scroll?

2. Yirmᵉyahu is a great scroll for learning about compositional history. How do the references to scrolls and writing and the various forms of Yirmᵉyahu in antiquity impact your historical understanding of prophets and writing in ancient Israel?

3. What religious and social conflicts of authority do you hear in passages such as Yirmᵉyahu, 2, 7, 8 and 14, and Isaiah 1 and 58? Investigate the social situation of these conflicts.

References

Blank, Sheldon H. *Jeremiah.* Philadelphia: Westminster, 1986.

Carroll, Robert J. *Jeremiah.* Philadelphia: SCM Press, 1986.

Ludrom, Jack R. "Jeremiah, Book of," in *The Anchor Bible Dictionary,* edited by David W. Freedman, 3:698–706. New York: Doubleday, 1992.

Rosenberg, Joel. "Jeremiah and Ezekiel," in *The Literary Guide to the Bible,* edited by Robert Alter and Frank Kermode. 184–206. Cambridge, MA: Harvard, 1987.

Silberman, Neil and Yuval Goren. "Faking Biblical History," *Archaeology 56* (2003): 20–9.

Swete, Henry Barclay. *An Introduction to the Old Testament in Greek.* Cambridge: Cambridge University, 1902.

Tov, Emanuel. *Textual Criticism of the Hebrew Bible.* 2nd ed. Minneapolis, MN: Fortress, 2001.

——. "The Literary History of the Book of Jeremiah in the Light of Its Textual History," in *Empirical Models for Biblical Criticism,* edited by Jeffrey H. Tigay, 211-38. Philadelphia: University of Pennsylvania 1985.

יחזקאל

Ezekiel *Y^ekhezqel*

SECTION OUTLINE

Y^ekhezqel the Prophet in His Setting
Literary Format and Movement
Y^ekhezqel the Entertainer
Text and Composition
Major Messages
Questions for Further Study
References

If there was ever evidence of superior imaginative powers and intellect among Israel's prophetic writers, this is it. This scroll comes from a creative mind full of unique ideas, images, visions, illustrations, and actions. Although it uses many traditional prophetic modes, such as frequent introductory claims of YHVH speaking, it often uses them with its own individual flair and personality. Ezekiel has always seemed "loud" to me. The rhetoric is strong, and the images are bold. Religiously, it is not very difficult to summarize the overarching messages of the scroll, which are expressed in many different ways. By the end of the scroll, having heard many distinct and inventive oracles, a reader is well aware of the writer's major concern for loyalty to YHVH and his ultimate hope in YHVH's ability to defeat all Israel's enemies and bring about a new and glorious kingdom.

The name of the scroll is that of the prophet mentioned in the opening lines, Y^ekhezqel. Pronounced as "y^ekhez-*kale*" (*kh* pronounced like *ch* as in *Bach*), this prophet is introduced as a priest and that identification matches major interests of the author(s) of this scroll. Scholars have found many connections between this scroll and Leviticus, a scroll he likely used. The audience is the people of Judah and Jerusalem, now exiled in Babylon. However, the writer constantly refers to his audience as *Israel*, using the broader and more ancient term. Y^ekhezqel is clearly not using *Israel* in a restricted sense, referring to the Northern Kingdom that had come to an end well over a century before the time of our scroll.

Yekhezqel the Prophet in His Setting

The scroll of Y^ekhezqel provides us a lot of information about the dates and setting of the prophet after whom the book is named. He is a widowed spokesperson for YHVH and lived and lectured in Babylon in the early years of the Jewish

*L*ITERARY FORMAT AND MOVEMENT

The scroll of Yᵉkhezqel is both diverse and clearly organized, repetitive and surprising. Stepping back to describe a larger structure, most readers have divided the scroll into three large sections that present oracles against Judah and Jerusalem (Chapters 1–24), oracles against foreign nations, especially Egypt (Chapters 25–32), and oracles of hope and restoration for Jerusalem (Chapters 33–48). The scroll is presented as a first-person report of the visions and oracles received by Yᵉkhezqel from YHVH, and of Yᵉkhezqel's actions in response to them. Rhetorically there is a strong emphasis, perhaps more than any other prophetic scroll, on the divine origin of his message. It begins in the opening lines of the scrolls and never loses momentum. The scroll is composed of a long series of oracles that are routinely set off from one another with introductory formula such as "the word of YHVH came to me" and "thus says YHVH." Oracles are often closed with "declares YHVH," "says Master YHVH," or "for I YHVH have spoken." Visions often begin with "I looked and I saw . . ." Direct instructions often come from YHVH to the prophet beginning with "O mortal . . ." This last term, *Mortal*, is clearly the writer's preferred self-designation. It is literally *ben adam*, "**son of man**/Adam," and occurs over 90 times in the scroll, each time emphasizing the distance between the merely mortal prophet and the deity who speaks to him. All of these formulas serve as guidelines that divide the revelations and give the work a rhythmic regularity, despite the diversity of form of the oracles and visions.

Another literary mechanism used in the scroll is the giving of precise dates for many of the oracles, such as we find in 1.1–3. Fifteen times oracles are dated to the very day of their performance. Performance seems a very good word to use for Yᵉkhezqel's activity. This provides a sense of temporal progress that relates to the actual content of the oracles and also serves to emphasize for the reader a sense of orality and of the prophetic event. The scroll even opens with such a chronological stress. Unfortunately, the first date given, "in the thirtieth year" (1.1) and its relation to the next date of "the fifth year of exile of King Jehoiachin" (1.2) remains ambiguous, because we are not sure what the starting episode of the 30 years is.

It is an impossible task to briefly describe the style and form of the oracles and visions in an adequate manner. English Bibles present much of the scroll in prose, but many Hebrew scholars have noted that even in prose much of the scroll uses poetic stylistic features. In some sense Yᵉkhezqel precipitates the apocalyptic imagination of later Jewish writers. The book contains everything from mystical visions of the divine realm, to priestly records, allegories and crude parables, foreign mythologies, imaginary future battles, international historiography, obscure Israelite lore, popular proverbs and lyrics, and reports of out of body experiences. Yᵉkhezqel reports on YHVH-ordered dramas for his audiences with their strange antics and bizarre acts. The prophet of this scroll is colorful and creative, and nothing can surprise the reader by the end. One modern scholar has compared his imaginative power to the writers Dante, Milton, and Blake (Rosenberg 1987, 195).

1.1–3 Introduction of time, prophet, YHVH's oracles	1.4–24.27 Series of oracles against Jerusalem and Judah for unfaithfulness to YHVH

25.1–17 Oracles against Ammon, Moab, Edom, Philistia	26.1–28.26 Oracles against Tyre and Sidon	29.1–32.32 Oracles against Egypt

33.1–39.29 Oracles of Israel's restoration and destruction of enemies	40.1–48.35 Oracles of the new temple and cult and new land of Jerusalem

exile there. Yᵉkhezqel, an educated priest, was likely among those taken captive in 598 BCE with some 8,000 others, in the first Babylonian onslaught (see 2 Kings 24.16). He even describes his particular setting—his neighborhood—as on the Chebar River. This was a larger irrigation canal, known to us from other sources, which diverted water from the Euphrates just north of Babylon. The earliest oracles are dated to 593 BCE, followed by more in 591, 588, 587, 585, 573, and one, a prophetic "update" of sorts, to 571. The second and final Babylonian campaign against Jerusalem came about a decade later when Jewish rule in Jerusalem collapsed in 586 BCE. In those intervening years, Jews in exile and those still in Judah were not always in accord regarding the Babylonian empire. Some hoped for its demise, some actively looked to Egypt for military aid, and some were resigned to a Babylonian conquest. All these sides, and others, would have made religious arguments for their positions, and YHVH was undoubtedly enlisted on all sides. We might recall that around this time the prophet Jeremiah attempted to persuade people not to listen to some other prophets of YHVH whose message was counter to his own (see Jeremiah 29.8–23). Yᵉkhezqel, too, prophesied against other prophets (13.1–23). Like Jeremiah, he understood the Babylonian conquest as the work of YHVH to punish his people because of their disloyalty to their covenantal obligations. Yet this same covenant also provides the basis for Yᵉkhezqel's message of hope; we can see both sides of the coin vividly and crudely in Chapter 16. At this time of crisis, Yᵉkhezqel brings messages of challenge, imagination, and hope.

> . . . I pledged myself to you and entered into a covenant with you, declared Master YHVH . . . but you trusted in your beauty and prostituted yourself . . . Behold, I will put out my hand against you . . . Thus says Master YHVH, I will do to you even as you did, spurning the pact and covenant. . . . But I myself will remember my covenant with you in the days of your youth and I will uphold for you an eternal covenant. (EZEKIEL 16.8, 15, 27, 59, 60)

Yᵉkhezqel the Entertainer

The prophet that is presented to us in this scroll is a highly imaginative figure, and he is even self-conscious about it. His performance antics, which are usually part of his revelation from YHVH, include digging through walls of his house (12.1–20), cutting and burning hair (5.1–4), eating scrolls (2.8–3.3), and lying on his side for 390 and then 40 days (4.4–8), to name a few. The opening vision of the scroll describes him seeing a mystical throne chariot of YHVH with detailed descriptions of its movement and surrounding creatures, yet at the end the witness makes it clear that the vision only reveals a likeness, a semblance, a mystery. Try drawing a picture of what he describes! Another vision transports the prophet back to Jerusalem where he watches the glory of YHVH depart the temple of Jerusalem (10.1–11.25). The prophet's allegories are bold and may seem shocking, such as when Israel is portrayed as a prostitute lying on a stage in the city square spreading her legs for passersby and playing with phalluses (see Chapters 16 and 23). The prophet's expansive erudition is perhaps best shown in the oracles against the foreign nations, where he creates allegories using myths and lore from surrounding cultures. After all this and more, we are not surprised in Chapter 33.30–33 when the prophetic figure complains that people talk about him and love to come hear him as one might love an entertainer, "with a beautiful voice who plays well on the lute" (33.32). The complaint is that they love to listen but they don't bother to obey!

Text and Composition

Ancient textual evidence for this scroll shows some variety in textual form; the Greek translation—shorter in many places and omitting repetitions—shows clearly that not all Ezekiel scrolls in antiquity were the same. To complicate matters more, Josephus, a Jewish historian writing in Rome around 100 CE, credits two books to Yᵉkhezqel (*Jewish Antiquities* 10.79), though some scholars speculate that he was thinking of two large sections of our scroll, Chapters 1–24 and 25–48. For our purposes, we will concentrate on the Yᵉkhezqel of medieval manuscripts, which was also an ancient form of the composition. As far as the early history of the scroll's composition, most scholars conclude that behind the original written form stand oral presentations of a sixth-century prophet living in Babylon. He, or writers who came shortly after him in the same century, likely put the material in the format that we know.

Major Messages

Through its dating system, our scroll makes clear that even though Jerusalem had been attacked, YHVH's word, even to those in exile, is a message of denunciation and punishment of Jerusalem and Israel for what was seen as a history of unfaithfulness to YHVH. Rhetorically this aims to convince listeners not to expect a miraculous triumph or return from exile, as some prophets announced. For readers decades later, history had confirmed Yᵉkhezqel's words and the lesson of the importance of obedience was underscored. For anyone with priestly sensibilities, nothing could illustrate more chillingly the gravity of the situation than Yᵉkhezqel's temple visions that depict YHVH's glory, a mysterious symbol of his presence, departing from the temple (see chapters 8–11).

Sometimes the prophetic oracles are descriptive of just what constitutes unfaith-fulness to YHVH for the author. We find, for example, condemnations of violence (7.11; 11.6), worship of other deities (8.1–18; 14.1–5), treating aliens with con-tempt, profaning the Sabbath, and extortion (22.6–12). One oracle says that Jerusalem is being destroyed for the same reasons as Sodom (see Genesis 19), namely for their arrogance and lack of compassion for poor and needy (16.49). Chapter 18 lists numerous items that the prophet opposes: adultery, sex during a wife's menstrual period, oppression, not helping the hungry, and many others. This chapter also stresses individual accountability: sons are not punished for their father's sins, past generations cannot be blamed, and one's fate is not set by the misdeeds of one's parents. On this final matter, the argument is clearly polemical, and the author even cites opposing arguments. Indeed, Israelite literature, even within the priesthood, also represents those with divergent view points, as one can read in Exodus 20.5 and 34.7.

The second large segment of the scroll (Chapter 25–32) is dedicated to con-demning other nations—mostly neighbors within Syria-Palestine and also Egypt. This had become a typical practice of prophetic speech, and its audience is clearly made up of Israelites, not the courts and streets of the foreign nations. In our scroll, this section provides some of the finest illustrations of the author's literary and artis-tic brilliance. Condemning other nations and declaring that YHVH will soon pun-ish them may serve different purposes, but the one lesson that it teaches in all cases is that YHVH is in control of all nations; eventually his justice will be administered even to Israel's enemies. In the scroll of Yᵉkhezqel, what should we make of the fact that Babylon is *not* one of the nations that is condemned? Was not Babylon exiling YHVH's people in the scroll's timeframe? What might be the result of an anti-Babylon pronouncement? It is clear is that Egypt, Babylon's superpower nemesis of the time, and, more importantly, the power to which some Israelites were looking for military support against Babylon, is extensively condemned (Chapters 29–32). In highly creative ways, Yᵉkhezqel's parables and poetry paint fascinating images of YHVH's universal sovereignty. The prophet's boldness and confidence is under-scored by the overt admission of an erroneous prophecy in 26.7–21 and 29.17–20.

Even the early section of the scroll provides messages of hope for the exiles. But hope comes to dominate at the end of the scroll, where the oracles are dated after the final collapse of Jerusalem in 586 BCE. The most famous oracle of hope is the memorable "valley of dry bones" section in Chapter 37. Perhaps it got its most famous hearing in the modern era through the Negro spiritual whose chorus includes, "Dem bones, dem bones, dem dry bones." The passage is a powerfully ani-mated depiction of life from death, encouraging despondent exiles to be hopeful, because YHVH, by the power of his word (spoken by the prophet!), will bring them back from the dead and return them to their land. Other oracles give images of David returning as king (37.24) and a cataclysmic final battle against an imaginary foe representing all possible foes, Gog, King of Magog. YHVH will win, and the entire world will know that YHVH reigns as God (38.1–39.29). That battle segment is significant in the history of ancient Israel's literature because it anticipates and was likely influential for the development of apocalyptic literature, such as we find in the scroll of Daniel. Finally, in the last lengthy subsection of the scroll (40.1–48.35), we find a detailed blueprint for the building and operation of YHVH's new temple in Jerusalem and a geographical renewal of the earth so that Israel's kingdom is restored and Jerusalem is centralized with waters of life flowing out from it. And most importantly, our prophet-priest closes the scroll with a final resolution to the crisis of YHVH's leaving the temple first described in Chapters 8–11. The scroll closes with: "The name of the city from that day on is 'YHVH Is There.'" And so the final vision of encouragement ends. The final picture in the reader's mind, whether in exile or decades later in any other location, is of YHVH's temple in YHVH's city, where YHVH is present.

Questions for Further Study

1. Of the many colorful metaphors and images in Yᵉkhezqel, which do you find most interesting? How do these function rhetorically in the scroll?

2. Why would a prophet and a prophetic scroll speak as if they were directly addressing foreign and distant people, as Yᵉkhezqel often does?

References

Boadt, Lawrence. "Ezekiel, Book of," in *The Anchor Bible Dictionary,* edited by David N. Freedman, 2:711–22. New York: Doubleday, 1992.

Klein, Ralph W. *Ezekiel.* Columbia, SC: University of South Carolina, 1988.

Rosenberg, Joel. "Jeremiah and Ezekiel," in *The Literary Guide to the Bible,* edited by Robert Alter and Frank Kermode, 184–206. Cambridge, MA: Harvard, 1987.

Zimmerli, Walther. *Ezekiel,* 2 vols. Philadelphia: Fortress, 1979, 1983.

The Scroll of the Twelve

Twelve to One

This scroll clearly began its history as many separate documents, at least twelve or more separate scrolls. In fact, in manuscript tradition after the invention of the codex, these are separated into twelve separate books, just as other books such as Isaiah and Jeremiah. Within Jewish tradition, the rubric "The Twelve" has been retained. This tradition goes back at least to the early second century BCE when a Jewish writer referred to "the twelve prophets" as a group (Ben Sira 49.10). Furthermore, a few Dead Sea Scroll manuscripts—our only textual witnesses from the period before the invention of the codex—contain several of these writings on the same scroll.

Practical considerations likely had much to do with the anthologizing onto one scroll of these texts that span approximately 500 years. Some of the texts are so short—only a column or two that they would have been easily lost as single manuscripts. All twelve together are still shorter than any of the three "major" prophets. They are also naturally grouped, being prophetic oracles, with one exception. There were probably other prophetic writings that could have been used but were not. The final tally of twelve may have been motivated by the attractiveness of that number in the ancient Jewish tradition. Some have debated how the narrative book of Jonah fits in with the other writings that are all literature of prophetic oracle. Someone clearly decided to make an anthology, and at some point probably in the third century BCE the number was set at twelve. The order of the twelve, however, varies between the standard Masoretic Hebrew manuscripts and the standard Greek manuscripts. The oldest of the Dead Sea Scroll manuscripts (4QXIIa), though not complete, show an even different order. Most modern English Bibles follow the Masoretic order, and so we will, too. Although there are interesting investigations to be made about the combining of the compositions, in this chapter we will focus on each text as an individual composition—as they originally existed and as they are in most manuscript traditions today.

הושע

Hosea *Hoshea*

Section Outline

Hoshea's Time: Politics
Literary Format and Movement
Hoshea's Time: Religion
The Text
Questions for Further Study
References

The independent prophetic composition that was placed first on this scroll of twelve goes under the Hebrew name of *Hoshea*, pronounced "ho-*shay*-ah." This name is essentially the same as the name Joshua, *Yᵉhoshua*; both mean "YHVH's salvation." This is the second longest of the twelve minor prophets; only Zechariah is longer. Hoshea, who is not mentioned in our library outside of this composition and is not known from any other sources, lived in the Northern Kingdom of Israel during the second half of the eighth century. Thus he was a contemporary of the prophet Amos who came to Israel to proclaim his oracle. Hoshea's time as an active prophet, if the content of his oracles is an accurate indication, seems to have extended later than that Amos into the period when Israel was in the decades-long process of falling to the Assyrian Empire. Hoshea's favorite name for the Northern Kingdom is Ephraim, which was the name of the dominant northern tribe, even as Judah is the name of the dominant southern tribe.

Hoshea's Time: Politics

The only attempt by the scroll's final author to date the writing is found in 1.1, where the names of five kings are given. The editor who penned this superscription was most familiar with and most interested in matters of Judah, the Southern Kingdom, indicated by the fact that four of the five kings are of Judah, and only one is from Israel, the region of Hoshea's activity. Modern historians set the dates of that one, Jeroboam II to between 788 and 747 BCE. The four Judean kings mentioned run to nearly 70 years later, to beginning of the seventh century. Jeroboam II's reign was long and prosperous; he was fortunate that the

LITERARY FORMAT AND MOVEMENT

The organizer of this composition, who came after Hoshea, arranged it into two sections, Chapters 1–3 and 4–14. The first part, about one-quarter of the scroll, contains two prose sections and serves as an extended thematic introduction to the loosely arranged poetic oracles that follow. In startling prose, a narrator tells of Hoshea's marriage to a prostitute. The oracles of the second section are not tightly arranged by content and are not divided by the common prophetic introductory formulas common to many other prophetic texts, such as "thus says YHVH." In fact, only at 4.1 does the editor supply the common rhetorical opening. The thematic tie of the composition is faithfulness/unfaithfulness in the relationship of YHVH and Israel. There is movement in the oracles between prophetic proclamation referring to YHVH in the third person and first person speech of YHVH. The concluding oracles call for return and restoration. Unfortunately the verse numbering systems of traditional Hebrew and traditional Christian English Bibles do not match, so in the following outline I give both numbers when they differ, English numbers in parentheses.

1.1 Editorial superscription

1.2–9 Hoshea's marriage to prostitute Gomer

2.1–25 (1.10–2.23) YHVH's relations with Israel

3.1–5 Hoshea's second marriage to prostitute Gomer

4.1–14.1 (4.1–13.16) Oracles on the relations of Israel and YHVH: faithfulness/unfaithfulness; departure/return; condemnation/comfort

14.2–9 (14.1–8) Call for return and healing

14.10 (14.9) Reflective postscript

Assyrian empire was not yet advancing in the area of Syrian-Palestine during the first half of the eighth century and that Egypt was embroiled in long civil war. Jeroboam's capital was at Samaria, and his influence extended far beyond that to many parts of Syria-Palestine. Some of the oracles of Hoshea seem to reflect on this time of prosperity and security. For example, consider these segments: "Ephraim says, 'Ah, I am rich, I have found wealth. All my gain has not found in me guilt of sin'" (12.9 [or 12.8]).

But this good fortune was spent with the arrival of King Tiglath-Pileser III to the Assyrian throne (745 to 727 BCE), because his imperial designs were set on the small kingdoms and lands of Syria-Palestine. Annual brutal campaigns were made into the region, kingdoms fell, a program of exile was put into practice—local leaders were deported, and foreign populations were brought in. Kings of the region attempted to save their kingdoms by payment of large tributes, which were essentially forced bribes; at other times they attempted to resist the Assyrian onslaught by looking to each other or to Egypt for military aid. Such attempts proved futile, as many small nations who have been victims of superpowers, ancient and modern, could testify. The successors of Jeroboam II endured tremendous pressures externally and internally, and as a result the last 25 years of the Northern Kingdom saw six different kings, most of whom were assassinated; dynastic lines changed four times. Less than two years after Jeroboam's death, Israel under King Menahem was paying Assyria an exorbitant tribute of over 100,000 pounds of silver, which likely would have been raised in taxes (see 2 Kings 15). By 732 BCE the major regional power Damascus had fallen, and major portions of Israel's area of dominance were removed from her control and administered by Assyria. The last king of Israel, also named Hoshea, was merely a client king of Assyria, ruling by Assyrian whim and paying annual tribute. At the end he decided to rebel against Assyrian control, and he asked Egypt for help; the result was complete disaster. Archaeologists have found the Assyrian records: Samaria was destroyed, 29,290 Israelites were deported, and 200 chariots were captured (see also 2 Kings 17). The poems of Hoshea the prophet do not seem to reference an awareness of the final destruction, but they do show an awareness of the years of increasing confusion that preceded it.

Hoshea's Time: Religion

Religiously, the viewpoint of the scroll of Hoshea aligns with the attitude of several other books. The covenantal relationship with YHVH is emphasized, and for this relationship Hoshea presents a YHVH-only position. As we noted in Chapter Two, Israelite religion as it existed historically is not the same as Israelite religion as conceived of by individual authors of our library. In this period there is plenty of archaeological evidence that Israelites at Samaria honored the Canaanite God Baal. Worship of Baal and YHVH was mixed in some Israelite circles according to Hoshea 2.18 (16). Hoshea objected to the worship of Baal, to arrangements that combined Baalism and YHVHism, and to images of other Gods (2.15 [2.13]; 4.12, 17; 9.10; 11.2). Quite naturally then, Hoshea's anger seemed especially aimed at priests who would not strictly enforce YHVH-only practices (4.4–9; 5.1; 6.4–9).

For our poet, the strongest condemnation of honoring other Gods comes not in specific references to other deities, but by using the metaphor of marriage. YHVH is Israel's only legitimate partner, and repeatedly the prophet condemns Israel for forgetting the covenant with YHVH and for acting like a prostitute, going after other Gods. The entire introductory segment (Chapters 1–3) serves this purpose. Consider these selections from Chapters 3 and 4:

> YHVH said to me again go, love a woman who loves another man, an adulteress,
> Just as YHVH loves Israel and they turn to other Gods. . . .
> Hear YHVH's word, people of Israel,
> Because YHVH has an indictment against those who live in the land,
> Because there is no faithfulness or loving-loyalty,
> Nor knowledge of God in the land (3.1, 4.1)

This imagery of a prostitute is not unique to Hoshea; it's actually a fairly common literary trope in prophetic poems to speak of Israel's unfaithfulness. But Hoshea does illustrate the metaphor with an object lesson like none other. The beginning chapters tell of Hoshea and his prostitute bride Gomer; the opening lines are rather startling. Like other prophetic scrolls, this one opens with an announcement of the YHVH speaking to the prophet. But what YHVH commands is certainly unexpected: "Go, marry a woman of prostitution, have children of prostitution, for the land prostitutes itself away from YHVH" (1.2). Chapter 1 continues this narrative of Hoshea's marriage to a prostitute named Gomer in a third-person prose format; Chapter 3 shifts to a first-person format. Gomer and Hoshea have three children—though it is not clear they are all his—who are given religiously symbolic names, such as YHVH Plants, No-Mercy, and Not-My-People. Of course, it is impossible to say whether there is any historicity to these narratives. But it is not relevant for understanding the rhetorical purpose of this scroll. The overt and transparent message is a call for Israel to refuse to worship other Gods and live faithfully according to covenant laws with YHVH, who loves them exceedingly and will embrace them and restore them.

> I will heal their disloyalty
> I will love them abundantly/graciously
> For my anger has turned from them.
> (14.5 [OR 14.4])

In this and other passages, the author speaks as YHVH in the first person, tenderly and to great rhetorical effect. However this message in its current written form is not addressed to the Northern Kingdom, but to people of a much later time, the Southern Kingdom. As all prophetic oracles, this one, too, was updated as later scribes or prophets wrote the words of YHVH for their own generation, perhaps before and after the fall of the Southern Kingdom in 586 BCE. Thus, sometimes Judahites are explicitly addressed, as in 6.11.

Finally we should mention that Hoshea references many ideas from Israelite traditions about the past, and many modern students have found his use of older traditions a fascinating study. It cannot be assumed that authors whose books stand late in our library's order knew the scrolls that come before. It is possible that a prophet in the eighth century wouldn't know the same stories of Israel's past that we know from the scroll of Genesis, for example. But the poem in 12.2–6 refers to several events spoken of in Genesis from the life of Jacob: his wrestling with an angel and his interaction with YHVH. There are some interesting wordplays in his use of stories from Genesis 25, 28, and 32. The poet uses these stories to promote his own message of love and justice.

The Text

The Hebrew text of Hoshea contains many difficult passages, and, the Greek translations and Dead Sea Scrolls do not offer us better readings. In fact, many early translators had just as much difficulty as modern ones do, as evidenced by their translations. Hosea is full of unusual word forms and odd grammatical constructions. Scholars are not sure how much of this to attribute to the process of transmission,

Study Room 7.3

SEEING WOMEN, SEEING PROSTITUTES

The depiction of women in ancient texts, including those of our library, is not just a matter of literary or historical study but is also subject to other forms of research. Today there are many forms of study that focus on certain aspects of culture or on persons as members of a society—sometimes called ideological criticisms. They pursue specific lines of questioning, such as the depiction and role of women or the way a society or author uses socio-economic categories.

The common use of the female prostitute as a metaphor for religiously unfaithful people (e.g., Hoshea, Isaiah, Jeremiah, Ezekiel) has been widely investigated as a part of feminist criticism. This analogy casts YHVH as the always faithful husband who is cheated by his unfaithful prostitute wife, Israel. The metaphor is never reversed. What can be said about roles of women and views of women in these depictions? What can legitimately be surmised about the ideology of the authors or Israelite society? How do such depictions reflect or affect stereotypes, ancient or modern? Dozens of other questions could be asked. To investigate the discussions see Laffey 1988, Trible 1978, and Yee 2003.

as in the case of Samuel, or to dialectical idiosyncrasies of the poet, as in the case of Job. If you look at one of the two more candid translations, the New Revised Standard Version and especially the Jewish Publication Society's Tanakh, you will often see footnotes indicating that the meaning of the Hebrew is uncertain or that an emendation seemed necessary to make sense of the Hebrew words. Such honesty among translators is refreshing.

Questions for Further Study

1. What are the proper ethics of textual criticism and translation? Every modern translation is the work of people who make decisions about what to tell and not tell their audience. What things should a translator tell about an ancient text? For example, should a translator say that a translation may be doubtful, the text ambiguous, or that there may be problems with the manuscript? What principles would you use to answers such questions? What are the obligations to honesty?

2. Many have said that a major theme of Hoshea is YHVH's unconditional love for Israel. Read through the scroll looking for this theme and its nuances. What do you find?

References

Anderson, Francis I., and David N. Freedman. *Hosea.* Garden City, NY: Doubleday, 1980.

Campbell, Edward F., Jr. "A Land Divided: Judah and Israel from the Death of Solomon to the Fall of Samaria, in *The Oxford History of the Biblical World,* edited by Michael D. Coogan, 206–41. New York: Oxford, 1988.

Laffey, Alice. *An Introduction to the old Testament: A Feminist Perspective.* Philadelphia: Fortress, 1988.

Mays, James L. *Hosea.* Philadelphia: Westminster, 1969.

Seow, C.L. "Hosea, Book of," in *The Anchor Bible Dictionary,* edited by David N. Freedman, 3:291–97. New York: Doubleday, 1992.

Trible, Phyllis. *God and Rhetoric of Sexuality.* Philadelphia: Fortress, 1978.

Yee, Gale A. *Poor Banished Children of Eve: Women as Evil in the Hebrew Bible.* Minneapolis, MN: Augsburg Fortress, 2003.

יואל

Joel *Yoel*

Joel was apparently a prophet in Israel—that's about all we can say. There is a dearth of information about the person for whom the scroll is named and about the time in which he lived. His name, *Yoel*, means "YHVH is God," and it was a common name among ancient Jews, especially after the Babylonian exile. In Hebrew it is pronounced "yo-*ale*."

Dating the Composition

When we try to date a writing, what do we look for? Meaningful and verifiable dates mentioned in the writing would be helpful, of course, but often ancient writers do not put a date on their compositions. Any historical references can be helpful—references to people or events that can be dated using other sources, such as kings or wars, can be helpful. Among ancient Israelite documents a reference to a threatening Assyrian or Babylonian army helps us date the text to the times when Israelites and others in Syria-Palestine felt threatened by the mighty Assyrian or Babylonian empires. But when we come to Yoel we find very little to help us date the writing. Yoel's most extensive disaster reference is not to a war we can identify, but to a locust plague—a metaphor that would have been meaningful for all of Israel's history. Our best clue in the case of Yoel is the frequent use he makes of material we know of from elsewhere in our library, including earlier prophetic literature, such as Amos. So it seems best to place him after the eighth century. There are also a few references that seem to reflect a time after Judah's exile, that is, after 539 BCE, such as the mention of Jews living in Greek lands in Joel 4.6 (or 3.6). Most scholars today place the book in the fifth or early fourth century BCE.

LITERARY FORMAT AND MOVEMENT

The majority of this scroll is poetry, as we expect in prophetic writings, with a section of prose in the second half. Rhetorically, the composition moves back and forth from highly charged emotive announcements of coming disaster meant to induce repentance to formal calls for repentance and statements of hope. The final movement is a positive vision of the future restoration of Israel. Printed Hebrew texts divide Yoel into four chapters, whereas printed Greek texts divided it into three, despite the fact that the actual content of Greek and Hebrew manuscripts is nearly identical. Modern English Bibles, even those translated from Hebrew (KJV, NRSV, NIV), still follow the Greek numbering! This is another evidence of the profound influence Greek Bibles have had on English Christian versions.

1.1 Editorial superscription

1.2–20 Announces catastrophe and calls for repentance

2.1–17 Warns of catastrophe and call for repentance

2.18–27 YHVH promising of blessing on land

3.1–4.21 (or 2.28–3.21) YHVH promising the Day of YHVH; a great battle, defeat and desolation for enemies, salvation and restoration for Jerusalem/Judah

Today's Priestly-Prophetic Message, Yesterday's Words

The short poetic essay of Yoel appears fairly traditional in terms of its religious message. We encounter the ideas of judgment, repentance, future battles, the Day of YHVH, destruction of enemies, and restoration of Jerusalem in several of our prophetic scrolls. Yoel may well have been influenced by other apocalyptic writers, depending on where he is placed historically, for this work's depiction of the future seems to point to the fuller apocalyptic expressions such as we read in Zechariah and Daniel. The author appeals to his listeners to repent, gathering as a community for fasting and sacrifice. The author fully assumes the legitimacy of YHVH's temple and priesthood, and his calls to repentance repeatedly are calls to formal assembly, sacrifice, and prayer led by priests. For example see 1.8–10, 13–14; 2.15–17.

Prepare a fast, proclaim an assembly,
Gather elders, all those who live in the land
To the house of YHVH your God,
And cry out to YHVH.
(YOEL 1.14)

There is no "anti-temple" sentiment to found here. Yoel has often been called a cultic prophet, a prophet who may have been associated with the temple in one way or another and whose message is in harmony with priestly concerns. Writings such as this help us fill out the complex prophetic realities, and trying to understand the

Study Room 7.4

WHAT'S THE DAY OF YHVH?

The references to the Day of YHVH became a favorite concept among some of Israel's ancient prophets. Chronologically we find the phrase first used by Amos and then also in the scrolls of Isaiah, Jeremiah, Ezekiel, Yoel, Obadiah, Zephaniah, and Malachi. However, the phrase in not used by some prophets: Hosea, Jonah, Micah, Nahum, Habakkuk, Haggai, Zechariah. But what were they referring to when they speak of the Day of YHVH? Is it good or bad? A holiday or a doomsday? Based on the way Amos speaks of this momentous day (5.18–20), it is clear that most of his audience thought it was a good day and a day to look forward to, when YHVH would act to prove his might and make Israel victorious against her enemies and their Gods. The wording is similar to a phrase used to speak of the day of great military victory by ancient kings and their Gods. But Amos says that people should not look forward to the Day of YHVH because on it they will be the ones YHVH defeated and punished; "it is darkness, not light."

Literature from prophets of later centuries revives the positive use of the Day of YHVH. Consider, for example, Obadiah 15–17 and Zechariah 14.1–9.

But what about Yoel? What do you make of the uses in Yoel 1.15; 2.1, 11; 3.4 (or 2.31); 4.14 (or 3.14)? Is it a good or bad day? for whom? What are the events and themes of the day? What is their cause? How does Yoel's use fit with the other scrolls?

interaction of priests and prophets at various times in Israelite history makes for fascinating sociological study.

Another fascinating way for us to read Yoel is by a consideration of the many earlier traditions that he uses, some of which exist in written form in other scrolls. Let's look at two examples.

YHVH form Zion roars, And from Jerusalem he sends forth his voice.
    (Amos 1.2)
	And YHVH from Zion roars, And from Jerusalem he sends forth his voice.
	    (Yoel 4.16 [or 3.16])

He [YHVH] shall judge between the nations, And adjudicate for many people. And they shall beat their swords into plows, And their spears into pruning hooks.
    (Isaiah 2.4a and Micah 4.4)
	Proclaim this among the nations: "Prepare for war! . . . Beat your plows into swords, And your pruning hooks into spears."
	    (Yoel 4.9a, 10 [or 3.9a, 10])

In the first example, the poet of Yoel uses a vivid figure of YHVH roaring, borrowed from the opening words of Amos. In the second and much more startling usage, he borrows the now famous lines from Isaiah, which were repeated verbatim in Micah, about turning weapons of war into implements of peace and prosperity. All three texts, Isaiah, Micah, and Yoel, are speaking of the future in some visionary sense. Isaiah and Micah are picturing a time of peace; Yoel reverses the metaphors of the earlier prophet(s). This sort of creative use of past traditions likely caught the attention of anyone acquainted with the poem used by Isaiah (2.2–4) and Micah (4.1–4)—perhaps it was a famous one.

Questions for Further Study

1. As you read through Yoel as a sociological or form critic, looking for evidence about the social setting and origin of the material, what clues do you find? What kinds of language are used? What social authorities are assumed or appealed to?

References

Hibbert, Theodore. "Joel, Book of," in *The Anchor Bible Dictionary*, edited by David N. Freedman, 3:873–80. New York: Doubleday. 1992.

Marks, Herbert. "The Twelve Prophets," in *The Literary Guide to the Bible*, edited by Robert Alter and Frank Kermode, 207–33. Cambridge, MA: Harvard, 1987.

Wolff, Hans. *Joel and Amos*. Philadelphia: Fortress, 1977.

עמוס

Amos *Ahmos*

Of the classical Hebrew prophetic writings, Amos (in Hebrew *Ahmos,* "Ah-*mose*") is likely one of the oldest and most influential. If the minimal biographical details about Ahmos found in this scroll are basically accurate, as many scholars consider them to be, then Ahmos and Hosea are the only ones of the fifteen classical prophets whose are associated primarily with the Northern Kingdom. For that reason, it is important for us in the following discussion to distinguish between the Northern and Southern kingdoms.

Influence of Ahmos

Both in Israelite antiquity among prophetic thinkers and certainly among modern American social critics, the words and ideas of Ahmos have been repeatedly echoed and his courage frequently invoked. He appears to be the earliest of our classical prophets, and his ideas and expressions are borrowed by later prophets. Perhaps more than any other ancient Jewish prophet, he became a symbol of the audacious, outspoken socio-religious critic, willing to confront religious, political, and popular leaders and institutions of power. It is no wonder that the speeches of Martin Luther King, Jr., drew on the ideas and expressions of Ahmos for his own often rhetorically brilliant speeches. In light of the influent power of Ahmos's words, let's look first at the socio-religious message of these poems, and then we will consider the scroll's literary form.

LITERARY FORMAT AND MOVEMENT

The scroll of Ahmos consists mostly of poetic oracles with numerous rhetorical introductory formulas and two brief biographical passages regarding the life of Ahmos.

1.1–2 Editorial introductions

1.1 Biographical/Historical superscription

1.2 Poetic/Oracular introduction of YHVH

1.3–2.16 Oracles Condemning Israel and Her Neighbors

1.3–5 Damascus

1.6–8 Gaza

1.9–10 Tyre

1.11–12 Edom

1.13–15 Ammon

2.1–3 Moab

2.4–5 Judah

2.6–16 Israel

3.1–6.14 Series of Oracles Condemning Israel

3.1–4.12 Oracles

4.13 Praise interlude

5.1–5.7 Oracles

5.8–9 Praise interlude

5.10–6.14 Oracles

7.1–9.10 Five Visions of YHVH's Judgment

7.10–17 Narrative interlude

8.4–14 Sermon/Oracles against Israel

9.5–6 Praise interlude

9.7–10 Oracle on Israel's status

9.11–16 Concluding Oracle of Restoration

The Non—prophet's World and His Oracles

Historical investigation on the scroll of Ahmos will reveal that most scholars have concluded that Ahmos lived in the eighth century BCE and that major portions of the scroll directly reflect Ahmos's poetic addresses to his contemporaries. There are also clear indications that later poetic hands supplemented and arranged the scroll, in keeping with the prophetic and scribal values and practices of the day. Furthermore, many have found that understanding the eighth-century history and culture helps to illumine the messages of Ahmos.

An ancient editor presented biographical material Ahmos using a one-sentence preface:

The words of YHVH to Ahmos, who was among the shepherds of Tekoa, which he saw about Israel in the days of Uzziah, king of Judah and in the days of Jeroboam, son of Joash, king of Israel, two years prior to the earthquake (Ahmos 1.1).

Historical reconstruction of the state of the two kingdoms using the dates of these two kings is quite secure: Uzziah, also known in some texts as Azariah, reigned as the local king of the territory of Judah from 785 to 743 BCE (see also Isaiah 6.1; 2 Kings 15.1–7) and Jeroboam II in the northern and larger kingdom of Israel at approximately the same time, 788 to 747 BCE. These long and prosperous reigns for both nations were possible in part because the Assyrian empire was not advancing in Syria-Palestine during the first half of the eighth century, and Egypt was embroiled in a long civil war. With relief from international pressure, the Israelite kingdoms expanded and flourished. Jeroboam II, whose capital was at Samaria, extended his influence into the region of the Arameans to the North, as far as Lobo-hamath, more than 70 miles (112.65 km) northeast from the capital, and southeast to the eastern shore of the Dead Sea. Jeroboam also took advantage of favorable trade conditions to increase his power and wealth. Archaeologists working in 1910 CE found over 63 documents in Samaria from this period testifying that a generous supply of wine and oil was being supplied from estates in the Israelite countryside to persons living in Samaria, likely court officials. Others found in Samaria more than 200 beautiful imported ivory carvings, symbols of luxury of which Ahmos was aware (Ahmos 6.4).

It is in this successful Northern Kingdom that we find the prophet Ahmos active, even though he was actually from the village of Tekoa, which most scholars identify as the Tekoa of the Southern Kingdom. And, if the story in Chapter 7 represents more than a rhetorical stance, Ahmos was not even an official prophet; it was not his profession. Instead Ahmos says, "I am a shepherd whom YHVH sent to Israel to prophesy" (7.14–15). But if the oracles in this scroll are any indication, Ahmos's journey to the North was difficult: his words were a jarring, discordant denunciation in the placid harmony of prosperity in Samaria for his audiences of royal, religious, and civic leaders.

Ahmos the Social Critic

We do not have to read between the lines to hear Ahmos's top priority: social justice. In clear but rich poetic metaphors, he condemns wealthy Israelites for their economic exploitation of the needy (2.6–8), rich women for their abuse of the poor (4.1), landowners who commit injustices against the poor (5.11), the affluent who demonstrate no concern for others (6.4–7), and the priests for trying to silence the prophets (2.12; 7.16). He brings a message of doom and downfall for Jeroboam (7.9). But all of that comes in colorful outrageous language: calling women cows, accusations of head trampling, and images of the priest's wife as a prostitute. No wonder such diatribes did not go unnoticed or ignored, for according to the other biographical passage of the book (7.10–15), Ahmos raised the ire of a leading priest, Amaziah, the temple at Bethel, one of two important shrines to YHVH in the Northern Kingdom and the one closest to the capital Samaria. The priest ordered Ahmos to go back to his native land of Judah. Ahmos responded with a defense of his calling by YHVH, and the next oracle in the text brings a message of doom upon Amaziah (7.10–17). If we step back and consider the situation, it is no surprise that this Yahwist priest, whose name means "YHVH is strong," would be so opposed to this traveler from the South claiming to speak for YHVH. The priest was in a position of divine and royal authority, an official of the king, and, more importantly, a minister of YHVH. No dedicated priest could have abided the following words, which Ahmos is claiming to speak for YHVH:

> I hate, I spurn your holidays,
> And I am not moved by your celebrations.
> Even when you offer me sacrifices and offerings, I don't accept,
> And your fat animal sacrifices, I don't look at.
> Get away from me the noise of your songs,
> The music of your harps I don't hear
> But make justice roll like water
> And right-ness like a continuous river.
> (AHMOS 5.21–24)

It was, of course, the priests who oversaw the worship of YHVH, directed Israelites in the festivals, and performed the sacrifices under the aegis of long-standing tradition and divinely sanctioned law. Yet Ahmos had the audacity to speak of YHVH's hatred for these sacred rites. If we want a modern parallel, we would have to imagine a guest speaker in a synagogue, mosque, or church full of respectable civic leaders declaring, "God says to you, 'I hate what goes on in here, I hate your singing and won't listen to your prayers. Get out of here and work for justice!'"

According to the scroll's poems, repeatedly stated in dozens of unequivocal expressions, Israel's injustices will soon lead to its downfall. YHVH will punish, and the prosperous nation will be destroyed (see 2.6; 9.8). Ahmos's message of denunciation and doom is unrelenting and is softened only by a small ray of hope that Israelite leaders will reform and then YHVH, too, may change his mind and decide not to punish.

> Seek good and not evil,
> So that you will live
> And YHVH, God of armies, will be with you
> Even as you say.
> Hate evil, and love good.
> And establish justice in your gate-court
> Perhaps YHVH, God of armies, will be gracious for the remnant of Joseph.
> (AHMOS 5.14–15)

Ahmos the Revisionist

Whatever the origins and calling of the historical Ahmos, the person behind the poems of this book was no ignorant peasant. The author or speaker is well aware of standard Israelite religious ideas and traditions, and he is ideologically flexible enough to turn shrewdly the tradition against itself where he thought it necessary. For example, the expression *YHVH's Day*, often translated "Day of the Lord," is extremely common in Israelite literature from the time of the divided kingdoms and later, and in popular understanding it referred to Israel's triumph over YHVH's foreign enemies. YHVH, after all, according to many Israelites was the creator God who had chosen to dwell exclusively with Israel and would protect them, showing his military strength, fighting to victory against their enemies and granting them salvation. Ahmos works this widespread confidence into a couple other poems as well, such as in 5.14 and 9.10, and it is observed in many psalms, such as Psalms 46–47. But Ahmos mocks the hope of such triumph, picturesquely declaring that they are in for a dark surprise and will become victims, not victors (5.18–20). With the same intention, Ahmos turns to the common metaphor of YHVH as shepherd. Kings and Gods in the ancient Near East are often seen as the shepherds of their people, and famously today, that is how YHVH is pictured in Psalm 23.1:11: "YHVH is my shepherd." Ahmos's shepherd, however, is not so successful: "Thus says YHVH, 'just like a shepherd who rescues from the lion's mouth two shins or a tip of an ear, so shall be rescued the people of Israel who live in Samaria'" (3.12). Notice the sarcastic tone here—what a great rescue, not even a whole ear, just a piece!

One more example of Ahmos's willingness to oppose traditional ideas is found in 3.1–2. Here the poet rehearses the commonplace notion that YHVH had delivered the Israelites from Egypt and that he had a special, exclusive relationship with them. But if any of his listeners want to take comfort from this idea, Ahmos will not allow it. Instead, warns the poem, special choosing means special punishment for wrongs committed. Later in the book, in perhaps his most radical revisionist moment of all, Ahmos returns to what was for many the heart of Israelite religion, tradition, and life, namely, YHVH's deliverance from Egypt. The exodus story and its massive mythic value is crucial and central to the mindset of many in Israel, North and South. It is a story of Israel's special protection, exclusive covenant, and relationship with the Creator. Ahmos is well aware of this so he, in YHVH's name, asks two questions,

"To me, aren't you like the people of Cush, O people of Israel?" declares YHVH.
"Didn't I bring Israel out of Egypt
and the Philistines out of Caphtor,
and the Armeans out of Kir?" (AHMOS 9.7)

To the first question Ahmos implies the answer, yes. But any Israelite versed in the traditions and stories of the past would have answered no, and then appealed to the exodus tradition as evidence that Israel is *not* like any other nation to YHVH. And so Ahmos's second question hits even harder because in it the very exodus is subverted, and YHVH declares that he has provided exodus for the Philistines and Arameans as well, both common enemies of the Israelites (see 1.3–5; 6–8). And the poet even uses the grammar of the last question to stress the point; all three nations, Israel, Philisitia, and Aram, have to share one verb!

The poetry preserved on our scroll does not further expound on issues of exclusivity and the relativity of Israel's salvation/exodus stories, though the opening two chapters do reflect a similar multinational concern for justice. Commentators and readers have been running in different directions, exploring the various meanings and theological implications. But the purpose of Ahmos's poetry is not to theorize about theological topics such as Israel's election, its exclusive relationship with YHVH, or its sacred stories about its past, though as a matter of principle Ahmos is clearly willing to challenge, even undermine cherished traditions. The thrust of this poetry and of the eighth-century prophet was to denounce the social injustice of a prosperous society, perpetrated by wealthy families, royalty, and priests.

POSTER 7.4

GOING TO CUSH, CAPHTOR, OR KIR?

Cush is the ancient Hebrew name for Ethiopia or ancient Nubia, the area in Africa south of Egypt. Forms of it are used in numerous places in biblical literature, such as Numbers 12.1, Jeremiah 13.23, and Daniel 11.43. Cush was a country only on the fringe of Israelite consciousness—not important at all—and that seems to be important for driving home the point in Ahmos 9.7.

Caphtor likely refers to one of two islands, either Crete or Cyprus. Historians are unsure of which island, but the same name seems also to be used in Akkadian (from Mesopotamia), Ugaritic (from Syria), Egyptian, and Greek. The Philistines, whom Ahmos says are from Caphtor, were a non-Semitic people who moved south to Canaan around 1200 BCE (see Chapter 3).

Kir's location is still unknown. Ahmos knows it as the origin of the Arameans, but modern scholars of ancient geography have not been able to trace the Arameans to their land of origin. *Kir* might be Ahmos's way of referring to an important city, possibly Nineveh, because the same word can mean simply "city." Others think it refers to an area of desert oases in north Arabia, others to a river in Armenia, and still others to a mountain range in northern Syria.

As you can see, there is still a lot of historical investigation to be done. Solving these sorts of questions involves fascinating treks through ancient languages, manuscripts, libraries, archaeological reports, and maybe travel to towns and villages in search of clues. For more information, see Hess 1992 and Mattingly 1992.

Construction of the Scroll

As with all prophetic books, we have these poems of Ahmos because later generations of prophets and scribes thought the words worth recording, arranging, editing, and passing on. The resulting scroll is not a transcript of the eighth-century prophet's speeches in the order that he gave them, and, of course, there is no such claim to that effect. It is not surprising that Ahmos's words would have been remembered and valued in light of the Northern Kingdom's subjugation and destruction at the hands of the Assyrian Empire only decades after he delivered his words of doom. On the other hand, ultimately all of the Jewish literature preserved in our library was kept and passed on by survivors and heirs of the Southern Kingdom, and so it is not surprising

Study Room 7.5

MAINSTREAMING A RADICAL?

Few would deny a certain antiestablishment tone in Ahmos's words, yet ultimately it is establishment that preserves them. It was in institutions full of sacrifices, songs, and prayers, such as temples, later synagogues, and churches, that preserved words such as these of Ahmos: "I hate, I spurn your holidays, And I am not moved by your celebrations. Even when you offer me sacrifices and offerings, I don't accept, And your fat animal sacrifices, I don't look at. Get away from me the noise of your songs, The music of your harps I don't hear."

About the issue of the antiestablishment prophet and the institution, sociologist Peter Berger has written the following:

Imagine that originally, prophets roamed freely all over the place. They would appear at all times and in different locations, even in sanctuaries, and shriek out their messages of divine instruction, often if not always accompanied by the spasms of possession; a most disturbing situation. Priests are in the business of managing disturbances. Who knows what priestly genius first invented what in retrospect appears as the obvious solution: Because we cannot get rid of these characters, let's put them on the payroll. We'll allow them to do their thing on Tuesdays and Thursdays, from noon till sundown, and we'll restrict them to the courtyard in front of the sanctuary's side entrance; this way we'll be able to keep an eye on them. And perhaps we can even charge admission. This operation has been successfully performed by sundry priesthoods ever since. (BERGER 1993, 174)

Berger's humorous scenario raises interesting questions. What happens to the radical when enfolded into the institution? If we apply this to a textual situation, who controls the radical texts? And would they still exist without the institutions? What might be said about institutions that are willing to embrace such dangerous texts? Are there less self-serving purposes than that suggested by Berger? Today, who now controls the words of Ahmos? What would Ahmos say about that?

to us if we perceive what seem to be supplements that speak to Southern concerns, whereas the Ahmos's biographical material and poetry seem focused on the Northern Kingdom of Israel. Literary-historical scholars who have attempted to reconstruct the various stages of its composition have come to various conclusions, seeing one, two, three, or up to six major periods of editing. Finally, prophetic scrolls were not preserved because their predictions came true. Prophetic doomsayers clearly seem to have been more concerned about affecting present conditions than about future predictions. If we judge from what is preserved as a whole, it has more to do with the perceived enduring value of the power and message of Ahmos's prophetic poetry.

So what are some clues to the composition? Look how the scroll begins with two editorial introductions—we have a biographical superscription (1.1) followed by a thematic statement, or motto (1.2): YHVH roaring certainly sets the appropriate tone for all the poems to follow. The Southern perspective is evident here: YHVH's base is in Jerusalem. The prophetic speech proper begins in 1.3 using the scroll's most common formula, "thus says YHVH." The scroll repeatedly enforces to the reader that the words spoken are YHVH's, and many speeches are given in the first person, where *I* refers to YHVH.

A rhetorically brilliant poem is found in 1.3–2.16. Here the prophet "surrounds" Israel by marching around her, denouncing her enemies, before finally turning in on Israel herself. The section 3.1–6.14 is a series of smaller units showing interesting poetic variety. For example, notice the series of questions in 3.3–8, the parallel opening and concluding lines in five sections of 4.6–11, and the conclusion drawn in 4.12. The next major section presents five visions, or illustrations, of YHVH's judgment. Interspersed among these is the narrative of Ahmos's dispute with the priest Amaziah and other oracles. In three places, 4.13, 5.8–9, and 9.7–10, we find verses of a poem or song praising the creative power of YHVH, which were likely drawn from an already existing composition. The book ends (9.11–15) with a promise not of doom but restoration, and not of Israel, but of Judah. It is likely that these words come from a later author from the South and from a time after the fall of the Southern Kingdom in 586 BCE.

Questions for Further Study

1. Do you think Ahmos was a real prophet? (What is a real prophet?) Might his nonprophet status be just a rhetorical device of the person or author? What evidence could you look for to help you decide? What questions would you ask?

2. What people in world of Ahmos would have been unfavorable to Ahmos? What people in the world of the scroll's readers? What people in your society parallel them?

References

Aharoni, Yohanan, et al. *The Macmillan Bible Atlas*. 3rd ed. New York: Macmillan. 1993.

Andersen, Francis I. and David N. Freedman. *Amos*. New York: Doubleday, 1989.

Berger, Peter. *A Far Glory*. New York: Free Press, 1993.

Campbell, Edward F., Jr. "A Land Divided: Judah and Israel from the Death of Solomon to the Fall of Samaria," in *The Oxford History of the Biblical World*, edited by Michael D. Coogan, 206–41. New York: Oxford, 1988.

Hess, Richard. "Caphtor", In *The Anchor Bible Dictionary*, edited by David N. Freedman, 1.869–70. New York: Doubleday, 1992.

Marks, Herbert. "The Twelve Prophets," in *The Literary Guide to the Bible*, edited by Robert Alter and Frank Kermode, 207–33. Cambridge, MA: Harvard, 1987.

Mattingly, Gerald L. "Kir." in *The Anchor Bible Dictionary*, edited by David N. Freedman, 4.83–4. New York: Doubleday, 1992.

Mazar, Amihai. *Archaeology of the Land of the Bible 10,000–586 B.C.E.* New York: Doubleday, 1990.

עבדיה

Obadiah *Ovadyah*

Section Outline

Structure and Message
Literary Format and Movement
Ovadyah's Times
Ovadyah and Other Poems
Questions for Further Study
References

Obadiah is far shorter than most modern sermons and not much more than a letter to the editor. This small poetic composition would have fit quite easily into one column of an ancient scroll. It only has 388 words, fewer than most pages of the book you are reading now. Perhaps at some time it circulated as a stand-alone document, but whether a single sheet could have survived the centuries without being physically attached to or incorporated into another larger document is hard to say.

The poet-prophet named *Ovadyah* in Hebrew, pronounced "oh-*vad*-yah," is otherwise unknown and no biographical information exists in the text. Even his name, which means "servant of YHVH," is commonplace among ancient Jews. It could even be simply a title, because "servant of YHVH" is a common way of referring to prophets (e.g., 2 Kings 9.7). Some scholars, looking at the text as a whole and comparing it to similar oracles in other books, have wondered if this single oracle might have become separated from a larger text. Some of these scholars have suggested possible sources for various parts of the text.

Structure and Message

The content and literary expression of this brief scroll is not unique among the classical prophetic collection of scrolls in our library. In many ways this one-page scroll reads as a sort of generic prophetic classic and so would serve as an excellent and manageable object of study for someone wanting a short sample to investigate and discover more about Israelite prophetic literature. The heading or title that was give to the piece in antiquity, Vision of Ovadyah, uses a standard term for a prophetic oracle (see also Isaiah 1.1 and Nahum 1.1). Structurally there are a few textual markers: At the beginning we find a common form of prophetic heading:

*L*ITERARY FORMAT AND MOVEMENT

Ovadyah is presented as one piece, a single poetic oracle, and it has one introductory rhetorical announcement, "Thus says YHVH." It has one two-part theme: YHVH's judgment on the neighboring nation of Edom and his eventual restoration of Israel's preeminence.

1–14 YHVH's judgment on Edom for her treatment of Israel

15–21 YHVH's establishment of Israel's dominance

"Thus says YHVH concerning Edom"; verse 4 ends with "declares YHVH"; and verse 18 ends with "for YHVH has spoken." But these do not seem to mark the major movements within the content. The oracle also exhibits slight internal rhetorical movement among speakers and addressees. The second half of verse 1 is in the first person plural as Israelites, or perhaps all the nations, then verse 2 shifts to YHVH addressing Edom directly, mostly in second person. Even when the speaker shifts the focus to the future of Israel, Israel remains always in the third person. Directing oracles to outsiders is a common rhetorical device in prophetic literature: clearly the intended audience of the speech—whether in an oral or written form—is the nation of Judah. The device gives voice to what the author believes should be said to such outsiders. In the case of Ovadyah, the speaker does not use vague generalities but instead fills his text with names of cities, regions, mountains, and ancestors that all serve as meaningful symbols of the Israelite and Edomite peoples.

It is not hard to summarize the basic message. The oracle condemns the nation of Edom, Israel's neighbor directly east of the kingdom of Judah, for aiding and abetting the downfall of Judah. The author knows of traditions that the Edomites and Israelites are kin and for this reason the intensity of feelings, good or bad, is magnified. The pain and bitterness of the author is clear and memorably expressed:

You should not have watched . . . you should not have rejoiced . . . you should not have boasted . . . you should not have invaded . . . you, especially you, should not have watched . . . you should not have looted . . . you should not have stood at the passes to cut down fugitives . . . you should not have betrayed . . . (12–14).

The response the oracle presents to these betrayals is familiar from many prophetic writings: the coming *Yom YHVH*, Day of YHVH. The concept of this day of the future we first saw in Ahmos, from the eighth century BCE. In Ovadyah it serves as the temporal working out of the author's conception of international justice: YHVH's revenge against those nations that have ill treated his own people, Edom in particular. "As you have done, it will be done to you" (15). In the end, according to this straightforward vision of this poet, Edom will be devoured and the now exiled Israelites will possess their land and the resulting kingdom will belong to

Poster 7.5

Ovadyah 1–4	Jeremiah 49.14–16
The vision of Ovadyah.	
Thus says the Lord YHVH concerning Edom:	
A report we heard from YHVH and a messenger among the nations has been sent,	**A report I heard from YHUH, and a messenger among the nations has been sent,**
"Rise up! Let us rise against her for battle!"	"Prepare yourselves together and come **against her, and rise up for battle!"**
Behold I will make you least among the nations; **despised.** you shall be utterly.	For behold **I will make you least among the nations,** despised by humankind.
The pride of your heart has deceived you,	The terror you inspire and the **pride of your heart** have deceived you,
you that live in the clefts of the rock,	**you who live in the clefts of the rock,**
whose dwelling is in the **heights.**	who hold the **height** of the hill.
You say in your heart,	
"Who will bring me down to the ground?"	Although you make your nest as high as the **eagle's,**
Though you soar aloft like the **eagle,** though your nest is set among the stars,	
from there I will bring you down, declares YHVH.	**from there I will bring you down,** declares YHVH.

YHVH (20–21). No major political or religious details, such as kings or priests, are painted into this picture of the future.

Ovadyah's Times

Though the text of Ovadyah gives few clues to specific events that historians can locate in the historical record, most scholars are convinced that this small oracle is best situated shortly after the destruction of Jerusalem and exile of many Judeans around 586 BCE. Along with Ovadyah, numerous Jewish poets-prophets from the period of Jerusalem's fall speak bitterly against the Edomites for their complicity with the Babylonian conquerors. You can read similar sentiments in Psalm 137.7, Isaiah 34.5–7, Lamentations 4.21, and Ezekiel 25.12–14. This seems the most plausible period, but we should also be aware that similar condemning attitudes toward Edom can be found before the destruction of Judah in the early sixth century

(Ahmos 1.11-12) and long after (Isaiah 63.1–6, Malachi 1.2–5). (2 Kings 14.7 contains a record of an eighth-century military victory over Edom. Also, archaeologists, discovered a military communication, known as the Arad Ostracon #24, from an Israelite commander in Jerusalem sent to Arad, on the southeastern border with Edom, in preparation for an Edomite attack in approximately 598 BCE, just as Babylonian armies were invading. Like many other prophetic oracles, Ovadyah's poem gives voice not only to the pain and bitterness of a defeated and desperate people, but also gives words to their longings of release and restoration, and in so doing gives hope.

Ovadyah and Other Poems

In addition to formulas such as Yom YHVH and "thus says YHVH," Ovadyah shows similarity of expression with other prophetic texts. Compare the segments of Poster 7.5, one from our scroll and one from the scroll of Jeremiah. The parts that correspond are marked in bold, and other segments are very similar.

The similarities are easy to see, and it would be stretching credulity to suggest that two separate poets arrived at these words independently. We recall that this type of textual borrowing, whether it came at an early or late stage of a manuscript, was common and acceptable in antiquity. In such situations we are usually faced with three possible explanations: author A used B, B used A, or both A and B used a common source C. In this case, most scholars argue that the poem found now in Jeremiah was used as a basis for the altered and slightly expanded poem found in Ovadyah. Other textual similarities in Ovadyah, none as long as this one, can be explored in Isaiah, Ezekiel, Zephaniah, and Joel.

Questions for Further Study

1. How would readers or hearers for whom Edom was a known enemy respond to this poetic condemnation? How would readers who know no Edomites centuries later respond? Why would this composition be kept by a community?

References

Ackroyd, Peter R. "Obadiah, Book of," in *The Anchor Bible Dictionary*, edited by David N. Freedman, 5:2–4. New York: Doubleday, 1992.

Marks, Herbert. "The Twelve Prophets" in *The Literary Guide to the Bible*, edited by Robert Alter and Frank Kermode, 207–33. Cambridge, MA: Harvard, 1987.

Wolff, Hans W. *Obadiah and Jonah.* Minneapolis, MN: Augsburg, 1986.

יונה

Jonah *Yonah*

Section Outline

This scroll is most curious and one of the most famous short stories or in the world. It is the story of Jonah, or *Yonah* in Hebrew, pronounced "yo-*nah*." It is the story of the great fish and serves as the text of the preacher's sermon in Chapter 9 of *Moby Dick*. Before we say more, recall a time when you were browsing a library's shelves, picked up a book, and wondered, "What is this book doing *here,* in this section?" That's the question many ask after studying this scroll, because Yonah is totally unique among all the prophetic books in our collection. It starts out with a completely typical prophetic introduction in the first eight words (1.1), but what follows is completely atypical. First of all, unlike others, it is not a collection of prophetic speeches by Yonah as we expect. Instead it is a story about Yonah. Actually, there is no prophetic oracle; just five words in Hebrew serve as the prediction in the narrative (3.4). This lacks all the usual prophetic introductory formulas, divine claims, such as "thus says YHVH," and poetic forms. In the other 14 classic prophetic books the clear interest of the author or compiler is the *words* of the prophet while the *person* of the prophet is at least secondary: sometimes he is all but ignored. But in Yonah, the interest is just the opposite. Unlike the usual collection of oracles, we find a literary prose story about the person Yonah. Unlike all the other classic prophetic books, the hero, Yonah, acts distinctly unlike a prophet, so much so that we might call him an anti—prophet. In fact, he never is actually called a prophet in the book. In

*L*ITERARY FORMAT AND MOVEMENT

Because we have already introduced the scroll as a short story, there is not too much left to say. Though the narrative hardly needs to be divided into chapters—it is less than 1,000 Hebrew words—in this case the standard modern chapter divisions are sensibly placed. They represent four basic scenes in this drama. This short little scroll is a masterpiece bubbling with humor, irony, and sarcasm. It is also clear that the author uses his considerable literary skills for asking serious theological questions of Israelite traditions.

1.1–17 Yonah, called by YHVH to condemn Nineveh, flees and is swallowed by a large fish.	2.1–10 Poem: Yonah prays to YHVH and is vomited onto land.	3.1–10 Yonah preaches in Nineveh, Nineveh repents, God repents of plan to destroy Nineveh.	4.1–11 Yonah is outraged at YHVH's mercy to Nineveh; YHVH questions Yonah.

other books, prophets are those who seek and experience YHVH's voice or presence, obey divine words, and deliver divine messages; but Yonah runs away from God, disobeys divine commands, and refuses to speak for God. Even more importantly, whereas other prophets see themselves as agents of YHVH's mercy, Yonah complains about YHVH's mercy. The reason for his complaint raises the religious crux of the story. Surely in most prophetic books of our library, whether the classical oracles of Isaiah or the stories of Elijah, the reader is intended to side with the prophet whose message or story is recounted, because, of course, the prophet has sided with God. But with Yonah, the book concludes with a rhetorical question in which YHVH sets himself against Yonah, and the reader must choose between God and the so-called prophet. Unusual indeed!

Questions of Genre and Origin

Most modern Bibles print the scroll as a prose narrative with a poem found about one-third of the way into to story (2.2–9). In the nineteenth and twentieth centuries there were some debates about whether the narrative is parabolic, a fictional story intended to teach, or whether it is a historically accurate recounting of an event in the life of a prophet named Yonah. There was an urban legend in circulation concerning a man named James Bartley who lived for days in a whale, a story calculated to prove Jonah's historicity (Davis 1991). But ancient Jewish and Christian interpreters were less interested issues of historicity, and most modern academic interpreters—many finding the book's purpose in matters other than history—have noticed numerous nonhistorical traits in the story: Nineveh depicted as much larger than its actual size (3.3); the comical picture of animals wearing sackcloth and fasting (3.7–8); the fantastical growth of a plant (4.6); and the spectacular notion of being eaten by a fish and living in its belly for three days and there composing a beautiful psalm of thanksgiving (1.17–2.1). On the other hand, it is plavsible that there was a historical prophet named Yonah who lived during the reign of Jeroboam II, king of Northern Israel (786 to 46 BCE) and prophesied Israel's expansion (see 2 Kings 14.25) at least 250 years before the composition of our book. A likely scenario is that an author of many generations later, perhaps using existing material about Yonah, composed this subtle, didactic, pious, and even subversive story. In all its simplicity, the book is remarkable, even profound, regardless of the genre in which it falls.

Compositional Date

This scroll gives few clues for its date of composition, and so scholarly historical estimates have varied by as much as 400 years, but most contemporary scholars would put it somewhere in the late sixth to forth centuries BCE. The social questions of Jewish relations to outsiders and the religious questions of YHVH's relations with other peoples were asked and answered variously at various times in Israel's history. However, the date is suggested by forms of the Hebren.

The International Times

One item of background information is important for understanding the message of Yonah. The nation of Assyria, with one of its capitals at Nineveh, was in many ways the quintessential evil empire to its enemies. Since the ninth century BCE Assyrian armies had frequently marched west from Mesopotamia, devastated cities and villages, and taken many captives into slavery or moved whole populations with a policy of mass deportation (Roux 1980, 284). They were the aggressive superpower for several centuries in the Fertile Crescent, exercising control through a vast military machine. In the late eighth century (722 BCE), they had utterly wiped out the largest and most prosperous of the Israelite kingdoms, the Northern Kingdom, and for all practical purposes they controlled the fate of Judah, which was forced to pay huge sums of tribute for its continued subservient existence. The Assyrian reputation, apparently part of their propaganda campaign against enemies, was one of fierce cruelty. Remember the cruel boast of one king, Ashurnasirpal II (883 to 859 BCE) that we discussed in Chapter 3 (Poster 3.2)?

It is no wonder that other nations, including Jews, rejoiced when the Assyrian Empire came crashing down with the destruction of Nineveh in 612 BCE and when the Babylonian armies, led by Nebuchadnezzar, delivered a death blow in 605 BCE. Listen to the Jewish prophet Nahum's poem about Nineveh as the empire falls:

> Ah! You bloody city,
> utterly deceitful, full of plunder—
> no end to the prey!
> Crack of whip and rumble of wheel,
> horse galloping and chariot bounding!
> Horsemen charging,

flashing sword and glittering spear,
piles of slain, heaps of corpses,
dead bodies without end—
they stumble over the bodies! . . .
I am against you,
declares YHVH of Armies,
and I will lift up your skirts over your face;
and I will have the nations stare at your genitals,
and kingdoms on your shame.
I will throw filth at you
and treat you with contempt,
and make you a spectacle.
Then all who see you will shrink from you and say,
"Nineveh is destroyed."
Who will feel sorry for her?"
Where shall I seek comforters for you?
(NAHUM 3)

Now we can begin to imagine the story of Yonah as it may have been felt in the ancient world where Assyrian power was long remembered. Because the story is set during the years of Assyrian supremacy, it is no longer surprising that the character Yonah would have been reluctant to go to Nineveh—what would they do to him? Running away might have been the wise thing to do! But now comes the twist. As it turns out, Yonah was not concerned for his own safety. He was deeply troubled that YHVH would have mercy even on the Assyrians: "Is not this what I said while I was still in my own country? That is why I fled to Tarshish at the beginning . . ." (4.2).

Just as the Assyrians had a reputation for outrageous cruelty, causing Yonah to want to see them destroyed, the author presents YHVH as having a reputation for outlandish mercy, which would result in grace being shown even to Nineveh: ". . . for I know that you are a gracious God and merciful, slow to anger, and abounding in steadfast love, and ready to relent from punishing" (4.2). This favorite description of YHVH's merciful character (see Exodus 34.6; Numbers 14.18; Joel 2.13; Psalm 86.15, 145.8; Nehemiah 9.17, 31) becomes ironically bitter in the mouth this anti—prophet. Yonah may have been written with the poetry of Nahum in mind, because the rhetorical questions that YHVH asks at the end of the Nahum's poem, "Nineveh is destroyed; who will feel sorry for her?" "Where shall I seek comforters for you?" are here ironically answered. Where shall YHVH go to find someone who cares about Nineveh's suffering? Not far at all, for this story, too, ends with a question by YHVH: "And should I not care about Nineveh . . . ?" (4.11). YHVH is the one who cares.

Yonah's own desire to see the destruction of the Assyrians is so intense that he would rather die, as he repeats three times in 3.3, 8, 9, than witness Israel's God showing mercy to Nineveh, which had now repented of its violence (3.8). It seems as if Yonah is saying that YHVH's mercy, patience, love, and forgiveness are fine for *us*, but not for *them*. Yonah becomes obsessed, even melodramatic, and hopes YHVH will change his mind again, this time in favor of destroying the enemy.

But the story raises an even larger national-religious question: Whose side is YHVH on? For whom does YHVH care? Even YHVH's object lesson of the magic one-day plant—should you really care more about a plant than all those people?—seems to have no effect on the prophet, and the story closes with a haunting question of human vengeance and rhetorically as declaration of the scope of YHVH's care. The pointed criticism and irony are profound and not easy: an Israelite prophet disgusted with his own God's mercy. Here is an Israelite eager to bring his sacrifice (2.10) to YHVH with a gracious reputation, but he is unwilling to countenance YHVH's pity for the enemy, even the children. The moral of the story is never propounded overtly to the audience—the masterpiece is far too good for that—but YHVH's question to Yonah, and all the issues of loyalty it raises, is the author's last question to his readers.

Foreigners

Careful readers of the scroll have noted that there are two sets of foreigners in relation to YHVH. In the first chapter the foreign sailors are so noble they do everything in their power to avoid jettisoning Yonah. And when at last they have no other choice but to throw him overboard, they pray to YHVH, Yonah's God, and worship him, both before and after they throw him overboard. These foreigners certainly seem religiously commendable—was that a major point of the author? The second episode, in Chapter 3, similarly presents *all* of Nineveh, every single person, from king to beggar and even all the animals—a delightful comic exaggeration—fasting, wearing sackcloth, special clothing to signify sorrow, and repenting of all their wrongs. Significantly what is not a part of this second episode is any turning of the Ninevites to the particular Israelite God YHVH. If we read carefully even in an English translation, we will notice that the author seems to carefully distinguish the identity of God based on the viewpoint of the characters in the story. Although Yonah prays to YHVH and is a piously loyal Yahwist, YHVH is never on the lips of the Ninevehites. What might we see in this distinction and sensitivity?

The Poem

The poem of the second chapter has often been mentioned for its seeming inappropriateness to the context. Why is Yonah praying a thanksgiving psalm and not a cry for rescue from the bottom of the fish? It is possible, as many have suggested, that the poem was inserted at a later time, though we do not have manuscript evidence for that. However, when the poem came to the prose narrative, apparently the author or editor of the scroll as we have it approved of this anticipatory psalm of thanksgiving for deliverance. Perhaps it is much like a Greek drama chorus, an opera, or even the choruses of modern songs, which often anticipate the plot narrative of the verses. But perhaps there is more to it. Because the vocabulary and themes of the psalm echo those of the prose sections, the placement seems much less haphazard. There are several wordplays, for example, that could exist even in English if translators take the time to replicate them: YHVH commands Yonah to "cry out" against Nineveh (1.1)—but he refuses. But Yonah eventually does "cry out" (2.1)—from the belly of the fish. And then we notice that his prayer, which starts out somewhat humbly, though there is no remorse or confession, quickly becomes assured of YHVH's salvation and mercy. Perhaps there is tremendous irony here. He has great confidence in YHVH's mercy—and them in just a few lines he will be cursing YHVH's mercy! Is this man presumptuous? Perhaps there is a touch of humor in YHVH's having the fish vomit this prophet who is sure of YHVH's salvation for himself, but resentful of it for others (Ackerman 1987, 242).

A True Prophet?

The book provides further opportunity to reflect on the perception of prophets in ancient Israel. It is the premise of Yonah that his message of certain doom—"In 40 days Nineveh will be destroyed!"—was not really certain at all. Doomsday prophecy seems to be thought of as always conditional. This is the case in other prophetic books as well, such as Jeremiah 26.16-19. The plot of Yonah operates on the basis of this assumption about true prophets. We could put it this way: A true prophet in ancient Israel hopes that his announcement of disaster does *not* come true. The purpose of the announcement of doom is to cause repentance, and because YHVH is considered merciful, he will change and not bring the punishment or disaster. Yonah, in contrast, as anti—prophet, would rather see his message of destruction come true. Ought one want to see enemies destroyed like Yonah, or, like YHVH, ought one want to have compassion on them?

A Strange Ending

The closing line of the book is a great curiosity. The persons who "do not know their right hand from left" are likely the children, but why mention the "many animals" (4.11)? Commentators have long considered this puzzle. Is this a winking glance back to the pious, repenting animals of 3.7–9? Or is it perhaps a sarcastic remark to Yonah, who may not like people so much, but maybe he can find some mercy in his heart for animals? After all, he was strongly attached to the plant. Or maybe there is something else that escapes the modern interpreter. In any case, it seems a delightfully peculiar ending to a delightful and provocative story.

Questions for Further Study

1. As a religion scholar, what are religious assumptions and teachings of this story?

2. If we ask religious and ethnographic questions, what would we say about the categories of "other" and "foreigner" and "enemy" in this scroll?

3. As a literary critic, what are some of the subtleties and ironies of the scroll?

4. How does this story of divine mercy sit among other prophetic messages? How does this scroll compare and contrast with other scrolls of the library and canon?

References

Ackerman, James S. "Jonah," in *The Literary Guide to the Bible*, edited by Robert Alter and Frank Kermode, 234–43. Cambridge, MA: Harvard, 1987.

Davis, Edward B. "A Whale of a Tale," *Perspectives on Science and Christian Faith* 43 (1991): 224–37.

Fretheim, Terence E. *The Message of Jonah.* Minneapolis, MN: Augsburg, 1977.

Ginzberg, Lovis. *The Legends of the Jews.* 7 vols. Philadelphia: Jevish Publication Society, 1990.

Magonet, Jonathan. "Jonah, book of," in *The Anchor Bible Dictionary*, edited by David N. Freedman, 3:936–42. New York: Doubleday, 1992.

Roux, Georges. *Ancient Iraq.* 2nd ed. London: Penguin, 1980.

Trible, Phyllis. *Rhetorical Criticism: Context, Method, and the Book of Jonah.* Minneapolis, MN: Fortress, 1994.

מיכה

Micah *Mekhah*

SECTION OUTLINE

Who and When
Literary Format and Movement
Composition of the Scroll
Mekhah's Opposition
A Court Case and Mekhah's Priorities
Questions for Further Study
References

Many people who have studied this poetic writing, which would have comprised four to six columns of a scroll, have seen in it connections to the scroll of Isaiah. Micah, pronounced *Mekhah* in Hebrew, "mee-*khah*," is compared to Isaiah because of thematic similarity. According to an editor who prefaced our scroll with biographical information, Isaiah and Mekhah lived at about the same in the Southern Kingdom of Judah, towards the end of the eighth century BCE. Mekhah seems to have been a younger contemporary of the now famous Isaiah and, while Isaiah was from the more urban Jerusalem, Mekhah was from the small village of Moreshet. Because the scroll of Mekhah is only one-twelfth the size of Isaiah, he has sometimes been called the "little Isaiah."

Who and When

Like the beginnings of several prophetic scrolls, an editor placed at the beginning the names of the kings that were thought to have been reigning while Mekhah was composing and speaking his public poems. In the case of Mekhah, three kings are mentioned—Jotham, Ahaz, Hezekiah—all of the Southern Kingdom of Judah, and modern historians set them as consecutive kings from ca. 742 to 687 BCE. That would mean that Mekhah was alive while Assyrian kings such as Tiglath-Pileser, Sargon II, and Sennacherib were conquering villages, cities, and whole territories in Syria-Palestine. He and all those he lived with would have seen the realities of warfare and known the fear of the aggressive Assyrian armies; the Northern Kingdom of Israel was destroyed in 722 BCE, and in 701 BCE much of Judah's territory was ripped away from the control of the

LITERARY FORMAT AND MOVEMENT

It is difficult to find an overall plan for the scroll based on themes, repetitions, or organizational indicators to help us determine how we might lay out these poems and what movements we might describe. When you read this rather short scroll, you will sense the difficulty. Regarding its content, most scholars have linked Chapters 1–3 with 6 and Chapter 4–5 with 7. Chapters 1–3 and 6 can be characterized as challenges to societal leaders—royal, economic, religious—for what the poet-prophet perceives as their injustices and disloyalty to YHVH, whereas Chapters 4–5 and 7 present poetic visions of a glorious future for Jerusalem. But a careful reading shows that these divisions do not fit exactly; remember that the medieval chapter divisions should not be allowed to impose breaks upon the text, as if they were original or natural. There are shifts of voice throughout the scroll—YHVH in first and third person, the prophet in first person, and Jerusalem in first and third person—but again, a clear comprehensive pattern does not emerge and should not be forced. Perhaps the scroll is best read as a series of related poems.

1.1 Editorial introduction	4.1–8 Vision of a future dominant and just Jerusalem	6.1–16 YHVH's courts case against Israel; condemnation of injustice, religious priorities, cheating	7.1–7 Personal lament over injustices and fate of city
1.2–7 Announcement of YHVH's coming doom	4.9–14 (or 5.1) Current humiliation contrasted with future glory		7.8–13 Personal confession and future hope
1.8–3.12 Condemnation of leaders, rulers, priests, prophets for corruption, injustice	5.1–16 Vision of future blessings from YHVH		7.14–20 Prayer for future care and forgiveness

government in Jerusalem. Mekhah knew what it was to live in a small vulnerable nation under the constant threat of much larger international forces. This is the stage for the prophet Mekhah, whose name stands behind this scroll. It seems that Mekhah addressed his poetic messages to people of both Israelite kingdoms.

For Mekhah we have a bit more information to add, because he is mentioned in the scroll named for the prophet Jeremiah, and a brief story is told about Mekhah's work as a prophet. His historical importance seems to have been significant. In the story, Jeremiah has been arrested because he has outspokenly condemned religious and other social leaders and has declared that YHVH would punish the nation with destruction. Jeremiah had a very unpatriotic opinion of and message for the officials of his day, so they attempted to silence him. Priests, prophets, and others wanted to put him to death. But some the officials attempted to save Jeremiah by invoking the memory of Mekhah.

POSTER 7.6

AN ASSYRIAN INVASION OF JUDAH

Assyrian Record

Assyrian kings often recorded their military exploits on large monuments. Here is a part of a monument that some believe to be of King Sennacherib who invaded Judah in ca. 701 BCE. Some Assyriologists argue that it comes from a different king, slightly earlier. In any case, it reports an Assyrian invasion during Mekhah time.

> [Ashur, my Lord, support]ed me and to the land of Ju[dah I marched. In] the course of my campaign, the tribute of the ki[ngs of . . . I received]. [by the mig]ht of Ashur, my Lord, the district [of Hezek]iah of Judah, like [ ] the city of Azekah, his stronghold, which is between my [ ] and the land of Judah . . . I conquered, I carried off its spoil. I tore down . . [ ] . . a royal [city] of the Philistines, which He[zek]iah had taken and fortified for himself . . .
> Translated by M. Cogan in Hallo 2003, 2:304

Judean Record

Accounts of Senacherib's 701 BCE campaign are also found in Jewish sources, namely 2 Kings 18–19 and Isaiah 36. The story there begins this way:

> In the fourteenth year of King Hezekiah, Sennacherib, king of Assyria invaded against all the fortified towns of Judah and seized them. King Hezekiah sent a message to the king of Assyria at Lachish saying: "I have erred; withdraw from me, and I shall bear whatever you impose on me." (2 Kings 18.13–14; see Isaiah 36.1)

Mekhah of Moreshet who was a prophet in the days of Hezekiah, king of Judah and who said to all the people of Judah, "Thus says YHVH of Armies, 'Zion shall be plowed as a field, Jerusalem shall be a ruin, And the temple mountain shall be a forest.'" But did Judah's King Hezekiah and all of Judah put him to death? Instead, did he not fear YHVH and seek out YHVH and did not YHVH change from bringing the evil he had pronounced against them?
(JEREMIAH 26.18–19)

This passage is fascinating for many reasons. What does it suggest about the perceived purpose of doomsday or negative prediction prophecy? How does the actual quote of Mekhah compare with the words in the scroll of Mekhah? We can check out this very early usage of the words of Mekhah by comparing Mekhah 3.9–12 with this text from Jeremiah. But for our purposes here, we will simply observe that a century after Mekhah, he is still remembered as an outspoken and negative prophet, and looking through much of our scroll we can see why. As you read through these poems, which parts do you find that match this description?

Composition of the Scroll

If we keep in mind the compositional practices of that time, we will not assume that the entire scroll is simply a report of the historical Mekhah's words. References to historical events *after* the time of Mekhah, such as the Babylonian exile (3.10), some hundred years away, were later additions, but are also completely in keeping with the dire words of Mekhah the prophet. Many scholars believe that the more positive visions of the future (see 4.1–5.15; 7.8–20) are likely additions from a much later time, even after the exile of Judah in the sixth century BCE. Although most of these additions are not known from texts outside of Mekhah, one of them can be found near the beginning of the scroll of Isaiah. Check out carefully the parallel versions in Poster 7.7.

We said earlier when looking at the scroll of Joel (p. 269) that part of this poem found in Isaiah and Mekhah was radically reedited, subverted even, by the author of Joel, who "beat plowshares into swords." But here we have the poem reproduced in nearly identical fashion in the two scrolls of Isaiah and Mekhah. Who copied whom? Or did both of them extract the poem from an earlier writing that we no longer have? The answers have varied among people studying the texts. No matter what explanation one chooses, these passages and Joel's usage, clearly demonstrate ways in which Israel's writers made use of other author's writings—and all without one footnote. Finally, we should be aware of some difficulties in the textual transmission of Mekhah; in Hebrew there are numerous words that are difficult to understand and seem to have been copied improperly. The worst section is near end of Chapter 1. The JPS version is commendably honest in this regard, noting, for example, that the meaning of much of 1.10–13 is uncertain.

Mekhah's Opposition

Recall from our introductory discussion about historical prophets in Israel (p. 227) that prophets of YHVH sometimes spoke contradictory messages and opposed each other, denouncing others as wrong—deceived, disingenuous, and fraudulent. Mekhah is one more prophet who apparently opposed religious leaders, such as priests, and also other prophets. Mekhah's message of coming judgment of YHVH was the opposite of others who gave a more positive assessment. Mekhah lambastes them as mercenary, willing to speak words that will make the people who pay them to feel happy and satisfied:

> Thus says YHVH about the prophets,
> Who mislead my people,
> "When they have food, they cry 'Peace,'

POSTER 7.7

Mekhah 4.1–4	**Yᵉshayahu 2.2–4**
In the days to come,	In the days to come,
The Mount of YHVH's House	The Mount of YHVH's House
Shall stand firm above the mountains;	Shall stand firm above the mountains
And it shall tower above the hills.	And tower above the hills;
The peoples shall gaze on it with joy,	And all the nations shall gaze on it with joy.
And the many nations shall go and shall say: "Come,	And the many peoples shall go and say: "Come,
Let us go up to the Mount of the YHVH,	Let us go up to the Mount of YHVH,
To the House of the God of Jacob;	To the House of the God of Jacob;
That He may instruct us in His ways,	That He may instruct us in His ways,
And that we may walk in His paths."	And that we may walk in His paths."
For instruction shall come forth from Zion,	For instruction shall come forth from Zion,
The word of YHVH from Jerusalem.	The word of YHVH from Jerusalem.
Thus He will judge among the many peoples,	Thus He will judge among the nations
And arbitrate for the multitude of nations, however distant;	And arbitrate for the many peoples,
And they shall beat their swords into plowshares	And they shall beat their swords into plowshares
And their spears into pruning hooks.	And their spears into pruning hooks:
Nation shall not take up sword against nation;	Nations shall not take up sword against nation;
They shall never again know war;	They shall never again know war.
But every man shall sit	
Under his grapevine or fig tree	
With no one to disturb him.	
For it was YHVH of Hosts who spoke.	
JPS Tanakh, modified	JPS Tanakh, modified

Community Reflections 7.2

☰ ⅄ ✝

SUMMARIES OF GOD'S REQUIREMENTS

In many religious traditions one can find summaries of God's requirements that are brief, easy to remember, and often profound. Such statements say a lot about the religious priorities or orientation of their author. In our library several summaries can be found.

The Ten Commandments (Exodus 20, Deuteronomy 6) are often thought to be such a summary.

Micah has it down to three: "YHVH requires from you; just this: Doing justice, loving mercy, humbly walking with your God" (6.8)

Jewish

According to a traditional story, the Jewish sage **Hillel** of the first century BCE put it down to one. A potential convert asked Hillel to teach him the entire set of God's instructions while he stood on one foot; in other words, he was asking Hillel to keep it short. Hillel used an inverse form of the so-called golden rule: "What is hateful to you, do not do to your fellow man. This is the whole Torah, all of it, the rest is commentary. Go and study it" (Talmud Shabbat 31a; see early form of this rule in Proverbs 24.29 and Tobit 4.15).

Christian

According to the Christian Gospel Matthew, when Jesus was asked what was the greatest commandment, he summarized God's law in two commands, replying,

"Love the Lord your God with all your heart and all your soul and all your mind. This is the first and great commandment [quoting from Deuteronomy 6.5]. And a second is like it, Love your neighbor as yourself [quoting from Leviticus 19.18]. On these two commands the whole law and the prophets depend." (Matthew 22.37–40)

But Matthew also has Jesus giving another summary in one rule, the so-called golden rule:

"All that you desire others to do to you, so you should do to them; for this is the law and the prophets."

(MATTHEW 7.12)

The Christian writer Paul summarizes in one rule this way:

"Owe nothing to anyone, except to love others. For anyone who loves another has fulfilled the entire law."

(ROMANS 13.8)

But when someone does not fill their mouths
They declare a war on him. . . ."
(MEKHAH 3.5)

And what do you think religious and social leaders would have thought of the following words?

Listen to this you heads of the House of Jacob,
And leaders of the House of Israel,
Who hate justice, and twist what is right.
Who build Zion with blood and Jerusalem with wrong.
Her rulers for bribes make judgments,
Her priests for a price give rulings,
Her prophets for money speak oracles.
Yet they all depend on YHVH, saying,
"YHVH is with us and no evil shall come upon us."
(MEKHAH 3.9–11)

It is clear that this scroll not only denounces social injustices (throughout Chapters 1–3 and 6–7); it also vigorously contests those who do such things and yet still have confidence that YHVH is with them and will protect them—as it might be said today, "God is on our side". It is crucial for us to recall that the later editors and pre-servers of the prophetic scrolls were willing to retain these passages that on a deep level call into question claims of God's presence and the legitimacy of religious and social leadership of any period.

A Court Case and Mekhah's Priorities

Mekhah 6.1–8 is an interesting poem for study, with its extended metaphor of YHVH taking his people to court to sue them for not fulfilling their obligations. The courtroom dialogue created shows awareness of traditions now recorded in Numbers, and it is a fascinating to see the rhetorical strategies involved and the sort of arguments that Mekhah represents YHVH as making and the way the people are presented as responding. At the end, the poet's religious priorities are succinctly and memorably stated. Instead of formal religious acts such as sacrifices, the prophet declares "YHVH requires from you; just this: Doing justice, loving mercy, humbly walking with your God (Mekhah 6.8).

Such a summary of YHVH's requirements is noteworthy and might be under-stood many different ways. What would its author make of the many requirements written in the scrolls of Exodus, Leviticus, and Deuteronomy? How might each of Mekhah's three requirements be defined?

Questions for Further Study

1. Mekhah is sometimes called the rural Isaiah. As an ecocritic, how does Mekhah speak of things having to do with nature and land?

2. As a religion scholar, what are benefits and liabilities of summarizing a religion? How would you define religion, and would that category fit Mekhah? What intellectual, ethical, and civil categories does the scroll use?

References

Anderson, Francis I. and David N. Freedman. *Micah.* New York: Doubleday, 2000.

Hallo, William W. *The Context of Scripture.* 3 vols. Leidin: E.J. Brill, 2003.

Hillers, Delbert. "Micah, Book of," in *The Anchor Bible Dictionary,* edited by David N. Freedman 4:807–10. New York: Doubleday, 1992.

Wolff, Hans W. *Micah.* Minneapolis, MN: Augsburg, 1990.

נחום

Nahum *Nakhum*

SECTION OUTLINE

The Times of Nakhum
Literary Format and Movement
National and Religious Overtones
Poetic Video
Questions for Further Study
References

Composed of fewers than 800 words and the second shortest of all the writings in our library, Nahum would only have taken a column or two of an ancient scroll. Historically we know nothing about the person for whom the scroll is named, *Nakham* in Hebrew, and the town he is said to come from, Elkosh, has not been identified with any certainty. His name is pronounced "Nah-*khum*," with the *kh* sounding like *ch* in *Bach*. We can easily see that the content of the scroll is quite straightforward; it is about the fall of the Assyrian empire as represented by its capital Nineveh, and, however much the poet's identity is unclear, his poetry is vivid and single-minded. Nakhum, with Obadiah and sections of other prophetic scrolls, such as Amos and Jeremiah, is an example of the oracles against the nations genre of prophetic poetry. This is nationalistic and patriotic poetry, and in the case of Nakhum the purpose is to celebrate the downfall of Assyria as a great triumph of YHVH and extremely good news for oppressed Israel.

The Times of Nakhum

Recall that the story of Jonah was clearly written against the background of Assyria; Nakhum shares the same backdrop. Beginning in the second half of the eighth century BCE, the well-documented Assyrian empire began expanding westward into Syria-Palestine. The small kingdoms of the region were in turmoil, attempting to organize resistance and survive by submitting to the aggressive superpower. Assyria's efficient army, with its mercenaries, engineers, war machines, propaganda, cruelty, and policy of deportation, was widely feared. Throughout these decades, both Israelite kingdoms paid large tributes and submitted to Assyrian demands, but even that was not enough. The Northern Kingdom of Israel fell in 722 BCE, and much of the Southern Kingdom

LITERARY FORMAT AND MOVEMENT

The poetry of Nakhum seems particularly vivid and lively; it is a kind of poetic live-action shot of the fall of Nineveh. The main poem of Nineveh's fall is the final two-thirds of the composition. The first line contains an editor's superscription identifying the oracle as Nakhum's, but with no reference to a time period for him, in contrast to other scrolls, such as Amos, Hosea, and Micah. Then we find an incomplete alphabetic acrostic poem running from the Hebrew letter *aleph* to the letter *kaf,* which would be like an English acrostic running from *A* to *K.* Did the rest of the poem exist somewhere else? Why did an author or editor choose to insert or write only a partial acrostic? The answers are currently unknown. In any case, the acrostic poem and the verses that follow serve as a general exposition of YHVH's reign over the world, his general goodness and patience, and his anger at and his sure triumph over his and Israel's enemies. After this general introductory poem, the vivid portrayal of Nineveh's fall begins. The chapter divisions do not seem satisfactory, and in English versions are slightly different than in Hebrew texts so I will list separate numbers when necessary.

1.1 Editor's superscription

1.2–8 Acrostic on YHVH's greatness

1.9–14 YHVH's victory over enemies

2.1 (or 1.15)–3.19 The good news to Israel: the fall of Nineveh and Assyria

DISPLAY 7.6 | JEHU, KING OF ISRAEL, BOWS AND GIVES TRIBUTE TO ASSYRIAN KING SHALMANESAR

succumbed by 701 BCE. In the seventh century, Assyria set her sights on the grand prize of Egypt and invaded Africa, seizing first lower (northern) then upper (southern) Egypt. More than 1,300 miles (2,092.15 km) from home, this Assyrian army had conquered the known world. But its many campaigns were not a humanitarian triumph of liberty. Assyria now had enemies everywhere, and Egyptian revolts in the West and Mesopotamian revolts in the East soon revealed the Assyrian giant's clay feet and brought about its welcomed demise before the end of the seventh century BCE. After years of war to quell Babylonian revolts in Mesopotamia, Nineveh fell to the armies of Babylonians and Medes, a nation from the East, in modern Iran, allied with Babylon against the Assyrians. In 613 BCE Nineveh fell, and in 605 BCE the Assyrian army was finally defeated at the massive battle of Carchemish, which pitted the Babylonians, led by Nebuchadnezzar, and Medes against Assyrian and her Egyptian allies. The Assyrian Empire had fallen.

With Assyria's death throes plainly in the vision of the poet Nakhum, most scholars date the composition of scroll or at least its main poem to the last half of the seventh century BCE or early in the sixth. The author writes ironically of Egypt's defeat (ca. 663 BCE) in 3.8–12 and relishes the notion of Assyria's demise. No doubt celebrations all over the Fertile Crescent were common wherever people had endured the onslaught of Assyria. Jerusalem was not the only place people were relieved and now longed for better times. Listen to the poetic invitation to celebrate:

> Look here on the hills,
> The footsteps of the herald announcing peace!
> Celebrate your festivals, Judah,
> Fulfill your vows.
> For never again shall the villain invade you,
> All of him is cut down.
> (NAKHUM 2.1 [OR 1.15])

National and Religious Overtones

We would miss a major thrust of this poetry if we spoke only of the defeat of Assyria. This poetry is both nationalistic and religious. According to the introductory poem, it is YHVH who is raging against his adversaries. The poet is not overt, with something banal like, "YHVH is defeating Assyria," but the implications are nonetheless clear: "YHVH takes revenge upon his enemies" and "does not clear those who are guilty" (1.2–3). Verse 3 is an interesting use of one of the most commonly quoted traditions about YHVH that we saw in the scroll of Exodus (34.14), that he is "slow to anger" but certainly not forgetful of guilt. The poem applies this tradition directly to the foreign nation of Assyria from a distinctly Israelite viewpoint. The invaders from the East are not just enemies of the Israelite kingdoms, as any observer could see: they were YHVH's enemies and had plotted against him. This is in keeping with many ancient and modern ideas of national warfare: the defeat of one's enemies is read as the direct result of a God's protection and might.

For the sake of comparison within our library, we find several different expressions of this mix of nationalism and religion. In the scroll of Amos, YHVH's punishment of the enemy is rhetorically turned against Israel, and in story of Jonah, YHVH's mercy extends to the Ninevehites. Here in Nakhum, the defeat of Assyria is simply YHVH's triumph.

Poetic Video

If you read Chapters 2–3 of Nakhum, you will encounter bold and vivid poetry. It is loud, and bustling, and full of blood and gore. It stinks of dead corpses, and it rings with the shouts of warriors. It is dark, sickening, and sexually crude. Amid his verbal pictures of live devastation, the poet stops just long enough to notice that none are mourning for or comforting Nineveh as she falls; there is only relief and gladness. This poem is a monument to that relief. Interestingly, the scroll closes with a question even as the story of Jonah did, but here the question is addressed to Assyria, so that even to the end the contrast between these two works is clear:

> No relief from your rupture,
> Your wound is incurable.
> All who hear of your news clap their hands about you!
> For is there anyone upon whom your endless evil did not come?
> (NAKHUM 3.19)

Questions for Further Study

1. If the authors of Nakhum and Jonah met, imagine what their conversations might be. How would they talk to each other about Israel's destruction, enemies, evil, and God? How might a religious community include them both, and how might they be used?

2. Compare the poetry of Nakhum with that of another prophet, such as Obadiah. How do you describe the differences in form, metaphor, style, and the like?

References

Cathcart, Kevin. "Nahum, Book of," in *The Anchor Bible Dictionary,* edited by David N. Freedman, 4:999–1000. New York: Doubleday, 1992.

Marks, Herbert. "The Twelve Prophets" in *The Literary Guide to the Bible,* edited by Robert Alter and Frank Kermode, 207–33. Cambridge, MA: Harvard, 1987.

Roberts, J. J. M. *Nahum, Habakkuk, and Zephaniah.* Louisville, KY: Westminster/John Knox, 1991.

Robertson, O. P. *The Books of Nahum, Habakkuk, and Zephaniah.* Grand Rapids, MI: Eerdmans, 1990.

חבקוק

Habakkuk *Khabakkuk*

SECTION OUTLINE

A Poet's Question-and-Answer Time with YHVH
Literary Format and Movement
Question for Further Study
References

This little scroll—of fewer than 900 words—is yet another piece of poetry associated with a prophet who is unknown. There is no biographical material about this person who is mentioned twice in the scroll, in 1.1 and 3.1. Most scholars set the date of composition around the end of the seventh century BCE, but it is difficult to speak with much certainty because there are not many clear historical details that we can identify. The end of the seventh century seems best because Babylon appears to be the superpower that is on the rise, and her reach is beginning to be felt. The scroll's name is supplied by the first line, "The oracle/vision that Khabakkuk the prophet saw." Khabakkuk is pronounced "khah-bah-*kook*," with *kh* like *ch* in *Bach*. The lack of historical specifics may be deliberate, for then the scroll becomes less-time bound and perhaps more open to being read as expressive of later readers' feelings.

A Poet's Question-and-Answer Time with YHVH

It takes little time to read through this scroll, and at the beginning one will be reminded of the book of Job, that great work of literature known for its many questions:

> How long, YHVH, shall I cry, and you not listen?
> Shall I shout to you, "Violence!" and you not save? (1.2)

YHVH's first answer directs the questioner into the realm of international politics to see that Babylon, or Chaldea, is on the rise and is coming to destroy many. But the questioner is not satisfied. Here the poet shows no sign of accepting the promise of more violence as an adequate response. One violent conqueror has replaced another, but those who are living rightly will still suffer.

LITERARY FORMAT AND MOVEMENT

Two editorial notations divide the book into two main segments. The first and longest is the one labeled as the oracle and the second is the prayer. Many readers investigating the compositional history have suggested that the prayer is a later addition, and this may be the case. However, thematically it is related to the first section and is a fitting pious conclusion. The oracle section is not in the common "thus says YHVH" format. Instead, the author in poetic form asks questions of YHVH about the injustice of Judah's suffering and then YHVH replies again in poetic form. This question-and-answer format is then repeated; the second time the questions become more intense and pointed. After the second answer section, the poetry moves into a segment of woes against oppressors—perhaps still a part of the last answer of YHVH. These woes might have been originally independent, but they fit quite well thematically, giving voice to the questioner's wishes and reinforcing YHVH's answer. The last section, the prayer, is a musical-liturgical psalm, complete with musical notations at beginning and end. As Khabakkuk's prayer, it concludes the scroll with a long expression of praise for YHVH's power and eventual victory, and of patience to wait for that coming day when the just persons will be saved and the oppressors removed.

1.1–2.20 The oracle of Khabakkuk	3.1–19 A prayer of Khabakkuk
1.2–4 Question	3.1–15 Praise of YHVH
YHVH's answer 1.5–11	3.16–19 Patience of poet
1.12–2.1 Question	
2.2–5 YHVH's answer	
2.6–20 Five woes	

Too pure are your eyes to see evil/and to observe wrongdoing you are not able.
So why do you observe the treacherous and stay silent while the wicked devours the right? (1.13)

The poet speaks of his expectation of YHVH's answer, and the second answer of YHVH does come with a formal announcement and fanfare (2.2–3). That answer again looks to the future and addresses the problem of injustice. We would be wrong not to point out that the first words of this answer, in 2.4, are difficult to understand in the Hebrew text, so much so that many scholars have resorted to emending the text to help it make sense. The JPS Tanakh rightly footnotes the difficulty: "meaning of Hebrew uncertain." In some sense the proud (oppressors) are in the wrong and then it is said that "the one who is right through his fidelity will live" (2.4).

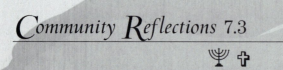

Community Reflections 7.3

TWO EARLY INTERPRETATIONS

Jewish

The community that wrote the Dead Sea Scrolls was a group of Jews who lived near the northwest end of the Dead Sea at a site known now as Qumran during the last centuries BCE and the first century CE. This community produced some of the earliest commentaries on scrolls of our library. Many of our scrolls, as well as others that are not in our library, were respected and in some sense authoritative for this community of Jews. A commentary is a writing that expounds on another text, usually explaining its meaning. We have copies of their line-by-line commentaries, called a *pesher* in Hebrew, of the books of Isaiah, Hosea, Micah, Nahum, Khabakkuk, Zephaniah, Malachi, and Psalms. What dominates nearly every line of these commentaries are two central ideas: 1) The scrolls refer not to the time of the prophet, such as Khabakkuk or Nahum, but instead to the time and experience of the present day Qumran group; 2) the present days of the Qumran community were the last days, and soon YHVH will bring the current world order to an end. Such ideas are seen elsewhere among Jews of this period and also in early Christian writings. Here is an example from the Qumran *pesher* to Khabakkuk.

> And God said to Khabakkuk to write down the things coming on the last generation, but the end of the age he did not reveal. And when it says "so that the one who reads it may run" (Khabakkuk 2.2), its interpretation concerns the True Teacher (the group's leader), to whom God revealed all the mysterious words of his servants the prophets. (column VII)

Christian

As the Qumran author used our scroll to speak to and about his own generation, so also the early Christian writer Paul, writing in about 55 CE, also used a line from Khabakkuk (2.4) for his own message. Attempting to draw a distinction that was vital for him, namely, a difference between living by faith and living according to Torah, Paul says the following in a letter to Christians in Galatia:

> That no one is justified before God by law is clear, because "the just one from faith will live"

(GALATIANS 3.11).

In other words, says YHVH according to the poet, the oppressors will not endure, and those who are just should continue to live faithfully. Continuing in this future-looking mode, the poetry moves into five statements of woe for oppressors. In many prophetic texts, woe oracles are addressed to specific nations, usually foreign ones. Remember Nahum? At one time these, too, might have been used against a particular foe, but here they take aim at an unnamed nation. Certainly Babylon would have been a prime suspect for some, but the door is wide open for application by readers of another time and place to apply the words to other oppressors, and not simply nations.

Though it does not explicitly make the point, it would seem that the closing prayer or hymn is meant to show that the questioner has changed stances and is now turning to YHVH in praise and trust for future salvation. An autobiographical writing style that was used in the questions continues in the hymn, and one could hardly find a more heartfelt pledge of faithfulness to YHVH despite every road-block than what one reads in the closing section of the poem. There is a realism of pain and suffering and a nearly incongruous yet genuine expression of confidence and even joy.

Questions for Further Study

1. Words from this scroll have been interpreted in interesting ways by widely divergent communities through history. What experiences, assumptions, and hopes might an ancient Israelite in exile have brought to the reading or hearing of this scroll?

2. What would be the rhetorical advantage of constructing a scroll as questions and answers?

References

Marks, Herbert. "The Twelve Prophets." In *The Literary Guide to the Bible*, edited by Robert Alter and Frank Kermode, 207–33. Cambridge, MA: Harvard, 1987.

Roberts, J. J. M. *Nahum, Habakkuk, and Zephaniah.* Louisville, KY: Westminster/John Knox, 1991.

Sweeney, Marvin A. "Habakkuk, Book of," in *The Anchor Bible Dictionary*, edited by David N. Freedman, 3:1–6. New York: Doubleday, 1992.

Szeles, M.E. *Habakkuk and Zephaniah: Wrath and Mercy.* Grand Rapids MI: Eerdmans, 1987.

צפניה

Zephaniah *Ts^efanyah*

In our day Zephaniah is one of the most obscure and least read scrolls of our library. It is brief—slightly more than 1,000 words—and in many ways its content and themes are typical of classical prophetic literature. Because Hebrew does have a real *z*, as in the name *Zechariah*, it seems much better to spell names that begin with the Hebrew letter *tsade* (צ) by using the English *ts*, pronounced like "ts" in *nets*. The entire Hebrew name *Ts^efanyah* is pronounced "ts^efahn-*yah*."

The Times of Ts^efanyah

Again in this scroll we find that an editor has provided some basic biographical information about the prophet to whom the oracles of this scroll are attributed. The period of his work, according to the editor, was during the reign of King Yoshiyahu, or Josiah, of Jerusalem, who reigned from 639 to 609 BCE. Josiah is known from other books to have instituted important religious reforms in his kingdom that favored the temple and priests in Jerusalem and those who advocated a YHVH-only cult and worship in Judah. Other texts in our library inform us that many kings before Josiah accepted other deities (e.g., 2 Kings 21.1–23.30), and the material culture revealed by archaeological excavations has shown extensive worship of numerous deities in Judah.

Curiously and uniquely in this case, the editor takes the prophet's genealogy back four generations to Hezkiyahu, or Hezekiah. Why would he do this? One explanation is that, the editor may be enhancing the prophet's status by showing royal lineage for him, because Hezekiah was a well-known king of Judah some 70 years before Josiah. In any case, the period to which the editor assigns the poet-prophet Ts^efanyah is decades after the fall of the Northern kingdom, a fate that weighed heavy in the mind of many Judeans during the decline of the Assyrian empire and before the invasion of Babylonian forces into the small kingdom of Judah.

*L*ITERARY FORMAT AND MOVEMENT

After the typical editorial introductory superscription (1.1), the entire scroll of Ts^efanyah is one continuous poetic oracle and content sections are not generally marked with definite signals of breaks, such as formulas or editorial remarks at the beginning or end of sections, such as we saw in Amos 1.3, 6, 9, 11, and 13. But there are shifts in content that show movement of theme and focus in the scroll. Most of the scroll is written with YHVH in the first person, though at times the rhetoric moves smoothly in and out of YHVH in the third person. Ts^efanyah's style is somewhat agitated, perhaps even frantic in places.

1.1 Editorial superscription

1.2–2.3 Coming universal destruction and Judah's destruction by YHVH

2.4–15 YHVH's punishment of foreign nations

3.1–20 Judah's punishment and future glory

The Urgent Poetry of Ts^efanyah

The poetry we find here is not given to soft-spoken, nuanced, highly qualified expression. It opens with a broad destructive sweep.

> Destructively I will destroy everything from the face of the earth,
> Declares YHVH.
> I will destroy human and animal;
> I will destroy bird of the air and fish of the sea,
> And the stumblings of the evil ones.
> I will cut down the human from the face of the earth,
> Declares YHVH.
> (1.2–3)

After this broad stroke, leaving little untouched, he moves immediately to his primary target: "I will lift my hand against Judah and against all the inhabitants of Jerusalem" (1.4a).

Not until the final segment of the scroll does this theme of destruction give way to a sustained positive theme. Echoing earlier prophetic speech, Ts^efanyah picks up the military figure of the Day of YHVH (see 1.7, 14) and proclaims it to be near. What is this day for Ts^efanyah?

> Day of wrath is that day,
> Day of distress and trouble,
> Day of disaster and calamity,
> Day of darkness and gloom,
> Day of clouds and dense darkness,
> Day of blasts and shouts against fortified towns and against high towers.
> (1.15–16)

This is YHVH's day of invincible battle against all his enemies.

Why all of this denunciation and destruction? According to the oracle of this scroll, YHVH is angry because those of Judah, as well as those outside, have "sinned against YHVH" (1.17). Numerous foreign nations, including Moabites, Canaanites, Ethiopians, Ammonites, and Assyrians, are mentioned, as is common in Israel's prophetic literature. Here in the poetry of Tsᵉfanyah they are invariably depicted as YHVH's enemies who either have been or will be destroyed. Descriptions of their destructions by YHVH serves the rhetorical purpose of placing YHVH as the God over all others, and, in fact this signals a prominent concern of the scroll, the worshiping of other Gods by people in Judah. It is the participation in and adoption of the rites and practices of other cults that is most specifically denounced in the scroll (see 1.4–9). The destruction of other nations also serves as a warning for the audience as to the fate that awaits them if they do not change.

> Seek after YHVH, all humble of the land, who do his laws.
> Seek justice,
> Seek humility.
> Perhaps you will be hidden on the day of the wrath of YHVH. (TSᵉFANYAH 2.3)

But the poet moves smoothly from foreign nations to Judah, such as the move from Nineveh to Jerusalem in 2.13–3.5. Tsᵉfanyah is a strong YHVH-only prophet, and he places the blame for Judah's current religious situation, which he finds so deplorable, squarely and quite broadly on Judah's leadership, its royal officials, social leaders, prophets, and priests (see 1.8; 3.4).

We cannot leave the scroll without mentioning its closing positive vision. Scattered throughout the scroll are occasional words of encouragement, but they are prominent in 3.11–20. Tsᵉfanyah envisions a day of proper worship of YHVH, victory over all Judah's enemies and oppressors, Judah's glorious restoration in the land, YHVH's forgiveness and mercy, and YHVH's reign as king in Jerusalem.

Questions for Further Study

1. Where would you place the author within his society? royalty? priest? wise man? Why? What are your clues and evidence?

References

Berlin, Adele, *Zephaniah*. New York: Doubleday, 1994.

Kselman, John S. "Zephaniah, Book of," in *The Anchor Bible Dictionary*, edited by David N. Freedman, 6:1077–80. New York: Doubleday, 1992.

Marks, Herbert. "The Twelve Prophets," in *The Literary Guide to the Bible*, edited by Robert Alter and Frank Kermode, 207–33. Cambridge, MA: Harvard, 1987.

Roberts, J. J. M. *Nahum, Habakkuk, and Zephaniah*. Louisville, KY: Westminster/John Knox, 1991.

Szeles, M.E. *Habakkuk and Zephaniah: Wrath and Mercy*. Grand Rapids, MI: Eerdmans, 1987.

חגי

Haggai *Khaggai*

Section Outline

The Times of Khaggai
Literary Format and Movement
Khaggai's Encouragements
Questions for Further Study
References

With fewer than 900 words and the third-shortest scroll overall, we have here a compact, tightly organized, and mostly straightforward composition. Most readers find it fairly easy to comprehend. Furthermore, its author seems to have one clearly defined mission, namely, encouraging the Jewish community of Jerusalem, many of whom had recently returned from exile in Babylon, to rebuild YHVH's temple there in Jerusalem. No biographical information is given for the man credited with these oracles; he is only called *Khaggai* the prophet. This name in Hebrew is pronounced "khag-*gai*" with the *kh* sounding like *ch* in *Bach*.

The Times of Khaggai

The Jewish community exiled to Babylon in 586 BCE by Nebuchanezzar's armies survived. Such survival is not to be taken for granted. The Israelites exiled by Assyrian forces in 722 BCE were lost in the historical record; what become of them we simply do not know. The Babylonian Empire itself fell to the invading Persian armies under the control of Cyrus in 539 BCE, and in the following year Cyrus issued a decree allowing displaced persons to return to the lands from which they were exiled. Many Jews returned to Judah; many stayed in Babylon and maintained their Jewish identity there. With Persian support and Persian-appointed Jewish governors, Jews began to rebuild their homeland, now the Persian province of *Yehud*. At the time of the oracles of Khaggai, the name the Jewish governor was Zerubbabel, a descendent of the last Jewish king Zedekiah, and thus of the great hero King David, too. But the new community was not without its problems. They had local enemies, there was tension among various groups within the returned exiles, and they did not experience agricultural and broad economic prosperity. Their difficulties were enormous.

LITERARY FORMAT AND MOVEMENT

Unlike much of Israel's prophetic literature, the scroll of Khaggai is not written in poetic form. It consists of four sermons, each of which is formally introduced as YHVH's message to Khaggai. In addition, an even stronger literary division is made at each of these four points by an editorial indication of the date—year, month, day—for each of the four oracles. In the case of the first sermon only, a brief narrative follows the oracle. There is confusion regarding the date indications found in 1.15 and 2.1, and some scholars have suggested that text has been misplaced, though currently available manuscripts do not confirm this. Within the oracles, Khaggai writes a direct prose of exhortation, including direct questions to the audience and calls to imagine a splendid future. Finally, some scholars argue that at one time this short composition was a part of the composition that we now know as Zechariah 1–8 (our next scroll). Historically and literarily this seems a possibility, but we lack manuscript evidence for this configuration, so our presentation we will consider the works as separate.

1.1–11 First oracle, call to build YHVH's house	2.1–9 Second oracle, encouragement and promise of future splendor	2.10–19 Third oracle, criticism of unclean offerings and unclean temple workers; bad harvests are signs of YHVH's disfavor.	2.20–23 Forth oracle, encouragement and promise of glorious political future for Zerubbabel the governor
1.12–15 Leaders and people obey call.			

The dates given in the scroll give the very day for each of the oracles. They all occur in second year of King Darius I (521 to 485 BCE) within a three-month period. The dates given, translated into our modern calendrical system are

- Haggai 1.1: 29 August, 520
- Haggai 1.15: 21 September, 520
- Haggai 2.1: 17 October, 520
- Haggai 2.10: 18 December, 520
- Haggai 2.20: 18 December, 520

Historians have determined that the rebuilt temple was completed five years later, and another book in our library, Ezra 6.13–15, narrates that completion in the year 515 BCE. It seems likely that this scroll was completed prior to 515 BCE and not substantially supplemented after that because it does not contain any indication that the Jerusalem temple has already been completed.

Khaggai's Encouragements

Each of the four sermons of Khaggai makes a different rhetorical appeal to its hearers or readers. The first sermon (1.1–15) asserts directly that the community had failed to prosper because, "says YHVH, my house lies ruined, while each person runs off to his own house" (1.4). According to the narrative that follows, the charge hit home, and work on the temple led by the governor Zerubbabel and the head priest Yehoshua (Joshua), began within weeks. The second oracle (2.1–9) addresses those who recognize that the temple they have begun is not as grand a construction as the earlier temple destroyed in 586 BCE. Khaggai declares for YHVH that "in a little while" I will shake up all creation and all nations, and make Judah prosperous, and the splendor of YHVH's new house will be greater than that of the former house (2.6).

Perhaps the oddest argument to modern ears comes in the third oracle of 2.10–19. This oracle includes a conversation with a priest about a couple of specific concerns of ritual purity. The basic point seems to be that the current sacrifices to YHVH are ritually unclean, and it implies that this situation can be remedied with the completion of the new temple. The text shifts somewhat abruptly in 2.15 and again repeats the argument that prosperity will come to the community once the work on the temple is underway. The last and shortest oracle (2.20–23) Khaggai addresses directly to the governor Zerubbabel. Here the encouragement comes again in the form of a glorious image of Judah's future in YHVH's plan. YHVH is said to be about to shake the kingdoms of the world and overturn their governments and armies. Then come this remarkable promise to Zerubbabel:

> "On that day," declares YHVH of armies, "I will take you Zerubbabel, son of Shealtiel, my servant," declares YHVH, "and I will set you as signet because I have chosen you," declares YHVH of armies. (2.23)

A signet is a stamp that marks a piece of clay that seals a treaty or contract with the identification of the owner, so the document that is sealed with a signet authentically represents the owner, often a king. Khaggai declares that in some manner, Zerubbabel is to be YHVH's representative. The scroll ends there, leaving the reader to ponder just what may be envisioned for Zerubbabel by this figure. It seem likely that the speaker expected zerubbabel's time to see the glorious future spoken of in the oracles.

We can make one final observation about the assumed relationships among prophet, priest, and governor here. Unlike some other prophetic scrolls, we find no tension; the prophet assumes and supports the priestly purity system and speaks highly of the civil governor as a part of YHVH's plan.

Questions for Further Study

1. How does this prose text strike its readers as opposed to the more common prophetic poetry?

2. As a historian of religion, how would you characterize the religion of this post-exilic scroll as compared to the religion of a mostly pre-exilic scroll such as Hosea or Amos? What are priorities and main categories?

References

Ackroyd, Peter R. *Exile and Restoration: A Study of Hebrew Thought in the Sixth Century B.C.E.* Philadephia: Westminster, 1968.

Marks, Herbert. "The Twelve Prophets," in *The Literary Guide to the Bible*, edited by Robert Alter and Frank Kermode, 207–33. Cambridge, MA: Harvard, 1987.

Meyers, Carol and Eric M. Meyers. "Haggai, Book of," in *The Anchor Bible Dictionary*, edited by 3:20–23. New York: Doubleday, 1992.

——. *Haggai, Zechariah 1–8*. Garden City, NY: Doubleday, 1987.

Petersen, David L. *Haggai and Zechariah 1–8*. Philadelphia: Westminster, 1984.

זכריה

Zechariah Z^ekharyah

This section of The Twelve is the longest of all and comprises 22 percent of the entire scroll. In its earlier form as an independent scroll, it would have been longer than several of the shortest nonprophetic scrolls in our library, such as Ruth or Song of Songs. In this case length also reflects difficulty—Z^ekharyah is certainly not the easiest scroll for us modern readers and scholars to read and understand. The first half of the book (Chapters 1–8) relates very much to the scroll we just finished, Haggai, for its oracles urge faithfulness to YHVH and support for YHVH's temple shortly after many Jews had returned from Babylon to Jerusalem. The second half (Chapters 9–14) has related but different concerns. Regarding the name of the scroll, which is the name of the prophet in the first line, you recall that in the case of Zephaniah a better English rendering of the name would replace the *z* with a *ts*, but in the case of Zechariah the *z* is the best English choice for the first letter of the Hebrew name, *Z^ekharyah*. The name is pronounced "z^ekhar-*yah*," with the *kh* sounding like *ch* in *Bach*.

The Times of Z^ekharyah and the Composition of the Scroll

This scroll's beginnings seem to be precisely in the same period as the previous scroll, Haggai, that is, during the years of the expansive Persian Empire under King Darius I (521 to 485 BCE). These two prophets are linked in the work known as Ezra (5.1; 6.14). Many Jews had returned from exile in Babylon in the last 20 years, and the new Jewish community of Syria-Palestine existed in the province of the Persian Empire called Yehud, around Jerusalem. As in Ezra-Nehemiah and Haggai, the Jewish leaders who are mentioned and held up for pious respect are Joshua, a priest, and Zerubbabel, a governor. Three times the scroll explicitly

LITERARY FORMAT AND MOVEMENT

Literarily the scroll called Z⁽ᵉ⁾kharyah easily divides into two segments, Chapters 1–8 and 9–14, the first half stemming from the sixth to fifth centuries BCE and the second from a century or two later. The first section is entirely in prose and is a distinct literary unit. After a brief introduction, which in some sense summarizes the oracular message of Z⁽ᵉ⁾kharyah, the first half of the scroll presents a narrative of conversations among YHVH, the prophet, and an angel. This narrative constitutes a series of eight visions of Z⁽ᵉ⁾kharyah and generally follows this basic literary pattern: Z⁽ᵉ⁾kharyah speaks in the first person of what he saw ("I looked and I saw . . ."), then he asks an angel about the meaning of the vision ("Then I asked . . ."), and then he reports what the angel answered ("And he answered me . . ."). After these eight visions, the scroll presents a series of short prose oracles regarding obedience to the instruction and words of YHVH, constantly repeating introductory formulas, such as "thus says YHVH." The rhetoric clearly attempts to persuade the reader of the legitimacy of the scroll's message. The second half of the scroll (Chapters 9–14) is more mixed in its literary form. Some clear structuring devices are found in the appearance of the heading "oracle: the word of YHVH," first in 9.1 and again at 12.1. These divide the last half of the scroll into two units, the first of which (9–11) is mostly poetry with some prose near the end, and the second of which (12–14) is mostly prose with a couple of small segments of poetry, as you can see in English Bibles such as the NRSV and the JPS Tanakh. In both of these sections, some passages presents YHVH speaking in the first person and other passages speak of YHVH in the third person.

1.1–6 Introduction and summary of YHVH's word to Z⁽ᵉ⁾kharyah	1.7–6.15 Eight visions of Z⁽ᵉ⁾kharyah interpreted by angel, encouraging faithfulness to YHVH and reestablishment of the temple in Jerusalem	7.1–8.23 Short prose oracles urging obedience to YHVH's instruction through priests and prophets

9.1–11.17 First oracle, poetic; the defeat of oppressors and enemies, restoration of Judah, and the triumph of YHVH	12.1–14.21 Second oracle, prose; the reestablishment of Israel/Jerusalem, and the final defeat of enemies and final triumph of YHVH

indicates dates of oracles from YHVH (1.1, 7; 7.1), which would correspond to 520 to 518 BCE. An oral presentation likely stands behind the writing of this part of the scroll sometime in the late sixth or early fifth century.

But that is just half the story, because dating the second half of the scroll, Chapters 9–14, has proven much more difficult. Most scholars think that these later chapters, which make no mention of Z⁽ᵉ⁾kharyah and are significantly more diverse in their makeup, were written more than one or two centuries later, during the period of Greek rule (see 9.13), in the late fourth or third century. Detailed study of

Chapters 9–14 has convinced many scholars that Chapters 9–11 and 12–14 have separate and complex compositional histories, but we'll have to pursue this fascinating compositional history at another time. All we can say here is that sometime, probably in the late fourth or third century BCE, someone put the last two segments of the scroll, 9–11 and 12–14, together and then linked them with the first section (1–8). Such a scenario is completely in keeping with concrete evidence of the practice of scroll composition at this time in Jewish societies.

The Visions and Message of Z^ekharyah Chapters 1–8

When you read Z^ekharyah, it will remind you of things you have read elsewhere in our library. The long section of the eight visions is similar to the scroll of Daniel (see Chapters 8), because both of them report visions that are interpreted by angels. In fact, literary scholars interested in tracing the history of the genre of writing known as apocalyptic literature understand this scroll of Z^ekharyah as representing a major developmental stage among earlier prophetic scrolls and later full-blown apocalyptic literature, such as Daniel and dozens of other Jewish works that were not later included in the Jewish sacred library. I've saved our discussion of apocalyptic literature for the scroll of Daniel, but it is here in Z^ekharyah that we first have the repeated motif of visions interpreted by angels. Many have wondered about the rise of this motif and apocalyptic literature and what they might signal about the society that produced them. Are the authors representing a cultural feeling of growing distance from the deity, so that a superhuman intermediary is needed? What might explain the rise of this intermediary interpreter in this narrative, when in older prophetic texts and narratives the prophet seemed to have direct access to deity and no need of interpreters? Does this emphasis on the need for interpretation relate to the growing status of written documents as vehicles of divine words? These questions demonstrate that anyone interested in the history of religion and in key developments about the nature of divine revelation in Judaism, Christianity, and Islam will want to look carefully at Z^ekharyah and numerous studies that have been done regarding these fascinating issues.

The eight visions themselves are quite interesting and fast paced. We might describe them as busy.

- In the first (1.7–17), a man is riding a red horse in a myrtle tree glen who has news of peace and eventual prosperity for Jerusalem.
- The second (2.1–4 or 1.18–21) is of four horns, representing conquering nations, that are themselves to be opposed by four blacksmiths.
- The third (2.5–17 or 2.1–13) is of a man with a measuring line who is measuring Jerusalem for future building.
- The fourth (3.1–10) is of the high priest Joshua and an adversary, sometimes poorly translated as a proper name, *Satan*; the adversary is rebuked, and Joshua is outfitted in festal clothes and exhorted to obey YHVH.
- The fifth (4.1–14) is of lamp stands, bowls, olive trees, and YHVH-chosen leaders Joshua and Zerubbabel, rebuilder of the temple.

- The sixth (5.1–4) is of a gigantic flying scroll that punishes people who disobey the commands of YHVH.
- The seventh (5.5–11) is hovering basket with a woman representing sin sitting in it. The basket is carried away to Babylon by two stork-winged women, and so Jerusalem is purified.
- The eighth (6.1–8) is of four chariots, representing the four winds of heaven, drawn by various colored horses coming out of two copper mountains and going in all directions. The significance is ambiguous.

As you can see there is great variety in these images, but the meanings presented are mostly messages calculated to encourage (1) support for the temple and Jerusalem's leaders and (2) obedience of YHVH's instruction (*torah*) in the traditions of prophets and priests. These are the repeated messages of the material before and after the eight visions as well, and they include specific instructions about obedience to prophets: justice and mercy for the poor, widows, orphans, and aliens; speaking truth; and working for peace (7.1–8.23).

The Themes of Z^ekharyah Chapters 9–14

The last part of the scroll is more traditionally prophetic literature in its format—oracles without angelic interpreters and with significant amounts of poetry. The mood also changes dramatically; we no longer see a focus on current needs to rebuild. Instead, the authors are looking mostly to the future and envisioning universal wars, attacks on Jerusalem, and YHVH's protection and ultimate triumph. Thematically then, this section, too, is related to dozens of later Jewish, and eventually Christian, apocalyptic compositions with their depictions of future battles and the eventual victory of their God and salvation of his people. Many nations are mentioned in these last two oracles, including the Greeks (9.13), who became the political rulers in the entire Western Mediterranean and Near Eastern area by 323 BCE with the lightning conquest of Alexander the Great. But unlike the first half of the scroll, a modern historian has difficulty determining the actual historical context out of which these words arise, because they give few identifiable clues to their current setting; even current leaders are unnamed, simply being called shepherds. The envisioning of great conflicts may represent current anxieties of the author's community. The oracles also speak with great confidence of YHVH's eventual victory, the cataclysmic changes on the earth, and the future universal greatness of Jerusalem and acknowledgment of its king and its God. This universality picks up the theme with which the first half of the scroll closes.

> And there will be continuous day—it is known to YHVH
> Not day, and not night, and even evening will be light.
> And on that day fresh water will flow out of Jerusalem;
> Half to the Eastern Sea, and half to the Western Sea.
> In both the summer and the winter this will be.
> And YHVH will be king over all the earth;
> In that day YHVH will be one and his name will be one. . . .

And it will be that all the survivors of the nations that came against Jerusalem will come up to Jerusalem year by year to worship the King, YHVH of armies, and to celebrate the festival of Sukkot.
(Zᴇᴋʜᴀʀʏᴀʜ 14.7–9, 16)

But such envisioning of these oracles is not an exercise in crystal-ball gazing or simple entertainment. The oracles make it abundantly clear that YHVH will rescue those who are faithful to his covenant, and they are intended to inspire faithfulness. There is even a highly ironic—for a scroll claiming the mantle of divine prophecy for its speaker (see especially 1.1–6; 7.1–14)—denouncement of prophets of a later time (13.2–6); a time when new prophetic words were not accepted, apparently because YHVH's instructions were considered already clear in the words of former prophets. So you can see that studying this book would also be of great value to the religious historian who is interested in the history of prophetic speech among ancient Judaism. Why would the author of the scroll think so poorly of prophets? What dangers did they pose for him? What is suggested about prophetic claims of this period?

To conclude, the scroll of Zᵉkharyah is fascinating for many different reasons. I once had a student tell me that it was his favorite because of all the different things that were going on in it and all the interesting questions it raises about the history and religion of Jews of this time. It is likely that this scroll was preserved in the library to provide the same sort of exhortation to generations of hearers as an original audience heard, but it has also provided generations of readers and writers with colorful expressions and a wealth of ideas for religious, literary, and historical consideration.

Questions for Further Study

1. What can a historian learn about the history of ancient Jewish ideas about prophets and prophecy from this scroll? What has changed? How are older prophets viewed? How does this scroll fit into that history?

2. What links to scrolls like Daniel and Revelation, in the Christian New Testament, do you see here? What other apocalyptic writings do you know? How are they similar?

References

Ackroyd, Peter R. *Exile and Restoration: A Study of Hebrew Thought in the Sixth Century B.C.E.* Philadephia: Westminster, 1968.

Hanson, Paul D., *The Dawn of Apocalyptic.* Rev. ed. Philadelphia: Fortress, 1979. 280–401.

Meyers, Carol and Eric M. Meyers. *Haggai, Zechariah 1–8.* Garden City, NY: Doubleday, 1987.

Meyers, Carol Eric M. Meyers, and David L. Petersen "Zechariah, Book of," in *The Anchor Bible Dictionary,* edited by David N. Freedman, 6:1061–8. New York: Doubleday, 1992.

Petersen, David L. *Haggai and Zechariah 1–8.* Philadelphia: Westminster, 1984.

מלאכי

Malachi *Malakhi*

SECTION OUTLINE

> Date and Setting of The Messenger
> Literary Format and Movement
> Message and Tradition
> Questions for Further Study
> References

In Jewish Bibles this writing is the last of the scroll of the twelve and so concludes the library section of *Neviim*, Prophets. In Catholic, Orthodox, and Protestant Christian Bibles, Malachi is the final book of the Old Testament. The scroll contains fewer than 1,200 words, about the size of a four-to-five-page writing assignment. The origin title *Malakhi*, pronounced in Hebrew as "mall-ah-*khee*," (*kh* as *ch* in *Bach*), is unclear. It comes from the first line of the scroll, an editor's superscription to the body of the work. But is Malakhi an actual personal name, or is it a title? The meaning of the word is "my messenger," and in this scroll at 3.1 and in other scrolls (Exodus 23.23; 32.34; Isaiah 42.19) it is not taken as a name. The early Jewish translators who put this scroll into Greek did not assume the occurrence in 1.1 to be a personal name, though other Jewish traditions, such as rabbinic literature, did take it as such. There is a certain sense in which our choice does not make much of a difference, for regardless of whether his name is Malakhi or he is an anonymous "messenger," we know nothing else about the person behind this scroll.

Date and Setting of The Messenger

The scroll is usually dated to the fifth century BCE, during the period when the Jews of Syria-Palestine have returned from exile in Babylon and are living in and around Jerusalem under Persian control. This would have made the author a near contemporary of the Jewish leaders Ezra and Nehemiah, though historians have been unable to agree on the relationships and sequence of the three. Many other Jews lived elsewhere in the Persian Empire, spread in groups from Egypt to Mesopotamia. There was a certain security of existence for those around Jerusalem, but for any who had hopes and dreams of a grand kingdom or a glorious independent Jewish state, the reality was certainly a disappointment.

LITERARY FORMAT AND MOVEMENT

Unlike most of the prophetic oracles in our library, this scroll is not written in poetry. Its literary style is unique among the traditional prophetic compositions of our library. The scroll also lacks the common introductory formula, "Thus says YHVH," that we know from many other prophetic scrolls. The superscription of an editor identifies the work as an oracle and the text itself presents a conversation or dispute. In most of this conversation the author places the "I" of the scroll, YHVH, in dialogue with a plural "you," the Israelites. The "you" is undoubtedly thought of as the scroll's audience by the author, and most likely was at some point the audience of an oral address by a prophet. The author also reports the words or thoughts of this group of addressees. Even while maintaining the conversational mode, occasionally the writer moves to referring to YHVH in the third person, and the prophet seems to be the speaker, such as in 2.13–17. This style creates very direct rhetoric and, to the extent that the questions and sentiments of the "you" passages are reflective of the questions and sentiments of the audience, the rhetoric is also personal. Here is YHVH, directly answering "your" concerns.

As with a natural conversation, it is not always easy to determine where formal divisions should be placed. I have traced the conversational movement in six major sections that are signaled by questions in the text, but these divisions are not hard and fast. The medieval chapter divisions of Malakhi are difficult to understand, and the Greek and Hebrew medieval manuscripts diverge on the numbering. The Greek manuscripts, followed by Christian English translations, have a Chapter 4 with six verses, whereas Hebrew manuscripts, followed by Jewish English translations, do not separate these last six verses and so have only three chapters.

1.1 Editorial Superscription	1.2–5 First dispute: YHVH's love for Israel over Edom	1.6–2.9 Second dispute: Proper temple worship in YHVH's covenant	2.10–16 Third dispute: YHVH's covenantal demands on marriage
2.17–3.7 Fourth dispute: YHVH coming punishment	3.8–12 Fifth dispute: Devotion to YHVH	3.13–21 (or 3.13–4.3) Sixth dispute: What is the benefit of serving YHVH?	3.22–23 (or 4.4–5) Final reminders: Obey the teachings of Moses; the day of YHVH is coming.

Even success as a minor Persian territory had proved difficult in the decades following the return to Jerusalem, which began in 538 BCE, thanks to the decree of Cyrus. Although this is the most plausible setting of the scroll's author, certainly those who decided to retain and copy the scroll for later readers or hearers saw here a message that could go beyond the confines of the immediate situation.

Community Reflections 7.4

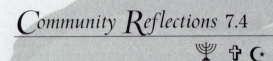

THE LIFE AND AFTERLIFE OF ELIJAH

The figure Elijah ("aelee-*yah*" in Hebrew) is one of the most famous prophets of all in our library. We first encounter him in the scroll of Kings—there he is presented as YHVH's nemesis of King Ahab. His story (1 Kings 17–2 Kings 2) is fascinating in many ways and full of action, suspense, passion, and danger. His death is no less dramatic, for, as the famous story goes, he never died. In the middle of a walk and conversation with his understudy Elisha, he was suddenly a fiery chariot drawn by flaming horses rumbles past and whisks him out of sight. Well, the answers differ in a variety of traditions. One of the most interesting things to notice is that Elijah is often spoken of as returning at a future time. And why not, no story ever says he died?

Judaism

Right here in Malakhi we find perhaps the oldest tradition about Elijah's return in 3.23 (or 4.5). Here he is a prophet whose message, YHVH promises, will bring family reconciliation before the great Day of YHVH. This is a standard prophetic role. In later Jewish tradition, a scroll was composed called the Apocalypse of Elijah that tells of the angel Michael describing to Elijah the end of Rome and wicked rulers and the triumph of YHVH and Jerusalem. In this tradition Elijah becomes the great prophetic harbinger of the Jewish Messiah, a promised rescuer whose work is to rescue from oppression and evil and usher in a period of peace for all. In this role Elijah shows up in many places of traditional Jewish liturgy, including Shabbat, circumcision ceremonies, and the Pesach (Passover) service, where an extra place at the table is set, an extra cup of wine is used, and the door is left open for his entrance.

Christianity

In Christian traditions, Elijah is also prominent. In the synoptic Gospels there is a story of Elijah mysteriously appearing on mountaintop along with Moses to have a conversation with Jesus. John the Baptist, a New Testament figure who functions as a precursor and announcer of Jesus, is presented as an Elijah, fulfilling the role of Messiah harbinger. Jesus even refers to John as Elijah (Matthew 11.14). And in Christian tradition there is a different Apocalypse of Elijah writing that has been preserved in Coptic and Greek, and other early Christian writers make reference to other books by Elijah that are no longer preserved.

Islam

In Muslim tradition in the Qur'an, we find both the Jewish and Christian traditions reflected. Elijah first appears (6.85) in a text that reflects the Christian Gospels, giving a list of righteous prophets, prophets of truth including Zachariah (the father of John the Baptist), John, Jesus, and Elijah. In another place (37.123–132) the author refers to Elijah's stories in the book of Kings and Elijah is held up as a great prophet who challenged the worship of false Gods.

For more on Elijah, see Wright 2004.

Message and Tradition

Malakhi's prose question-and-answer format sets it apart from other prophetic books and demonstrates yet another example of the literary creativity of an ancient Jewish prophetic writer. Though unique in form, the message of the scroll is one of continuity with widespread and established covenant traditions of Israelite literature. If we had to condense Malakhi's message into one statement, which is always a dangerous thing to do, the scroll of Malakhi may be considered an exhortation stressing a long-established theme: faithfulness to the covenant between Israel and YHVH. The scroll is also traditional in the sense that although it stands in the prophetic tradition, it is also supportive of the temple cult of YHVH, though it can also be critical of priestly actions it deems unworthy of YHVH. Expanding our summary a bit, we can say that the author is interested in

- promoting personal religious attitudes of faithfulness to YHVH's covenant;
- larger social reforms, such as stopping divorce, ending marriage of Jews to non-Jews, and ensuring the well-being of widows, orphans, and foreigners; and
- cultic reforms, such as insuring proper temple offerings and ending laxity of priests

One other by now traditional theme that Malakhi engages is the idea of the Day of YHVH. In this scroll the day is invoked as an unspecified time in the future of YHVH's judgment, for which one should prepare now by living according to the requirements of the covenantal relationship. See especially 2.17–3.5 and the last verse of the scroll. And of course we should not miss the final overt reminder of the scroll to not forget the teachings of Moses (3.22 or 4.4). These teachings, whatever the form in which the author knew them, were clearly authoritative instructions for this author. All in all one might say that this last composition of The Twelve stresses a great deal of continuity with earlier writings and traditions of our library.

Questions for Further Study

1. Considering a wide range of topics, such as religion and literary form, what continuities and discontinuities do you find Malakhi and earlier prophetic scrolls?
2. What earlier traditions of Israel does the author assume his audience knows? How does he use these traditions?

References

Hill, Andrew E. *Malachi.* Garden City, NY: Doubleday, 1998

——. "Malachi, Book of," in *The Anchor Bible Dictionary,* edited by David N. Freedman, 4:478–5. New York: Doubleday, 1992.

Petersen, David L. *Zechariah 9–14, Malachi.* Louisville, KY: Westminster/John Knox, 1995.

Wright, J. Edward. " Whither Elijah? The Ascension of Elijah in Biblical and Pseudepigraphic Traditions," in *Things Revealed: Studies in Early Jewish and Christian Literature in Honor of Michael E. Stone,* edited by Esther G. Chazon, David Satran, and Ruth A. Clements, Leiden: E. J. Brill, 2004.

Writings *Ketuvim*

CHAPTER OUTLINE

Overview

This final division of the Hebrew Bible is in some sense the most miscellaneous of the three. *Ketuvim,* pronounced "keh-tu-*veem*," simply means "writings" in Hebrew, which is a rather generic title. The eleven scrolls of this section are quite diverse, more so than the Torah and Neviim. We find here poetry and historical narrative, liturgy, and proverb collections, international wisdom and Israelite song lyrics, philosophical reflections and entertaining stories, and both pious and sensual passion. There's something for everyone. Some of these books are among the most famous and most used of the entire library, such as Psalms and Job, and others might be considered the most beautiful and passionate. On the other hand, some are little used or known, such as Ezra-Nehemiah or Chronicles. Such was the case in antiquity, too: among the Dead Sea Scrolls, we found parts of nearly 40 copies of Psalms and only one of Chronicles.

The scrolls of the Ketuvim tend to be the youngest of all those of the library, many stemming from the fourth to second centuries BCE. Because some might consider these works as less important or secondary, it seems particularly important to read them carefully for the form and content that the ancient authors carefully crafted. Certainly modern individuals and communities may value these scrolls as they see fit, but when the scrolls were composed the authors surely did not envision being relegated to the literary equivalent of an attic. Equally important for us as we proceed is the reminder that just because we are coming to these scrolls at the end of our study does not mean they were intended to be fit into or subsumed under any system of thought or theology that we might have developed from the earlier scrolls. Respecting each author and the integrity of each scroll will lead us to listening carefully to the individual creation and content of each presentation. It will also be most interesting that way!

Psalm Literature in the Ancient Near Eastern World

It's no surprise that many other cultures in the ancient world also composed religious poetry and songs. Egyptian compositions, which are now often called hymns, have become quite famous among examples of ancient literature. We can appreciated the beauty of expression and piety found in Egyptians songs preserved from many centuries, some dating before 2000 BCE, and many from later centuries of Egyptian greatness, the 1500s to the 1200s. "Hymn to Amon-Re," "Hymn to the Nile," and "Hymn to Aton" are some of the poems praising and thanking particular deities. Many Hebrew Bible scholars and students of literature have seen many close and specific parallels between the Akenaton's "Hymn to Aton" and the Israelite Psalm 104 in our scroll; it is often concluded that the psalmist made use of some form of the older Egyptian hymn from the 1300s.

Even closer to the culture and location of Israel, archaeologists have found other Canaanite psalms, especially at an ancient cite called Ugarit, in literature dating from the fourteenth and thirteenth centuries BCE. The language of Ugarit is closely related to Hebrew, and the poetic forms of the two literatures also have much in common. Hallmarks of Hebrew poetry, parallelism especially, similar or identical similes, titles for deity, imagery, and recurring identical word pairs are all found in abundance in the two traditions. What is clear, as Jonas Greenfield puts it, is that the Israelites were "active participants in a broader literary culture: they were participants and also innovators" (Greenfield 1987, 560).

Songs and singing are mentioned in many scrolls of our library. In cultures of today, as well as in those of the Fertile Crescent, music, singing, chanting, and performance poetry are associated with divine worship and cultic ritual (e.g., Psalm 38.1), royal court performance (e.g., 1 Samuel 16.16–23, 2 Samuel 19.35), prophetic activity (e.g., 1 Samuel 10.5, 1 Chronicles 25.1–5), funeral rites (e.g., 2 Samuel 1.18), dancing, (e.g., 2 Samuel 6.14), feasting (e.g., Amos 8.10), sensuality, and all levels of society (e.g. Isaiah 5.12). The scrolls that are dedicated in their entirety to poetry of this kind are Psalms, Lamentations, and Song of Songs, all contained here in the Ketuvim.

Wisdom Literature in the Ancient Near Eastern World

We should also say a few words about a different type of literature, what we call wisdom literature. Our scrolls of Proverbs, Job, and Ecclesiastes are often designated wisdom literature in modern discussions. And that is not a bad name for the three of them, because together they use Hebrew terms for "wisdom" far more than any books of our library. Wisdom is their subject, and it was the subject of many writings outside of Israel too. Actually, *wisdom literature* is a term used by modern scholars to describe certain writings of Syria-Palestine, ancient Mesopotamia, and Egypt. Wisdom literature shares general traits of perspective, ways of considering life and viewing the world.

- Wisdom literature focuses on the experience of life and how the individual ought to live in a wise and rewarding way, how one can excel, and how one is to cultivate virtues and eradicate vices.

- Wisdom literature is noticeably universal, not nationalist, in scope; it speaks of human experience generally and does not depend on nationalist categories.

- Its purview is all of life and creation, and it is concerned with what gives life order and justice.

- Because wisdom is seen as residing beyond national and ethnic borders, wisdom literature is therefore quite international in flavor and outlook. It often speaks of deities, but not in exclusivist or particularist terms. In Egypt for example, where there were many Gods and Goddesses, wisdom literature rises above particularity and cultic differences and is much more generic in its references to deities, more like a modern generic use of *God* for any deity.

- Wisdom literature seems to stem from educational, scribal social settings, which were often dominated by men and boys of royal courts, so despite what I said about a universal viewpoint, women's perspectives and concerns are not well represented. In this literature a very common trope is that of a father addressing his son, which may have literal application in some cases, but more generally applies to the teacher and his pupil. You will see the son, or in some translations the child, addressed frequently in Proverbs.

References

Alter, Robert. *The Art of Biblical Poetry.* New York: Basic Books, 1985.

Brown, William P. *Character in Crisis: A Fresh Apporach to the Wisdom Literature of the Old Testament.* Grand Rapids, MI: Eerdmans, 1996.

Brueggemann, Walter. *In Man We Trust.* Richmond, VA: John Knox, 1972.

Crenshaw, James L. *Old Testament Wisdom.* Louisville, KY: Westminster/John Knox, 1998.

Gammie, John G. and Leo G. Perdue. *The Sage in Israel and the Ancient Near East.* Winona Lake, IN: Eisenbrauns, 1990.

Greenfield, Jonas C. "The Hebrew Bible and Canaanite Literature," in *The Literary Guide to the Bible,* edited by Robert Alter and Frank Kermode, 545–60. Cambridge, MA: Harvard, 1987.

Murphy, Roland E. *Responses to 101 Questions on the Psalms and Other Writings.* New York: Paulist, 1994.

———. *The Tree of Life: An Exploration of Biblical Wisdom Literature,* 2nd ed. Grand Rapids, MI: Eerdmans, 1996.

The New Interpreter's Bible. Vols. 4, 5. Nashville, TN: Abingdon, 1996, 1997.

תהלים

Psalms *T^ehelim*

Section Outline

In 1640 CE in Cambridge, Massachusetts, the first book ever printed in the so-called New World came off the press. It was *The Whole Booke of Psalms Faithfully Translated into English Metre*, commonly known as the Bay Psalm Book. The popularity of Psalms long preceded the seventeenth century and is still in evidence today. From choirs and pulpits in churches and synagogues to rock concerts (U2's "Forty") and popular movies and rap (Coolio's "Gangsta's Paradise"), lines from this scroll have been echoing through the ages. It is a favored and much quoted text in both Jewish and Christian liturgy and tradition.

The English name comes from the Greek word *psalmos*, "sound of the harp, song sung to a harp," or more generally "song." But the Hebrew name, *T^ehelim*, pronounced "t^ehe-*leem*," means "praises" and is not necessarily a musical term. It should be noted, however, that although the title is understandable—many of the poems are praises to YHVH—a large number of the poems are not encomiums of the God; they are laments or cries of distress.

Because it is the largest collection of individual poems in our library and quite a famous book even in the modern world, we probably know something about what we should expect. At the beginning of our tour (chapter 4), we mentioned that poetry is a creative, intricate art, the work of imaginative wordsmiths. Hebrew poetry is dynamic; there is no formula, no exact science, and no unbreakable logic to its construction. We must be willing to grant poetic license, and leave room for ambiguity and subtle wordplay. We must expect a range of

DISPLAY 8.1 | TITLE PAGE OF THE BAY PSALM BOOK, CAMBRIDGE, MASSACHUSETTS, 1640

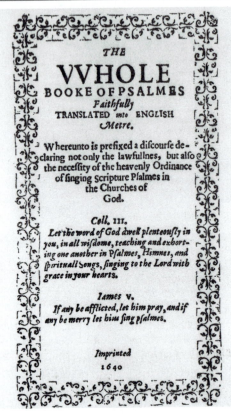

poetic expression, including metaphor, simile, shifting devices, changes in voice, exaggeration, and unusual vocabulary.

Collecting Poems in Ancient Israel

We already saw that psalm literature was common outside of Israel, and we should now add that this scroll of T^ehelim was by no means the only collection of songs in ancient Israel. The writer of 2 Samuel (1.18) refers to and quotes a certain song entitled "Bow," contained in a scroll he calls the Scroll of Yashar. You probably recall that we saw another poem cited from this Yashar collection in our scroll of Joshua (10.12–13). Remember too that the scroll of Numbers (21.14) quotes a poem from the Scroll of YHVH's Wars. We also find intriguing evidence of earlier poem collections within our own scroll of T^ehelim. For example, all of the poems in book one (Chapters 1–41) are described in the opening editorial remark as psalms "of David" except for 1, 2, 10, and 33. Might this have been a Psalms of David collection at one

*L*ITERARY FORMAT AND MOVEMENT

As an anthology of individual poems—many likely having musical associations for ancient users—this Hebrew scroll is made up of 150 independent chapters. This independence is illustrated by the fact that there are variations in arrangement of the 150 (or more) psalms in some ancient manuscripts. So we could justify 150 columns in our layout of the literary organization. On the other hand, there are clearly various groupings among the poems, several of which we will mention later. One of the oldest ways of arranging the 150 psalms is to group them into five sections, or books. In some medieval Jewish literature the division into five is said to mirror the five books of the Torah, but we do not have evidence from the period of the scroll's formation that suggests a reason for these division. The divisions do have internal textual support, instead of simply being late externally applied divisions. At the end of Chapters 41, 72, 89, and 106 are verses that scholars call doxologies—formulas of praise that conclude the section and were not simply the last verse of the psalm. In each case the formula uses the Hebrew particle *amen,* and it is only in these concluding formula that the word occurs in this scroll. The JPS Tanakh translation shows by it textual layout the concluding nature of these verses. At the end of the second segment (72.20), we even find an editorial remark about the end of the collection.

The concluding lines at the end of the first four books read this way:

41.14: Blessed is YHVH, God of Israel from beginning to end; amen, amen.	72.18–20: Blessed is YHVH, God of Israel, who alone does wonders. Blessed is his glorious name forever; his glory fills all the earth; amen, amen. Prayers of David, son of Yeshai are ended.	89.53: Blessed is YHVH forever; amen, amen.	106.48: Blessed is YHVH, God of Israel from beginning to end. And all the people say, "Amen." Praise YH(VH).

We should also here observe that many scholars now believe that the first two poems of the scroll were not originally part of the first book—notice that they lack the typical Davidic editorial opening—but were placed there to in order to set front and center the themes of happiness through obedience to the instruction of YHVH (Psalm 1) and of the rule of YHVH through his king in Zion (Psalm 2). It is interesting to ask what effect such placement might have on the usage of poems that come later in the scroll, if any.

Of course the literary form of all 150 psalms is poetic, and, because it is a collection of many independently composed poems, we expect to find a variety of

Hebrew poetic forms and style. We will describe these later. A helpful analogy for understanding this scroll is to think of a prayer book or hymnal that many worshiping communities use today. They are anthologies of prayer or songs with long histories of growth over time. There is some logic to their organization—usually loose subject matter connections or liturgical ordering—but other prayer books or song books may have many of the same entries but in a differing order. Each prayer or song has its own integrity and stands on its own; its origin, use, and contextual frame are independent.

Finally, in modern Bibles there are two different conventions for dividing and numbering individual verses within chapters. The Hebrew manuscripts followed by modern Jewish versions number the editorial information at the beginning of many poems (all but 22 psalms have such information) as the entire verse 1, but modern Christian editions generally begin verse 1 after the editorial information. The result is that in many psalms a Christian translation will have one—sometimes two—fewer verse numbers, even though the actual text is the same. I have tried to clarify this for you by putting both numbers where necessary, as in "5 (or 4)." Additionally, in the study of this scroll we usually use the term *psalm*, instead of *chapter*, because each poem, or psalm, represents a separate unit, or chapter.

1–41	42–72	73–89	90–106	107–150
Book 1	Book 2	Book 3	Book 4	Book 5

time? And notice the editorial remark at the end of Psalm 72: "Prayers of David son of Yeshai are ended." Obviously at some point this line was the end of a Psalms of David collection—but it's not anymore; after Psalm 72, there are 37 more psalms that are associated with David. So it seems clear that a collection of David psalms, roughly corresponding to Psalms 1–72, was incorporated into, or formed the basis of, our scroll and then was later supplemented.

Other collections are also in evidence: There is the Korah collection of 44–49 and the Asaph collection of 73–83. Some poems are tied together by opening editorial remarks and themes, such as the Psalms of Pilgrimage (120–134) and the similar and formal praise poems, all of which begin and end in exactly the same way (146–150). Careful readers have also observed that the bulk of books 2 and 3, Chapters 42–83, refer to Israel's God almost exclusively with the Hebrew title *Elohim*, instead of the personal name *YHVH*, whereas in psalms outside of the grouping Elohim is found much less often. To be exact:

- Outside of T^ehelim 42–83, Elohim is used 119 times; YHVH is used 650 times in 108 psalms.
- In T^ehelim 42–83, Elohim is used 245 times; YHVH is used only 45 times in 42 psalms.
- Intriguingly, one poem is used twice in our scroll, once in its mostly Elohim version, T^ehelim 53, and once in its mostly YHVH version, T^ehelim 14.

DISPLAY 8.2 | A SECTION OF THE MOST FAMOUS DEAD SEA T^eHELIM
SCROLL, 11Q5, FROM CAVE 11

What best explains these curious facts? Many scholars have concluded that at one time there was an Elohim collection of poems, perhaps produced by someone who took already existing poems and edited out most occurrences of the name *YHVH* and substituted the title *Elohim*. Some scholars think that this may have been done for reasons of piety—to remove the sacred name from the text and thus from the lips of readers as a show of respect and devotion. More recently, Ziony Zevit has argued that the removal of the personal name and replacement with a generic word allowed for a broader use among those Israelites who did not focus exclusively on YHVH (Zevit 674–87). But regardless of the reason, which cannot be determined with existing evidence, it seems clear that these poems using mainly Elohim were at one time a distinct group that has now been incorporated into our larger T^ehelim scroll and that the one case of overlap (T^ehelim 14 and 53) was not removed by an editor.

Finally, it has been known for many centuries that some manuscripts of T^ehelim had more than 150 psalms. Greek versions, for example, have 151 and Syriac versions have 155 psalms. Because of the discovery of the Dead Sea Scroll we now have hard evidence from the last centuries BCE of additional poems and other forms of the scroll we know of as T^ehelim, and, the discoveries teach us a lot about the process of formation for our scroll. There were more manuscripts found of T^ehelim than any other single composition, 36 in all. We find that they have many differences and that this one community used and preserved several different editions of T^ehelim scrolls. For example, one Qumran scroll (11Q5), of which only the final 27 columns are preserved, has a form that has poems in a different order than our T^ehelim; contains poems we only knew about from Greek or Syriac versions or other scrolls; and contains poems we had never seen before.

Scrolls scholars James VanderKam and Peter Flint show the contents of the end of 11Q5, using the traditional numbers:

> 101, 102, 103, 109, 118, 104, 147, 105, 146, 148, 120, 121, 122, 123, 124, 125, 126, 127, 128, 129, 130, 131, 132, 119, 135, 136, 145, 154, unique, 139, 137, 138, Ben Sira 51, unique, 93, 141, 133, 144, 155, 142, 143, 149, 150, unique, 2 Samuel 23.7, prose section (unique), 140, 134, 151A, 151B. (VANDERKAM AND FLINT, 123, SIMPLIFIED)

Looking at all the Dead Sea Scroll evidence and other manuscripts, we can see that in the last centuries BCE, psalms scrolls varied in form and content and included the basis for the version that we know as Tᵉhelim. We find several differing editions in use by one Jewish community at the site of Qumran. Our 150-poem version is the one that much later was chiefly used in Rabbinic Jewish circles and is the basic form behind modern Jewish, Roman Catholic, and Protestant Bibles. Early Christian communities, however, and the Orthodox churches today use a longer version of Tᵉhelim.

Authors and Dates

As an ancient anthology, we would expect that the scroll of Tᵉhelim was changed and expanded over time, and ancient manuscript discoveries have demonstrated exactly that. Our scroll may well include poems dating back to the tenth or ninth centuries BCE, whereas others come from the sixth century (see Tᵉhelim 137) and some even later. Many of the poems are associated with David, the Jewish king who lived in the tenth century; he is mentioned in the editorial introduction of more than 70 psalms. But this mention is not a clear designation of authorship, because the Hebrew phrasing may be understood several different ways, such as "for," "according to," or "in the manner of David." Other names are mentioned too, such as the Korahites, a priestly family active in the Jerusalem temple (e.g., Tᵉhelim 44), and Asaph, another family associated with temple music (e.g., Tᵉhelim 73). These editorial notes at the beginning of so many of our poems come from a compiler at later time, and they show us how particular poems were linked with certain poem collections, traditions, and stories, some of which we know from other scrolls (e.g. Tᵉhelim 18, 34, 51, 52). The editorial introductions do not, however, tell us much about the poem's author or original setting. In their anonymity they are typical of Israelite literature.

Music and Tᵉhelim

It is most unfortunate that there are no recordings of the ancient Jewish music preserved in Tᵉhelim. We have no clear evidence that all of the poems had musical settings, but many of them surely did. Scholars have counted nearly 60 terms of musical significance throughout the scroll. Tᵉhelim 150 lists numerous instruments apparently available in the culture. Look at the first lines of Tᵉhelim 4 and 5; they mention stringed instruments and flutes. Unfortunately, because we do not have adequate remains of musical instruments from the material culture of Israel, we often do not know just what the instruments actually were. We do find frequently used words for a musical poem, or song, including *mizmor* (see first line of Tᵉhelim 3) and *shir* (see first line of Tᵉhelim 45). Many terms that we find could be musical cues to inform a musician of the tune or style, such as the editorial opening of Tᵉhelim 22. One word that is used more than 70 times, *selah*, is still of unknown significance to modern scholars, but many believe that it is a notation marking a pause, perhaps signaled by a musical action such as a cymbal clang (see Tᵉhelim 24.6, 10). As you can see, there is still a lot we don't know, and more archaeological discoveries would help us learn about ancient instruments.

DISPLAY 8.3 | NINTH OR EIGHTH-CENTURY BCE ISRAELITE FIGURINES OF MUSICIANS FROM ACHZIV

Larger Poetic Structures

You recall that when we started our tour we talked about the hallmarks of Hebrew poetry (Chapter 4), cadence, and especially parallelism. Beyond those major building blocks, there are larger structural forms used by the ancient Jewish poets represented in T^ehelim. For example, we have acrostic psalms in which successive lines or groups of lines begin with successive letter of the Hebrew alphabet (25, 34, 37, 111, 112, 119, 145). If you have ever written an acrostic, you know that it can require a good deal of ingenuity and creativity to think of appropriately meaningful words for each letter of the alphabet with which to begin your lines. Consider the poet of T^ehelim 119, a lengthy psalm extolling the virtues of YHVH's instructions and the longest of all the poems in our scroll, who started eight consecutive lines with each of the 22 letters of the Hebrew alphabet, and so produced a poem of 176 lines. Unfortunately, all the artistic labor that went into that aspect of the poem is completely lost on modern English readers. A translation completed in the 1940s by Ronald Knox rights this wrong by valiantly translating using an English acrostic format.

Some of these acrostic psalms raise other interesting issues. T^ehelim 9–10, when joined together form a broken acrostic—three letters of the 22-letter alphabet are missing their lines and some lines of the poem do not fit the model. But could 19 lines of acrostic form be merely coincidence? In fact, in ancient Greek manuscripts T^ehelim 9–10 are written as one poem, but our medieval Hebrew manuscripts divide them. Unfortunately, we have no evidence among the preserved Dead Sea Scrolls to help us in this case. This may have been one psalm that was later divided because its text and poetic form was corrupted in transmission. Or it may have been two distinct poems, each dealing with a different theme (9: YHVH's triumphant reign over enemy nations; 10: a lament for the poor), which at some time were linked because of textual coincidence or intentional alteration. How would you argue the point? What investigative questions should be asked?

Although the Dead Sea Scrolls do not help us in the case of T^ehelim 9–10, they are a major aid for T^ehelim 145. In our medieval Hebrew translations this, too, was a broken acrostic lacking Hebrew letter *nun*—equivalent of English *n*—between verses 13 and 14. Again, ancient Greek and Syriac translation have a complete verse here that is not in Hebrew versions, but was there a Hebrew original behind these translations? This psalm occurs in one Qumran text, and the apparently missing *n* line is there, and so, if we follow our oldest manuscript of this poem, we can restore the line as follows:

N ever failing is YHVH in all his words, and graciously loyal in all his deeds.

This Qumran scroll demonstrates something else about the potential flexibility of the ancient poetry, because after every acrostic line there is this refrain:

Bless YHVH and bless his name from beginning to end.

This refrain likely indicates that the poem was used in a liturgical context when one group responded with the words of the refrain after another speaker recited or read each line of the acrostic. Another example of the usage of a refrain is found in T^ehelim 136.

Study Room 8.1

"FIXING" SOME PSALMS

As a teacher I enjoy giving and reading a "fix it" assignment regarding acrostic psalms, which stretches some poetic muscles of students, and improves many modern translations that totally ignore this poetic device. Choose either T^ehelim 25, 34, 37, 111, 112, 119, or 145 or Lamentations 1, 2, 3, or 4, and carefully paraphrase each line, being careful to start each verse (as indicated by the numbering system) with a successive letter of the alphabet. (Your teacher should be able to help you find the Hebrew acrostic lines.) Because English has four more letters than Hebrew, you have some flexibility; perhaps you will want to throw out any four letters you can't use. A thesaurus is a good tool to use and it is often enjoyable to do this in small groups. If you want to work on this for a long time, choose T^ehelim 119!

There are other types of letter games besides acrostics that can be played at the beginning of lines. T^ehelim 103 uses a form of alliteration. In most of the poem, lines in groups of two, three, or four begin with the same letter, and the first two lines begin the same as the last four.

Several poems in T^ehelim are narrative poems. Each separate verse follows typical forms of Hebrew parallelism, but the entire poem tells a story. Some of the longer poems in our collection, for example 78, 105, 106, 135, and 136, provide a basic poetic retelling of Israel's past and her relationship to her God. Students of ancient Jewish traditions have found these fascinating because they show a poet's retelling of Israel's past and provide a basis for comparison with other retellings found in other scrolls of our library. Other narrative poems speak not of the community or national level, but for the individual. The now famous T^ehelim 23 opens with a narrative (T^ehelim 23.1–4) metaphorically describing YHVH's care for his sheep, the speaker. Near the end (23.5–6), the narrative shifts from describing YHVH as the great shepherd to YHVH as the great host for the speaker. T^ehelim 104 is a different kind of story, not so much a narrative of human historical affairs, but of YHVH's great works of creation, past and present, from the stretching out of the skies and placing of the earth's foundations to the daily care for animals. It is this beautiful poem that has many striking parallels with the famous Egyptian poem known as Hymn to the Sun or Hymn to Aton.

Many poems of our scroll utilize some form of what is called *inclusio,* a form of repetition that uses words to set up bookends that begin and close a poem or a section of a poem. Perhaps the most obvious examples are found in T^ehelim 146–150, each of which begins and ends with the call to "Praise YHVH." Many other kinds of repetition are also used, including repeated phrases (e.g., T^ehelim 136) and key words or motifs.

Kinds of Psalms

How would you categorize these many different poems? Depending on what kind of investigation we are interested in doing, we could try to do it by date, poetic type, editorial remarks, musical associations, or content. Because we have already talked quite a bit about issues of scroll formation and poetic style, let's turn and look at the content of some poems and consider their rhetorical stance. How does the poet seek to influence his God, his hearers, and even himself? What stance or identity does the speaker adopt? And if we are interested in content, what are the subjects these poems address, and what purposes are presented for them? All these questions can be broken down for independent and expansive analysis, but here we will find it useful to treat them together.

The following five genres represent a typical categorization of the poems of our anthology, but be aware that these classifications were created by later readers, not category headings supplied by the scroll. Most importantly, there are not clear divisions between the groupings, and we should never restrict the poet's freedom to cross all boundaries; we find many mixtures. The categories are intended purely as descriptive tools of typical patterns. The chapter numbers are from Anderson (213–17).

1. Praise Poems (Ch 8, 19, 33, 66, 95, 100, 103, 104, 111, 113, 114, 117, 145, 146, 147, 148, 149, 150)

The first type of poems, praise psalms, are perhaps the ones modern readers first think of most readily when they hear the word *Psalms*. Praise poems are just what you would expect, poems that praise and celebrate the God of Israel. They usually open with an invitation from the poetic voice to the group or community to join in praising YHVH. It is this genre of psalm that gives us the most widely spoken Hebrew word, *hallelujah,* which in Hebrew is two words: an imperative verb "to praise," *hal-lou,* and an abbreviated form of the divine name, *YH.* Frequently the themes of these poems are creation and redemption, YHVH's creating and rule of the world (physical and historical), and YHVH's rescuing of Israel.

2–3. Lament Poems (Individual—3, 4, 5, 7, 9–10, 13, 14 (or 53), 17, 22, 25, 26, 27, 28, 31, 35, 36, 39, 40, 41, 42, 43, 52, 53, 54, 55, 56, 57, 59, 61, 63, 64, 69, 70, 71, 77, 86, 88, 109, 120, 139, 140, 141, 142, Community—12, 44, 58, 60, 74, 79, 80, 83, 85, 89, 90, 94, 123, 126, 129, 137)

The second and third categories are corporate (2) and individual (3) laments. Laments are poetic cries to God: complaints and prayers for aid and comfort. They may be bitter or hopeful, despairing or angry. Some of them appear confident of coming relief; some are haunting questions. They usually speak from one of two points of view, that of the individual, using the first person singular, or that of the community, using the first person plural. They address Israel's God (YHVH) directly. These prayers describe an array of troubles encountered in human existence either as an individual or as a group, and they plead with God to respond, often providing supportive arguments as to why he should. Near the end of these poems, there is frequently an expression of trust or a vow to praise YHVH or to perform a sacrifice. Although a modern reader may find the praise psalms more familiar, the complaint poems outnumber all the others. The supplicant is in need of salvation from enemies or disaster; often the shadow of Sheol, that murky dark place of death, is reaching into the domain of life through sickness and disaster, and the speaker of the poem cries out for YHVH to hear and to rescue. It is the intensity of their emotion and openness of expression that seems most remarkable to modern ears, and yet in some sense has always been contemporary.

> My God, my God, why did you abandon me? . . .
> My God, I cry out in the day, and you do not answer . . .
> (TᴇHELIM 22.2)

The pathos of the speaker is clear, and in the poetry of Tᵉhelim the pathos of YHVH can be equally vivid. The God of these poets, whether called YHVH or Elohim, is not the image of a distant abstract philosopher's God, nor a theologian's God who is changeless, beyond criticism, and passionless. Instead, the God we find in the mind of these poets is seen as one who can listen (or should!), change, be moved (or should!), lead armies (or should!), take revenge on ene- mies (or should!), and rescue his beloved from their personal struggles. Over and over the picture is of a dynamic deity envisioned many ways. The poetic imagery often gives the reader a vision of the personal anguish and range of emo- tions of the speaker and also a lively array of images of YHVH projected by the poets. In T^ehelim 82, using a common ancient Near Eastern motif of an assembly of Gods with one of them as the king, Elohim is the chief in the council of Gods (literally, "divine assembly, in the midst of Gods") and holds them all responsible for justice. In T^ehelim 44, a national lament for a loss in battle, the writer does not shy away from directly taking Israel's God to task for the loss and yells for him to wake up.

> Elohim we praise all day long,
> And your name we thank continuously.
> Yet you rejected and disgraced us,
> And did not go out against our armies . . .
> You gave us up like sheep for devouring,
> And among the nations you scattered us.
> You sold your people for nothing,
> Not even getting a high price for them!
> You made us a disgrace to our neighbors,
> Scorn and derision to those surrounding us. . . .
> Wake up! Why do you sleep, Master?
> Get up! Do not abandon us forever!
> Why do you hide your face from us?
> And forget our anguish and distress?
> (T^EHELIM 44.9–10 [OR 8–9], 13–14 [OR 12–13], 24–25 [OR 23–24])

The passionate plea is clear, even painful, for a reader with empathy. The visions of divine realities in the author's mind are equally apparent and must be seriously attended. This writer seems desperately to awake YHVH to action. (For a contrast- ing use of the sleeping metaphor, see T^ehelim 121.)

Perhaps the most haunting of the lament poems is T^ehelim 89, which displays a unique poetic form—an apparent praise song at the beginning turns out to be a bit- ter cry of breathtaking rhetorical courage. Here the story of YHVH's covenant with Israel is rehearsed and celebrated (89.1–37), only to set up the accusation that YHVH has unfaithfully renounced the covenant (89.38–45). The depiction of the covenantal relationship here is not the same as the scrolls of Kings or prophetic writers who blame Israel for breaking the covenant. Such honest sentiment on the part of the poet is remarkable today because it is often not properly acknowledged and is rarely a part of Israelite expression.

What is even more remarkable, in light of widespread but inaccurate notions of some supposed biblical unity of pious thought, is that later editors of T^ehelim and eventually of the entire library included this contrarian's reading of YHVH's covenant story. Using pieces of T^ehelim to construct a supposed systematic religious ideology or systematic theology of YHVH seems a disrespectful and grotesque violation of this poetic literature. What T^ehelim offers us are windows into the imaginations of some ancient Jewish poets who reflect deeply and uniquely on their traditions and their experience of life. In the poetic vision of one, the God of Israel sleeps and ought to wake up (Psalm 44.24 [or 23]); for another he awakes, shakes off his sleep like a drunk warrior, and routs his enemies (Psalm 78.65); for another he is Israel's guardian and never sleeps (Psalm 121.4). These pictures retain their own artistic and imaginative integrity for modern readers only when we allow each one to fully articulate its own images.

Another community lament—beautiful and exquisite—found in T^ehelim 90, is perhaps my favorite in the entire anthology. It is the only poem associated with Moses (see first line) but curiously has no other specific mention of Israel. Is it an imagined prayer of Moses, as if he were watching the destruction of Jerusalem? Is it an imagined reflection on human loss, disappointment, and death by Israel's greatest leader, who was barred by YHVH's anger from entering the promised land? (See Deuteronomy 3.26.) Or is it a community lament for the human community about the brevity of life? It is perhaps all these and more? Reflecting the fragility of life, the poet also demonstrates the fragility and inadequacy of our poetic categories, gliding from praise, to wise reflection, to petition, to lament, and plea. This poem is also a fine example of a nonhistorical trait of many of the poems in T^ehelim. Although they eschew abstract expression by using concrete language and lively metaphors, the poems generally do not use historically specific language that would tie the poem to one time or place. Thus, for example, opponents are not usually Assyrians or Babylonians, but warriors or enemies. One result of this trait is to allow the listeners to associate troubles and situations of their own times with the poetic expression. No doubt this characteristic has done much to keep the poems alive for thousands of years.

4–5. Thanksgiving Poems (Individual—18, 21, 30, 32, 34, 40.1–11; 66.13–20; 92, 103, 108, 116, 118, 138, Community—65, 67, 75, 107, 124, 136)

Like the lament poems, thanksgiving poems can be divided by their point of view into individual (4) and community (5) types. Thanksgiving psalms have things in common with our first category, praise poems, and perhaps the distinction is not always useful. Scholars usually distinguish thanksgiving poems by their descriptions of trouble and distress from which the speaker has been delivered. There is usually testimony to God's saving acts and then an exhortation for others to join in the praise to YHVH. We find an interesting example in this category in T^ehelim 107, where YHVH's gracious loyalty is being recounted in a long poem of thanksgiving. YHVH's *khesed*, a Hebrew word meaning something close to "loving loyalty," forms a kind of *inclusio* for the poem, ending the first and last lines. A call to gratitude begins the poem.

> Thank YHVH for he is good,
> For forever is his loving loyalty.
> Those whom YHVH rescued should speak,
> Whom he rescued from the hand of trouble (107.1–2)

Community Reflections 8.1

☰ ✝ ☾

PROPHETIZATION OF PSALMS

By the late centuries bce, the Israelite king David had been dubbed the traditional author of our scroll of Tehelim. In these years and those that followed, groups within the three large religious traditions that developed out of Israelite history all made appreciative and considerable use of Tehelim as a source of poetic praise to God. One aspect of their appreciation, beginning prior to the rise of Christianity or Islam, was what has been called prophetization. As scholar John Reeves describes it, this refers to the "bestowal of prophetic rank upon a number of literary or even historical figures who do not normally enjoy such status within the traditional scriptures" (Reeves 1999, 72). David, for example, who is never called a prophet in scrolls from our library and who in fact looks to others for divine instruction from professional prophets such as Gad (1 Samuel 22) and Nathan (2 Samuel 7), is by later traditions dubbed a prophet. A text from the Dead Sea Scrolls says that David composed his songs "through prophecy" (11Q5). This tradition continued and become wider and stronger as later Jewish, Christian, and Muslim texts refer to David as a prophet, and equally importantly, the scroll of Tehelim is prophetized and is often read as if its poetry is referring to future events or even to the end of time. In Christian traditions, this prophetization opened the way for many psalms to be thought of as messianic psalms, that is, psalms that are interpreted as speaking of Jesus, the Christian Messiah. (Based on Reeves 1999, 72–74 and Kugel 1990, 45–55.)

The poem moves to giving four narrative illustrations of troubles into which people had the misfortune of falling; two innocently, two not without guilt.

They were lost in the wilderness . . . (107.4)
They sat in darkness and gloom . . . (107.10)
They became fools by their guilty ways . . . (107.17)
They went out to sea in ships . . . (107.23)

These are the opening lines of four stories of rescue by YHVH. Each story is told using repetitive vocabulary and forms. And each rescued group, after their rescue, is instructed by the speaker with these words:

They must thank YHVH for his loving loyalty,
And his wonderful works for all humankind (107.8, 15, 21, 31)

The four stories are followed by a hymn celebrating YHVH's earthly creations and care (107.33–42), and the poem ends with a call, an appeal to the poet's imagined audience, to be wise and to stop and consider these things. Maybe the poet is gently suggesting to the audience, these things could happen to you.

There are other genres of poems, too, such as those that take up the theme of living wisely and understanding the world and thus have much in common with wisdom literature as preserved in our scrolls of Proverbs, Job, and Qohelet. These are not presented as prayers, but as poetic instructions for proper conduct. Royal poems are those that clearly have their origin in the royal court, perhaps penned for a particular celebration such as a coronation (Tᵉhelim 2) or military victory (Tᵉhelim 18). These psalms engage matters of statecraft, politics, warfare, religion, and personal well-being. The king might be presented as YHVH's son (2.7) or one whom YHVH protects in war (110.1–3). Not infrequently Israel's poets take a royal theme and apply it to their God, depicting him as king of Zion and the entire world. This occurs in Tᵉhelim 29, 47, 93, 95, 97, 98, and 99.

> All the peoples, you must clap your hands!
> Shout to God with a loud voice!
> For Highest YHVH is awesome,
> Great King over all the earth.
> (Tᴇʜᴇʟɪᴍ 47.2–3 [ᴏʀ 1–2])

Psalms and Prayers

Many poems of Tᵉhelim are overtly addressed to Israel's God, by name (YHVH) or by title (e.g., Elohim). As such they are expressions of their authors to their God, and many are infused with deeply personal sentiments. But they are also artistically constructed, not raw personal outbursts. Many exhibit deep and carefully construed religious reflections and expressions. Furthermore, when poems become part of the anthology, something of their original individual expression moves to the corporate domain of whatever community gathers and uses these psalms. On the other hand, poems that were originally composed for corporate liturgical use can also be used differently once they enter the anthology. In short, no matter how personal in origin, these psalms may become corporate expressions in communal acts of worship, and no matter how corporate or formal in their liturgical context, psalms may also become personal expressions whenever individuals make use of them in their own experience.

Questions for Further Study

1. From a comparative religions standpoint, how do these formal expressions to YHVH compare to modern public expressions (hymns, songs, prayers, etc.) in a religious service? What is the breadth of expression? What are the boundaries? What expressions of feelings are considered acceptable or unacceptable?

2. Because many of these poems were likely set to music, how does that change your reading of them? Is the musical component important for understanding such poems?

3. Asking as a form critic, what is the evidence for various formal social settings for the oral use of these poems?

References

Alter, Robert. "Psalms," in *The Literary Guide to the Bible*, edited by Robert Alter and Frank Kermode, 244–62. Cambridge, MA: Harvard, 1987.

Anderson, Bernhard W. *Out of the Depths,* 3rd ed. Louisville, KY: Westminster/John Knox, 2000.

Greenfield, Jonas C. "The Hebrew Bible and Canaanite Literature" in *The Literary Guide to the Bible,* edited by Robert Alter and Frank Kermode, 545–60. Cambridge, MA: Harvard, 1987.

Holladay, William L. *The Psalms Through Three Thousand Years.* Minneapolis, MN: Fortress, 1996.

Kugel, James. "David the Prophet," in *Poetry and Prophecy,* edited by J. Kugel, 45–55. Ithaca: Cornell, 1990.

Miller, Patrick D. *They Cried to the Lord: The Form and Theology of Biblical Prayer.* Minneapolis, MN: Fortress, 1994.

Reeves, John C. "Scriptural Authority in early Judaism," in *Living Traditions of the Bible,* edited by James E. Bowley, 72–4. St. Louis: Chalice, 1999.

Sarna, Nahum M. *Songs of the Heart: An Introdtion to the Book of Psalms.* New York: Schocken, 1993.

VanderKam, James and Peter Flint. *The Meaning of the Dead Sea Scrolls.* San Francisco: HarperCollins, 2002.

Zevit, Ziony. *The Religions of Ancient Israel.* London: Continuum, 2001.

מִשְׁלֵי

Proverbs *Mishlei*

SECTION OUTLINE

Literary Format and Movement

Wisdom in Mishlei

What is a proverb?

Lady Wisdom

Wisdom and the Fear of YHVH

A Jewish "Patron Saint" of Wisdom?

Collecting Proverbs

A Final Poem

Questions for Further Study

References

Everybody knows what a proverb is and almost everyone has seen a collection of proverbs or witty and wise sayings. That's what we have here in this scroll. People of many different cultures have been remembering, collecting, and passing on wise sayings for millennia and this is Israel's premiere example. The scroll of Proverbs is an anthology of wisdom sayings collected in ancient Israel. Its Hebrew name, *Mishlei*, pronounced "*mish*-lay," is an abbreviated form of *mishlei-shᵉlomo*, "proverbs of Solomon," the scroll's first words. Actually leaving *Solomon* out of the title is better because the collectors explicitly credit many others besides Solomon for the proverbs in the scroll. The author immediately reveals what content the reader should expect, and he states explicitly the purpose of the scroll: to teach wisdom.

> For knowing wisdom and training, for understanding words of understanding;
> For grasping training of insight, right-ness, justice, fairness;
> For giving the simple-minded shrewdness, the youth knowledge and prudence;
> a wise man will listen and increase his grasp, and the understanding will gain skill;
> For understanding a proverb and a literary figure, sayings of wise men and riddles.
> (MISHLEI 1.2–6)

LITERARY FORMAT AND MOVEMENT

Successful anthologies of proverbs can be organized in a variety of ways, some with tight structures (alphabetic or by author), some with much looser structures (thematic), or perhaps almost randomly. In the case of Mishlei, a rather loosely organized collection, there are some textual structural signals, such as editors' titles to sections, that provide segmentation for the collection, though it is not always easy to tell where a named collection ends. (For example, do sayings of Agur end in 30.9 or 14 or 33?) These titles likely reflect earlier collections of proverbs that were utilized in the composition of this work. But we would not call the larger structure haphazard. Mishlei begins with a long appeal to consider wisdom, an advertisement of sorts, trying to convince the reader to finish the rest of the scroll. This long early section has many proverbs and longer segments of poetry that describe the great value of wisdom and illustrate wise living. Structurally it is the most complicated of all sections, moving back and forth between longer poems and proverbs and sometimes embedding proverbs in poems. It is here that we find Lady Wisdom standing to entice readers to join her (Chapter 8–9). Later sections of the scroll are quite loose in their internal collection of proverbs, and sometimes there is some grouping of proverbs by themes. Thought was also put into concluding the scroll, for at its end (31.10–31) we find an acrostic poem that is a formal and extended riddle about the finding of wisdom.

1.1–9.18 Proverbs of Sh^elomo, Son of David, King of Israel (1.1–6 Purpose of collection Long poems in 5,7,8,9)	10.1–22.16 Proverbs of Sh^elomo	22.17–24.22 Sayings of the Wise Men	25.1–29.27 More Proverbs of Sh^elomo Transmitted by Officials of Hezekiah, King of Judah
30.1–33 Sayings of Agur, Son of Yakeh	31.1–9 Sayings of Lemuel, Taught by his Mother	31.10–31 Concluding acrostic poem	

Wisdom in Mishlei

This Israelite collection of proverbs shares many characteristics of wisdom writings in cultures surrounding Israel, as we described them at the beginning of this chapter. Wisdom—in Hebrew *khokhmah*—is its theme and its highest value. If we seek a definition, we might say, wisdom is good thinking for good living. Having wisdom means thinking deeply about the arrangement of order and justice in creation and living in accordance with that order. Gaining wisdom means striving to understand the myriad relationships in one's life—God, rulers, wives, friends, employers, slaves—and to conduct oneself appropriately in each case. Wisdom means knowing one's limitations and weaknesses—the foibles of humanity in general—and acting prudently in light of those human realities. As you can see, wisdom in Mishlei is both theoretical and practical.

When we ask about the categories that operate in Mishlei to describe wisdom, again we find common ground with non-Israelite literature. Mishlei operates in universal categories, not national ones. We do not find references to Israel's particular stories, such as the Exodus from Egypt, wilderness, or exile. Proverbs does not trade on distinctions between Israel and non-Israelite cults, morals, religion, land, or stories. We find no intent to preserve separateness from non-Israelites here, such as we find in scrolls such as Leviticus, Deuteronomy, and Kings. There is nothing to be found here of the laws of Moses versus foreign customs. *Torah* in Mishlei refers to the instruction of wisdom, whatever its origin. Mishlei has no outsiders. It does not know the distinctions of Jew/Gentile, Israelite/non-Israelite, or elect/non-elect; there is no "us versus them." The enemies are not Egyptians, Canaanites, or Babylonians. Here the enemies are folly and simplemindedness, and the distinctions are between the wise and the fool and the simple-minded and the discerning. What we see repeatedly are not modern categories such as believer/ nonbeliever, religious/secular, or faith/nonfaith. The categories and vocabulary that dominate the outlook of Mishlei are wisdom, knowledge, learning, virtue, right-ness (righteousness), ignorance, folly, vice, and wrong. We can describe Mishlei as religious, because YHVH is frequently mentioned, but aside from the name of the deity, there is nothing peculiar to the Israelite cult or historical traditions that closes this wisdom off from non-Israelite wisdom traditions. In the same way Egyptian wisdom writings often invoke the God Thoth, but the references are generic and easily transferred to another deity.

Mishlei, like other wisdom literature, is broadly pious. In its Israelite form, wisdom literature advocates the fear of YHVH, and YHVH appears throughout as the deity of creation, order, providence, and ultimate judge of right-ness. But Mishlei does not polemicize against other Gods. It does not even mention, much less celebrate, Israelite national traditions about escape from Egypt, but instead it shows deep respect for Egyptian wisdom by heavily borrowing from it. To underscore this broad perspective and demonstrate its international character, our scroll of Mishlei quotes and credits foreign wisdom traditions explicitly. The two sections Sayings of Agur (in Chapter 30) and Sayings of Lemuel (in Chapter 31) are likely non-Israelite in origin, and the Sayings of the Wise Men section (in Chapters 22–24) freely quotes repeatedly from a famous wisdom tradition of Egypt, The Instruction of Amen-em-ope. Mishlei even makes a veiled reference to Amen-em-ope's famous book of thirty chapters in Mishlei 22.20. Amen-em-ope lived in Egypt sometime between 1250 and 1000 BCE, and his thirty chapters were handed down in Egyptian scribal circles.

This breadth and universal human scope is further underscored by the methods of discovering wisdom presented in Mishlei. These methods, what they are and what they are not, speak volumes about the underlying intellectual and religious ideology of the compilers. There is no reason to think that all those formally interested in wisdom in ancient Israel had the identical attitudes toward religion (a modern term) or toward Israel's traditions about YHVH. But in Mishlei there is a strong general approach to gaining wisdom. Some clearly thought wisdom was fully compatible with Yahwism but we certainly cannot assume that their sense of Yahwism was the same as that of other authors from our library. In Mishlei, wisdom is not found by seeking special revelations from God; one is not urged to pray for wisdom. The author of proverbs does not speak as a prophet, declaring, "Thus says YHVH!" Wisdom does not come in the form of oracles or supernatural visions. Instead, wisdom is learned by study, reflecting on experience, listening to those who are wise, and going to foreign lands and culling proverbs from their traditions. Wisdom speakers appeal to the listeners' self-interest and their sense of order and justice; they do not back up their teachings with claims of divine authority. Sure, wisdom may be thought of God's gift (2.6), but it is a gift available universally in different cultures and finding it is not a matter of accepting a prophets or priests or wise man's divine claim. Lady Wisdom does have a voice, but it may be heard in Egypt or anywhere else. To summarize Mishlei's approach, we might say that wisdom must be sought and thought.

Finally, we must say something about the seriousness of wisdom in Mishlei. This scroll does not play a central role in many religious traditions that use this library, and so we might think that its content is secondary or not as crucial as the other seemingly more important and centralized scrolls. I think the author would take serious exception to this opinion. We should first recall that such rankings of value of the various scrolls in the library—Which are more important? Which are allowed to shape a community's or individual's priorities and language and categories?—are external valuations of individuals and communities; they are not intrinsic to the library. Second, the compiler of Mishlei loudly and repeatedly appeals to his readers to regard the attainment of this wisdom as the highest of all values. The rhetoric could hardly be stronger. Mishlei is not a back-page advice column about how to get a job or be a friend. Wisdom is not presented as something the reader might want to consider if he has time left after he has mastered Israel's other literature. Wisdom is the key to all existence in Mishlei. If we could interview our author and ask what is at stake with wisdom, he would respond that wisdom is the tree of life (3.18), the fountain of all that is good and just and right. YHVH operates according to wisdom, and upon wisdom the order of the world is founded (3.19). This universal wisdom is the key to pleasing God and having just relations with all. In fact, as we mentioned above, the first nine chapters, nearly a third of the scroll, are essentially an appeal in proverbial and poetic form to value wisdom above all else. So in this scroll of Mishlei we have a presentation of international learning and wisdom as the most important engagement of all of life.

What is a Proverb?

The compiler of Mishlei did not write an essay about wisdom; he compiled wisdom poems, hundreds of pithy wise sayings, and riddles. Like proverbs in many cultures, these are short. In fact the essence of a proverbial form is brevity, and of course this is because of the function of proverbs in most every society. Proverbs reside in oral culture, being repeated generation after generation. They must be easily remembered, and they must be worth remembering. They must have pith, brevity, and punch. Hebrew proverbs exemplify the most severely restrictive literary art form in our library. Compactness is so highly valued that the artistry of a proverb is shown in how much nuance, creativity, ambiguity, subtleness, surprise, and meaning one can pack into a tight space. A good proverb tries to get big ideas into a few words and attempts to maximize the meaning of each word. In Hebrew, most of the proverbs are one-liners, and each line is split into two or three parts. Each line usually has only seven to nine words, so each half-line is usually only three or four words. This brevity is crucial and intrinsic to proverbial poetry. This presents a major problem with translations, because not many translators seem to value brevity with the result that few English translations of Mishlei translate these proverbs as proverbs. Let's look at these translations of Mishlei 13.24, a seven-word proverb that I have listed here from shortest to longest.

> *King James Version (1611):* He that spareth his rod hateth his sonne; but he that loveth him chasteneth him betimes.
> *Jewish Publication Society, Tanakh (1985):* He who spares the rod hates his son but he who loves him disciplines him early.
> *New International Version (1977):* He who spares the rod hates his son but he who loves him is careful to discipline him.
> *Revised Standard Version (1952):* He who spares the rod hates his son, but he who loves him is diligent to discipline him.
> *New Revised Standard Version (1989):* Those who spare the rod hate their children but those who love them are diligent to discipline them.
> *Good News Bible (1976):* If you don't punish your son you don't love him. If you do love him, you will correct him.

Now I recognize that different translators may adopt different goals. Aiming for a lower reading level or attempting to be nonsexist for example, will make a large difference in how one translates. At the same time I would suggest that if we are attempting to translate a *proverb* we should do our best to make our translation a real proverb by striving for the essential characteristic, brevity. None of these translations seem like very good proverbs to me, and the last one especially is not a proverb at all. It is hardly memorable, and all artistry has been completely lost. Translations that attempt to explain the content without paying attention to the literary form are woefully inadequate. Now the reason I chose this example is because there is an old English proverb that is a true proverb and comes right from this verse in Mishlei:

> Spare the rod, spoil the child.

Now regardless of what we think of this advice, it illustrates perfectly how proverbs in the real world exist and survive. This old English form is succinct and poetic, using only six words, alliterated *sp* at the beginning of each half, and *d* concluding each half. Its proverbial form is perfect, and so it has been remembered and passed on for generations. Do you know the English proverb "Birds of a feather flock together"? What about its "academic" explanatory translation: "Feathered biped vertebrates tend to be gregarious according to their respective types of plumage"? Which one of those will be passed on as a famous proverb?

The proverbs of Mishlei exhibit many clever and memorable literary traits, and they do this as compactly as possible. Let's look at a few more examples. The major characteristic of Hebrew poetry generally is parallelism, or the use of twin and occasionally triplet lines. In the scroll of Mishlei, these twins are usually one line's worth of text. These parallel lines are related in a variety of ways, sometimes antithetically, such as in Mishlei 10.1:

> Wise son makes dad glad, silly son makes mom sad.

The antithesis lies in the poet's use of contrasting pairs in the two lines: wise/silly, dad/mom, glad/sad. Antithetical parallelism dominates in Chapters 10–15 of Mishlei.

A different kind of relationship might be called developmental parallelism, where the second half of the line intensifies, focuses, concretizes, finishes, or nuances the first half. Take 19.29 for example:

> Penalties are prepared for boasters, beatings for backs of fools.

Here the second half is more concrete, and more painful! In another kind of developmental parallelism, the two halves form a short narrative and may show cause and effect or results. In 19.24, we have a picturesque narrative, complete with comic exaggeration:

> Lazy digs his digits into the dish, but doesn't even get them to his mouth.

Now I'm not going to argue too loudly for my alliterations; maybe you can improve it. But clearly this is a delightful image of a guy so lazy he can't even bring his food to his mouth; any translation must be careful not to ruin the proverbial picture.

There is another category, quite entertaining, that Robert Alter calls riddle parallelism. Here, the first half gives a perplexing or startling notion or image that raises a question; then the riddle is resolved in the second half of the line. Look at 11.22:

> A golden ring in the snout of a pig [=] a woman with beauty but without sense.

The Hebrew does not need to express explicitly the implied "is like" between the two halves. The riddle might be put this way: "What is like a pig with a gold ring?" Or look at 26.14 and ask, "How is a door like a lazy person?"

There are many more techniques we could discuss. There are numerical proverbs (e.g., 30.15–33) and sets of proverbs that all begin with the same word (e.g., 30.11–14). There are "better than" proverbs (e.g., 15.16–17), and proverbs with rhyming, alliteration, and cadence. Of course, not all the proverbs seem equally creative or clever to a reader, but we can simply stress in closing that Mishlei's proverbs are true proverbs, terse and artfully crafted.

Lady Wisdom

If we read through Mishlei asking about repeated tropes and themes, we will notice that though the collection of proverbs shows a definite male-centered orientation, it does frequently speak of women, although in a rather limited range of identities. In the early chapters, two of the longer poems contrast two women: Chapter 7 tells the story of a simple-minded man seduced by a prostitute: "Like a bird rushing into a trap, and he does not know it is his life" (7.23).

Now on one level there is little doubt that the author is warning his young male students against prostitutes, but on a larger level of this book of wisdom, this prostitute is Dame Folly, and the readers are being urged to avoid foolishness and simple-mindedness. Dame Folly is the foil for Lady Wisdom of the next chapter. Wisdom is

POSTER 8.1

PROVERBS IN TENSION

All cultures have proverbs that are in some sense contradictory or at odds. That is because, of course, life is complicated and no single rule of thumb can take into account all the factors of situation. Consider the differences of perspective and insight of these common proverbs. Then consider Mishlei 26, 4–5.

Look before you leap.

or

He who hesitates is lost.

Many hands make light work.

or

Too many cooks spoil the broth.

You're never too old to learn.

or

You can't teach an old dog new tricks.

Absence makes the heart grow fonder.

or

Out of sight, out of mind.

Beware of Greeks bearing gifts.

or

Never look a gift horse in the mouth.

personified here as a beautiful woman who walks the streets and calls to passing men. In Hebrew grammar, where all nouns have gender and there is no neuter, the word wisdom, *khokhmah,* is a feminine term, and so wisdom is naturally personified as the figure Lady Wisdom. Chapters 8 through 9 are a delightful enticement to come and learn from Lady Wisdom. The author deftly describes her own seductions for intelligence and instruction: "Wisdom is better than jewels. No desires equal her!" (8.11)

Wisdom and the Fear of YHVH

Part of the general piety of Mishlei is expressed in the admonishment to fear YHVH, an appropriate attitude and behavior toward God. This word *fear* is typically used as an expression of awe and worship. After the poetic introduction to the scroll, the first statement is that knowledge begins with the fear of YHVH (1.7), and a parallel expression is seen at 9.10 where it says that wisdom starts with the fear of YHVH. But it does not take much more reading to understand that the scroll's author is not suggesting a hard and fast hierarchy, because elsewhere the roles are reversed. The poem of 2.1–6 sees the fear of YHVH coming from the learning of wisdom. Another way to look at the matter comes in 4.7 where "the beginning of wisdom is 'Get wisdom!'" This surprising poetic line leads one to expect a noun at the end, like this: "The beginning of wisdom is _____"; but instead there is an imperative. This poet says to his listener, wisdom begins when you get busy and get it, work for it, and study it. The attainment of wisdom is presented in myriad ways in the proverbs and poems of Mishlei, some more religious than others, and there is no systematic formulation of a hierarchy of wisdom. In Israel some wisdom writers clearly saw the fear of YHVH as the best starting place; the aggregate implication of the collection of proverbs is that one might start just about anywhere and, more importantly, one should start now.

This same sense of wisdom as a pervasive entity that one might approach from various directions comes through in other location metaphors. Where is wisdom? She is with YHVH the creator (8.22–31) and is to be found calling in streets and highways, in mountains, at gates, and in towns (8.1–4). And although Mishlei is generally optimistic about the ability to live a wise and rewarding life, there are moments when the hiddenness of wisdom is also a reality, as in 30.1–4.

A Jewish "Patron Saint" of Wisdom?

As you no doubt noticed the name Solomon, *Sh^elomo* in Hebrew, appears on the first line of our scroll, as it does in 10.1 and 25.1 also. Formal wisdom was often associated with royal courts and scribes in the days of ancient Israel. In some sense, as we can tell from the preponderance of the topics, this literature is written for the benefit of the male elite of the court. In Israel, Solomon is the Israelite king who is most strongly associated with wisdom. Though we have no records from the time, it does not seem impossible that there are historical reasons for this association, and perhaps there were some records from near Sh^elomo's time that were kept. 1 Kings 3–5 has stories of Solomon's wisdom and his writing of proverbs and songs. Mishlei also mentions the court of Hezekiah (25.1), centuries after Solomon, as maintaining wisdom traditions. All we can say with supporting evidence is that wisdom collections in Israel existed prior to this scroll of Mishlei and this scroll reproduces at least parts of those collections. As we read through our collection, we see many signals of earlier collections, including the various titles and the numerous proverbs that are repeated in different sections. And just as our scroll represents a later stage in proverbial compositions, there are other stages that come after it. By the time our scroll was written, Solomon had become the "patron saint" of wisdom in many Jewish circles, and we will see later examples of texts invoking the name Solomon. Our scroll dates probably to the fifth to third centuries BCE. The Greek translation of our scroll exemplifies a text with significant growth and some rearrangement of content. Our scroll is one stage in the development of a changing and expanding collection of proverbs.

Solomon's status as Israel's great wise man seemed to grow with time. A scroll known as the Wisdom of Solomon was composed in the first century BCE and is now

POSTER 8.2

SAYINGS OF AMEN-EM-OPE AND MISHLEI

If you go to the British Museum you might be able to see a beautiful complete papyrus manuscript of this wonderful scroll of wisdom, consisting of 30 short paragraphs. Mishlei 22.20 mentions its 30 segments. By the time of the composition of Mishlei, this writing was well over 500 years old and apparently quite famous. Mishlei uses and modifies them in the section that runs from 22.17 to 24.22. Below are some passages from it that are mirrored in Mishlei.

Amen-em-ope, from Saying 1:
Give your ears, hear the sayings, Give your heart to understand them.
It profits to put them in your heart, Woe to him who neglects them!

Mishlei 22.17–18:
Turn your ear and hear the sayings of the wise, set your heart for my understanding
For it will be worthwhile if you keep them close, if they are in your body, may they stick strongly on your lips.

Amenemope, from Saying 9:
Do not befriend the heated man, Nor approach him for conversation.

Mishlei 22.24:
Do not befriend the man of anger, and the man of hot temper, do not approach.

Amenemope, from Saying 6:
Beware of destroying the borders of fields, lest a terror carry you away.
One pleases God with the might of the lord when one discerns the borders of fields.

Mishlei 22.10–11
Do not remove the ancient landmark, and onto the fields of the orphan do not move.
For their defender is strong, he will plead their case with you.

Amenemope, from Saying 30:
The scribe who is skilled in his office, He is found worthy to be a courtier.

Mishlei 22.29
You see the man skilled in his work? He will be set before kings.

Translated by Miriam Lichtheim in Hallo 2003, 1:115–22

part of Roman Catholic and Orthodox Bibles. We will consider it in the next chapter. Another scroll we will deal with later is called Sirach, or Ben Sira; it comes from the second century BCE. I mention it here because, like Mishlei, it contains many proverbs, but unlike Mishlei, it brings together the Torah of Moses and the wisdom tradition. Within our library, we already saw that the scroll of Deuteronomy speaks quite often of wisdom, and of course Deuteronomy is presented as Moses's direct teachings.

Collecting Proverbs

The business of collecting proverbs into a scroll and including with it numerous appeals for wisdom and discernment creates a document that is more than the sum of its parts. Proverbs normally exist independently as single sayings, but here they are rubbing shoulders in a kind of artificial context. The collector has provided that context and has stressed repeatedly the need to seek out wisdom and to think carefully. Each proverb brings a different perspective, a different angle to the calling of Lady Wisdom to think and live wisely. As they stand together in the scroll, each proverb is not just a rule of thumb or a common sense directive to be followed. Each proverb becomes an invitation to reflection on a given aspect of the human experience for the sake of wise living. The collection of proverbs reflects a view of life and experience that desires to see things from many angles; experience needs to be turned around and considered from different perspectives, and there is not just one rule on any given subject that suffices for all situations. For example, look at 26.4–5: "Don't answer a fool foolishly, or you will be a fool! Do answer a fool foolishly, or he will think he's wise!"

These two proverbs give exactly opposite advice. If they existed independently, one might be tempted to take each as a rule or general law. But here, side by side in the collection, taking them both as a rule becomes impossible. Instead the reader is compelled by their proximity to reflect, think, and consider when it is wise to answer a fool and when it is not. To put the matter more starkly and dramatically, one proverb is a law; two proverbs are a subversion of law. Here in 26.4–5 the author does not tell the reader what to do. Just the opposite is true: The author creates a dilemma and does not give the answer. Instead, the reader is compelled to think for him- or herself. This collection of proverbs does not put many directly contradictory proverbs together like it does here in 26.4–5, but it does contain many different perspectives on single topics that create tensions. The result is an ideology of critical thinking and discernment that infuses the entire collective scroll and calls the reader to think carefully and not to obey blindly. Mishlei is not so much about memorizing proverbs—a proverb is worthless to a person who doesn't think, says 26.7. Mishlei is about thinking about proverbs; seeking to discern and decide their relevance and application for life. Using some modern categories of education, Mishlei as a whole is more about encouraging careful critical thinking than about providing the definition or the content of wisdom.

This ideology of critical thinking recognizes the complexities of life and conforms perfectly to the spirit of the universal search for wisdom. If the search is a truly liberal one, it will not result in banal platitudes, easy answers, and simple cookie-cutter solutions for all of life. Mishlei is focused on human experience, and the compiler knows that the world and human experiences in it are enormously complex. The result is contradictory proverbs and many different perspectives. Mishlei recognizes there are things humans don't understand (30.18–19), that an action may seem right and wise and turn out to be wrong (14.12; 16.25), and that there are dark mysteries and uncontrollable realities (17.4; 17.8; 20.6, 9). It seems quite appropriate that near the end of our scroll we have a riddle that still seems unsolved (30.1–4). Mishlei is an undermining of simplistic, either/or, dogmatic thinking, and directs a great deals of attention to showing the simpleminded the complexities of experience (1.4, 22; 8.5; 9.6; 22.3): "How long, simple mind, will you love the simple?" (1.22)

A Final Poem

Mishlei closes with an alphabetic acrostic (31.10–31) and another personification. Here we have a description of a wife/woman, in Hebrew the term can mean either. As we saw with the woman personified in Mishlei Chapter 7, this woman of the acrostic may refer on one level to a certain kind of woman, in this case, a valiant wife. But on a larger scale it refers to the wisdom that all the readers should be seeking. It describes in great detail the great things that wisdom can do for the person who finds her. It also seems that the author subtly underscores the difficulty of finding her with his first line: "A heroic woman, who can find?"

In any case it is most interesting to note that though this book is thoroughly male in its orientation, its greatest value, wisdom, is personified as a woman, Lady Wisdom, and its greatest poems, including this concluding composition, are dedicated to personifying her.

Questions for Further Study

1. As a religion scholar, in what ways to you see Mishlei and individual proverbs as religious, and how have you defined religion? In what ways is it philosophical or pragmatic?
2. Proverb collections usually seem to have originated among males. What are the male perspectives and assumptions that you clearly see? What would be a female view on some of those proverbs?

References

Alter, Robert. *The Art of Biblical Poetry*. New York: Basic Books, 1985.

Brown, William P. *Character in Crisis: A Fresh Apporach to the Wisdom Literature of the Old Testament*. Grand Rapids MI: Eerdmans, 1996.

Crenshaw, James L. *Old Testament Wisdom*, Louisville, KY: Westminster/John Knox, 1998.

Hallo, William W., ed. *The Context of Scripture*. 3 vols. Leiden: E. J. Brill, 2003.

McKane, William. *Proverbs*. Philadelphia: Westminster, 1970.

Murphy, Roland E. *The Tree of Life: An Exploration of Biblical Wisdom Literature*, 2nd ed. Grand Rapids MI: Eerdmans, 1996.

אִיּוֹב

Job *Eyyov*

SECTION OUTLINE

Literary Format and Movement

The Basic Drama

Date and Composition

The Ancient Hebrew Text of Eyyov

Historical Names and Places

Eyyov as Wisdom Literature

The Prologue

The Poetic Disputes

The Epilogue

Eyyov in the Library

Questions for Further Study

References

As I pull this scroll off the shelf, I am reminded of its accolades as a classic of world literature. The nineteenth-century English poet Tennyson praised it as "the greatest poem of ancient and modern times." G.K. Chesterton once said, "The 'Iliad' is only great because all life is a battle, the 'Odyssey' because all life is a journey, the Book of Job because all life is a riddle." Job in Hebrew is *Eyyov,* pronounced "ee-*yov,*" is one of the most famous scrolls in this library. It is also, for many who actually read it, one of the most surprising, because they are often expecting something quite different. Job is a favorite and basic text for passionate discussions—maybe you have had them—that try to get a handle on how the existence of a good God relates to the reality of a world where unspeakably terrible things happen. In this regard the character of Job has become a universal symbol of innocent suffering.

As residents of a modern world, our lives are full of dangers—nuclear weapons, huge military forces, and fears of random violence. And of course we hear reports daily of horrendous deaths from famine, airplane crashes, cancer, AIDS, car wrecks, and floods. As I write this, the newspapers are reporting more than 50 deaths in the northeastern United States from the President's Day Blizzard of 2003. (As I make final edits in January of 2005, more than 150,000 people are dead in southern Asia because of tidal waves triggered by a powerful earthquake on December 26, 2004. And now I must add the disaster of katrina.) And between today and the day you read this, there will be a litany of mayhem and disasters snuffing out innumerable human lives. And that's just a few of the deaths—what about all the other injustices and tragedies of life?

A look at some of the titles in the religion or reflection section of a bookstore will reveal that people have often reflected on how all this pain and misfortune squares with ideas of God; best known, perhaps, is Rabbi Harold Kushner's, *When Bad Things Happen to Good People.* In religious theism, such as in Judaism, Christianity, and Islam, these issues are often discussed as the problem of **theodicy,** and they bring together questions that many theists have. Have you ever wondered why so many terrible things happen in this world if God is at once completely good and completely sovereign? Or, to put the question in broader terms, is there a moral order in the world where cause and effect is felt or where good behavior or piety leads to divine blessing? Is(are) God(s) involved, responsible for, or implicated by the evils of the world? What do the answers mean for the character of God? But, of course, tragedy and human reflection on it was not invented in the twentieth century. More than 200 years ago, Voltaire observed, "Indeed, history is nothing more than a tableau of crimes and misfortunes" (*L'Ingénu,* ch. 10), and he was echoing the deep thoughts of many through the centuries.

In the ancient world, tragedy was no less common, but surely that is not news to any one. Warfare, natural disasters, diseases, much shorter life expectancy, and personal tragedies of every sort were as present then as now. And from the rich literary cultures of the Fertile Crescent we can read their literary musings on the injustices and tragedies of human existence and the role of God or Gods. We will read profound and provocative Egyptian and Mesopotamian examples later on.

But Eyyov is not merely a story of suffering, and it is not a propositional and theoretical monograph on the issue of God and suffering. A look at Eyyov through a literary lens shows that most of the book is soaring poetry, a poetic drama or dramatic reading, in which the poetic artistry corresponds in magnificence to the painful depths of the questions about evil in the world. In modern literature Eyyov has inspired other dramas; for example, there is Archibald MacLeish's *J.B.,* Neil Simon's *God's Favorite,* Elie Wiesel's *The Trial of God,* and Robert Frost's poetic drama *A Masque of Reason.* It is especially in the poetry that the learning and genius of the author shines. At every turn the careful reader will find something fascinating, perhaps disturbing or shocking, curious or comical, but always deeply moving and profoundly human. I'm not sure that anyone has described Eyyov's general literary quality and sophistication better than Carol Newsom:

> The book of Job is an immensely learned and cosmopolitan work. One recognizes this quality in the texture of the language itself, which is full of rare vocabulary and archaic verbal forms. The complex and beautiful poetry contains numerous mythological allusions, some of which appear to be based on Egyptian and Mesopotamian traditions. Furthermore, the poetic dialogue presents Job in terms of a sophisticated reworking of the Mesopotamian tradition of the righteous sufferer. This same command of cultural and literary forms is evident in the author's treatment of genres and stylistic features drawn from Israelite tradition. The speeches of Job and his friends are largely shaped as disputations and make use of a rich variety of rhetorical devices one finds in

wisdom, prophetic, and legal argumentation (e.g., rhetorical questions, wisdom sayings, appeals to ancient tradition). The author also displays a similar command of the genres of Israelite piety, in particular the hymn, the psalm of praise, and the complaint psalm. Not only are these forms cited in their traditional modes, but in the speeches of Job they are also rendered as exquisite parodies. Legal vocabulary, categories, and practices are similarly drawn upon for the development of a forensic metaphor through which to explore Job's relationship with God. The overall impression is of an author who has remarkable command of the religious literature and traditions of Israel and its neighbors." (NEWSOM 326)

LITERARY FORMAT AND MOVEMENT

Eyyov is a drama consisting of long exquisite poetic disputes among Eyyov, four friends, and YHVH, sandwiched between a brief prose prologue and an even briefer epilogue. In this case the traditional chapter and verse numberings are more confusing than helpful, and there are some minor numbering differences between Hebrew and English editions.

1.1–2.13 Prologue	Poetic Cycle 1	Poetic Cycle 2	Poetic Cycle 3
Setting the stage for the poetic dialogue	**3.1–26 Eyyov** curses his birth, laments his suffering.	**12.1–14.22 Eyyov** maintains his integrity, accuses friends of lying to protect God, laments.	**21.1–34 Eyyov** rebuts, argues that those who pay no heed to God or goodness prosper.
Eyyov's exceptional perfection, YHVH's boast, accuser's skepticism, YHVH's test	**4.1–5.27 Eliphaz** criticizes Eyyov, defends God's discipline of Eyyov.	**15.1–35 Eliphaz** condemns Eyyov for not accepting traditional wisdom.	**22.1–30 Eliphaz** defends God's justice and calls Eyyov to repent of his evil.
Eyyov's continued perfection; YHVH's boast, accuser's skepticism, YHVH's test	**6.1–7.21 Eyyov** maintains his innocence.	**16.1–17.16 Eyyov** maintains his innocence and God's violence.	**23.1–24.17[a] Eyyov** seeks to find God, remarks on prosperity of evildoers.
Eyyov's continued perfection, Eyyov's three friends arrive to comfort him.	**8.1–22 Bildad** defends God's justice in punishing Eyyov	**18.1–21 Bildad** describes the punishment of evil doers.	**25.1–6[a] Bildad** questions how anyone can be justified before God.
	9.1–10.22 Eyyov presses case of God's injustice, appeals to God for trial.	**19.1–29 Eyyov** names God's injustices and calls friends to have mercy in like God.	**26.1–27.23[a] Eyyov** criticizes friends, refuses to lie to protect God.
	11.1–20 Zophar defends God, calls Eyyov to repent.	**20.1–29 Zophar** describes God's punishment of evildoers.	**(Zophar?)[a]**

28.1–28 Poetic Interlude

The inaccessibility of wisdom for humanity

29.1–31.40 Eyyov's closing arguments; recalls happiness, laments suffering, cries out to God, and affirms his innocence.

32.1–5 Prose segue introducing dialogue with the young Elihu

32.6–33.33 Elihu tells of his own wisdom and God's justice.

34.1–37 Elihu again; defends God's justice, lambastes Eyyov's sin.

35.1–16 Elihu again; defends God for not hearing evil-doers.

36.1–37.24 Elihu again; defends God's justice, calls Eyyov to repent.

38.1–39.30 YHVH answers Eyyov: questions about power in creation and nature.

40.3–5 Eyyov's brief response

40.6–41.34 YHVH answers Eyyov: more questions about power in nature.

42.1–6 Eyyov answers YHVH, ceases questions.

42.7–17 Epilogue

YHVH rebukes friends, Eyyov is comforted, Eyyov gains new family and wealth; dies old and contented.

[a]See "Textual Issues."

The Basic Drama

A prose narrative, Chapters 1–2, introduces the main characters and provides the action that is the backdrop for the dialogue in Chapters 3–42. There are two different stage scenes or sets in this backdrop. The first is at Eyyov's large estate in the land of Uz. The protagonist is introduced here as a morally and piously perfect man with all the material and familial success one could hope for, including great wealth, three daughters, and seven sons (1.1–5). The second scene (1.6–10) is YHVH's divine court, where YHVH presides over a pantheon of lesser divine beings, literally "sons of God[s]." Among them is the accuser, who is not an angel or demon named Satan (see Study Room 8.2) to whom YHVH brags about Eyyov, pointing out his moral and pious perfection. The accuser is unimpressed—"Does Job serve Elohim for nothing?"—contending that Eyyov is devoted to God only because God has blessed Eyyov with so much success and that if YHVH were to remove these blessings, Eyyov would turn and curse God. YHVH takes the accuser up on the bet and grants him power over Eyyov, though the accuser is not allowed to harm him physically.

Now the scene shifts to Job's estate, where four disasters strike, one after another. The author tells of these in a patently absurd, comical, and effective manner. In about one minute, Job's hears the news of the death of his slaves, the theft of oxen and donkeys at the hands of the attacking Sabeans, the burning up of his sheep and servants by a fire from God, the capture of his camels and murder of slaves by the Chaldeans, and the killing of all his children by a great wind. Job mourns but also speaks the now famous words, and his first poetic lines:

> Naked I came from my mother's womb,
> And naked shall I return there.
> YHVH gave, and YHVH took,
> The name of YHVH be blessed (1.21).

And the narrator confirms that despite all this, "Eyyov did not sin nor did he give offense to God" (1.22).

So the scene shifts back to the divine court (2.1–6) where YHVH again brags to the accuser of Eyyov's perfect piety even though "you [the accuser] incited me [YHVH] against him." But the skeptical accuser points out that Eyyov is still physically healthy and argues that if YHVH should significantly harm his body, Eyyov would then curse God. And again, YHVH without hesitation puts Eyyov into the accuser's hands.

The final scene (2.7–13) of the prologue depicts Eyyov afflicted with painful sores from the "sole of his feet to the top of his head" (2.7), scraping himself with pottery shards and mourning. He continues to maintain his pious frame of mind, refusing to curse God as his wife suggests. He is then visited by three friends, Eliphaz, Bildad, and Zophar, who come to comfort him but are so astounded by his grotesque appearance that they are speechless for seven days. And now the stage is set for the extended aria to begin, the great poetry of Eyyov.

Date and Composition

It is a difficult task to determine a date of composition for a book like Eyyov for several reasons. As a fictional piece of literature with very few historical reference points, the explicit data is slim. Based mostly on linguistic analysis, scholars usually date the composition in the basic form we have it to the sixth to fourth centuries BCE. Furthermore, scholars have long recognized that the book likely combines materials that may have had an earlier and independent existence, though there are differences regarding which sections came to be written first. There are several interesting issues for anyone with investigative tendencies. Consider these questions raised by a careful reading of Eyyov: Why do the prose prologue and epilogue usually refer to the deity as YHVH, whereas the dispute cycles always use Elohim, with one exception, 12.9? Why does the accuser, so central to the plot of the prologue never appear again, neither in the poetry nor in the concluding narrative? Why is Elihu never mentioned in the prologue or epilogue, especially in 42.7 where only three disputants are rebuked, when the dialogue section has four? Is the angry Eyyov of the dialogue the one in the prologue and epilogue? Is Eyyov actually rewarded in the end, which would seem to contradict the observations in Eyyov's poetry sections and the implications in the poetry of YHVH?

Many scholars pursuing source-critical questions have come to the conclusion that the story of Eyyov, an innocent, pious sufferer, may have circulated orally long before this scroll was written, perhaps in different forms. An author or editor may have inserted the poetic debate into the middle of the preexisting narrative. That a story of Eyyov was already well-known literature seems to be confirmed by

POSTER 8.3

"I'M INNOCENT!"

Anyone who has visited tombs in Egypt or read from the so-called Egyptian Book of the Dead has likely seen a long list of negative confessions recorded on behalf of the deceased. Such lists usually include dozens of sins that the speaker says he did *not* do. There is a similar lengthy denial in Eyyov Chapter 31. This sort of list was very common in several formats in Egypt, beginning as early as 2300 BCE and continuing through the middle of the last century BCE, at the time the book of Eyyov was written.

> From the Book of the Dead
>
> I have not committed evil against men.
> I have not mistreated cattle.
> I have not committed sin in the place of truth.
> I have not known that which is not.
> I have not see evil.
> I have not blasphemed a God.
> I have not done violence to a poor man.

Translated by John A. Wilson in Pritchard 1967, 34, modified.

Ezekiel's mention of Eyyov as a famous righteous person (Ezekiel 14.14, 20), a reference likely written prior to our book of Eyyov. Perhaps this older version told of Eyyov the patient sufferer who was later rewarded by YHVH for his endurance. If so, that original story of a pious, longsuffering, and uncomplaining Eyyov has certainly been transformed—parodied even—by the flood of bold accusations and an attitude of questioning God in superlative poetry. When the poetic dispute, from the hand of a poet who preferred using Elohim to YHVH, was grafted into the popular story, parts of the prose, such as the accuser in the epilogue, may have been omitted and some parts modified or added. Or, conversely, it is possible that an original prologue depicted YHVH alone as testing Eyyov and that only later the accuser character was added to the prologue, just as an accuser has been added to another Israelite writing (compare 1 Chronicles 21.1 to 2 Samuel 24.1). Similarly, it may be that a later writer then inserted the Elihu section (32.1–37.24), without bothering to alter the epilogue. This sort of reconstruction of the composition is educated speculation—there are no manuscripts of the proposed older form— but it certainly fits with the hard evidence that is available for the production of written works in ancient Israelite culture, and it helps to explain some of the perceived difficulties in the text.

The Ancient Hebrew Text of Eyyov

As exquisite as the poetry may be, the Hebrew text of Eyyov seems to have suffered in its transmission over the centuries. As investigators we would attempt to use the tools of textual criticism to make some conclusions, but in this case the textual evidence does not help us out much. The early Greek translation seems of little help because the translator omitted much, making the book one-sixth shorter, and was influenced by classical Greek poetic models. Eyyov is difficult to begin with; the vocabulary of the poetic section strains modern readers and translators because Eyyov contains more rarely used words than any other book of our library. I admire the Jewish Publication Society's translation for many reasons, including the honesty of the translators who have not infrequently added the footnote, "meaning of Hebrew uncertain." Regarding modern translations, if translators are attempting to give their readers an accurate sense of the poetic form and meaning, then their resulting translations should exhibit an expansive vocabulary and a fair degree of difficulty. Thus, Eyyov is not elementary school reading.

In addition to language issues, there are other basic structural problems perceived by many readers. For example, 1) in such a highly structured work, where a particularly literary shape is clearly being followed, there are some peculiar departures or missing texts and 2) some of the content seems out of place in its textual placement. In the first case, the third poetic cycle does not contain a speech of Zophar as one would expect. Why not? Has there been a textual disruption? Similarly, Bildad's speech in third cycle (25.1–6) is curiously much shorter than any other speech of the three cycles. Why? For the second problem, there are two parts of Eyyov's speeches that seem not to match Eyyov's claims and arguments in all other places. Specifically, 24.18–25 and 27.7–23 sound more like the speeches of Eyyov's friends. One solution scholars have proposed solves both problems at once. The words of 24.18–25 could be credited to Bildad simply by moving the introductory clause of 25.1 back to 24.18, and 27.7–23 could be read as the misplaced speech of Zophar. I personally find this highly attractive, but I wish there were an ancient manuscript to support it. On the other hand, given the extreme rarity of ancient manuscripts, it is not too surprising that we do not have one that predates a possibly very early copyist error. Still, some scholars for good reason are very reluctant to alter the text as it stands, because that sort of solution could certainly be overdone.

Historical Names and Places

In case anyone wonders, there is no connection between Job's Uz and Oz, the home of Frank Baum's Wizard! Although the Eyyov story in its current form is dramatic fiction, it does have a real historical setting. Uz is mentioned in four other scrolls in our library (Genesis, Chronicles, Jeremiah, Lamentations), and in those places is certainly an actual location. It seems best to locate it in Arabia, but not much else is clear. The places of origin, for Eyyov's three friends (2.11) Shuah, Naamah, and Tema, and the location of the Sabeans (1.15) are generally better known, being attested in ancient literature outside the scrolls of our library. These can also be placed on the inhabited edges of Arabia. But more significant than the actual places is the fact that all the characters of the story, including Eyyov himself, are non-Israelites. We would be mistaken if we thought all the scrolls in this ancient Jewish library were of limited in outlook to strictly Jewish or Israelite concern.

Finally, a brief word about our protagonist's name. The name *Eyyov* may be significant for its possible meaning or for its sound association. The Hebrew consonants are the same for the word that means "to be hostile, to treat as enemy." Perhaps such a name was chosen for its associations, even its ambiguity. Is God treating Eyyov as an "enemy" or is "the accuser"? Perhaps Eyyov is the hostile one.

Eyyov as Wisdom Literature

True to its character as a piece of wisdom literature, Eyyov has an international outlook. It is true that the name of the Israelite God, YHVH, is used regularly in the beginning and ending, but there is no distinct Israelite characterization given to him and no connections made to Israelite history or distinct Israelite traditions. Tellingly, the drama's characters also have no Israelite associations. Eyyov is not suffering as an Israelite, he is suffering as a sort of "everyman," and there is no recourse to exclusively Israelite traditions of prophets, laws, or revelations. The usage of YHVH in a more generic, international setting, especially on the lips of the Uzite Eyyov and his non-Israelite friends goes far to subvert the Israelite/non-Israelite distinction and for a Jewish reader does as much to internationalize Israel's YHVH as it does to connect the experience of foreign individuals with the experience of Israelites.

In this international vein, we should also mention that surrounding cultures also bequeathed to us literature filled with the pain of suffering and the cry of the injustice (Study Room 8.3). Even the structure of Eyyov, poetry encased in prose, finds parallels in other literatures. But these similarities in no way diminish the sublime literature and expression of Eyyov.

The Prologue

If we move beyond the interesting sources critical and historical-critical questions that attempt to explain how the book was composed, we could ask how this story unfolds as a literary drama in its present form. What sort of things does the artist highlight? The prologue is a daring, humorous, painful, prose beginning that rapidly sets the stage for the poetic meditations to follow and gives the readers much to ponder. Eyyov is unequivocally presented as perfectly pious and upright; the narrator's four-fold description of him, "perfect, upright, fearing God, turning from evil," is repeated twice by YHVH (1.8, 2.3). Eyyov even goes so far as to sacrifice—a traditional pious act in the ancient world, intended to cover sin—for his children on those occasions when he thinks they might have had an offensive thought toward God (1.5). The narrator underlines Eyyov's extreme observance by remarking that he always did this (1.5) and that he did not sin (1.22, 2.10). This stress is easy to understand, because the entire drama depends on the reader's understanding that Eyyov was an innocent, blameless man.

Study Room 8.2

WHO IS SATAN?

In our entire Hebrew library, the noun שׂטׂן, *s-t-n* (pronounced "sah-*tahn*") is used just 26 times and always as a common noun, *not* as a proper name. Fifteen of those uses are here in the prologue of Eyyov. In the centuries in which this literature was being written, Jews did not have a concept of a Satan anything like the one common today. The *sah-tahn* of biblical Hebrew is not the personal name of the leader of demonic forces, a fallen angel, or the devil. A *sah-tahn* is someone (human or divine) who is an opposer, enemy, adversary, or accuser. So, for example, the Philistines do not want David's help in battle because they fear he will turn and become their adversary (1 Samuel 29.4) and later David refers to those offering political advice that he considers erroneous as his opposition (2 Samuel 19.23). Songwriters of Israel sometimes refer to a political or personal enemy as their accuser, using this word (see Psalms 38.20; 71.13; 109.4, 6, 20, 29). In a story in Numbers (22.23–25), YHVH sends an angel in order to block the path, literally to be the adversary of Balaam, so YHVH's obedient angel can be called a *sah-tahn*. Here in the prologue of Eyyov (see also Zechariah 3.1–2 and 1 Chronicles 21.1), *sah-tahn* refers to an adversary who is more than human, is a member of the YHVH's divine court, has no independent authority over humans, and is not pictured at all as a leader of evil angels. Furthermore, *sah-tahn* is certainly not a proper name because in ancient Hebrew proper names are not preceded by the definite article, and in Eyyov *sah-tahn* always has the definite article. We should also remember that Hebrew has no capital letters and so when modern English translations translate with *Satan*, the capitalization that makes it appear as a proper name is purely a modern English convention and error. Here in the story of Job, this *sah-tahn* is accusing Eyyov of serving God just for personal gain and more generally serves as Eyyov's adversary. His function in the divine court seems to be as an earthly patrol, "going back and forth, walking up and down."

But later, in the third century BCE through the first and second centuries CE, concepts of heavenly beings among some Jewish and later Christian groups changed. Evil and good supernatural beings were named and their origins, careers, and actions described in stories from this period. During this time, many evil demons began to be important characters in some popular Jewish and Christian religious thinking and psychology. And it is during this time that we see the word *sah-tahn* begin to be used as a name of a leader of evil forces. Other names and titles were use also: Belial (or Beliar), Mastemah, Apoloyon, Sammael, Asmodeus, Beelzebub, Prince of Evil, Devil. There are various explanations for the origins of these beings in different texts. The most common stories of origin in these centuries used an obscure passage from Genesis (6.4) to depict these evil beings as the illicit offspring of divine male beings mating with human women (see the book of 1 Enoch for this view). Others told of Satan being thrown out of heaven for insubordination, and this view came to dominate modern Western Christian tradition through John Milton's poem *Paradise Lost*, written in 1667, where the Latin Bible's *lucifer,* "light bearer" (see Isaiah 14.12) is used as a proper name for Satan. Other ancient Christian literature told of Satan's refusal to bow down to Adam, as ordered by God (see the *Life of Adam and Eve.*). This story has deeply influenced Islamic tradition. Another interesting twist excerpt from is that the link was made between the wicked Satan and the tempting snake in the Garden of Eden story of Genesis 2–3 fairly recently. Genesis gives a story of a snake, not of a supernatural evil being. But in late antiquity, Jewish and Christian writings view the Genesis story through the lens of the later traditions of evil angels and so came to identify the snake with Satan (For Jewish texts see Talmud, Sota 9b, Sanhedrin 29a and for Christian texts, see *Life of Adam and Eve,* 14–16). Many modern presentations of Genesis read the story the same way, assuming that the snake is Satan, though the text itself gives no support for the idea.

So, what do you make of this history of Satan? What understanding(s) of *satan* have been presented to you? What are the roles of Satan in religious teachings of various religious communities today? How does the personification of evil as a supernatural being change a religious system or personal religious psychology?

Based on Pagels 1995

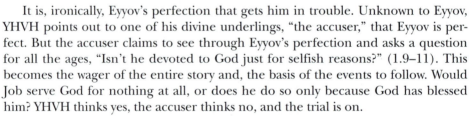

It is, ironically, Eyyov's perfection that gets him in trouble. Unknown to Eyyov, YHVH points out to one of his divine underlings, "the accuser," that Eyyov is perfect. But the accuser claims to see through Eyyov's perfection and asks a question for all the ages, "Isn't he devoted to God just for selfish reasons?" (1.9–11). This becomes the wager of the entire story and, the basis of the events to follow. Would Job serve God for nothing at all, or does he do so only because God has blessed him? YHVH thinks yes, the accuser thinks no, and the trial is on.

Eyyov's day of extreme misfortune flashes past (1.13–19) as comically tragic. But reading carefully one notices that of the four disasters which befall Eyyov that day, two are the work of enemies (Sabeans, Chaldeans), and two are direct acts of the divine (fire from God, wind). Yet Eyyov assumes that God is responsible for all of the calamites (1.21; 2.10). After all, God is in complete control. Repeatedly the book continues to stress this divine control—notice how the accuser can only touch Job with YHVH's permission—in the prose and poetic sections.

Careful literary readers have noted the ironies of this book. Between the two different stage sets of the prologue, the heavenly courtroom and the earthly home of Eyyov, there is a one-way mirror. YHVH and the accuser can see Eyyov, but Eyyov cannot see and hear the heavenly sparring upon which his fate depends. But—and this is crucial—the audience sees and hears both. This is called dramatic irony, the literary device of allowing the audience to see and know things that some members of the cast do not. Thus, Eyyov is completely unaware of the wager hanging over his head. YHVH's triumph in his bet depends on Eyyov's action, but Eyyov has no idea. The reader, God, and the accuser know, but Job and all the cast members on the earthly side of the stage do not have this knowledge.

Another kind of irony is found in the singular remark of Eyyov's wife, suggesting he curse God and die. She first quotes YHVH's second boast of Eyyov, "still he hangs on to his integrity" (2.3, 9) but then finishes by advising Eyyov to curse God, exactly what would make the accuser win the wager (2.5, 9). Except to the ears of the unbelievably pious Eyyov, her advice likely sounds very reasonable.

But an even greater irony is beginning to unfold. With the wager comes the testing of Eyyov, the trial of the protagonist. One could then imagine the story as a grand drama of Eyyov's "trial by fire," how he was tested and how he triumphed. But that is not the trial in which our author is interested. Eyyov proves true (1.22; 2.10), but the real trial of this scroll, we are soon to find out, is not of Eyyov but of YHVH. This is a bold and ironic twist, for to the readers the questions that are presented in the rich poetry of Eyyov are questions for YHVH. Can YHVH prove himself just? Eventually Eyyov himself summons God to the courtroom (13.3).

As the opening act draws to a close, Eyyov sits silently in abject misery with three friends, who have come to console him and are speechless before him for seven days. The literary effect of this is equivalent to having a stage absolutely quiet—all eyes focused on Eyyov— a long still silence, until suddenly the silence is ripped by the crash of Eyyov's lament, long, and furious, and bitter—for which the audience, is completely unprepared. After hearing of Eyyov's patient acceptance and pious ability to hold his tongue, his long and beautiful harangue, starting in 3.1, is a shocker. Remember, in the ancient scrolls of this book, there were no marking to indicate where a new section started.

The Poetic Disputes

Eyyov's first speech begins as a lament, a complaint, for his life. Literary scholars attempting to understand how this literature "works" have attempted to describe many things, including

- its poetic forms, such as figures of speech, metaphors, parallel structures, repetitions;
- its use of Hebrew language, such as vocabulary and unusual word formations;
- its movement of the argument, such as the content and rhetoric of each speaker and their relationship to other speakers; and
- its relationship to other comparative works from the ancient Near East

The results are most interesting. Let's examine the third line of questioning and display in a separate note some of the other ancient literature that compares to Eyyov. The argument begins on a note of depression. At length Eyyov laments his very life (3.1–26), cursing his birth—"Perish the day I was born on"—and longing

Study Room 8.3

COMPARATIVE LITERATURE

Egypt

Archaeologists have found several Egyptian texts dating from the second millennium BCE that share commonalities with Eyyov. Interestingly, three of them are, like Eyyov, a mixture of poetry with prose. More importantly, they lament the injustice that a God or Gods allow. Almost in passing, one author's work, titled "The Admonitions of Ipu-Wer," wonders if God is asleep, neglecting to direct the course of events so that evil is punished (ANET, 441–4). In two other Egyptian texts, "Dispute over Suicide" and "Protests of the Eloquent Peasant," the protagonist is driven by misfortune and injustice to prefer death to his miserable existence. Read the selections below and then recall Eyyov's frequent wish to die (Eyyov 3.1–26; 7.1–21; 10.18–22).

> From "Dispute over Suicide"
>
> To whom can I speak today?
> Hearts are rapacious
> No man has a heart upon which one may rely
> To whom can I speak today?
> There are no righteous,
> The land is left to those who do wrong
> To whom can I speak today?
> There is lack of an intimate friend
> One has recourse to an unknown to complain to him . . .
> To whom can I speak today?
> I am laden with wretchedness
> For lack of an intimate friend
> To whom can I speak today?
> The sin which treads the earth,
> It has no end.
> Death is in my sight today
> Like the recovery of a sick man,
> Like going out into the open after a confinement.
> Death is in my sight today
> Like the odor of myrrh
> Like sitting under an awning on a breezy day . . .
> Death is in my sight today
> Like the longing of a man to see his house
> After he has spent many years held in captivity (ANET, 406–7)
>
> Translated by John A. Wilson in Pritchard 1969, 406–07

Mesopotamia

One text originating probably in ancient Babylon (ca. 1000 BCE) has even been dubbed "The Babylonian Job" or "Babylonian Theodicy." It contains the poetic complaints of a sufferer to the God and the responses of a friend who attempts to defend the God and the moral ordering of the world.

From "The Babylonian Theodicy"

Sufferer:
Those who do not seek the God go the way of prosperity,
While those who pray to the Goddess become destitute and impoverished.
In my youth I tried to find the will of my God;
With prostration and prayer I sought my Goddess . . .
My God decreed poverty instead of wealth for me . . .
The rogue has been promoted, but I have been brought low.

Friend:
My just, knowledgeable friend, your thoughts are perverse.
You have now forsaken justice and blaspheme against your God's plans.
In your mind you think of disregarding the divine ordinances . . .
Unless you seek the will of the God, what success can you have? . . .

Sufferer:
I have looked around in the world, but things are turned around
The God does not impede the way of even a demon . . .
What has it profited me that I have bowed down to
　　my God? . . .

Translated by Robert D. Biggs in Pritchard 1969, 602–3,
　　modified

for death—"Why did I not die from the womb?" Retaining its everyman sensitivity, Eyyov's first great outburst remains less personally directed, except for its deeply personal misery; neither his friends nor God are addressed. But God is clearly considered responsible (3.23), and it will not be long before Job is looking for answers.

Answers are not hard to come by in the dispute; Eyyov's friends are full of them. Eliphaz answers that Eyyov is only reaping what he has sown in God's moral world (4.8) and advises Eyyov to seek God and not to reject the "discipline of the Almighty" (5.17). Eyyov retorts, defending his innocence and the propriety of his longing to die, which he repeats in 6.8–10, and he does in fact turn to God (7.17–21) but not in the manner Eliphaz advised. Bildad repeats the common sense platitude that sin leads to suffering, because God surely does not "pervert justice" (8.1–7). But Eyyov maintains his protestations that he is innocent (9.21), reviews in his mind the conundrums of divine justice, recognizing that he has no way of assessing God's justice or of appealing to a unbiased judge (9.3–35).

Nevertheless, Eyyov, still in pain and misery, advances the argument by seeking directly to question God:

> My soul is revolted by my life,
> I will vent my complaint,
> I will in the bitterness of my soul.
> I say to God: "Do not declare me guilty; tell me why you contend against me!"
> Does it seem good to oppress me? . . .
> Although you know I am not guilty? . . .
> Why from the womb did you bring me out? . . .
> Turn away from me that I may find a little happiness. (10.1–22)

Zophar, believing he knows precisely how things stand in the God's sight, responds that Eyyov's babble is worthless and that God in fact has mercifully punished Eyyov with less than he deserves (11.2–6). Eyyov's next response, which both concludes the first cycle and may be said to begin the second, is the longest and deepest so far (12.1–14.22). It is a lengthy diatribe against his friends ("your maxims are proverbs of ash" 13.12) and an extended contemplation of the justness of Eyyov's case with an awareness of the hopelessness of winning a judgment against God in court. Eyyov maintains his integrity and accuses his friends of lying in order to defend God (13.7–8). Honesty is his guiding principle, and he alone has the courage to speak the truth no matter what the consequences it may have for theology. Eyyov returns to the contemplation of death.

The remainder of the cycles (Chapters 15–31) do not really bring new information to the argument. All the participants maintain their views. Even the newcomer, Elihu (32.1–37.24), though he promises much and is very long-winded, delivers nothing to substantially advance the repeated arguments of the friends. Chapter 28 does provide a brief and intriguing respite from the argument—a beautiful poem on the elusiveness of wisdom. This is, after all, wisdom literature.

Finally, in Chapter 38 Eyyov gets his interview with YHVH. But it turns out to be different than Eyyov might have imagined. YHVH does not answer the questions and criticisms of Eyyov; instead, YHVH responds, "from a tornado," with a whole series of his own mind-blowing questions, such as:

> Where were you when I was founding the earth?
> Do you understand the expanse of the world?
> Can you make it rain?
> Can you provide food for the raven?
> Do you give the horse its strength?

You will notice that these questions—there are about 40 of them—have nothing to do with the specifics of Eyyov's case! One scholar has written that God's response is "striking for it irrelevance" (Murphy 1990, 42). What's going on here? Eyyov's questions get answered with questions. In Chapters 38 and 39 God shows Eyyov the huge world that God somehow controls. Using language and imagery from Eyyov's own speeches, God reveals though this series of rhetorical questions and descriptions a massive creation and the wonder of its intricacies. The intricacies are mirrored in the intricate and dazzling poetry of the divine voice, the most exquisite and poetically brilliant of the scroll. God is not in the courtroom answering questions about justice; the world he reveals is not a world under the control of a system of morality that makes sense to humans. In fact, humans do not figure into God's speech at all.

Perhaps your mind has been boggled by an impressive show in a planetarium on the size of the universe or you have been overwhelmed at an Imax theater show on the vastness of the under sea world. That overwhelming effect seems to be what the author of Eyyov is after in these speeches of God. What we have is information overload combined with a relentless personal, direct questioning of Eyyov.

Eyyov answers; or better, he says he will not answer (40.3–5). Now it is Eyyov who will not speak. Why does he declare his speechlessness? Is he submitting somehow? Is he overwhelmed somehow? Is he protesting the divine irrelevance? As with much great literature, the author does not here explain his meaning; ambiguity remains, multivalency surrounds its interpretive legacy. But God is not close to being finished. YHVH continues in the same vein, as if the divine questioning and information program were unfinished. Again the venue is the huge natural world, unknown and uncontrolled by humankind but dominated by God. The questions come with descriptions of two wondrous monsters, Behemoth and Leviathan, by some taken as ancient mythological monsters, by others as a massive hippopotamus and a wild crocodile. It hardly matters though; it is the effect that is important. Again, humans in general are irrelevent; Eyyov and his questions of justice are not God's topic for the day.

Eyyov's final words bring the dénouement to the entire dialogue: Eyyov acknowledges God's control of all things, something he never doubted. He admits he has spoken of things unknown that he does not understand. Eyyov had spoken of God's rule in the world and called into question God's ways because of their seeming injustice, but having seen a larger picture, he falls silent. Eyyov does not admit sin, nor does he repent of all that he had said in the preceding chapters. Every commentator worthy of the name will point out the intriguing ambiguity of Eyyov's final words and syntax (42.6). Quite literally, the last four lines of this grand poetic dispute can be put like this:

> By my ear, I had heard you,
> Now, by my eye, I have seen you,
> For thus I refuse [despise, reject?] and take comfort [feel sorrow?]
> For dust and ashes.

The shift in Eyyov's behavior is caused by his seeing. But what has he seen? Had YHVH really appeared? (See 38.1; 40.6.) Does this seeing refer to his sense of sight only—what his eyes saw in the grand imaginative tour of the world? Or has this grand vision brought a deeper sense of understanding? And what was the object of Eyyov's sight?—"I have seen *you*." In what sense did Eyyov see YHVH?

Oh, the questions the reader would love to ask Eyyov! Was that the author's intent? The loquacious Eyyov is now silent. He has had a mesmerizing lecture about the massive creation—*not* about YHVH's justice. Eyyov has walked out of the lecture hall of the universe—with its stores of rain clouds, sea monsters, rock badgers, wild donkeys, bloody stallions, cruel ostrich mothers—and he is overwhelmed by

YHVH's power, and profoundly aware of his own human condition as mere dust. He falls silent.

The Epilogue

The closing narrative ties up a few loose ends but still leaves plenty of questions unanswered. In case any readers had thought that Eyyov's friends were to be commended for defending YHVH and Eyyov was to be chastised for questioning YHVH's justice, the concluding narrator indicates that the reverse is the case. YHVH condemns Eliphaz and his friends for "not speaking correctly of me as my servant Eyyov has" (42.7, 8).

It is then, only by Eyyov's willingness to offer a sacrifice, that they are spared divine wrath. The author could not make it clearer, the defenders of YHVH are lambasted, the honest questioner is praised as right.

In the end YHVH restores Eyyov's fortune. YHVH's wager with the accuser, which was the cause of the whole trial of Eyyov, is never mentioned here at the end. We are left asking if the accuser has lost, and if YHVH has won. But what of the larger trial, Eyyov's trial of his God? Perhaps the dispute could be said to have been canceled on account of the gross inequality of the participants or the refusal of one to engage the questions of the other. Eyyov's questions of YHVH are still on the table. And so are YHVH's of Eyyov. But the dispute is left behind because the narrator removes the readers from the gallery of the imagined divine courtroom, and Eyyov finally gets the comfort he deserves.

> "Then his brothers and sisters and all those who knew him came . . . and sympathized and comforted him for all the evil YHVH had brought upon him" (42.11).

Note well who does comfort Job—none was forthcoming in YHVH's speech—and to whom the narrator credits the grievous evils of job's life.

What Eyyov now obtains is double his original possessions and a new family. His family is new, but the original ten are still dead. His three new daughters are intriguingly named and remarked for their beauty. But in light of the point of the entire composition, why does he get anything back? Was it not the erroneous friends who argued that the righteous are rewarded and the wicked punished? The literary scholar sensitive to the themes of the poetry must ask, if the author has rescinded his thesis, lost his nerve, and resorted to popular opinion. Is Eyyov now being rewarded? How does this reversal work in relation to the poetry? Eyyov's exquisite poetry stressed the notion that humans cannot see disaster and assume its cause is sin or see blessing and assume righteousness. We must first carefully notice that the epilogist never says that Eyyov was rewarded, though the deduction would not be hard to make. But perhaps this author has a final ironic point to make in his scroll. He has already destroyed the certainty of those so confident of YHVH's justice in their theology. Might he now be narrating a rebuttal to the doctrinaire cynic who believed that good people always suffer and never get what they deserve? So, in this ambiguous and almost nonchalant, comical manner, Eyyov the righteous is blessed. The God, in this scroll, is free to confound all.

Eyyov in the Library

It would not take a trained religion scholar to see why this beautiful piece of literature with its unflinching questioning of the God is often thought to be at odds with ideas found within the religious traditions related to biblical literature. How a tradition may stifle a book or attempt to overcome it is not my concern here, except to point out that such has often been the case. Other scrolls within our library have statements expressing the very notions of reward and punishment against which Eyyov forcefully argues, such as Deuteronomic history of kings. What would the character Eyyov say about the entirety of Psalm 37, which assures "that the righteous are never abandoned"? However, Eyyov is not alone. In the spirit of Eyyov Abraham questions YHVH's justice in Genesis 18.24–5. Psalm writers know of the unjust realities of life (see Psalm 74 and 89), and we will soon see that Qohelet (Ecclesiastes) may be said to agree wholeheartedly with Eyyov and go further. Even so, Eyyov's unrestrained questioning and his unmatched resolve might still sound scandalous, and so it is important to repeat our library principle: if the scrolls are to be read with integrity as the singular and original compositions that they were, then we must not distort the content of one to harmonize it with another or to make it palatable to modern sensibilities or systems of theology. If readers today are surprised by the profound theological ideas of Eyyov, it may say much about the inadequacy of modern biblical education and the imposition of simplistic systems of religious ideology.

POSTER 8.4

QUESTIONS, QUESTIONS, QUESTIONS

Abraham approached [YHVH] and said, "Will you indeed wipe out the righteous people with the evil? . . . How awful of you to do this thing, to kill the righteous with the evil, so that the righteous ones fare the same as the evil! How awful of you! Shall not the judge of all the earth do justice?"
—Genesis 18.23, 25

How long, YHVH? Will you always hide yourself?
Always will your wrath burn like fire?
Remember what my life span is!
Why have you created every life for nothing?
—Psalm 89.46–47

There is a foggy mystery that happens on the earth, namely that righteous people get treated in accordance with the conduct of evil people, and evil people get treated in accordance with of righteous! I say this is a foggy mystery . . .
—Qohelet 8.14

Perhaps even more important than this specific issue of divine reward and punishment is a recognition of that the author of Eyyov does not entertain or even suggest any involvement with many themes found elsewhere in our library's literature; themes such as covenant, Jewish redemption, and Israelite identity or election. These and other themes that are often considered the dominant strain in ancient Jewish and later Christian religion are not in play here. In the end, for many people accustomed to hearing about biblical teaching in religious or nonreligious settings, this scroll of Eyyov does not sound much like Bible is supposed to sound! But that is not Eyyov's problem; it's the modern problem of not recognizing the diversity of this ancient library. Some might seek to honor this diversity, and others might ignore it or even try to squelch it by burying it under a preferred religious ideology. And that, of course, is exactly what Eyyov's friends tried to do!

Questions for Further Study

1. Recent interpretations by literary critics have tried to make sense out of what others have called the missing Zophar speech. What strategies do you see for making this case? Which seems most plausible to you and why?

2. In your experience, has this ancient poetic work ever been used to address the so-called problem of evil or innocent suffering? What aspects of Eyyov were chosen for usage?

3. Considering the many flora, fauna, and cosmic references in YHVH's speeches, what can be said about the poet's learning and literary style? What does he know about the natural world? How might he know these things?

References

Alter, Robert. *The Art of Biblical Poetry.* New York: Basic Books, 1985.

Crenshaw, James L. "Job, Book of," in *The Anchor Bible Dictionary,* edited by David N. Freedman 3:858–68. New York: Doubleday, 1992.

Chesterton, G. K. "A Defence of Nonsense" in *The Defendant.* London: R. Brimley Johnson, 1901.

Crenshaw, James L. *Theodicy in the Old Testament.* Philadelphia: Fortress, 1983.

Ginzberg, Louis. *The Legends of the Jews.* Philadelphia: Jewish Publication Society, 1909.

Greenberg, Irving. "Cloud of Smoke, Pillar of Fire," in *Auschwitz: Beginning of a New Era?* Edited by Eva Fleischner. New York: KTAV, 1977.

Greenberg, Moshe. "Job," in *The Literary Guide to the Bible,* edited by Robert Alter and Frank Kermode 283–304. Cambridge, MA: Harvard, 1987.

Levi, Primo. *Survival in Auschwitz.* New York: Simon & Schuster, 1986.

Murphy, Roland E. *The Tree of Life.* Grand Rapids, MI: Eerdmans, 1990.

Newsom, Carol A. "The Book of Job," in *The New Interpreter's Bible,* 4:317–637. Nashville, TN: Abingdon, 1996.

Pagels, Elaine. *The Origin of Satan.* New York: Random House, 1995.

Pritchard, James B. *Ancient Near Eastern Texts,* 3rd ed. Princeton: Princeton University, 1967.

Voltaire, F. M. Arouet. *L'Ingénu.* Translated by John Butt. London: Penguin, 1978.

Zukerman, Bruce. *Job the Silent.* New York: Oxford, 1991.

שִׁיר הַשִּׁירִים
Song of Songs
Shir Hashirim

SECTION OUTLINE

Link to Solomon
Literary Format and Movement
Who Is Speaking?
What Are They Saying?
Specific Metaphors
Female and Male
Reflection on Love
Religious Literature?
Questions for Further Study
References

"The Greatest Song!" That's really the name of this scroll. According to Hebrew idiom the best king would literally be called the king of kings and the best book would be the book of books. In this case the title actually comes from the first line of the scroll: "The Greatest Song, which is of Solomon." This Song of Songs is a scroll of imaginative, reflective poetry describing sensual longing and an encounter between two lovers. The lovers are anonymous, the only identification used for one of them is the obscure reference "Shulamite," used of a woman in Chapter 7.1; but the significance of this designation is unclear to us. In short, this scroll fits well into an ancient genre that we can label erotic poetry. It can be found in Mesopotamian and Egyptian cultures long before Israel's advent and in Hellenistic cultures of the fourth and third centuries BCE. Like the noble poetry of love and desire of many cultures, *Shir Hashirim*—pronounced "sheer-ha-shee-*reem*,"—overflows with metaphors; for the ancient reader they were no doubt a chief source of delight. But for the modern reader, far removed from the culture, they are frequently hard to understand and require explanation. But explanations can ruin poetry, so we must be careful.

Link to Solomon

The title line of the scroll links the work to Solomon, but not necessarily as its author. The Hebrew employed could be translated, "to Solomon," "for Solomon," or "by Solomon." Solomon is mentioned six times in the poems, but never as an

*L*ITERARY FORMAT AND MOVEMENT

Beyond the first title line, Song of Songs consists entirely of poetry. It is a work of art, with a distinct feel. But scholars disagree about the overarching structure of this sensual poetry. Is it a drama/dialogue with a beginning, middle, and end; one unified poem moving in a linear fashion; or more of an anthology of loosely connected but complimentary poems? Clearly there are some distinct segments, and different speakers in them—male, female, narrator, and chorus. For our purposes it seems best to mark out these individual units without tying them all together into a comprehensive scheme. This follows the literary conclusion of scholars who think the poetry of Shir Hashirim is best understood as a "string of separate moments" (Falk 1982, 133) or as lyrics of songs strung together. They are united by their general theme of amorous desire, as well as by repetition and by subtle linguistic connections and shifts. There are often beautiful connections between individual poems. This string of poetry does not have a formal introduction nor a formal conclusion. It starts at a pitch of high intensity and ends with an equally intense expectation of more to come, perhaps pointing one back to the beginning (Bloch 1995, 18; Falk 1982, 133). The divisions I use here are those of Falk, though I recognize the work of Bloch as well. In some sense all the poems are about sensuous love and desire, and all are imaginative, even idyllic. As you read them all together, you will observe that shifts in metaphor, it is scene, speaker, and perspective are frequent. Because Hebrew verbs have gender, it is often easy to identify the speaker. Unfortunately, English verbs are not assigned gender, and most modern translations do not give us this information. In my estimation, this seems a serious and easily remedied oversight of most modern translations; it's like reading a Shakespearean play but not knowing who is talking to whom. Perhaps you might want to correct this deficiency in your personal English copy of Song of Songs, as I've done in mine, by marking in the margin the speakers. In only a few cases is it not clear.

1.1 Editor's title	2.15 Group	7.1–6 Group and female
1.2–4 Female to lover	2.16–17 Female to lover	7.7–10a Male to lover
1.5–6 Female to group (women)	3.1–5 Female to group (women)	7.10b–14 Female to lover
1.7–8 Lovers' dialogue	3.6–11 Group	8.1–4 Female to lover
1.9–11 Male to lover	4.1–7 Male to lover	8.5a Group
1.12–14 Female to lover	4.8 Male to lover	8.5b Female to lover
1.15–17 Lovers' dialogue	4.9–11 Male to lover	8.6–7 Female to lover
2.1–3 Lovers' dialogue	4.12–5.1 Lovers' dialogue	8.8–10 Group and female
2.4–7 Female to group (women)	5.2–6.3 Female/Male/Group	8.11–12 Male monologue
2.8–13 Lovers' dialogue	6.4–10 Male to lover	8.13–14 Lovers' dialogue
2.14 Male to lover	6.11–12 Male monologue	

author; always to evoke royal imagery (see 1.5; 3.7, 9, 11; 8.11–12). The work was composed long after the days of King Solomon, who ruled in the tenth century BCE. Most scholars place the composition five, six, or even seven centuries after that, but there is little to go on because the poems have little historical orientation. As early as the sixth century Solomon is known a composer of songs, as we can see in 1 Kings 4.32. By the fourth and third centuries he had become for some Jews a sort of "patron saint" of wisdom and music, and so it was a common literary device for whole books to be attributed to him, such as the Greek compositions the Wisdom of Solomon (first century BCE, see Chapter 9), the Psalms of Solomon (first century BCE), and the Odes of Solomon (first or second century CE). In a similar manner this collection of songs, Shir Hashirim, could be using the name Solomon as its author. The very real possibility is that, like the collection of poems in the scroll of Psalms, Shir Hashirim contains poems from several different periods. The individual poems themselves likely existed first in oral form, as songs or parts of songs, and then were collected by an author for this collection and extended poem.

Who Is Speaking?

The poems we have here display several different speaker formats.

1. Monologue of female or male speaking about her/his lover; sometimes the lover is directly addressed as "you"; sometimes the lover is spoken of in third person as "he" or "she" (e.g., female: 1.2–4; male: 1.9–11).
2. Dialogue between lovers. (e.g., 1.7–8; female speaks inverse 7, male speaks in verse 8).
3. Monologue of female that includes address to group; group may be an imagined construct of speaker (e.g., 2.4–7); this type of monologue is never done by a male speaker.
4. Monologue by unidentifiable speaker or a group to an unspecified audience (e.g., 2.15).
5. Trilogue among female, male, and group (e.g., 5.2–6.3); this is the single longest poem.

In one sense, the whole book is one long poem with all the different speakers joining in one grand exchange. Commentators trace the movement of this one large conversation in a variety of ways. On the other hand, the divisions into plausible smaller units can be helpful for understanding the interactions in specific conversations.

What Are They Saying?

Shir Hashirim is a poetic celebration of sensual love but not in an abstract manner. It is a multivoiced artistic expression of love and desire for one's lover. The speakers describe the yearning for their lover and describe and praise their lover's body. There are dramatic episodes of one lover chasing another. A specific scene is imagined for a sensuous encounter, as if in a dream. The lovers speak with anticipation or even anxiety but sometimes with full satisfaction. What they say is more often than not sensuous, involving the five senses. Words of seeing, smelling, tasting, touching, and hearing are frequent. All the speakers in their various expressions constantly utilize metaphor and simile, which by nature evoke comparisons. Because of the extensive use of them in Shir Hashirim, it is worth our while to address metaphor here.

The comparisons that metaphors invoke are always partial, never complete, in this or any other work. They never completely identify one thing as the other. My son or daughter may be the Babe Ruth of his or her baseball team, but no one actually mistakes him or her for Babe Ruth. Metaphors and similes present a kind of equation and guessing game. They equate one thing to another, but they do not usually spell out the likeness. The nature of the comparison is left to the reader's imagination, and for reading Shir Hashirim, the ancient reader undoubtedly had a distinct advantage over the modern one, because meaningful comparisons assume cultural understandings. In Shir Hashirim some comparisons are easy to understand. Others may be multifaceted, but still others may seem extremely subtle, or even slight—involving only a single aspect. A metaphor may be transparent or purposefully ambiguous. Some comparisons may refer not to a specific physical aspect but to a comparable sensation derived from both sides of the equation. Sometimes it may be only connotations that are comparable. Some of the metaphors are mixed so as to produce synesthesia, where the sensation of one sensory organ is associated with another one, such as in "delicious song" (2.14). Naturally in a work of this sort, many metaphors will include sexual innuendo and double entendre. Sometimes we might have to admit the nature of the comparison is lost on us. But before giving up, let me suggest that perhaps the most common mistake is the tendency to attempt to always make the metaphors visual, when in fact there are many other possibilities.

Additionally, the metaphors in this scroll are constantly shifting. Even in single episodes the speakers are constantly changing figures of speech, and this characteristic not only keeps the poetry moving and the reader alert, but also emphasizes the nonliteralness, mystery, and ineffability of the entire enterprise of trying to describe the delights of passionate love and one's lover. Though metaphors require abstract thought to create and interpret, the metaphors of Shir Hashirim themselves are concrete and sensual.

Specific Metaphors

A few metaphors require special comment. The first is that familial images are often used in ways that a modern reader may find unusual at first. The male speaks of his lover as "my sister, my bride" (4.9), and she desires him to be as "a brother" (8.1). She also speaks of being alone with her lover in her mother's room (3.4). These and other examples in Shir Hashirim, as well as many from other ancient cultures, show how familial bonds and contexts were appropriate sources of imagery and metaphor, and we cannot assume that all words are meant literally. She may not be his biological sister, and in fact not his legal bride, either. Both are terms of endearment evoking familiarity and intimacy. In the same way, modern American love songs often use the term *baby* to refer to one's lover, but there is no suspicion or suggestion of incest. Generally we find frequent references to family and family contexts in ancient erotica from Israel and surrounding nations.

POSTER 8.5

ANCIENT EGYPTIAN LOVE SONGS

(Thirteenth Century BCE)

> The love of my sister is on yonder side,
> A stream lies between us,
> And a crocodile waits in the shallows.
> But when I go down into the water,
> I wade the current,
> My heart is great upon the steam,
> And the waves are like land unto my feet.
> It is the love of her that makes me steady,
> For it makes a water-charm for me!
> When I see my sister coming,
> My heart dances,
> And my arms open wide to embrace her, . . .
> When my lover comes to me.

Translated by John A. Wilson in Pritchard 1969, 468

Female Song

> Mix your body with mine . . .
> As honey mixes with water,
> As mandrake mixes with gum,
> As dough mixes with yeast . . .
> Come to your lover,
> Like a horse charging onto the field of battle,
> Like a falcon swooping toward the marsh . . .

Male Song

> My lover is a marsh,
> My lover is lush with growth . . .
> Her mouth is a lotus bud,
> Her breasts are mandrake blossoms.
> Her arms are vines,
> Her eyes are shaded like berries.
> Her head is a trap built from branches . . . I am the goose.
> Her hair is the bait in the trap . . . to ensnare me.

Translation of Matthews and Benjamin, 1997, 298.

Of the scores of metaphors that are used in this scroll, one certainly stands out as the most common, and that is the garden or orchard. At times this idyllic setting is a place where both lovers may go for sensual pleasure, a sort of Garden of Eden image (8.13). At other times the woman is the garden into which she invites the man (4.16). He speaks of her as "my garden" (5.1) into which he enters, he gathers, pastures, and eats. Once he is a tree under which she sits and eats his fruit (2.3). The most extended treatment of the garden figure occurs in 4.12–5.1, where sights and smells and fresh breezes and tasty fruits are all evoked for erotic effect. A similar and common metaphor is the vineyard. There is actually a group of related words here—vines, vineyard, grapes, wine—all of which are associated in numerous poems with erotic experience, female breasts, and female sexuality.

It would of course be natural that fertility images would be common in this kind of poetry. Thus the landscape of Shir Hashirim bursts with flowers and fruit, nuts, spices, young animals, and lush countrysides. Some of the poems are brief narrative episodes that occur outdoors in pastoral settings. It is interesting to note that the climate is always one of springtime. Yet, at the same time, Shir Hashirim never invokes child-bearing or conception as a goal or even outcome. These poems of lovers and love-making are celebrations of loving pleasure, not of children or posterity.

Female and Male

Shir Hashirim stands out among the scrolls of our library not only because of its unique subject matter, but also because of the perspective through which it takes up that subject. "My lover is mine and I am his" (2.16), she declares with complete mutuality. Shir Hashirim exhibits no obvious male sexism. The woman speaks more than the man and asserts her own interests and desires. Both lovers praise each other's bodies and initiate activity with one another. In short, as Phyllis Trible has put it, in Shir Hashirim, "there is no male dominance, no female subordination, and no stereotyping of either sex" (Trible 161).

Reflection on Love

As we have already mentioned these poems are not so much about the subject of love, as they are about a lover; statements of desire for and enjoyment of him or her. We do not find abstract ideas about love or eros, but concrete manifestations of desire and passion. There is one exception to this rule of concreteness near the end of the scroll in 8.6–7. The female is speaking to the male and says:

> Place me as a seal on your heart,
> As a seal on your arm,
> Because fierce as death is love,
> Hard as Sheol is passion.
> Its arrows are arrows of all consuming fire,
> Vast floods of water not able to quench love,
> And rivers will not drown it.
> If a man offered all the money of his house for love, he would be completely scorned.

Community Reflections 8.2

☙ ✝

INTERPRETING LOVE SONGS

Many centuries after the writing of Shir Hashirim, an interesting tradition of interpretation developed in Jewish and Christian circles that flourished especially in medieval times. This tradition began in the Jewish community, which read Shir Hashirim as if it were an allegory that described the love between God and Israelites. In the Christian community the love was applied to the relationship between Christ and the Church or individual Christians. Although the scroll itself does not mention God and traditional religious categories and does not point to that line of interpretation, it is easy to see how the tradition arose among those seeking traditional spiritual insights in the text. Furthermore, other books in the library, such as Hosea, do speak of the relationship between God and Israel as a marriage. Allegorical interpretation is still used in many places, though the basic underlying sensual meaning is usually also recognized.

Judaism

The Jewish forms of this allegorical interpretation are usually called historical allegories because they identify phrases in Shir Hashirim with particular events in traditional Jewish history. Some of these writings, in the form of commentaries, line-by-line explanations, or *targumim,* explanatory translations into Aramaic, tell the story of Jewish history from the rescue of Israel from Egypt to Mt. Sinai, through the time of exile and restoration. The authors of these texts attempt to find hidden meanings and possible connections with other biblical texts. Here is a sample section from the medieval rabbinic commentary known as *Midrash Rabbah.* It understands God to be the male of Shir Hashirim 1.2, and it associates God's mouth with the giving of God's words at Mt. Sinai.

> "Let him kiss me with the kisses of his mouth" (Song of Songs 1.1) Rabbi Johanan said. An angel carried each one of the divine sayings [at Mount Sinai] from the Holy One, blessed by He, to each of the Israelites and said to him, "Do you take upon yourself this commandment? There are this many rules attached to it, and this many penalties, and this many precautionary measures, and this many precepts, and this may lenient and strict applications, and this reward." The Israelite would answer him, "Yes." He then said, "Do you accept the divinity of the Holy One, blessed by He?" and he answered, "Yes, yes." Thereupon he kissed him on the mouth. . . . Other Rabbis, however, say, The commandment itself went in turn to each of the Israelites and said to him, "Do you undertake to keep me? These are my rules and penalties, precautionary measures, regulations, relaxations and rigors, and this reward." And he would reply, "Yes, yes." And straight away the commandment would kiss him.
>
> —MIDRASH RABBAH, SONG OF SONGS, 1983, MODIFIED

Following this allegorical line of interpretation, Shir Hashirim was selected as one of the **Five Megillot** (scrolls) that are read at the spring holiday of Pesach, Passover, which celebrates the rescue of the Jews from Egypt and the special loving relationship between God and God's people.

Christianity

In Christian interpretation, allegorical interpretation also became very traditional. In the fourth century the scholar Origen preached and wrote a ten-volume commentary on Shir Hashirim that shows awareness of the underlying sensual meaning but focuses on the pastoral concerns of the relationship between Christ and the Christian soul. Many Christian commentators followed Origen, and in the medieval period there were more commentaries written on Shir Hashirim than any other book of the Christian Old Testament. The sixteenth-century Spanish Christian mystical writer, St. John of the Cross, composed a Spiritual Canticle, a poetic abridgement and paraphrase of the Canticle of Canticles, the Latin derived title of Shir Hashirim. He read the book as a mystical explanation of the love between the soul and Jesus Christ, its Spouse. Here is a sample in which he uses the idea of the hidden male lover from Shir Hashirim 6.1:

THE BRIDE

Where have You hidden Yourself,
And abandoned me to my sorrow, O my Beloved!
You have fled like the hart,
Having wounded me.
I ran after You, crying; but You were gone.

In this first stanza the soul, enamored of the Word, the Son of God, the Bridegroom, desiring to be united to Him in the clear and substantial vision, sets before Him the anxieties of its love, complaining of His absence. And this the more so because, now pierced and wounded with love, for which it had abandoned all things, even itself, it has still to endure the absence of the Beloved, Who has not released it from its mortal flesh, that it might have the fruition of Him in the glory of eternity. Hence it cries out, "Where have You hidden Yourself?"

Here is our scroll's longest reflection on the meaning of love in the abstract. She begins with a command to the male to set her deeply into his person; internally and externally he is marked as hers. The reason for this depth of marking? Because the love of which she partakes is deep and fierce as death, the power that defeats everyone. "Love is as strong as death," she says. The explanation goes no further in the abstract. Instead metaphors rush back in. How is love as strong as death? We could speculate and perhaps the author would encourage the reader to do so. The poetry here suggests, prods, and gives us pause, but it does not continue with an abstract explanation of love. The next lines suggest power, inextinguishability, and even danger. This entire scroll has been at play in the world of sensuous love. But here the love is a dangerous fire, and the poet seems self-consciously aware of the seriousness of it all. This poem concludes that this passion is a danger that no sane person would give up, even for the wealth of the whole house.

But for the end of the scroll, it is not the *danger* of love that is allowed to remain on the reader's mind. This serious moment is not allowed to last or to dampen the spirit. In 8.8 the poet plunges right back into the sensuous world of vineyards, breasts, and gardens, and the scroll ends with a dialogue of longing and expression for more!

Male:	O lady of the gardens,
	Friends listening for your voice,
	Let me hear you!
Female:	Hurry my lover,
	Be like a gazelle or young stag,
	Upon the hills of cinnamon.
	—SHIR HASHIRIM 8.14

Religious Literature?

For whatever reason, the author or compiler of Shir Hashirim felt no need to speak of God in this scroll. There are no references to YHVH or even a more generic reference to deity. There are many different definitions of religious, and some of them might be broad enough to include this scroll under the caption, but this scroll of poetry hardly matches what most people think of when they hear the word *Bible* or *religion*. It is not my goal here to confound definitions of *religious,* though I would encourage reading and thinking about such things; surely modern distinctions between religious and secular are problematic and do not match ancient Israelite categories well. However, it is a goal of mine in this *Guided Tour* to present the scrolls of this ancient Jewish library now called Bible as they really are. Shir Hashirim is erotic poetry, and that basic fact should not be obscured. If we had never read Shir Hashirim in Bibles before, and an archaeologist had discovered a copy, everyone would say that it is clearly sensuous literature. In the long history of interpreting Shir Hashirim, some have attempted to deny the erotic sense of the scroll. But there have also been some even among those who practiced allegorical or religiously symbolic interpretations, who acknowledged its original erotic character.

Surely this scroll stands as testament to a certain broad-mindedness of the compilers of this library. Some have speculated that Song of Songs was included in the collection only because allegorical interpretation turned it into a pious religious book. But this is just speculation, and it assumes a certain narrowness of perspective that we should not impose from a later time. It also ignores the fact that even with allegorical interpretation the underlying plain sensuality is still on display, even for those who wish to use it as a stepping-stone to some other meaning. Rabbi Akiba in the early second century CE is quoted as defending its inclusion, but there is no mention of a particular interpretation, and there are a variety of ways to account for Akiba's valuation of the book. There is no evidence to suggest that it was interpreted allegorically in its earliest centuries of existence, the fourth to first centuries BCE. Ultimately it was decided that this scroll, which has no reference to Israel's God and no traditionally religious language or content, ought to be included on the shelves of the library. This scroll is one of the most obvious reasons why it is useful and more accurate to think of a Bible as a diverse library instead of as a single book with a monolithic message or outlook. Would Shir Hashirim be in the Bible if the books were chosen today?

Questions for Further Study

1. If we tried to do a study of comparative sexuality, what would we see as the similarities and differences between Shir Hashirim and the love lyrics of other times and places, such as ancient Greece, China, medieval or modern Europe, or the modern United States? What are the ideologies and cultural assumptions that underlie these differences and similarities?

2. How do these poems relate place, such as countryside, urban, pasture? What is idealized? What is the attitude of the poet to nature?

3. What poetic images and metaphors in Shir Hashirim do you find most delightful, intriguing, and evocative? Why?

References

Bloch, Ariel and Chana Bloch. *The Song of Songs*. Berkeley CA: University of California, 1995.

Falk, Marcia. *Love Lyrics from the Bible*. Sheffield, England: Almond, 1982.

Midrash Rabbob, *Song of Songs*. London: Soncino press, 1983.

Matthews, Victor and Don Benjemin. *Old Testament Parallels*. 2nd ed. Mahwah, NJ: Paulist, 1997.

Murphy, Roland E. "Song of Songs, Book of," in *The Anchor Bible Dictionary*, edited by David N. Freedman, 6:150–55. New York: Doubleday, 1992.

Pope, Marvin H., *Song of Songs*. Garden City, NY: Doubleday, 1977.

Pritchard, James B. *Ancient Near Eastern Tests*. Princeton: Princeton University, 1969.

Trible, Phyllis. *God and the Rhetorie of Sexuality*. Philadelphia: Fortness, 1978.

Walsh, Carey Ellen. *Exquisite Desire*. Minneapolis, MN: Fortress, 2000.

רות

Ruth *Rut*

This artistically composed short story—only four to five columns or pages in most editions—may seem a lot like one you might find in an anthology of literature. It has given great pleasure to many readers. It is a story of loyalty, love, fate, and graciousness. Its literary style is rich, subtle, and carefully crafted, and its perspective and subject matter are refreshing and unique in our library. The name of the scroll derives from its most active character, *Rut*, pronounced in Hebrew as "*root.*" Its tight prose brims with wordplays, symbolic names, thematic words, use of echoes, innuendo, *inclusios*, and intimate dialogue. This story about two women is set in the male-dominated society of ancient Israel, and another remarkable uniqueness is that the women's actions drive the story. Although the males are always reacting to their initiatives, the women make their own decisions and initiate conversations and events; their perspective is central to the telling.

Dramatic Setting and Date

If you recall the scroll of Judges that we looked at earlier, you'll remember vivid stories of Israelites neck deep in murder and mayhem. Ironically, the author of Rut situates her story right in the middle of those days "when judges ruled" (1.1) Could we have more of a contrast? Rut has no villains in sight, characters and villages alike display respect for foreigners and live lives of dignity and courage in loving loyalty to others.

Literary scholars have found reason to think that this story, like many of those in Judges, also existed in an oral form prior to its splendid written form. But considering the purpose of the composer of Judges to illustrate the social breakdown among Israelite tribes, it is no wonder that the story of Rut would not be included in that anthology, even if the author of Judges had been acquainted

LITERARY FORMAT AND MOVEMENT

Rut was written with careful attention to detail and a style at once both gentle and powerful in its economy. Well over half of the work is conversation among characters, all of whom are sympathetically presented, which lends it a warm intimacy. Its structure has been described different ways, but the model we'll use presents the story as four movements, each of which calls for a character to make a life-changing decision for the well-being of another. In this case the movements correspond to the chapter divisions that were added much later.

1.1–5 Prologue: an ill-fated Israelite family moves to Moab.	2.1 Prologue: Boaz	3.1–5 Naomi's plan for Rut to obtain Boaz.	4.1–2 Prologue: Boaz at court
	2.2–22 Rut obtains food and minimal status.		4.3–12 Rut obtains legal status as wife of Boaz.
1.6–21 Naomi, cursed, returns with Moabite Rut.	2.23 Summary: Provision	3.6–15 Rut enacts the plan.	
		3.16–18 Rut and Naomi wait for results.	4.13–17 Marriage, a child, Naomi blessed
1.22 Summary: Return			4.18 Epilogue: Line of David

with it. These two completely different narratives, both painting pictures of the same period of Israel's past, stand together as a good reminder that a single work cannot be taken to represent all aspects of a given time. The Judges editor was selective and desired a certain kind of story. Rut's story provides us with a balance to that selectivity. There is also nothing in the story itself or in external sources that can demonstrate that the story is historical by modern standards. The author writes with a definite realism, but historicity is another matter altogether. A modern historian will need to consider all available sources for the period and take into account the purposes and biases of all literary texts. But of course the story's value is not dependent it historicity.

Dating the actual period of composition proves very difficult for Rut: scholars date it from the tenth to fifth century BCE, that is, either in the times of monarchy, exile in Babylon, or after exile. The language of Rut has some divergent forms, possibly colloquialisms, but not necessarily good indicators of antiquity. Some have argued that Rut's open attitude to foreigners suggests that it was written to counteract more xenophobic attitudes, such as one encounters in Ezra-Nehemiah. But Rut is hardly polemical, and the loosely organized Israelites no doubt exhibited a variety of attitudes about outsiders for much of their history.

A Simple Story, Well Told

The narrative begins abruptly and darkly; four words set the timeframe, and then comes a famine. Ironically, the famine drives a man and his family, wife and two sons, from the breadbasket of Israel, *Bethlehem*, ("pronounced "*bait-le-chem*"), which means "house of bread/food." They seek sustenance in a foreign land to the east, Moab, a land of foreign clans, language, and Gods. They live there about ten years, long enough for their sons, named Machlon, "sick," and Chilion, "failing," to marry two Moabite girls, Orpah "very uncertain," and Rut, "refreshment." But the three father and both sons all die unexpectedly and three childless widows remain, a desperate situation in male-dominated cultures. Naomi, "lovely," upon hearing that YHVH had taken pity and relieved her homeland of famine, decides to return to her land, and naturally she counsels her daughters-in-law to return to their own Moabite homes instead of facing the plight of a foreign widow among Israelites. Here the narrative gives way to rich, intimate dialogue (1.8). A moving scene of tears and loving affection among all three follows. Reluctantly Orpah submits to the wise pleadings of her mother-in-law and is not in the least castigated by the narrator, but Rut declares her ultimate loyalty is to Naomi, and she swears a beautiful oath forever linking her life to that of Naomi:

> Wherever you go, I will go,
> and wherever you lodge, I will lodge,
> Your people—my people
> Your God—my God
> Wherever you die, I will die,
> There I will be buried.
> (Oath) May YHVH do this or more to me [probably accompanied by a gesture indicating death]
> If even death comes between me and you. (1.16–17)

The somber scene continues as the two desperate women return bereft to Bethlehem, which is abuzz with news of Naomi's return. The women of the village, who function something like a chorus in a Greek drama, ask, "Is this Naomi ('Lovely')?" And so she responds with her own bitter poem that minces no words about YHVH's treatment of her:

> Do not call me Naomi!
> Call me Mara ("bitter"),
> For bitter indeed has the Almighty been to me.
> I was full when I left,
> Empty YHVH has brought me back.
> Why call me lovely?
> YHVH tells against me
> And the Almighty does evil to me. (1.20)

The narrator begins the second movement with the introduction of a potential benefactor, a relative of Naomi's husband, for the destitute women. Notice how the narrator stretches out his description and builds up to his name Boaz, which means "strong" or "noble." But however prominent he may be and however hopeful the reader may become upon learning about him, the next line returns to dialogue and returns the readers back to reality—Rut is Moabite, a foreigner; she has no standing among these clans. So she sets out to change her status, by becoming a lowly maidservant. Because it is barley harvest season, she sets out for the fields, aiming to win someone's favor and permission to follow behind the hired harvesters and gather what has been left, according to custom. This secondary harvesting is called gleaning. (At some point in Israelite history this was a legally instituted provision for the poor; see Leviticus 19.9–10; 23.22; Deuteronomy 24.19–22.) In this story where fate has been so hard to this point, matters appear to be taking a turn for the better as Rut happens upon the field of Boaz and requests and receives from the servant in charge permission to work. And that is when Boaz notices her and assumes she is a servant of someone else but is told that her status is even less, she is "the Moabite who returned with Naomi" (2.6). But the noble Boaz takes a liking to her, and tells her to remain in his fields, follow his reapers, and even gives access to their provisions. Rut is full of gratitude, but still concerned for her long-range welfare. She asks Boaz why she, a foreigner, has received such kind treatment. Boaz replies that he has heard just how lovingly loyal she had been to her mother-in-law, and he hoped that YHVH would reward her for "seeking refuge under his wings." The Hebrew word for "wings," *canaf*, will be important later. But Rut is not content with the good wishes, however pious, so she subtly and gently presses on, remarking to Boaz that although he has treated her like a maidservant, he has not actually made her such. Boaz then moves to give Rut a more formal standing; she is placed among the workers for meals, and Boaz serves her and instructs his servants to provide extra grain for her from their own sheaves. At the end of the day, Rut processes her grain with the servants and returns to Naomi with nearly a bushel full of grain. It is only then that the storyteller allows Rut to learn from Naomi what the reader already knows, namely, that that man Boaz who had treated Rut so nobly and kindly, is a kinsman of Naomi (20). Here the author puns on Boaz's name, saying that he (*boaz*) has not *azab*-ed (forsaken) her.

It is important that Boaz is a kinsman because in ancient Israel kinsmen were male relatives who had the first right and responsibility of purchase of property in the clan and so potentially this noble Boaz could be the one to purchase the land once owned by Naomi's deceased husband, thereby giving Naomi a means of survival. But as scene three opens, we learn that Naomi is thinking less about herself than about the future of her lovingly loyal daughter-in-law. Sensing Boaz's interest in Rut, she moves to find out what might become of it. Might Rut be able to convince him to make her a concubine or even a wife? Is this possible for Rut, a Moabite? Naomi tells Rut of her plan to send Rut—looking beautiful and smelling good—to the threshing floor, where the grain was pounded out of the stalks, late at night after Boaz had had plenty to drink and had lain down. This scene, taking place at night, is delicately sensuous, replete with suggestively sexual double entendres, euphemisms, and, at least for the author, in keeping with the nobility and integrity of the actors. The sexuality is unmistakable in the ancient Hebrew figures of speech and words for "coming," "knowing," "spreading over," and uncovering "feet," a common euphemism for genitals. "Then go to him," says Naomi, "and uncover him and lie down. He will then tell you what to do." Rut responds to this daring plan, "I will do all that you say." But of course, Rut does not just do as Naomi says; she does even more. Rut acts out her noble seduction beautifully, instructing Boaz to "spread his cloak over her," a phrase which in the context is literal and carries the implication of betrothal. "Betrothal" is word we don't use much, but it's perfect here. (See Deuteronomy 23.1 and Ezekiel 16.8 for the figure of speech.) The Hebrew word for "cloak" used is *canaf*, the same as for "wing" in 2.12.

Study Room 8.4

WOMEN AND A FOREIGN WOMAN

In most of our ancient library the narratives, laws, proverbs, the lives of women are secondary. Feminist criticism, a methodology of study that asks questions about the characterization and roles of women in history, culture, and literature, has greatly added to the exploration of Israelite and biblical subjects. The case of the scroll of Rut turns out to be quite exceptional. So much so that many scholars consider that that the author may have been a woman. Clear proof seems lacking, but it is an intriguing possibility. What do you think? Read through the text carefully and notice all the things women do. An interesting study of Rut along these lines has been made by Phyllis Trible in Chapter 6 of her book, *God and the Rhetoric of Sexuality*.

But Rut is not only a woman in a male-dominated society, she is also a foreign woman in an Israelite society. Look the scroll over again and notice how many times the storyteller reminds the audience that Rut is a Moabite. How does this affect her standing? How do people react to her? What stereotypes or cultural conventions may be in play? How does she make herself at home among her new chosen people? Israelite literature of our library does not have a monolithic ideology of foreign peoples. The book of Rut is one example. What viewpoint does it offer? Do you observe other viewpoints in other scrolls? What does that say about the library's collectors?

Boaz had wished divine blessing upon Rut for seeking shelter under "his wings," referring to YHVH. But the lovingly loyal and ever industrious Rut seeks to turn his wish for YHVH to act into a responsible action of Boaz; she gently and sensuously asks him to move her from the status of maidservant and to make her his wife. Boaz is even more impressed by this courageous and loving deed of loyalty, for he is aware that if he should marry Rut, according to an apparently active custom, their son would inherit the land that would have belonged Naomi's sons, but that land would be retained in Naomi's family by future generations not in Boaz's family.

What will he decide? Who is in charge in this scene? At the planning stage Naomi had told Rut, "He will tell you what to do" (3.4). Rut had responded, "Everything that you say I will do" (3.5). But in the end it is not Boaz who tells Rut what to do, but Boaz who accepts her instructions and declares to her, "Everything that you say I will do for you" (3.11). As the final scene resolves the story, Boaz indeed does it all, legally declaring Rut his wife and redeeming the land of Naomi, but not before one last moment of suspense. A relative nearer to Naomi than Boaz appears on the scene and is given his legal option of redemption ahead of Boaz. The narrator names him only "So-and-so." In a story where names are symbolic of the character, this is clearly a comment about his nonparticipation in this story of individuals working out lovingly loyal relationships. Rut the Moabite has been

Community Reflections 8.3

ॐ

The scroll of Rut is the second of the Five *Megillot*, "five scrolls" from the Ketuvim. These are the five books that are read at specific holidays of the Jewish calendar. Rut, a story of loving loyalty set amid the fields of grain at harvest time in Israel, is read during the spring harvest holiday of *Shavuot*, or "weeks." We can read about the origins of this holiday in Exodus 23.16; 34.22; Leviticus 23.15-21; Numbers 28.26–31; and Deuteronomy 16.9–12. In the late spring, the first grain crops planted during the winter, such as wheat and barley, were harvested.

When and why Rut was selected for this holiday is simply not known today, but the harvest motif was likely part of the reason for the connection. Beyond that we can only observe that this story of a foreigner, who models perfect love of family and who casts her lot with people of YHVH, becomes an integral part of this Jewish celebration. For this reason, in Jewish literature Rut is often considered the model convert and a reminder to always embrace one who deeply desires to join the people of Israel.

married, Naomi the widow has been redeemed, and even her dead husband's line will continue, for the child of Rut and Boaz is considered hers. The people of the village embrace Rut as one of them. The chorus of women reappears in the final scene, blesses YHVH for his provision, and praises Rut as a loving daughter who is better than seven sons (4.15). A final epilogue, which is perhaps a later addition, gives a brief genealogy—as it turns out this son of the Moabite widow is the grandfather of Israel's most celebrated king David.

The Point?

What was the author's purpose when she put her stylus to her scroll? The story is worked out with a natural acknowledgement of YHVH as Israel's God, yet would we characterize the story as religious? YHVH is distant, never speaking or doing miracles. Characters never wait for him to act. Yet *khesed*, which I have translated as "lovingly loyal" or "loving loyalty," is a richly religious term in ancient Jewish literature, and is a key *leitwort*, theme-word, in Rut. But this should not be considered the sole purpose; the author may have several purposes, Phyllis Trible puts it well:

> Attempts to specify a single purpose falter in light of the book's richness and complexity. Many levels of meaning intertwine—social, political, religious, and aesthetic. A representative list includes: to maintain Israelite customs, inculcate legal duties, integrate law and daily life, legitimate David and his monarchy, tell a good story, encourage proselytes, promote universalism over against nationalism, elevate the virtues of friendship and loyalty, glorify family ties, preserve women's traditions, and witness to God at work. (Trible 1992, 847)

Questions for Further Study

1. As a social and ethnographic critic, what do you find about social relationships, boundaries, and hierarchies in this story?

2. As a feminist critic, what do you find about women and their relationships to men and to each other?

3. As a religion scholar, what role does religion and deity play in the narrative? How would you characterize God in the story? How do characters speak about God?

References

Brenner, Athalya, ed. *A Feminist Companion to Rut.* Sheffield, England: Sheffield Academic Press, 1993.

Campbell, Edward F., Jr. *Rut, The Anchor Bible Commentary.* New York: Doubleday, 1975.

Sasson, Jack M. "Rut," in *The Literary Guide to the Bible,* edited by Robert Alter and Frank Kermode, 320–28. Cambridge, MA: Harvard, 1987.

Trible, Phyllis. "Rut, Book of," in *The Anchor Bible Dictionary,* edited by David N. Freedman 5:842–47.New York: Doubleday, 1992.

Trible, Phyllis. *God and the Rhetoric of Sexuality.* Philadelphia: Fortress, 1978.

איכה

Lamentations *Eikhah*

SECTION OUTLINE

This scroll almost deserves a moment of silence as we unroll it. Lamentations contains five sorrow-filled poems written in exile after the Babylonian armies destroyed Jerusalem and took many captives back to Babylon in 586 BCE. I've never been a refugee; I've never been displaced from my home or forced to flee for my life to another land. What about you? Our world has many who could answer yes to that question, and the ancient world did, too. In this scroll that reality of exile, death, and loss is inscribed in formal communal mourning poetry. It is strikingly beautiful and overwhelmingly heartbreaking. I'm not sure what the word *Lamentations* conjurs in your mind, but if you are thinking along the lines of "mourning" and "bitter complaint" then we're on the right track. The English title comes originally from the Greek translation. The Hebrew title, *Eikhah*, pronounced "ei-*khah*" (*kh* like *ch* in *Bach*) is the first word of the first poem and of the second and fourth poems. It is a term of questioning and desperation and dejection, such as *alas!* This is poetry for the survivors of tragedy, the lucky ones who don't feel lucky. It is also deeply religious, often speaking of YHVH and addressing him directly.

We do not know the author of this anonymous scroll, though there were traditions that assigned the scroll to the prophet Jeremiah, but there is no strong evidence for this. Of course each of the poems may come from a different poet.

LITERARY FORMAT AND MOVEMENT

Eikhah is a fascinating study in dissonance. It is at once rigidly formal and powerfully emotive. Probably the most structured and controlled of any scroll from our library, yet it is a commemoration of chaotic destruction and uncontrollable grief. This is mourning poetry, thoughtfully and artfully composed. It consists of five separate highly ordered poems. The first four are alphabetic acrostics, with the first letter of each verse beginning with consecutive letter of the 22-letter Hebrew alphabet. The middle poem, Chapter 3, follows this pattern in the most rigid manner of all; each line of the poem begins with the prescribed letter, thus forming a triple acrostic, because each letter is assigned to three consecutive lines of poetry. Unfortunately most popular modern English translations make no attempt to translate this clear and obvious aspect of the Hebrew text. There is one exception in English, the translation of Ronald Knox from the middle of the last century. It is also commendable that the Jewish Publication Society's Tanakh does at least indicate the Hebrew letters at each verse. The last poem, Chapter 5, has been called a false acrostic, in that it consists of 22 poetic verses but is not an acrostic. On the other hand, the last chapter is more structured than the other four in regard to standard Hebrew parallelism. The dominant poetic rhythm of the poems generally follows the *qinah*, or mourning meter. It is followed closely in poem three, observed also in two and four, and partially observed in one. In *qinah* meter each poetic line is divided into two parts. The first part follows a normal rhythm, but the second is shorter, usually by one beat. The effect is "a peculiar limping rhythm, in which the second member as it were dies away and expires" (Budde 1903, 4:5). Eikhah does not use *qinah* meter exclusively, and *qinah* is not a rhythm exclusively for mourning, because it is used in other non-mourning poems, such as Jonah 2 and Song of Songs 1.9–11, and it is not used in some mourning poems, such as 2 Samuel 1.17–27. *Qinah* is like a minor key in western music, especially associated with sadness but not exclusively so. The perspective of the poems shifts even within the poems and sometimes YHVH is addressed directly in the second person and sometimes in the third person; sometimes Jerusalem speaks, and sometimes she is spoken for or described; sometimes the poetic speaker is singular, and sometimes the communal plural is used.

1.1-22 The desolation of Lady Jerusalem	2.1-22 Dialogue on Jerusalem's destruction by her master and foe, YHVH	3.1-66 A personal mourning	4.1-22 Jerusalem before and after	5.1-22 Concluding prayer of and for remembrance

A Poetic Monument of Sorrow

Military invasion and brutal defeat, loss of family and home, and forced removal to a foreign land: surely such an experiences are among the most disorienting, chaotic, and mournful a human may ever face. How does a survivor cope? How does a community now in disarray survive? The poetry of Eikhah clearly represents careful reflection. It is not raw. The scroll of Eikhah is a well-ordered poetic monument to chaos and an ironic, artistic exercise in form that commemorates chaotic disaster. The poet restricts himself to an elemental arrangement—the alphabet. The poems thus become predictable; life may be in upheaval, but at least one's poetry is dependable. At the same time, does such poetic confinement mirror the harsh confinements of Jewish survivors forced to exist in foreign territory? The alphabetic form creates a strong beginning in each of those lines and when combined with the *qinah* meter, which creates a certain weakness at the ends of lines, the effect is significant. Each of these lines has a certain anticlimax of form; a defeat of sorts. This is the poetry of a well-planned funeral. Finally, in the last short poem (Chapter 5), the alphabetic form breaks down, which may in fact be artistically significant, as we will discuss.

We can say a few things about the general content of the poems before we look at each one individually. Here Jerusalem is personified often as daughter Zion or virgin Zion. These metaphors, used in this story of warfare and violence, heighten the sense of helplessness and violation. At times Jerusalem herself speaks in the first person. This calamity of Jerusalem, of course, is the reality experienced by Jewish individuals and the community as a whole. There is nothing theoretical here. Although Jerusalem is personalized in this manner, the poems otherwise are not individual, personal laments. No names or personalized stories of Judeans, victims or survivors, are utilized. This is poetry of the community.

Beside the obvious distraught sorrow apparent in many painful descriptions of disaster, realistic and metaphorical, other emotions and sentiments also come to the fore. Religiously, we can observe a wide range of nuanced sentiment. YHVH is called upon to see the suffering of his people and to be compassionate. He is the hope of the future in one section and called upon to avenge Judah. Conversely, he is pictured as being pitiless, an enemy of his own people, and the ultimate cause of the destruction. On one hand, the people's moral failure is considered to have aroused YHVH's anger and brought his punishment, so we find a call to repentance. On the other, there are clear expressions questioning this moralistic explanation; the suffering innocents cry out. A notion of despair is present in some places, and troubling questions for a person trusting in YHVH conclude the scroll.

I do not want to overplay the negativity of this scroll—it is intriguing and beautiful in many respects. In modern popular usage of Eikhah, the ray of hope that is found in the middle of poem three often receives the most attention. However, hope is certainly not the primary message of the scroll, nor is it the primary religious idea or sentiment. Eikhah cannot be adequately characterized as hopeful. It can be characterized as an honest, exquisitely beautiful, and painful expression of a community reflecting on their experience and their God.

Poem One

This poem is a heart-wrenching expression of disconsolation of Lady Jerusalem. There she sits, weeping, tears on her cheeks. She has no comforters. In verses 1–11 a narrator details her disaster, interrupted once by Jerusalem's own outcry, "Look, YHVH, on my misery! . . ." (1.9). In verses 12–22, Jerusalem speaks and weeps and

POSTER 8.6

SORROW AS FAR AS THE EYE CAN SEE

As far back as the historian's eye can see, human beings have been suffering, and some of the earliest preserved literature is lament—bitter, sad cries to the God(s). In about 2004 BCE, an army of Elamites from the east destroyed the city of Ur, in modern Iraq. After its destruction, a poet writing in Sumerian composed a long lament poem of 436 lines, divided into eleven songs. As is common, the author considers the destruction as the will of the Gods, laments to the Gods, and prays to the Gods for a brighter future for Ur. The poet writes that the Gods, Anu and Enlil had ordered the destruction of Ur against tearful appeals from the Goddess Ningal. Prayers for the future to Ur's patron, Nanna, come in the last song.

> O city, a bitter lament set up as thy lament;
> Thy lament which is bitter—O city, set up thy lament.
> His righteous city which has been destroyed—bitter is its lament;
> His Ur which has been destroyed—bitter is its lament . . .
> The storm ordered by Enlil in hate, the storm which wears away the land
> Covered Ur like a garment, enveloped it like linen.
> The raging storm has attacked unceasingly; the people groan;
> On that day . . . the city into ruins was made; the people groan. . . .
> Its walls were breached; the people groan.
> In its lofty gates, where they were wont to promenade, dead bodies were lying about;
> In its boulevards, where the feasts were celebrated, scattered they lay.
> In all its streets, where they were wont to promenade, dead bodies were lying about;
> In its places, where the festivities of the land took place, the people lay in heaps. . . .
> Ur—its weak and its strong perished through hunger;
> Mothers and fathers who did not leave their houses were overcome by fire;
> The young lying on their mother's laps, like fish were carried off by the waters . . .
> From distant days, when the land was founded,
> O Nanna, the humble who have taken thy path,
> Have brought unto thee their tears of the smitten house; before thee is their cry!
> O Nanna, may thy city which has been returned to its place, step forth gloriously before thee! . . .
> Upon that which the man of offerings has brought, gaze with steadfast eye! . . .
> May every evil heart of its people be pure before thee!
> May the heart of those who dwell in the land be good before thee!

Translated by S. N. Kramer in Pritchard 1969, 455–63.

prays to YHVH for herself, interrupted once by the narrator (1.17). The poem's subject moves back and forth among topics of desolation, hunger, enemies, YHVH's punishment, exile, and prayers. But there is no real progress, no resolution, no sustained argument:

> B itterly weeping in the night, a tear is on her cheek.
> There is none to comfort her of all who loved her.
> All her friends betrayed her; they are her enemies.
> (EIKHAH 1.2)

Poem Two

The second poem, the longest of the five, is a pain-filled dialogue about Jerusalem's destruction by her foe—and her master—YHVH. Using the same poetic and acrostic form as poem one but increasing the lines under each letter, it begins blatantly noting YHVH's treatment of Jerusalem in the third person and explicitly declaring that YHVH has become Israel's enemy:

> The master [YHVH] has humiliated in anger daughter Zion . . . thrown down . . . not remembered . . . destroyed without pity . . . razed in anger . . . consumed . . smashed into ruins . . . destroyed . . . abolished festival and sacrifice . . . scorned . . . determined to destroy . . .
> (EIKHAH 2.1–10)

Then Jerusalem responds briefly with despair (11–12), exhausted by the painful recounting, recalling the deaths of the babies in her midst but not remarking on the status of YHVH. The narrator answers, addressing Jerusalem directly (13–19), and calls her to pray to YHVH. She takes up the invitation (20–22), the poet beautifully smoothing almost imperceptibly the transition from narrator to Jerusalem; they are, after all, the same, in historical reality. And Lady Jerusalem rises to the challenge, not with confession or repentance, but with a challenge to YHVH, and by extension to all who would blithely accept the moralistic conclusion that this destruction is justified by anyone's sin. She commands YHVH to look at the innocent children, women, and elderly he has slaughtered:

> R eview reality, YHVH, and consider to whom you have done this.
> Alas, women ate their babies, the ones they bore.
> Alas, in the sanctuary, priest and prophet were killed.
> (EIKHAH 2.20)

Poem Three

Nearly as long as poem two, poem three is the most structured, with its triple acrostic and its extensive use of the *qinah* mourning rhythm. The medieval verse numbering system most translations use started a new verse with each line, thus tripling the number of verses, though the actual number of words is two less than the previous poem. Because every single line begins with the predetermined letter, there is a strong, artificial stiffness to the structure. But the poet subtly diminishes that rigidity by crossing the boundaries with carry-over themes and sentence subjects. Specifics of Jerusalem's calamity are absent, and the "I" who begins the poems is not Lady Jerusalem but an everyman figure. The poem begins with personal distress, rises like a mountain in the middle to an expression of hope, and returns to sorrow and cries for revenge. More than half (3.1–39) of the poem is a first person "I am the man" speaking of YHVH's affliction, then of his loving loyalty, and finally of his promise for a future of goodness. Such sentiments of hope are the exception in this scroll as a whole, but in the movement of this poem they seem to have had quite an effect, for the speaker shifts to a plural "we" addressing YHVH as "you" and calling for a return to YHVH (40–47). But by the end the tears return and a single person, possibly Jerusalem, speaks again of God in the third person (48–54). In conclusion, YHVH is appealed to that he might bring justice and revenge (55–66). But whether the author thought YHVH even heard is a question to be asked.

Shrouding yourself in anger you pursue us; you kill without pity.

Shrouding yourself in a cloud; prayer passes by.

Scum and rubbish you have made us among the nations.
(EIKHAH 3.43–45)

Poem Four

The fourth poem returns to the acrostic style of poems one and two, though it is only two-thirds the length because each stanza consists of two lines instead of three. Details of Jerusalem's calamity also return in grotesque detail: children begging, burned bodies, and women boiling their children for food. Many of these lines present a picture of Jerusalem before and after disaster hit. In the end, revenge on Edom is contemplated. Unlike the others, this poem contains no prayer and seems decidedly less passionate, though very aware of the horrors.

Consumed with anger is YHVH, he poured out his wrath
He kindled a fire in Zion, and it consumed its foundations.
(EIKHAH 4.11)

Poem Five

Finally, the last poem is the short false acrostic that is perhaps the most personal of all. It is a prayer of the community, written in the plural. It is a prayer of remembrance—recalling the calamities that have come upon them, and a prayer for remembrance—calling YHVH to remember them. Is it significant that the acrostic form has been abandoned? Has the disciplined sense of order been lost? Has the author symbolically given up? Is the attempt at control abandoned? Has the structured, ordered mourning given way to uncontrolled sobbing? But even here one wonders about the ironic thinking of the author or compiler, for in this last poem the classic structure of Hebrew parallelism is the strongest of any of the poems. Has some sense of normality returned? The scroll closes with questions for YHVH.

Community Reflections 8.4

THE USE OF THE EIKHAH

This scroll of Eikhah is another of the five *megillot* from the Ketuvim that are used at specific Jewish sacred times. The observance of Tisha b'Av, **"Ninth of Av,"** falls in the late summer. It is a remembrance and commemoration of the fallen Temple, which was destroyed by Babylonian armies in 586 BCE, and of the **Second Temple,** which was destroyed by Roman armies in 70 CE. Traditionally Tisha b'Av involves fasting and mourning, and the evening service ends with a reading of Eikhah.

> Why have you forgotten us completely?
> Why have you forsaken us?
> Return us, YHVH, to you! And we will return.
> Renew our days as in the past.
> Or have you rejected us forever?
> (EIKHAH 5.20–22)

This final line has been variously translated. With many others, I think it is likely meant as a question, as in verse 20. In any case—statement or question—our scroll leaves the matter of YHVH's rejection open. There is no resolution, happy ending, easy comfort, or promise. Yet the address is still to YHVH. The community takes up its scroll and recites. The community preserves this scroll for future generations and in doing so chooses to preserve their own honest and painful questions for the consideration of future generations. When might they be needed again?

Questions for Further Study

1. For a community recently exiled, what is the value of this kind of lament literature? What might be the value centuries later?

References

Budde, K. "Poetry (Hebrew)," in *A Dictionary of the Bible*, edited by James Hastings, 4:2–3, New York: Scribner's Sons, 1903.

Hillers, Delbert R. "Lamentations, Book of," in *The Anchor Bible Dictionary*, edited by David N. Freedman, 4:137–41. New York: Doubleday, 1992.

Landy, Francis. "Lamentations," in *The Literary Guide to the Bible*, edited by Robert Alter and Frank Kermode, 329–34. Cambridge, MA: Harvard, 1987.

Linafelt, Tod. *Surviving Lamentations: Catastrophe, Lament, and Protest in the Afterlife of a Biblical Book*. Chicago: University of Chicago, 2000.

Pritchard, James R. *Ancient Near Eastern Texts*. Princeton: Princeton University, Press, 1969.

Slavitt, David R. *The Book of Lamentations*. Baltimore: Johns Hopkins, 2001.

קֹהֶלֶת

Ecclesiastes *Qohelet*

Section Outline

Now this just might be the book that can capture the attention of a modern reader, even if nothing else in our library has. It is a book of great paradox—simple and straightforward and at the same time complex and enigmatic. I suppose it's only fitting then that we are not quite sure just what the Hebrew name *Qohelet*, pronounced "Ko-*heh*-let" means. It comes from a common Hebrew verb meaning "to gather, assemble," and it seems to be used as a personal name or title in the first line: "the words of Qohelet, son of David . . . (1.1).

But the form of the word seems to be a feminine singular, as if it might refer to the "assembly" of people or things that are being gathered, though exceptions have been found of other masculine words that also take this similar form in Hebrew. So maybe it's best to see the title as meaning a "gatherer" or "collector" of wisdom, people, or something else. The English title, *Ecclesiastes*, is a direct transliteration of the ancient Greek title, which means "one who summons or assembles a gathering of citizens." Much later Christian translations, especially Protestant, took this as meaning "preacher," but that does not really reflect the word well. Going back to the Hebrew title, I'm not sure what *Qohelet* might have conjured up in an ancient reader's mind, but we can see from the use of the word in this scroll that Qohelet is involved in a search (1.12–13; 7.27; 12.9–10). Qohelet is presented as a seeker who also teaches. This scroll then is a research report, written by an explorer.

LITERARY FORMAT AND MOVEMENT

Literarily, Qohelet is interesting and elusive to describe. The scroll is presented as the autobiographical personal reflections on the experience of life by a wise man. The scroll at times has a conversational manner—a conversation that the reader is allowed to overhear—as the figure Qohelet talks about and to himself (e.g., 1.12; 2.1). We might think of the written form almost at a personal journal or travel book. These personal reflections or thematic musings incorporate several different literary forms. We find poems, long and short a variety of proverbs and traditional sayings; anecdotes; direct instruction; rhetorical questions; and theme mottos. Like many conversations, the design or flow is nearly impossible to outline according to some clear logical plan, and modern scholars chart its movements in many different ways. Therefore, I have not charted the arrangement of the large middle section of the scroll. As soon as you start reading it, I think you'll see how the writing is smooth but not systematic. This conversation flows easily from one topic to another and often circles around and takes up a thematic thread in another way. One scholar and careful reader, Jacques Ellul, had used an analogy of weaving: The scroll has threads of various colors moving in and out. Some are distinct, some are common, and they form a united whole cloth, but the appearance of any one thread is unpredictable.

There are some literary landmarks in the book that stand out in the flow of the writing. After a narrator's superscription or title (1.1), we find immediately the controlling thesis and motto of Qohelet in 1.2: Everything is *hevel. Hevel* is the Hebrew metaphor that dominates the entire scroll. It occurs throughout the work nearly 40 times and is the grand conclusion in 12.8. Thus, as introduction and conclusion, it forms bookends, known as an *inclusio,* around the whole composition. After the conclusion there is an explicitly denoted epilogue; another narrator makes a few parting comments on Qohelet's already completed composition. In the course of the large central section of reflection we find not only numerous short poems, but also three major ones, all of which are beautiful and memorable themed compositions that relate directly to the prose material around them. The first and last poems are prominently placed just inside the thesis bookends. Finally, careful readers have noted that event the loose prose of Qohelet rings with poetic forms and style.

| 1.1 Narrator's superscription | 1.2–3 Thesis poem and driving question | 1.4–12.7 Exploring question, discoveries, and conclusions; major poems at 1.4–11; 3.1–8; 12.3–7 | 12.8 Restatement of thesis | 12.9–14 Narrator's epilogue |

Qohelet is another Jewish example (with Job and Proverbs) of ancient wisdom literature. Qohelet has a personal and universal perspective; its themes and concerns are not distinctly Israelite. Qohelet operates in universal categories, not national ones. We do not find references to Israel's particular traditions, such as the Exodus, wilderness, or exile, and there is no concern of Israelite versus non-Israelites. The values that dominate Qohelet consist of wisdom, knowledge, searching, right-ness (righteousness), ignorance, folly, vice, and wrong. Qohelet is certainly not secular, if by that we mean not concerned with God or religion—Qohelet frequently refers to God, but not in a way that is peculiar to the Israelite cult or Israelite historical traditions.

Date and Authorship

Most likely Qohelet was composed in the Persian period of Israel's history when Jews lived both in Syria-Palestine and other places of the empire and even beyond it, around the late fifth or early fourth century BCE. The late form of the Hebrew used and a few Persian words make the dating fairly clear, though it is possible that it may be even later, as some scholars argue. By this time it was a well-established and non-controversial literary convention to compose a work in the name of a great sage or person of the past. Our scroll never uses his name, but Solomon, the "patron saint" of Jewish wisdom, is presented as the author in a slightly veiled fashion. We recall from earlier that Solomon's name is behind parts of the scroll of Proverbs, and we will see later that another book, the Wisdom of Solomon, is attributed to him as well. Therefore, our learned author Qohelet takes on the persona of Israel's wisest king. The royal imagery is then wonderfully exploited in the scroll by giving Qohelet, the exploring and searching character, all the available resources for his exploration. Solomon is the perfect character for Qohelet to assume, not only because he was perceived as wise, but also because his wealth allows Qohelet to explore everything under the sky for his quest (1.13, 16; 2.1, 9). The scroll of Kings illustrates well the reputation for learning that Solomon had (1 Kings 10).

The Quest

We have already noted that our scroll is written as the reflections of a wise man with a quest. This searching imagery is prevalent throughout the scroll. But, a quest for what? To put it succinctly in modern terms, we might say Qohelet is searching for meaning, humanly fulfilling knowledge, and wisdom in the experience of life, which is always lived in the shadow of death.

> What is the benefit for a human in his toil that he toils at under the sun? . . .
> I, Qohelet, when king over Israel in Jerusalem, set my mind to search out and understand with wisdom all that is done under the sun.
> (QOHELET 1.3, 12)

Qohelet the searcher narrates his extensive search to understand what is good and what makes one happy (2.3, 24) and to discover how human life fits with the ways of God (9.1). The presentation of Qohelet's exploration indicates that he will search exhaustively. He explores subjects such as wealth, wisdom, justice, pleasure, labor, nature, and human relationships. I would even add religion, but religion is not a distinct category for Qohelet. What we might call religion imbues all of Qohelet's writing; God is a part of the entire equation of Qohelet's quest and its results.

The Findings

What Qohelet finds is the theme of the work and is so often explicitly described as the result of searching that no one could miss it. There is no suspense. Qohelet finds *hevel:* "*Hevel* of *hevels,* says Qohelet, *hevel* of *hevels*; all is *hevel,*" or "So much vapor, says Qohelet, so much vapor, all is vapor" (1.2).

In our scroll, *hevel* is a metaphor; the literal meaning of the word can be "air," "vapor," "breath," "mist," or "steam." It conjures up images of fog and clouds. Most modern translators of Qohelet opt to explain the metaphor whenever it is used in our scroll, and so they go with an abstract English word such as *vanity, futility,* or *meaninglessness,* all connotations that the metaphor can have. But in such a poetic book I prefer to leave the original metaphors intact, honoring the artistry of the author and also allowing the reader to hear the text as ancients would have heard it, leaving the original open-ended metaphor intact. English translators should follow their own example of translating another metaphor, "chasing after the wind":

> All is vapor,
> and chasing after the wind.

In all nine places that the "chasing wind" metaphor occurs, with or without the "vapor" metaphor (1.14, 17; 2.17, 26; 4.4, 6, 16; 5.16; 6.9), modern translators don't explain the second metaphor, "chasing after the wind." "Chasing the wind" is no more literally intended than "vapor," and to attempt to explain it would diminish the depth, openness, and beauty of the poetic expression.

So, just what does this vapor found by Qohelet encompass? Put negatively, we can say what Qohelet did not find. Qohelet did not find the secret to what makes life good or to happiness. He searched high and low, and he did not find a wonderful plan that gave meaning to human experience and history. He did not find a way to make sense of and understand all that goes on under the sun, in life, experience, and nature.

> All this I tested by wisdom. I had said, "I will understand."
> But it (understanding) is too far from me.
> What happens is far and so very deep; who can find it out? (7.23–24)

> When I set my mind to know wisdom, and to understand the business going on on the earth . . . I saw all the work of God, that no human is able to find out the happenings that happen under the sun.
> No matter how much the human works to discover it, he will not find out, and even if someone says he is wise (enough) to know, he cannot find out (8.16–17).

In these passages, Qohelet declares that the understanding of life, its meaning, and God's ways in it are elusive; he is not able to understand. This is the human predicament according to the author: we cannot know, and those who claim to have it all figured out, don't. This is also the major irony and paradox of the scroll. By using his wisdom, the author undermines traditional wisdom's claims to knowing. Who can possibly know what is best for a man to do in life (6.12)? Who can discover the secret of what happens (7.23–24)? God's actions cannot be foreseen or understood (11.1–5). Time and chance happen to all (9.11). As a wisdom writer, Qohelet exhibits a brutal honesty within the wisdom tradition, and he does value wisdom above all else. But he is willing to follow his observations wherever they lead, even if they subvert his own tradition. For Qohelet, wisdom is wise only when it knows what it does not know.

The results of Qohelet's search are also put positively in the scroll. There is one theme under which all others (including the negative result), can be subsumed: *hevel.* Over and over again the seeker declares that no matter where he looked he found life under the sun to be *hevel.* If we look at Qohelet's prose, it is not difficult to explain the metaphor, because he often spells it out! Qohelet finds

- his experience and understanding of life under the sun to be insubstantial and unsatisfying;
- human existence and its goodness to be transient and short lived; and
- life so often to be foul and vexing; injustices and evils abound. (Miller 1997, 449)

Often getting very specific, Qohelet sees life as full of contradictions, such as events that don't make sense according to rules of justice (e.g., 4.1–6). Who can understand? Who can grasp the wind? And, according to Qohelet, God is in control of all, and humans have little or no control. Who can direct the fog? Qohelet finds that the world is an endless repetition with no ultimate gain. Nothing is ever new; all people are eventually dead and forgotten. Death brings everything—just or unjust, dog or lion—to Sheol, that dark, foul place of being forgotten (3.19–22; 9.4–10). It is, in the end, death that overshadows all and brings all to *hevel* (2.14–15; 3.20).

In his subversion, negativity, and sensation of realities of life, Qohelet has not infrequently been compared to other writers throughout history, such as Albert Camus with his concept of the absurdity of life. As one author puts it, this sense of the world "has occurred at intervals throughout history, whenever a thinker or a literary artist has become acutely aware of the gap between the human power of understanding and the unintelligibility of the universe. Its basic principle is that man has no access to the so-called 'transcendent.'" [Weightman 1998, 26] Biblical scholar Michael Fox writes of Camus and Qohelet, "The two thinkers are aligned also in their unflinching determination to strip away illusions and to face life's harsh irrationality" (Fox 1999, 10).

Method of the Search

How does Qohelet know? What was his research method? What is his epistemology? Of course, the scroll's poetic author does not articulate precise scientific or philosophical propositional declarations, but he does, in his own artistic way, speak of his method of knowing. Overtly stated, his method is the "way of wisdom" (see 1.13; 7.23–25; 8.16). This includes experiential testing (2.1), observation of natural events and human behavior (3.10; 4.1, 4, 7; 9.11, 13), study and reflection (8.16), and drawing conclusions based on those reflections (1.14; 3.10–12; 9.1). To put it in modern terms, Qohelet follows a basic theistic, rational empiricism. What he does not depend on are special divine revelations, prophetic words, divinely inspired or authoritative texts. There is no assumption or use of Israelite traditions about Moses or YHVH's words to ancestors.

Resulting Advice

Qohelet never advises despair from living, and he does not shy away from giving instruction. Perhaps nothing is clearer in this scroll than Qohelet's teaching to enjoy life. Whatever stage of life you are in, Qohelet advises that one makes the most of it, for soon it will be gone. The examples are numerous: See 3.9–13; 5.17–18 (or 18–19); 8.15; 9.7–9; 11.7–12.2.

> So I myself praise enjoyment. For the only good for a human under the sun is to eat and drink and to enjoy; and it will be with him in the toil of the days of his life that God gives to him under the sun. (8.15)

In fact, Qohelet has plenty of explicit advice. Another general teaching would be would be to think wisely. Even knowing the profound limitations of human knowledge, Qohelet is still extolling the virtues of wisdom:

- Think about God and God's ways (7.13–14; 12.1).
- Think about death (7.2).
- Think critically about what people say (7.21–22).

Qohelet includes some generic religious instructions:

- Fear God (7.18).
- Don't be overly pious (7.14–18).

Finally, we could say that Qohelet, in a spirit similar to the Latin poet Horace (65 to 8 BCE), advises his reader to seize the day. *Carpe diem!*

- Take risks (11.1–6)
- Enjoy what you have while you have it (2.24; 5.17 [or 18]; 7.14; 8.15).

> Anything that your hand finds to do, do it with all your might, for there is no doing, or thinking, or knowing, or wisdom in Sheol where you are going (9.10).

God and *Hevel*

The Jewish author of Qohelet never uses the particular Israelite name for God, YHVH. But Elohim, as a single sovereign but inscrutable deity over all humankind, is referred to often. For Qohelet—this is extremely important to make clear— Elohim does not save life from its *hevel*-ness, its transience, and all its vexing characteristics. God does not provide the happy answer to Qohelet's relentless questioning nor the positive resolution to his negative conclusions. But God is always a part of Qohelet's equation and cannot be extracted from his arguments, expressions, or rhetoric. It would be disingenuous to argue that Qohelet contrasts a life of *hevel*-ness with a life lived with God. For Qohelet, all of life is lived with God, and all of life under the sun is lived in *hevel*-ness. In this sense, Qohelet is deeply religious, even if his views of what constitutes proper religion and acceptable conclusions differ from what others at his time had chosen to accept. Qohelet never refers to his God as *hevel; hevel*-ness is the pervasive phenomenon of human experience. Yet Qohelet leaves little doubt as to who is ultimately in charge:

> All this I took to my mind to ascertain: the right-doing person and the wise one, and all their actions are in God's power, and also love, and also hate! And a human does not know any of this beforehand. (9.1)

The Epilogue

The end of the scroll, 12.9–14, contains one or more distinct epilogues. Scholars have differed as to whether or not the end was added by a later author or if it may have been an epilogue of the original composition. Because it reads more traditionally in religious terms, some have thought that it was added to tone down the earlier radical and skeptical words of Qohelet, though the praise for Qohelet and his words is clear and direct in 12.9–10. Others have interpreted the few words of the epilogue to be later observations that are not in conflict with the central teachings of the scroll, finding parallels to the epilogue in the body of the scroll. Other scholars have seen contradictions between the epilogue and body but noted that Qohelet, even in the body of the work, is at home with paradoxes and contradictions of life and thought. Still others have seen it as another persona of the original author, distancing himself from the words of Qohelet. In any case, nothing in the epilogue, much less in the body of the scroll, indicates that Qohelet was intended to be read as some sort of negative lesson; as what might happen to you if you pursue this impious way. Qohelet's words may be difficult, but after all, "The sayings of the wise are like goads and nails!" (12.10). Indeed, these nails have made many people uncomfortable!

Qohelet in the Library

There is little doubt that the teachings of Qohelet contrast with ideas of some other scrolls of our library; there are also some parallels too. But overall, Qohelet is not what many people have been trained to expect from biblical literature. Commentators have been commenting on that fact for thousands of years. I have often wondered if Qohelet would be valued and included in some religious traditions if it were freshly discovered by an archaeologist today, instead of being in the Bible. In the end, Qohelet's readers are left with choices about what impact Qohelet will have and how his words will be perceived. There are many modern

Community Reflections 8.5

THE USE OF QOHELET (ECCLESTIASTES)

As one of the five *megillot*, Qohelet is read at Sukkot (Tabernacles), the most joyous of Judaism's fall holiday season, akin to Thanksgiving Day in many cultures. This reading tradition developed long ago, and the reasoning behind the choices is not clearly known today. Modern Jewish writers have wondered why a negative, skeptical book such as Qohelet is read time of joy. One author has answered that it is precisely for the irony and contrast:

> The juxtaposition of piety and skepticism, irreconcilable as they may appear, seems to belong to the whole paradox of the Jewish mind. Faith and Reason write one upon the other in the palimpsest of our past. Perhaps it was to strike the balance of sanity that the Fathers of the Synagogue chose the recital of Ecclesiastes, with its melancholy refrain "Vanity of vanities, all in vanity," on the Festival of Tabernacles when the Jew is commanded to rejoice. At all events, it is hard to escape the judgment that the major emphasis of Jewish thinking has indeed been that of setting our shoulders joyously to the world's wheel. That we have spared ourselves some unhappiness by, beforehand, slipping the Book of Ecclesiastes beneath our arm, seems like wise truth.

—Abraham Cohen, 1952, 105.

books that seek to turn Qohelet into some sort of negative lesson or seek to make it somehow appear that he is in agreement with the other scrolls. That exercise always seems to muzzle Qohelet and only demonstrates what the authors want to hear. As with all the other books, we do not know why this scroll was included in our library, because we lack all records of those decisions. At the very least we can say that those who selected the scrolls for this library were open to including even such a scroll as this. Perhaps our library imagery is most important here, so that we can allow this scroll to speak with its own singular integrity and not smother it with external systems of thought.

Questions for Further Study

1. What are the primary religious teachings of the wise man Qohelet? How do they relate in detail to religious teachings else where in our library?

2. As a literary critic, how would you characterize and describe the format and "plan" of this scroll?

3. What thinkers and authors of other cultures and times most remind you of Qohelet?

References

Cohen, Abraham. *The Five Megilloth.* London: Soncino, 1952.

Crenshaw, James L. "Ecclesiastes, Book of," in *The Anchor Bible Dictionary,* edited by David N. Freedman, 2:271–80. New York: Doubleday, 1992.

———*Ecclesiastes, Old Testament Library.* Philadelphia: Westminster, 1987.

Fox, Michael V. *A Time to Tear Down and A Time to Build Up: A Rereading of Ecclesiastes.* Grand Rapids, MI: Eerdmans, 1999.

Miller, D. "Qohelet's Symbolic Use of הבל," *Journal of Biblical Literature* 117 (1998): 437–54.

Seow, C. L. *Ecclesiastes, The Anchor Bible.* New York: Doubleday, 1997.

Weightman, John. *The Outsider* [Review of *Albert Camos: A Life*]. New York Review of Books 45.1 (1998): 26–29.

Williams, James G. "Proverbs and Ecclesiastes" in *The Literary Guide to the Bible*, edited by Robert Alter and Frank Kermode, 262–82. Cambridge, MA: Harvard, 1987.

אסתר

Esther *Estar*

SECTION OUTLINE

If you like fast paced, bold, comical or farcical drama with a powerful villain, a doltish king, a noble hero, and a beautiful and shrewd heroine, you will like this scroll. This story is like no other in our library. Esther and the next scroll, Daniel, are examples of what we call diaspora literature works composed by a Jew about living a Jewish life in a foreign land (see Chapter 3, p. 59). In historical terms, we would say that diaspora literature is set in the period of exile, after the Southern Kingdom of Judah fell to the Babylonian armies in the first decades of the sixth century BCE and many Jews were transported to Babylon. After Jews were allowed to return to the area of Syria-Palestine by the policy of the new Persian conquerors (539 BCE), many did go back to their land in Judah and Jerusalem, and their stories are told in books such as Ezra-Nehemiah. However, many others who still maintained their Jewish identity preferred to remain in Babylon where they had now been settled for several generations. Some of the exiles moved to other places in the Persian Empire, and so from at least the middle of the sixth century BCE the Jewish diaspora was a significant reality of Jewish life, and Jewish culture produced literature reflecting that reality. In our library, the scrolls of Daniel and Esther are stories set in diaspora contexts. Esther is placed in the Persian Empire, and the stories of Daniel are set in either Babylonian or Persian locations. Another example of diaspora literature is the scroll of Tobit, which is in Catholic and Christian orthodox biblical libraries.

Estar, besides being a unique and entertaining story with a clear didactic purpose, is also an interesting specimen to see how the content of a scroll can change and develop over time. For many scrolls of our library we only have one

*L*iterary Format and Movement

The Hebrew Estar scroll fits well into a loose genre of Jewish literature that has been called diaspora novella. This is a short story about a Jews living in a foreign country who encounter a crisis because of a threat from the larger culture to their life or well-being. The crisis places the Jew(s) in a dilemma that calls upon her or him to act for or against her/his Jewish identity, usually at substantial personal risk. The stories normally do not present the Jewish antagonists as powerless victims, but rather as strong, astute, and highly successful, even when measured by the standards of the larger foreign culture. Besides having a literary entertainment value, these stories provide models of successful Jewish life in a foreign culture for the thousands of Jews who lived throughout Greek cultures. The story of Joseph in Egypt, found in Genesis 39–50, has many similarities to this genre. Estar is another such story, with four main characters, two of whom are Jewish, Mordecai and Estar, and two of whom are foreign, the Persian king and his anti-Jewish head of state, Haman. Estar is not a subtle, erudite work of literature, such as the scroll of Job. It seems a work more popular than sophisticated, clever, and comical, with characters painted in bold strokes. Though combining elements of mortal threat, violence, hatred, and suspense, it manages to maintain a distinct lightness. The narrative action vocabulary is small but still has descriptive specifics. The story contains a more descriptive content and less dialogue than we are accustomed to in classical Hebrew narrative. You can see this for yourself just by comparing a couple pages in the scrolls of Estar and Rut. Estar's settings are royal and always places of power. The narrative cleverly moves among six royal banquets—beginning, middle, and end—to tell its tale of crisis, courage, reversal, and triumph. Reversal is perhaps the leading theme; the end of the story turns nearly everything around!

1.1–24 Banquets 1 and 2; King Ahasuerus's banquet; Queen Vashti's fall from throne	2.1–23 Estar the new, beautiful, loyal queen and her cousin Mordecai	3.1–15 Haman wins over Ahasuerus in plot to kill all the Jews.	4.1–17 Mordecai pleads with Estar to appeal to Ahasuerus.
5.1–8.8 Banquets 3 and 4; Estar's plan; Ahasuerus honors Mordecai; Haman unmasked and executed; triumph of Estar and Mordecai	8.9–9.17 Banquet 5; triumph of the Jews over enemies; celebrations	9.18–32 Banquet 6; instructions for celebration of Purim for all Jews	10.1–3 Appendix on Ahasuerus and Mordecai

basic version of the scroll, and if we are interested in the textual history we are left to speculate from clues in that one version what earlier versions may have looked like. In some cases though, like this scroll of Esther, very different ancient versions still exist, and we can see clearly the changes that editors and authors made over time. In this case, it is not because of the discovery of the Dead Sea Scrolls that we have an alternative version; it is because the two different Greek versions of Esther preserve later alternative editions. The most well-known Greek version presents the same basic story, but it has a very different overall character by making substantial additions and deletions. You might recall that with the scroll of Jeremiah, the older version is to be found in Greek Bibles as confirmed by Dead Sea manuscripts. For Esther, the situation is reversed. The younger alternative version exemplified in Greek manuscripts exists in Roman Catholic and Christian Orthodox Bibles, and the older version exemplified in Hebrew manuscripts is in Jewish and Protestant Bibles.

For once, the name of the book in English is pronounced almost identically to the name in Hebrew, *Estar*. The irony is that the name Estar, pronounced "ehs-*ter*," is not her Hebrew name. We learn in Estar 2.7 that her Hebrew name is Hadassah, but the story uses her foreign name. Like Jews in other diaspora tales (see Daniel 1.6–7) and mirroring actual practice of many Jews, Estar has two names; each one denotes one of the cultures in which she lives. Her story is very much about how she self-identifies, negotiates, and thrives both as Jewa and as a member in a larger foreign culture. The author of Estar writes not only to provide reason for celebration but also for emulation.

Dramatic Setting and Plot

Many Jewish communities existed in various places in the Persian empire for more than 200 years; from 539 BCE, when the powerful Persian king Cyrus conquered Babylon, until late fourth century when the Macedonian Alexander the Great replaced the Persian Empire with his own. Many Jews did not leave Babylon to return to their homeland in Syria-Palestine even when they were allowed to do so by Cyrus and his successors. They had attained some measure of success and also maintained their Jewish identity and traditions. The scroll of Estar is a part of their legacy. It is set at the highest levels of Persian society at the winter palace in the city of Susa, a famous city of antiquity, now in Iran, where a significant Jewish population lived. The king, who in our English texts is Ahasuerus, is better known to us in other history writing as Xerxes I, who ruled from 485 to 464 BCE. The story begins at a 180-day party! thrown by Ahasuerus for all officials, governors, and the army. All goes well until Queen Vashti refuses to come perform as a spectacle at the command of a drunken Ahasuerus. The author develops the character of the king almost completely—impulsive, misogynist, extreme, easily swayed, and not so bright—by the end of the first episode. Vashti is deposed, and the king is persuaded to hold a beauty pageant, Persian style, to choose a new queen. At this point the orphaned Estar and her cousin Mordecai, who raised her, are introduced.

Mordecai was a government official and at one time had saved the king's life. Estar, of course, is beautiful, and she is among all eligible beautiful virgins from across the empire brought to Susa and given a twelve-month beauty treatment. Each virgin went by turn to king, spent the night with him, and then was taken to the harem. Needless to say, the king selected Estar, who was "admired by everyone who saw her" (2.15), and she became the new queen. This all happened without Estar making known that she was Jewish.

And now comes the crisis in the person of Haman, the megalomaniac whom the king has just promoted above all other officials. Mordecai had refused to bow down in obeisance to Haman, and so Haman decides to take revenge on this one Jew by having the entire Jewish population of the empire destroyed. By smooth rhetoric and a large bribe he manages to convince the king to issue such the empire-wide order. However, the king is still ignorant of his queen's Jewish identity. **Lots,** a kind of dice, and known here by their Babylonian name, *pur,* are thrown to determine the date of the Jewish extermination, and Haman has a gallows built for Mordecai that is 75 feet (22.86 m) high. In the remainder of the story Haman's sinister plot unravels suspensefully, but only because of the astute planning and actions of Mordecai and especially Estar, who must try to change the immutable order of Ahasuerus. In the end, everything is reversed; Mordecai is raised in position, Haman is hung on the gallows he built for Mordecai, and the Jews of the empire are given permission to kill their enemies on the very day that they were supposed to be killed by them. The reversals and ironies pile up, including the name of the holiday that was instituted to celebrate the Jewish triumph, *Purim*—named after the lots that were cast to determine the date of their destruction.

Date and Composition History

If Estar is a story set during the reign of Xerxes I (485 to 464 BCE) then it must have been written after that. Because the work has many Persian words with Hebrew spellings in it but no Greek ones, many scholars believe it was written prior to the fall of Persian Empire and the spread of Greek culture, which started around 323 BCE. Others suggest that the lack of Greek words does not necessarily rule out a Greek period dating, because the author may simply have been true to the Persian setting in telling his story. In any case, the Hebrew form of Estar that we have in our scroll is usually dated somewhere in the late fifth to third centuries BCE, though some put it even later. The reality of Jews living as foreigners in another culture is continuous, beginning in the sixth century BCE until today.

Estar and History

The scroll of Estar is not subtle, restrained, or modest. It is full of easily recognized exaggerations, and though replete with colorful facts and details, it hardly comes across as historical. Although the ancient author did use some actual facts of the

Persian customs, he also gave his imagination great liberty to create numerous nonhistorical details to make his story lively and entertaining. For example, in case anyone thought it serious history, Persian kings did not choose their queens by having sex with virgins night after night. This imaginative trait is characteristic of the diaspora novella genre as a whole and can be easily observed in Judith and Tobit (see Chapter 9), parts of Daniel, and other diaspora novellas. Just a few of the details that are false or unproven can be mentioned here: Persia was not administratively divided into 127 satrapies, Persian laws were not unchangeable, the 180-day party for all the leaders was unlikely, there is no record of Xerxes's wives Vashti and Estar or of governmental permission for ethnic slaughter. Of course, there is no need to think that the scroll is somehow less worthy of our time because it is not a historical report.

On the other hand, there are likely other important historical realities behind the story. These would include realities of

- successful Jews in non-Jewish settings,
- retaining and maintaining Jewish identity as distinct from other citizens,
- successful individual Jews advocating for their Jewish community,
- encountering anti-Jewish persons, and
- general pro-Persian attitudes among Jews.

Estar is about Jews who succeed at the highest levels of society but who also have the highest sense of responsibility for their people, the entire Jewish community. Therefore they use their positions of power and their acumen and savvy to save the entire Jewish population when it is threatened. It is both entertaining and didactic. The scroll is by no means anti-Persian, though it pokes some fun at the king. The storyteller's only real enemies are those people who hate Jews, and Haman himself is non-Persian. Interestingly, the author makes Haman the nationality of an ancient proverbial enemy of Israel, long before the Persians were involved with Jews. Haman is an Agagite, that is, a descendant of the Amalekite king Agag. You can read about that tribe's fights with the Israelite tribe of Benjamin, Mordecai's tribe, in 1 Samuel 15.

Estar and Religion

In all our discussion so far it is interesting to note that we have not mentioned God or YHVH. That is because the Hebrew scroll of Esther has absolutely no mention of God. Mordecai and Esther maintain their Jewish identity, but even that is not overtly defined in religious terms in our story. Religious customs or practices are not mentioned either; there are no prayers; no talk of YHVH's blessing, covenant, or revelation. They are not concerned with eating kosher food (compare Daniel 1) or following divine rules or Mosaic laws. The author pictures Jews as having distinct customs (3.8), but they are not noted in a manner that we could describe as religious. The rather generic and cross-cultural practice of fasting is mentioned twice (4.16, 9.31) but that is the extent of the religious activity.

Shouldn't Mordecai and Estar have prayed at such a time of crisis? Shouldn't the celebrations be thanksgiving to God for his protection? Some readers have found a hint of religion in Mordecai's general question to Estar of her life's purpose: "Who knows? Maybe for this time, you have arisen to the throne" (4.14). But religious implications are hardly obvious in the question, and it is certainly not robustly religious.

Of course, part of the difficulty here is our modern category of religious, which will differ among us and would certainly differ from the ancient categories of the author of Estar. Would he be able to understand what we mean by religious? But we do not have to solve this issue in order to make the point strongly that Hebrew Estar does not fit well into common modern conceptions of religious, especially those informed by the institutions of the Abrahamic religions. Many will be surprised to find here among biblical literature a scroll that doesn't even mention Israel's God and is not religious in modern terms. A second equally strong point that can be made is that Estar contrasts sharply with many other books in our library. It shares with Song of Songs the distinction of not mentioning God, but it is the only narrative scroll to not do so. Estar is a fine demonstration of the willingness of the founders of this Jewish library to include diverse perspectives and approaches. This library is not religiously monolithic and not all of it is even religious. One final comment: If you're interested in a religious Estar, don't stop here; make sure examine the Greek version of Estar.

A Later Version

As with all the other scrolls of our library, modern readers have tried to figure out the compositional history of Estar. There are several ideas about how the Hebrew Estar came to be in the form in which we now have it. In the case of Estar, there is irrefutable evidence confirming the idea that these ancient documents were often shaped and supplemented and edited over time, because we also possess from antiquity a later version of Estar. In this case it is not from the Dead Sea Scrolls. In fact, Estar is the only scroll of the Hebrew Bible that was not preserved among the Dead Sea Scrolls. Instead we turn to Greek texts. The later version of Estar has six large insertions in the text comprising 107 verses. This represents a substantial addition, because in the earlier version of our Hebrew Bible there are only 167 verses, and some of these have been shortened in the later Greek version. The later version is preserved today in Greek manuscripts, but that does not mean that the additions were composed in Greek. In fact, scholars have determined that four of the six were written in Hebrew prior to the scroll being translated into Greek, and two were composed in Greek after the translation was made. The Greek version also has many omissions when compared to the older Hebrew, and there are some places where smaller additions are made to the story. In modern Bibles, you will find that the Roman Catholic and Orthodox Christian churches use the longer version, whereas Jewish and Protestant Bibles contain the shorter version.

POSTER 8.7

Estar 2.20, Older Version	**Estar 2.20, Later Version**
But Estar did not mention her kin and her people as Mordecai instructed her; for Estar did what Mordecai said, even as she did when she was with him.	But Estar did not reveal her country; for thus Mordecai had commanded her to fear God and to keep all his laws, even as when she was with him, and Estar did not alter her mode of life.

The later and longer version gives additional background material at the beginning of the book and supplies some of the official correspondence of the King Ahasuerus. But by far the most dramatic change is to the religious character of the scroll. In this late version Israel's God is everywhere, appearing over 50 times in both the six large additions as well as in other places. Furthermore, Estar and Mordecai become much more religious: They pray, observe kosher rules of eating, and refer to traditions about Jerusalem and Abraham. See, for example, the following textual comparison in Poster 8.7, which is just one of the hundreds that could be mentioned. In this case, the narrator mentions God and Estar's keeping of God's commands.

In other places the newer edition also refers to the sins of Israel as the cause of the Jewish crisis and says God intervenes on behalf of Estar. In many ways, especially religiously, it is a different story.

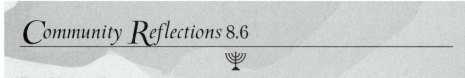

Community Reflections 8.6

THE USE OF ESTAR

Estar is the scroll of the *Five Megillot*, which is read for the early spring festival of Purim. The historical origins of Purim are debated by historians and, frankly, are somewhat lost in the fog of history. But the scroll of Estar provides a story for its origin, and this story is central in Jewish celebrations of Purim.

For a modern American unfamiliar with Purim celebrations, this might help: Purim feels a bit like a combination of Halloween, Mardi Gras, and April Fool's Day. It is a time of happiness, fun, and even silliness. It is a celebration of good out of bad, reversals, salvation, and a spirit of community, with revelry and generosity, even as Mordecai himself had instructed (Estar 9.20–23).

Questions for Further Study

1. As a historian, what sources would you use to investigate the Persian historical setting of Estar?
2. As a feminist critic, what would you make of how are men and women depicted in this story? What is surprising, traditional, or ironic?

References

Berg, Sandra Beth. *The Book of Esther: Motifs, Themes, and Structure.* Missoula, MT: Scholars Press, 1979.

Clines, David J. A. *The Esther Scroll: The Story of the Story.* Sheffield, England: Sheffield University, 1984.

Moore, Carey A. "Esther, Book of," in *The Anchor Bible Dictionary,* edited by David N. Freedman, 2:633–43. New York: Doubleday, 1992.

Moore, Carey A. *Esther.* Garden City, NY: Doubleday, 1975.

Sasson, Jack M. "Esther," in *The Literary Guide to the Bible,* edited by Robert Alter and Frank Kermode, 335–42. Cambridge, MA: Harvard, 1987.

דניאל

Daniel *Daniyel*

SECTION OUTLINE

Literary Format and Movement

Ancient Daniyel Stories

The Longer Version

Daniyel's Dramatic Settings, History, and Date of
  Composition

Apocalyptic Literature and Daniyel

Where to Put Daniyel?

Questions for Further Study

References

One of the most famous stories from our library is probably "Daniel in the Lion's Den." Daniel stories were probably very popular in antiquity as well, but we'll get to that a little later. For now we'll simply say that this scroll is a collection of stories about a young Jewish male named *Daniyel,* pronounced in Hebrew as "dah-nee-*yale*"; only one story in the scroll does not mention Daniyel. All of the stories are set in a Jewish community outside of the Jewish homeland. Like Esther, there is more to these writings than a good story. The rhetorical purpose seems clearly didactic; how should one self-identify, negotiate, and even thrive as a Jew living as a minority in a larger foreign culture?

Similar to Estar, in the case of Daniyel we first have to determine which scroll of Daniyel to use. Religious communities have preserved two—the shorter form used in Jewish and Protestant traditions and the longer form found in Roman Catholic and Christian Orthodox Bibles. The shorter form is preserved in Hebrew texts–the Dead Sea Scrolls and Masoretic Texts—and the longer form is preserved in the Septuagint. Below we will actually look at both short and long versions because both have survived and made it into modern day Bibles.

*L*ITERARY FORMAT AND MOVEMENT

In the case of Daniyel, we could approach the literary form in a couple of ways. If the scroll is a collection of individual Daniyel stories, then maybe we should consider them as individual units. On the other hand, maybe there are connections and developments across the individual units that act as unifying elements. Of course, this is not strictly an either/or proposition, and readers asking literary questions have made fruitful observations from both approaches. The ancient manuscript evidence shows that Daniyel stories existed independently and were sometimes added as single units to larger collections of Daniyel stories. However, in whatever way the units at one time existed independently, they were obviously put together on the same scroll at some point and, with the exception of Chapter 3, they all share one main character, Daniyel.

Looking more closely, we can naturally divide the Hebrew scroll of Daniyel in two, because the first six chapters present six separate narratives about Daniyel's experiences as a highly respected young Jewish wise man in the service of foreign kings. Chapter 3 is a similar story about Daniyel's friends. The last half of the scroll, also in six chapters in modern Bibles, is a different literary genre: a thin narrative with four strong and well-developed apocalyptic visions of Daniyel and their interpretation. The two halves of the scroll are linked by certain religious ideas but not by any continuative plot lines. The two halves share a strong notion of the God of Israel's control of world history and teach in their own respective ways that Jews of the diaspora, even in the face of cruel opposition, should strive to be faithful to their God by keeping his laws because they have confidence in his sovereignty in the past, present, and future.

The first six stories of the Hebrew version are all court tales, stories of Jews who have risen to the top of a foreign government, just below the king, because of their wisdom and skills. In some stories they demonstrate that their wisdom is superior to others in the court, and this superiority is credited to their God (Chapters 1, 2, 4, 5). In others, a crisis develops that involves overwhelming pressure to compromise the hero's loyalty to his God. But at great personal risk he stands firm and his God rescues him from the difficulty (Chapters 3, 6).

In some sense, the court tales about Daniyel in the first half of the scroll, which have shown him to be exceptionally wise, gifted with dream interpretation, and pious, have proven him worthy to be the recipient and proclaimer of his God's revelations in the second half. In another sense, there is a disruption for the Daniyel of the second half of the scroll. Though still wise and pious, he is unable to directly discern the meaning of his own dreams, and an angel must interpret them for him. Perhaps the difference represents an ideological shift.

There are numerous literary shifts in the scroll that likely demonstrate the differing origins of various stories and show the looseness of the collection. For example, 1.1–2.4a and Chapters 8–12 are in Hebrew, but the stories in between are in Aramaic, a language commonly spoken by Jews in the last centuries BCE. Another literary shift occurs in Chapter 7.2, where the scroll moves to a first person narrator style with Daniyel as the narrator; previous stories had been third person narratives about Daniyel. There are also numerous chronological shifts in the various dramatic settings backwards and forwards, putting Daniyel under different kings and empires.

1.1–21 Daniel and his three friends succeed at court; from Nebuchadnezzar to Cyrus	2.1–49 Daniel interprets Nebuchadnezzar's political dream.	3.1–33 Three friends thrown into furnace by Nebuchadnezzar for their piety and are rescued by God. *Long Version: Azariah's prayer and the song from the furnace after verse 23*	4.1–34 Daniel interprets Nebuchadnezzar's second political dream	5.1–29 Daniel reads mysterious writing on wall at Belshazzar's feast.	6.1–29 Daniel is thrown to lions by Darius the Mede for his piety and is rescued by God.
7.1–28 Daniel's vision of four beasts; interpreted by angel	8.1–27 Daniel's vision of ram and goat; interpreted by angel	9.1–27 Daniel reads Jeremiah; interpreted by angel	10.1–12.12 Daniel's fourth vision; interpreted by angel	*Long Version: Daniel exposes Bel as worthless idol, kills dragon, and is rescued by God in lions' den.*	*Long Version: A young Daniel saves Susanna from two lustful Jewish elders.*

Ancient Daniyel Stories

We have quite a number of Daniyel stories preserved from antiquity, besides the ones on the Hebrew scroll. First, we know of three more from Greek manuscripts of this scroll:

- Daniyel exposes the idol of Bel, another name for Marduk, a God of Babylon, to be nothing but a fraud.
- Daniyel kills a dragon/snake that Babylonians revered as a God.
- A young Daniyel rescues a Jewish woman named Susanna from lustful Jewish elders by his wisdom.

These stories were composed in Hebrew or Aramaic and then added at a later time to a Hebrew Daniyel scroll before being translated into Greek. Even in our Greek manuscripts they are not always added in the same place. Often the Susanna tale is placed at the beginning of the scroll, where it makes a good introduction to the wise and virtuous young Daniyel. There are actually two different versions of this story preserved in different Greek manuscripts, and two more different versions of Daniyel 3–6 are also preserved in Greek.

The Dead Sea Scrolls also preserve four Aramaic manuscripts (4Q243–4Q246) with stories of Daniyel that have similarities with those in our scroll. Though the copies are quite fragmentary and likely contained several different episodes, one scroll indicates that Daniyel appeared before King Belshazzar and gave a review of history from the time of the Flood.

Another scroll likely represents an earlier stage of the tale in Daniyel Chapter 4 (VanderKam 1994, 139–41). It states that the Babylonian king Nabonidus is punished by the Jewish God and so converts to worshiping him upon learning that he is the one true God.

The picture that clearly emerges from a great deal of manuscript evidence is that there were many different Hebrew and Aramaic compositions, versions, collections, and Greek translations of Daniyel stories. Much later library builders of Judaism and Christianity selected such collections for their sacred library, and so the Hebrew Bible has a shorter collection, and the Catholic and Orthodox form of the Christian Bibles have a longer version. The Protestant Bible reverts back to the Hebrew form in the case of Daniyel.

But our history of the stories of Daniyel is still not over. A figure named Daniyel was written about long before our scroll's stories were composed. The prophetic book of Ezekiel refers twice to a famous wise man named Daniyel, whom he associates with Noah and Job (Ezekiel 14.14; 28.3). Furthermore, as far back as the thirteenth century BCE a neighboring Semitic people who lived at Ugarit in present-day Syria also told stories of a Daniyel, in their language, *Dnil*, who was a pious judge. The Jewish book of Jubilees, composed during the same centuries as stories in our Daniel scroll was being written, also refers to a Daniyel who lived before the Flood and was the uncle of Enoch (Jubilees 4.20). Though we are not sure of the relationship of all these Daniyel traditions, clearly Daniyel was a widely known literary hero about whom people from Jewish and non-Jewish cultures composed stories.

The Longer Version

The longer version of Daniyel is the form used by the Roman Catholic and Orthodox Christian churches today. The first major addition is today known as "Susanna." It is the story of beautiful Jewish maiden in Babylon who is spied on while bathing by two aging despicable Jewish judges. The villains attempt to convince her to have sex with them, threatening to lie about her in court and bring her to disgrace and death. But she refuses, and they follow through on their threat. Only after being sentenced to death is she saved by the wisdom of Daniyel, whom God had inspired. The old Jewish judges are made to look like doltish rogues by the wiser Jewish youth. In contrast to the other stories of Daniyel, which have their critical arrows aimed at non-Jews, this one involves only Jews and demonstrates that this Jewish author felt free enough to teach and entertain at the expense of Jewish elders and leaders.

The second addition is known as the "Prayer of Azariah" and the "Song of the Three Young Men." If you look at your copy of Daniyel, you'll see in Chapter 3 that three youths get thrown into a fiery furnace. According to the longer addition, added between 3.23 and 34, one of them prays a beautiful poetic prayer for deliverance after which all three sing a long ornate song of praise, blessing their God as the great creator and sustainer of nature and anticipating his salvation.

The final addition, "Bel and the Snake," or "Bel and the Dragon," is a story in two episodes about Daniyel, at the risk of great personal harm, outwitting the priests of Babylon and the Persian King Cyrus. Because it pits a pious Jew against not-so-bright non-Jews, it is in keeping with the stories of Daniyel found in the first six chapters of the version in the library of the Hebrew Bible. One scholar has called this tale "the world's first detective story" (Moore 1992, 27), and it reads in such an entertaining, simplistic fashion. The clear didactic purpose is to entertainingly teach its Jewish audience that their God will protect those who are wise and worship the one and only God instead of the worthless statues and mortal animals that other people worship. It goes without saying that we shouldn't read these stories as if they accurately reflected the religious ideas and beliefs of Persian or Greek priests and temples.

Daniyel's Dramatic Settings, History, and Date of Composition

The stories of Daniyel in our library's collection all begin by stating the time and setting of the story. They range from the third year of King Jehoiakim of Jerusalem, "when Nebuchadnezzar besieged it" (ca. 605 BCE), according to Daniyel 101, to the reign of the Persian king Darius, probably Darius I, 522 to 486 BCE). The first four chapters take place in Babylon under Nebuchadnezzar (604 to 562 BCE; Chapter 5 is set in the final days of Babylon before it fell to the Persians (539 BCE); Chapter 6 seemingly moves ahead to the Persian king Darius (522 BCE); Chapters 7 and 8 go back to Belshazzar (554 to 551 BCE); Chapter 9 again goes to Darius (522 BCE); Chapter 10 moves back to the third year of Cyrus in Babylon (535 BCE); and Chapters 11 and 12 are again with Darius (522 BCE).

It seem highly unlikely to me that ancient readers and composers would have understood this literature as anything close to what we think of as serious documented history. We have no good reason to assume that their obvious religious didactic purpose depended on some sort of modern sense of historicity. The world then and now is full of fictional stories that use real settings to teach what authors and audiences value. Like the scroll of Judith, which we'll come to later, our stories of Daniyel are full of unmistakably non-historical details that would not in the least have bothered authors or hearers, and we have no reason to judge this ancient work by criteria from our modern genre of academic history. For example, no invasion of Jerusalem by Nebuchadnezzar is known to have occurred in 606 or 605 BCE (Daniel 1.1) and in fact a later date is reported in 2 Kings 24.10. Belshazzar was not the last king of Babylon (Daniel 5.30); his father Nabonidus was, and the Persian king who conquered Babylon was not Darius (Daniel 6.1 [or 5.31]); Cyrus was, as attested in dozens of ancient sources, including Ezra-Nehemiah 1.1–3. The king Darius was not a Mede (i.e., from Media) as in Daniel 6.1; 9.1; 11.1; he was a Persian. The kings Nebuchadnezzar and Darius were not converts to the Jewish God (Daniel 2.47; 3.28–33; 4.34; 6.26–28). If we want to consider these stories as an ancient reader might have, we should also recognize that they follow stereotypical literary patterns of a group of writings from the ancient world known as adventures in a foreign royal court. They can be found in Egyptian, Greek, Jewish, Canaanite, and Mesopotamian cultures. One internationally famous story from middle of the first millennium BCE is the "Tale of Ahikar," and in our library we have the scroll of Esther and the story of Joseph, contained in the scroll of Genesis.

Clearly our stories of Daniel were composed after the beginning of the Jewish exile in the sixth century. Precisely when the first six stories (Chapter 1–6) may have originated is hard to say, though King Darius (522 to 486 BCE) is used in Chapter 6, so it must have come after that. Based on the complicated manuscript tradition, many scholars believe that these first chapters were collected in the fourth or third centuries BCE.

The last six chapters (Chapters 7–12), which are a different kind of literature, come quite clearly from the middle of the second century BCE, because they reflect many details of the Jewish conflict and war with their Syrian-Greek rulers in the years 167 to 164. Some of the events of these years are spoken of as revelations to Daniyel, in accord with the common practices of this apocalypic genre. For example, Chapter 11 shows knowledge of actions of numerous Ptolemaic (Southern) and Seleucid (Northern) kings. Most attention is given to Antiochus IV Epiphanes (Daniel 11.21–45), who ruled from 175 to 164 BCE. In 11.31 we read of his desecration of the Jerusalem temple in 168 BCE, also recounted in the book of 1 Maccabbees. In 11.37 we read of Antiochus's failure to respect the Gods of his ancestors, and indeed, Antiochus did much to exalt his own divine status and to replace the Seleucid worship of Apollo with Zeus. But Antiochus's life did not end the way our author predicted, between the Mediterreanean and Jerusalem (11.45). Instead he died in 164 BCE fighting far to the east in Parthia. Clearly, our author's political history—presented as revelation before the event—is right to about 165 BCE but is wrong after that, indicating that at least this part of the scroll was likely composed in those years 167 to 164 BCE.

We must also include in this history of composition the additional stories that are present in all the ancient Greek manuscripts, which we referred to above as part of the longer versions of Daniyel. These sections must have been composed and made a part of a Hebrew version of Daniyel sometime prior to 100 BCE, the approximate date of the oldest Greek translation of Daniyel.

Apocalyptic Literature and Daniyel

The English word *apocalypse* comes from a Greek word for "revelation," and it appears in many Jewish scrolls and later Christian ones, the most famous being the last book of the Christian New Testament, the Revelation (Apocalypse) of John.

And of course the word *apocalypse* has lived a long life in modern American culture in movies such as *Apocalypse Now!* and in hundreds of evangelical Christian books, seminars, and websites. Scholars studying a large group of ancient Jewish and Christian writings have used the term *apocalyptic literature* to describe an entire genre. An apocalypse is a writing with a narrative framework that reports a highly symbolic divine message to a human, (often by dream or vision) that is mediated/ interpreted (often allegorically or mythically) by an otherworldly being (usually an angel), that reveals supernatural events relating to the future, that and is meant to influence the thinking and behavior of the reading audience. (Based on Collins 1984, 4) This descriptive definition applies quite well to the four visions in the last half of Daniyel. In these visions Daniyel sees successions of wild animals, strange beasts, supernatural beings, and huge statues. He puzzles over their meaning, and then an angel explains them to him. The meaning always has to do with how the nations of the world (such as Babylon, Persian, or Greece) are playing their parts in the plan of the God of Israel for judging the wicked and bringing a kingdom of justice. Many of the symbolic details of the visions have been correlated by scholars to actual events up until 164 BCE, after which point correspondence seems to be lost. This is significant because not only does it help historians date the writing of this part of the scroll, it also helps us understand the intensity of the writing. Jews living in Syria-Palestine during the second century at one point endured oppressive, measures from the Greek king Antiochus Epiphanes, ruler of the Seleucid kingdom (175 to 164 BCE). These apocalyptic stories react to that persecution with a message of encouragement and hope.

There is also no denying the entertainment value of apocalyptic literature in general and that of these visions of Daniyel in particular. Their popularity even today testifies to that. We might think of ancient apocalyptic literature as a kind of pious fantasy literature with a religious purpose. The authors' objectives were certainly not just entertainment. The character Daniyel throughout is a prayerful and pious Jew, and the culminating lesson of each story is that his fellow Jews should remain faithful to their God even in the face of persecution because in the end the just God of Israel, their God, will triumph.

Where to Put Daniyel?

Jewish medieval tradition declares that Daniyel is not a prophet (Talmud Sanhedrin 93b), and he is not grouped with the prophets in Hebrew Bibles. Christian tradition grouped him with the prophets. Such categorizations are the decisions of later communities and reflect their understandings and priorities. Perhaps the two different categorizations also reflect the two halves of the scroll, with Chapters 7–12 seeming the most prophetic given their divine revelations (Talmon 344).

Questions for Further Study

1. In Daniyel 9 the author shows an awareness of written material credited to Jeremiah. As a historian, how would you investigate the relation of Daniyel's

author to the earlier scroll? How does the author of Daniyel value the Jeremiah material? What are his principles of interpretation?

2. How would Jewish readers who live as minorities in non-Jewish places engage the various stories of Daniel? Do different stories reflect different views of foreign governments? What would readers under different kinds of government bring to the stories?

References

Collins, John J. *The Apocalyptic Imagination.* New York: Crossroads, 1984.

———"The Jewish Apocalypses," *Semeia* 14 (1979): 21–59.

Goldingay, John E. *Daniel.* Dallas, TX: Word Books, 1989.

Hartman, Louis F. and Alexander A. Di Lella *The Book of Daniel.* Garden City, NY: Doubleday, 1978.

Moore, Carey A., "Daniel, Additions to," in *The Anchor Bible Dictionary,* edited by David N. Freedman, 2:633–643. (New York: Doubleday, 1992).

———. "Daniel, Book of," in *The Anchor Bible Dictionary,* edited by David N. Freedman, 2:29–37. New York: Doubleday, 1992.

Talmon, Shemaryahu. "Daniel," in *The Literary Guide to the Bible,* edited by Robert Alter and Frank Kermode 343–56. Cambridge, MA: Harvard, 1987.

VanderKam, James. *The Dead Sea Scrolls Today.* Grand Rapids, MI: Ferdmans, 1994.

עזרא–נחמיה

Ezra-Nehemiah

Ezra-N^ekhemyah

SECTION OUTLINE

Literary Format and Movement

History and Ezra-N^ekhemyah

Stories with a Purpose

Questions for Further Study

References

There are all sorts of complications in dealing with this scroll, perhaps first of which is deciding if it is one scroll or two. In many English Bibles Ezra and Nehemiah are presented as two separate books, but this has not always been the case. No Hebrew manuscripts until the fifteenth century CE divide the writing into two separate documents. In Greek translations it seems that the division began with Origen, a third-century Christian scholar. Jerome, the fourth-century Christian whose Latin translation of the Bible became standard in churches in the West, divided the two but still linked them by calling the first 1 Ezra and the next 2 Ezra. This practice of dividing the work into two had a widespread influence in English editions of Bible, even on modern Jewish English translations. Today, some will treat them as two separate books (JPS-Tanakh) and others print the two together as if it were one book, except that they will use a chapter numbering system that starts over at Nehemiah. Thus, for ease and uniformity in referencing, instead of Ezra-Nehemiah Chapters 1–23, we have Ezra 1–10 and Nehemiah 1–13. Unfortunately the Dead Sea Scrolls do not lend any aid in this matter, because none of the preserved copies contains the section of the scroll that would be helpful. For our purposes, let's consider Ezra-N^ekhemyah as one work but as a practical measure, we will use the standard English chapter divisions.

So far we have only seen some of the complications. There were several works going by the name Ezra, or the Greek form, Esdras, in the years before and after the turn of the era and several of them are related to our scroll of Ezra-Nehemiah. In Greek manuscripts, a book known as 1 Esdras contains portions of 2 Chronicles, Ezra 1–10, parts of N^ekhemyah 7 and 8, and a fairly long narrative not found in Ezra-N^ekhemyah. 1 Esdras is a literary edition that is obviously different from but related to our scroll Ezra-N^ekhemyah. It was widely used in antiquity among Jews and later by Christians. Eventually Jewish tradition selected what we now call

LITERARY FORMAT AND MOVEMENT

Ezra-Nᵉkhemyah is essentially a prose narrative about the leadership of three persons, Zerubbabel, Ezra, and Nᵉkhemyah. These three are presented as devout Jews who returned from Babylon to Judah during the years of Persian control in the Fertile Crescent. These leaders, as best we can tell with little evidence, were likely distanced from each other historically by several decades, but the scroll links them and creates a sense of continuous uninterrupted history—they are all part of the same story of reestablishing Jewish temple and society under the relatively benevolent policies of Persian rule. For the story of each leader, the author supplements his narrative with the texts of personal letters or official royal decrees pertinent lists and pious religious addresses clearly meant to inspire the hearer to faithful service to YHVH. Part of the text is actually in a different language: Ezra 4.8–6.18 and 7.12–26 are in Aramaic, which was the language of international correspondence and widely used by Jews in both vernacular and literary composition. The shift in language makes particular sense for the official documents, though its significance for parts of the narrative is less understood. It may reflect a different source, and it evidences the bilingual skills of author and readers. The author also uses dialogue effectively to make key points and advance the narrative. In the Ezra sections there is some first person narrative with Ezra speaking (Ezra 7:27–9:15), and there is a large amount of first person style in the Nᵉkhemyah section (Nehemiah 1–7.5). This is often referred to as Nehemiah's memoir and reads as a very personal account. It is punctuated by brief personal prayers of Nᵉkhemyah, such as "Remember me, o my God, for goodness," which give the readers a feel for the author's personal sense of piety and this matches a wider sense of the scroll, for it closes with such a prayer (Nehemiah 6.9,14; 13. 14, 29, 31).

The narrative contains some shifts that prove difficult to understand. The Nᵉkhemyah story is broken up by the insertion of material about Ezra (Nehemiah 8–10), which may seem out of place to many modern readers; 1 Esdras contains much of the same content as our scroll but in a less-disrupted order. For these reasons many have proposed that originally Nehemiah Chapter 8 was placed immediately after what is now Ezra Chapter 8 and that Nehemiah 9.1–5 stood between what is now Ezra 10.15 and 10.16. There is no doubt that such major shifts of material were possible in ancient scroll making—the variant ancient editions provide obvious proof. Even within Ezra-Nᵉkhemyah we find a case of obvious copying in Ezra 2.1–70, which is nearly identical to Nehemiah 7.6–72 (or 73). In any case, as our scroll Ezra-Nᵉkhemyah stands now the storyline moves from Ezra to Nᵉkhemyah, back to Ezra, and concludes with Nᵉkhemyah. Perhaps the objective was to more closely link and interrelate the missions of the two leaders.

Ezra 1.1–6.22	Ezra 7.1–10.44	Neh.1.1–7.72a	Neh. 7.72b–10.40	Neh. 11.1–13.31
First Jews to return under Seshbazzar and then Zerubbabel	Return and work of Ezra	(or 73a) Return and work of Nehemiah	(or 7.73b–39) Work of Ezra continued	Work of Nehemiah continued

Ezra-Nᵉkhemyah as the literary edition for the Jewish library, whereas some Christian traditions kept both. Greek manuscripts of Bible used by the Orthodox churches preserve 1 Esdras and 2 Esdras. 2 Esdras is a Greek translation of Ezra-Nᵉkhemyah. To add to the confusion, in many Latin manuscripts 2 Esdras is a translation of just Nehemiah, and some manuscripts have up to five different books of Esdras.

The relationship of all the various texts is extremely complex, and scholars have still not been able to sort out the puzzles to everyone's satisfaction. It is actually a fascinating study to try to discover the ins and outs of these various literary versions of Ezra. It is likely that there was an earlier form of this work that no longer exists, and all we have are these later literary editions, which are nearly identical in some places yet have major differences in others. But we won't go any further in explaining the various possibilities; instead we will concentrate on one of these literary editions, the scroll of Ezra-Nᵉkhemyah as it stands in Hebrew manuscripts of the Masoretic tradition. However, in order to be aware of the extent of the version of Ezra that developed within Judaism and early Christianity, we should mention other writings as well, such as 4 Ezra, Apocalypse of Ezra, Questions of Ezra, Revelation of Ezra, and Vision of Ezra. Finally, for a brief discussion of how the beginning of Ezra-Nᵉkhemyah relates to the ending of Chronicles, we'll wait until we come to the scroll of Chronicles.

In Hebrew, *Ezra* is pronounced just as you usually hear it in American English, "ehz-*rah*," and Nehemiah is pronounced as "nᵉkhem-*yah*" (*kh* as *ch* in *Bach*).

History and Ezra-Nᵉkhemyah

A large contingent of Jews was exiled approximately 1,000 miles (1,609, 34 km) from home to the other side of the Fertile Crescent by the Babylonian armies at the beginning of the sixth century BCE, but they did not simply disappear into Babylonian culture. Though we have little by way of straightforward historical evidence, we can be sure that many Jews living there maintained their unique cultural identities, preserving old and creating new Jewish traditions. Then, thanks to the liberating conquest of the Persian king Cyrus, approximately fifty years after being exiled they were allowed to return to their homeland in Israel, which was now a small subunit in a western satrapy of the massive Persian Empire. (Display 8.4)

Archaeologists in the nineteenth century recovered the now famous Cyrus cylinder, on which Cyrus declares that he has pleased the Babylonian Gods, Marduk in particular, by ousting the impious and unjust Babylonian king Nabonidus. In fact, Cyrus claims that Marduk had especially chosen and called Cyrus for this purpose. The inscriber is also proud to proclaim that Cyrus restored the temples of other Gods outside of Babylon also, allowed their temple objects to be returned, and repatriated people to their homelands. This is precisely the policy that made possible the stories of Ezra-Nᵉkhemyah. Many episodes of our scroll lack chronological markers, but it seems that the first section corresponds to early returns of Jewish groups during the time of Cyrus, who ruled until 530 BCE, under two Jewish leaders who had the Babylonian names Sheshbazzar and Zerubbabel. Now Zerubbabel we know from two other scrolls in our library, the prophetic writings of Haggai and Zechariah, both of whom encourage Zerubbabel to rebuild the temple of YHVH (see Ezra 5.1). But Sheshbazzar is completely unknown outside of Ezra Chapters 1

DISPLAY 8.4 | INSCRIPTION COMMEMORATING CYRUS'S LIBERATION
OF BABYLON

and 5, and there has been much speculation about his identity and relation to the
apparent governor Zerubbabel. Since the first century he has been variously identified as Shethar-bozenai (Ezra 5.6), Daniel (the one for whom the scroll is named),
or Shenazzar (1 Chronicles 3.18), and some have thought that Sheshbazzar was second name for Zerubbabel. Look at Ezra 3.8–10 and then read Ezra 5.16, and you
will see the historical dilemma that is resolved by identifying the two men. Of
course, other problems are raised, and this solution is not preferred by many.

The historical ambiguity extends to the persons of Ezra and Neᵏhemyah too.
Our scroll gives a date for Ezra, during the reign of Artaxerxes (Ezra 7.1), who
reigned from 464 to 423 BCE. Dates given for Neᵏhemyah are much later. Historians
are most satisfied with dating him to the twentieth year of Artaxerxes I's reign,
around 445 to 444 BCE (Nehemiah 2.1). So between the Seshbazzar and Zerubbabel
episodes and the Neᵏhemyah episodes we have jumped nearly 100 years. The dating
of Ezra is extremely problematic for historians—some date him before Neᵏhemyah,
some see him as a contemporary, and some put him long after Neᵏhemyah. Because
this *Guided Tour* is not a book mostly about history, I won't attempt to explain the
various positions. Our author is clearly writing a kind of history, though it is not a
precise, chronologically arranged account that we might expect from modern historians. This scroll is very episodic, skipping many decades without notice; it does
not include the names of many Jewish leaders of the time that we know of from

Display 8.5 | YEHUD COINAGE

Two sides of a Jerusalem Yehud coin from the Persian period, ca. 350 BCE. The inscription reads *YHD*, *Yehuda* in Aramic and Hebrew.

other sources, indicating that it is highly selective; it creates an important religious story that does not have the goals and values of straightforward chronicles of events.

Stories with a Purpose

A writer in the fourth century most likely set down these stories about the recent past. Within a relatively short time span, different literary editions of these stories existed, our scroll of Ezra-N^ekhemyah being one sample and 1 Esdras being another. But the underlying and general purpose of the authors seems to have been to present for their Jewish audience stories of how Jews of the preceding generations had been preserved by YHVH in Babylon, how YHVH had directed the course of international political history to bring about their release and return, and how such men as Sheshbazzar, Zerubbabel, Ezra, and N^ekhemyah had led their own grandparents and parents not only in rebuilding the temple but in rebuilding a community to be faithful to covenant traditions of Moses. For all the newness of this community, the underlying theme of our scroll is one of continuity. Ezra is presented as one who reads the scroll of the teaching of Moses, which is explicitly equated with the teaching of YHVH:

> And all the people gathered together as one person at the square which is in front of the Water Gate and they said to Ezra the scribe to bring the scroll of instruction of Moshe which YHVH commanded to Israel. And Ezra the priest brought the instruction before the assembly of men, and women, and everyone who understood to listen from. . . . And he read it . . . from dawn until midday in front of all the men and women and those who understood; and the ears of all the people were given to the

scroll of instruction. . . . And Ezra the scribe stood on the wooden podium which they made for this . . . and he opened the scroll in the sight of all the people . . . and as he opened it all the people stood. And Ezra blessed YHVH the Great God and all the people answered, "Amen, amen" with lifted arms and bowed and prostrated themselves to YHVH, faces to the ground.

(N^{e}KHEMYAH 8.1–6)

In fact, Moshe is brought up by name ten times in Ezra-N^{e}khemyah and always with reference to the instruction from YHVH now written on a scroll, so it is accurate to say that both Moshe and this instruction from YHVH is presented here as the supreme written authority for the community. Of course there are those such as Ezra and other priests and scribes who copy, write, and interpret the instruction, and then teach it and apply it—for one such example, see N^{e}khemyah 8.8–9.5— and they therefore maintain the human authority that always has the power over the written medium.

Just what was this instruction of Moshe? Was it the five books that later became known as the Five Books of Moses, the Torah? You might recall that we asked the same question when we were just beginning our tour (Chapter 1, "Building a Library"), and we discovered that when Ezra-N^{e}khemyah actually quotes the instruction of Moshe (N^{e}khemyah 8.15), the quotation does not match any passage that we have in our Books of Moses. This should not be surprising because in antiquity there were numerous writings that were known as teachings of Moshe, some of which no longer exist, such as the one quoted in N^{e}khemyah 8.15. Others have only been discovered with the appearance of the Dead Sea Scrolls; still others have been known for centuries but were not selected for most biblical libraries. On the other hand, the content of the scroll of Moshe mentioned in Ezra-N^{e}khemyah is similar to material in Leviticus and Deuteronomy, and so we have some sense that Ezra's scroll of the instruction of Moshe was similar to written scrolls we have.

Much more important for understanding the thrust of Ezra-N^{e}khemyah than knowing the precise scroll of Moshe that was used is seeing what specific teachings the author stresses. The early chapters deal with the rebuilding of the temple, and clearly proper temple worship by a priesthood of proper pedigree and purification was crucial for our author. Many of the lists that are included are relevant for these cultic and priestly matters. Also important and obvious was the position of the instruction of YHVH through Moshe as the written authority to be read, taught, and obeyed (Ezra 3.2; 6.18; 7.6–26; N^{e}khemyah 1.7–8; 8.1–14; 9.14; 10.29; 13.1). Perhaps the author was most successful on this point, for in a great deal of later Jewish tradition, Ezra is thought of as the great scribe who wrote and taught the torah of Moshe. He is a second Moses of sorts and towers above nearly all other figures in forms of Judaism in which Torah was and is central.

We should also note here that according to our author even the Persians are supportive of the law of YHVH and the authority of Ezra (Ezra 7.11–26), and our scroll significantly has no sentiment against Persian rule. Living by YHVH's instructions in the torah of Moshe is seems perfectly possible even while living under the Persian government. There is no hint of wishing for a successor to David and a separate state.

POSTER 8.8

CYRUS AND THE GODS

The Cyrus inscription and a couple of scrolls from our library provide a fine example for us of the various ways people interpreted historical events and directed others through their rhetoric to interpret them. In the royal Persian rhetoric to a Babylonian audience, Cyrus is presented as one chosen and called by the Babylonian God Marduk to restore the temple of Marduk in Babylon and to restore prosperity to that city, which was suffering the punishment of Marduk and other Gods due to the impious and last Babylonian king, Nabonidus. The inscription also presents Cyrus as the one who reestablished the temples and worship of Gods of non-Babylonians, though the Judahites are not mentioned. These ideas are to be compared with the Jewish writings from around the same period that refer to this event, namely Ezra-Nᵉkhemyah, repeated in Chronicles, and Isaiah. These texts are also laudatory of Cyrus—and no wonder, because it was Cyrus who freed Jews from their exile. We should also notice that for a Jewish audience Cyrus is not presented as one called by Marduk but rather as one charged by YHVH to rebuild the temple in Jerusalem. If someday as an archaeologist you discover an actual copy of Cyrus's decree, how do you think it will read? And notice what happens to the political events of Cyrus's liberation when the Israelite poetic and prophetic artist of the scroll of Isaiah presents them.

In the following texts there are not direct parallels to be read between the columns. They are arranged this way only for the sake of easy comparison and to show how the same event is understood in two very different ways.

Cyrus, Persian King for Babylonian Audience

... Upon (hearing) their cries, the Lord of the Gods (Marduk) became furiously angry [and he left] their borders; and the Gods who lived among them forsook their dwellings, angry that he (Nabonidus) had brought (them) into Babylon. Marduk [ ] turned (?) towards all the habitations that were abandoned and all the people of Sumer and Akkad who had become corpses; [he was recon]ciled and had mercy (upon them). He surveyed and looked through-out all the lands, searching for a right-eous king whom he would support. He called out his name: Cyrus, king of Anshan; he pronounced his name to be king over all (the world). . . . And he (Cyrus) shepherded with justice and

Jewish Authors for Jewish Audience

And in the first year of Cyrus, King of Persia, for the fulfillment of the word of YHVH by the mouth of Jeremiah (see Jeremiah 29.10), YHVH moved the spirit Cyrus, king of Persia, and he (Cyrus) sent a proclamation to all his kingdom and also a document saying:
"Thus says Cyrus, king of Persia, all the kingdoms of the earth YHVH, the God of the Sky/Heavens, has given to me and he summoned me to build for him a house in Jerusalem which is in Judah. Any among you of all his people—may his God be with him—let him now go up to Jerusalem which is in Jerusalem and let him build the house of YHVH, the God of Israel, who is the God who is in Jerusalem; and all who remain in their places, wherever one (going up) may

righteousness . . . . Marduk, the great lord, guardian (?) of his people, looked with gladness upon his good deeds and upright heart. He ordered him to march to his city Babylon. He set him on the road to Babylon and like a companion and friend, he went at his side. His vast army, whose number, like the water of the river, cannot be known, marched at his side fully armed. He made him enter his city Babylon without fighting or battle; he saved Babylon from hardship. He delivered Nabonidus, the king who did not revere him, into his hands. All the people . . . greeted him with gladness and praised his name.

I am Cyrus, king of the world, great king, mighty king, king of Babylon . . . whose rule Bel (i.e., Marduk) and Nabu love, whose kingship they desire for their hearts' pleasure. . . . As for the citizens of Babylon, upon whom he[a] imposed corvée, which was not the god's will and not befitting them, I relieved their weariness and freed them from their service (?). Marduk, the great lord, rejoiced over my [good] deeds. He sent gracious blessings upon me, Cyrus, the king who worships him . . .

I returned the (images of) the gods to the sacred centers [on the other side of] the Tigris whose sanctuaries had been abandoned for a long time, and I let them dwell in eternal abodes. I gathered all the inhabitants and returned (to them) their dwellings. . . .

Translated by Mordechai Cogan in Hallo 2003, 2:314–315, modified

[a]Nabonidus

live, let the people of his place provide silver and gold and possessions, and livestock, along with donations for the house of the God who is in Jerusalem." (Ezra-Neᵏhemyah 1.1–4; 2 Chronicles 6.22–23)

Thus says YHVH to his messiah, to Cyrus:
"Whose right arm I have picked, . . .
I myself will go before you and level mountains,
Bronze doors I will break and iron bars I will cut down.
And I will give you concealed treasures and secret riches
So that you will know that I, YHVH, who calls you by name, am God of Israel;
On behalf of my servant Jacob, and Israel my chosen,
I call you by your name
I hail you, (though) you do not know me.
I am YHVH and there is no other,
Besides me there are no Gods.
I strengthen you, (though) you do not know me.
So that they will know from the rising of the sun to its setting
That there is no other besides me.
I am YHVH and there is no other.
Forming light and creating darkness,
Making peace and creating evil,
I YHVH am doing all these. . . ."
Thus says YHVH, Holy One of Israel and his Maker,
"Question the destiny of my children,
And about the work of my hands you will instruct me.
I myself made the earth and on it I created man.
I, my hands, stretched the skies and all their armies/hosts I marshaled.
I myself moved him (Cyrus) in justice and all his roads I straighten.
He will rebuild my city and my exiles he will send out;
Not for a price and without payment,"
Says YHVH of Armies.
(Isaiah 45.1–7, 11–13)

Important social concerns for the author of Ezra-N^ekhemyah were certain social and religious separations of Jews from non-Jews. This included calling for divorces of Jews who had married non-Jews. (Ezra 10; Nehemiah 13.1–3). What the author thought or knew of the traditions of Moshe himself marrying a foreigner (see Exodus 2.15–22) we can only speculate. The author is also concerned for the practical matters of daily life, such as the repair of Jerusalem's walls and other city structures (Nehemiah 1–4) Finally, we must add that the author is also concerned for economic conditions of the people, and he stresses the need to ensure that the wealthy of society are not taking advantage of the poor (Nehemiah 5). Near the end of our stories the Jews of Jerusalem commit themselves to maintaining the covenant with YHVH by obeying YHVH's instructions to Moshe (Nehemiah 10.29), and this is the great message of our author.

Questions for Further Study

As a religious scholar and social historian, what is the role of Mosaic text to this author? What can we learn about the social setting(s) in which Moses or Mosaic literature in invoked? How do the texts of Moses relate to the Persian authority? How do they relate to authorities such as kings, priests, and prophets?

References

Blenkinsopp, Joseph. *Ezra-Nehemiah*. Philadelphia: Westminster, 1988.

Hallo, William W. *The Context of Scripture*. 3 vols. Leiden: E.J. Brill, 2003.

Klein, Ralph W. "The Books of Ezra and Nehemiah," in *The New Interpreter's Bible*, 3:661–851. Nashville, TN: Abingdon, 1999.

Myers, Jacob M. *Ezra, Nehemiah*. Garden City, NY: Doubleday, 1965.

Talmon, Shemaryahu. "Ezra and Nehemiah," in *The Literary Guide to the Bible*, edited by Robert Alter and Frank Kermode, 357–64. Cambridge, MA: Harvard, 1987.

דברי הימים
Chronicles *Devrei Hayamim*

Section Outline

Literary Format and Movement
A Historical Review
Ancient Source Citation
Watching the Writer
The Writing Continues
The End of the Story
Questions for Further Study
References

It makes sense that this scroll is so long—second only to Kings in our library—because it is a narrative of nearly the entire length of Jewish history, as seen by a Jewish author writing sometime in the fourth century BCE. It is a peculiar summary of the past, encompassing traditions that are covered in Genesis, Exodus, Leviticus, Numbers, Deuteronomy, Joshua, Judges, Ruth, Samuel, and Kings. For that reason too, it is in some sense a fitting last book of our library. However, it is not always last; we do have Hebrew manuscripts in which it is the first book of the Ketuvim, not the last. In Greek manuscripts this book usually follows Kings, and that is where you will find it in Roman Catholic, Orthodox, and Protestant Bibles. There are also good reasons for these different arrangements, and the differences underscore the variety within our collection. Different groups arrange their libraries differently.

A similar situation exists regarding the title. The Hebrew name for the book, *Devrei Hayamim,* is pronounced "deev-*ray* hah-yah-*meem*," and it means "things/events of the times/days." In this case it does not come from the first line of the scroll; it was a much later descriptive title from Jewish literature. The Greek title, *Paralipomenon,* means "things omitted" and reflects the inaccurate notion that the scroll serves as a sort of appendix to other scrolls, especially in Samuel and Kings. The English name *Chronicles* comes from A Christian scholar from the fourth a fifth century CE named Jerome, who in Latin referred to the book as a "Chronicle of all the divine history."

*L*ITERARY FORMAT AND MOVEMENT

Because so much of Devrei Hayamim reviews material that is covered in earlier scrolls of our library, we can readily see this author's priorities and interests by comparing his story with other earlier works. The chronicler, as this author is often called, is interested in painting a sweeping landscape of Jewish history and placing in the center of it a grand portrait of King David, serving as the model of a king who pleases and worships YHUH. These priorities are shown in the literary format: the space that is given to David—nearly 30 percent of the scroll—and the space that is given to the building of the temple in Jerusalem and the worship of YHVH. The story of Israel before David, which begins with Adam, is done in the form of genealogical lists and is clearly introductory to the reign of David. The story of Israel that comes after David, which included more than 500 years for the author, is a story of the decline of the Jerusalem temple-centered kingdom and its exile to Babylon; the Northern Kingdom of Israel is ignored completely. A final brief narrative conclusion brings the dark story to a close with a ray of light—the king of Persia has released the Jews and heard a call from YHVH to rebuild that temple of Jerusalem. Along the way we find several fascinating additions made to the story, which were not found in the earlier scrolls, such as some beautiful inspiring orations (2 Devrei Hayamim 13.4–12; 20.5–12) and stories about prophets (2 Devrei Hayamim 15.1–7; 21.12–15). If we imagine this work as a great pictorial canvas, we would see on the left a long line of small people from Adam leading to a large central portrait of David holding the blueprints for YHVH's temple. On the other side of David would be series of kings becoming smaller and smaller, beginning with Solomon the temple builder and ending with Zedekiah, the last exiled king. At the extreme right end would be the Persian king Cyrus, holding a commission from YHVH for building a house for YHVH in Jerusalem and calling on Jews to return there.

1 Devrei Hayamim 1–9 Annotated Jewish genealogies from Adam to David	1 Devrei Hayamim 10–29 David, YHVH's great king and temple planner	2 Devrei Hayamim 1–9 The temple of YHVH built by Solomon and his great reign	2 Devrei Hayamim 10–36.21 The decline and fall of the kings and kingdom of Judah	2 Devrei Hayamim 36.22–23 YHVH's plan through Cyrus to release Jews and rebuild temple

A Historical Review

Devrei Hayamim is another review of the Jewish past, a Jewish world history of sorts, and one with a decisive angle. The chronicler looks back into the Jewish past knowing many traditions of Israel's origin and history and fully aware of the demise of his people's kingdom, and he chooses to write its history focusing on David and the sacred temple of Jerusalem. For him, hundreds of years later, most important of all

Study Room 8.5

EVALUATING KINGS

Just what is your opinion of presidents Jefferson, Taft, Eisenhower, and Bush? How do historians evaluate them? The answers will vary. Answers varied among ancient Jewish writers too, and it makes for a fascinating study to see the differences. If one reads carefully through Kings and Devrei Hayamim together, one will see each king of Judah evaluated, though the chronicler's evaluation is not always as explicit and formal and Kings. Read king by king and compare at the end of each section. What is different about the accounts? What is the same? On what are the evaluations based and how do they differ? For starters consider these three kings: Jehoshaphat in 1 Kings 22.1–22.46 and 2 Devrei Hayamim 17.1–21.1; Jehoash in 2 Kings 12.1–21 and 2 Devrei Hayamim 24.1–27; and Manasseh in 2 Kings 21.1–18 and 2 Devrei Hayamim 33.1–20.

were religious-political concerns, and his narrative is an idealized story with particular emphases and omissions. Obedience to YHVH and the proper honoring of his presence are vital issues. He was interested in depicting David as the great model of piety who established the temple of Jerusalem, which was then built by his son Solomon. Unlike the more balanced portrait of David in Samuel and Kings, the chronicler removes the negative and presents what he considers a shining example of YHVH-pleasing leadership. David is the perfect pious worship leader of Israel. His military prowess is mentioned, but much more important are his actions for the temple. He establishes the priests, formulates all the building plans, arranges for supplies, and organizes the musicians, gatekeepers, and treasures. He even procures the land with fantastic sums of gold and silver—much higher than the parallel version in Samuel—which signals the great value of the temple in the author's mind (compare 1 Devrei Hayamim 21.25 with 2 Samuel 24.18–24). We will look at more of these differences below, but the point here is that YHVH's temple in Jerusalem is a key to the entire scroll. It is David's focus and Solomon's pride. It is the only place where true temple worship of YHVH occurs. Because the Northern Kingdom left it, they essentially abandoned YHVH according to the chronicler, and so he all but ignores the history of the larger Israelite kingdom in the North. The author of this scroll clearly wanted to exalt Jerusalem's temple, perhaps because of disputes in his own day. There are myriad possibilities that might have motivated this author, probably doing his writing in Jerusalem during a period when Judea was a small struggling community controlled by Persian-appointed governors. How might this scroll have been accepted, and what affect might it have had on the community?

Poster 8.9

An Ancient Bibliography

General Royal Histories

Record of the Kings of Israel and Judah (1 Devrei Hayamim 9.1; 2 Devrei Hayamim 35.27)

Record of the Kings of Judah and Israel (2 Devrei Hayamim 25.26, 28.26)

Royal Record of Judah and Israel (2 Devrei Hayamim 16.11)

Record of the Kings of Israel (2 Devrei Hayamim 20.34)

Deeds of the Kings of Israel (2 Devrei Hayamim 33.18)

Prophetic Writings

Deeds of Samuel the Seer (1 Devrei Hayamim 29.29)

Deeds of Nathan the Prophet (1 Devrei Hayamim 29.29, 2 Devrei Hayamim 9.29)

Deeds of Gad the Visionary (1 Devrei Hayamim 29.29)

Prophecy of Ahijah the Shilonite (2 Devrei Hayamim 9.29)

Visions of Iddo the Visionary (2 Devrei Hayamim 9.29)

Deeds of Shemiah the Prophet and Iddo the Visionary (2 Devrei Hayamim 12.15)

Vision of Isaiah, Son of Amoz, the Prophet (2 Devrei Hayamim 32.32)

Stories or Commentaries

Story *(Midrash)* of the Prophet Iddo (2 Devrei Hayamim 13.22)

Story *(Midrash)* of the Record of the Kings (2 Devrei Hayamim 24.27)

Other works are mentioned but without a description or title, such as writing by Isaiah about Uzziah (2 Devrei Hayamim 26.22). Others can be found in 1 Devrei Hayamim 27.24; 28.19, and 2 Devrei Hayamim 35.4; 35.25.

Ancient Source Citation

No other author in our library names as many sources does the author of Devrei Hayamim. Some 20 books seem to be given, some of which you can see from Poster 8.9. Citation of sources seems to be of major importance to this author; he does it extensively. Most of the writings are cited in a formulaic way; usually at the end of an episode the author writes that additional material about the king or episode can be found in a certain scroll. For example,

> And more of the deeds of Manasseh and his prayer to his God and the words of the visionaries who spoke to him in the name of YHVH God of Israel are in the Deeds of the Kings of Israel
> (2 Devrei Hayamim 33.18)

This reminds us of the similar practice by the author of Kings. My translation is a bit deceptive, because the ancient Hebrew has no capital letters to indicate an official title. Furthermore, not all scrolls seem to have had official titles as we tend to have today, and many scholars believe that the many sources referred to may be different descriptions for just a few different works. This is certainly a possibility and without the actual ancient sources we probably cannot know exactly how many different sources are cited. We should also mention the curious fact that the chronicler extensively used Samuel and Kings, but he doesn't seem to name them at all.

Watching the Writer

Have the many times we've talked about sources in this book made you want to actually see just how an ancient Israelite author might have used his sources to create his scroll? The book of Devrei Hayamim provides a good opportunity to observe the process. For most of the scrolls in our library, the sources that were used have long since disappeared, but for Devrei Hayamim we still have the major source for his work on David and his successors: the scrolls of Samuel and Kings. Scholars and any curious persons asking questions about how authors use sources have a great deal of hard factual information about the process because of the many parallel accounts of these three scrolls. I have found that this type of study is usually new to students and that they usually enjoy it a great deal. It is a great way to see firsthand the work of an ancient Jewish writer. Read carefully and side by side, if possible, 2 Samuel II and 2 Devrei Hayamim 20, and then compare 2 Samuel 24 with 2 Devrei Hayamim 21. Finally, compare also 2 kings 21.1–18 with 2 Devrei Hayamim 33.1–20.

The Writing Continues

I'm sure you noticed in reading the comparison of Kings and Devrei Hayamim that although the scroll of Kings contains no good word about Judah's longest reigning King Manasseh, the scroll of Devrei Hayamim presents him as one who repented of his evil ways, prayed fervently to YHVH, and was restored. And the chronicler even states that his prayer can be found in another source (2 Devrei Hayamim 33.18). Whatever that source was at the time Devrei Hayamim was written, later Jewish tradition did have a prayer of Manasseh. Sometime in the first century CE or perhaps somewhat earlier, a Jewish author composed a prayer of repentance that fills in the gap left by Devrei Hayamim: Devrei Hayamim mentions the prayer twice (2 Devrei Hayamim 33.13,18) but never quotes it. This was a common practice among religious Jews throughout the centuries before and after the turn of the era. In the centuries following its composition, this prayer was been preserved only in Christian circles and was copied into many Christian Bible manuscripts. I here cite a few lines from James Charlesworth's translation. The entire work can be seen in Charlesworth 1983, 2:625–37.

> And now behold I am bending the knees of my heart before you;
> and I am beseeching your kindness.
> I have sinned, O Lord, I have sinned:

and I certainly know my sins.
I beseech you;
forgive me, O lord, forgive me!

The End of the Story

If you look at the very last verse of Devrei Hayamim (36.22–23) and the very first verses of the scroll called Ezra-N^ekhemyah (1.1–3), you will see that they are virtually identical accounts of Cyrus's liberation of his Jewish subjects. Clearly one was copied from the other, or perhaps both came from a third source. Scholars have argued all sides of this question, and it is clear that Devrei Hayamim and Ezra are elsewhere very different in style and language. Therefore, it seems unlikely that Ezra is a sequel to Devrei Hayamim by same author. So, did an author or later editor of Devrei Hayamim insert this ending that had originally be the beginning of Ezra-N^ekhemyah, or did an author of Ezra-N^ekhemyah decide that the way Devrei Hayamim ended would be a perfect way to start his story? What is clear is that these lines signaled to any reader who happened to know the content of the scroll of Ezra, that Ezra follows Devrei Hayamim in sequence (Talmon 1987, 371). Perhaps more importantly for the story of Devrei Hayamim, these final words bring a positive and hopeful ending to this long narrative of YHVH's people Israel. There is a future.

Questions for Further Study

1. If we ask a historiographic question, what might be the motivations for writing a history like Devrei Hayamim when Samuel and Kings have already been written?

2. Because Devrei Hayamim comes from a time long after the existence of Israelite kings, what is the attitude toward kingship of this author? What is the attitude toward other institutions and positions of power?

3. How does Devrei Hayamim relate to prophets? Do they play a role his story? Does he mention any of the prophets whose scrolls we have read? Why or why not?

References

Allen, Leslie C. "The First and Second Books of Chronicles," in *The New Interpreter's Bible*, 3:299–659, Nashville, TN: Abingdon, 1999.

Charlesworth, James H. *The Old Testament Pseudepigrapha*, 2 vols. New York: Doubleday, 1983.

Klein, Ralph W. Chronicles 1–2, Book of," in *The Anchor Bible Dictionary*, edited by David N. Freedman, 1:992–1002. New York: Doubleday, 1992.

Meyers, Jacob M. *1 Chronicles*. Garden City, NY: Doubleday, 1965.

———. *2 Chronicles*. Garden City, NY: Doubleday, 1965.

Talmon, Shemaryahu. "1 and 2 Chronicles," in *The Literary Guide to the Bible*, edited by Robert Alter and Frank Kermode, 365–72. Cambridge, MA: Harvard, 1987.

Additional Scrolls

CHAPTER OUTLINE

More Scrolls?

As we learned at the beginning of our tour, the Jewish Bible ends with the 24 scrolls already surveyed. The scrolls in this chapter are not part of modern Jewish Bibles because all current Jewish communities have followed the lead of those second-century CE Jewish rabbinic leaders who apparently confirmed the limitation of their most sacred writings to the 24 scrolls that we have just studied. The great war of Rome against the Jews of Palestine in 68 to 73 CE and the second war in 132 to 135 at least in part precipitated the rise of those rabbinic leaders to prominence. These were the religious and social leaders who survived and emerged in those devastating generations. Their importance for later generations of Jews could hardly be overstated, for their work resulted in the **Mishnah** a milestone record of Jewish traditions, written about 200 CE under the direction of Judah HaNasi. In the Mishnah we find some evidence about the designation of some scrolls as sacred. We'll say more about those Jewish leaders in the next chapter.

However, before the first and second centuries CE, Jewish communities wrote and sometimes collected more than the 24 scrolls we just surveyed on our tour. Since 586 BCE, many Jews lived outside of what was the land of Israel. Some lived in Mesopotamia (2 Kings 25); some went to Egypt (Jeremiah 42). When the Persians conquered Mesopotamia and the eastern Mediterranean world in the mid-sixth century BCE, Jews moved to various places in the expansive Persian Empire (539 to 323 BCE). Two centuries later, Jewish movement continued to the East and West under the Greek empires (ca. 323 to 63 BCE) and then under the Roman Empire, which oversaw the final destruction of the temple in Jerusalem in 70 CE. During these periods some Jews also lived in the land that was once the kingdom of Israel. For most of those years that land was under the direct control of the parade of empires—Babylonian, Persian, Greek, Roman—and so in a very real sense they too were living in a foreign country. Only for a short time between 142 to 63 BCE was there an independent Jewish kingdom, which started with a revolt against the Syrian-Greek rule in 167 BCE, led by a family known as the Hasmoneans, or Maccabees. We will say more about this brief period of independence later when we discuss the scrolls known as 1 and 2 Maccabees.

So all during these centuries, Jews in various locations continued to compose and collect scrolls. Some of the newer scrolls came to be of high importance to some Jewish groups and communities in some parts of the Roman world. The considerable influence of some of these groups can be seen in many Christian communities who, inheriting their sacred writings from local Jewish practice, included some of these scrolls in their own collections of sacred and most important writings. Other scrolls were also written by Jews but ended up not surviving in any modern forms of Bible, either because the writings themselves were not deemed worthy or because the communities that cherished them did not survive. Some of these scrolls have been forever lost, some have been preserved in ancient manuscripts by scribes, and still others have been unearthed by archaeologists.

For the historian, literary critic, sociologist, or simply an ordinary curious person, whose fields of exploration are not restricted by later canon makers of a religious community, these works may be just as interesting and valuable as any of those that are in the traditional Jewish canon. Many of them are fascinating reading and all of them reveal a great deal about the way Jews lived, thought, followed Jewish traditions, reformed and discarded traditions, interacted with other peoples and cultures, thrived or suffered, and much else during the crucial centuries of 300 to 1 BCE. If we tried to survey all of the literary writings of ancient Israelite or Jewish communities, this *Guided Tour* would never end. There are literally hundreds of them. On the other hand, at the very least we should consider those writings that are found in some modern Bibles, namely the Bibles of the Roman Catholic and Eastern Orthodox traditions, even though they are not in Jewish Bibles and are not formally part of what in academic parlance we call the Hebrew Bible.

Deuterocanonicals

Books that are canonical in Roman Catholic and Orthodox Christian traditions but not in other traditions are now often called the Deuterocanonicals, a term that comes from sixteenth-century Roman Catholic tradition and means books of the "second canon." The adjective meaning "second" *(deutero)* does not imply lesser status, just as it does not imply lesser status in the name *Deuteronomy*, which is translated "second law." For Roman Catholic and Eastern Orthodox Christians, these books of

POSTER 9.1

ADDITIONAL BOOKS

Roman Catholic	Orthodox
Tobit	Tobit
Judith	Judith
1 Maccabees	1 Maccabees
2 Maccabees	2 Maccabees
	3 Maccabees
	4 Maccabees
Wisdom (of Solomon)	Wisdom (of Solomon)
Ecclesiaticus (Sirach)	Ecclesiaticus (Sirach)
Baruch (including Letter of Jeremiah)	Baruch
	Letter of Jeremiah
Additions to Daniel: Bel and the Dragon, Song of the Three Young Men, Susanna Additions to Esther	Additions to Daniel: Bel and the Song of the Three Young Men, Susanna Additions to Esther

the Deuterocanonicals are equal in status to other biblical books and they are interspersed among the other books in the Old Testament portion of those churches' Bibles. Eastern Orthodox communions have a few other writings as well (see the list on page 9). In Protestant Christian tradition, these books are often referred to as the Apocrypha, a somewhat derogatory term meaning "hidden" or "spurious." The history of the differing books in Christian Bibles is a long and fascinating one and well worth exploring in its many complexities. But we can summarize by saying that the books in this section were part of sacred scriptures for most Christian communities for many centuries. Some Christian writers occasionally questioned the status of these writings, and sometimes the books were deemed of lesser value, but not until well after the Protestant Reformation (sixteenth century CE) were they completely removed from Christian Bibles by some Protestant Christians. In early Protestant traditions we can see these writing being considered worthy of inclusion in Bibles but of lesser status. For example, in the earliest editions of the King James Version (1611), the seven books of the Deuterocanonicals and 1 and 2 Esdras are included in a separate section, called Apocrypha, between the Old and New Testaments. However, in the following decades they are explicitly excluded by official Protestant teachings, such as the Westminster Confession of Faith of 1646, and so for several centuries Protestants did not produce Bibles that include them. In the late twentieth century, Protestant scholars and publishers became more aware and interested in the books of the Apocrypha, and so some editions of Bibles from Protestant publishers, such as the New Revised Standard Edition (1989), began appearing with these books included in a separate section between the Old and New Testaments.

In the following pages we review the scrolls of the Deuterocanonicals, and we will generally follow the order in which they appear in Roman Catholic Bibles, with the exception that 3 and 4 Maccabees will be inserted. In the case of the additions to Esther and Daniel, we have already considered that material in the previous chapter, when we were looking at those two books in our Hebrew Bible library. In the titles I have provided a Hebrew form for those scrolls that were originally composed in Hebrew.

Questions for Further Study

As a scholar of sociology and religion, what are the functions of canons in religious communities? How do they support or subvert a human authority? How do they change over time? How do communities work with and around them?

References

Charlesworth, James H., ed. *The Old Testament Pseudepigrapha*, 2 vols. Garden City, NY: Doubleday, 1983–1985.

Cohen, Shaye J. D. *From the Maccabees to the Mishnah*. Philadelphia: Westminster, 1987.

Collins, John J. *Between Athens and Jerusalem: Jewish Identity in the Hellenistic Diaspora*, 2nd ed. Grand Rapids, MI: Eerdmans, 2000.

Harrington, Daniel J. *Invitation to the Apocrypha*. Grand Rapids, MI: Eerdmans, 1999.

Nickelsburg, G. W. E. *Jewish Literature between the Bible and the Mishnah*, 2nd ed. Philadelphia: AugsburgFortress, 2005.

VanderKam, James. *Introduction to Early Judaism*. Grand Rapids, MI: Eerdmans, 2000.

טוֹבִי

Tobit *Tovi*

Like Esther and Daniel, Tobit is another diaspora tale, a story told by a Jew about living as a Jew in a foreign land. These stories of Jewish life in a foreign land provide us an interesting glimpse into the religious and social ideals of various Jewish communities in the last centuries BCE. Most commentators sense entertainment motivation in the story of Tobit. In Hebrew or Aramaic, the scroll's name would be Tovi pronounced "toe-*vee*," but our English versions follow the Greek manuscripts by using the name Tobit.

The scroll was written in Aramaic probably between the late fourth and early second century BCE, during a period when Hellenistic rulers were holding sway in most parts of the Mediterranean world. Among the Dead Sea Scrolls we have five editions in Aramaic and one in Hebrew, but the editions that survived in Christian communities were Greek and Latin translations. The author sets his story in a much earlier time—in the late eighth century BCE when Assyrian power ruled the Fertile Crescent and the Northern Kingdom of Israel had been destroyed and the surviving Israelites had been resettled in the in Mesopotamia (see the scroll of 2 Kings 17). This is a fictional short story with realistic characters set in Nineveh during the days of Shalmanesar, Sennacherib, and Esarhaddon, Assyrian kings of the eighth and seventh centuries BCE. For the place of the story's composition, many locations have been proposed—Egypt, Syria, Persia, and Hellenistic Palestine. No location can claim consensus among scholars, but it is not crucial for us to know in order to appreciate the composition.

Tovi is a pious Jew from Israel who was exiled by Shalmanesar to Nineveh. He faithfully follows the laws of Moses, gives generously to the poor, and shows respect for the dead by always ensuring a proper burial for fellow Jews, even when it has been forbidden by the king for those executed by the state. He has a son named Tobiah (Tobias in Greek) and a wife named Hannah. But bad fortune comes his way: he is impoverished when he looses his eyesight in a bizarre accident involving sparrow droppings. His situation becomes desperate and he prays to God to die. Meanwhile, across the empire his kinfolk, Raguel and his daughter Sarah live in the city of Ecbatana. Sarah has had her own disasters: a series of seven husbands have died on their wedding night because her bridal chamber is plagued by the demon Asmodeus. She too, at the same time as Tovi, prays to die.

Tovi decides to send his son Tobiah to the distant city of Rages, in order to recover some needed family wealth from a kinsman named Gabael who lives there. Tobiah sets out on his journey with his dog and with a hired guide named Azariah ("YHVH helps"), who is really the angel Raphael in disguise. On their way, Tobiah catches a large magical fish in the Tigris. Later Raphael teaches Tobiah that burning its heart will drive away demons and that its gall will cure blindness. The next stop on the way to Rages is Ecbatana, where they stay at the house of Raguel and Sarah. Tobiah and Sarah are married, and the demons are defeated. Later the wealth of Tovi is recovered, and when the travelers return to Nineveh, his blindness is cured.

Of course, that brief retelling does the story no justice—it really is quite entertaining and full of curious details. Beyond being a delightful tale, it is also quite clearly didactic. The author is not subtle about his lessons: Remain faithful to our Jewish customs and our divine laws, and our God will remain faithful to us by acting to save and prosper us, perhaps best summarized in 4.5–6. Generosity and compassion to the needy and destitute, and respect for parents and the dead are especially stressed. These lessons, of course, were traditional, reflecting many earlier passages in our library (e.g., Deuteronomy 28) and also in accord with other diaspora literature. The book also uses many common literary formulas and folklore motifs, such as pious deathbed instructions or testament from father to son (4.1–21; 14.1–15), a journey to a distant city for treasure and marriage (4.1–11.18), active angels and an angel in disguise (5.1–22; 12.11–22), a demon in the bridal chamber (3.7–9; 8.1–9), and pious burial of the dead (1.3–2.10). Literary and historical scholars are interested in how the author of Tovit uses traditions from earlier Jewish literature, for there are unmistakable connections in this work with earlier books in our library. The author clearly promotes traditions attributed to Moses.

These features, the entertaining story, and the many clear religious teachings of the story give us an excellent picture of popular religious values, social customs, and cultural ideas of some Jews living as minorities in Hellenistic environments. Jewish identity and a sense that success and blessing are possible are strongly maintained, and the Jewish God is active and dependable within a non-Jewish environment. The work is filled with praises to Israel's God, the God of the whole world (14.6), and ends with a long hymn of praise (13.1–17) and hopeful predictions for the future in which, for example, the just will be rewarded, the wicked destroyed, and all Israel will live in safety in Jerusalem (14.3–9).

Questions for Further Study

1. After reading Tovit, what do you see as its entertainment value for an ancient Jewish reader?
2. What is the attitude toward non-Jewish government?

References

Moore, "Tobit, Book of," In *The Anchor Bible Dictionary,* edited by David N. Freedman, 6:585–94. New York: Doubleday, 1992.

Moore, Cary. *Tobit.* New York: Doubleday, 1996.

Nowell, Irene. "The Book of Tobit," in *The New Interpreter's Bible,* edited by 3:973–1971. Nashville, TN: Abingdon, 1999.

יהודית

Judith *Yehudit*

This fascinating composition, originally in Hebrew, is another entertaining fictional story about a pious and heroic woman named Judith who rescues her small village and all Jerusalem from the invading armies of a powerful empire and king. The story was likely composed toward the end of the second century or beginning of the first century BCE. This is during the time of independence of a small Jewish kingdom centered in Jerusalem, under the leadership of the Hasmonean kings, also known as the Maccabees. Just as the Maccabees—led by Judah, who died in 161 BCE and was succeed by his brothers—defeated the much larger invading foreign armies, Judith also defeats the overwhelming threat of Nebuchadnezzar.

From nearly the first word, the author seems to make it quite clear that he is writing a fictional story set in a fictional time:

> It happened in the twelfth year of the rule of Nebuchadrezzar, who reigned over the Assyrians . . .

The historical Nebuchadnezzar was the Babylonian king who destroyed Jerusalem and exiled many of its inhabitants in 586 BCE. He lived and ruled after the days of the Assyrian empire. This scroll presents a literary rematch with an archenemy of the Jews. Perhaps the Assyrians are included because it was the Assyrian Empire that destroyed the Northern Kingdom of Israel back in the eighth century BCE.

Using the name Judith for the story's heroine is highly significant. Judith, or the Hebrew form *Yehudit* pronounced "yeh-hu-*deet*," is simply the feminine name form of the masculine name Judah; she is "Jewess," or "woman of Judea," the female personification of the Jewish nation and people. Thus the clever writer of this Jewish hero story pits the nations of Assyria and Babylon, represented by Nebuchadezzar, king of Assyria, against the "Jewess" Yehudit. They will find out that they are no match for her.

The story divides neatly into two sections (Chapters 1–7, 8–16), and Yehudit is not introduced until the second half, beginning in Chapter 8. The first half describes the threat: Nebuchadnezzar with a vast army is easily marauding through the entire land of Syria-Palestine. He sends his ruthless general Holofernes to plunder and destroy Jerusalem and to make captives of all its inhabitants. This Holofernes is the archvillain of our story. Although most other towns and cities submit voluntarily to the Assyrian forces, the Israelites of Jerusalem and surrounding towns are instructed to resist by their high priest and the Jewish senate. The term *senate* is one of the many clues that point to the Hellenistic dating of the composition; it was only in the Hellenistic era that there was a

Jewish senate. Holofernes is forced to march against Jerusalem and to get there he must pass the village of Bethulia, where the pious widow Yehudit lives a solitary, God-fearing, and devout life. Holofernes, with nearly 200,000 troops, sets up a blockade of Bethulia, which includes cutting off its water supply. After 34 days the townspeople are ready to surrender, scolding the leaders for not making peace with Assyria earlier. The leaders bow to the pressure and decide to hold out for five more days, hope for a miracle, and surrender if necessary. This is where Yehudit enters the story. She chastises the leaders of Bethulia for not trusting their God and not fervently praying to him. They yield and ask the pious Yehudit to pray for them.

After this excoriation, she announces that she "will work an action" (8.32), and it is this action that saves her town, all of Jerusalem, and makes her famous. Yehudit, who is also extremely beautiful, goes out to the camp of Holofernes with her maid and through a series of lies and flirtations gains his confidence. He takes the bait and anticipates a night of pleasure. Once he is drunk, Yehudit uses his own sword to sever his head and then returns to Bethulia. The ruse is later discovered and when proclaimed in the camp, all the Assyrians flee in fear and trembling. "One woman of the Hebrews has made an embarrassment of the house of King Nebuchadnezzar" (14.18).

Thus, in this grand rematch of Israelites vs. Assyrians and Babxlonians, the Israelites, having been admonished by the praiseworthy widow, have been rescued by God through her piety and shrewd resourcefulness. God has delivered them from their worst enemy.

Of the many ways to approach this scroll, readers have found that literary questions provide interesting lines of inquiry. If we ask about genre, literary antecedents, and similar works, we will soon recognize that the author has written a story in which the heroine is patterned after heroes of other Jewish stories. These are individuals who represent or embody all their fellow Jews and save all of Israel by their heroism; Jael over Sisera (Judges 4, 5), David over Goliath (1 Samuel 17), Esther over Haman (Esther), and Daniel over the Persian wise men (Daniel 6). In Roman Catholic Bibles, Judith is found immediately before Esther, and they are very similar tales of Jewish heroines who save their people. Literary critics have also noted another prominent feature: the scroll is entirely ironic, much like Esther, but even more so. All the major characters and main events see eventual reversals; the first become last, the powerful become weak, the exploiters become the exploited, and the weak weaponless widow cuts the head off the powerful, armed general.

If we approach the story asking questions about religion, we also have a great deal of data to consider, and the author is not subtle. The author values and teaches, often by the mouth of the heroine Yehudit, a deeply felt Judaism of honoring and worshiping only the God of Israel, trusting in him for protection, following the ways of faithful ancestors, properly observing Sabbaths and holidays, and maintaining moral purity (e.g., especially Chapters 5, 8, 16). We clearly recognize here what is known as Deuteronomic theology, a historically powerful religious ideal that confidently states that

> as long as they [Israelites] did not sin before their God, good things happened to them, because the God who hates iniquity is with them. But when they departed from the path that he set for them, they were defeated in many wars and taken captive . . . (5.17–18)

This religious viewpoint is unmistakably clear throughout the entire work and echoes scrolls we read earlier, such as Deuteronomy and Kings.

Questions for Further Study

1. What are some of the questions a feminist critic would ask about this scroll, especially regarding Yehudit and her relationship to male figures in the story?
2. Compare Yehudit to other Jewish female heroes, such as Estar and Rut.

References

Craven, Toni. *Artistry and Faith in the Book of Judith.* Chico, CA: Society of Biblical Literature, 1983.

Moore, Carey A. "Judith, Book of." In *The Anchor Bible Dictionary,* edited by David N. Freedman, 3:1117–25. New York: Doubleday, 1992.

Wills, Lawrence M. "The Book of Judith." In *The New Interpreter's Bible,* edited by 3:1073–183. Nashville, TN: Abingdon, 1999.

מקב׳

1 Maccabees

Perhaps this is the most famous of all the Additional Scrolls, not so much because the writing itself is well known, but because it contains the story of the Maccabees. This is the story celebrated at the Jewish holiday of Hanukkah, even though the scroll itself is not in the Jewish Bible. It is a narrative of religious suppression and temple desecration by an occupying power, the Syrian-Greek Seleucids Empire, against the Jews living in region of Jerusalem, who successfully revolt against the empire and win their freedom. This revolt is led by a family who became known as the Hasmoneans—probably from the name of a town—or even more famously as the Maccabees—probably from a nickname meaning "hammer" applied to a son named Judah, or, in its anglicized Greek form, Judas (2.4).

We need to make another clarification regarding the name of this scroll and the next three we will consider. There are four books with the name Maccabees, and one might naturally think that they are related in origin, much as 1 and 2 Samuel are really part one and two of the same work. In fact, the four Maccabees books are all separate compositions, and 3 Maccabees is really misnamed because its story is unrelated to the Maccabees. 1 Maccabees is likely the oldest of these compositions, written in Hebrew around 100 BCE, and it covers in a fairly detailed fashion events of approximately 175 to 132 BCE. Because its original composition was in Hebrew, I have included one Hebrew form of "Maccabee" at the beginning of the section. (There is another spelling as well.) However, no Hebrew manuscripts remain; the oldest texts are Greek and Latin translations.

Looking at 1 Maccabees from a modern historian's perspective, we would say that the author provides a great deal of credible historical information about the battles between the declining Seleucid Empire and the rising Hasmonean Jewish leaders, who fought for and secured their own small kingdom. The writing style and explicit religious concerns will remind you of the scroll of Kings. The story begins with the ominous rise to the throne of the Seleucid king Antiochus Epiphanes ("God Revealed") in 175 BCE (1.10). During this time, there was a minimally documented internal Jewish conflict: there were Jews who adopted certain Greek ways of living that the author rejects as completely against the Jewish covenant with their God (1.11–15).

To summarize, Antiochus, desperate for money and harmony in his empire, raided and desecrated the Jerusalem temple, plundered the city, and attempted to ban local religious customs and enforce unifying Greek religious customs (1.20–63). Needless to say, this ban gave rise to a revolt that was headed by a priestly family from a village called Modein led by Mattathias and his five sons

Poster 9.2

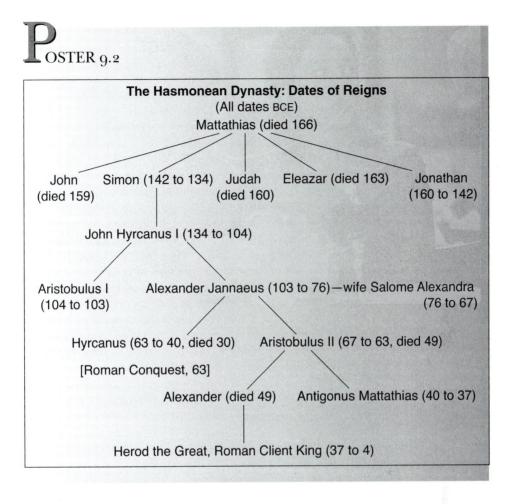

The Hasmonean Dynasty: Dates of Reigns
(All dates BCE)

Mattathias (died 166)

John (died 159)   Simon (142 to 134)   Judah (died 160)   Eleazar (died 163)   Jonathan (160 to 142)

John Hyrcanus I (134 to 104)

Aristobulus I (104 to 103)   Alexander Jannaeus (103 to 76)—wife Salome Alexandra (76 to 67)

Hyrcanus (63 to 40, died 30)   Aristobulus II (67 to 63, died 49)

[Roman Conquest, 63]

Alexander (died 49)   Antigonus Mattathias (40 to 37)

Herod the Great, Roman Client King (37 to 4)

(2.1–48). Later authors refer to the family as the Hasmoneans. Mattathias and his sons refused to sacrifice to foreign Gods in Modein, declaring

> I and my sons and my brothers will walk by the covenant of our fathers; far be it from us to abandon the law and commands; the words of the king we will not hear to be turned aside at all from our pious service. (2.20–22)

With those words, Mattathias attacked and killed a fellow Jew who was sacrificing on the foreign altar, and the revolution was begun. A group of like-minded compatriots then gathered in the wilderness; among them is a religiously zealous group known as the Hasidim (2.42). Led by Mattathias and his sons, they carry out a series of successful attacks against the Greek armies over the course of three years. Jerusalem and the temple are recaptured in 164 BCE and the holy site is reconsecrated and dedicated exactly three years to the day since it was violated by foreign sacrifice (4.36–61). The name *Hanukkah,* which is still celebrated by Jews on this day the twenty-fifth of Kislev, comes from the Hebrew word for "dedication." We should also note that this scroll does not refer to the miracle of a one day's supply of oil lasting eight days—that story is not recorded until many centuries later in the Babylonian Talmud (shabbat 21b). The successful revolt led by the Hasmonean brothers spread geographically, and the Hasmoneans, while retaining their identity as priests, changed from renegade military leaders to political leaders who established a dynastic succession and gained independence from a faltering Greek Empire in 142 BCE (13.41–42): "In the one-seventieth year, the yoke of the Gentiles/nations was cast off from Israel . . ."

The work ends with a mention of the death of the last of the five sons of Mattathias, Simon, in 134 BCE and the beginning of the rule of his son John, 134 to 104 BCE.

1 Maccabees is written as a religious story. The chief motive for the revolt is to promote faithfulness to the laws of the God of Israel and to the righteous ways of Jewish ancestors. Although the author does not use miracles as part of his narrative, his God is his constant concern. Prayers, divine worship, priestly purity concerns, prophetic expressions of righteousness, religious poetry—all these permeate the narrative to such an extent that one is reminded of narratives of Samuel, Kings, and Chronicles. One unmistakable and primary religious objective of the author, especially at the beginning of his work, is to oppose the adoption of Greek cultural ways among Jews. Those who do so are considered unfaithful renegades who are on the side of the invading army of the Seleucids. For modern readers interested in studying the history of Judaism or sociological religious issues, we have much to consider here. Hellenistic cultural forms pervaded many parts of the Greek empires beginning in the third century BCE, and a great deal of Jewish literature of these centuries displays the variety of ways in which Jews interacted with Greek culture. Jews argued and advocated for different positions vis-à-vis different aspects of Greek culture, such as education, religious ideas, dress, diet, and government. 1 Maccabees strikes a particularly challenging stance against foreign influence and presents the Hasmoneans as the swift and great champions of the ways of the Jewish God and people. It is interesting then to realize that within only a few decades, some Jews of the region thought that the Hasmoneans were faithless compromisers of Jewish ways and traditions. In fact, as a ruling family they successfully expanded Jewish land holdings, made treaties with other nations, and worked with various Jewish factions to consolidate their own power, along the way making compromises and enemies.

DISPLAY 9.1 | COINS OF HASMONEAN KING ALEXANDER JAMAEUS

Questions for Further Study

What can be said about the function of canon when a Jewish tradition that does not admit 1 Maccabees canon celebrates Hanukkah, whereas Roman Catholic and Christian Orthodox traditions that do have 1 Maccabees in the canon do not celebrate the holiday? What are the complexities involved? What are historical changes in tradition that need to be taken into account?

References

Bickerman, Elias J. *The God of the Maccabees.* Leiden: E. J. Brill, 1979.

Doran, Robert. "1 Maccabees" in *The New Interpreter's Bible,* 4:1–178. Nashville, TN: Abingdon, 1996.

Goldstein, Jonathan A. *I Maccabees.* Garden City, NJ: Doubleday, 1976.

Harrington, Daniel J. *The Maccabean Revolt: Anatomy of a Biblical Revolution.* Wilmington, DE: Glazier, 1988.

Tcherikover, Victor. *Hellenistic Civilization and the Jews.* Philadelphia: Jewish Publication Society, 1959.

2 Maccabees

As we would expect, the scroll now called 2 Maccabees is also about the revolt of the Jews in the region around Jerusalem against the Syrian-Greek Empire of the Seleucid Dynasty. But it is not a sequel to 1 Maccabees, nor do we find simple repetition or even the same chronological frame. Instead, 2 Maccabees presents a fuller account of Jewish disagreements regarding proper attitudes toward Greek cultural practices. Like 1 Maccabees, the author of this scroll is also opposed to the Hellenizers, those Jews, including leading priests, who adopted foreign attitudes and actions that the author considered violations of divinely ordained Jewish law (4.11–17). But this author spends a good deal more space describing the internal conflicts among Jews of this time. We find here various parties among the priests and rulers who have varying views of authentic Jewish practice and varying allegiances to the rival political will of the Seleucid Empire, based in Syria, and the Ptolemaic Empire, based in Egypt (3.1–6.17). Such information gives the political and religious historian a good deal of data regarding the contesting forms of Judaism that were being practiced in the mid-second century BCE in Jerusalem. Appropriately then, it is here in 2 Maccabees that we have the first known use of the term *Judaism* (2.21), a term that has been used ever since to label particularly the religious traits of Jews.

With this greater influence on internal Jewish disputes, the author covers a significantly shorter time span than the approximately 45 years covered in 1 Maccabees. The scroll opens in approximately 180 BCE and concludes with the defeat of the Seleucid Greek general Nicanor by Judah the Maccabee in 161 BCE (15.1–39).

The history of composition for this scroll is quite unique among the scrolls in our library. First, 2 Maccabees reads in some ways much like a Greek historical work and less like the Israelite and Jewish histories such as Samuel, Kings, and Chronicles. Like Greek historians such as Herodotus and Thucydides, the author speaks in the first person and tells of his writing project. He writes in the introduction (2.19–32) that is work is an epitome, a literary condensation or summary, of a larger five-volume work by an otherwise unknown author, Jason of Cyrene. He describes his own goals not only of brevity and easy of reading but also making a work pleasurable to read (see 15.38–39), and the stories are told with considerable flare and vivid drama. The modern reader will also notice that two letters from Jewish leaders in Jerusalem to leaders in Egypt have been affixed at the beginning of the work, thus creating the situation where the epitome's introduction actually begins in 2.19.

If we wanted to study 2 Maccabees in an effort to understand its religious point of view, we would soon notice several characteristics. Unlike 1 Maccabees, the narrative contains many miracles and divine appearances. High drama

POSTER 9.3

A JEWISH TEMPLE IN EGYPT?

Jewish religious and cultural diversity in the last centuries BCE is quite remarkable, more so than many realize. Not only were there many different scrolls that were valued differently and different attitudes toward the Jewish God and torah, there were also different temples outside of Jerusalem. Already in the fifth century BCE, when the Persians were in charge, there was a Jewish colony in southern Egypt on the island of Elephantine that had a Jewish temple where sacrifices to the Jewish God were performed. Archaeologists in the late 1900s made some great discoveries of archaeological remains, and Jewish texts there that attest to this temple and some of community's correspondence with Jews in Jerusalem.

There was also another Jewish temple. In the early second century BCE, there was major civil unrest, at times war, among Jewish priests and leaders in Jerusalem. One priest, Onias IV, son of the Jerusalem high priest Onias III, had moved to Egypt. At a site called Leontopolis in the region of Heliopolis, near modern Cairo, he requested and was given an abandoned Egyptian temple that he made into a Jewish temple where he presided as high priest for Jews in the region. The Jewish historian Josephus tells us about this temple in his works *Antiquities of the Jews* (13.62–73, 12.387–88; 20.236) of the late first century CE.

It is also necessary to mention the attitude of one group toward the Jerusalem temple. This is the community of Jews who wrote the sectarian works among the Dead Sea Scrolls during the last century BCE. This group did not build their own temple, but they did object so strongly to the leadership of the Jerusalem temple that they refused to participate in or support it in any way. Instead, they looked forward to the day when their own proper ways of conducting temple sacrifices and manners of worship would replace the current abomination.

comes to the fore in scenes where an aged teacher of Torah spits out the pork that has been forcibly placed in his mouth and is then beaten to death, but not before giving a rousing speech (6.18–31). There follows a story of the martyrdom of seven brothers who would rather die than transgress the laws of their ancestors by eating pork. They too, before being gruesomely killed, proclaim their allegiance to their God (7.1–41). It is in the speech of the second brother that we encounter clearly for the first time in Jewish literature the idea that the righteous dead will be raised up for a new life (7.9), an idea that is less clearly spoken of in Daniel 12.2, which was written only several decades before 2 Maccabees. Of course, the idea of the **resurrection** of the dead will become supremely important in later forms of Judaism and Christianity. Finally, the religious investigator will notice that 2 Maccabees does have religious ideas in common with 1 Maccabees, Samuel, Kings, and some classical prophets of the Hebrew Bible. For our author, the God of Israel rules the world, uses all the nations to accomplish his purposes, and intervenes constantly to do so. This includes punishments and lessons for his people the Jews administered through the hand of foreign armies and generals. Furthermore, just as it was taught unequivocally in the scroll of Judith, proper observance of God's laws will ensure political and military protection, just as disobedience will ensure defeat (e.g., 11.13; 13.8). Finally, it is of great interest to many that 2 Maccabees is the first Jewish text that teaches an older Greek idea that God created the world *ex nihilo* "from nothing" (7.28).

Questions for Further Study

As a religion scholar, in what ways is the Judaism represented in this work (or any other!) a religion? a culture? an ethnicity? a civilization? a tradition? How are these terms related?

References

Doran, Robert. "2 Maccabees." In *The New Interpreter's Bible*, 4:179–299. Nashville, TN: Abingdon, 1996.

Doran, Robert. *Temple Propaganda: The Purpose and Character of 2 Maccabees*. Washington D.C.: Catholic Biblical Association, 1981.

Goldstein, Jonathan A. *II Maccabees*. Garden City, NJ: Doubleday, 1983.

Tcherikover, Victor. *Hellenistic Civilization and the Jews*. Philadelphia: Jewish Publication Society, 1959.

3 Maccabees

This fairly brief story will remind you thematically of several scrolls you have already read, such as Esther, 2 Maccabees, and Judith. The first thing to say, however, is that the title is truly a mistake; the work has nothing to do with the stories of the Maccabees. Instead it is about the persecution and humiliation of Jews in Alexandria, Egypt, and it is set in the days of the Ptolemaic king Philopator who reigned from 221 to 203 BCE, several decades before the Maccabean rise to power in 167 BCE. The work itself was likely written in the early part of the first century BCE by a Jew who lived in Alexandria, Egypt, which had a large Jewish population at the time. It was composed in Greek.

The story begins in Jerusalem with the Egyptian king Philopator (Ptolemy IV) requesting an entrance into the inner sanctuary of the holy temple, as was his standard practice in many temples. But the Jews do not permit him to enter due to the sanctity of the site: it is off limits to any one but the high priest, and he enters only once a year (1.11–12). But the king protests, and a major contest of royal will and Jewish piety ensues. Philopator makes his plans; the Jews of Jerusalem, led by the high priest, mourn, make supplication and are prepared to die to defend the holiness of the site and of their God. In the end, their God strikes the king with a violent illness, and he leaves Jerusalem enraged (1.1–2.24). This anger he takes out on the Jews of Alexandria by decreeing that Jews must bring a sacrifice if they ever enter another temple; they must pay poll tax and are made the status of slaves. Those who object will be killed. Jews can escape this treatment by being initiated into Greek mystery religions. Some Jews make the compromise, but most resist (2.25–33). The king seeks to kill them but several attempts are divinely thwarted. Finally, after the rounding up of a great many Jews, a mass slaughter is planned involving 500 drunken elephants. Again the Jews pray, this time led by a piously famed Eleazar, and again their God intervenes by showing his holy face to the king along with two frightful angels. At that point the elephants turn on their Greek forces, "the king's wrath [is] changed to pity and tears," and he testifies to the magnanimity of the Jews and their God (6.16–22). The story ends with grand reversals: The Jews are given a royal banquet by the king, who has had a complete change of heart, and their enemies are shamed (6.22–41). Finally, the Jews request of the king to be allowed to execute those Jews who had compromised by transgressing God's laws, and their request is granted (7.1–16).

If we come to this scroll asking historical questions, we will soon realize that it does not reflect real events of the time of Philopator. On the other hand, in the first century BCE when Roman interests were playing an expanding role in Egypt, the legal status of Jews was not always secure in Alexandria. Combining historical and religious inquiries, we can see that this story, which borrows many episodes and themes from earlier literature, was written to encourage the Jews of Alexandria to remain faithful to the God of their ancestors and to strongly make the point that that faithfulness must be defined in particular manners of social interaction. There is certainly a clear internal Jewish polemic in this story—the author's Jewish enemies end up being put to death. Although the story certainly emphasizes that Jews must live distinctly from non-Jews in particular ways, it also says that this arrangement can be respectful, mutually beneficial, and even friendly.

From a literary standpoint, the work is written in a bombastic Greek style—full of unusual words, phrasing, and exaggerations. Scholars have noted that its tone and style resemble popular Greek novels or romances. It is best understood as fictional work that is set in a historical context, not dissimilar to stories of Daniel, Esther, Tobit, and Judith. Therefore, it can be considered a diaspora tale. In addition, its entertainment value is not to be discounted.

Questions for Further Study

Describe the internal religious polemics of this work. What other works in and out of our library do they bring to mind?

References

Anderson, Hugh. "Third Maccabees," in *The Anchor Bible Dictionary*, edited by David N. Freedman, 4:450–52. New York: Doubleday, 1992.

Gruen, Erich S. *Heritage and Hellenism*. Berkeley: University of California, 1998.

Hadas, Moses. *The Third and Fourth Books of Maccabees*. New York: Harper, 1953.

4 Maccabees

The fourth and final work named for the famous Maccabees is another Greek composition and likely comes from the end of the last century BCE or from the beginning of the first century CE. The author's location is also hard to determine—some have argued for Alexandria, others for Jerusalem, and others for Antioch. Fortunately, our quest is not merely one for historical facts about the specific historical context of the author; when we start asking other kinds of questions, including rhetorical and philosophical, we are rewarded with more solid answers.

The scroll of 4 Maccabees is an excellent example of the fruitful interaction between the Jewish heritage and Greek traditions. The author uses stories known to us from 1 Maccabees and especially 2 Maccabees, namely, the executions of Eleazar, the seven brothers, and their mother by the Greek army for remaining true to their Jewish traditions. The scroll is a narrative that begins with a philosophical introduction and then moves to a retelling the stories of the final speeches of these nine heroes. These inspiring speeches fill up most of the content of the scroll.

Anyone familiar with the scrolls of the library will immediately see that the author of 4 Maccabees is also familiar with many of the characters and traditions found in those earlier scrolls: Abel and Cain, Abraham, Isaac, Jacob, Joseph, Torah, Moses, David, Prophets, Isaiah, Psalms (18.10–19). Many other stories are mentioned also, and so it is clear that Jewish stories and texts were alive and active in the author's writing culture and the lesson present in the scrolls of the other Maccabees, Judith, and Tobit: remain faithful to the traditions and God of our ancestors. What might surprise some readers is that 4 Maccabees is equally informed and inspired by the Greek philosophical school known as Stoicism, which was itself influenced by platonic thought. For example, from the very opening we find Greek philosophical terminology, including an explanation of the four cardinal virtues of Platonic and Stoic thought: rational thought, self-control, justice, and courage. Plato (ca. 429 to 347 BCE) lived in Athens, and stoicism developed a widespread following after its founder Zeno (335 to 263 BCE) came to Athens from Cyprus. The four virtues are just the beginning of the evidence of Greek influence, because 4 Maccabees overtly teaches, as did the Greek schools, that all passions and desires for comfort must be ruled by reason; the mind must control the body. This basic teaching is presented not as the teaching Plato or other Greek thinkers, but as the teaching of Jewish laws, prophets, ancestors, and traditions. In harmony with this philosophy of reason over body, the scroll also assumes the immortality of the rational mind, often called the soul, so that the death of the martyrs is really an escape of the rational soul from the body (7.19; 9.22; 14.5; 16.13, 25; 17.12; 18.23). We are not saying that the author's main goal is to teach Stoicism—in fact he sometimes has ideas counter to stoic notions—but his work is wholly informed by Platonic and Stoic ideals and language, and he understands them as the truth of commands of his God.

Finally, the author presents a theological notion about the martyrdom of Eleazar, the seven sons, and their mother that we did not encounter in 1 and 2 Maccabees. In 4 Maccabees we learn that the deaths of these brave martyrs is actually vicariously beneficial—it brings redemptive credit with God, or atonement—for other individuals of the faithful community, both in the present and future (6.28–29; 17.21–22).

So in the end, 4 Maccabees is a fascinating piece of rhetoric that adds a new kind of work to our library. Here we have a Greek narrative teaching its audience faithfulness to ancient Jewish tradition and doing so through the teachings of Greek philosophy. Rhetorically, the author makes these points through a first person narrator but most forcefully through the speeches of the great martyrs.

Questions for Further Study

As an anthropologist or historian of religion, how would you describe and account for the growing importance of martyrdom in works of this period?

References

Anderson, Hugh. "Third Maccabees," in *The Anchor Bible Dictionary,* edited by David N. Freedman, 4:452–54. New York: Doubleday, 1992.

Hadas, Moses. *The Third and Fourth Books of Maccabees.* New York: Harper, 1953.

Wisdom of Solomon

Reading Greek philosophical categories in 4 Maccabees prepares us well for this next scroll. Tradition has understandably credited the book to Solomon, though his name never occurs in the scroll, and in fact it was written in Greek sometime in the first century BCE, most likely in Alexandria, Egypt. It is referred to as Wisdom of Solomon or simply Wisdom, and the Jewish author certainly aims to present his work in the wisdom tradition of Solomon, who had become the "patron saint" of Jewish wisdom writings. Looking in Wisdom 7.1–9.18, we see the figure of Solomon and his prayers for wisdom (1 Kings 3.6–9, 2 Chronicles 1.8–10) echoing in the text. Numerous other passages and the poetic form recall the content and form of the scroll of Proverbs. In Greek style, again we find ethical instructions to practice the four key moral virtues of Platonism and Stoicism (Wisdom 8.7). If we are to categorize this literature by its theme or content, we would obviously say that it is a later Hellenistic example of Jewish wisdom literature, in the vein of Proverbs, Job, and Qohelet (Ecclesiastes).

This interesting composition is a didactic poem that teaches about wisdom. Like 4 Maccabees, it combines Jewish and Greek cultural heritage, specifically Jewish religious and wisdom traditions with Greek philosophical traditions. Like Proverbs, this scroll personifies wisdom as a woman (6.12–16) and adds the idea that wisdom is a divine spirit loving humanity (1.6–7). Also like Proverbs, the poetry is somewhat diverse, moving from proverbs (e.g., 6.17) and pithy sayings (e.g., 1.15) to longer meditations (e.g., 7.1–8.21), exhortations (e.g., 6.1–11), prayers (e.g., 9.1–18), Jewish biographical history lessons (e.g., 10.1–11.4), and even expansive arguments (e.g., 1.12–4.19). Unlike Proverbs, Job, and Qohelet (Ecclesiastes), Wisdom makes use of peculiarly Jewish historical and religious traditions, such as the stories of the Israelites' sojourn in and exodus from Egypt (especially 11.5–19.22). In this way, Wisdom of Solomon is less international in its outlook than the earlier wisdom literature contained in our library.

Wisdom of Solomon is not just a general exhortation to be ethical and live wisely. Instead, it is poetry that makes specific moral and theological points and arguments and in so doing it is significant in the history of Jewish thought. Here we find for the first time the clear indication of future immortality of those who live justly; in fact, there is an extensive argument for such a view (1.12–5.23). Our author even cites the arguments of his opponents (2.1–120) in order to counter them. Again, it seems clear that Greek ideas about the immortality of the soul are influencing the author, in contrast to most of the writings in the Hebrew Bible that envision no such afterlife. Sounding like Plato, our author describes the soul as being weighted down by the body and awaiting release (9.14–18). Remember how the scroll of Daniel, which also comes after extensive Jewish contact with Greek culture, referred to a resurrection to a future life for the righteous

(Daniel 12.2)? This long section of Wisdom spells out an afterlife position quite fully, making the case that those who are righteous will live forever. You will also recall that this is contrary to Qohelet (Ecclesiastes) (3.19–22; 9.4–10), who explicitly denied a future existence in any place other than the undesirable Sheol. So too, our next scroll, Ben Sira (ca. 200 BCE), has no suggestion of an afterlife. Thus we are witnessing a fascinating development in our scroll, namely that Wisdom of Solomon, written a century or two later than these earlier wisdom texts, signals a strong new position within Judaism by arguing for life after physical death, a tradition that will become important in later forms of Judaism and Christianity.

Of further interest is an intriguing link that is made between ancient Jewish and Greek traditions. We see a creative mind at work forging a link between a Greek idea of the *logos*, word which that can mean "reason," "sense," "word," "reasoning," "principle," or "power," and the idea of *Sophia*, "wisdom," which our author personifies, as did the author of Proverbs. To some Greek philosophers, *logos*, was the divine emanation that knit the cosmos together and infuses the world with order and reason. This ordering principle is now associated with the personified and active wisdom of the Jewish God (9.1–2; 18.15) who creates the world and aids those who are just. About a century later, this idea of the *logos*, as the saving emanation of God will be a key concept for the early Christian writer of the Gospel of John (1.1–4).

Questions for Further Study

What ideas in Wisdom of Solomon are comparable to specific religious teachings that you know of in our time? What ideas are significantly different from ideas in works of the Hebrew Bible?

References

Kolarcik, Michael. "The Book of Wisdom," in *The New Interpreter's Bible*, 5:435–600. Nashville, TN: Abingdon, 1997.

Winston, David. *The Wisdom of Solomon*. Garden City, NY: Doubleday, 1979.

Winston, David. "Wisdom of Solomon," in *The Anchor Bible Dictionary*, edited by David N. Freedman, 6:120–27. New York: Doubleday, 1992.

חומת בן סידא
Wisdom of Ben Sira
Homat ben Sira

This scroll continues in the vein of Jewish wisdom literature written in the Hellenistic period, when Greek empires controlled the regions around Mediterranean and the Fertile Crescent. This scroll is by far the longest of all those in this category of Deuterocanonicals, and it is about twice as long as Proverbs, the composition it most resembles. The work has a long, influential, and fascinating history of translation and transmission in various Jewish and Christian communities, and it is this variety that produced the three or four different names by which we know the scroll. Wisdom of Ben Sira is the more complete title for which Ben Sira and Sirach (a variation of Sira) are abbreviations. The name Ecclesiasticus, meaning "book of the church," comes from Latin manuscripts used by the Roman Catholic tradition.

For many centuries we only possessed this composition in Greek, Latin, and Syriac translations. But several modern discoveries have turned up sizeable fragments of the original Hebrew. First was the discovery of old manuscripts in the Ben Ezra Synagogue of Old Cairo in the late 1800s, and then came archaeological discoveries at Qumran and later at the fortress of Masada, also near the Dead Sea. As you would expect by now, these various manuscripts do not all have identical texts. For example, Hebrew manuscripts contain a poem that we don't have in Greek, which is now printed in most English editions between Ben Sira 51.12 and 13. Perhaps even more interesting is that we actually have in our Hebrew and Greek manuscripts information about the original author of the Hebrew scroll and about when the Hebrew was translated into Greek and by whom. Like almost no other scroll we have considered, Ben Sira contains a straightforward account of its own production; after seeing so many scrolls that were written anonymously or pseudonymously, we are happily quite confident that we even know the author's name.

The original Hebrew composition was written around 200 to 180 BCE by a certain Yeshua son of Eleazar son of Sirach (50.27). *Yeshua* transliterates into English as *Joshua* or *Jesus*. The "son of" is a translation of the Hebrew word *ben*. It was not uncommon for Jewish males of this time to be called the son of a grandfather; thus, Yeshua ben Sirach. This Yeshua was a teacher and scribe, probably in Jerusalem, who put his wisdom into the written form of this scroll, most likely his magnum opus. Several decades later, around 130 BCE, his grandson, who had moved to Egypt, took it upon himself translate his grandfather's work into Greek and to commend it to a much wider Jewish audience. This is all explained in the Greek preface to the scroll (see also 51.24).

This preface, written by the grandson in Egypt, is one of the most valuable historical disclosures we have about ancient Jewish writings from the last centuries BCE. The grandson mentions his travel to Egypt and the purpose of his translation and its shortcomings. He also refers to older Jewish writings, to which his grandfather "was devoted," calling them "the law, the prophets, and the other ancestral scrolls," and he knows that they, too, have been translated into Greek. From this preface we gain many clues about Jewish cultures in Jerusalem and Egypt that were highly valuing written texts of their Jewish heritage, collecting them, categorizing them, studying them, translating them, and writing more of them for future generations. Yeshua himself, in the body of his work, highlights the importance of the written instructions from Moses by presenting all-encompassing Wisdom as identical with "the scroll of the covenant with the greatest God, the law that Moses commanded us as an inheritance for the peoples of Jacob" (24.23).

So what do we find in this scroll by Yeshua that caused his grandson to value it enough to translate it? The answer is wisdom poetry. Like Proverbs, like much of Job and Qohelet (Ecclesiastes), and like Wisdom of Solomon, Yeshua wrote within a known literary tradition of wisdom literature. This teacher's writing, which is completely in poetic form, is not clearly in a developed arrangement; it seems to be a collection of reflections and instructions. In many ways, like Proverbs, Yeshua is writing to praise wisdom and commend it to his students, whom he speaks to quite personally in the second person as his son. Thus he instructs his reader, "my son," about honesty; hard work; discipline; guarding one's tongue, wealth, and temper; and controlling sexual passions.

Yeshua's wisdom, unlike Proverbs—and far different from Job and Qohelet (Ecclesiastes)—combines traditional wisdom themes with particular Jewish ideas about history and religion. In this way the scroll is much like Wisdom of Solomon. Most impressive is a long and detailed history poem in honor of famous Jewish ancestors—mostly characters from the scrolls of the Hebrew Bible—which runs from pre-flood heroes down to the high priest of Yeshua's own day, Simon (44.1–50.26). Yeshua's poetry also includes what we might call liturgy, that is, praises and prayers to the God of the Jews (42.15–43.33; 51.1–12). But in contrast to Wisdom of Solomon, which was written perhaps a century and a half after Yeshua wrote, our scroll speaks of the future without even remotely envisioning an afterlife for those who die. Instead, in keeping with earlier Jewish conceptions, Sheol is the future abode of everyone (14.12–19; 38.16–23) and Israel lives forever only in the sense of future generations who are faithful to their God (44.13–15).

There is one more fascinating fact about Ben Sira. The scroll, after a brief first person postscript by Yeshua (50.27–29), closes with some prayers praising Israel's God, one of which was also found as a psalm in one of the many Psalms scrolls among the Dead Sea Scrolls. What is usually printed as Ben Sira 51.13–20 is found as a separate poem in a psalm collection completely separate from Ben Sira. This provides an excellent case for textual detective work! Where was the poem first?

Who borrowed from whom? You can see that for someone with a healthy curiosity about the history of the scrolls of our library, this could make for a absorbing investigation.

Questions for Further Study

1. Ben Sira is another work combing older Jewish traditions and some Greek traditions, but with different results. If you were to construct a continuum of Jewish cultural and religious positions in the Hellenistic period, what would it look like? How much variety would you see?

References

Crenshaw, James L. "The Book of Sirach," in *The New Interpreter's Bible*, 5:601–867. Nashville, TN: Abingdon, 1997.

Skehan, Patrick W. and Alexander A. Di Lella, *The Wisdom of Ben Sira*. Garden City, NY: Doubleday, 1987.

Di Lella, Alexander A. "Book of Ben Sira," in *The Anchor Bible Dictionary*, edited by David N. Freedman, 6:931–45. New York: Doubleday, 1992.

ברוך

Baruch

The name Baruch may sound familiar, and if you look back at our discussion of the scroll of Jeremiah you will recall why (see the section "Baruch, Scribe and Associate"). Baruch, pronounced in Hebrew as "bah-*rookh*" (*kh* as *ch* in *Bach*), was the name of a scribe who worked for or with the prophet Jeremiah in the sixth century BCE during the downfall of the Southern Kingdom of Israel. In the scroll of Jeremiah, especially in the shorter version, Baruch is an important figure and prophet in his own right. In later centuries his reputation grew, at least in some Jewish circles, and we are not surprised to see literature being composed as if Baruch himself wrote them; therefore, this scroll is a pseudepigraphon. It was likely written in Hebrew sometime in the late second century BCE, some four centuries after the historical Baruch.

The work is quite short—six to eight pages in most English versions—and is easily divided into two halves. The first half (1.1–3.8) is in prose and details some of the traditions about Baruch. It begins with the tradition that Baruch went to Babylon with the exiles in 586 BCE when Jerusalem was conquered by Babylon, and while there he wrote this work (1.1). What Baruch writes is a long prayer of confession of sins that he instructs the new exiles to pray (1.15–3.8). Clearly the second-century BCE author looking back at the fall of Jerusalem interprets it as God's fulfillment of his warnings to Moses, namely that he would punish his people for disobedience and for not listening to his words through the words of Moses and the prophets. Our author also sees a hopeful ending to this story of the eternal covenant between his God and his people (2.30–35). This view of God's activity is not uncommon for this period, and in fact the unknown author of Baruch seems to borrow directly from Daniel Chapter 9.

The second half of the scroll is made up of several poems, which were probably separate compositions originally. The first is in praise of wisdom (3.9–4.4) and reminds us of passages in Proverbs, Job 28, Ben Sira, and Wisdom of Solomon. Nearing the end of his extolling of wisdom, who is personified as a woman, the author indicates that wisdom is "the scroll of the commands of God" and that the instruction that exists forever (4.1). There are similar sayings in Ben Sira. We might say, however, if we judge from a modern sense of thematic continuity, that this section on wisdom does not seem to mesh so well with the rest of Baruch. But perhaps this last segment on the *torah* of Israel's God is the linchpin that links the segments.

The next poem returns to the subject of Jerusalem and exile. It begins with Jerusalem speaking words of encouragement to the exiles as her children now scattered but soon to return (4.5–29). A response by an external voice comes next, and Jerusalem is comforted and told that she can look forward to days of renewal and peace and glory (4.30–5.9). Clearly this second-century BCE author was looking forward to days ahead when Jerusalem could again hold her head high and was prophetically seeking to encourage others, whether living outside of Judah or in it, with this vision.

Questions for Further Study

Studying the figure of Baruch in Jewish and Christian traditions is fascinating; sometimes he is praised as a true Jewish prophet and in others is denounced as the founder of Zoroastrianism. Read about this in some standard encyclopedias. How do such contrasts develop? What is their value for historical study? for religion?

References

Mendels, Doron. "Baruch, Book of," in *The Anchor Bible Dictionary,* edited by David N. Freedman, 1:618–20. New York: Doubleday, 1992.

Tov, Emanuel. *The Book of Baruch Also Called I Baruch.* Missoula, MT: Society of Biblical Literature, 1975.

Wright, J. Edward, *Baruch Ben Neriah.* Columbia: University of South Carolina, 2003.

סֵפֶד יִרְמִיָהוּ

Letter of Jeremiah
Sefer Yirm^eyahu

Sometime in the third or perhaps fourth century BCE, a devout Jew composed this two- or three-page piece in either Hebrew or Aramaic. The scroll is introduced as a letter written by Jeremiah, the famous prophet of the sixth century BCE. According to the introduction, Jeremiah sent the letter from Jerusalem to Babylon to give the exiles a message that God commanded him to deliver. The inspiration for setting the work as a letter is the report of a message sent by Jeremiah in Jeremiah 29.1. Similarly, the scroll of Baruch is presented as a letter—it was not an uncommon form of pseudepigraphic writing. This short work appears variously in ancient manuscripts. We have no Hebrew manuscripts of it, and in Greek or Latin translations it is sometimes attached to Baruch as the last chapter of that work. Thus, in the Roman Catholic tradition it is the last chapter of Baruch, whereas in tradition of the Orthodox Christian churches it is a separate work.

But once you get past the opening verse, the scroll will not strike you much like a letter. It is really a rhetorically organized sermon, a rant even, against idolatry, the making and worshiping of physical images of Gods. The author scoffs at the caricatures of Babylonian Gods, which he describes as worthless stones served by foolish priests. The scroll is structured around two refrains that occur at the ends of thematic paragraphs. The first refrain, "Therefore, it is clear that they are not Gods; don't fear them!" occurs in the opening and closing sections of the scroll five times. The second refrain, "Why then would anyone think they are Gods or call them Gods?" occurs fives times in the middle of the scroll.

It is perfectly clear that the author sensed that Jews of his day, who lived as a minority amid peoples with temples with impressive representations of Gods, were tempted to worship these other Gods. Appealing to Jewish traditions of their God's work in creation, he makes the impassioned appeal to not turn to powerless idols. The author's theme and polemic is in accord with earlier Jewish writings that also criticize images of foreign Gods as worthless. We see this not only in Jeremiah (e.g., 10.1–16), from which this scroll derives its inspiration, but also in other Israelite literature (e.g., Isaiah 46.1–7 and Psalms 115.4–8). Our letter seems to have been known by some later authors, such as the writer of 2 Maccabees. In 2 Maccabees 2.2, written a century or more after the Letter of Jeremiah, the author refers to

Jeremiah's instructions to exiles in Babylon not to be taken in by the statues of foreign Gods.

Questions for Further Study

What might be the internal Jewish polemic regarding the way other Gods are to be conceptualized? Is Aristotle's Prime Mover an idol? (The Prime Mover was Aristotle's idea of a supreme being: an unchanging, impersonal, eternal, ultimate cause of all. See his *Metaphysics*.) Is Zeus?

References

Harrington, Daniel J. *Invitation to the Apocrypha*. Grand Rapids, MI: Eerdmans, 1999.

Moore, Carey A. *Daniel, Esther and Jeremiah: The Additions*. Garden City, NY: Doubleday, 1977.

——. "Jeremiah, Additions to," in *The Anchor Bible Dictionary*, edited by David N. Freedman, 3:684–98. New York: Doubleday, 1992.

Chapter 10

Meeting the Librarians: The Communities of the Scrolls

Religious Communities and Biblical Literature

A library is impossible without librarians. The preservation of any document beyond the lifespan of its author(s) requires that later individuals and groups decide to keep the writing, maybe supplementing, copying, or translating it to a different language for contemporary readers. From the first person or group who preserved a biblical scroll until the most recent form today, these writings have been preserved for a variety of reasons. Why does a person keep some books or papers and not others? Obviously because we value them enough to keep them and obviously there are many different reasons for valuing the writings of the library we just left. Consider these purposes:

- preserving records for a king's or priest's archive
- preserving ancient Jewish traditions about the past and God
- preserving instructions considered divine
- preserving ancient wise sayings in order to teach them to contemporary students
- preserving enjoyable and entertaining stories or beautiful poetry
- preserving provocative intellectual literature

Of course, all of these reasons might be combined in various ways by different preservers over time. All of them may be motivated by strong religious or cultural attitudes. At different points in time in various communities, the preservation of certain writings became a tradition itself, and to formally remove a writing became hard, though not impossible. For example, many Jews in the second and first centuries BCE choose to preserve writings such as Genesis, Deuteronomy, Ben Sira, and Tobit in Greek translations, while other Jewish groups were preserving these same books in Hebrew. Later, by the second to fourth centuries CE, most Jewish groups no longer choose to preserve their sacred writings in Greek, but instead preserved them mostly in Hebrew. Many Christian communities were just the opposite: They kept the Hebrew writings that they valued enough to preserve mostly in translated forms such as Greek, and they preserved other documents that we now know as New Testament writings in their original Greek. Today, of course, Jews and Christians have chosen to preserve these writings in myriad modern languages and forms.

In our world today there are three major religions, Judaism, Christianity, and Islam, that are directly related to the literature of the library we have just toured. We might think of two of them, Judaism and Christianity, as the religious communities that visit and use this library a lot and also as those who work to maintain it in good usable condition. In some ways it is more accurate to say that they have built up their own separate libraries. The library is a very active, living place for them. But all three of these religions value and employ biblical literature, though they do so in quite different ways. For essays about this variety of attitudes and uses among Jews, Christians, and Muslims, see Bowley 1998. People in each of these religions have some sense of continuity or connection with these writings. At the most basic level, some of them say they are today worshiping the same God we read about in Genesis and Psalms. Many would also describe themselves as physical or religious descendants of the characters we read about, especially Abraham. Jews trace their religious lineage back to Moses and Abraham. In the Qur'an we find the idea that "the nearest of kin to Abraham are those who follow him" in his submission (*islam*) to God (*sura* 3.67–68), and in early Christian writings we have the notion that even Gentiles (non-Jews) may become the descendants of Abraham (Romans 4.16) by religious faith. Thus, these three world religions are sometimes called the Abrahamic religions, or the biblical religions, and are studied together because of this common heritage. Finally, we certainly should not overlook the many people in our world who may not consider themselves a part of these three religions but who still highly value and admire literature from our library for a variety of reasons; they see themselves as heirs to treasured writings of a common human heritage.

DISPLAY 10.1 | THE GUTENBERG BIBLE BROUGHT ABOUT A REVOLUTION IN BIBLE PRODUCTION

Johann Gutenberg (ca. 1396 to 1468) of Mainz was the first to print Bibles, beginning in 1453. He printed for both Christian and Jewish clients. Book production became substantially cheaper, faster, and more accurate.

As you know, Jews, Christians, and Muslims are often very different from each other in their religious ideas and practices, and this is not the place for an introduction to these three religions with which about half the population of our world are affiliated. Before we leave our tour we can make some brief generalizations about the major groups of Bible users that will be helpful as we seek to understand the wide variety of biblical interpreters today. It is the historical experiences and differing religious ideas of the communities that have produced varied understandings of the value, role, and meaning. All of these groups demonstrate many religious developments from the time period of the writing and collecting of the biblical library. For each community, and each individual, biblical literature is only one component in a larger system of thought about reality, the world as we experience it, and God(s).

Jewish Practice

There are some 14 to 15 million Jews in the world today, some of whom are religious, some are not. Those Jews who affiliate with the major, formal Jewish religious organizations can be classified as Reform, Conservative, Reconstructionist, or

Traditional (Orthodox). If you know many different Jews, especially ones from various backgrounds and branches of Judaism, you will already know that each group views and values the Tanakh differently. Some stress that it is divine in origin, others will see it as fully human, and there are several intermediate viewpoints. Generally speaking, among all Jews today, the Torah takes precedence over and above the other scrolls of the Tanakh. This priority and the identification of *Torah* with the first five scrolls and not with other ancient scrolls attributed to Moses was a historical development of the last few centuries BCE and first two centuries CE (see Chapter 1 for a review). These five books, now traditionally handwritten on one very long, large scroll for synagogue use, are the textual centerpiece of Jewish life.

- The Torah is spoken of as the covenant and central story of Jewish religious life.

- Commentaries, summaries, expansions have continuously been written about the Torah.

- The Torah is read though consecutively once a year in synagogues, and a special festival and service marks the ending and starting over of the reading.

- The physical scroll of the Torah is granted meticulous care and ritual honor.

But the primacy of the Torah does not mean that all Jews agree about how to think about its authority, interpretation, or relevance. One Jew will value the Torah as a supremely important part of her heritage but not as an authoritative voice of God for today. Another Jew will value it as the written word of God delivered to Moses, to be interpreted and applied as taught by a particular Jewish group.

The Jewish heritage today owes a great deal to Jewish leaders, called rabbis, who produced the writings known as the Mishnah (ca. 200 CE) and the Babylonian Talmud (ca. 500 CE) in the second century CE through the fifth century CE, as well as many commentaries on the Torah. We should not think that Judaism is the same as the religion of the Torah or Hebrew Bible. Remember how so much of the library we toured is about priests, the temple, sacrifices, and prophets? The various Judaisms today really have none of that. Like Islam and Christianity, modern Judaism is a development from those ancient Israelite traditions. We could say that developments in Judaism led to a religion centered on texts, specifically the Torah: reading, discussing, debating, studying, commenting, arguing, and loving. The two large multivolume writings of Mishnah and Talmud (over 6,000 pages) provide a sort of written conversation and guide by scholars and teachers about Jewish practice, ideas, and interpretation of the Torah and other sacred scrolls of Tanakh. For those Jews known as Traditionalists or Orthodox, the Mishnah and Talmud serve as the practical guide for studying and understanding the Torah and for practicing Judaism today, and these writings are also considered sacred and divine. For other Jews, especially Reform or Reconstructionist Jews, the Mishnah and Talmud usually play a less central or authoritative role. These movements are not intellectually or religiously committed to affirming agreement with earlier Jewish teachers whose words are found in the Torah, Mishnah, Talmud, or later commentaries. Leaders of the Conservative movement tend to steer a middle path between the Reform and Traditionalists.

Poster 10.1

Many Jewish Ways of Reading

In the twenty-first century, Jews use many different methods of interpreting, researching, and enjoying the ancient texts of our library, such as those described in Chapter 2. In Jewish tradition long before the modern period, Jewish methods of interpretation were often grouped into the following four categories that formed a hierarchy from the least to the most valuable:

1. *Peshat:* the simple, plain, or surface meaning of words and narratives
2. *Remez:* the allegorical meaning that usually served to produce philosophical meanings
3. *Derash:* the meanings that edify and instruct; inspiring morals and teaching rules for living
4. *Sod:* the mystical and secret messages of a passage as revealed through the study of Kabbalah, Jewish mysticism.

Since the Enlightenment and rise of modern scientific and historical methods, the simple and plain meaning of texts has certainly become more valued by many Jewish readers and researchers, and for some Jews, modern archaeological findings that call into question the historicity of biblical (or even Talmudic) events are highly problematic. However, the value of multiple ways of reading and multiple interpretations within Judaism remains as strong as ever.

Jews of the Reform movement today also give pride of place to the Torah, but Reform Jews have also emphasized the Neviim scrolls, especially in their ethical calls for justice. In all branches of Judaism, other scrolls of our library outside of the Torah are regularly read or studied. Some are formally part of synagogue services, such as Psalms, Esther, Ruth, Qohelet (Ecclesiastes), and Song of Songs. But books outside of the 24 scrolls of the Hebrew Bible, such as Mishnah, Talmud, Midrashim, and Commentaries, which have accumulated over the centuries, are constantly being used to engage the more ancient texts of our library. It is as if there were a great conversation going on across the ages about the meaning and importance of all these texts, and the conversation is just as lively today as ever. The conversation is about almost anything imaginable—God, ethics, religious practices and ideas, folklore, parables, and much more. This conversation itself is so highly valued that it becomes a part of the Torah. Let me explain. The word *torah* can refer to a single teaching or lesson, but it also refers to the first five books of the Hebrew scriptures. But it also can be used in Judaism to refer to all the books of the Hebrew Bible. Beyond that, torah can be used to include later works of Jewish learning and tradition, such as the Talmud—sometimes referred to as the **Oral Torah.** And finally, all Jewish learning and study are sometimes called *torah.* As one modern rabbi puts it, "Torah in the broadest sense is what happens whenever two or more Jews get together to discuss sacred matters" (Wylen 2005, 42). Most Shabbat (Saturday) mornings I join in a delightful conversation/discussion/argument in my local synagogue and though we always launch from the Torah, the five books, we never know just where our conversation might end up.

A central feature of this centuries-long conversation within Judaism is that the table is open to a range of interpreters—rabbis and others who understand the meaning of the texts of the Torah and other scrolls very differently. It has long been recognized—even emphasized and celebrated—that the Torah or any other Jewish book is interpreted differently by different people, and many Jewish texts pass on a wide variety of interpretations and the arguments of all sides of debates. These differences are often seen as inherent in the text itself. According to one ancient rabbi, "there are seventy faces to the Torah," by which he means to emphasize that any line of Torah study may have dozens of different interpretations, all of which may be insightful and valid (*Midrash Rabbah*, Numbers 7.19). This recognition of multiple meanings has much in common with modern literary appreciation for ambiguity and multivalency that we talked about in Chapter 2.

Christian Practice

The religion that we today call Christianity, involving nearly 2 billion adherents, arose first among Jews and then among non-Jews in the first and second centuries CE. The religious devotion and beliefs were centered around a Jewish teacher named Jesus (ca. 5 BCE to 28 CE) who lived in the region of Galilee during a time of Roman control. Because of the strong Jewish presence in the earliest period of Christianity, Jewish religious writings were of great importance to Christian ideas and practices. Thus, many of the scrolls of our library were already highly valued by the earliest Jewish Christians, and they also became vital to the new religious life of later Christians. Open up a New Testament to almost any page and you will see the inspirational and often authoritative use that these authors make of earlier Jewish writings. This is not insignificant, because it represents the victory of one side of an argument among second- and third-century Christians. There were some Christians, most famously a Christian leader named Marcion (ca. 110 to 160 CE), who argued that the Christian message and beliefs were not closely tied to old Jewish ideas, and so Christians ought not to accept or use the old Jewish books. Eventually Marcion's arguments lost out, and so all forms of Christianity still officially maintain the older Jewish writings, usually referred to as the Old Testament.

Because Christian ideas were at first spread primarily in the Greek-speaking environment of the Roman Empire, Christians naturally used Greek editions of the Jewish writings. These Greek editions included writings originally composed in Hebrew or Greek that were not included in the official Jewish canon, which was fully settled for most Jews by 200 CE. It is also during this period that the codex was invented, and Christian groups seem to have taken to the new technological invention and began to use it for making copies of their sacred writings.

Among early Christians there was not a standardized collection of sacred writings, and to this day there is no universally accepted list of authoritative books common to all Christians, even though there is a large central core of works that all Christian canons share. We talked about this in Chapters 1 and 9, and you can turn back to see the various lists. The first evidence of Christian interest in defining a precise Christian set of sacred scriptures comes with Melito, bishop of Sardis, who around 180 CE traveled to Palestine and inquired about which books were valued as sacred. Later Christians composed lists of these books, and there is a striking lack of unanimity regarding the books of the inherited Jewish library (Lewis 1991, 168). Since the time of the great Christian scholar Jerome (342 to 420 CE), some Christian leaders and bodies have acknowledged the impreciseness of the Christian canon by creating an intermediate category of books that are deemed good, but not as good; that is, good for reading and moral teaching but not for the establishment of Christian orthodox belief. An example of this is found in the 1611 of the King James Bible: it includes the lesser books, which it calls Apocrypha, in a separate section between the Old and New Testaments. There are still differences among Christians today in the lists of books that comprise the Old Testament.

In certain ways this is not an important issue within Christianity. Much more decisive than the number of books accepted for the Old Testament is the addition of specifically Christian writings to the collection of books valued as sacred and authoritative. The Christian New Testament, containing 27 different Christian writings, is the most important part of the Bible for all Christian groups, because here we can see the centrality of Jesus Christ, *Christ* being the Greek translation of the Hebrew word *messiah* or *meshiach* (actual Hebrew pronounced m^e-*she*-akh), a Jewish title for a heroic rescuer (see page 240). To understand how biblical literature functions within Christianity, we should first recognize that at the center of the Christian ideas stands Jesus. As you might realize from different Christians you know or from the sheer number of different Christian groups, Christianity is very diverse, even in its views about Jesus. This has actually been the case from the beginning, as a great deal of evidence in hundreds of early Christian writings demonstrates. But what is common to all is the prime importance of Jesus, and this has had a major impact on the way Christians read and value the scrolls of our library.

This centrality of the Christian figure of Jesus Christ means that the New Testament is at least to some degree more important than the scrolls of the Hebrew Bible, or Old Testament. Some Christian leaders have attempted to change the title *Old Testament* to something less denigrating, such as *First Testament*. One way of putting it is that for Christians, Jesus Christ is God's most important message and revelation to humanity, and so all earlier messages from or understandings of God should be understood in the light of Christ. The teachings of Jesus written in the New Testament Gospels and the theology about Jesus in many Christian writings function as a religious interpretive framework that guides Christian readings and understandings. Many Christian interpreters through the centuries have read the writings of our library looking for ways in which their content might relate to Christian ideas about Jesus. For example, Jesus is frequently spoken of as being the fulfillment of promises that God made in the ancient Jewish writings. Or, allegorical

POSTER 10.2

MANY CHRISTIAN WAYS OF READING

In the twenty-first century Christians use many different methods of interpreting, researching, and enjoying the ancient texts of our library, such as those described in Chapter 2. In Christian tradition, especially in the Western Catholic regions, the following four categories formed the standard medieval description of ways to interpret biblical passages:

Literal: the factual, simple meaning

Allegorical: the meaning obtained by reading of stories allegorically; guides theological beliefs

Moral: the meanings that teach a person what to do and how to live

Anagogical: the meaning that relates the passage to the future—end of time or eternity—through symbolism

Do you notice some similarities with the four Jewish forms, described in Poster 10.1? Just as in Judaism, the Enlightenment and rise of modern scientific and historical methods have had an effect on Christian interpreters, especially by emphasizing historical matters and ancient contexts. For some Christians who are committed to certain beliefs about the past, these modern discoveries and methods have been problematic, although others have adapted their ways of thinking to the new scientific and historical ideas.

interpretation can be used to see Christ in stories of the Hebrew Bible; recall the story discussed in Chapter 5, Community Reflections 5.4, page 168.

If Judaism's 14 to 15 million adherents can display many different religious ideas and practices, just think what might be true of nearly 2 billion Christians. If we were to attempt to describe the many differences, we might decide that we should talk about Christianities, not just a single group. These differences affect the way people interact with biblical literature. For example, some Christian groups have clearly designated hierarchies that have official authority in the group for interpreting scriptures and, more importantly, for setting the agenda of that group's discussions about the meaning of scriptures. In Roman Catholicisms the ultimate authority is the Pope, though in practice there is a good deal of diversity among Catholics. In many Protestant groups, leaders must subscribe to a particular written document, often called a confession or statement of faith, which is intended to dictate what beliefs about Jesus and scriptures are acceptable; this document is a general guide for acceptable interpretations of biblical literature. The Eastern

Orthodox churches stress the need for interpretation to be done in keeping with the broad outlines of the official decisions early Christian councils. Another large group of Christians, known as the Church of Jesus Christ of Latter Day Saints, or Mormons, is guided in its in interpretation by its acceptance of another book of revelation, the Book of Mormon, and other particular Mormon teachings.

Christians have found many different way to make the biblical texts meaningful to their own lives and minds. At many levels within Christian denominations, people regularly interact with writers and speakers from outside their own group, and in this way a many boundary-crossing conversation occurs, and people become aware of the variety of interpretations.

Muslim Practice

The religion of Islam arose in the seventh century CE on the Arabian Peninsula. Today it spans the globe and has around 1 billion adherents. The religious practices of Muslims are also quite varied, as one would expect. Generally speaking, Islam has elements that resemble both Judaism and Christianity, and Muslims believe in the God of the Jews and Christians. The founder of Islam, Muhammad (570 to 632 CE), grew up in an area influenced by both Jewish and Christian thought. Muslim leaders consider many of the great persons in the stories of the Hebrew Bible such as Adam, Abraham, Moses, and David, to be God's prophets. Jesus is also considered a great prophet, and the sacred books of Jews and Christians are spoken of as containing God's message. It is in the Qur'an that we first encounter the respectful term *people of the book,* which is used to refer to Jews and Christians.

However, central to Islam is a new and final written revelation from God. This revelation is of course the Qur'an, which, according to Muslim ideas, eclipses all other revelations. The degree of textual finality for Muslims is generally seen as absolute, so much so that great stress is placed on the original language of the Qur'an, and translations are often not formally thought of as Qur'an. Furthermore, Muslims do not generally deal directly with Bibles, whether Jewish or Christian. It is not like Christianity, which decided to use the older books of the Old Testament and add its own in the form of the New Testament. The Qur'an alone functions as holy scripture in Islam, and for this reason we would say that the biblical library or libraries is more important for Jews and Christians than it for is Muslims.

But that does not mean our library is not important for understanding Islam. In fact, it is the Qur'an itself that has hundreds, probably thousands of references, direct and indirect, to stories, persons, and ideas in the Hebrew Bible and Christian New Testament, as reflected in the "Community Reflections" sections in the preceding chapters. On the one hand, biblical literature is not formally studied or interpreted directly in an Islamic religious setting. On the other hand, biblical literature is constantly being reflected in the pages of Qur'an. A description of the various Islamic forms of interpretation of the Qur'an is just as complex as the Jewish and Christian methods for their sacred texts, but because they would apply only to the Qur'an, we will not explore this here. But in regard to biblical literature, we can say that the Qur'an presents interpretations that are mostly interested in matters of God's revelation, religious beliefs, divine actions, and moral teachings.

Study Room 10.1

METHODS AND POLITICS

Tied to the American evangelical Christian position on proper biblical interpretation and the use of modern science is the story of the famous 1925 U.S.
trial of John Scopes, who was arrested for violating a Tennessee law prohibiting
the teaching of "any theory that denies the story of the Divine Creation of man
as taught in the Bible, and to teach instead that man has descended from a
lower order of animals" (Butler Act, 64th Tennessee General Assembly, 1925).

Read the stories in Genesis 1–3 and consider the various Christian and
Jewish interpretive strategies that could be applied to them. What kind of biblical interpretation must have been assumed as exclusively correct in order
for Scopes to be convicted for violating the Tennessee law? What interpretive
methods would not be against this law? What is literalism? How does this trial
relate to the situation of Galileo Galilei in the seventeenth century and of the
debates in Kansas and elsewhere about the teaching of evolution in 1999 and
2005? Why are certain exclusivist ways of reading Genesis so influential in the
United States? Are they in other nations? How have Jews or Muslims reacted
to these Christian readings? How have other Christians reacted?

Consider the following quote from an early Christian leader, Origen (185
to 254 CE). How might he have responded to the Tennessee law? What type of
interpretation does he advocate? Would he have been arrested, too?

> Now what man of intelligence will believe that the first and the second
> and the third day, and the evening and the morning existed without the
> sun and moon and stars? And that the first day, if we may so call it, was
> even without a heaven? And who is so silly as to believe that God, after
> the manner of a farmer, "planted a paradise eastward in Eden," and set
> in it a visible and palpable "tree of life," of such a sort that anyone who
> tasted its fruit with his bodily teeth would gain life; and again that one
> could partake of "good and evil" by masticating the fruit taken from the
> tree of that name? And when God is said to "walk in the paradise in
> the cool of the day" and Adam to hide himself behind a
> tree, I do not think anyone will doubt that these are
> figurative expressions which indicate certain mysteries
> through a semblance of history and not through actual
> event.

—*On First Principles* 1936, 289.

The Library in Our Pluralistic World

There have been other pluralistic times and places in world history when people of
different cultures and religions lived together as neighbors, but probably not to the
degree that is true of the twenty-first century. So many people of the world are no

longer isolated to communities made up of one religion or ethnic group. I currently live in the relatively small city of Jackson, Mississippi—not exactly the world's leading cosmopolitan center—and yet I have regular face-to-face interaction with Jews, Christians, Muslims, Hindus, Buddhists, Unitarians, Sikhs, Bahais, and many nonreligious people. Within those religious groupings there are huge practical and ideological differences among members of the same religion. Then we need to consider all the ethnic and cultural differences of those from China, Egypt, India, New Orleans, New York, Nebraska, or Natchez. Despite these differences, the cultures of our world interact through instant news, the Web, phone technology, and email. It's really quite astonishing just how direct, fast, even intimate, our global connections are. The potentials for greater and greater conflicts, as well as for greater and greater peaceful cooperation, are numerous.

This interconnected world affects the biblical library in many different ways. One of the most important is the way in which pluralistic conversations take place. We all have choices to make. Will only voices of one religion be allowed to study and interpret biblical texts? Will people who may value and interpret the Bible so differently be allowed to participate in our conversations about the meaning of biblical texts? Will one religion dominate or control the conversation? What are the qualifications for participation in the conversation? Should a Buddhist be allowed to teach about these ancient Hebrew scrolls? What makes a teacher or author qualified? Are there religious requirements?

If we look around our world we can see that there is a range of answers to these questions among different groups in various places. Some would allow only for listening to insiders, people who are of the same religious tradition. There are many schools and other institutions that maintain such controls. However, other places and institutions practice listening to and engaging people of many different religious or cultural viewpoints, and they often demonstrate that healthy religious identity and free interaction with other viewpoints go hand in hand. Many people today who study biblical literature actually take advantage of many different kinds of conversations, including study sessions, books, online resources, as well as those in a church or synagogue and those in broader academic settings. This is a great advantage and gift for all of us—we have the freedom and right to study and learn from the people and perspectives of our own choosing.

The rise of intellectual and academic freedom in many countries is a historical development of incalculable worth that has revolutionized the serious and deep study of biblical texts in many ways. This is a long and fascinating story, and much of it concerns the Bible and involves fascinating figures, such as Origen, Jerome, Abraham Ibn Ezra, Spinoza, Voltaire, and Wellhausen. The study of biblical literature is no longer tightly tied only to Jewish and Christian institutions. Biblical studies now attract people of all different beliefs and values, and nonsectarian and nonreligious institutions are heavily involved in the preservation and serious study of biblical literature. If our institutions of learning are intellectually free, and if the relentless pursuit of knowledge and understanding is the task we have set for ourselves, then our schools will value the efforts of all those who would join in the conversation and enterprise for understanding and learning about our ancient Hebrew library and its history and contexts. From personal experience, my own biblical learning is often enhanced by students and scholars of many different religious and cultural identities. And it has made for some lively classroom discussions. We learn about ancient texts and times, and upon reflection we learn about our ourselves and about our common humanity that brought us here. When at our best, we display the common humanitarian values of honest and fair research, intellectual freedom and hospitality, and respectful interaction in agreement and disagreement.

All in all, in Jewish, Christian, Muslim, or open academic environments, the conversations around our biblical scrolls are so often meaningful, a lot of work, and a lot of fun.

References

Barton, John. *People of the Book? The Authority of the Bible in Christianity.* Louisville, KY: Westminster/John Knox, 1988.

Bowley, James E. *Living Traditions of the Bible: Scripture in Jewish, Christian, and Muslim Practice.* St. Louis, MD: Chalice, 1999.

Brown, Raymond E. *The Critical Meaning of the Bible.* New York: Paulist, 1981.

Carroll, Robert P. *Wolf in the Sheepfold: The Bible as Problematic for Theology.* London: SCM Press, 1997.

Davies, Phillip. *Whose Bible is it Anyway?* 2nd ed. London: T. & T. Clark, 2004.

Kaltner, John. *Ishmael Instructs Isaac: An Introduction to the Qur'an for Bible Readers.* Collegeville, MN: Liturgical Press, 1999.

Lewis, Jack. "Some Aspects of the Problem of Inclusion of the Apocrypha," in *The Apocrypha in Ecumenical Perspective,* edited by S. Meurer, 161–207. New York: United Bible Society, 1991.

Midrush Rabbah 10 vols. Edited by H. Freedman. London: Soncino, 1983.

Origen, *On First Principles.* Translated by G. Buttreworth, London: SPCJ, 1936.

Pelikan, Jaroslav. *Whose Bible Is It? A History of The Sacred Scriptures Through the Ages.* New York: Viking, 2005.

Reeves, John C. *Bible and Qur'an.* Atlanta: Society of Biblical Literature, 2003.

Visotzky, Burton L. *Reading the Book: Making the Bible a Timeless Text.* New York: Schocken, 1996.

Wylen, Stephen M. *The Seventy Faces of Torah.* New York: Paulist, 2005.

Checking Out

Goodbye!

I hope that you have enjoyed this *Guided Tour* through the fascinating ancient library of Israel and that you have considered facts, viewpoints, and ancient realities about the Bible that you didn't know before we began. What did you find most interesting? Where do you think we should have spent more time? Send me a note if you would like to help me improve future editions of this tour. What scroll of our library will you go and study now? Would you like to become an archaeologist? A Hebrew scholar? A Dead Sea Scroll investigator? There's a lot more for us to learn. How will you read and study this literature differently now? How will you value it in your life, and how will you look at it differently in your culture?

My greatest hope is that here at the end of our tour you are more curious about this literature than you were at the beginning and that you are eager for more deep, critical, and reasoned learning about these living texts of our heritage. Please come back for further fun, study, and reflection in the generous spirit of intellectual freedom. Long live curiosity! And so, as one of our ancient Israelite authors might say, *shalom!*

Glossary

absolute law In ancient legal codes this type of law or rule is stated as an absolute requirement without giving qualifications, specific cases, or penalties. An example is "You must not murder" and others of the Ten Commandments in Exodus 20 and Deuteronomy 5. Contrasts with **"case law."**

Adam In the first creation story of Genesis 1, the term *adam* is used generically for humans, male and female (see Genesis 1.27). In the creation narrative of Genesis 2, Adam, a male, is the first human created. The name Adam links the human to the earth or ground, *adamah*.

allegory A literary genre of narrative that uses symbolism—where subjects, objects, or events in stories represent abstract ideas, such as religious or philosophical meanings. Ezekiel 16 contains an allegory with its explanation. Allegorical interpretation has been applied to various writing by Jewish, Christian, and Muslim interpreters, whether or not they were originally intended as an allegory.

apocalypse From a Greek word that means "revelation," the term has a more specific meaning in biblical study. Apocalyptic literature is a genre that claims to reveal divine knowledge, usually about the future and ending of the current world, often uses highly symbolic language, and always teaches that Israel's God is sovereign and would ultimately triumph. The revelation is made to a human recipient and often requires supernatural travel, communication, or interpretation, often by an angel. See Daniel 7–12 for examples of apocalyptic literature. This kind of literature became popular first in Judaism (starting in second century BCE), then in Christianity (second century CE), and then in Islam (seventh century CE).

apocrypha From a Greek word meaning "hidden," the word in Christian circles became a term of disparagement for writings that were deemed spurious, heretical, or at least of secondary value, and were therefore not part of the canon of sacred scripture. The term was applied collectively in Christian Protestant circles to the book that Roman Catholics refer to as Deuterocanonicals. See page 438.

Apsu In Mesopotamian mythology, Apsu was the divine male personification of subterranean freshwaters. In Babylonian creation stories, Apsu existed at the beginning with his wife/lover Tiamet, salt water, and fathered with her the first generation of Gods.

Aram In the time of the Israelites, this name applied to a region now making up much of Syria and western Iraq. The name also applies to the Semitic people who inhabited the region, the Arameans. Their most important city was Damascus. They were historically powerful in the region and figure prominently in the scroll of Kings. Their language, Aramaic, became one of the most widely spoken languages in Asia during the periods of Persian, Greek, and Roman empires. Israelite authors were aware of Israel's kinship with Arameans (Deuteronomy 26.5).

Ark of the Covenant The sacred large wooden box overlaid with gold that figures into several Israelite narratives. Its dimensions were between 3 and 4 feet (.91 and 1.22m) long, and about 2.5 feet (.76 m) wide and high. Outside on both ends stood an image of a winged cherub (Exodus 25.10–22). Inside it is said were the store tablets containing YHVH's commands (Deuteronomy 10.2, 1 Kings 8.9). The area above the box between the **cherubim** was considered the throne or place of YHVH (1 Samuel 4.4). Despite many reports from Ethiopia and elsewhere, there is no verified evidence that this sacred box exists today.

Armageddon This name comes from the Christian book of Revelation (16.16), which says that God's enemies will gather "at a place that in

Hebrew is called *Harmagedon.*" Most scholars think it refers to the hill (*har*) of Megiddo, a strategic site of many battles in the region of **Galilee** (see Judges 5.19, 2 Chronicles 35.22). The name does not have the symbolic importance in Israelite or Jewish texts that it came to have in the Christian tradition.

Baal   This word in Hebrew and other **Semitic** languages can be a common noun meaning "lord, master, owner, husband" or the proper name of a widely worshiped chief Canaanite God (1 Kings 18) often associated with storms. Baal is sometimes worshipped by Israelites (1 Kings 16.31–32), sometimes the title is used for YHVH (Hosea 2.18 [16]).

Babylon   The name of the great southern Mesopotamian city, capital of the Babylonian civilization and empire, one of the dominating cultures of the region before and during the time of the Israelites. It was the Babylonians who conquered the mighty Assyrian Empire (ca. 610 BCE) and also Judah and Jerusalem, exiling Jews to the land of Babylonia in 586 BCE (2 Kings 25, Psalms 137).

Bible   From a Greek plural word that means "books" or "scrolls." At a much later time, long after the invention of the codex, this word came to be used for a collection of sacred writings placed between two covers as a single object. It is anachronistic to use it to refer to events or objects prior to the third century CE. See page 1.

Book of the Covenant   See **Covenant Code.**

calendar   The writings in the Israelite library give evidence of several different calendar systems, which is not surprising because the literature reflects divergent periods, places, and influences. What came to be know and is used today as the Jewish calendar is a lunar–solar system of 12 lunar months, which is adjusted every 9 out of 17 years by adding a thirteenth month. The month names are Babylonian in origin, adopted by Jews after their exile there in the sixth century BCE. See page 141.

canon   The official collection of writings deemed sacred or especially valuable by a group; the writings usually considered authoritative by the group, though that authority may be understood differently. For information on various canons, see page 5. Note the important spelling difference from *cannon.*

case law   In legal codes this type of law or rule, also known as casuistic law, is stated with qualifi-

cations, specific situations, and/or penalties, such as, "If a man does *x* to his neighbor, then the penalty shall be *y.*" Compare Leviticus 5.21–24 to the **absolute law** of Exodus 20.13.

Canaan   A name used in Egyptian, Mesopotamian, and Israelite texts that refers to the geographical region between the Mediterranean Sea and the Jordan River. Its inhabitants were called Canaanites. In texts of our library, it approximates the area that was at times under Israelite control and comprised the kingdom(s) of Israel (Genesis 12.5).

chaos   Many ancient creation stories, including the Israelite story of Genesis 1, involve a God or Gods creating order out of the previously existing material chaos of the world.

cherubim   The Hebrew plural form of *cherub;* refers to winged creatures or beasts with mixed animal and/or human characteristics that are found in the art and literature of Israel and other surrounding cultures. Sometimes they are part of two- (1 Kings 6.9) or three-dimensional art (Exodus 25.18–22), visions (Ezekiel 1.5–14), or narratives (Genesis 3.24). They certainly are not the chubby, cute cherubs of Western art.

Christ   The English word that represents the Greek *Xristos,* "anointed" one. The Greek term is a translation of the Hebrew word *m^eshi-akh,* often spelled **"messiah"** in English. The Greek term is used throughout the Christian New Testament for the Christian divine savior, Jesus. In the Hebrew Bible the word usually refers to the Israelite kings because they were anointed in a ceremony that involved pouring olive oil their heads. See page 240.

Christianity   A religion that arose in the middle of the first century CE among followers of Jesus the Jew after his death. Christianity, now a world religion, considers the Hebrew writings of the Jewish Bible as sacred and in corporates these books into the Old Testament.

church   The English word is likely derived from a Greek word meaning "of the Lord," which was used since the third century CE to refer to Christian houses of worship. The term is not used for Israelite or Jewish houses of worship or prayer and is not found in the Hebrew Bible.

circumcision   The practice of cutting off the foreskin of the penis. This was a custom of several ancient cultures, including Egypt and Israel. In Israelite texts the practice is a sacred religious rite first associated with Abraham, performed the eighth day after birth and is a sign of Israel's covenant with YHVH. The rite came to be known as *B'rit-milah,* meaning "covenant of circumcision" in Hebrew (Genesis 17.9–14).

covenant　A formal agreement or treaty between two parties. The Hebrew word for treaty, *b'rit,* is used by many Israelite authors to describe and explain YHVH's special relationship with the Israelites. In Judaism the idea of an eternal covenant between the Jews and their God became central.

Covenant Code　Used mostly by scholars to refer to the collection of rulings found in Exodus 20.19[22]–23.33, based on the phrase in Exodus 24.7. This collection may have been an older group of laws that was incorporated into the scroll of Exodus.

creation　The term creation has come to be a caption for literature about the origin of the world, most famously in Genesis 1 and 2, but also elsewhere, such as Job 38–39 and Psalms 104. It is often thought that creation accounts in many ancient cultures are significant indicators of a culture's over-arching views of itself, humanity, and deity.

criticism　From a Greek verb meaning "to discern, separate, assess"; in general academic terms, criticism means to read and study with care and attention to details. More specifically, a certain kind of criticism, such as textual criticism, refers to a specific set of issues and questions about a text or other object of study. For various kinds of criticism, see page 35.

cubit　A unit of length measurement used in ancient Israel and other societies that is roughly equivalent to the span from the elbow to the fingertips of a man's arm, approximately 18 inches.

cult　From a Latin word for "worship," this term does not have negative connotations when used in the academic fields that study religion. It refers to the organized worship of a deity, usually involving priests, temples, **sacrifices,** praises, and prayers.

Cyrus the Great　A strong Persian king (559 to 530 BCE) who led the Persian conquest of Babylon (539 BCE) and expanded the Persian Empire to include Syria-Palestine and Egypt. He allowed and encouraged Jews and other exiles of the Babylonians to return to their homelands. For this reason Jewish authors looked favorably upon him (Isaiah 45.1, 2 Chronicles 36.22–23).

Day of Atonement　A solemn, holy day in the ancient Israelite cultic calendar, known in Hebrew as *Yom Kippur.* Cultic rites of the day included special sacrifices, and the religious focus is centered on human repentance for wrongs and divine forgiving, covering, or atoning of sins (Leviticus 23.26–32). It remains an important autumn fast day in Judaism on 10 Tishri.

Day of the LORD or **Day of YHVH**　A phrase found in several prophetic writings in our scrolls that picture YHVH as a warrior, sometimes fighting against Israel (Amos 5.18) and sometimes against other nations (Ezekiel 30.2–4). It is the day of YHVH's victory.

Dead Sea Scrolls　A cache of ancient Jewish writings from approximately 200 BCE to 50 CE, discovered from 1947 to 1956 CE in 11 caves near the northwest tip of the Dead Sea, close to the archaeological site of Qumran. The collection includes more than 900 different manuscripts, most of which are fragmentary. Approximately one-third of them are manuscripts of works that were already known to us, such as scrolls of the Hebrew Bible.

Decalogue　A Greek term meaning "ten words" taken from Exodus 24.28. It refers to the groupings of instructions found in Exodus 20.1–14[17] or Deuteronomy 5.6–18.

Deuterocanonicals　From a Greek term meaning "second canon." It is the name used in Roman Catholic teaching for those books of the **Old Testament** that are not contained in the Jewish Hebrew Bible. Protestants removed these writings from their canon and designated them as Apocrypha. See pages 438–440.

Deuteronomic　Characteristic of the ideology/theology of the scroll Deuteronomy. The author of Deuteronomy presents the history of Israel as defined by obedience or disobedience to YHVH's laws and covenant—the former leads to success, the latter to disaster. The scrolls Joshua, Judges, Samuel, and Kings are often called the Deuteronomic history by scholars because they use the same guiding ideology to frame their narratives.

Edom　The region southeast of the Dead Sea, inhabited by the sometimes-powerful Edomites, who, in Israelite reckoning, are the descendents of Esau, the brother of Jacob (Genesis 25.19–26; 36.1). Israelite literature has many references to these neighbors, including the writing of the scroll of Obadiah, which focuses on sixth-century negative relations between the Israelites and

Edomites. In later centuries many Edomites moved west and south of the Dead Sea into the area called the Negev. There they became known as Idumeans.

El   The personal name of a Canaanite God who was widely worshiped. El was also used in a more generic sense, as "God" or "deity." It was used by Israelites in reference to YHVH (Exodus 15.2) and was often combined with other words to make a title (*el-shaddai*, "Mountain God," Genesis 17.1). It is an element in many personal and place names (e.g., Eleazar, *el-azar*, "God helps," Exodus 6.23; Bethel, *bet-el*, "house of God" Genesis 28.16–19)

Elohim   A Hebrew word for "God," or "Gods," frequently used by Israelite authors to refer to the God of Israel, YHVH. The word is formally a plural in Hebrew grammar, and it sometimes refers to the plural "Gods" (Exodus 18.11) or to lower divine beings (Psalms 8.6; 97.7). Most frequently the plural form refers to the God of Israel singularly, and grammatically it is a form that signifies intensity or magnification.

Emanuel   See **Immanuel.**

Enuma Elish   The ancient Babylonian story that tells of the creation of world out of the chaotic mass of water by the God Marduk, who conquered the Goddess Tiamet and used her body for the subsequent division of the land from water and set in order the rest of the world. He then created humans out of the blood of the defeated God Kingu to serve the Gods.

eponym   The name of a group of people, such as *Israel*, that is said to derive from the name of an ancestor or significant member of the group. Israel, the son of Isaac, is the eponymous ancestor of the Israelite nation. Israelite literature uses eponyms for many people groups.

eschatology   The study of or ideas about the end of world history. The word comes from a Greek word, *eskaton*, meaning "last, end." It is often used in connection with apocalyptic literature, which gives a literary picture of the ending of history. Eschatology became particularly important in Christian thought.

Essenes   A group of Jews at the last century BCE and first century CE who were known for their deep piety, study of texts, and careful ritual purity. They are often identified as identical to or similar to the Jews living near the Dead Sea and as those responsible for the **Dead Sea Scrolls**.

etiology   An etiological story offers an explanation for why something is the way it is. Hebrew literature has many such stories, many of them explaining the purported reason for names (e.g., Genesis 3.8–19; 21.25–31).

ex nihilo   A Latin phrase meaning "from nothing," which became very important in parts of Christian theology. It refers to the creation of the world from nothing. The creation story of Genesis 1, like other ancient Near Eastern creation stories, does not posit that God created from nothing. The earliest known clear statement of God creating the world from nothing is in 2 Maccabees 7.28. See page 452.

First Temple   The Jerusalem temple described in 1 Kings 5.1–8.66 built by Solomon; historians use the term *First Temple Period* for the period of the Judean monarchy from the tenth century BCE to 586 BCE, when Babylonians invaders destroyed the temple and exiled the Jews.

Five Megillot   *Megillot* is Hebrew for "scrolls." Five small scrolls of the Ketuvim of the Hebrew Bible are grouped in Jewish tradition because they are traditionally read at five different holidays: Song of Songs at **Passover,** Ruth at **Shavuot,** Lamentations at **Ninth of Av,** Qohelet (Ecclesiastes) at **Sukkot,** and Esther at **Purim.**

Galilee   A region in the northern part of ancient Israel near a large natural lake fed and drained by the Jordan River, especially the region northwest of the lake (1 Kings 9.11). The lake in Hebrew is called *Kinneret,* or later the Sea of Galilee or Sea of Tiberias. The region was home to many different people groups in antiquity, even during the periods of Israelite nationhood (Isaiah 9.1). It was a fertile region and important for trade routes.

genre   A word meaning "kind," or "type," which is used especially to refer to the different forms of literature. Understanding the rules or characteristics of a composition's genre is important for understanding the meaning for the author and original audience.

Gentile   From a Latin word, it is used in many Bible translations to refer to anyone who is not Jewish or Israelite. The Hebrew equivalent is *goy.* Later Christian writers also used it to refer to those who were non-Jews and non-Christians.

Gilgamesh Epic   One of the most famous and wide-spread ancient epics, existing in different versions and predating Israelite literature. It features Gilgamesh, a king from Mesopotamia, who seeks immortality. In one episode he finds out that a certain Utnapishtim attained immortality after surviving a massive flood sent by the Gods by building a boat and riding the storm out with his family and many animals. In this epic there are notable similarities with stories in the early chapters of the Israelite book of Genesis. See page 126.

Hanukkah   A Jewish holiday that celebrates the military victory of the Jews against the Syrian-Greek forces led by the Maccabees and the rededication of the Jerusalem temple after it had been desecrated (164 BCE). The English name derives from the Hebrew word for "dedication." Narratives of the military victory are found in 1 and 2 Maccabees (see pages 446–452), and the legend of the miraculous oil is found in the Talmud. The holiday was sometimes called the Feast of Lights.

Hebrew   The name of the central nation or people group in biblical literature, traditionally derived from a patriarch mentioned in Genesis 10.21 and 11.14 who was seven generations before Abraham. Generally speaking in the narratives of Israel, the word *Hebrews* is used for this tribal group until the name *Israel* begins to be used, roughly at the beginning of the scroll of Exodus. The word *Hebrew* also refers to the language of these people and their descendants.

Hellenism (Hellenistic)   From the Greek word for "Greek," this refers to the culture of the Greeks (including language, political institutions, religion, literature, philosophy, and architecture) that was spread throughout the eastern Mediterranean and through and beyond Mesopotamia after the conquests of Alexander the Great (333 to 323 BCE).

Hillel   An important and favorite Jewish teacher who lived at the end of the first century BCE and whose teachings helped shaped **rabbinic Judaism.**

Holiness Code   A term applied by scholars to Leviticus 17–27, a collection of ethical, cultic, and ritual laws which many consider to have a distinct origin or author, as compared to other parts of Leviticus. The title comes from the frequent appeal to YHVH's holiness as the basis and motivational inspiration of the instructions.

Holy Spirit   A term used mostly in Christian tradition for the divine being present in the world and separate from God the Father and God the Son. In the Hebrew Bible, where the term is much less prominent, a divine spirit is said to come on prophets or others for special purposes. The term

can also refer to the personal sense of the deity being present with a person (Psalm 51.13 [11]).

Immanuel   An English rendering of a two-word Hebrew term, *emanu el,* in a poem of Isaiah (7.14) that the author uses as a name for a coming son of King Ahaz. The name means "with us [is] God."

Intertestamental Period   A Christian term for the time between the composition of the last major writings of the **Old Testament** and the events of the **New Testament.** It roughly corresponds to the Hellenistic and early Roman Period of Jewish history, or the last four centuries BCE.

Israel   The name for the central people group of biblical literature that is usually used in the narrative period from the exodus from Egypt to the exile to Babylon, after which they are called Jews. Sometimes it refers more specifically to the Northern Kingdom, which lasted from the end of the tenth century to the end of the eighth century BCE. The meaning of the name, according to the wordplay of a story in Genesis 32.23–33, is "strives with God" or "God strives," though modern etymological study is inconclusive.

Jew   An Anglicized form of *Judahite.* It refers to people group from the period of the Exodus to the Babylorian exile. Judah was the name of the Southern Kingdom of Israelites, which lasted from the end of the tenth century until the early sixth century BCE. The kingdom it was centered around the hill country of Jerusalem. Judah also was the name of an important patriarch in the stories of Genesis and the name of one of the traditional tribes of Israel. The name *Jew* came to designate the ethnic, religious, or cultural group descended from Judah.

Jubilees   An important Jewish writing composed in the third or second century BCE. It is a "work of Moses," that is, it claims to have been written by Moses and includes much material from the works of Genesis and Exodus, also traditionally associated with Moses. Jubilees was an authoritative and sacred writing for the Jews who composed the **Dead Sea Scrolls.** The name of the book derives from the Hebrew word *yovel,* meaning "jubilee," which refers to a 50-year period of time. The work is concerned with the division of history into Jubilee periods (see Leviticus 25).

Judaism   Usually used as the name of the religion of Jews from the period of about the fifth century BCE until the present. The term is derived from the name Judah, the name of a patriarch, tribe, and kingdom of the ancient Israelites. In existing literature, the term *Judaism* as a reference to the religion was first used in the Greek work of 2 Maccabees (2.21, 14.38).

Ketuvim Hebrew word meaning "writings," which became the title for the third section of the Hebrew Bible. See page 325.

kosher From a Hebrew word that means "proper, fit"; in Jewish tradition it is a general term that applies to proper diet, ritual, and practices; all acts that are done following Jewish rules are considered kosher. Many ancient laws of diet and ritual are to be found in the books of Exodus, Leviticus, Number, and Deuteronomy.

lots Devices used in ancient Israel and other cultures in order to make decisions in a way that the result could be attributed to the deity, much like the throwing dice or drawing straws. A form of divination (e.g., Joshua 18.8–10).

LXX Roman numeral for 70. Greek translations of the scrolls of the sacred Hebrew scrolls collectively came to be known as the translation of the seventy, or Septuagint, due to a legend contained in the Jewish composition called the *Letter of Aristaeus* where seventy-two elders of Jerusalem go to Alexandria, Egypt, to translate the scrolls.

Maccabees Name meaning "the hammer" that derives from the nickname of one of five brothers of the Hasmonean family, who led the successful revolt against the Syrian-Greek overlords in the first half of the second century BCE.

Masoretes From a Hebrew word meaning "transmitters"; this title is used to refer to Jewish copyists who copied and manufactured manuscripts of Jewish works, especially copies of Tanakh. They worked from the sixth through the ninth centuries CE in **Palestine,** and the oldest existing Masoretic manuscripts are from the last ninth and early tenth centuries CE.

menorah A seven-branched candlestick or lamp that became the most common symbol of Judaism. It was a light stand in the Jerusalem temple in ancient Israel. See Exodus 25.31–40. A nine-branched menorah, sometimes called a hanukkiah, is used to celebrate the holiday of **Hanukkah.**

Mesopotamia From a Greek word meaning "between the rivers"; a geographical term referring to the land between the Tigris and Euphrates rivers. It forms the eastern half the Fertile Crescent and was the birthplace and home to important ancient civilizations, such as Sumer, Babylon, and Assyria.

messiah An Anglicized form of the Hebrew *meshiach*, an Israelite title that means "anointed" and usually referred to any Israelite king who had be designated as the king. In the last centuries BCE some Jews applied the term to a Jewish hero that they hoped would come in the future. Early Christians applied the title in its Greek form, *Kristos*, to Jesus (i.e., Christ).

midrash Hebrew term for "interpretation, exposition, commentary." It refers to Jewish practice and texts that interpret biblical literature, often providing many different meanings, stories, and instructions.

Mishnah A document of Judaism that mostly contains rules and discussions of them, organized loosely by topic. It was produced around 200 CE and is traditionally associated with the rabbi Judah *Ha-Nasi*, Judah the Prince. The work formed the basis of the later larger commentary, the **Talmud.**

mitzvah A Hebrew word for "command" that in the Hebrew Bible usually refers to any ethical or ritual instructions from YHVH (e.g. Exodus 20.6). In later Judaism it became the standard term for all ethical duties and good deeds.

monotheism The belief that there is only one God. On Israelite beliefs, see page 47. Judaism, Christianity, and Islam are often referred to as the three major monotheistic religions.

Nebuchadnezzar II A great Babylonian king (604 to 562 BCE) who invaded and conquered Jerusalem and the kingdom of Judah around 586 and then took many Judahites as captives to Babylon (2 Kings 25).

Negev The large southern region of Syria-Palestine that encompassed both ancient and modern Israel, south of the hill country around Jerusalem and Hebron and between the Mediterranean and Jordan Rift. It is mostly arid, dotted by settlements where wells are found, such as Beer-sheva and Arad.

Neviim Hebrew word meaning "prophets," which became the title for the second section of the Hebrew Bible. See page 185.

new covenant A phrase used by the prophet Jeremiah (31.31–36) referring to a reality he envisioned in the future when all Israelites would naturally live according to the requirements of the covenant with YHWH because the laws of the covenant would be "written on their hearts."

New Testament A phrase used in Christianity that means "new covenant." It refers to the Christian idea of a new arrangement between God and humans for salvation through Jesus Christ. It also refers to the collection of twenty-seven books that are sacred to Christianity.

Ninth of Av A summer fast day in the Jewish month of Av that commemorates the destructions of Jerusalem and the temple in 586 BCE by the Babylonians and in 70 CE by the Romans. The scroll of Lamentations provides the reading for the day.

Old Testament A Christian theological term originating in the second century CE that refers to the collection of books of the Hebrew Bible and for Roman Catholics and Orthodox churches the Deuterocanonicals as well. The term obviously assumes the existence and significance of the **New Testament.**

oracle A message or saying believed to come from a God, delivered through a messenger, a **prophet,** to humans. Belief in such messages was common in the ancient world and was required for the existence of prophets. The word *oracle* tends not to be used in English Bible translations, though it could often be used for the term *word,* in the common phrase, "the word of YHVH came . . ." The scrolls of the classical prophets are mostly filled with poetic oracles (e.g., Zephaniah 1.1; see also Isaiah 17.1; 19.1; 21.1; 22.1; 23.1).

Oral Torah In Judaism, since the first or second century CE, this term has been used to refer to the idea that Israel's God revealed two forms of instruction on Mt. Sinai, a written form, contained in the **Torah** of the Hebrew Bible, and an oral form, which was handed down orally and only much later was written down as later Jewish literature, such as the **Mishnah** and **Talmuds.**

oral tradition Any intellectual material, such as stories, customs laws, that has been passed through generations by word of mouth. Some oral traditions are later written down; those that are not are often lost as cultures evolve or die out. Ancient Israel, like surrounding cultures, depended on oral traditions, even during the beginning of the ninth century BCE, when written traditions became more valued.

orthodox From Greek, the word means "correct opinion" and was used especially in Christian

history by various authorities, to designate persons, groups, or ideas as correct in doctrine and to distinguish them from others considered incorrect or heretical. In modern Judaism the term is used to refer to a wide variety of Jewish sects that accept as authoritative the great rabbinic collection known as the Babylonian **Talmud.** In Christianity Orthodox can refer to the churches of the Orthodox Communion.

Palestine The English name roughly approximates the Greek form of *Philistine,* known in Egyptian and Israelite sources as *p-l/r-sh-t.* The Philistines arrived in the region of eastern coast of the Mediterranean and Egypt in the late thirteenth and early twelfth century BCE. They settled mainly in the region along the coast, north of Egypt and south of modern Tel Aviv. Already in antiquity their name was used to designate the larger geographic area, sometimes considered part of Syria, between Egypt and Phoenicia. See the Greek historian Herodotus, 3.91.

Passover A Jewish spring holiday, know in Hebrew as *Pesach,* that primarily celebrates the story of the Israelites being rescued from slavery in Egypt and escaping to the desert to become an independent nation. The name derives from a crucial event in the story where the angel of YHVH goes from door to door in Egypt killing all first-born sons but passes over the homes of Israelites. See Exodus 1–15.

Pentateuch From a Greek word meaning "five scrolls"; it refers to the first five scrolls of the Hebrew Bible, also called the **Torah.**

Pesach See **Passover.**

Pharisees A movement or loose group of religious Jews, especially in Palestine, during the first century CE, with roots going back well into the first century BCE. The name likely comes from Hebrew *perushim,* "separatists." Pharisees were known for their support of the **Oral Torah,** their attempts to extend observance of instructions of the Torah into all areas of life, and their belief in a resurrection of the dead and afterlife. They were often opposed by the more traditional and conservative **Sadducees.**

Philo A very important Jewish philosopher, interpreter, and statesman who lived in Alexandria, Egypt, ca. 20 BCE to 50 CE. His surviving writings demonstrate Jewish and Greek learning and how they were applied to the interpretation of **Torah** by Hellenistic Jews. Philo used a Greek translation of the Torah for all of his study.

priest A person in ancient Israel and surrounding countries who was an official administrator of a temple or cult. The Hebrew word for priest is *kohen.* Israelites priests were usually descendants from a particular family, Aaron, and tribe, Levi. After the destruction of the Jerusalem temple in 70 CE, Judaism did not maintain a priesthood.

prophet From a Greek word, it refers to a messenger of a God. The most common Hebrew equivalent is *navi.* Israel and surrounding cultures had a prominent role for a class of spokespersons of their Gods. See page 226.

pseudepigraphy From a Greek word meaning "false writing." The designation as used today is not intended to have negative connotations. It refers to a large and loosely defined body of Jewish literature that was produced especially in the last centuries BCE but is not part of the Hebrew Bible. The title was applied because many of these writings explicitly claim to be written by a great sage or leader of the distant past, such as Abraham or Joseph.

pseudonymity (pseudonymously) From a Greek word meaning "false name," it refers to the practice of purposefully ascribing the authorship of a composition to someone other than the actual author(s). In Jewish antiquity it was at times an accepted and widespread literary practice to present a writing as if it were the work of an ancient worthy.

Purim A Jewish holiday celebrated in the late winter that commemorates the events or ideas of the scroll of Esther, namely the triumph of the Jews over Persian enemies who were trying to kill them all by intrigue. The name means "lots," which are used in the story.

Qumran The site name of the location where the **Dead Sea Scrolls** were found in nearby caves, more specifically called *Khirbet Qumran,* Arabic for "ruins of Qumran."

Qur'an The Arabic name of the Muslim sacred book. The name means "recitation" and is presented as the words of God (*Allah* in Arabic) to the prophet Muhammad.

rabbi A Hebrew term of respect that means "my great one." It became the commonly used designation for Jewish teachers and **Torah** scholars probably in the first or second century CE.

rabbinic Judaism A general term for the form of living a Jewish life that was advocated by Jewish leaders especially in Palestine after the destruction of the Jerusalem temple in 70 CE. Jewish leaders formulated their traditions into a form of Judaism that did not require a temple. They saw themselves in continuity with earlier **Pharisees,** prophets, and the Torah of Moses. Fruits of their labors include **Mishnah, Talmud,** and the dominant forms of Judaism throughout late antiquity and medieval periods.

Ramses A number of Egyptian kings were called by this name, which means "son of Ra," a chief deity of Egypt. The most famous and powerful was Ramses II, who ruled from about 1290 to 1224 BCE. No Ramses is mentioned by name in biblical texts.

redactor A scholarly word for an editor who creates a document by selecting content from other sources, arranging, editing, and perhaps supplementing it with his or her own writing. In ancient Israel the activity of redaction seems to have been a typical way of working with texts.

resurrection One idea about an afterlife that was influential among Jews in the last centuries BCE and later among Christians and Muslims, which posits that at a time in the distant future God will raise the dead to life. This idea is not a part of the majority of the scrolls in the Hebrew Bible, though it is mentioned in one of the latest books, Daniel (12.2–3). The scroll of Qohelet (Ecclesiastes) is dismissive of ideas of resurrection or afterlife. The ongoing argument in early **Judaism** (last centuries BCE) can also be observed in Sirach (44.1–15) and Wisdom of Solomon (1–6). The impetus for advocating resurrection and an afterlife within Judaism seems clearly to have been the desire to see final justification and reward for the righteous.

Rosh Hashanah A Hebrew phrase that means "first of the year" and is the name for a Jewish fall harvest and new year festival on the first of the month of Tishri. In extant biblical texts it is not called a new year holiday (Numbers 29.1–6).

Sabbath The Anglicized pronunciation of the Hebrew *sha-baht,* the seventh day of the week and the most referenced and arguably important Jewish holy day. The name is from the Hebrew verb meaning "to stop, cease." It is a day for resting and ceasing from labor. It is referred to in numerous scrolls of the Hebrew Bible, including Genesis 2.1–3 and Exodus 20.8–11. Later in Christian tradition some elements of the Jewish Sabbath were transferred to the first day of the week, which was then called the Christian Sabbath.

sacrifice In ancient Israel, an expression of thanksgiving or worship or a plea for forgiveness or favor offered to a deity in the form of a slaughtered animal that was burned on a sacred altar and whose blood was splashed onto the altar. Grains, produce, and liquids were also used. The Israelites, like nearly all surrounding nations, had a religious cult system involving numerous sacrifices. Such sacrifices were thought to be means of communicating human devotion to and of pleasing the God (Leviticus 1.1–3.17).

Sadducees A leading group of Jews with ancient roots who were influential in the temple and among political leaders in the first century CE. They opposed religious and social innovations and the Oral Law of their major rival group, the **Pharisees**, and they argued for maintaining traditional temple practices and religious ideas, in opposition to newer notions such as the idea of an afterlife. The name may derive from *Zadok-im*, an important priestly family.

Samaria Anglicized form of the Hebrew city name *Shomron*, which was the capital of the Northern Kingdom of Israel from the ninth century until its destruction by Assyria in 722 BCE. The term is also applied to the entire large surrounding region north of Judah and south of Galilee.

Samaritans Named used for people from the region of Samaria, especially used in the last centuries BCE and later. Samaritans still live in this area in modern times. Samaritans claimed descent from survivors of the destruction of the Northern Kingdom of Israel by Assyria in 722 BCE, though many Jews did not accept their claims. Samaritans hold as sacred the Torah or Five Books of Moses.

Second Temple In Israelite and Jewish history this refers to the temple of Jerusalem that was completed in the late sixth century, after the return of Jewish exiles from **Babylon.** The Second Temple Period lasted until 70 CE, when the temple was destroyed by invading Roman armies.

seder A Hebrew word meaning "order"; this has become the term for the formally ordered and liturgical **Passover** dinner, celebrated by Jews on the first night of Passover.

Semitic A word that, when speaking of languages, refers to a large language family that includes Hebrew, Arabic, and Aramaic. When used of modern people it applies only to Jews. See page 79.

Septuagint See **LXX.**

Shabbat See **Sabbath.**

Shavuot A spring holiday beginning on 6 Sivan that celebrated the spring harvest of the late winter/early spring crops. The Hebrew word means "weeks" and refers to the counting of seven weeks after **Passover.** See Exodus 34.22 and Deuteronomy 16.9–12. In Christian tradition this became known as pentecost, which celebrated a particular Christian tradition.

She'ma A Hebrew word meaning "Listen!" that begins a Jewish liturgical statement, commonly translated, "Hear, O Israel, Lord is our God, the Lord is One" from Deuteronomy 6.4.

Sheol A dark, shadowy, mostly unknown place of all the dead that is referred to in several scrolls of the Hebrew Bible; it is the most common conception of an afterlife in the Hebrew Bible. Although not a place of life and hope, it was also not a place of torment or pain. See 1 Samuel 2.6, Job 7.9, and Qohelet (Ecclesiastes) 9.10.

shofar A Hebrew word for the horn of a ram that could be prepared and then used as a trumpet. It was utilized in some holiday and cultic settings, such at **Rosh Hashanah.**

sin In Hebrew Bible scrolls, an error, mistake, or moral failing, especially considered displeasing to the God.

son of man A phrased used frequently in Ezekiel to refer to the human prophet and in Daniel 7 to refer to a divine being who appears as a human. In later Christian usage it refers to the Christian Christ, or Jesus.

Sukkot A annual Israelite and now Jewish autumn seven-day holiday, beginning on 15 Tishri. The word *sukkot* means "booths," temporary structures, and the holiday combines a harvest festival with commemoration of days of wandering in the wilderness and living in temporary shelters. See Leviticus 23.39–43.

synagogue A Greek term meaning "gathering" that became the standard name for a local Jewish place of worship and study outside of the temple in Jerusalem.

Talmud A Hebrew word meaning "teaching"; it is the title of a massive commentary on the **Mishnah** (ca. 200 CE) that was compiled in the third to fifth centuries CE. There are two forms, the smaller Jerusalem Talmud and the larger and more widespread Babylonian Talmud.

Ten Commandments See **Decalogue.**

tent of meeting   A frequently used term in Exodus, Leviticus, and Numbers for a tent where Moses and others met together and, more importantly, where Moses would meet with YHVH, the God of Israel.

tetragrammaton   A Greek word meaning "four letters" that in Judaism refers to the personal name of the God of Israel, YHVH. In most modern English translations it is represented as "LORD," in contrast to "Lord," which represents a Hebrew noun meaning "master." See page 25.

theodicy   A term that comes from two Greek words meaning "God's justice." It refers to the theological dilemma within monotheistic systems of trying to reconcile or justify the idea of a caring, good, sovereign God with fact of horrible and innocent suffering of humans. The book of Job deals quite directly with this issues. See page 355.

theophany   English form of an ancient Greek word meaning "appearance of a God." Ancient Israelite and many other religious traditions have narratives about their God(s) appearing on the earth. Genesis 2 and Exodus 3 and 20 contain examples.

Tiamat   A Babylonian Goddess, identified with the deep sea, and the female of the original pair of Gods. With Apsu her husband she becomes the mother of all deities. She is eventually killed in battle by Marduk, and her body is used to create the great dome of the sky over the earth.

Torah   A Hebrew word that means "instruction." In the late centuries BCE and early CE it came to be used of teachings and scrolls associated with Moses, who by that time was revered as Judaism's great teacher and recipient of divine instructions. With the solidification of a collection of Jewish sacred literature, the term then became used for the first five books of the Hebrew Bible. In Jewish tradition the term was and is used with broader meanings also: it can refer to the entire collection of biblical literature, or it may include all of later Jewish teachings, such as **Mishnah** and **Talmud.**

Finally it sometimes even refers to all of Jewish learning and study.

unleavened bread   Bread that has no rising agents in it so that it remains flat even when baked. According to the narrative Exodus, the Israelites only had time to bake this kind of bread on the night of their escape from Egypt (Exodus 12.14–20; 33–39). An ancient feast day was called the Feast of Unleavened Bread and was eventually identified at a part of the **Passover** holiday.

Ur   A Mesopotamian city, traditionally the native home of Abraham (Genesis 11.28–31). There are two possible sites for Ur. Archaeological evidence locates Ur, a very important Sumerian and early Babylonian city, in southern **Mesopotamia,** now in Iraq. The other traditional location is in northern Mesopotamia at the Turkish city of Urfa.

YHVH   An English attempt at representing the four consonants of the personal name used for Israel's God. In the scrolls of the Hebrew Bible, this is by far the most common way to refer to the Israelite God. For the sake of pronunciation, "ah" and "eh" vowels are added resulting in *yah-veh.* In Jewish tradition it became the custom to never pronounce the name because of its sacredness.

Yom Kippur   See **Day of Atonement.**

ziggurat   From an Akkadian word meaning "mountain top, tower"; a temple structure used in ancient Sumer and Babylon that resembles a stepped pyramid. The most famous still stands today in Iraq near Babylon. It is likely that the tower of Babel story envisions this sort of structure (Genesis 11.1–9).

Zion   A place name in Hebrew literature that in the earliest cases refers to a small hill or mountain captured and settled by the Israelite king David (2 Samuel 5.7, 1 Kings 8.1). It became a name for the entire city of Jerusalem and came to be frequently used as a symbol for a Jewish home and homeland (Psalm 137), even as it is in the modern use of *Zionism.*

Index